Strategic Advancements in Utilizing Data Mining and Warehousing Technologies:
New Concepts and Developments

David Taniar
Monash University, Australia

Laura Irina Rusu
Latrobe University, Australia

INFORMATION SCIENCE REFERENCE

Hershey · New York

Director of Editorial Content:	Kristin Klinger
Senior Managing Editor:	Jamie Snavely
Assistant Managing Editor:	Michael Brehm
Publishing Assistant:	Sean Woznicki
Typesetter:	Michael Brehm, Michael Killian
Cover Design:	Lisa Tosheff
Printed at:	Yurchak Printing Inc.

Published in the United States of America by
Information Science Reference (an imprint of IGI Global)
701 E. Chocolate Avenue
Hershey PA 17033
Tel: 717-533-8845
Fax: 717-533-8661
E-mail: cust@igi-global.com
Web site: http://www.igi-global.com/reference

Library of Congress Cataloging-in-Publication Data

Strategic advancements in utilizing data mining and warehousing technologies :
new concepts and developments / David Taniar and Laura Irina Rusu, editors.
     p. cm.
  Includes bibliographical references and index.
  Summary: "This book presents and disseminates new concepts and developments
in the areas of data warehousing and data mining, in particular on the
research trends shaped during the last few years"--Provided by publisher.
  ISBN 978-1-60566-717-1 (hardcover) -- ISBN 978-1-60566-718-8 (ebook) 1.
Data mining. 2. Data warehousing. I. Taniar, David. II. Rusu, Laura Irina,
1973-
  QA76.9.D343S6852 2010
  005.74'5--dc22
                              2009047893

British Cataloguing in Publication Data
A Cataloguing in Publication record for this book is available from the British Library.

Advances in Data Warehousing and Mining Series (ADWM)

ISBN: 1935-2646

Editor-in-Chief: David Taniar, Monash Univerisy, Australia

Research and Trends in Data Mining Technologies and Applications
David Taniar, Monash University, Australia

IGI Publishing • copyright 2007 • 340 pp • H/C (ISBN: 1-59904-271-1) •
E-Book (ISBN: 1-59904-273-8)

Activities in data warehousing and mining are constantly emerging. Data mining methods, algorithms, online analytical processes, data mart and practical issues consistently evolve, providing a challenge for professionals in the field. Research and Trends in Data Mining Technologies and Applications focuses on the integration between the fields of data warehousing and data mining, with emphasis on the applicability to real-world problems. This book provides an international perspective, highlighting solutions to some of researchers' toughest challenges. Developments in the knowledge discovery process, data models, structures, and design serve as answers and solutions to these emerging challenges.

The Advances in Data Warehousing and Mining (ADWM) Book Series aims to publish and disseminate knowledge on an international basis in the areas of data warehousing and data mining. The book series provides a highly regarded outlet for the most emerging research in the field and seeks to bridge underrepresented themes within the data warehousing and mining discipline.
The Advances in Data Warehousing and Mining (ADWM) Book Series serves to provide a continuous forum for state-of-the-art developments and research, as well as current innovative activities in data warehousing and mining. In contrast to other book series, the ADWM focuses on the integration between the fields of data warehousing and data mining, with emphasize on the applicability to real world problems. ADWM is targeted at both academic researchers and practicing IT professionals.

Hershey • New York

Order online at www.igi-global.com or call 717-533-8845 x 10 –
Mon-Fri 8:30 am - 5:00 pm (est) or fax 24 hours a day 717-533-8661

Editorial Advisory Board

Table of Contents

Detailed Table of Contents

Maurizio Pighin, University of Udine, Italy
Lucio Ieronutti, University of Udine, Italy

The design and configuration of a data warehouse can be a difficult task, especially when the initial databases are very large and characterized by redundant information. In particular, the choice of which attributes have to be considered as dimensions and measures can be not trivial and it can heavily influence the effectiveness of the final system. This chapter proposes a methodology targeted at supporting the design and deriving information on the total quality of the final data warehouse. This proposal was tested on three real-world commercial ERP databases.

Gerasimos Marketos, University of Piraeus, Greece
Yannis Theodoridis, University of Piraeus, Greece
Ioannis S. Kalogeras, National Observatory of Athens, Greece

Earthquake data composes an ever increasing collection of earth science information for post-processing analysis. Earth scientists, local or national administration officers and so forth, are working with these data collections for scientific or planning purposes. This chapter discusses the architecture of a so-called Seismic Data Management and Mining System (SDMMS) for quick and easy data collection, processing, and visualization. The SDMMS architecture includes, among others, a seismological database for efficient and effective querying and a seismological data warehouse for OLAP analysis and data mining. The authors provide template schemes for these two components as well as examples of their functionality towards the support of decision making. This chapter also provides a comparative survey of existing operational or prototype SDMMS.

Chapter 3

Marko Banek, University of Zagreb, Croatia
Boris Vrdoljak, University of Zagreb, Croatia
A Min Tjoa, Vienna University of Technology, Austria
Zoran Skočir, University of Zagreb, Croatia

A federated data warehouse is a logical integration of data warehouses applicable when physical integration is impossible due to privacy policy or legal restrictions. In healthcare systems federated data warehouses are a most feasible source of data for deducing guidelines for evidence-based medicine based on data material from different participating institutions. In order to enable the translation of queries in a federated approach, schemas of the federated warehouse and the local warehouses must be matched. This chapter presents a procedure that enables the matching process for schema structures specific to the multidimensional model of data warehouses: facts, measures, dimensions, aggregation levels and dimensional attributes. Similarities between warehouse-specific structures are computed by using linguistic and structural comparison. The calculated values are used to create necessary mappings.

Chapter 4

Franck Ravat, Université Toulouse I, France
Olivier Teste, Université Toulouse III, France
Ronan Tournier, Université Toulouse III, France
Gilles Zurfluh, Université Toulouse I, France

This chapter deals with multidimensional analyses. Analyzed data are designed according to a conceptual model as a constellation of facts and dimensions, which are composed of multi-hierarchies. This model supports a query algebra defining a minimal core of operators, which produce multidimensional tables for displaying analyzed data. This user-oriented algebra supports complex analyses through advanced operators and binary operators. A graphical language, based on this algebra, is also provided to ease the specification of multidimensional queries. These graphical manipulations are expressed from a constellation schema and they produce multidimensional tables.

Chapter 5

Michael Lawrence, Dalhousie University, Canada
Andrew Rau-Chaplin, Dalhousie University, Canada

In a data warehousing environment, aggregate views are often materialized in order to speed up aggregate queries of online analytical processing (OLAP). Due to the increasing size of data warehouses, it is often infeasible to materialize all views. View selection, the task of selecting a subset of views to materialize based on updates and expectations of the query load, is an important and challenging problem. This chapter explores dynamic view selection in which the distribution of queries changes over time and the set of materialized views must be tuned by replacing some of the previously materialized views with new ones.

Frank Dehne, Carleton University, Canada

Todd Eavis, Concordia University, Canada

Andrew Rau-Chaplin, Dalhousie University, Canada

This chapter addresses the query performance issue for Relational OLAP (ROLAP) data cubes. The authors present RCUBE, a distributed multi-dimensional ROLAP indexing scheme which is practical to implement, requires only a small communication volume, and is fully adapted to distributed disks. Their solution is efficient for spatial searches in high dimensions and scalable in terms of data sizes, dimensions, and number of processors. Their method is also incrementally maintainable. Using "surrogate" group-bys, it allows for the efficient processing of arbitrary OLAP queries on partial cubes, where not all of the group-bys have been materialized. Experiments with RCUBE show that the ROLAP advantage of better scalability, in comparison to MOLAP, can be maintained while providing, at the same time, a fast and flexible index for OLAP queries.

Chapter 7

Xiaodan Zhang, Drexel University, USA

Liping Jing, The University of Hong Kong, China

Xiaohua Hu, Drexel University, USA

Michael Ng, Hong Kong Baptist University, China

Jiali Xia, Jiangxi University of Finance and Economics, China

Xiaohua Zhou, Drexel University, USA

This chapter conducts a comparative study on how different term semantic similarity measures including path-based, information-content-based and feature-based similarity measure affect document clustering. Term re-weighting of document vector is an important method to integrate domain ontology to clustering process. In detail, the weight of a term is augmented by the weights of its co-occurred concepts. Spherical k-means are used for evaluate document vector re-weighting on two real-world datasets: Disease10 and OHSUMED23. Experimental results on nine different semantic measures have shown many useful findings.

Xiaodan Zhang, Drexel University, USA

Xiaohua Hu, Drexel University, USA & Jiangxi University of Finance and Economics, China

Jiali Xia, Jiangxi University of Finance and Economics, China

Xiaohua Zhou, Drexel University, USA

Palakorn Achananuparp, Drexel University, USA

This chapter presents a graph-based knowledge representation for biomedical digital library literature clustering. An efficient clustering method is developed to identify the ontology-enriched k-highest density term subgraphs that capture the core semantic relationship information about each document cluster. The distance between each document and the k term graph clusters is calculated. A document is then assigned to the closest term cluster. The extensive experimental results on two PubMed document sets (Disease10 and OHSUMED23) show that this approach is comparable to spherical k-means. The contributions of this approach are the following: (1) it provide two corpus-level graph representations to improve document clustering, a term co-occurrence graph and an abstract-title graph; (2) it develops an efficient and effective document clustering algorithm by identifying k distinguishable class-specific core term subgraphs using terms' global and local importance information; and (3) the identified term clusters give a meaningful explanation for the document clustering results.

This chapter takes advantage of using fuzzy classifier rules to capture the correlations between genes. The main motivation to conduct this study is that a fuzzy classifier rule is essentially an "if-then" rule that contains linguistic terms to represent the feature values. This representation of a rule that demonstrates the correlations among the genes is very simple to understand and interpret for domain experts. In this proposed gene selection procedure, instead of measuring the effectiveness of every single gene for building the classifier model, the authors incorporate the impotence of a gene correlation with other existing genes in the process of gene selection. That is, a gene is rejected if it is not in a significant correlation with other genes in the dataset. Furthermore, in order to improve the reliability of this approach, the process is repeated several times in these experiments, and the genes reported as the result are the genes selected in most experiments. This chapter reports test results on five datasets and analyzes the achieved results from biological perspective.

A new approach to vertical fragmentation in relational databases is proposed using association rules, a data-mining technique. Vertical fragmentation can enhance the performance of database systems by reducing the number of disk accesses needed by transactions. By adapting Apriori algorithm, a design methodology for vertical partitioning is proposed. The heuristic methodology is tested using two real-life databases for various minimum support levels and minimum confidence levels. In the smaller database, the partitioning solution obtained matched the optimal solution using exhaustive enumeration. The application of this method on the larger database resulted in the partitioning solution that has an improvement of 41.05% over unpartitioned solution and took less than a second to produce the solution. This chapter provides future research directions on extending the procedure to distributed and object-oriented database designs.

Chapter 11

The data quality of a vector spatial data can be assessed using the data contained within one or more data warehouses. Spatial consistency includes topological consistency, or the conformance to topological rules (Hadzilacos & Tryfona, 1992, Rodríguez, 2005). Detection of inconsistencies in vector spatial data is an important step for improvement of spatial data quality (Redman, 1992; Veregin, 1991). An approach for detecting topo-semantic inconsistencies in vector spatial data is presented. Inconsistencies between pairs of neighboring vector spatial objects are detected by comparing relations between spatial objects to rules (Klein, 2007). A property of spatial objects, called elasticity, has been defined to measure the contribution of each of the objects to inconsistent behavior. Grouping of multiple objects, which are inconsistent with one another, based on their elasticity is proposed. The ability to detect groups of neighboring objects that are inconsistent with one another can later serve as the basis of an effort to increase the quality of spatial data sets stored in data warehouses, as well as increase the quality of results of data-mining processes.

Chapter 12

Sequential patterns mining is an important data-mining technique used to identify frequently observed sequential occurrence of items across ordered transactions over time. It has been extensively studied in the literature, and there exists a diversity of algorithms. However, more complex structural patterns are often hidden behind sequences. This chapter begins with the introduction of a model for the representation of sequential patterns—Sequential Patterns Graph—which motivates the search for new structural relation patterns. An integrative framework for the discovery of these patterns–Postsequential Patterns Mining–is then described which underpins the postprocessing of sequential patterns. A corresponding data-mining method based on sequential patterns postprocessing is proposed and shown to be effective in the search for concurrent patterns. From experiments conducted on three component algorithms, it is demonstrated that sequential patterns-based concurrent patterns mining provides an efficient method for structural knowledge discovery.

Chapter 13

This chapter considers a new kind of temporal pattern where both interval and punctual time representation are considered. These patterns, which the authors call temporal point-interval patterns, aim at capturing how events taking place during different time periods or at different time instants relate to each other. The datasets where these kinds of patterns may appear are temporal relational databases whose relations contain point or interval timestamps. The authors use a simple extension of Allen's Temporal Interval Logic as a formalism for specifying these temporal patterns. The authors also present the algorithm MILPRIT* for mining temporal point-interval patterns, which uses variants of the classical levelwise search algorithms. In addition, MILPRIT* allows a broad spectrum of constraints to be incorporated into the mining process. An extensive set of experiments of MILPRIT* executed over synthetic and real data is presented, showing its effectiveness for mining temporal relational patterns.

Chapter 14
    Rong She, Simon Fraser University, Canada
    Ke Wang, Simon Fraser University, Canada
    Ada Waichee Fu, Chinese University of Hong Kong, Hong Kong
    Yabo Xu, Simon Fraser University, Canada

This chapter proposes a privacy-preserving protocol for computing aggregation queries over the join of private tables. In this problem, several parties wish to share aggregated information over the join of their tables, but want to conceal the details that generate such information. The join operation presents a challenge to privacy preservation because it requires matching individual records from private tables without letting any non-owning party know the actual join values or make any inference about the data in other parties. The authors solve this problem by using a novel private sketching protocol that securely exchanges some randomized summary information about private tables. This protocol (1) conceals individual private values and their distributions from all non-owning parties, (2) works on many general forms of aggregation functions, (3) handles group-by aggregates, and (4) handles roll-up/drill-down operations. Previous works have not provided this level of privacy for such queries.

Chapter 15
    Junping Zhang, Fudan University, China
    Guo-Zheng Li, Shanghai University, China

The PAKDD Competition 2007 involved the problem of predicting customers' propensity to take up a home loan when a collection of data from credit card users are provided. It is rather difficult to address the problem because 1) the data set is extremely imbalanced; 2) the features are mixture types; and 3) there are many missing values. This chapter gives an overview on the competition, mainly consisting of three parts: 1) The background of the database and some statistical results of participants are introduced; 2) An analysis from the viewpoint of data preparation, resampling/reweighting and ensemble learning employed by different participants is given; and 3) Finally, some business insights are highlighted.

Mingjun Wei, Zhejiang University and Sherpa Consulting, China
Lei Chai, Sherpa Consulting, China
Renying Wei, China Mobile Group Zhejiang Co., China
Wang Huo, China Mobile Group Zhejiang Co., China

The authors of this chapter won the Grand Champion (Tie) of PAKDD-2007 data mining competition. The data mining task is to score credit card customers of a consumer finance company according to the likelihood that customers take up the home loans offered by the company. This report presents their solution for this business problem. TreeNet and logistic regression are the data mining algorithms used in this project. The final score is based on the cross-algorithm ensemble of two within-algorithm ensembles of TreeNet and logistic regression. Finally, some discussions from their solution are presented.

Hualin Wang, AllianceData, USA
Xiaogang Su, University of Central Florida, USA

This chapter presents an award-winning algorithm for the data mining competition of PAKDD 2007, in which the goal is to help a financial company to predict the likelihood of taking up a home loan for their credit card based customers. The involved data are very limited and characterized by very low buying rate. To tackle such an unbalanced classification problem, the authors apply a bagging algorithm based on probit model ensembles. One integral element of the algorithm is a special way of conducting the resampling in forming bootstrap samples. A brief justification is provided. This method offers a feasible and robust way to solve this difficult yet very common business problem.

Paulo J.L. Adeodato, NeuroTech Ltd. and Federal University of Pernambuco, Brazil
Germano C. Vasconcelos, NeuroTech Ltd. and Federal University of Pernambuco, Brazil
Adrian L. Arnaud, NeuroTech Ltd. and Federal University of Pernambuco, Brazil
Rodrigo C.L.V. Cunha, NeuroTech Ltd. and Federal University of Pernambuco, Brazil
Domingos S.M.P. Monteiro, NeuroTech Ltd. and Federal University of Pernambuco, Brazil
Rosalvo F. Oliveira Neto, NeuroTech Ltd. and Federal University of Pernambuco, Brazil

This chapter presents an efficient solution for the PAKDD-2007 Competition cross-selling problem. The solution is based on a thorough approach which involves the creation of new input variables, efficient data preparation and transformation, adequate data sampling strategy and a combination of two of the most robust modelling techniques. Due to the complexity imposed by the very small amount of examples in the target class, the approach for model robustness was to produce the median score of the 11 models developed with an adapted version of the 11-fold cross-validation process and the use of a combination of two robust techniques via stacking – the MLP neural network and the n-tuple classifier. Despite the problem complexity, the performance on the prediction data set (unlabeled samples), measured through KS2 and ROC curves was shown to be very effective and finished as the first runner-up solution of the competition.

    Dan Steinberg, Salford Systems, USA
    Nicholas Scott Cardell, Salford Systems, USA
    John Ries, Salford Systems, USA
    Mykhaylo Golovnya, Salford Systems, USA

Today's credit card issuers are increasingly offering a broad range of products and services with separate lines of business responsible for different product groups. Too often, the separate lines of business operate independently and information available to one line of business may not be used productively by others. This study examines the potential of using information from customers of multiple products to identify customers most likely to respond to cross-sell product offers. Specifically, the authors examine the potential for offering home loans to a population of credit card holders by studying individuals who do hold both a credit card and a mortgage with the card issuer. Using real world data provided to the 2007 PAKDD data mining competition, this chapter employ Friedman's stochastic gradient boosting (MART™, TreeNet®) for the rapid development of a high performance cross-sell predictive model.

    Thierry Van de Merckt, VADIS Consulting sa, Belgium
    Jean-François Chevalier, VADIS Consulting sa, Belgium

This chapter presents VADIS Consulting's solution for the cross-selling problem of the PAKDD_2007 competition. For this competition, the authors have used their in-house developed tool RANK, which automates a lot of important tasks that must be done to provide a good solution for predictive modelling projects. It was for them a way of benchmarking their 3 years of investment effort against other tools and techniques. RANK encodes some important steps of the CRISP-DM methodology: Data Quality Audit, Data Transformation, Modelling, and Evaluation. The authors have used RANK as they would do in a normal project, however with much less access to the business information, and hence the task was quite elementary: they have audited the data quality and found some problems that were further corrected, they have then let RANK build a model by applying its standard recoding, and then applied automatic statistical evaluation for variable selection and pruning. The result was not extremely good in terms of prediction, but the model was extremely stable, which is what the authors were looking for.

    Dehong Qiu, Huazhong University of Science and Technology, P.R.China
    Ye Wang, Huazhong University of Science and Technology, P.R.China
    Qifeng Zhang, Huazhong University of Science and Technology, P.R.China

The task of the 2007 PAKDD competition was to help a finance company to build a cross-selling model to score the propensity of a credit card customer to take up a home loan. The present work tries to increase the prediction accuracy and enhance the model comprehensibility through efficiently selecting features and samples simultaneously. A new framework that coordinates feature selection and sample selection together is built. The criteria of optimal feature selection and the method of sample selection are designed. Experiments show that the new algorithm not only raises the value of the area under ROC curves, but also reveals more valuable business insights.

Chapter 22
    Vladimir Nikulin, Suncorp, Australia

Imbalanced data represent a significant problem because the corresponding classifier has a tendency to ignore patterns which have smaller representation in the training set. This chapter proposes to consider a large number of balanced training subsets where representatives from the larger pattern are selected randomly. As an outcome, the system will produce a matrix of linear regression coefficients where rows represent random subsets and columns represent features. Based on the above matrix an assessment of the stability of the influence of the particular features is made. It is proposed to keep in the model only features with stable influence. The final model represents an average of the single models, which are not necessarily a linear regression. The above model had proven to be efficient and competitive during the PAKDD-2007 Data Mining Competition.

Chapter 23
    Zhi-Zhuo Zhang, South China University of Technology, China
    Qiong Chen, South China University of Technology, China
    Shang-Fu Ke, South China University of Technology, China
    Yi-Jun Wu, South China University of Technology, China
    Fei Qi, South China University of Technology, China
    Ying-Peng Zhang, South China University of Technology, China

Ranking potential customers has become an effective tool for company decision makers to design marketing strategies. The task of PAKDD competition 2007 was a cross-selling problem between credit card and home loan, which can also be treated as a ranking potential customers problem. This chapter proposes a 3-level ranking model, namely Group-Ensemble, to handle such kinds of problems. In this model, Bagging, RankBoost and Expending Regression Tree are applied to solve crucial data mining problems like data imbalance, missing value and time-variant distribution. The chapter verifies the model with data provided by PAKDD Competition 2007 and shows that Group-Ensemble can make selling strategy much more efficient.

Preface

INTRODUCTION

In the context of the dynamic business environment which exists nowadays, it is increasingly critical that organizations use only quality and up to date information, in order to make successful business decisions. Data warehouses are built with the aim of providing integrated and clean chronological data. Additionally, they are accompanied by tools which allow business users to query and analyse the warehoused data. These reporting tools are often seen as the finality of data collected in the warehouse. However, data mining applications do more than using simple or complex statistical functions often used in reporting; they try to discover interesting hidden information from the data collected, by looking at patterns, relationships, clusters of data, outrigger values, etc.

The purpose of this book is to present and disseminate new concepts and developments in the areas of data warehousing and data mining. The focus is on latest research discoveries and proposals in these two areas, in particular on the research trends shaped during the last few years.

Web applications' usage in particular continues to see a dramatic increase, especially in the areas where customer interaction is sought after by business, but not only. The language of choice for web applications is XML (eXtensible Markup Language). It is then very important that a data warehouse is built with a supporting technology that allows global information interactions and management—this is the reason for the emergence of XML representation for web data warehousing. The hierarchical nature of XML within an XML data warehouse and the fact that it represents a document warehouse rather than a traditional table-based relational warehouse, have raised the need for new methodologies in dealing with warehousing issues. Also, performing data mining by extracting knowledge from web (XML) data has proved to be a challenging task. The dynamicity of the web data, together with the complexities brought in by the XML's flexible structure, required new techniques to deal with data mining issues.

This chapter is split in two main sections: the first section first gives an overview of the data warehousing and discusses its importance in providing support for the decision making process, followed by a discussion about the state of the art research work in this area; the second section presents the importance of extracting profound knowledge from data by employing data mining tools, followed by an analysis of the current trends and research work in this area. As mentioned, web XML data is a growingly significant presence in various types of applications, therefore an important fraction of this chapter will be dedicated to discussing current research trends in web XML data warehousing, respectively web XML data mining.

CURRENT TRENDS IN DATA WAREHOUSING

This section first gives an overview of the data warehousing generic concepts and then it looks at the latest trends and advancements of the research work in this domain.

Data Warehousing: An Overview

The concept of data warehouse was defined by [Inmon, 2005] as a "[…] subject-oriented, integrated, time-variant and non-volatile collection of data in support of management's decisions". Another definition was given by [Marakas, 2003], that a data warehouse is "[…] a copy of transaction data specifically structured for querying, analysis and reporting".

It has been shown that for relational database systems, the operational and historical data cannot exist within the same structure because neither of them would perform well. Several reasons have been enumerated to support the need for a separate data warehouse to collect data for decisional support [Han & Kamber, 2006]:

- A data warehouse is subject-oriented, which means that it is built around the major focus of an application: customer, product, sales etc. Conversely, an operational system contains all data produced by daily transaction processing and, depending on the application, might include data not required by the decision process;
- A data warehouse might contain information integrated from multiple sources (e.g. relational database, other files of different formats, emails etc), whereas operational systems always contain data produced by the application, most usually in the form of data in relational tables;
- A data warehouse is time variant and reflects the collection of data during a large period of time (e.g. 5-10 years or more), while operational systems do not keep data for such a long period of time;
- A data warehouse is used for the decision process only, and not for daily transaction processing. This means that a low number of queries are applied on larger volumes of data, compared with operational systems which are queried very often but for low volumes of data (e.g. to respond customer enquires);
- Finally, a data warehouse is non-volatile, which means that after the warehouse is built, data is uploaded and never deleted; new data arrives periodically and expands the data warehouse; queries are usually applied by the data analysts and therefore a data warehouse does not require concurrent transaction processing features; comparatively, operational systems are updated frequently, should allow multiple users, and hence should allow concurrent transaction processing.

Generic data warehouse architecture as proposed by [Kimball & Ross, 2002] contains the following four main areas (see Figure 1):

- ***Operational source systems:*** these contain the transactional data, used in day to day operations, by a large number of users (possible hundreds or thousands in large applications). The data in these systems needs to be current, guaranteed up to date and the priority is high performance and high availability of the information;
- ***Data staging area:*** this is the area where the ETL (Extract – Transform – Load) process takes place. As the name says, the data is extracted from the operational source systems, then it is cleaned, transformed and integrated, and finally it is sent to be loaded into the data warehouse.

Figure 1. Data Warehouse Architecture as proposed by [Kimball & Ross, 2002]

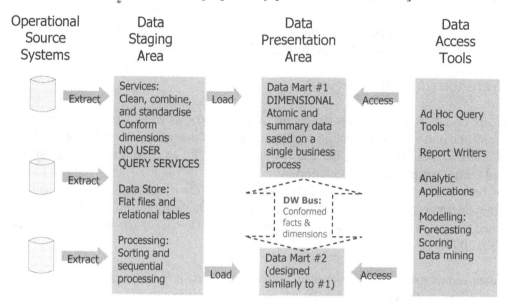

Note that data staging area does not provide presentation services to the business users, in other words business users are not the direct consumers of the ETL process' output;

- **Data presentation area:** this is where the data is organised and stored, ready to be accessed by the business users. The storage is modelled as a series of data marts, depending on the specific business requirements, all conforming to the data warehouse bus architecture. For more details on *data marts* and *bus architecture* we refer the reader to [Kimball & Ross, 2002], whose authors have actually introduced these concepts in the warehousing literature;
- **Data access tools:** this is a collection of ad hoc query tools, report writers, data mining applications etc, all designed to query, report or analyse data stored in the data warehouse;

The data warehouse architecture described above was proposed for traditional relational databases, where the data is structured and therefore easier to manipulate. In the case of other types of complex data though, this architecture might need some alterations to support the complex scenarios (for example the case of warehousing dynamic and temporal web XML data).

Latest Trends and Advancements in Data Warehousing

Nowadays the information is very dynamic and many applications create huge amounts of data everyday. For example, millions of transactions are completed continuously in large online shops (e.g. Amazon, EBay etc), many banking systems, share markets etc. Companies in the entire world are in a tight competition to provide better services and attract more clients. Hence, an easy customer access to web applications and the ability to perform transactions anytime from anywhere has been the fastest growing feature of the business applications in the last few years.

More, the data itself cannot be labelled as "simple" anymore (that is, numerical or symbolic) but it can now be expressed in different formats (structured, unstructured, images, sounds etc), it can come from different sources, or can be temporal (that is, it would change its structure and/or values in time) [Darmont & Boussaïd, 2006]. Consequently, different types of storage, manipulation and processing are required in order to manage this complex data. New visions on data warehousing and data mining are therefore required.

During the last few years we could witness a growing amount of research work, determined by the growing size of the data warehouses which need to be build, the more and more heterogeneous data which needs to be integrated and stored, and the complex tools needed to query it. This section discusses therefore some of the trends in the area.

Spatial Data Warehousing

This is an area concerned with integration of spatial data with multidimensional data analysis techniques. The term 'spatial' is used in a geographical sense, meaning data that includes descriptors about how objects are located on Earth. Mainly, this is done using coordinates.

There are quite a few types of data which can be considered as spatial, as follows: data obtained via mobile devices (e.g. GPS), geo-sensory data, data about land usage etc. These types of data are collected either by private companies (e.g. mobile data) or by public governmental bodies (e.g. land data). Because this type of information could be used to take security decisions, spatial data warehousing becomes therefore a key techniques in enabling access to data and data analysis for decision making support.

Spatial data warehousing can be seen as an integration of two main techniques: spatial data handling and multidimensional data analysis [Damiani & Spaccapietra, 2006].

Spatial data handling can be done using two types of systems:

- **Spatial database management systems:** these extend the functionality of regular DBMS by including features for efficient storage, manipulation and querying of spatial data. Two such commercial spatial DBMS are Oracle Spatial and IBM DB2 Spatial Extender [Damiani & Spaccapietra, 2006]. Note that spatial DBMS are not for direct end-user usage, but would be interrogated by database specialists to produce reports, various analyses etc;
- **GIS (Geographical Information System):** is an integration of computer programs written to read and represent information from a spatial DBMS, and present it in a nice visual way to the end-user. Note that, in this case the end-user would be the direct consumer of the GIS output, without the need of a database specialist's help;

Multidimensional data analysis is a leading technique in many domains, where various quantitative variables are measured against dimensions, such as time, location, product etc. Information is stored in cubes, at the intersection between selected dimensions, and offers the possibility of analysis by drilling-down, rolling-up, slicing, dicing etc.

By integrating spatial data with multidimensional data analysis technique, spatial information can be studied from different perspectives, including a spatial dimension. This integration is already very powerful in existing business systems, for example in warehousing enterprise information, where localisation of data could be decisive. Figure 2 shows graphically the benefits of a spatial data warehouse for a national supermarket in US in answering business queries about the customer habits, sales breakup on regions, stores etc.

Nevertheless, spatial data warehousing is still a young research area, where multidimensional models are yet to be determined and implemented. The reason why this area is a step behind the business domains is because spatial data is peculiar and complex, and spatial data management technology has only recently reached maturity [Damiani & Spaccapietra, 2006].

Figure 2 Benefits of a spatial data warehouse – updated from [ESRI, 1998]

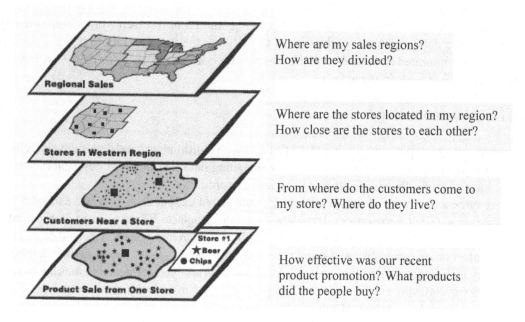

Research work in this area started ten years ago with the introduction of concepts of 'spatial dimension' and 'spatial measure' by [Han et al, 1998]. Following that, most recent research literature in spatial data warehousing includes: Rivest et al (2001), Fidalgo et al (2004), Scotch & Parmantoa (2005), Zhang & Tsotras (2005) and many others. As at 2006, a comprehensive and formal data model for spatial data warehousing was still a major research issue. The authors of [Damiani & Spaccapietra, 2006] proposed a novel spatial multidimensional data model for spatial objects with geometry, called Multigranular Spatial Data Warehouse (MuSD) where they suggest representing spatial information at multiple levels of granularity.

Future work and trends identified in spatial data warehousing are related to storage, manipulation and analysis of complex spatial objects. These are objects that cannot be represented using geometries such as lines, polygons etc, but they are spatio-temporal and continuous object: an example is the concept of trajectory of a moving entity. Research is focused nowadays on obtaining summarised data out of database of trajectories, by using the concept of similarity and proposing new methods of measuring this similarity.

Text Data Warehousing

Recently, this area has known more and more research interest, because in an enterprise setting the data which needs to be stored in a data warehouse does not usually come only from the operational database systems, but also from a range of other sources (such as email, documents, reports). Generally, it can be said that in an enterprise environment the information lives in structured, unstructured and semi-structured sources. In order to integrate data from structured systems (relational databases) with the structured or unstructured data, current approaches use Information Retrieval techniques. Other approaches propose to use Information Extraction paradigms. We present here some of the research work which use these approaches.

In order to incorporate text documents into a data warehouse where the data from structured systems is also stored, the same components and steps of the warehousing process, including ETL (Extract-Transform-Load), need to be followed [Kimball & Ross, 1996; Kimball & Ross, 2002]. The source documents need to be identified, then the documents need to undergo some transformations (e.g. striping emails of their header and storing them as separate entities, or striping documents of their format and storing only the text component); eventually, the documents are physically moved into the data warehouse.

For each document, two components need to be stored in the data warehouse: the document itself and the metadata (this is, information about the document which can be read by the computer, e.g. size, title, subject, version, author etc). The metadata is stored in the data warehouse in a separate section, called metadata repository. Kimball (2002) deems that, for highly complex metadata, even a small star schema can be constructed, where the fact table would store the actual documents, while the different types of metadata would be stored in dimensions.

To store the document content itself, Information Retrieval approaches treat it as a "bag of words". Each word from the document is scanned and tokenised, the linking and stop words are removed, and the output of the procedure is a list of words—where each word receives a weight, based on the number of its appearances in the initial text. The output is used in so called "inverted index", where an index is created by sorting the list of terms and, for each term, a list of documents which contain each term is kept. Other more complex indexes also keep the number of appearances, or the position(s) where the term appears, in order to support proximity queries [Badia, 2006]. In a vector-space approach, queries are represented as vectors of query terms (where the non-content words have been removed) and answering those queries actually means to find the document vectors of terms which are closest to the query vector.

The IR (Information Retrieval) approaches are criticised because they only utilise the physical terms appearing in the documents, while these terms are "(at best) second-order indicators of the content of a document". More, the vector-space approach has some issues related to the usage of words as such, especially where synonyms, homonyms, and other relationships can appear (research work has proposed to solve these issues by employing the concept of 'thesaurus') [Badia, 2006].

Information Extraction (IE) is another approach employed to solve text data warehousing problem. In this case, the input collection of documents are analysed using "shallow parsing" to perform entity extraction (to determine which entities are referred to in the text), link extraction (to determine which entities are in any sort of relationships) and event extraction (to determine what events are described by the entities and links discovered). The information extracted would then be integrated into a data warehouse.

It is possible that IR-oriented techniques would dominate the text warehousing area for a while, because there is still a lot of research work proposing solutions to deal with the identified issues. However, it is prognosed that IE approaches will see a rapid growing in the near future, fuelled by the boost in requests for text mining and consequently for more efficient text warehousing techniques [Badia, 2006].

Web Data Warehousing

As mentioned in the Introduction section, web data has been an increasing presence nowadays, because the World Wide Web offers the foundation for many large scale web applications to be developed.

The language of choice for web applications is XML (eXtensible Markup Language). It is a well-known fact that the industry has lately started to use XML heavily in a wide range of areas such as data exchange, as a vehicle for straight-through-processing (STP) in the online banking system, for data exchange between various layers in a multi-tiered system architecture, for development of web services, standard representation of business requirements for reporting purposes, etc. The domains where XML

Figure 3. Distribution of XML sites by zone (from [Mignet et al, 2003])

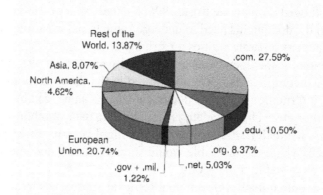

is used are very diverse, from technology to financial services, medical systems, bioinformatics, etc. Consequently, we have witnessed a rapid increase in the amount of information being represented in XML format, which has triggered the need for researchers to investigate a number of issues associated with XML storage, querying and analysis.

One area of research is *XML warehousing*. It has been predicted that soon most of the stored data will be in XML format [Pardede E., 2007]. Other authors also predict that XML will become the 'lingua franca' of the web [Mignet et al, 2003]. It is therefore critical that efficient and scalable XML warehousing techniques should exist. At the same time, the great flexibility of the XML format for data representation and the dynamicity of available XML data increase the difficulty which is naturally associated with the task of storing huge amounts of information.

In this section we first look at the growing popularity of XML, and then at some issues and research requirements brought in recently by the XML warehousing.

XML Format Popularity

A study dated 2003 concluded that, despite its infancy at that time, XML had already permeated the web [Mignet et al, 2003]. That is, at the time of the study, XML documents could be found in all major internet domains and in all geographic regions of the globe. In 2003, the '.com' and '.net' domains combined contained 53% of the documents and 76% of the volume of the XML content on the web (see Figure 3).

More, only 48% of the documents referenced a Document Type Definition (DTD) [W3C-XML 1.0] and a surprising figure of only 0.09% of the analysed XML documents were referencing an XML schema.

The same study showed that generally the XML documents were small (with an average size at that date of 4kB), but they were shallow (with 99% of the XML documents having fewer than 8 levels of elements nesting). Moreover, the volume of markup tags was very large compared with the actual content of the documents.

Naturally, things have evolved since 2003, and nowadays the volume of data formatted using XML is even higher. While there are no certain figures to tell the XML data size and usage distribution as at 2009 (the current year), the extent to which XML is used as a standard format for data exchange and representation in many domains indicate its wide usage nowadays. A few representative examples are as follows:

- *GPX* (the GPS Exchange Format) – this is a light-weight XML data format for the interchange of GPS data between application and Web services on the Internet [GPX, 2008];
- *HL7* (Health Level Seven) – this is an ANSI-accredited organisation in the domain of clinical and administrative data, which uses XML since 1996. A special 'XML interest group' exists within HL7, with the declared objective to employ XML to create standardised templates of healthcare documentation [HL7, 2008];
- *FIX* (Financial Information eXchange) – this is a standard communication protocol for equity trading data. The FIXML (FIX Markup Language) creates business messages for the FIX protocol using XML format [Ogbuji, 2004];
- *XBLR* (eXtensible Business Reporting Language) – this is an XML-based specification for preparation and exchange of financial reports and data [Ogbuji, 2004];
- *XPDL* (XML Process Definition Language) – this uses XML to represent the BPM (Business Process Management) processes. It is considered the most widely deployed process definition language, and is used in many applications such as ERP (Enterprise Resource Planning), CRM (Customer Relationship Management), BI (Business Intelligence), workflow, etc [WfMC, 2008];
- *BPEL* (Business Process Execution Language) – this is an entirely different standard but complementary to XPLD. BPEL is an 'execution language' which uses XML to provide a definition of web services orchestration (the executable aspects of a business process, when the process is dealing with web services and XML data) [WfMC, 2008];

The above list gives just a small number of examples indicating how widely used XML is nowadays.

XML Data Warehousing

In line with the increasing use of XML documents for the exchange of information between different legacy systems and for representing semi-structured data in web applications, XML data warehousing has started to pose diverse issues to the researchers and practitioners [Buchner et al., 2000; Marian et al., 2001; Xyleme, L., 2001]. As in traditional data warehousing, the design of the most suitable and efficient structural storage systems has been one of the main focuses of XML data warehousing.

In a number of previous research works we proposed to distinguish between static and dynamic XML documents [Rusu et al, 2005; Rusu et al, 2006; Rusu et al, 2008], based on the representation of temporal coverage and persistency of the rendered information. In other words, a static XML document does not contain an element which indicates how long the document is valid. Conversely, a dynamic XML document inherently contains at least one element which indicates the temporal coverage of the specific version of the document. Hence, the analysis of the state of the art work in the area of XML data warehousing can be also split in two: first we will discuss the problem of warehousing data from static XML documents, and then we will examine existing work and issues identified in warehousing data from dynamic (multi-versioned) XML documents.

Warehousing static XML documents first became a research focus as early as 2001-2002. Few major directions have started to emerge, as follows:

- *Design of XML warehouses based on user requirements and needs*—In this case, researchers look at the issue of warehousing XML documents by taking the user's point of view. That is, the user's needs in terms of possible future queries on the XML data warehouse are considered to be most critical. [Zhang et al., 2003, Boussaid et al., 2006];

- *Design of XML warehouses based on XML schema or Document Type Definition (DTD)*—In this case, the structure of the XML documents is considered to be the most important aspect which needs to be carried into the XML warehouse's structure. That is, the parent-child and sibling relationships in the XML structural hierarchy need to be also found in the final XML data warehouse. Few works in this area are [Golfarelli et al., 2001, Vrdoljak et al., 2003; Pokorny, 2001; Pokorny, 2002];
- *Conceptual design of XML document warehouses*—Conceptual modelling is widely used for database design or software engineering. The most frequent used methods are ER (entity-relationships) diagrams, data flow diagrams, system flowcharts, UML (Unified Modeling Language), etc. Two works which present a conceptual design for an XML warehouse are [Nassis et al., 2004] and [Nassis et al., 2006];
- *Design of XML warehouses as XML data summary*—Some researchers believe that the amount of XML data which needs to be warehoused will increase so much that it will be huge and almost impossible to warehouse and query. Therefore, they propose to warehouse a summary of the XML data instead of actual data, in such a way that the result of queries is not affected. [Comai et al., 2003];
- *Analysis of XML warehouses using OLAP*—In this case, researchers look at the traditional multidimensional warehousing, which has fact document(s) and dimensions, and try to apply the same OLAP techniques, traditionally applied to the relational data, on the warehoused XML data. Several works in this category are [Huang and Su, 2002; Hummer et al., 2003; Park et al., 2005].
- *Integrated XML document management*—In this case, researchers investigate how different XML documents can be integrated with other type of data (text documents, media files etc), or how the information from geographically dispersed XML warehouses can be combined. Two works in this category are [Hsiao et al., 2003; Rajugan et al., 2005].

However, during the last several years, it has become clear that, due to the specific characteristics of the dynamic XML documents (temporality, unpredictability), they require a different warehousing solution from the static XML documents.

The research work in this area is still at the beginning. In our previous work [Rusu et al, 2006a], we proposed a framework for warehousing dynamic (multi-versioned) XML documents (see Figure 4). As it can be noticed in this framework, three main stages are involved in the warehousing process: Stage A identifies the changes between the incoming successive versions of the dynamic XML documents—the output of this stage is a collection of historical data and changes; in Stage B the data is cleaned and integrated, then in Stage C the final XML data warehouse is built by constructing the fact XML document(s) and the required dimensions. Note that the resultant warehouse is native XML, where all documents are stored in XML format.

Other works in the same area focus mostly on the management of changes between multiple versions of XML documents, and propose some storage policies for dynamic (multi-versioned) XML documents, as follows:

- *Representing changes from dynamic (multi-versioned) XML documents*—In this case, researchers looked at how the changes between consecutive versions of multi-versioned XML documents can be calculated and represented [Marian et al., 2001; Cobena et al., 2002; Chien et al., 2001; Chien et al., 2002; Wang et al., 2003]. In our earlier work [Rusu et al, 2005], we proposed a different solution to represent changes from multi-versioned XML documents, by using the concept of 'consolidated delta', which responds better to versioning queries;

Figure 4. General process of building XML data warehouse for dynamic XML documents [Rusu et al, 2006a]

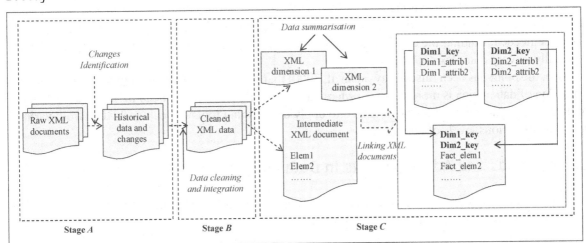

- *Storage policies for dynamic (multi-versioned) XML documents* – This focuses on finding efficient ways of storing data from multiple versions of XML documents, considering the constraints of similarity between consecutive versions and hence the possible high redundancy of information. Some proposals in this area are [Marian et al., 2001; Chien et al., 2002; Wang & Zaniolo, 2003]. Four different storage techniques were critically analysed and compared in [Rusu et al, 2008a] based on two efficiency indicators.

CURRENT TRENDS IN DATA MINING

This section will first give a high-level overview of data mining, followed by a discussion of some of the latest trends and research work advancements in this domain.

Data Mining: An Overview

As mentioned earlier in this chapter, modern days' data cannot be labelled as 'simple' anymore. The more and more heterogenous, complex and peculiar data in various domains, the more and more intelligent techniques required to mine it and extract interesting knowledge out of it.

Data mining is a compilation of techniques, methods and algorithms utilised in order to extract knowledge hidden in huge amounts of data, being therefore much more than a list of statistical formulas applied on a collection of data. Few major groups of data mining tasks are [Fayyad et al, 2000]:

- Predictive modelling (classification, regression)
- Descriptive modelling (clustering)
- Pattern discovery (discovering association rules, frequent sequences etc)
- Dependency modelling and causality (graphical models, density estimation)
- Change and deviation detection/modelling

Each data mining tasks would usually reveal a different type of interesting knowledge from the mined data; hence at one point only one task is applied in order to find a specific type of information. For example the task of discovering relationship between data items would require an association rules algorithm, while for grouping data in sets (clusters) based on their similarity a clustering algorithm would be needed. Finding the actual algorithm which suits better to a specific problem is a challenge, especially in very complex applications.

Also, the point has been raised [Fayyad et al, 2000] that research study of data mining tasks assume a collection of data which is more cleaner, ordered and correctly labelled than can be found in real world applications. Hence, there is a growing need to apply data mining tools on real world data from various domains, of various levels of complexity.

Latest Trends and Advancements in Data Mining

Current research work in data mining focuses on complex applications of data mining tasks; this section discusses therefore some of the trends in this area.

Knowledge Discovery from Genetic and Medical Data

During the last few years, bioinformatics has attracted a lot of attention, from both biologists and data mining specialists. The most critical application in this domain has been extracting patterns (that is, full biological information) from gene expression data.

Typical tasks in gene expression data mining include clustering, classification and association rules discovery, on extensive microarray data [Han et al, 2006]:

- Clustering techniques can be used to identify genes which are co-regulated in a similar manner under different experimental conditions. One-way clustering groups the genes separately, while two-way clustering groups the genes by taking the relationship between them in consideration.

Some of the work in gene expression clustering is focused on: K-ary clustering [Bar-Joseph et al, 2003], dynamically growing self-organisation trees [Luo et al, 2004], fuzzy K-means clustering [Gasch & Eisen, 2002], and many others.

- *Classification* helps in identifying differences between cells, for example healthy (normal) cells from cancer cells. Most current approaches attempt to differentiate groups of genes with similar functionality in an unsupervised mode (that is, without prior knowledge of their true functional classes).

Some of the work in genes expression classification is focused on: support vector machine [Furrey, 2000], Bayesian classification [Moler et al, 2000], emerging patterns [Boulesteix et al, 2003], and many others.

- *Association rules* can show how some genes influence the expression of other genes in regulatory pathways.

Some of the work in discovering association rules in gene expression data investigates distance based association rule mining [Icev et al, 2003], finding association rule groups [Cong et al, 2004], frequent pattern mining [Pan et al, 2003], etc.

Text Mining

This category of data mining focuses on extracting useful patterns from text data. Text is the most available option for everyday people of storing and exchanging data: an important part of information exchanged in any company would be via e-mails, reports, notes, memos, etc. Hence, a lot of the specialists' knowledge might not get to be stored formally in a database or a document storage system, but it can be 'hidden' in piles of unstructured or semi-structured text. More, we witness everyday an exponential growth of the text information publicly available on the web, in electronic databases, libraries, discussion forums etc.

Due to the widespread use and exponential growth of this type of information, a manual analysis would be an unrealistic task. Text mining comes therefore to automate the search, filtering or clustering large amounts of text data (text- or hypertext databases) in order to make use of the hidden information with it.

Several possible applications of text mining are as follows (and the list is not exhaustive):

- *Analysis of customer profile* – this can be extracted from complaints, suggestion/feedback forms, etc;
- *Personalised information service* – for example the distribution of newsletters, invitations etc based on customer profile;
- *Personal or national security* – scanning emails and messages to identify spam, information leakage, possible threats etc;
- *Plagiarism detection* – identifying text repeated in multiple publications, without acknowledging the contribution of the original author.

During the last few years, Academia has put in a lot of effort in text mining research. For example, a Text-Mining Research Group has been established at the University of West Bohemia (Czech Republic) with the long-term objective of creating "a robust system to extract knowledge from semi-structured data in a multi-language web environment in order to infer new information / knowledge that is not contained explicitly in the original data" [TMRG, 2009]. Their research work has been around automatic text summarization [Ježek & Steinberger, 2008; Steinberger, 2007], plagiarism detection [Češka, 2008; Češka et al, 2008], detection of authoritative sources [Fiala, 2007], etc.

Due to the increased accessibility of people to various resources on the web, future work in text mining will very likely continue to be around plagiarism detection, social networks mining, filtering and classifying web sites based on the text content, etc.

XML Data Mining

Another emerging area of data mining research is *XML mining*. The effort of storing a huge amount of data in XML format into an effective warehouse structure should not be rewarded only by a number (albeit a high number) of successful queries applied on the warehoused data. Hence, researchers have identified an opportunity to consider various mining tasks which could be applied to the XML data to discover hidden interesting information such as association rules, clusters, classification, frequent patterns etc.

XML mining includes both *mining of structures* as well as *mining of contents* from XML documents [Nayak et al., 2002; Nayak, 2005]. Mining of structure is seen as essentially mining the XML schema and it includes *intra-structure mining* and *inter-structure mining*. Mining of content consists of *content analysis* and *structure clarification* (see Figure 5).

Figure 5. Main types of XML data mining tasks (updated from [Nayak, 2005])

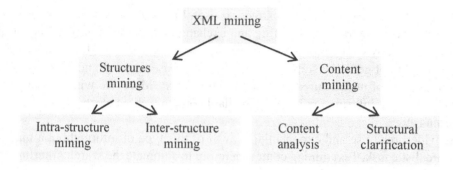

The concepts in Figure 4 can be explained as follows:

- *Intra-structure mining* is concerned with mining the structure inside an XML document, where tasks of classification, clustering or association rules discovering could be applied;
- *Inter-structure mining* is concerned with mining the structures between XML documents, where the applicable tasks could be clustering schemas and defining hierarchies of schemas on the web, and classification applied with namespaces and URIs – Uniform Resources Identifiers;
- *Content analysis* is concerned with analysing texts within the XML document;
- *Structural clarification* is concerned with determining the similar documents, based on their content.

As mentioned previously in the 'XML data warehousing' section, XML documents can be static or dynamic. Therefore during the last few years, research work in mining XML documents has focused on mining both static and dynamic (multi-versioned) XML data, for example: discovering association rules, clustering, finding frequent structural patterns, mining changes between XML document versions etc. We mention here few of the works in these domains:

- *Discovering association rules from static XML documents*—Most of the work done in the area of mining association rules from static XML documents use XML-oriented algorithms based on the Apriori algorithm [Agrawal, 1993, 1998]. However, a number of non Apriori-based approaches have been also developed. Few works worth mentioning here are [Wan & Dobbie, 2003; Wan & Dobbie, 2004; Braga et al., 2002a; Braga et al., 2002b; Braga et al., 2003; Feng et al., 2003] and others;
- *Clustering static XML documents*—this type of clustering focuses on grouping XML documents in clusters based on their similarity. Clustering can be based on structural similarity [De Francesca et al., 2003; Liang et al., 2004; Costa et al., 2004], or structural and semantic similarity [Yoon et al., 2001; Shen & Wang, 2003]. Some XML clustering techniques are distance-based [Nierman & Jagadish, 2002; Dalamagas et al., 2004, Dalamagas et al., 2006; Xing et al., 2007];
- *Discovering association rules from dynamic (multi-versioned) XML documents*—The work in this area is still in its infancy, and only a limited number of existing works have addressed the issue of discovering association rules from multi-versioned XML documents. Few existing proposals in this area are [Chen et al., 2004; Rusu et al, 2006b, Rusu et al, 2006c].

- *Clustering dynamic (multi-versioned) XML documents* – This focuses on techniques to re-cluster collections of XML documents after some of the document have changed. One work which proposes such a technique is [Rusu et al, 2008b]. Also, some work has been done on clustering a series of XML documents, when each incoming XML document is different from the previous one and needs to be placed in the correct cluster. One work in this category is [Nayak and Xu, 2006];
- *Extracting patterns of structural changes from XML documents* – This type of works try to extract frequently changing structures from sequences of versions of dynamic XML documents, or sequences of deltas (that is, differences between versions). Few works in this category are [Zhao et al., 2004a; Zhao et al., 2004b; Zhao et al., 2006];

In our opinion, future work in XML mining will continue the research trends in discovering patterns and frequent changing structures from dynamic (multi-versioned) XML documents, and will also need to look at mining tasks which have not been extensively researched so far, such as clustering or classification dynamic XML documents.

CONCLUSION

The purpose of this chapter was to highlight some of the trends and advancements made by the research work in data warehousing and data mining. We showed that these trends are not limited to one area, but they are spread across multiple domains. That is, there is extensive research work in warehousing and mining text, spatial or medical data, and also in warehousing and mining XML data, which is increasingly used by many business applications.

Certainly, the applicability of data warehousing and mining research is not limited to the domains mentioned in this chapter. The other chapters of this book will detail more on such trends and advancements in other modern areas.

David Taniar
Clayton School of Information Technology
Monash University, Australia

Laura Irina Rusu
Department of Computer Science and Computer Engineering
La Trobe University, Australia

REFERENCES

Agrawal R., Imielinski, T. and Swami, A.N., Mining Association Rules between Sets of Items in Large Databases, In the *Proceedings of the 1993 ACM SIGMOD International Conference on Management of Data (SIGMOD 1993)*, pp. 207-216, Washington D.C., U.S., ACM Press, 1993

Agrawal R., Srikant, R., Fast Algorithms for Mining Association Rules, *Readings in Database Systems (3rd Edition.)*, pp.580-592, Morgan Kaufmann Publishers Inc, 1998

Badia, A., Text Warehousing: Present and Future, In *Processing and Managing Complex Data for Decision Support*, Idea Group Publishing, 2006

Bar-Joseph, Z., Demaine, E.D., Gifford, D.K., Srebro, N., Hamel, A.M. & Jaakkola, T.S., K-ary clustering with optimal leaf ordering for gene expression data, *Bioinformatics*, 19(9), pp. 1070-1078, 2003

Boulesteix, A., Tutz, G., & Strimmer, K., A CART-based approach to discover emerging patterns in microarray data, *Bioinformatics*, 19(18), pp. 2465-2472, 2003

Boussaid, O., Messaoud, R.B., Choquet, R. and Anthoard, S., 2006, X-Warehousing: An XML-Based Approach for Warehousing Complex Data, In Proceedings of the *10th East European Conference on Advances in Databases and Information Systems (ADBIS 2006)*, LNCS 4152, pp. 39-54, Springer, 2006

Braga, D., Campi, A., Klemettinen, M., and Lanzi, P.L., Mining Association Rules from XML data, In *Proceedings of the 4th International Conference on Data Warehousing and Knowledge Discovery (DaWak 2002)*, Lecture Notes in Computer Science, Volume 2454, pp.21-30, Springer, 2002

Braga D., Campi A., Ceri S., Klementinen M., and Lanzi P.L., A tool for extracting XML association rules, *Proceedings of the 14th International Conference on Tools with Artificial Intelligence (ICTAI '02)*, pp.57, Washington, DC, USA, 2002

Braga, D., Campi, A. and Ceri, S., Discovering Interesting Information in XML with Association Rules, *Proceedings of 2003 ACM symposium on Applied Computing (SAC'03)*, pp.450-454, Melbourne, Florinda, USA, 2003

Chen, L., Bhowmick, SS. and Chia, L.T., Mining Association Rules from Structural Deltas of Historical XML Documents, In Proceeding of the *8th Pacific-Asia Conference on Advances in Knowledge Discovery and Data Mining (PAKDD 2004)*, Lecture Notes in Computer Science, vol. 3056, pp.452-457, Springer, 2004

Comai, S., Marrara, S., and Tanca, L., Representing and Querying Summarised XML Data, In Proceedings of the *14th International Conference on Database and Expert Systems Applications (DEXA 2003)*, Lecture Notes in Computer Science, vol. 2736, pp.171-181, Springer, 2003

Cong, G., Tung, A.K.H., Xu, T.X., Pan, F., & Yang, J., Finding interesting rule groups in microarray datasets, Proceed of the ACM SIGMOD *Intl. Conf. on Management of Data*, pp. 143-154, ACM 2004

Costa G., Manco G., Ortale R. and Tagarelli, A., A Tree-Based Approach to Clustering XML documents by Structure, *Proceedings of the 8th European Conference on Principles and Practice of Knowledge Discovery in Databases (PKDD 2004)*, Lecture Notes in Computer Science, vol. 3202, pp. 137-148, 2004

Česka, Z., Free-text plagiarism detection based on latent semantic analysis, Technical Report no DCSE/TR-2008-01, Pilsen, Czech Republic, April 2008

Česka, Z., Toman, M., Ježek, K., Multilingual Plagiarism Detection, Proceedings of the *13th International Conference on Artificial Intelligence: Methodology, Systems, Applications (AIMSA 2008)*, Varna, Bulgaria, Lecture Notes in Artificial Intelligence, 5253, pp. 83-92, Springer, 2008

Dalamagas, T., Cheng, T., Winkel, K.J. and Sellis, T., Clustering XML documents by Structure, *In Proceedings of the 3rd Helenic Conference on AI (SETN 2004)*, Lecture Notes in Computer Science, vol. 3025, pp. 112-121, Springer, 2004

Dalamagas, T., Cheng, T., Winkel, K.J. and Sellis, T., A methodology for clustering XML documents by structure, *Information System Journal*, vol. 31, 187-228, 2006

Damiani, M. L. & Spaccapietra, S., Spatial Data Warehouse Modelling, In *Processing and Managing Complex Data for Decision Support*, Idea Group Publishing, 2006

Darmont, J. & Boussaïd, O., *Processing and Managing Complex Data for Decision Support*, Idea Group Publishing, 2006

De Francesca, F., Gordano, G., Ortale, R. and Tagarelli, A., Distance-based Clustering of XML Documents, *1st International Workshop on Mining Graphs, Trees and Sequences (MGTS '03)*—in conjunction with PKDD '03, pp. 75-78, Croatia, September 22-26, 2003

Environmental Systems Research Institute (ESRI), Spatial Data Warehousing, White paper, March 1998, online at www.geoweb.dnv.org / Education / whitepapers

Fayyad, U., Chaudhuri, S. & Bradley, P., *Data Mining and its Role in Database Systems*, Tutorial at the International Conference on Very Large Databases, 2000

Feng, L., Dillon, T., Wiegand H. and Chang E., An XML – Enabled Association Rules Framework, *In Proceedings of International Conference on Database and Expert Systems Applications (DEXA 2003)*, Lecture Notes in Computer Science, vol. 2736, pp.88-97, Springer, 2003

Fiala, D., Web Mining methods for the detection of Authoritative Sources, PhD thesis, University of West Bohemia in Pilsen, Czech Republic and Louis Pasteur University Strasbourg, France, 2007, online at http://textmining.zcu.cz

Fidalgo, R.N., Times, V.C., Silva, J., & Souza, F. (2004), GeoDWFrame: a framework for guiding the design of geographical dimensional schemas, Proceedings of the *6th International Conference on Data Warehousing and Knowledge Discovery (DaWaK 2004)*, LNCS 3181, pp. 26-37, 2004

Furrey, T., Cristianini, N. Duffy, N., Bednarski, D., Schummer, M. & Haussler, D., Support vector machine classification and validation of cancer tissue using microarray expression data, *Bioinformatics*, 16(10), pp. 906-914, 2000

Gasch, A.P. & Eisen, M.B., Exploring the conditional regulation of yeast gene expression through fuzzy k-means clustering, *Genome Biology*, 3(11), 2002

Golfarelli, M., Rizzi, S. and Vrdoljak, B., Data Warehouse Design from XML Sources, In Proceedings of the *4th ACM International Workshop on Data Warehousing and OLAP (DOLAP'01)*, pp.40-47, ACM 2001

GPS Exchange Format (GPX), available online at http://www.topografix.com/gpx.asp, 2008

Han, J., Gruenwald, L. & Conway, T., Data Mining in Gene Expression Data Analysis: a Survey, In *Processing and Managing Complex Data for Decision Support*, Idea Group Publishing, 2006

Health Level Seven (HL7), online at http://www.hl7.org/about/hl7about.htm, 2008

Hsiao, H., Hui, J., Li, N. and Tijare, P., Integrated XML Document Management, In *Proceedings of EEXTT and DIWeb 2002*, Lecture Notes in Computer Science, vol. 2590, 47-67, Springer, 2003

Huang, S.-M. and Su, C.-H., The Development of an XML-Based Data Warehouse System, In *Proceedings of the 3rd International Conference on Intelligent Data Engineering and Automated Learning (IDEAL 2002)*, pp.206-212, Lecture Notes in Computer Science, vol. 2412, Springer, 2002

Hummer, W., Bauer, A. and Harde, G., XCube: XML for data warehouses, In *Proceedings of the ACM 6th International Workshop on Data Warehousing and OLAP (DOLAP 2003)*, New Orleans, USA, ACM 2003, 33-40, 2003

Icev, A., Ruiz, C. & Ryder, E.F., Distance-enhanced association rules for gene expression, Proceed of 3rd ACM SIGKDD *Workshop on Data Mining in Bioinformatics*, ACM 2003

Inmon, W.H., *Building the Data Warehouse*, Wiley, 2005

Ježek, K., & Steinberger, J., Automatic Text Summarization (The state of the art 2007 and new challenges), In Proceedings of Znalosti 2008, Bratislava, Slovakia, pp. 1–12, 2008

Kimball, R., *The Data Warehouse Toolkit*, Wiley & Sons, 1996

Kimball, R., Ross, M., *The Data Warehouse Toolkit*, Wiley & Sons, 2002

Liang, W., Cheung, D.W., Mamoulis, N. and Yiu, S-M., An Efficient and Scalable Algorithm for Clustering XML Documents by Structure, *IEEE Transactions on Knowledge and Data Engineering*, 16(1), pp. 82-96, IEEE Computer Society, 2004

Luo, F., Khan, L., Bastani, F., Yen, I. & Zhou, J., A dynamically growing self-organisation tree (DGSOT) for hierarchical clustering gene expression profiles, *Bioinformatics*, 20(16), pp. 2605-2617, 2004

Marakas, G. M., *Modern Data Warehousing, Mining, and Visualisation*, Prentice-Hall, 2003

Mignet, L., Barbosa, D. and Veltri, P., The XML Web: A first study, In *Proceed. of the 12th International World Wide Web Conference (WWW 2003)*, Budapest, Hungary, pp. 500-510, ACM 2003

Moler, E.J., Radisky, D.C. & Mian, I.S., Integrating naïve Bayes models and external knowledge to examine copper and iron homeostasis in S. cerevisiae, *Physiol Genomics*, 4(2), pp. 127-135, 2000

Nassis V., Rajugan, R., Dillon, T. And Rahayu, W., Conceptual Design of XML Document Warehouses, In Proceedings of *the 6th International Conference on Data Warehousing and Knowledge Discovery (DaWaK 2004)*, Lecture Notes in Computer Science, vol. 3181, pp. 1-14, Springer , 2004

Nassis, V., Dillon, T., Rajugan R. and Rahayu, W., An XML Document Warehouse Model, In Proceedings of the *11th International Conference on Database Systems for Advanced Applications (DASFAA 2006)*, Lecture Notes in Computer Science, vol. 3882, pp. 513-529, Springer , 2006

Nayak, R., Witt, R. and Tonev, A., Data Mining and XML documents, *Proceedings of the 2002 International Conference on Internet Computing (IC 2002)*, pp.660-666, June 24-27, Nevada, USA, CSREA Press, 2002

Nayak, R., Discovering Knowledge from XML Documents, In Wong, J. (Ed.), *Encyclopaedia of Data Warehousing and Mining*, Idea Group Publications, 2005

Nayak, R., Xu, S., 2006, XCLS: A Fast and Effective Clustering Algorithm for Heterogeneous XML Documents, In *Proceedings of the 10th Pacific-Asia Conference on Advances in Knowledge Discovery and Data Mining (PAKDD 2006)*, Singapore, Lecture Notes in Computer Science, vol. 3918, pp. 292-302, Springer, 2006

Nierman, H. and Jagadish, V., Evaluating Structural Similarity in XML documents, In *Proceedings of the 5th International Workshop on Web and Databases*, June 2002

Ogbuji, Uche, Thinking XML: A glimpse into XML in the financial services industry, Fourthought, Inc., 2004, online at http://www.ibm.com/developerworks/xml/library/x-think22.html, 2008

Pan, F., Cong, G. & Tung, A.K.H., Carpenter: finding closed patterns in long biological datasets and data mining, Proceed of the 9th ACM SIGKDD *Intl Conf on Knowledge Discovery and Data Mining*, pp. 637-642, ACM 2003

Pardede, E., 2007 – *eXtensible Markup Language (XML) Document Update in XML Database Storages*, PhD thesis, LaTrobe University, Australia, 2007

Park, B.K., Han, H. and Song, I.L., XML-OLAP: A Multidimensional Analysis Framework for XML Warehouses, In Proceedings of the *7th International Conference on Data Warehousing and Knowledge Discovery (DaWaK 2005)*, LNCS 3589, Springer, 32-42, 2005

Pokorny, J., Modelling Stars Using XML, *Proceedings of the 4th ACM Workshop on Data Warehousing and OLAP (DOLAP 2001)*, pp.24-31, Atlanta, ACM 2001

Pokorny, J., XML Data Warehouse: Modeling and Querying, In Proceedings of the *5th International Conference on Databases and Information Systems II (Baltic DB&IS 2002)*, pp. 67-80, Estonia, Kluwer Academic Publishers, 2002

Rajugan, R, Chang, E. and Dillon, T., Conceptual Design of an XML FACT Repository for Dispersed XML Document Warehouses and XML Marts, In Proceedings of the *5th International Conference on Computer and Information Technology (CIT 2005)*, 141-149, IEEE Computer Society, 2005

Rivest, S., Bedard, Y. & Marchand, P., Towards better support for spatial decision making: Defining the characteristics of spatial on-line analytical processing (SOLAP). *Geomatica*, 55(4), pp. 539-555, 2001

Rusu, L.I., Rahayu, W. and Taniar, D., D., Maintaining Versions of Dynamic XML Documents, In Proceedings of the *6th International Conference on Web Information Systems Engineering (WISE 2005)*, New York, USA, Lecture Notes in Computer Science, vol. 3806, pp.536-543, Springer , 2005

Rusu, L.I., Rahayu, W. and Taniar, D., Warehousing Dynamic XML Documents, In Proceedings of the *8th International Conference on Data Warehousing and Knowledge Discovery (DaWaK 2006)*, Lecture Notes in Computer Science, vol. 4081, Springer, 175-184, 2006

Rusu, L.I., Rahayu, W. and Taniar, D., Extracting Variable Knowledge from Multi-Versioned XML Documents, Workshop Proceedings of the *6th IEEE International Conference on Data Mining (ICDM 2006)*, IEEE Computer Society, pp. 70-74, Hong Kong, China, 2006

Rusu, L.I., Rahayu, W. and Taniar, D., Mining Changes from Versions of Dynamic XML Documents, Proceedings of the *1st International Workshop on Knowledge Discovery from XML Documents (KDXD 2006)*, LNCS 3915, Springer, pp. 3-12, Singapore, 2006

Rusu, L.I., Rahayu, W. and Taniar, D., Storage Techniques for Multi-versioned XML Documents, *In Proceedings of the 13th International Conference DASFAA 2008*, New Delhi, India, March 19-21, Lecture Notes in Computer Science, vol. 4947, 538-545, 2008

Rusu, L.I., Rahayu, W. and Taniar, D., Intelligent Dynamic XML Documents Clustering, Proceedings of the *22nd International Conference on Advanced Information Networking and Applications (AINA 2008)*, IEEE Computer Society, pp. 449-456, Okinawa, Japan, 2008

Scotch, M. & Parmantoa, B., SOVAT: Spatial OLAP visualisation and analysis tool, Proceedings of the *38th Hawaii International Conference on System Sciences*, 2005

Shen Y. and Wang B., Clustering Schemaless XML Documents, *On the Move to Meaningful Internet Systems*, pp. 767-784, Lecture Notes in Computer Science, vol. 2888, Springer 2003

Steinberger, J., Text summarization within the LSA Framework, PhD Thesis, University of West Bohemia in Pilsen, Czech Republic, January 2007, online at http://textmining.zcu.cz

Text-Mining Research Group, University of West Bohemia, Czech Republic, online at http://textmining.zcu.cz/, January 2009

Vrdoljak, B., Banek M. and Rizzi S., Designing Web Warehouses from XML Schema, In Proceedings of the *5th International Conference on Data Warehousing and Knowledge Discovery (DaWaK 2003)*, Lecture Notes in Computer Science, vol. 2737, pp. 89-98, Springer 2003

Xing, G., Xia, Z. and Guo, J., Clustering XML Documents Based on Structural Similarity, *In Proceedings of the 12th International Conference on Advances on Databases (DASFAA 2007)*, Lecture Notes in Computer Science, vol. 4443, pp.905-911, Springer, 2007

Zhao, Q., Bhowmick, S.S., Mohania, M. and Kambayashi, Y. Discovering Frequently Changing Structures from Historical Structural Deltas of Unordered XML, *Proceedings of the 2004 ACM International Conference on Information and Knowledge Management (CIKM 04)*, pp.188-197, November 8-13, Washington, US, ACM 2004

Zhao, Q., Bhowmick, S.S. and Mandria, S., Discovering Pattern-based Dynamic Structure from Versions of Unordered XML Documents, In Pr*oceedings of the 6th International Conference on Data Warehousing and Knowledge Discovery (DaWak 2004)*, Lecture Notes in Computer Science, vol. 3181, pp.77-86, Springer 2004

Zhao, Q., Chen, L., Bhowmick, S. and Mandria, S., XML structural delta mining: issues and challenges, *Data Knowledge Engineering*, 59 (3), pp. 627 – 651, Elsevier Science Publishers, 2006

Zhang, D., & Tsotras, V., Optimising spatial Min/Max aggregations, *The VLDB journal*, 14, pp. 170-181, 2005

Zhang J., Ling T.W., Bruckner R.M. and Tjoa A.M., 2003, Building XML Data Warehouse Based on Frequent Patterns in User Queries, In Proceedings of the *5th International Conference on Data Warehousing and Knowledge Discovery (DaWaK 2003)*, Lecture Notes in Computer Science, vol. 2737, pp. 99-108, Springer, 2003

Wan, J.W. and Dobbie, G., Extracting Association Rules from XML documents using XQuery, *Proceedings of the 5th ACM international workshop on Web information and data management (WIDM 2003)*, pp.94-97, ACM Press, 2003

Wan, J.W. and Dobbie, G., Mining association rules from XML data using XQuery, In *Proceedings of International Conference on Research and Practice in Information Technology (CRPIT 2004)*, pp. 169-174, Australian Computer Society, 2004

World Wide Web Consortium (W3C), XML 1.0 specifications, online at http://www.w3.org/TR/2000/ REC-xml-20001006

Workflow Management Coalition (WfMC), online at http://www.wfmc.org/standards/ publicdocuments. htm, 2008

Yoon, J. P., Raghavan, V., Chakilam, V., and Kerschberg, L., BitCube: A Three-Dimensional Bitmap Indexing for XML Documents. *Journal of Intelligent Information Systems, vol.* 17, 2-3, pp. 241-254, 2001

Chapter 1
A Methodology Supporting the Design and Evaluating the Final Quality of Data Warehouses

Maurizio Pighin
University of Udine, Italy

Lucio Ieronutti
University of Udine, Italy

ABSTRACT

The design and configuration of a data warehouse can be difficult tasks especially in the case of very large databases and in the presence of redundant information. In particular, the choice of which attributes have to be considered as dimensions and measures can be not trivial and it can heavily influence the effectiveness of the final system. In this article, we propose a methodology targeted at supporting the design and deriving information on the total quality of the final data warehouse. We tested our proposal on three real-world commercial ERP databases.

INTRODUCTION AND MOTIVATION

Information systems allow companies and organizations to collect a large number of transactional data. Starting from this data, datawarehousing provides architectures and tools to derive information at a level of abstraction suitable for supporting decision processes.

There are different factors influencing the effectiveness of a data warehouse and the quality of related decisions. For example, while the selection of good-quality operational data enable to better target the decision process in the presence of alternative choices (Chengalur-Smith, Ballou, & Pazer, 1999), poor-quality data cause information scrap and rework that wastes people, money, materials and facilities resources (Ballau,

Wang, Pazer, & Tayi, 1998; English, 1999; Wang & Strong, 1996a, 1996b).

We have recently started at facing the problem of data quality in data warehouses (Pighin & Ieronutti, 2007); at the beginning of our research, we have considered the semantics-based solutions that have been proposed in the literature, and then we moved towards statistical methods, since in a real-world scenario data warehouse-engineers typically have a partial knowledge and vision of a specific operational database (e.g., how an organization really uses the operational system) and related semantics and then they need a support for the selection of data required to build a data warehouse. We then propose a context-independent methodology that is able both to support the expert during the data warehouse creation and evaluate the final quality of taken design choices. The proposed solution is mainly focused on statistical and syntactical aspects of data rather on semantics and it is based on a set of metrics, each one designed with the aim of capturing a particular data feature.

However, since most design choices are based on semantic considerations, our goal is to propose a solution that can be coupled with semantics-based techniques (for instance the one proposed by Golfarelli, Maio, and Rizzi (1998)) to effectively drive design choices. In particular, our methodology results effective in the following situations:

- During the construction phase, it is able to drive the selection of an attribute in the case of multiple choices (i.e., redundant information); for example, when an attribute belongs to different tables of a given database or belongs to different databases (that is the typical scenario in these kind of applications). Additionally, it is able to evaluate the quality of each choice (i.e., the informative value added to the final data warehouse choosing a table and its attribute as measure or dimension).

- At the end of the data warehouse design, it measures in quantitative terms the final quality of the data warehouse. Moreover, in the case of data warehouses based on the same design choices (characterized by the same schema), our methodology is also able to evaluate how data really stored into the initial database influences the informative content of the resulting data warehouse.

To evaluate the effectiveness of our methodology in identifying attributes that are more suitable to be used as dimensions and measures, we have experimented proposed metrics on three real ERP (Enterprise Resource Planning) commercial systems. Two systems are based on a DB Informix running on Unix server and one is based on a DB Oracle running on Windows server. In the experiment, they are called respectively *DB01*, *DB02* and *DB03*. More specifically, our metrics have been tested on data collected by the selling subsystems.

In this article, we refer to measures and dimensions related to the data warehouse, and to metrics as the indexes defined in the methodology we propose for evaluating data quality and reliability. Moreover, we use DW and DB to identify respectively a decisional data warehouse and an operational database.

RELATED WORK

In the literature, different researchers have been focused on data quality in operational systems and a number of different definitions and methodologies have been proposed, each one characterized by different quality metrics. Although Wang (1996a) and Redman (1996) proposed a wide number of metrics that have become the reference models for data quality in operational systems, in the literature most works refer only to a limited subset (e.g., *accuracy, completeness, consistency* and *timeliness*).

Literature reviews (e.g., Wang, Storey, & Firth, 1995) highlighted that there is not a general agreement on data quality metrics; for example, *timeliness* has been defined by some researchers in terms of whether the data are out of date (Ballou & Pazer, 1985), while other researchers use the same term for identifying the availability of output on time (Karr, Sanil, & Banks, 2006; Kriebel, 1978; Scannapieco, Virgillito, Marchetti, Mecella, & Baldoni, 2004). Moreover, some of the proposed metrics, called *subjective metrics* (Wang & Strong, 1996a); require an evaluation made by questionnaires and/or interviews and then result more suitable for qualitative evaluations rather than quantitative ones. Jeusfeld, Quix, and Jarke (1998) adopt a metamodeling approach for linking quality measurements to different abstraction levels and user requirements, and propose a notation to formulate quality goals, queries and measurements.

Some researchers have been focused on automatic methods for conceptual schema development and evaluation. Some of these approaches (e.g., Phipps & Davis, 2002) include the possibility of using the user input to refine the obtained result. However, these solutions typically require to translate user requirements into a formal and complete description of a logical schema.

An alternative category of approaches employs statistical techniques for assessing data quality. For example, analyzing the statistical distributions of data it can provide useful information on data quality. In this context, an interesting work has been presented in (Karr et al., 2006), where a statistical approach has been experimented on two real databases; their work provided us with interesting cues and gave a strong motivation for our research.

A different category of techniques for assessing data quality concerns Cooperative Information Systems (CISs). In this context, the DaQuinCIS project proposed a methodology (Scannapieco et al., 2004) for quality measurement and improvement. The proposed solution is primarily based on the premise that CISs are characterized by high data replication (i.e., different copies of the same data are stored by different organizations). From data quality prospective, this feature offers the opportunity of evaluating and improving data quality on the basis of comparisons among different copies. Data redundancy has been effectively used not only for identifying mistakes, but also for reconciling available copies or selecting the most appropriate ones.

With respect to operational systems, additional factors influence the effectiveness of data warehouses and the quality of related decisions. For example, while in the context of operational systems the quality of data mainly depends on the design and production processes generating and integrating data, in data warehouses the choice of which attributes have to be considered as measures and which as dimensions heavily influence the data warehouse effectiveness.

PROPOSED INDEXES

In this Section, we describe the set of indexes we propose for evaluating how much an attribute of a given DB is suitable to be used for correctly building a DW.

Considering the whole set of definitions and metrics that have been proposed in the literature for assessing data quality of an operational DB, we identified the concepts *relevance* and *value-added* proposed by Wang (1996a) as the most appropriate ones for our analysis. Indeed, we are interested in identifying the set of attributes of a given DB storing relevant information and that could add value in decision processes. For such purpose, we identified a set of indexes referring to the following two types of DB entities:

- **Tables of a DB:** At a general level, we define a set of metrics highlighting which tables of a given DB could contain more/less relevant data.

- **Attributes of a table:** At a level of a single table, we define a set of metrics that help users in identifying which attributes of a given table would be more relevant for data analysis purposes.

All proposed indexes are normalized into the interval *[0, 1]*, where *0* indicates that the set of data belonging to the considered entity (attribute or table) does not provide value added from the data analysis point of view, while *1* indicates that it can play a fundamental role in supporting decision processes. In the following Sections, we separately present indexes referring to the above types of entities.

Indexes for Tables

In this section, we describe the set of metrics $M_{e=1..k}$ and corresponding indexes we propose for DB tables. With these metrics, we aim at taking into account that different tables could play different roles and then result more/less suitable for extracting measures and dimensions.

The global indicators $S_{m,j}$ and $S_{d,j}$ measuring how much the table t_j is suitable to extract measures and dimensions are derived by combining the indexes computed by the metrics $M_{e=1..k}$ using respectively the coefficients $C_{m,e}$ and $C_{d,e}$. These global indicators are used: (i) to support the selection of the tables for the DW construction, (ii) to differently weight the indexes computed on the attributes belonging to different tables.

In particular, the two indexes $S_{m,j}$ and $S_{d,j}$ are derived as described in Formula 1.

$$S_{p,j} = \frac{\sum_{e=1}^{k} \left(C_{p,e} * M_e(t_j) \right)}{k} \tag{1}$$

where: (i) $p = d$ or m (d = dimension, m = measure); (ii) $e = 1, ..., k$ identifies the metric; (iii) $j = 1,...,q$ identifies the table; (iv) $C_{p,e}$ is the coefficient of the table-metric e.

In the following, we first introduce two elementary functions, and then we describe the metrics we propose for DB tables and corresponding coefficients:

- $cRec(t_j)$. It counts the number of records actually stored into the table t_j.
- $cAttr(t_j)$. It counts the number of attributes in the table t_j.

Percentage of Records

This metric measures the percentage of records stored into the considered table with respect to the total number of DB records (or the considered subset), using the function $cRec(t_j)$. It is important to note that into the original DB, different tables can store data referring to different time intervals (typically, the most recent transactional data). For example, into a real DB old transactional data are generally either deleted or moved into other secondary tables. Then, to correctly compare the number of records stored into different tables, a first normalization based on temporal intervals is useful (*TNORM*). More specifically, if a table does not store transactional data (e.g., it stores information on customers and/or suppliers), the number of records considered for this metric corresponds to the number of records actually stored into the table. On the other hand, the time-normalization is required if the table stores information related to transactional activities; in such case, our methodology asks the designer to specify the temporal attribute of the table related to transactional activities on which apply the *TNORM* function.

Being q the total number of tables, the final index for the table t_j is computed as described in Formula 2.

$$M_1(t_j) = \frac{TNORM(cRec(t_j))}{\sum_{j=1}^{q} TNORM(cRec(t_j))} \tag{2}$$

Figure 1. Percentage of records stored into different tables

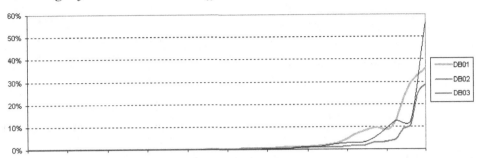

Figure 2. Percentage of attributes stored into different tables

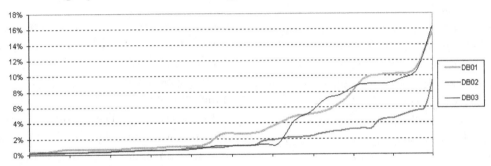

If the analysis concerns the identification of the tables that are more suitable to extract measures, the corresponding coefficient is positive ($C_{m,1} > 0$) since tables storing transactional and operational information are generally characterized by an higher number of records with respect to the other tables. On the other hand, the coefficient for dimensions is negative ($C_{d,1} < 0$) since, for example, tables pertaining to business objects definitions (e.g., products and clients) are typically characterized by a lower number of records than transactional archives.

Figure 1 shows the percentage of records for the tables of the three real commercial DBs of the experiment. It is interesting to note that the distribution of records into different tables is similar into the considered DBs; most tables (about 80%) store a limited percentage of records (less than 5%), while only few tables (less than 5%) are characterized by a large number of records. In other words, there are several tables contributing positively to the quality of the attributes from dimensions point of view, while from measures point of view the number of table is more limited.

Percentage of Attributes

This metric measures the percentage of attributes belonging to the considered table with respect to the total number of DB attributes. The index for this metric is computed as described in Formula 3.

$$M_2(t_j) = \frac{cAttr(t_j)}{\sum_{j=1}^{q} cAttr(t_j)}$$

(3)

The coefficient for this metric is positive for measures ($C_{m,2} > 0$) since, for example, tables storing information on business objects are typically characterized by an high number of attributes. A negative coefficient is used in the case of dimensions ($C_{d,2} < 0$) because tables storing information concerning transactional activities are generally characterized by a lower number of attributes.

Figure 2 shows the percentage of attributes for the same tables of the experiment; one can easily note that the attributes are more distributed on DB tables with respect to the number of records.

List of Coefficients for Table-Metrics

Table 1 summarizes the set of coefficients we have employed for evaluating the DB tables.

By changing that coefficient of a given metric, one can modifies the weight of the corresponding index. In our experiment, the absolute value of all coefficients belongs to the interval [0, 1]; when the coefficient of a given metric is close to 0, the corresponding index (independently from its value) barely influences the indicators $S_{m,j}$ and $S_{d,j}$ of the table t_j. On the other extreme, metrics characterized by coefficients that are close to 1 heavily influences these indicators.

Since the percentage of records stored into a table is a feature that is more relevant with respect to the percentage of attributes characterizing the table, in our experiment the coefficient for the second metric is smaller that the one assigned to the first metric. In particular, while the coefficient for M_1 equals 1, for M_2 equals 0.5 (while the sign of the coefficient depends on the role considered for the analysis, i.e., dimensions or measures point of view).

Indexes for Attributes

In this Section, we describe the set of metrics $m_{h=1..r}$ and corresponding indexes we propose for DB attributes. The aim of these metrics is to highlight different proprieties and features of data.

The global indicators $s_{d,i}$ and $s_{m,i}$ measuring how much the attribute a_i is suitable to be used respectively as measure and dimension are derived by differently combining the indexes derived by the metrics $m_{h=1..r}$ using respectively the coefficients

Table 1. List of coefficients for table-metrics

	C_d	C_m
M_1 - Percentage of records	-1	1
M_2 - Percentage if attributes	-0.5	0.5

$c_{m,h}$ and $c_{d,h}$. In particular, the two indexes $s_{d,i}$ and $s_{m,i}$ are derived as described in Formula 4.

$$s_{p,i} = \frac{\sum_{h=1}^{r}\left(c_{p,h} * m_h(a_i)\right)}{r} \tag{4}$$

where (i) $p = d$ or m (d = dimension, m = measure); (ii) $h = 1, ..., r$ identifies the metric; (iii) i identifies the attribute; (iv) $c_{p,h}$ is the coefficient of the attribute-metric h considering the role p of the attribute.

In the case of a DW attribute derived as a combination of more than one DB attributes, the corresponding index is derived as the mean of the indexes related to the DB attributes.

In the following, we first introduce a set of definitions and elementary functions, and then we describe in proposed metrics and corresponding coefficients:

- *cNull(a)*. It counts the number of null values of the given attribute a_i.
- *cValue(a, v)*. It counts the number of occurrences of the value v into the given attribute a_i (more generally, the number of instances of a given value into an array).
- *cValues(a)*. It counts the number of different values of the considered attribute a_i.
- *inst(a, nIntervals)*. This function returns an array of *nIntervals* integer values. In particular, it first subdivides the domain into *nIntervals* intervals and then, for each interval, it counts the number of data falling into the corresponding range of values.
- *Pkey(t)* identifies the set of attributes belonging to the primary key of the table t_j.

- *cPkey(t_j)*. It counts the number of attributes constituting the primary key of the table t_j.
- *cPkey(t_j, a_i)*. It returns 1/ *cPkey(t_j)* if the attribute a_i belongs to *cPkey(t_j)*, 0 otherwise.
- *Dkey(t_j)* identifies the set of duplicable keys of the table t_j.
- *cDkey(t_j)*. It counts the total number of attributes belonging to duplicable keys of the table t_j.
- *cDkey(t_j, a_i)*. It counts the total number of instances of the attribute a_i in *Dkey(t_j)* (the same attribute can belong to more than one duplicable key).

Percentage of Null Values

Given the attribute a_i belonging to the table t_j, this metric measures the percentage of data having null values as described in Formula 5.

$$m_1(a_i) = \frac{cNull(a_i)}{c\,\mathrm{Re}\,c(t_j)} \qquad a_i \in t_j \tag{5}$$

Although simple, this metric provides an important indicator concerning the relevance of an attribute since, independently from its role, attributes characterized by a high percentage of null values are not suitable to effectively support decision processes. For example, an attribute having a percentage of null values greater than 90% is characterized by a scarce informative content

from the analysis point of view. For this reason, both coefficients for this metric are negative ($c_{m,1}$ and $c_{d,1} < 0$), highlighting that the presence of an high number of null values is an undesirable feature for both dimensions and measures.

Concerning the order in which different metrics are applied, it is important to note that the percentage of null values is the first-computed index and the computation of the other indexes is constrained to the value provided by this metric. Indeed, the other indexes are computed only if the percentage of null values is below a given threshold (e.g., in our experiments = 95%).

Experimenting our methodology on real commercial databases, we have measured a percentage of null values that is considerably higher than expected. For example, the overall percentage of null values for the databases considered in the experimental evaluation reported in the Experimental Evaluation section are 41,36%, 42,62% and 51,53%, respectively, for the first, second, and third DB. Figure 3 shows the ranked indexes (increasing order) computed for the attributes belonging to the considered DBs. It is interesting to note that the three DBs show similar distributions of null values; about one third of the attributes do not contain null values, another one third stores only null values, and the remaining one third of attributes is characterized by different (linearly distributed) percentages of null values.

Figure 3. Percentage of null values for the attributes

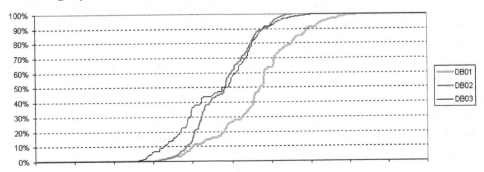

Box 1.

$$m_2(a_i) = \begin{cases} 0 & \text{if } (m_1(a_i) > threshold) \text{ or } (c\,\mathrm{Re}\,c(a_i) - cNull(a_i) < 2) \\ 1 & \text{if } (c\,\mathrm{Re}\,c(a_i) - cNull(a_i) = 2) \\ \left(\cos\left(\dfrac{cValues(a_i) - 2}{c\,\mathrm{Re}\,c(t_j) - cNull(a_i) - 2} * 2\pi \right) + 1 \right)/2 & \text{otherwise} \end{cases}$$

$$(6)$$

Number of Values

Given the attribute a_i belonging to the table t_j, the index computed by this metric concerns the extent in which the attribute assumes different values on the domain. In particular, the metric returns an index that is close to 1 in two different (and opposite) cases: (i) the attribute assumes a limited number of different values or (ii) it assumes a wide range of different values. Values ranging from 0 to 1 are computed for intermediate situations.

The index for this metric is computed as described in Formula 6, see Box 1.

If the percentage of null values is above the chosen threshold, or if the domain is represented by a single value, then index equals 0. On the other extreme, the index equals 1 when the attribute is characterized only by two different values. In the other cases, this metric behaves like the cosine function. As a result, if an attribute assumes a small number of different values (e.g., in the case of units of measurement where only a limited number of different values is admitted), this metric derives a value that is close to 1. A similar value is derived when an attribute is the primary key of a large table, since in this case the number of different values equals the total number of records stored into the table.

If the analysis concerns the evaluation of how much an attribute is suitable to be used as dimension, the corresponding coefficient is positive ($c_{d,2}$ > 0), since both attributes assuming a limited number of different values and ones characterized by a large number of different values can be effectively used for exploring the data. For example, an attribute storing information on the payment type (e.g., cash money or credit card) is suitable to be used as dimension and typically it is characterized by limited number of different values. On the other extreme, an attributes storing information on product or customer codes is also suitable to be used as dimension and typically it is characterized by a high number of different values.

With respect to the measures choice, the coefficient is negative ($c_{m,2}$ < 0) because attributes characterized by (i) a few values are generally not suitable to be used as measures, since they do not contain discriminatory and predictive information, and (ii) a large number of different values can correspond to keys and then result unsuitable to be used as measures. On the other hand, attributes storing information related to transactional activities (then, suitable to be used as measures) are characterized by a number of values (e.g., purchase money or number of elements sold) that is lower with respect to the total number of records. Figure 4 shows the ranked indexes (increasing order) computed for the attributes belonging to the three different commercial DBs of the experiment. Also in this case, it is interesting to note that the computed indexes exhibit similar distributions.

Figure 4. Number of values for the attributes

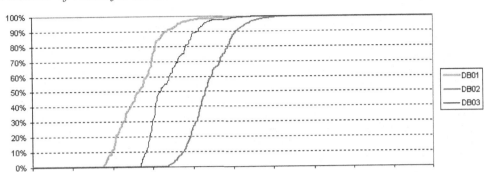

Box 2.

$$m_3(a_i) = 1 - \frac{cValue(inst(a_i, sqrt(c\operatorname{Re}c(t_j) - cNull(a_i)), 0)}{sqrt(c\operatorname{Re}c(t_j) - cNull(a_i))} \qquad a_i \in t_j$$

$$(7)$$

Degree of Clusterization

Given the attribute a_i belonging to the table t_j, this metric measures the extent in which the attribute assumes similar values on the domain. The index for this metric is computed as described in Formula 7, see Box 2.

This metric works at follows. First, using the $inst(a_i, sqrt(cRec(t_j)-cNull(a_i)))$ function, it discretizes the domain of a_i by equally subdividing it into a number of intervals equals to the square root of the number of not-null values of a_i. As a result, the more the number of not-null values, the more the number of intervals used for the discretization. With respect to the choice of having a number of intervals linearly proportional to the number of values, the square root function allows one to reduce the complexity of the computation in the case of a huge number of records (that is the typical scenario for the attributes belonging to tables that store information on transactional activities). Then, the index is derived by counting the number of intervals having at least one value falling in them. If there are several empty

intervals, this means that data are clustered on the domain and then the computed index is close to 1. On the other hand, if values are spread on the domain, it is probable that most intervals have at least one value falling in them; in this case, the computed index is close to 0. It is important to highlight that this metric does not consider the distribution of values into different intervals, but only the number of empty intervals.

If the analysis concerns the evaluation of how much an attribute is suitable to be used as dimension, the corresponding coefficient is positive ($c_{d,3} > 0$), since typically attributes that are suitable to be used as dimensions (e.g., numerical codes and names of products, customers and supplier) are clusterizable. On the other hand, the coefficient for measures is negative ($c_{m,3} < 0$), since attributes suitable to be used as measures generally are characterized by values that tend to spread over the domain. Figure 5 shows the ranked indexes (increasing order) computed for the attributes belonging to the three considered commercial DBs.

Figure 5. Degree of clusterization for the attributes

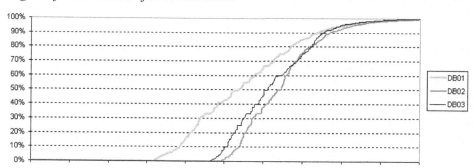

Box 3.

$$m_4(a_i) = \frac{-\displaystyle\sum_{k=1}^{nIntervals} \frac{inst(a_i, nIntervals)[k]}{\displaystyle\sum_{t=1}^{nIntervals} inst(a_i, nIntervals)[t]} \log_2 \frac{inst(a_i, nIntervals)[k]}{\displaystyle\sum_{k=1}^{nIntervals} inst(a_i, nIntervals)[t]}}{-\log_2 \frac{1}{nIntervals}} \qquad nIntervals = sqrt(cNull(a_i))$$

$$(9)$$

Uniformity of Distribution

This metric measures how much the values of an attribute are equally distributed on the domain. More specifically, this metric use the general meaning of *entropy* for characterizing the distribution of data of a given attribute. With this metric we aim at automatically distinguishing a uniform distribution from other types of distribution.

The concept of entropy is used in a wide range of different application domains. For example, in physics, the entropy quantifies the amount of disorder of a system while, in the field of information theory, the concept of entropy relates to the amount of *uncertainty* about an event associated with a given probability distribution. In this context, Shannon defines entropy in terms of a discrete random event x, characterized by a set of possible states $i=1...n$ as described in Formula 8.

$$H(x) = \sum_{i=1}^{n} p(i) \log_2\left(\frac{1}{p(i)}\right) = -\sum_{i=1}^{n} p(i) \log_2 p(i) \quad (8)$$

where $p(i)$ indicates the probability of i.

We used the concept of entropy for characterizing the distribution of values of a given attribute. In particular, the index $m_4(a_i)$ for the attribute a_i is computed as follows. First of all, similarly to the previous metric, this one uses the $inst(a_i, sqrt(cRec(t_j)-cNull(a_i)))$ function to discretize the domain of a_i and count the number of values falling into different intervals. The metric then normalizes these values, deriving for each interval the value $p(k)$ corresponding to the percentage of values falling into the kth interval. Then, the index for this metric is derived using the above definition of entropy and normalizing the computed value. As a result, the index measuring the uniformity of distribution is computed as described in Formula 9, see Box 3.

Where

$$-\log_2 \frac{1}{n}$$

is used for normalization purposes (the maximum value is obtained in the case of uniform distributions).

Figure 6. Uniformity of distribution for the attributes

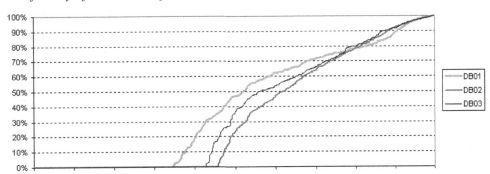

Box 4.

$$m_5(a_i) = \begin{cases} cPkey(t_j, a_i) & \text{if } cDkey(t_j) = 0 \\[2em] \dfrac{cPkey(t_j, a_i) + \left(\dfrac{cDkey(t_j, a_i)}{cDkey(t_j)} * w \right)}{(1 + w)} & \text{otherwise} \end{cases}$$

$$(10)$$

The possibility of highlighting uniform distributions enables our methodologies to effective evaluating attributes that are suitable to be used as measures, since typically these attributes are characterized by other types of distribution (e.g., normal distribution). For example, it is more probable that the distribution of values of an attribute storing information on the customer is more similar to a uniform distribution with respect to the distribution of values of an attribute storing information on the bill (typically characterized by a Gaussian distribution of values).

For this reason, if the analysis concerns the evaluation of how much an attribute is suitable to be used as a measure, the corresponding coefficient is negative ($c_{m,4} < 0$) since the attributes suitable to be used as measures are generally characterized by values that are not equally distributed on the domain. On the other hand, if the analysis

concerns dimensions, the corresponding coefficient is positive ($c_{d,4} > 0$) since the more values are uniformly distributed on the domain (or in the considered subset), the more effectively the analyst can explore the data. Figure 6 shows the ranked indexes (increasing order) computed for the attributes belonging to the three commercial DBs.

It is important to highlight the difference between this metric and the previous one; although both based on the same domain discretization, while the uniformity of distribution considers the number of times the values falls into different intervals, the degree of clusterization takes into account only the number of intervals that have at least one value falling in them. As a result, while this metric provides information on the distribution of values, the previous one indicates if the values stored into the attributes can be clustered.

Figure 7. Keys for the attributes

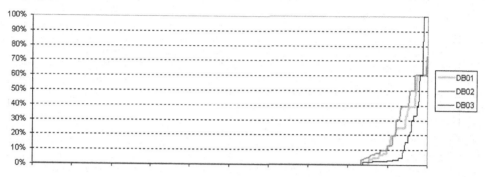

Box 5.

$$m_6(a_i) = \begin{cases} 0 & a_i \text{ stores boolean values or alphanumerical strings of various type} \\ 0.5 & a_i \text{ stores whole numbers of various type} \\ 1 & a_i \text{ stores decimal values of various type} \end{cases}$$

$$(11)$$

Keys

This metric derives a value both taking into account if the considered attribute belong or not to primary and/or duplicable keys and considering the total number of attributes constituting the keys.

The primary key of a given table t_j can either correspond to a single attribute (in this case, $cPkey(t_j) = 1$) or can be composed by a set of attributes ($cPkey(t_j) > 1$). Moreover, it is important also to note that in a given table t_j (i) more than one duplicable key can exist, each one (potentially) characterized by a different number of attributes, (ii) an attribute can belong to more than one duplicable key (in this case, $cDkey(t_j, a_j) > 1$).

For combining the information on primary and duplicable keys, we introduce the additional parameter $w \in [0, 1]$; more specifically, w is used for differently weighting attributes belonging to the primary key and ones belonging to secondary keys. In our experiments, we assign the same weight to primary and secondary keys (i.e., $w = 0.5$).

Given the attribute a_i belonging to the table t_j, the index for this metric is computed as described in Formula 10.

On one extreme, if a_i is the primary key of the table t_j and the table does not contain duplicable keys, the index for a_i equals 1, while all the indexes for the other attributes equal 0.

The coefficient for dimensions is positive ($c_{d,5} > 0$) since attributes belonging to the primary or secondary keys often identify look-up tables and then they are the best candidates for dimensions into a DW. On the other hand, the coefficient for measures is negative ($c_{m,5} < 0$) since attribute belonging to primary or secondary keys typically are not suitable to be used as measures. Figure 7 shows the ranked indexes (increasing order) computed for the attributes belonging to the three commercial DBs.

Type of Attribute

This metric returns a float value according to the type of the attribute. More specifically, the index

Table 2. List of coefficients for attribute-metrics

	c_d	c_m
m_1 - Percentage of null values	-1	-1
m_2 - Number of values	1	-1
m_3 - Degree of clusterization	1	-1
m_4 - Uniformity of Distribution	1	-1
m_5 - Keys	1	-1
m_6 - Type of attribute	-1	1

for such metric is derived as described in Formula 11, see Box 5.

Typically numerical attributes are more suitable to be used as measures rather than being used as dimensions; for this reason, the coefficient for measures is positive ($c_{m,6} > 0$). On the other hand, in the case of dimensions, the corresponding coefficient is negative ($c_{d,6} < 0$) since business objects definitions are often coded by alphanumerical attributes. Moreover, alphanumerical attributes are rarely use in a DW as measures due to the limited number of applicable mathematical functions (e.g., count function).

List of Coefficients for Attribute-Metrics

Although coefficients can take arbitrary values, we actually assign unitary values to the related coefficients (i.e., -1 or +1); as a result, in our experiments we have equally weighed the indexes computed by our metrics for deriving the global indexes s_d and s_m.

However, we intend to investigate in our future work if an accurate tuning of the coefficients may lead to more effective results. Table 2 summarizes the set of coefficients we have employed for the attributes.

DW-QUALITY METRIC

Our methodology characterizes each attribute with a couple of global indexes $G_{m,i,j}$ and $G_{d,i,j}$

indicating how much the attribute a_i belonging to the table t_j is suitable to be used respectively as measure and as dimension. These indexes are computed as described in Formula 12.

$$G_{p,i,j} = S_{p,j} * s_{p,i} \qquad a_i \in t_j \qquad (12)$$

where: (i) $p = d$ or m (d = dimension, m = measure); (ii) i identifies the attribute; (iii) j identifies the table; (iv) $S_{p,j}$ corresponds to a table-metric index; (v) $s_{p,j}$ corresponds to a attribute-metric index.

Once all these indexes are computed, our methodology derives two lists of attributes: the first list of attributes contains all DB attributes ordered according to G_d, while the second one is ordered according to G_m. We then define $rank_d(a_i)$ the function deriving the relative position of a_i into the first (ordered) list, while $rank_m(a_i)$ the function deriving the position of a_i into the second list. We use these ranking functions to evaluate the effectiveness of our methodology in correctly identifying the set of attributes that are more suitable for the DW construction (see section titled Experimental evaluation–Attribute indexes).

The global index $I(DW)$ measuring the total quality of the final DW is derived using the above indexes. More specifically, being A_d the set of n_d attributes chosen as dimensions and A_m the set of n_m attributes to be used as measures, the index measuring the total DW quality is computed as described in Formula 13.

$$I(DW) = \frac{\sum_{\substack{a_i \in A_m \\ a_i \in t_j}} G_{m,i,j} + \sum_{\substack{a_i \in A_d \\ a_i \in t_j}} G_{d,i,j}}{n_d + n_m} \qquad (13)$$

EXPERIMENTAL EVALUATION

As defined in the introduction, we have experimented our methodology on three subsets of DBs of two real world business systems. Considered subsets are characterized by hundreds of tables, thousands of attributes and millions of records.

In particular, while DB01 and DB02 correspond to different instantiations of the same DB schema (it is the same ERP system used by two different commercial organizations), DB03 has a different DB schema (it is based on a different ERP system).

For the experimental evaluation, we asked to an expert to build an unique (and relatively simple) schema for a commercial DW. The expert selected the attributes that are the most suitable to support decision processes. In particular, the DW build by the expert is characterized by a star schema where six attributes are used as measures ($n_m = 6$) and nine attributes as dimensions ($n_d = 9$). Starting from this schema, we build three DWs, filling them with the three different DB sources. As a result, the attributes chosen to build the first two DWs are physically the same (since they belong to the same DB schema), while a different set of attributes (characterized by the same semantics with respect to ones selected for previous DWs) are chosen for the DW03 construction.

Then, we have experimented our methodology for testing its effectiveness by considering the above three case studies. The analysis is mainly targeted at evaluating if the proposed metrics effectively support quantitative analysis by taking into account (i) the structure of the initial DB (in this experiment, two different DB schemas are considered), (ii) data actually stored into the initial DB (in this experiment, three different data sources are considered), and (iii) the DW schema (in this experiment, an unique DW schema is considered). We have then evaluated both if during the DW construction the proposed methodology can be effectively used to drive design choices and, at the end of the selection phase, if it can be used for deriving information on the total quality of the final DW.

Table Indexes

In the first phase of our experiment, we have considered the metrics we propose for the DB

tables and evaluated if they highlight tables that are more suitable to extract measures and dimensions. The global indexes S_d and S_m for the three DBs are summarized respectively in Table 3(a) and Table 3(b).

Derived quality measurements for the DB tables are consistent with our expectations; for example, for both DB01 and DB02, the procedure highlights that *xsr* and *art* are the most suitable tables for extracting measures. Indeed, while the first table stores selling information, the second one includes pricing information on products. It is also interesting to note that although based on the same DB schema, different indexes are computed for DB01 and DB02 due to different distributions of data.

With respect to measures, a similar result is obtained for DB03, where the table *MAG_COSTO* is semantically equivalent to *art*, and *VEW_V_BOLLA_RIGA_ADD* stores the same kind of information stored into *xsr*. Derived quality measurements also indicate that both in DB01 and DB02 *smag*, *zon* and *gum* are the most suitable tables for extracting dimensions, while they result less suitable for selecting measures. Indeed, *smag* and *gum* store information on categories respectively of products and customers, while *zon* stores geographical information on customers. Similarly for *COW_GRUPPO_IM-PREND*, *COW_ZONA_COMMERCIALE* and *MAG_TAB_RICL_DESCR*, where these tables store the same kind of information respectively of *gum*, *zon* and *smag*. In general, tables that are the best candidate to extract measures, are the worst ones to extract dimensions and vice versa.

It is also interesting to note that the expert selected as measures attributes belonging to *xsr* and *art* in the case of DW01 and DW02, while attributes belonging to *MAG_COSTO* and *VEW_V_BOLLA_RIGA_ADD* for building DW03. On the other hand, some of the dimensions chosen by the expert correspond to attributes belonging to *gum*, *zon* and *smag* in the case of DW01 and DW02, while the expert selected attributes belonging

Table 3. List of tables of DB01, DB02 and DB03 ranked according to (a) S_d *and (b)* S_m

(a) Dimensions		(b) Measures	
Tables of DB01	S_d	Tables of DB01	S_m
gum	0,7480	xsr	0,4996
zon	0,7461	art	0,3282
smag	0,7459	…	…
…	…	smag	0,2541
art	0,6718	zon	0,2539
xsr	0,5004	gum	0,2520
Tables of DB02	S_d	Tables of DB02	S_m
gum	0,7481	art	0,4220
zon	0,7463	xsr	0,4016
smag	0,7458	…	…
…	…	smag	0,2542
xsr	0,5984	zon	0,2537
art	0,5780	gum	0,2519
Tables of DB03	S_d	Tables of DB03	S_m
COW_GRUPPO_IMPREND	0,7494	MAG_COSTO	0,4577
COW_ZONA_COMMER-CIALE	0,7490	VEW_V_BOLLA_RIGA_ADD	0,3366
MAG_TAB_RICL_DESCR	0,7465	…	…
…	…	MAG_TAB_RICL_DESCR	0,2535
VEW_V_BOLLA_RIGA_ADD	0,6634	COW_ZONA_COMMER-CIALE	0,2510
MAG_COSTO	0,5423	COW_GRUPPO_IMPREND	0,2506

to *COW_GRUPPO_IMPREND, COW_ZONA_COMMERCIALE* and *MAG_TAB_RICL_DESCR* for building DW03.

Attribute Indexes

In the second phase of the experiment, we have considered the metrics we propose for the DB attributes. Using the indexes computed in the previous phase, for each considered attribute we derive the quality indexes G_d and G_m, summarized respectively in Table 4(a) and Table 4(b). The last column of Table 4(a) and Table 4(b) specifies respectively $rank_d$ and $rank_m$ (0 corresponds to the first position and then to the best candidate, while 1 corresponds to the last position and then represents the worst candidate). Also these computed indexes are consistent with our expectations; for example, in DB01 the attribute *ag_cod_agente* results the most appropriate one to be used as a dimension, and it results unsuitable to be used as a measure. This result is in line with our expectations, since the considered attribute stores information on sellers' codes. On the other hand, the attribute *xr_valore* results the most appropriate one to be used as measure, but unsuitable to be used as dimension.

Table 4. Attributes of DB01, DB02 and DB03 ranked according to (a) G_d and (b) G_m

(a) Dimensions				(b) Measures		
Attributes of DB01	G_d	$rank_d$		**Attributes of DB01**	G_m	$rank_m$
ag_cod_agente	0,5974	0,0000		xr_valore	0,3515	0,0000
zn_sigla	0,5661	0,0059		xr_num_ord	0,3006	0,0059
…	…	…		…	…	…
xr_valore	0,1426	0,7219		ag_cod_agente	0,0939	0,6982
…	…	…		…	…	…
xr_sconto_ex_vsc	0,0000	0,9941		xr_sconto_ex_vsc	0,0000	0,9941
zn_ragg_1	0,0000	1,0000		zn_ragg_1	0,0000	1,0000
Attributes of DB02	G_d	$rank_d$		**Attributes of DB02**	G_m	$rank_m$
ps_sigla_paese	0,5956	0,0000		xr_prezzo	0,2742	0,0000
gu_codice	0,5743	0,0056		xr_valore	0,2741	0,0056
…	…	…		…	…	…
xr_prezzo	0,1038	0,5307		ps_sigla_paese	0,0937	0,5251
…	…	…		…	…	…
xr_val_sco	0,0000	0,9944		xr_val_sco	0,0000	0,9944
zn_ragg_1	0,0000	1,0000		zn_ragg_1	0,0000	1,0000
Attributes of DB03	G_d	$rank_d$		Attributes of DB03	G_m	$rank_m$
COD_VOCE_RICL_ COD_IND_RICL	0,6849	0,0000		COSTO	0,2565	0,0000
COD_LINGUA	0,6375	0,0020		COSTO_CALCOLATO	0,2529	0,0020
…	…	…		…	…	…
COSTO	0,2131	0,6373		COD_VOCE_RICL_ COD_IND_RICL	0,0632	0,6529
…	…	…		…	…	…
VAL_SCONTO_TEST	0,0000	0,9980		VAL_SCONTO_TEST	0,0000	0,9980
VOCE_DI_SPESA	0,0000	1,0000		VOCE_DI_SPESA	0,0000	1,0000

Also in this case, this result is consistent with the semantics of data, since this attribute stores pricing information. Similar results are obtained for DB02 and DB03. Moreover, it is interesting to note that the attributes occupying the last positions are the same both in Table 4(a) and Table 4(b) (e.g., *zn_ragg_1* for DB01). This is due to the fact that these attributes are characterized by a high percentage of null values and then they result unsuitable to be used both as dimensions and measures in the considered DBs.

Indexes of Selected Measures and Dimensions

In the third phase of our experiment, we have considered the DW built by the expert and analyzed the rank of selected attributes in order to evaluate the effectiveness of our methodology in correctly measuring the quality of the attributes according to their role into the DW.

In Table 5, we report the measures chosen for building the three DWs and related ranks. With

Table 5. Ranking of DW01, DW02 and DW03 measures

DW	Source		G_m			$rank_m$		
	DB01 and DB02	DB03	DB01	DB02	DB03	DB01	DB02	DB03
product quantity	xr_qta	QTA_SPEDITA	0,2769	0,1725	0,1707	0,0179	0,2135	0,0452
product price	xr_valore	RIGA_PREZZO	0,3515	0,2741	0,1452	0,0000	0,0056	0,1454
broker commission	xr_prov_age	PROVV_AG1	0,2720	0,0000	0,1629	0,0238	0,9607	0,0766
customer discount	xr_val_sco	SC_RIGA	0,2617	0,0000	0,1685	0,0298	0,9888	0,0511
product last cost	a_ult_prz_pag	COSTO_F1	0,2060	0,2026	0,2565	0,1071	0,1236	0,0020
product std. cost	a_prz_pag_stand	COSTO_F2	0,1873	0,2105	0,2565	0,1667	0,0955	0,0000

Figure 8. Derived quality for measures

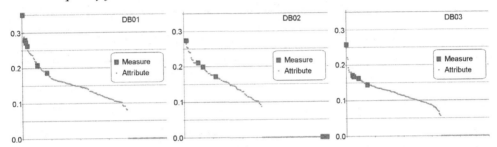

respect to the measures choice, our methodology evaluates differently the quality of the design choices for the three DWs. Indeed, the computed indexes does not depend on semantics of selected measures (that is the typical criterion adopted by the expert for the DW construction), rather than on the data actually stored into selected attributes and on the initial DB schema.

To better evaluate the obtained results, we illustrate in Figure 8 the whole set of DB attributes ranked according to G_m, highlighting the measures chosen by the expert to build the DW.

In the case of DW01, four out of six attributes selected by the expert rank under the 3% of the whole set of considered attributes, and the remaining two attributes rank under the 17%. A good result is also obtained for DW03, where five out six attributes rank under the 8% and the remaining attribute rank under the 15%. A different result is obtained for DW02, where four out of six attributes rank under the 22% of the whole set of DB02 attributes, while the remaining two attri-

butes are characterized by a low data quality. We have then analyzed *xr_prov_age* and *xr_val_sco*, discovering that these attributes are characterized by an high percentage of null values (> 90%) and then, although chosen due to their semantics by the expert to build the DW, in DB02 they are not useful to be used for analysis purposes. Also with respect to the dimensions choice, our methodology evaluates the attributes chosen to build the DWs. In Table 6, we report the dimensions chosen for building the three DWs and related ranks. In the case of DW01, five out nine attributes rank under the 6% of the whole set of considered attributes and three attributes under the 18%; moreover, our procedure correctly highlights that *xi_prov* has a scarce informative content being characterized by an high percentage of null values (>80%). A good result is also obtained for DW03, where all selected dimensions rank under the 4% of the whole set of considered attributes.

Like in the case of measures, also in the case of dimensions the expert build DW02 by

Table 6. Ranking of DW01, DW02 and DW03 dimensions

DW	Source		G_d			$Rank_d$		
	DB01 and DB02	DB03	DB01	DB02	DB03	DB01	DB02	DB03
product	a_sigla_art	COD_ARTICOLO	0,5513	0,4727	0,5828	0,0417	0,1236	0,0177
product class	smg_tipo_codice	COD_VOCE_RICL_ COD_IND_RICL_F1	0,5400	0,5666	0,6849	0,0536	0,0169	0,0020
warehouse class	a_cl_inv	COD_VOCE_RICL_ COD_IND_RICL_F2	0,5175	0,0000	0,6849	0,0833	0,6910	0,0000
customer	sc_cod_s_conto	CONTI_ CLIENTI_M_P	0,4715	0,4970	0,6335	0,1786	0,0787	0,0039
customer class	gu_codice	COD_GRUPPO	0,4987	0,5743	0,6224	0,1250	0,0056	0,0059
province	xi_prov	COD_PROVINCIA	0,3644	0,4894	0,5582	0,3750	0,0899	0,0314
country	ps_sigla_paese	ELENCO_STATI_ COD_ISO	0,5634	0,5956	0,6124	0,0179	0,0000	0,0079
broker	ag_cod_agente	CONTI_ FORNITORI_M_P	0,5974	0,0000	0,6098	0,0000	0,5449	0,0098
commercial zone	zn_sigla	COD_ZONA_COMM	0,5661	0,5662	0,5668	0,0060	0,0225	0,0275

Figure 9. Derived quality for dimensions

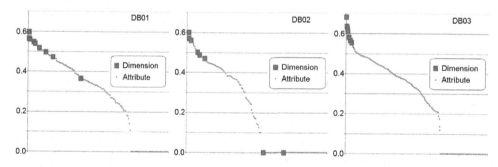

selecting some attributes that are semantically relevant, but they are actually not suitable to effectively support the analysis due to stored data (also in this case, the percentage of null values of *ag_cod_agente* and *a_cl_inv* is over a given threshold). These attributes inevitably affect the quality of the final DW. All the other selected dimensions rank under the 9% of the whole set of considered attributes.

A graphical representation of these results is depicted in Figure 9, where dimensions chosen by the expert to built the DWs are highlighted.

Indeed, the construction and configuration of an effective DW requires not only the knowledge of both the logical structure of the DB and semantic information on its attributes, but it

needs to know how an organization actually uses the business system (since it influences the data distributions).

The result confirms the effectiveness of the proposed methodology in supporting the design, creation and evaluation of DWs, since it is able to correctly highlight the attributes that are more suitable to be used as dimensions and measures.

DW Quality

The final phase of our experiment is targeted at comparing the derived global indicators measuring the quality of the three different DWs. Applying our methodology, we have obtained the global indicators *I(DW01)*=0.415, *I(DW02)*=0.308 and *I(DW03)*=0.448.

From computed measurements, DW03 results the better DW, while DW02 result the worst one, due to both the low quality of data stored into the selected DB attributes and the initial DB schema. In the following Section we discuss in more detail derived results.

ASSESSMENT

It is important to note that the final DW-quality measurement is influenced by three different factors:

- The DW design choices. For a given DB, the measured DW quality strictly depends on selected measures and dimensions.
- The schema of the initial DB. Some indexes depend only on the initial DB schema. For example, given two DBs characterized by the same schema (e.g., DB01 and DB02), the attribute metrics m_5 and m_6 derive the same measurements independently from the data actually stored into analyzed attributes.
- Characteristics and quality of data actually stored into the selected attributes. Most indexes depend on the features (e.g., percentage of null values and data distribution) of data actually stored into the selected DW attributes. As a result, given two DWs built starting from DBs characterized by the same schema, a metric can derive a different measurement depending on the values actually stored into the considered attribute.

Our methodology highlights that DW03 results the best DW, while DW02 results the worst one, due to both the low quality of data stored into the selected DB attributes and the initial DB schema. More specifically, in the case of DW01 and DW02 the first factor does not influence the evaluation since chosen measures and dimensions

are exactly the same. Then, we can easily derive that DW01 results better than DW02 since data stored into the attributes chosen for building the first DW are more suitable to be used for analysis purposes with respect to the ones chosen for the second DW. The evaluation of DW03 as the best DW depends on a multitude of aspects, and to precisely identify the strong points of the third DW it requires to separately analyze each computed index. For example, consider the index concerning the percentage of null values. Although DB03 is the DB characterized by the highest percentage of null values (as reported in Figure 3), the indexes concerning the attributes chosen for building DW03 highlight that these attributes store more valid values with respect to the attributes chosen for building DW01 and DW02.

It is important to note that the evaluation of the DWs depends on measures and dimensions chosen to build the DW. Different requisites can lead the expert to change selected measures and dimensions and then our procedure could produce a completely different result.

The selection of measures and dimensions is a semantic-dependent task, and our methodology is not designed for replacing the work of the expert (automatically proposing the attributes that are the best candidates for dimensions and measures), but our main goal is to propose a set of metrics targeted at helping the expert in selecting appropriate measures and dimensions (especially in the case of multiple choices) during the DW design phase and evaluating the quality of taken design choices at the end of the construction.

CONCLUSION

In this article, we have proposed a methodology that can be used (i) during the DW construction phase to drive the selection of measures and dimensions and (ii) to evaluate the final quality of design choices. Proposed methodology is mainly focused on statistical and syntactical aspects of data and can be effectively used paired with semantic-based solutions to support the DW construction and configuration. We have tested proposed metrics on three DWs; the experimental evaluation demonstrated the effectiveness of our methodology in evaluating the DW, e.g., our methodology correctly highlighted some inappropriate initial design choices (e.g., the expert chooses as a measure an attribute characterized by a percentage of null values greater that 90%).

The proposed method is actually based on a set of six indexes for attributes and two indexes for tables; although these indexes are able to highlight attributes that are more suitable to be used as measures and dimensions, in future work we intend to introduce additional indexes characterizing the attributes in order to improve the accuracy of the measurements. We are currently investigating if the conditional entropy and mutual information can be used for automatically discovering correlations among attributes in order to enable our methodology to suggest alternative design choices during the DW creation. For example, an attribute could represent a valid alternative to another attribute if (i) it is strongly correlated with the second attribute and (ii) its quality is higher with respect to the one measured for the second attribute. From this point of view, we are currently evaluating also the possibility of including metrics using information on DB relations (e.g., computing the rate between incoming and outgoing table relations). Finally, we plan to evaluate if an accurate tuning of coefficients allows the procedure to further increase its effectiveness.

We have recently started at testing our metrics on completely different contexts for evaluating if its effectiveness is independent from the specific application domain; we then shift from commercial business systems to a DB collecting University examinations and another DB collecting motorways car-crashes. This evaluation is also targeted at highlighting possible limitations of the proposed methodology and can elicit new requirements.

REFERENCES

Ballou, D. P., & Pazer, H. L. (1985). Modeling data and process quality in multi-input, multi-output information systems. *Management Science, 31*(2), 150-162.

Ballau, D. P, Wang, R. Y., Pazer, H. L., & Tayi G. K. (1998). Modelling information manufacturing systems to determine information product quality. *Management Science, 44*(4), 462-484.

Chengalur-Smith, I. N., Ballou, D. P., & Pazer H. L. (1999). The impact of data quality information on decision making: An exploratory analysis. *IEEE Transactions on Knowledge and Data Engineering, 11*(6), 853-864.

English, L. P. (1999). *Improving data warehouse & business information quality: Methods for reducing costs and increasing profits.* New York: Wiley.

Golfarelli, M., Maio, D., & Rizzi, S. (1998). The dimensional fact model: A conceptual model for data warehouses. *International Journal of Cooperative Information Systems, 7*(2/3), 215-247.

Jeusfeld, M. A., Quix, C., & Jarke, M. (1998). Design and analysis of quality information for data warehouses. In *Proceedings of the International Conference on Conceptual Modeling* (pp. 349-362).

Karr, A. F., Sanil, A. P., & Banks, D. L. (2006). Data quality: A statistical perspective. *Statistical Methodology, 3*(2), 137-173.

Kriebel, C. H. (1978). Evaluating the quality of information systems. In *Proceedings of the BIFOA Symposium* (pp. 18-20).

Phipps, C., & Davis, K. (2002). Automating data warehouse conceptual schema design and evaluation. In *Proceedings of DMDW* (pp. 23-32).

Pighin, M., & Ieronutti, L. (2007). From database to datawarehouses: A design quality evaluation. In *Proceedings of the International Conference on Enterprise Information Systems* (pp. 178-185).

Redman, T. C. (1996). *Data quality for the information age.* Norwood, MA: Artech House.

Scannapieco, M., Virgillito, A., Marchetti, C., Mecella, M., & Baldoni, R. (2004). The DaQuin-CIS architecture: A platform for exchanging and improving data quality in cooperative information systems. *Information Systems, 29*(7), 551-582.

Wang, R.Y., & Strong D. M. (1996a). Beyond accuracy: What data quality means to data consumers. *Journal of Management Information Systems, 12*(4), 5-33.

Wang, R.Y., & Strong D. M. (1996b). *Data quality systems evaluation and implementation.* London: Cambridge Market Intelligence Ltd.

Wang, R.Y., Storey, V. C., & Firth, C. P. (1995). A framework for analysis of data quality research. *IEEE Transactions on Knowledge and Data Engineering, 7*(4), 623-640.

This work was previously published in International Journal of Data Warehousing and Mining, Vol. 4, Issue 3, edited by D. Taniar, pp. 15-34, copyright 2008 by IGI Publishing (an imprint of IGI Global).

Chapter 2
Seismological Data Warehousing and Mining:
A Survey

Gerasimos Marketos
University of Piraeus, Greece

Yannis Theodoridis
University of Piraeus, Greece

Ioannis S. Kalogeras
National Observatory of Athens, Greece

ABSTRACT

Earthquake data composes an ever increasing collection of earth science information for post-processing analysis. Earth scientists, local or national administration officers and so forth, are working with these data collections for scientific or planning purposes. In this article, we discuss the architecture of a so-called seismic data management and mining system (SDMMS) for quick and easy data collection, processing, and visualization. The SDMMS architecture includes, among others, a seismological database for efficient and effective querying and a seismological data warehouse for OLAP analysis and data mining. We provide template schemes for these two components as well as examples of their functionality towards the support of decision making. We also provide a comparative survey of existing operational or prototype SDMMS.

INTRODUCTION

For centuries, humans have been feeling, recording and studying earthquake phenomena. Taking into account that at least one earthquake of magnitude $M < 3$ ($M > 3$) occurs every one second (every ten minutes, respectively) worldwide, the seismic data collection is huge and rapidly increasing. Scientists record this information in order to describe and study tectonic activity, which is described by recording attributes about geographic information (epicenter location and disaster areas), time of event, magnitude, depth, an so forth.

On the other hand, computer engineers specialized in the area of Information & Knowledge Management find an invaluable "data treasure", which they can process and analyze helping in the discovery of knowledge from this data. Recently, a number of applications for the management and analysis of seismological or, in general, geophysical data, have been proposed in the literature by Andrienko and Andrienko (1999), Kretschmer and Roccatagliata (2000), Theodoridis (2003), and Yu (2005). In general, the collaboration between the data mining community and physical scientists has been only recently launched (Behnke & Dobinson, 2000).

Desirable components of a so-called *seismic data management and mining system* (SDMMS) include tools for quick and easy data exploration and inspection, algorithms for generating historic profiles of specific geographic areas and time periods, techniques providing the association of seismic data with other geophysical parameters of interest, such as geological morphology, and top line visualization components using geographic and other thematic-oriented (e.g., topological and climatic) maps for the presentation of data to the user and supporting sophisticated user interaction.

In summary, we classify users that an SDMMS should support in three profiles:

- **Researchers of geophysical sciences**, interested in constructing and visualizing seismic profiles of certain regions during specific time periods or in discovering regions of similar seismic behavior.
- **Public administration officers**, requesting for information such as distances between epicenters and other demographical entities (schools, hospitals, heavy industries, etc.).
- **Citizens ("Web surfers")**, searching for seismic activity, thus querying the system for seismic properties of general interest, for example, for finding all epicenters of earthquakes in distance no more than 50Km from their favorite place.

The availability of systems following the proposed SDMMS architecture provides users a wealth of information about earthquakes assisting in awareness and understanding, two critical factors for decision making, either at individual or at administration level.

The rest of the article is organized as follows. Initially, we sketch a desired SDMMS architecture, including its database and data warehouse design. The section that follows, presents querying, online analytical processing (OLAP) and data mining functionality an SDMMS could offer, putting emphasis on the support of decision making. Furthermore, we survey and compare proposed systems and tools found in the literature for the management of seismological or, in general, earth science data. Conclusions are drawn in the last section.

THE ARCHITECTURE OF A SEISMIC DATA MANAGEMENT AND MINING SYSTEM

Earthquake phenomena are instantly recorded by a number of organizations (e.g., Institutes of Geodynamics and Schools of Physics) worldwide. The architecture of a SDMMS might allow for the integration of several remote sources. The aim is to collect and analyze the most accurate seismic data among different sources. Obviously, some sources provide data about the same earthquakes though with slight differences in their details (e.g., the magnitude or the exact timestamp of the recorded earthquake). SDMMS should be able to

Figure 1. A general SDMMS architecture proposed for seismological data management

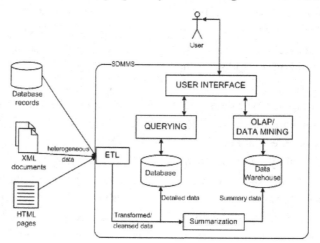

integrate the remote sources in a proper way by refining and homogenizing raw data.

Collected data can be stored in a local database and/or a data warehouse (for simple querying and analysis for decision making, respectively). In general, data within the database is dynamic and detailed, while that within the data warehouse is static and summarized (this is because the modifications of the former are continuous, while the latter are subjected to periodical updates).

Figure 1 presents the proposed abstract architecture that serves the task of collecting data from several sources around the world and storing them in a local repository (database and/or data warehouse). A mediator is responsible for the management of the process from the extraction of data from their sources until their load into the local repository, the so-called *extract-transform-load* (ETL) approach.

Formats for storing seismic data include SEG-Y and SEG P1-P4. SEG-Y (Barry et al., 1975) is used by the U.S. Geological Survey and consists of a header and a trace data block. SEG P1-P4 (SEG, 2006) has been developed by SEG Subcommittee on Potential Fields and Positioning Standards in order to standardize data exchange formats. The oil and gas industry in conjunction with PPDM, a not-for-profit organization that develops and

maintains standards for the resource industry, run a Data Exchange Project that will guarantee interoperability between businesses within the energy industry (PPDM, 2006). The aim of the project is to replace SEG-Y and SEG P1-P4 formats with new ones based in open source technologies (like XML and SOAP).

In the following subsections, we present efficient design proposals for the two components of the local repository of a SDMMS, namely the seismological database (SDMMS database subsection) and the seismological data warehouse (SDMMS data warehouse subsection).

SDMMS Database

Remote sources provide SDMMS with a variety of seismological information to be stored in the local database. Figure 2 illustrates the conceptual design (Entity-Relationship diagram) of a local database proposed for SDMMS purposes.

QUAKE contains the minimum information required to describe an earthquake event includes *timestamp* of its appearance, *location* (latitude / longitude coordinates) and *depth*. On the other hand, this information only is not adequate for user-friendly querying and further data analysis as one wish to know more about the geographical

Figure 2. The proposed E-R diagram of a seismological database for SDMMS purposes

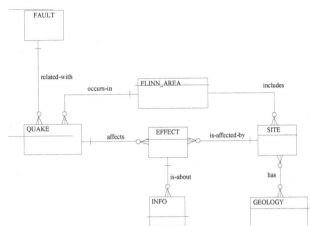

Figure 3. Faults and plates worldwide (Seismo-Surfer, 2006)

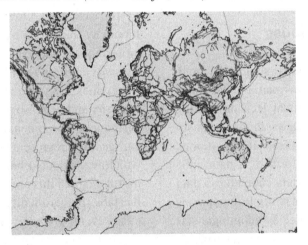

areas where an earthquake occurred. For this purpose, the addition of FLINN_AREA assists on the geographical positioning of both the earthquake epicenter and the affected sites using the Flinn & Engdahl geographical terminology (Young et al., 1996) that partitions world in disjoint polygons. Moreover, FAULT includes details about the *seismogenic fault* related with an earthquake (name of the fault, its characterization, strike, slip and rake of plates, etc.), extracted from bibliography, e.g. (Kiratzi & Louvari, 2003); see Figure 3 for an illustration of faults and plates worldwide.

SITE stores demographical and other information about the primitive *administrative partitions* of a country (e.g., counties or municipalities) with information about population and so forth, while GEOLOGY describes the *geological morphology* of a site so that we can discover how the different morphological classes are affected by earthquakes.

EFFECT records *macroseismic intensity* observed at a site as a result of an earthquake. Other attributes of this entity might include the *epicentral* and *hypocentral distance* and the *azimuth* (the angle between the site-epicenter line and the line of North). Finally, an auxiliary entity (INFO) might include complementary *multimedia material*, such

Figure 4. A spatial data warehouse design proposed for SDMMS purposes

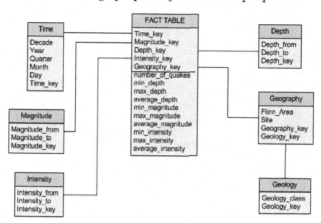

as pictures, audio/video descriptions, references and so forth. about earthquake effects.

SDMMS Data Warehouse

A *data warehouse* is defined as a subject-oriented, integrated, time-variant, non-volatile collection of data in support of management decision-making process (Inmon, 1996). Data warehouses are usually based on a multi-dimensional data model, which views data in the form of a data cube (Agarwal et al., 1996). A data cube allows data to be modeled and viewed in multiple dimensions and is typically implemented by adopting a star (or snowflake) schema model, according to which the data warehouse consists of a *fact table* (schematically, at the center of the star) surrounded by a set of *dimensional tables* related with the fact table. For SDMMS purposes, dimensional tables should maintain at least information (e.g., hierarchies) about *magnitude, intensity, geography, time dimension*, and so forth. (the so-called *dimensions* of the data cube), while the fact table should contain measures on seismological data, such as the *number of earthquakes, minimum/ maximum depth*, and so forth, as well as keys to related dimensional tables (Figure 4). Since geography is a key issue in SDMMS, involved in dimensions and/or measures, what we propose

here is a spatial data warehouse (Stefanovic et al., 2000).

In particular, dimension *time* consists of a hierarchy that represents time periods in which an earthquake happened. Dimensions *magnitude, intensity* and *depth* consist of intervals rather than hierarchies. They represent classes of *magnitude, intensity* and *depth* so that we can categorize the earthquake phenomena. Dimensions *geography* and *geology* represent the geographical area in which an earthquake happened and the geological morphology of this area, respectively. As for the fact table, the cardinality of a certain type of earthquake events (*number_of_quakes*) together with *min/max* and *average* information are stored.

In the following section, we present examples of operations that illustrate the usefulness of a database and a data warehouse that follow the schemes of Figure 2 and Figure 4, respectively.

QUERYING, OLAP ANALYSIS, AND MINING

Traditional database management systems (DBMS) are known as operational database or OLTP (online transaction processing) systems as they support the daily storage and retrieval needs of an information system. Apart from querying, they support three main operations (insertions, updates and deletions) that can be formalized and executed over a DBMS using a structured query language (SQL).

Nevertheless, maintaining summary data in a local data warehouse can be used for data analysis purposes. Two popular techniques for analyzing data and interpreting their meaning are OLAP analysis and data mining. An important aspect in decision making is the level of details that the decision-maker needs. Middle and upper management make complex and important decisions and therefore detailed data can not satisfy these requirements. Summarized data and hidden knowledge acquiring from the stored data can lead to better decisions. Similarly, summarized seismological data are of particular interest to earth scientists because they can study the phenomenon from a higher level and search for hidden, previously unknown knowledge.

Querying the Database

Querying seismological databases involves spatiotemporal concepts like snapshots, changes of objects and maps, motion and phenomena (Pfoser & Tryfona, 1998; Theodoridis, 2003). In particular, SDMMS should provide at least the following database querying functionality:

- **Retrieval of spatial information given a temporal instance:** This concept is used, for example, when we are dealing with records including position (latitude and longitude of earthquake epicenter) and time of earthquake realization together with attributes like magnitude, depth of epicenter, and so on.
- **Retrieval of spatial information given a temporal interval:** This way, evolution of spatial objects over time is captured (assume, for example, that we are interested in recording the duration of an earthquake and how certain parameters of the phenomenon

vary throughout the time interval of its duration).

- **Overlay of spatial information on layers given a temporal instance or interval:** The combination of layers and time information results into snapshots of a layer. For example, this kind of modeling is used when we are interested in magnitude thematic maps of earthquakes realized during a specific day inside a specific area (temporal instance) or modeling the whole sequence of earthquakes, including pre- and aftershocks (using the notion of layers in time intervals).

Examples of typical queries involving the spatial and the temporal dimension of seismological data are the following (Theodoridis, 2003):

- Find the ten epicenters of earthquakes realized during the past four months, which reside more closely to a given location.
- Find all epicenters of earthquakes residing in a certain region, with a magnitude $M>5$ and a realization time in the past four months.
- (Assuming multiple layers of information, e.g., corresponding to main cities' coordinates and population) find the five strongest quakes occurred in a distance of less than 100Km from cities of population over one million during the 20th century.

OLAP Analysis

Additional to (naïve or advanced) database queries on detailed seismological data, a data warehouse approach utilizes online analytical processing (OLAP). We illustrate the benefits obtained by such an approach with two examples of operations supported by spatial data warehouse and OLAP technologies:

- A user may ask to view part of the historical seismic profile, that is, the ten most destructive quakes in the past twenty years, over

Figure 5. Selecting parts of a cube by filtering a single (slice) or multiple dimensions (dice)

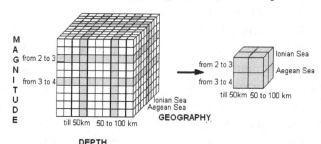

Figure 6. Alternative presentations: Views of a cube (pivot)

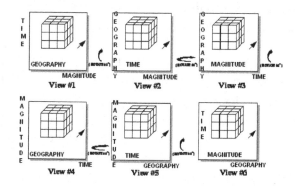

Europe, and, moreover, he/she can easily view the same information over Greece (more detailed view, formally a *drill-down* operation) or worldwide (more summarized view, formally a *roll-up* operation).

• Given the existence of multiple thematic maps, perhaps one for quake magnitude and one for another, non-geophysical parameter such as the resulting damage, these maps could be overlaid for the exploration of possible relationships, such as finding regions of high, though non-destructive, seismicity and vice versa.

Further to roll-up and drill-down operations described above, typical data cube operations include *slice* and *dice*, for selecting parts of a data cube by imposing conditions on a single or multiple cube dimensions, respectively (Figure 5), and *pivot*, which provides the user with alternative presentations of the cube (Figure 6).

Another important issue in data warehousing is the physical representation of a cube. Relational OLAP (ROLAP) and multidimensional OLAP (MOLAP) are the two principal models proposed in the literature. ROLAP actually uses relational tables that a relational DBMS is designed to handle, while MOLAP makes use of specialized structures (multi-dimensional arrays) designed especially for OLAP purposes. The advantage of ROLAP is that it can handle large volumes of data (since relational DBMS are perfect for this task). On the other hand, MOLAP is much faster for performing OLAP operations due to the extensive use of main memory structures.

For SDMMS purposes, where both requirements are there (large volume of data and fast OLAP operations), either ROLAP or MOLAP could be adopted for the implementation of the seismological data warehouse, or even a combination of the two (Hybrid OLAP – HOLAP), which has been recently supported by commercial DBMS, would be an alternative.

Data Mining

Integrating data analysis and mining techniques into an SDMMS ultimately aims to the discovery of interesting, implicit and previously unknown knowledge. The *knowledge discovery in databases* (KDD) process consists of the following steps, from the storage of interesting information in a data warehouse until the extraction, interpretation and understanding of useful, possibly hidden knowledge (Fayad et al., 1996; Han & Kamber, 2000):

1. Building a data warehouse from one or more raw databases (data warehouse building step)
2. Selecting and cleansing data warehouse contents to focus on target data (selection and cleansing step)
3. Transforming data to a format convenient for data mining (transformation step)
4. Extracting rules and patterns by using data mining techniques (data mining step)
5. Interpreting and evaluating data mining results to produce understandable and useful knowledge (interpretation and evaluation step)

Examples of useful patterns found through KDD process include clustering of information (e.g., shocks occurred closely in space and/or time), classification of phenomena with respect to area and epicenter, detecting phenomena semantics by using pattern finding techniques (e.g., characterizing the main shock and possible intensive aftershocks in shock sequences, measuring the similarity of shock sequences, according to a similarity measure specified by the domain expert, etc.). Recently, there have been proposals that expand the application of knowledge discovery

methods on multi-dimensional data (Koperski & Han, 1995; Koperski et al., 1998).

Association Rule Mining

Association rule mining aims at discovering interesting correlations among database attributes (Agrawal et al., 1993). Association rules are implications of the form $A \Rightarrow B [s, c]$, $A \subset J$, $B \subset J$ where A, B and J are sets of items (i.e., attributes), characterized by two measures: *support* (*s*) and *confidence* (*c*). The support of a rule $A \Rightarrow B$ expresses the probability that a database event contains both A and B, whereas the confidence of the rule expresses the conditional probability that a database event containing A also contains B.

As an example, an association rule on seismological data would be like the following (cf. discussion in SDMMS database subsection for attribute meanings):

location in $L \wedge depth \geq 100$ Km $\Rightarrow$ *magnitude* $\geq$ 5R [1%, 50%]

which is interpreted as follows: *whenever an earthquake occurs in location L at a depth of over 100 Km its magnitude is likely to be greater than 5R with a probability of 50%; this combination occurred in 1% of all recorded events.*

An interesting variation is that of temporal association rule mining (*sequencing*), which detects correlations between events with time as in the following example:

location in $L_1 \wedge magnitude \geq 7R \Rightarrow$ *location* in L_2 within [0, 30 days] [0.1%, 30%]

which is interpreted as follows: *whenever an earthquake occurs in location L_1 with a magnitude greater than 7R it is likely that another earthquake occurs in location L_2 within a month after the first event with a probability of 30%; this combination occurred in 0.1% of all recorded events.*

Figure 7. Discovering clusters of earthquake epicenters (Theodoridis, 2003)

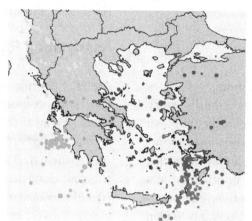

By identifying and analyzing event sequences (*seismic sequences*) seismologists can be assisted in studying this kind of earthquake behavior.

Clustering

Data clustering (Kaufman & Rousseeuw, 1990; Jain et al., 1999) is the unsupervised process of grouping together sets of objects into classes with respect to a similarity measure. Thus, it is the behavior of groups rather than that of individual events that is detected. Applications on seismic data could be for the purpose of finding densely populated regions (according to the Euclidean distance) between the epicenters, and, hence, locating regions of high seismic frequency or dividing the area of a country into zones according to seismicity criteria (e.g., low/medium/high seismic load) as illustrated in Figure 7.

Several clustering methods have been proposed in the literature. Using multi-dimensional correlations, local spatio-temporal clusters of low magnitude events can be extracted (Dzwinel et al., 2003). Also, correlations between the clusters and the earthquakes are recognized. Signal processing techniques can be applied to spatial data if they are considered as multidimensional signals (Sheikholeslami et al., 2000). A clustering approach based on wavelet transforms can identify clusters by finding dense regions in the transformed data. Finally, hybrid methodologies have been proposed (Guo et al., 2003) where spatial clustering is combined with high-dimensional clustering.

Data Classification

Classification is one of the most common supervised learning techniques. The objective of classification is to first analyze a (labeled) training set and, through this procedure, build a model for labeling new data entries (Han & Kamber, 2000). In particular, at the first step a classification model is built using a *training data set* consisting of database records that are known to belong in a certain class and a proper supervised learning method, e.g. decision trees or neural networks. In case of decision trees, for example, the model consists of a tree of "if" statements leading to a label denoting the class the record it belongs in. At the second step, the built model is used for the classification of records not included in the training set. Many methods have been developed for classification, including decision tree induction, neural networks and Bayesian networks (Fayad et al., 1996).

As an example, the (hypothetical) decision tree illustrated in Figure 8 tries to "predict" the

Figure 8. An example decision tree for seismological data

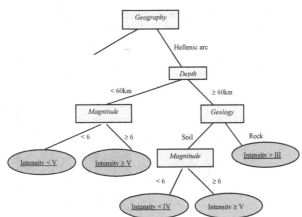

macroseismic intensity at a site given the depth and the magnitude of an earthquake, the geographic area and the local geology. Such an implication uncovers correlations among the attributes of the seismological database and decision trees of such a type are already used by local authorities to prioritize actions for response and relief of the population after a strong earthquake.

In this section, we presented querying, OLAP and data mining that could be used for extracting useful conclusions about seismological data stored in a SDMMS. These operations can be part of a system that manages seismological data in order to support the decision-making process.

SDMMS for Decision-Making Purposes

After having discussed the components of a SDMMS, we present alternative usage of such a system with respect to user profile:

- Citizens find a portal useful for getting information about past earthquakes and about protection against earthquakes.
- Geophysicists make data analysis for constructing and visualizing seismic profiles of certain regions.

- Public administration officers utilize information to improve emergency response and make decisions about the structural rules.

A system with these characteristics can be characterized as a Decision Support System (DSS) that will provide users with aggregated information and, even more, useful, interpretable and easily understood knowledge. Examples of decision making through collecting and analyzing seismological data are the following:

- Public administration officers utilize information to improve emergency response and make decisions about the structural rules. For example, PEADAB is a related EU-funded project towards this direction (Gerbesioti et al., 2001; PEADAB, 2006).
- Seismological events can not be isolated from the movement of plates that cause faults, the volcano activities, the site effects and many others. Seismologists need an integrated environment in which all this information can be presented and analyzed. So they can reach conclusions by collecting and analyzing seismological data using SDMMS, which can automate this process and provide strong analytical tools. As an example, an integrated seismic network, called CISN,

Figure 9. Descartes/Kepler functionality (Andrienko & Andrienko, 1999)

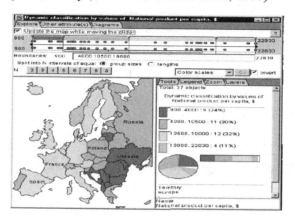

has been developed in California with ShakeMap and HAZUS being the two core tools of this network (Goltz & Eisner, 2003). ShakeMap is used to provide details about the earthquakes within five minutes after they happen. HAZUS, a methodology for earthquake, flood and wind hazards, generates estimates of population impacts in terms of deaths and injuries. Other provided estimates are damages to buildings, critical facilities and transportation lifelines.

A real challenge for the future could be the use of all the collected information to manage emergencies. Assume a DSS that could predict the level of destruction in urban areas and by taking under consideration the particular infrastructure (mass transport means, utility networks, locations of hospitals and schools, etc.) assist officers guide an emergency operation.

PROTOTYPE SYSTEMS AND TOOLS: A SURVEY

In this section, we present a number of prototype tools that have been proposed to collect, process and analyze seismological or, in general, spatial and earth science data. We also provide a short

comparison from the perspective of SDMMS architecture and objectives.

Descartes/Kepler

Andrienko and Andrienko (1999) proposed an integrated environment (Descartes/Kepler) where data mining and visualization techniques are used to analyze spatial data. Their aim is to integrate traditional data mining tools with cartographic visualization tools so that the users can view both source data and results produced by the data mining process.

Descartes provides mapping and visualization features. Furthermore, it supports some data transformations effective for visual analysis, and the dynamic calculation of derived variables. On the other hand, Kepler incorporates a number of data mining methods. It is an open platform and through an interface new methods can be added. Kepler supports the whole Knowledge KDD process including data input and format transformation tools, access to databases, querying, management of (intermediate) results, and graphical presentations of various kinds of data mining results (trees, rules, and groups).

Figure 9 illustrates a composite screenshot of the tool with maps and charts visualization.

Figure 10. Visualization capabilities in CommonGIS (CommonGIS, 2006)

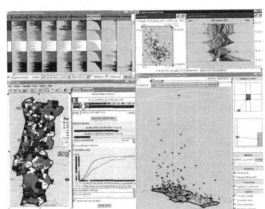

CommonGIS

CommonGIS (Kretschmer & Roccatagliata, 2000; CommonGIS, 2006) deals with geographical data and supports the visualization and analysis of statistical data that are related with spatial objects. The main features of CommonGIS are the following:

- Supports a variety of standard formats of map and table data
- Adopts a flexible client-server architecture that optimizes download time and supports integration of data from remote servers
- Combines interactive mapping techniques with statistical graphics displays and computation
- Includes comprehensive tools for analysis of spatial time-series
- Includes information visualization tools (dynamic query, table lens, parallel coordinate plots, etc.) dynamically linked to maps and graphics via highlighting, selection, and brushing
- Supports interactive multi-criteria decision making and sensitivity analysis
- Helps users to follow problem solving scenarios

- Applies multivariate graphics to the analysis of spatial data
- Displays spatio-temporal events and other kinds of multidimensional data
- Includes tools for interactive aggregation of grid data tightly coupled with dynamic visualization of aggregation results

Figure 10 illustrates a collection of visualization results supported by CommonGIS.

GEODE

Geo-Data Explorer (GEODE) is an ambitious and highly promising application developed by the USGS for providing users with geographically referenced data. The project aims in developing a portal which will provide real-time data and will support data analysis independently from special hardware, software and training (Levine & Schultz, 2002). The main features of GEODE include: simultaneous display of many data formats, possibility of downloading specific parts of datasets, illustration of data in real-time, support of multiple scales, unlimited dataset size; maps customization and support of image export.

Figure 11 illustrates the functionality of GEODE through a representative screenshot.

Figure 11. GEODE functionality (GEODE)

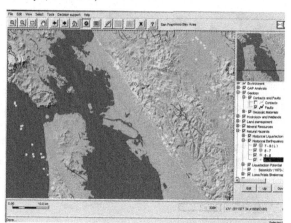

Figure 12. Querying capabilities of Seismo-Surfer (Seismo-Surfer, 2006)

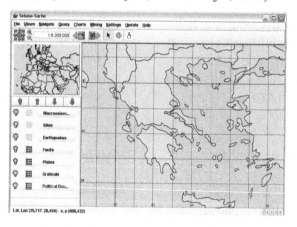

Seismo-Surfer

Last but not least, Seismo-Surfer is a tool for collecting, querying, and mining seismological data following the SDMMS concept (Theodoridis, 2003; Kalogeras et al., 2004; Seismo-Surfer, 2006). Its database is automatically updated from remote sources; querying on different earthquake parameters is allowed, while data analysis for extracting useful information is limited to a data clustering algorithm. Querying and mining results are graphically presented via maps and charts.

Seismo-Surfer architecture, in general, follows the SDMMS architecture illustrated in Figure

1. A number of filters cleanse and homogenize the datasets (mainly concerning about duplicate entries), which are available from remote sources and pre-processed datasets are stored in the local database. In its current version, Seismo-Surfer supports links with two remote sources: one at a national level for Greece (GI-NOA, 2006) and one worldwide (NEIC-USGS). Users interact with the database via a graphical user interface. Querying and data mining results are presented in graphical mode (maps, charts, etc.). Querying on earthquake parameters includes variations of spatial queries, such as range, distance, nearest-neighbor and top-N queries (illustrated in Figure 12).

Table 1. Comparing SDMMS prototypes

	Descartes/ Kepler	CommonGIS	GEODE	Seismo-Surfer
Web interface	No	Yes	Yes	Yes
Dynamic information (through Internet or Map load/retrieval)	Both	Internet	Both	Both
Commercial / prototype systems exploited	Descartes Kepler	Descartes PGS map server (Lava/Magma) Vizard	Informix PGS map server (Lava/Magma)	Oracle OpenMap
OLAP functionality	No	No	No	No
Data pre-processing	Cartographic visualization (Descartes) ETL techniques (Kepler)	Data characterization scheme	Image compression (MR SID), data transform unit	Filters for data cleansing & integration
Data mining techniques	Clustering, Classification, Assoc. rules	None	None	Clustering
Visualization techniques	Maps, Charts	Maps, Charts	Maps	Maps, Charts
Query formulation (via Interface or Query language)	Interface	Interface	Interface	Interface

A Comparison of SDMMS Prototypes

Table 1 presents a comparison between the different prototypes that were presented in this section. According to this table, all support dynamic loading of up-to-date information from remote sources, querying and visualization facilities; OLAP functionality is not provided at all, whereas data mining techniques are included in Descartes/ Kepler and Seismo-Surfer.

CONCLUSION

In this article, we discussed the architecture of a so-called *seismic data management and mining system* (SDMMS) for quick and easy data collection, processing (generating historic profiles of specific geographic areas and time periods,

providing the association of seismic data with other geophysical parameters of interest, etc.), and visualization supporting sophisticated user interaction.

The core components of this architecture include a seismological database (for querying) and a seismological data warehouse (for OLAP analysis and data mining). We provided template schemes for both components as well as examples of their functionality. Emphasis was put on the decision-making, since SDMMS could be used as a DSS by specialized earth scientists and public administration officers. We also provided a survey of existing operational or prototype systems following (at a low or high percentage) the proposed SDMMS functionality.

Interestingly, OLAP and data mining functionality vary from absent to quite limited. This is a hint for future work on the surveyed as well as new tools for seismological data management.

REFERENCES

Agarwal, S., Agrawal, R., Deshpande, P., Gupta, A., Naughton, J., Ramakrishnan, R., et al. (1996). On the computation of multidimensional aggregates. In *Proceedings of the 22nd International Conference on Very Large Databases, VLDB'96*, Bombay, India.

Agrawal, R., Imielinski, T., & Swami, A. (1993). Mining Association Rules between Sets of Items in Large Databases. In *Proceedings of ACM SIGMOD International Conference on Management of Data, SIGMOD'93* (pp. 207-216), Washington DC, USA.

Andrienko, G., & Andrienko N. (1999). Knowledge-based visualization to support spatial data mining. In *Proceedings of the 3rd Symposium on Intelligent Data Analysis, IDA'99*, Amsterdam, The Netherlands.

Barry, R., Cavers, D., & Kneale, C. (1975). Recommended standards for digital tape formats. *Geophysics, 40*, 344-352.

Behnke, J., & Dobinson, E. (2000). NASA workshop on issues in the application of data mining to scientific data. *ACM SIGKDD Explorations Newsletter, 2*(1), 70-79.

CommonGIS. (2006). *GIS for everyone...everywhere!*. Retrieved from http://commongis.jrc.it/index.html

Dzwinel, W., Yuen, D., Kaneko, Y., Boryczko, K., & Ben-Zion, Y. (2003). Multi-resolution clustering analysis and 3-D visualization of multitudinous synthetic earthquakes. *Visual Geosciences, 8*(1), 12-25.

Fayad, U., Piatetsky-Shapiro, G., Smith, P., & Uthurusami, R. (1996). *Advances in Knowledge Discovery and Data Mining*. MIT Press.

Gerbesioti, A., Delis, V., Theodoridis, Y., & Anagnostopoulos, S. (2001). Developing decision support tools for confronting seismic hazards. In *Proceedings of the 8th Panhellenic Conference in Informatics, PCI'01*, Nicosia, Cyprus.

GI-NOA. (2006). *Earthquake catalog*. Retrieved from http://www.gein.noa.gr/services/cat.html

Goltz, J., & Eisner R. (2003). Real-time emergency management decision support: The California integrated seismic network (CISN). In *Proceedings of the Disaster Resistant California 2003 Conference, DRC'03*, San Jose, CA, USA.

Guo, D., Peuquet D., & Gahegan, M. (2003). ICEAGE. Interactive clustering and exploration of large and high-dimensional geodata. *GeoInformatica, 7*(3), 229-253.

Han, J., & Kamber, M. (2000). *Data mining: Concepts and techniques*. Morgan Kaufmann.

Inmon, W. (1996). *Building the data warehouse*, 2nd ed. John Wiley & Sons.

Jain, A., Murty, M., & Flynn, P. (1999). Data clustering: A review. *ACM Computing Surveys, 31*(3), 264-323.

Kalogeras, I., Marketos, G., & Theodoridis, Y. (2004). A tool for collecting, querying, and mining macroseismic data. *Bulletin of the Geological Society of Greece, vol. XXXVI*.

Kaufman, L. & Rousseeuw, P. (1990). *Finding Groups in Data: An Introduction to Cluster Analysis*. John Wiley & Sons.

Kiratzi, A., & Louvari, E. (2003). Focal mechanisms of shallow earthquakes in the aegean sea and the surrounding lands determined by waveform modeling: A new database. *Journal of Geodynamics, 36*, 251-274.

Koperski K., & Han J. (1995). Discovery of spatial association rules in geographic information databases. In *Proceedings of the 4th International Symposium on Large in Spatial Databases, SSD'95*, Portland, MA, USA.

Koperski, K., Han, J., & Adhikary, J. (1998). Mining knowledge in geographical data. *Communications of the ACM, 26*(1), 65-74.

Kretschmer, U., & Roccatagliata, E. (2000). CommonGIS: A European Project for an Easy Access to Geo-data. In *Proceedings of the 2nd European GIS Education Seminar, EUGISES'00*, Budapest, Hungary.

Levine, M., & Schultz, A. (2002). *GEODE (Geo-Data Explorer)—A U.S. geological survey application for data retrieval, display, and analysis through the Internet*. U.S. Geological Survey, Fact Sheet 132-01, Online Version 1.0. Retrieved from http://pubs.usgs.gov/fs/fs132-01/

NEIC-USGS. *Earthquake search*. Retrieved from http://neic.usgs.gov/neis/epic/epic_global.html

PEADAB. (2006). *Post-earthquake assessment of building safety*. Retrieved from http://europa.eu.int/comm/environment/ civil/prote/cpactiv/cpact08a.htm

Pfoser, D., & Tryfona, N. (1998). Requirements, definitions and notations for spatiotemporal application environments. In *Proceedings of the 6th International Symposium on Advances in Geographic Information Systems, ACM-GIS'98*, (pp. 124-130). Washington DC, USA.

PPDM. (2006). *The data exchange project*. Retrieved from http://www.ppdm.org/standards/exchange/index.html

SEG. (2006). The Society of Exploration Geophysicists. http://www.seg.org

Seismo-Surfer. (2006). Seismo-Surfer Project. http://www.seismo.gr

Sheikholeslami, G., Chatterjee, S., & Zhang, A. (2000). WaveCluster: A Wavelet-based Clustering Approach for Spatial Data in Very Large Databases. *The VLDB Journal, 8*(3-4), 289-304.

Stefanovic, N., Han, J., & Koperski, K. (2000). Object-based selective materialization for efficient implementation of spatial data cubes. *IEEE Transactions on Knowledge and Data Engineering, 12*(6), 938-958.

Theodoridis, Y. (2003). Seismo-surfer: A prototype for collecting, querying and mining seismic data. In *Advances in Informatics—Post Proceedings of the 8th Panhellenic Conference in Informatics* (pp. 159-171*)*. Berlin: Springer Verlag.

Young, J., Presgrave, B., Aichele, H., Wiens, D., & Flinn, E. (1996). The Flinn-Engdahl Regionaligation Scheme: The 1995 Revision. *Physics of the Earth and Planetary Interiors, 96*, 223-297.

Yu, B. (2005). Mining earth science data for geophysical structure: A case study in cloud detection. In *Proceedings of 2005 SIAM International Conference on Data Mining, SIAM'05*, Newport Beach, CA, USA..

This work was previously published in International Journal of Data Warehousing and Mining, Vol. 4, Issue 1, edited by D. Taniar, pp. 1-16, copyright 2008 by IGI Publishing (an imprint of IGI Global).

Chapter 3
Automated Integration of Heterogeneous Data Warehouse Schemas

Marko Banek
University of Zagreb, Croatia

Boris Vrdoljak
University of Zagreb, Croatia

A Min Tjoa
Vienna University of Technology, Austria

Zoran Skočir
University of Zagreb, Croatia

ABSTRACT

A federated data warehouse is a logical integration of data warehouses applicable when physical integration is impossible due to privacy policy or legal restrictions. In healthcare systems federated data warehouses are a most feasible source of data for deducing guidelines for evidence-based medicine based on data material from different participating institutions. In order to enable the translation of queries in a federated approach, schemas of the federated warehouse and the local warehouses must be matched. In this paper we present a procedure that enables the matching process for schema structures specific to the multidimensional model of data warehouses: facts, measures, dimensions, aggregation levels and dimensional attributes. Similarities between warehouse-specific structures are computed by using linguistic and structural comparison. The calculated values are used to create necessary mappings.

INTRODUCTION

Increasing competitiveness in business and permanent demands for greater efficiency (either in business or government and non-profit organizations) enforce independent organizations to integrate their data warehouses. Data warehouse integration provides a broader base for decision-support systems, knowledge discovery and data mining than each of the separate independent warehouses could offer. Large corporations integrate their separately developed regional warehouses, newly merged companies integrate their warehouses to enable the business to be run centrally, while independent organizations join together their warehouses leading to a significant benefit to all participants and/or their customers.

In the field of healthcare the emergence of evidence-based medicine has made data integration a sine-qua-non topic. Evidence-based medicine (EBM) is the *conscientious, explicit, and judicious use of current best evidence in making decisions about the care of individual patients* (Sackett, Rosenberg, Muir Gray, Haynes & Richardson, 1996). It complements an existing clinical decision making process with the most accurate and most efficient research evidence. Application of its concepts speeds up the transfer of clinical research findings into practice, leading to a higher percentage of healed patients, to cost reduction, both for patients and health insurance organizations, as well as to the improvement of the healthcare process as a whole.

Successful application of evidence-based medicine is strongly related to the data it relies on. The central part of an evidence-based medical information system is a large data warehouse that unites all relevant internal healthcare data of an institution with the evidence-based guidelines coming mostly from outside scientific sources. In order to enhance the productivity of their administration, healthcare organizations practicing evidence-based medicine are striving to a better cooperation with other related organizations. The

more data is joined together and the larger and thus more reliable data patterns are created, the more knowledge can be gathered from them. Thus, healthcare organizations practicing evidence-based medicine need to join their data into a single data warehouse, which serves as the foundation of the knowledge discovery system.

The traditional approach to integrating two or more data warehouses (often called *component warehouses* or *local warehouses*) is to create a new warehouse, to which the data from all component warehouses are physically copied and thus joined into a single system. However, when independent organizations share their data for mutual purposes, their privacy policies or legal limitations may reduce the access to some data and restrict or completely forbid any physical copy of their data to be created in any system that is out of their full control. The highly confidential and legally protected healthcare records, whose integration has motivated this article, are a typical example of such data.

An alternative approach to a "fully" physical integration that is able to cope with the imposed restrictions could be based on the bus architecture (Inmon, 1996; Hackney, 1997). The local warehouses would contain both detailed and summarized data and a central, physical data warehouse containing exclusively summarized data would be used for OLAP. However, discovering rules in evidence-based medicine requires processing of detailed data that corresponds to the basic (i.e. most detailed) granularity level in the component warehouses. Thus, all data from the components should be transferred into the joint warehouse and not only the summarized data. Moreover, the bus architecture requires the component warehouses to be developed simultaneously, while in our case the integration of independently developed, heterogeneous warehouses is needed.

In our opinion, the proper solution to integrating healthcare data warehouses is a *data warehouse federation* (Sheth & Larson, 1990; Jindal & Acharya, 2004). The integration is performed from a logical point of view, using a *common conceptual model* (Jindal & Acharya, 2004), while only heterogeneous local source warehouses exist physically. The user of such a federated solution observes the whole federation as a single unit i.e. she must not notice that several heterogeneous parts of the warehouse actually exist (Sheth & Larson, 1990). The logical existence of the federated warehouse does not have any impact on the users of local component warehouses. In our previous work (Banek, Tjoa & Stolba, 2006; Stolba, Banek & Tjoa, 2006), we developed the conceptual model of a federated data warehouse that unifies data warehouses of different health insurance organizations.

Queries on the federated data warehouse must be translated into sub-queries that correspond to the conceptual models of local warehouses. Furthermore, results of the queries need to be translated to match the conceptual model of the federation and then merged into a single final answer. In order to perform query translation, a list of mappings between the structures of the federated multidimensional conceptual model and their corresponding counterparts in the multidimensional conceptual models of the local warehouses must be discovered. Since the multidimensional data model prevails in data warehouse design, the mappings must be defined for all particular structure types of the multidimensional conceptual model: facts, measures, dimensions, aggregation levels and dimensional attributes.

In this article, we introduce a mechanism that is capable to automate at the greatest extent possible the process of creating the mappings between the corresponding multidimensional structures in order to shorten the data warehouse integration process as a whole. Our mechanism is strictly aimed at matching complex multidimensional schemas consisting of multiple facts and shared dimensions. The contribution of our work is to propose a match discovery procedure for data warehouse-specific multidimensional structures, with special emphasis to aggregation levels. We

enhance the match discovery techniques for database and semi-structured data schemas, enabling their application to data warehouse schemas.

A schema matching process can never be fully automated, since no semantic model of an information system can match the real-world state completely. Moreover, the federated conceptual model and the conceptual models of the local warehouses may interpret the same real-world state in a different manner. Therefore, we introduce a semi-automated matching process, where a plan of mappings between the corresponding structures is created fully automatically and where then a warehouse designer checks and, if necessary, corrects the proposed plan. A software implementation of the integration process is provided and the entire procedure is verified on an example.

This article is an extended version of our DaWaK 2007 conference paper (Banek, Vrdoljak, Tjoa & Skočir, 2007). The DaWaK 2007 conference paper sketched the characteristics of our automated procedure for matching multidimensional warehouse schemas. In addition, this article describes in detail the problem of selecting optimal mappings between multidimensional structures and presents our heuristic solution implemented as a greedy algorithm. Moreover, we thoroughly illustrate the experiments performed in order to verify our approach and give a comparison between our approach and existing automated techniques for matching database schemas, XML Schemas and ontologies. Besides, the article provides an exhaustive study of the related work in automating the matching process for different kinds of schemas.

The article is structured as follows. Section 2 gives an overview of the related work. Basic strategies for matching multidimensional structures are presented in Section 3. Similarity functions for multidimensional structures are shown in Section 4, while the mapping strategies are explained in the Section 5. Section 6 evaluates the performance of the algorithm that matches data warehouse schemas and compares the algorithm with existing techniques for matching database schemas, XML Schemas and ontologies. Conclusions are drawn in Section 7.

RELATED WORK

There are two basic approaches to automated matching of database schemas, semi-structured data schemas and ontologies: *schema-based* and *instance-based* (Rahm & Bernstein, 2001). While schema-based matching considers only schema metadata and not instance data, instance-based matching uses both schema metadata and instance data (i.e. the content of a database, semi-structured documents or ontology instances).

Another classification of the matching techniques distinguishes between *rule-based* and *learning-based* approaches (Doan & Halevi, 2005). Rule-based techniques are based on hand-crafted rules (e.g. *two elements match if they have the same name and the same number of sub-elements*). In those approaches, the similarity of schema elements is generally regarded as a probability function, with values in the [0,1] interval, and is computed as a combination of the similarities of names, data types and/or substructures. Learning-based solutions employ a variety of learning techniques (e.g. neural network or naïve Bayes approach). Recent approaches involve domain ontologies, as well as various combinations of search, information retrieval or data mining techniques in order to produce complex matches. Schema-based matching techniques are rule-based, while instance-based techniques can either be rule-based or learning-based.

Some of the matching techniques search for mappings between two or more sources in order to define the integrated schema (e.g. the federated database schema from two source database schemas). Such approaches are called *mediators* (Madhavan, Bernstein & Rahm, 2001). Other tech-

niques are focused on creating mappings between the sources regardless of their final use.

Well known schema-based approaches designed for matching of database or semi-structured (particularly XML) schemas are *ARTEMIS-MOMIS* (Bergamaschi, Castano & Vincini, 1999), *Cupid* (Madhavan et al., 2001) and *similarity flooding* (Melnik, Garcia-Molina & Rahm, 2002). The first two approaches analyze names of schema elements (database tables and attributes; elements in XML documents) and also the relationships between them (table-attribute relationships; nesting in XML documents). A similarity coefficient is associated with all structure pairs. The similarity coefficient expresses the degree of equivalence between the structures (the maximal value of the coefficient is 1 for totally equivalent structures, while the minimal value 0 would denote that the structures are not related at all). Both in ARTEMIS-MOMIS and Cupid, the linguistic analysis of structure names does not include only string comparisons (a measure parameter called edit distance is calculated as the minimum number of token insertions, deletions, and substitutions required to transform one string into another, as defined by Levenshtein (1966)), but also additional semantic knowledge (synonyms, antonyms, related terms) from different thesaurus sources. On the other hand, the *similarity flooding* algorithm translates database tables or semi-structured sources into graphs and performs an initial string comparison of the graph vertices' names without using semantic knowledge. Later steps are based on calculations within the graph.

DIKE (Palopoli, Saccà, Terracina & Ursino; 2003) is a schema-based technique designed as a part of a database mediator tool, which uses entity-relationship diagrams as input. Database objects (entities, relationships, attributes and subschemes formed as clusters of entities, relationships and attributes) are translated into a graph and the similarity between the graph vertices is computed taking into account the lexical similarity of their names and the similarity of the related objects in their neighborhood. A thesaurus derived from WordNet is applied to calculate lexical similarity.

Rahm, Do and Massmann (2004) define a technique for matching large XML Schemas without additional analysis of the corresponding XML documents. They propose a fragment-oriented approach in order to decompose a complex matching problem into several simple problems. Reusing existing matching results at the level of schema fragments is regarded as a way to speed up the process.

Instance-based approaches apply various learning and mining techniques to compare instance data, together with schema metadata (thus being able to outperform schema-based techniques). iMAP (Dhamankar, Lee, Doan, Halevy & Domingos, 2004) is a comprehensive approach for semi-automatic discovery of semantic matches between database schemas, which uses neural networks and text searching methods. Doan, Lu, Lee and Han (2003) combine mining algorithms (decision trees and association rules) with manually created rules to analyze database tuples. In addition to a standard analysis of equal or similar content of joint attributes in tuples, disjoint attributes are also examined. The matching process is augmented by examining knowledge of the content domain. Embley, Xu and Ding (2004) convert database and ontology schemas to graphs and then apply decision trees over the object names and the data instance values. Particular relevance is given to mappings of cardinality n:1 and n:m, which are created by using the knowledge of the domain provided by ontology snippets.

Many techniques aimed at matching ontologies are graph-based or share basic principles with approaches for database schema matching. Recent techniques have been particularly focused on ontologies written in the OWL language, which became a W3C Recommendation in 2004. FCA-Merge (Stumme & Maedche, 2001) is a bottom-up approach for ontology mediation based on Formal Concepts Analysis. The input data are two source ontologies and natural language documents that contain instances of the ontology concepts. First a *formal context* is created automatically for each of the two ontologies and then the common context with its concept lattice is produced. The mediated ontology is extracted from the common concept lattice by manual analysis. Euzenat and Valtchev (2004) present a technique for automatically aligning OWL-Lite ontologies based on similarity computation. Ontologies are translated into graphs and similarity scores between ontology components produced as probability coefficients. The similarity measure is based on linguistic similarity between class names and on structural relations: the subsumption relation (superclass-subclass), the relation between classes and their instances and the relation between classes and their properties.

COMA++ (Aumueller, Do & Massmann, 2005) is a tool that matches relational schemas, XML Schemas and OWL ontologies. It offers a graphical interface, allowing a variety of user interactions. All data models are converted to directed graphs and then the matching process is performed using a combination of more than ten different matching algorithms proposed in the literature. COMA++ applies a fragment-based divide-and-conquer approach to matching and supports the reuse of previous matches.

There are two basic approaches to implementing query translation between the conceptual model of a federated database (or a federated warehouse as well) and the conceptual models of local databases (warehouses) once the mappings between them have been provided. Both approaches use the wrapper/mediator architecture. The mediator module (Beneventano & Bergamaschi, 2006; Beneventano, Bergamaschi, Guerra & Vincini, 2003) handles the queries on the federation and uses the mappings between the conceptual models to create sub-queries corresponding to the local sources. Wrappers provide an interface to local databases. The *local-as-view* (LAV) approach (Ullman, 1997) represents the content of each local source as a view over the *global virtual view* i.e. the federation. It is applicable when new sources are frequently added to the federation, but requires the federation itself to be well-defined (probably by hand, not created automatically from the sources). The *global-as-view* (GAV) approach (Halevy, 2001) represents the content of all federation components as a view over the local sources. GAV directs the system how to use the sources to retrieve data and thus significantly reduces the effort of defining the query processing policy. However, extending the system with a new source becomes complicated in the majority of cases, when it requires a redefinition of the views associated to the federation.

Semantic similarity of names is actually represented by the semantic similarity of words that stem from the names. Semantic similarity functions present the degree of relatedness of two input words (word senses). Similarity calculation is performed by exploring the relationships between concepts (terms) in thesauri. Some techniques (Resnik, 1999) additionally use information theory principles (terms appearing less frequently are considered more significant; concepts with a more "elaborate" meaning are more significant than their super-classes i.e. more general terms: e.g. *screwdriver* in comparison with *tool*). The technique described by Yang and Powers (2005) exploits WordNet (WordNet, 2007), a large thesaurus of English language hand-crafted by psycholinguists. WordNet organizes terms according to human, native speaker's perception, providing a list of synonyms, antonyms and homonyms, as well as the subordination-superordination hierarchy and part-whole relations. Words (word senses) in WordNet are interpreted as graph vertices, connected by edges representing subordination-superordination and part-whole relations (each edge is given a weight according to the relation type). All possible paths between two target vertices are constructed and weights are multiplied across paths. The highest weight

product represents the linguistic similarity between two target words.

To the best of our knowledge, none of the existing frameworks for automated schema matching has been successfully applied to match data warehouses, due to the specific features of the multidimensional conceptual model. An automated check of match compatibility between data warehouse dimensions is performed by Cabibbo and Torlone (2005), where however match candidates must first be proposed manually by the integration designer. Moreover, if a dimension of one warehouse is compatible to more than one dimension in another warehouse, it is not considered which of the two possible matches would be preferred, since the approach applies no semantic reasoning at all.

MATCHING STRATEGY FOR SOLVING HETEROGENEITIES AMONG MULTIDIMENSIONAL STRUCTURES

The goal of our research is to automate the process of matching data warehouse schemas in cases when the access to data warehouse content is prohibited (as in case of healthcare data warehouses). Hence, we develop a matching algorithm that is exclusively based on analyzing data warehouse schemas. The new algorithm combines some warehouse-oriented enhancements of the already mentioned standard database and XML schema matching approaches (Bergamaschi et al., 1999; Madhavan et al., 2001; Melnik et al., 2002) with the entirely new strategies specific to data warehouses and the multidimensional conceptual model.

Since our federated data warehouse for evidence-based medicine (Banek et al., 2006) needed to be based on an international standard for medical healthcare systems, we had to create it manually by analyzing both the international standard (Health Level Seven, 2008) and the source warehouses, which were all created before the existence of the standard. Hence, there was

Figure 1. Two compatible tables with different attribute and table conflicts

first_name (string)	last_name (string)	street_name (string)	street_number (string)	city (string)	country (string)	INSURANT
Robert	Brandt	Murgasse	5A	Graz	Austria	

given_name (string)	middle_name (string)	family_name (string)	address (string)	municipality (string)	country (characte)	PATIENT
Robert	Heinrich	Brandt	Murgasse 5A	Graz	A	

Table 1. Classification of conflicts among data warehouses

	Facts	Dimensions

Schema level	• different members of dimensions ("dimensionality")
	• naming conflicts (measures)
	• domain conflicts (measures)
		• diverse aggregation hierarchies
		  ○ inner level conflicts
		  ○ lowest level conflicts
		• domain and/or naming conflicts (dimensional attributes)

Schema-instance	• fact context as dimension instances	• dimension members as contextual dimensions

no need to develop a mediator tool such as AR-TEMIS/MOMIS or DIKE. Instead, we focused on automating the generation of mappings between the manually created federated warehouse and each of the source warehouses.

Classification of Schema Heterogeneities

Heterogeneities in data warehouse schemas arise either when:

1. different structures (relational, multidimensional etc.) are used to represent the same information, or
2. different specifications (i.e. different interpretations) of the same structure exist.

A survey of heterogeneities that arise in *multidatabase systems* i.e. the integration of different relational databases is given by Kim and Seo (1991). Attribute conflicts are due to different names and domains and can be categorized either as one-to-one or -to-many. Examples are depicted

in Figure 1. One-to-one conflicts are caused by different naming (attribute *city* in table *insurant* corresponding to attribute *municipality* in table *patient*) or different assignments to domains (the two *country* attributes with different data types). An example of-to-many conflict are two attributes in table *insurant*, *street_name* and *street_number*, which correspond to a single attribute in table *patient*, *address*. Table conflicts occur when two tables in different databases describe the same information, but different names, data types or constraints are used to represent the information (there is a table conflict between tables *insurant* and *patient* due to different naming).

Berger and Schrefl (2006) analyzed heterogeneities that appear in data warehouse integration. Apart from naming and domain conflicts (presented by Kim and Seo), they introduce additional conflicts that are specific to data warehouses and the multidimensional conceptual model. Their classification of conflicts is given in Table 1.

Diverse aggregation hierarchies can manifest either as a *lowest level conflict* or an *inner level conflict*. In the first case, two semantically

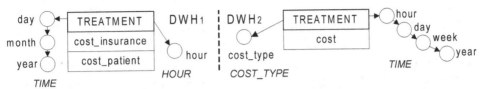

Figure 2. Data warehouses with heterogeneities specific to the multidimensional model

corresponding dimensions (e.g. *time* dimensions in DWH_1 and DWH_2 in Figure 2) have different lowest (i.e. basic) grain level (*day* and *hour*) which means that the granularity of their facts is also different. In the second case there is a common aggregation level (not necessarily the lowest), but the aggregation at the coarser grain levels takes different ways (levels *month* and *week* in DWH_1 and DWH_2, respectively).

The *dimensionality conflict* corresponds to a different number of dimensions associated with the same fact (the *hour* and *time* dimensions in DWH_1 corresponding to a single *time* dimension in DWH_2). Finally, *schema-instance conflicts* appear when some context of the fact in one data warehouse becomes the content (value) of dimensions in the other (*insurance* and *patient* are part of measure names in DWH_1, while being values of the *cost_type* dimension in DWH_2).

The Matching Algorithm

In this article we adopt the *Dimensional Fact Model*, a variant of the multidimensional conceptual model defined by Golfarelli, Maio and Rizzi (1998), with some extensions concerning complex dimension hierarchies as described by Mansmann and Scholl (2006). A multidimensional data warehouse schema consists of a set of *facts*, which describe the topic of interest for the decision-making process: $\mathcal{F} = \{F_1, F_2, ..., F_m\}$. Each fact F_i is described by a set of *measures*, continuous (usually numeric) attributes $m_i = \{m_{i1}, m_{i2}, ..., m_{in}\}$, as well as a set of mutually independent parameters called *dimensions*. Facts may share dimensions and therefore the set of dimensions $\mathcal{D}$ is not associated with each fact, but to the warehouse as a whole $\mathcal{D}$

$= \{D_1, D_2, ..., D_p\}$. Particular subsets of $\mathcal{D}$, $\mathcal{D}_i \subseteq \mathcal{D}$ are associated with each fact F_i.

A *hierarchy schema* $\mathcal{H}_j$ of dimension D_j is a four-tuple $(\mathcal{L}_j, \subseteq_{\mathcal{H}_j}, \top_{\mathcal{H}_j}, \bot_{\mathcal{H}_j})$, where $\mathcal{L}_j = \{L_{j1}, L_{j2}, ..., L_{jq}\}$ is the set of aggregation levels of $\mathcal{H}_j$, $\subseteq_{\mathcal{H}_j}$ is a partial order on the levels of $\mathcal{L}_j$, and $\top_{\mathcal{H}_j}$ and $\bot_{\mathcal{H}_j}$ are the top (most abstract) and bottom (most detailed) levels of the ordering, respectively. A hierarchy H (an instance of hierarchy schema $\mathcal{H}$) is a pair $(\mathcal{L}_H, \subseteq)$, where $\mathcal{L}_H = \{L_{jk}\}$ is a set of levels. Each aggregation level L_{jk} contains a set a_{jk} of associated attributes $a_{jk} = \{a_{jk1}, a_{jk2}, ..., a_{jkr}\}$.

The matching process determines whether two multidimensional structures S_1 and S_2, belonging to data warehouses DWH_1 and DWH_2, respectively, are mutually equivalent. The two structures, S_1 and S_2, may either be facts, measures, dimensions, aggregation levels or dimensional attributes, where we state that both of them must belong to the same type of multidimensional structures.

The mapping plan for structures of type S, $\mathcal{M}_S$, is actually a set of pairs: $\mathcal{M}_S = \{(S_1, S_2) \mid S_1 \in DWH_1 \wedge S_2 \in DWH_2\}$ where all structures must be of the same type. Mapping cardinalities can be one-to-one, one-to-many or many-to-many. Mappings of the type -to-many are more likely to be expected for attributes and measures than for aggregation levels, dimensions or facts.

The algorithm that automatically matches heterogeneous data warehouse schemas consists of two basic phases:

1. comparison of match target structures,
2. creation of mappings.

During the first phase the equivalence of multidimensional structures is determined as the value of a probability function called similarity function. Similarity between multidimensional structures is calculated (using a heuristic algorithm given in Section 4) by comparing their names as well as their data types (for attributes and measures) and substructures (for aggregation levels, dimensions and facts). While the same basic idea is used by ARTEMIS/MOMIS and Cupid, these frameworks cannot solve the heterogeneities that specifically occur in the multidimensional model of data warehouses, especially the hierarchical organization of aggregation levels in dimensions.

In the second phase, heuristic rules are applied to determine which structures should be mapped as equivalent, among a much larger number of possible matches. The result of the automated matching process must as much as possible be commensurate with the solution that a data warehouse designer would produce manually.

Our matching algorithm recognizes four levels of matching:

1. facts,
2. dimensions and measures (constructing the facts),
3. aggregation levels (constructing the dimensions), and
4. dimensional attributes (constructing the aggregation levels).

Similarity calculation (the first part of the matching algorithm) starts with atomic structures, dimensional attributes and measures, whose similarity is computed from the similarity of their names and data types. Similarity between aggregation levels is calculated next, taking into account their names and the already calculated similarity between attributes of which they consist. The process continues with dimension similarity, while similarity between facts is determined at the end.

On the other hand, we opine that mapping (the second phase of the automated matching process) must start with the most complex multidimen-

sional structures: the facts. If we determine that two facts are compatible (i.e. that they match), we map in parallel their measures and dimensions in the next step. The mapping candidates are only measures and dimensions of the two facts and no other measures and dimensions in the warehouse schema. Next, we proceed to aggregation levels (mapping aggregation levels is limited exclusively to the levels of the already matched dimensions) and then, finally, to attributes (attributes are mapped only within the already mapped aggregation levels).

Mapping Aggregation Levels

Mapping facts, measures, dimensions and dimensional attributes is similar to mapping database structures, as they form flat arrays. For instance, given two corresponding facts F_1 and F_2, a dimension D_{1i}, which belongs to F_1 can be mapped to any dimension D_{2j} belonging to F_2. Each dimension is mapped to its most similar counterpart according to the value of the similarity function.

Hierarchical structure imposes several inherent limits to aggregation level matching, as the existing partial order must be preserved. The limitations and additional heuristic recommendations are shown in the remainder of this section.

Prohibition of mappings that violate the partial order in hierarchies. Let D_1 and D_2 be two mapped dimensions, each of them (for reasons of simplicity) containing of a single hierarchy H_1 and H_2, respectively. Let L_{1i} be an aggregation level in D_1 (belonging to H_1) and L_{2j} an aggregation level in D_2 (belonging to H_2). Let L_{1i} and L_{2j} be equivalent, matching levels and let their mapping already be registered: $(L_{1i}, L_{2j}) \in \mathcal{M}_L$ (as depicted in the left part of Figure 3). In this case, no level in D_1 representing a finer granularity than L_{1i} (e.g. $L_{1(i-1)}$) can be mapped to a level in D_2 representing a coarser granularity than L_{2j} (e.g. $L_{2(j+1)}$). Similarly, no level in D_2 representing a finer granularity than L_{2j} (e.g. $L_{2(j-1)}$) can be mapped to a level in D_1 representing a coarser granularity

Figure 3. Illustrating restrictions to aggregation level matching

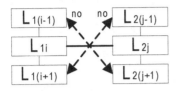 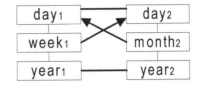

Figure 4. Prohibition of mapping unmatched levels to the counterparts of their descendants

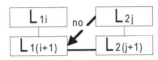 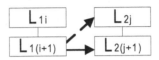

than L_{1i} (e.g. $L_{1(i+1)}$). The mapping between L_{1i} and L_{2j} is represented by a solid line. Invalid mappings $(L_{1(i-1)}, L_{2(j+1)})$ and $(L_{1(i+1)}, L_{2(j-1)})$ are showed as dashed lines. The coherence of partial orders in dimensions has also been stated as a necessary condition for dimension compatibility by Cabibbo and Torlone (2005).

Mapping unmatched levels to the counterparts of their parent levels. This strategy is used to solve inner level conflicts. Let us suppose that the equivalent levels day_1 and day_2, as well as $year_1$ and $year_2$ have already been mapped (see right part of Figure 3). The obvious incompatibility between levels $week_1$ and $month_2$ is noted by a low value of the similarity function between them. Week records in D_1 and month records in D_2 are both aggregations obtained by summing the day records. Since $week_1$ records can also be obtained by summing day_2 records, $week_1$ can be mapped to day_2, which is the counterpart of its parent (i.e. the nearest finer) level, day_1. Similarly, $month_2$ can be mapped to day_1. When a query on D_1 concerning $week_1$ is translated in order to correspond to D_2, records of the level day_2 need to be summed.

Prohibition of mapping unmatched levels to the counterparts of their descendants. This rule is not inherent to the multidimensional model as both previous rules (it would be possible to create valid mappings that are not in accordance with it), but is experience-based. Consider the left part of

Figure 4. Let there be a mapping between levels $L_{1(i+1)}$ and $L_{2(j+1)}$, i.e. $(L_{1(i+1)}, L_{2(j+1)}) \in \mathcal{M}_L$.

Mapping L_{1i} (or any of its ancestors, i.e. levels finer than L_{1i}) to $L_{2(j+1)}$, as well as mapping L_{2j} (or any of its ancestors) to $L_{1(i+1)}$ should be prohibited. An explanation can be obtained by watching the matching process in the other direction. The goal of the mapping process is to map every level to the coarsest possible counterpart that semantically corresponds to it (in order to preserve the richness of the hierarchy). Supposing that $L_{1(i+1)}$ is equally similar to L_{2j} and $L_{2(j+1)}$ we prefer mapping it to $L_{2(j+1)}$ (in the right part of Figure 4, the solid pointed line represents the "proper" mapping, while the dashed pointed line symbolizes the worse choice). Back to the initial problem, mapping L_{2j} to $L_{1(i+1)}$, can be viewed in the opposite direction, as mapping $L_{1(i+1)}$ to L_{2j}. $L_{1(i+1)}$ is already mapped to $L_{2(j+1)}$, which is coarser than L_{2j}, so mapping it to L_{2j} would be redundant and useless.

SIMILARITY FUNCTIONS FOR MULTIDIMENSIONAL STRUCTURES

As stated in Section 3, the process of schema matching starts with calculating similarities between multidimensional structures. Later we apply a match selection algorithm based on those similarities. The existing matching approaches where similarity between particular structures

Table 2. Data type (in)compatibility coefficients

Compatible data types		Incompatible data types	
Combination of reduced data types	**Coefficient value** *tcoeff*	**Combination of reduced data types**	**Coefficient value** *tcoeff*
string-string	0,95	string-numeric	0,80
numeric-numeric	0,95	string-datetime	0,75
datetime-datetime	1,00	string-boolean	0,75
boolean-boolean	1,00	numeric-datetime	0,75
		numeric-boolean	0,75
		datetime-boolean	0.70

is computed are described in the works of Bergamaschi et al. (1999), Madhavan et al. (2001), Melnik et al. (2002), Rodríguez and Egenhofer (2003) and Dhamankar et al. (2004).

The basic idea for similarity calculation is the fact that complex structures' similarity is computed from the similarities between their less complex substructures, by means of some mathematical expression. Therefore, the similarity between any two complex multidimensional structures of the same kind can be recursively translated into a set of calculations at the atomic level: the level of dimensional attributes and measures.

Similarity Calculation for Measures and Dimensional Attributes

We introduce a new formula for calculating similarity between two dimensional attributes or two measures. Their similarity is obtained from the similarity of their names (*nsim*) and the data type compatibility coefficient *tcoeff* raised to the power determined by a non-negative real number *texp* (the latter enables us to calibrate the formula):

$$sim_{atomic}(S_1, S_2) = nsim(S_1, S_2) \cdot tcoeff(S_1, S_2)^{texp},$$
$$texp \in [0, \infty). \tag{1}$$

Similarity of structure names is actually the semantic similarity of words that stem from the names. Semantic similarity functions present the degree of relatedness of two input words (word senses), which is calculated by using the technique developed by Yang and Powers (2005), briefly described in the Related work section.

We assume the notion of data type compatibility such that attributes sharing their data type are more related than those that do not. We reduce all data types to four basic ones: *numeric, string, datetime* and *boolean*. Infrequently appearing data types (*date, boolean*) are more indicative than the frequent *string* and *numeric* types, either when their compatibility indicates a higher similarity or when their incompatibility suggests that the attributes do not correspond. We empirically determine the value of *tcoeff* as shown in Table 2.

Complex Structure Similarity

We adopt the idea of similarity between complex structures as stated by Madhavan et al. (2001). Similarity between structures S_1 and S_2 is a weighted sum (i.e. linear combination) of their name similarity (*nsim*) and structural similarity (*ssim*), to which all substructures at the next lower level of matching (as expressed in Section 3) contribute (let Σ_{S1} and Σ_{S2} denote the substructure sets of S_1 and S_2, respectively; let w_{name} be the weight of name similarity):

$$sim(S_1, S_2) = w_{name} \cdot nsim(S_1, S_2) +$$
$$+ (1 - w_{name}) \cdot ssim(\Sigma_{S1}, \Sigma_{S2}),$$
$$w_{name} \in [0, 1]. \tag{2}$$

The structure similarity formula for aggregation levels (Equation 3) considers the already calculated similarities between dimensional attributes (as explained in Section 3, a_{li} denotes the attribute set of level L_{li}). Likewise, structure similarity formula for dimensions (Equation 4) considers aggregation levels, while the structure similarity formula for facts (Equation 5) deals both with dimensions and measures. Each of the three formulas is basically the same, but the values of the four weight factors w_{lname}, w_{dname}, w_{fname} and w_m may differ (their exact values will be determined in Section 6).

$$
\begin{aligned}
sim(L_{1i}, L_{2j}) = &\ w_{lname} \cdot nsim(L_{1i}, L_{2j}) + \\
&+ (1-w_{lname}) \cdot ssim(a_{1i}, a_{2j}) \\
&\quad w_{lname} \in [0, 1].
\end{aligned}
\tag{3}
$$

$$
\begin{aligned}
sim(D_1, D_2) = &\ w_{dname} \cdot nsim(D_1, D_2) + \\
&+ (1-w_{dname}) \cdot ssim(\mathcal{L}_1, \mathcal{L}_2) \\
&\quad w_{dname} \in [0, 1].
\end{aligned}
\tag{4}
$$

$$
\begin{aligned}
sim(F_1, F_2) = &\ w_{fname} \cdot nsim(F_1, F_2) + \\
&+ w_m \cdot ssim(m_1, m_2) + \\
&+ (1 - w_{fname} - w_m) \cdot ssim(\mathcal{D}_1, \mathcal{D}_2), \\
&w_{fname}, w_m \in [0, 1], \quad w_{fname} + w_m \le 1.
\end{aligned}
\tag{5}
$$

Madhavan et al. (2001) calculate structure similarity recursively, with some initial values being adjusted in several steps. We use a different approach, adapting the formula for calculating semantic similarity among entity classes of different ontologies (Rodriguez & Egenhofer, 2003). *Neighborhood similarity* between two entity classes takes into account not only their names, but also other classes surrounding them within a certain radius. We make an analogy between complex structures and entity classes. Their substructures can then be viewed as analogous to neighborhood classes, surrounding the target (i.e. the complex structure) within a radius of size one. Aggregation levels are surrounded by their attributes (there is an edge between each attribute and the target

aggregation level), dimensions are surrounded by their aggregation levels and facts are surrounded by their dimensions and measures.

MAPPING MULTIDIMENSIONAL STRUCTURES

Creation of mappings is the second main phase of the algorithm for an automated warehouse schema matching. It is performed after the accomplishment of the comparison between the target multidimensional structures. The comparison algorithms calculate similarity for the entire Cartesian product of the two target sets. Although these similarities are low for most of the pairs, there often exist several match candidates that are highly and approximately equally similar to a single target structure. Many of those high-similarity mapping candidates are still redundant. Moreover, some mappings may even be contradictory, as the existence of one of them can make some others incorrect and impossible (e.g. following the restrictions on aggregation level matching). The creation of mappings is determined by two basic factors:

1. constraints,
2. selection metrics.

The basic constraint applied is the *structure type constraint*. Multidimensional structures belonging to one of the five structure types (facts, measures, dimensions, aggregation levels, dimensional attributes) can be mapped only to the structures of the same type. On the other hand, we do not directly apply *data type constraints* for matching dimensional attributes and measures. Still, the data type affects the final value of similarity between two attributes or measures and thus also affects the result of the entire matching process (see Equation 1).

Cardinality constraints define whether a structure needs to be mapped to any counterpart (lower bound of cardinality) and whether it can be mapped to more than one counterpart (upper bound of cardinality). There are no constraints in our approach considering the upper bound of cardinality. A fact, measure, dimension, aggregation level or attribute in a data warehouse DWH_1 may always be mapped to more than one counterpart in some other warehouse DWH_2. The lower bound of cardinality is inherently bound to zero for aggregation levels. If two dimensions are correspondent and the lowest level conflict exists (see the classification of conflicts in Section 3), then the finest level in one of the dimensions must either remain unpaired (the lower bound of cardinality becomes zero) or be mapped to a semantically corresponding aggregation level that belongs to another dimension. Since there are no obligations that would require mandatory mapping of other structure types, their lower bound of cardinality is also zero. Consequently, the cardinality of mapping is [0, N] for all five types of multidimensional structures.

Additional constraints to aggregation level mapping are imposed by the three rules described in Section 3 in order to preserve the partial order in hierarchies.

Having applied all mentioned constraints, there are still much more possible mappings than those a designer would produce manually. A selection metric defines how the calculated similarity values are used to determine which candidates are the "best" among all possible mappings. "Being the best" means the best fit to reality and being a part of the optimal, manually created solution.

Selection Metrics and the Problem of Stable Marriage in Bipartite Graphs

The selection metric issue has long been studied in graph theory as the *problem of stable marriage* in *bipartite graphs* (Lovàsz & Plummer, 1986; Melnik et al., 2002).

A *bipartite graph* is a graph whose vertices form a partition of two disjoint sets such that no edge connects any two vertices of the same set. In the stable marriage problem the vertices belonging to the different sets correspond to members of opposite sexes while in the mapping selection problem they can be viewed as members of the two sets of (multidimensional) structures being mapped. An edge symbolizes a possible marriage and can thus exist only between vertices belonging to different parts of the graph (i.e. to opposite sexes). Each edge is given a weight coefficient from the interval [0,1], which describes mutual affinity between the partners. When bipartite graphs are applied to solve match selection problems, the coefficient corresponds to the similarity between the components of the match target sets. In our particular case, those are similarities between the multidimensional structures represented by the vertices. Thus, in the initial bipartite graph the vertices correspond to marriage (match) candidates, and the edges to all possible marriages (mappings). The list of mappings $\mathcal{M}$, which is the final product of our automated schema matching process, is a subset of this initial graph.

A selection metric defines an algorithm (which is also called a filter) that selects an appropriate subset of edges as mappings and eliminates all others. Melnik et al. (2002) test six different filter algorithms. We implemented three of them: *best sum*, *threshold* and *outer*. In the original version of the stable marriage problem (Lovasz & Plummer, 1986; Melnik et al., 2002), only one-to-one mappings (i.e. monogamous marriages) are allowed. For reasons of simplicity, only monogamous mappings will be allowed in the illustration of the three filters' work in the following paragraphs. However, we actually need algorithms that allow polygamy, although they will produce monogamous matches in the majority of cases.

The *best sum* filter maps combinations with the highest possible total sum of edge similarities. This means that the average total "satisfaction" of all men and women is maximized (although it is possible that there are marriages where one or both of the spouses have not declared the other

Figure 5. Mapping selection using the best sum filter

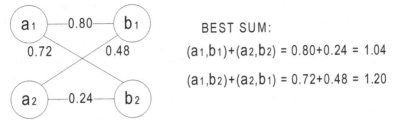

BEST SUM:

$(a_1,b_1)+(a_2,b_2) = 0.80+0.24 = 1.04$

$(a_1,b_2)+(a_2,b_1) = 0.72+0.48 = 1.20$

Figure 6. Mapping selection using the threshold and the outer filter

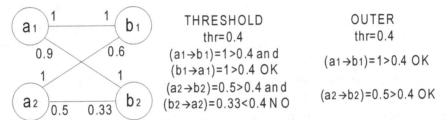

THRESHOLD
thr=0.4

$(a_1 \rightarrow b_1)=1>0.4$ an d
$(b_1 \rightarrow a_1)=1>0.4$ OK
$(a_2 \rightarrow b_2)=0.5>0.4$ an d
$(b_2 \rightarrow a_2)=0.33<0.4$ N O

OUTER
thr=0.4

$(a_1 \rightarrow b_1)=1>0.4$ OK

$(a_2 \rightarrow b_2)=0.5>0.4$ OK

spouse as the first choice in the preference list). We could say that the *best sum* filter is a "totalitarian" approach as it prefers the goals of the "community" as a whole to the personal "feelings" of its members. For the graph given in Figure 5, the *best sum* filter would produce combinations (a_1,b_2) and (a_2,b_1) as their sum, 1.20, is greater than the sum of the other possible combination (1.04).

The *threshold* and the *outer* filter are more "liberal". They allow each of the marriage candidates to make the choice of their own. The "personal" preference of each candidate a for a possible partner b_j can be mathematically expressed as relative similarity, i.e. the ratio of the absolute similarity between a and b_j and the highest absolute similarity the person a expresses to any of the candidates (i.e. similarity between a and its preferred partner):

$$sim_R(a, b_j) = sim(a,b_j) / \max_j sim(a,b_j) \qquad (6)$$

According to this definition, each mapping candidate will affine at least one possible partner with relative similarity 1. Relative similarities for the graph shown in Figure 5 are given in Figure 6. Obviously, relative similarity is asymmetric. The *threshold* filter forbids a mapping if relative similarities at any of the two sides of the selected edge are smaller than some predefined threshold *thr* (e.g. if we state that *thr* is equal to 0.4, then mapping (a_1,b_2) is allowed).

Certainly, if polygamy is not allowed, a problem arises either when person b_1 (see Figure 6), preferred by person a_2, herself prefers another person a_1, or when person a_1 is the first choice of two persons, b_1 and b_2. In our implementation of the *threshold* filter vertices with the highest relative similarity choose first. When there are several such vertices (as there always are at the beginning, when each of the vertices is adjacent to at least one edge with relative similarity 1), one of the vertices that are adjacent to the edge with the highest absolute similarity will take the lead. In the particular case shown in Figure 6, this would be a_1 or b_1 (with absolute similarity 0.80). The *threshold* filter first creates the pair (a_1,b_1), since the relative similarity at both sides of the edge is higher than the threshold (1 > 0.4). Assuming that only monogamous mappings are allowed, the only remaining candidate pair is (a_2, b_2). The vertex with the highest similarity, a_2 ($sim_R(a_2, b_2)$ = 0.5), proposes a mapping. However, $sim_R(b_2, a_2)$ = 0.33 < 0.4 = thr, and thus the mapping (a_2, b_2) is not created.

The *outer* filter works rather similarly to the *threshold* filter. In general, the *outer* filter is polygamous and constructs [1, N]:[1, N] mappings so that no candidate remains unmapped. While the *threshold* filter allows each candidate to refuse a marriage proposal (the threshold is checked at both sides of the selected edge), the *outer* filter forbids refusals. Thus, if a prefers b, b cannot refuse (but can also make a proposal to another person according to b's own choice, which results in polygamy). Like the *threshold* filter, the monogamous version of the *outer* filter would first create the mapping (a_1, b_1). Next, a_2 proposes mapping (a_2, b_2) and b_2 cannot refuse.

We implement all three filters as greedy algorithms. A greedy algorithm is a heuristic algorithm that assures a good-quality solution of the problem in a reasonably short time for a large majority of cases, but neither the solution is necessarily the optimal one, nor the algorithm will surely produce a good-quality solution in all cases. A greedy algorithm divides the problem into a set of mutually dependent parts, which follow one after another and the results of the previous parts are the inputs to the next parts. Thus, a possibly bad choice at the beginning influences the final result, but the algorithm is much faster than algorithms that search for an optimal solution. The latter may in some cases be extremely complex and hence too slow and impossible to be executed in practice. An example of a wrong choice can be seen in Figure 7.

If we falsely map aggregation level *quarter₁* to *day₂* (dashed line in Figure 7), the restriction rules will forbid us to produce the correct mapping between *month₁* and *month₂* (denoted by a solid line in Figure 7).

All three greedy algorithms first make a list of absolute similarity values between all members of the match target sets A and B. Next, the lists are sorted in descending order. The *threshold* and the *outer* filter algorithms also make two sorted relative similarity lists (one from the perspective of A and the other from the perspective of B). Furthermore, the lists of unmapped members of A and B are created (containing the whole sets at the beginning). All filters take the candidate pairs from the top of the similarity list and create a mapping if the pair satisfies all general requirements and constraints (e.g the three restriction rules for aggregation level mapping), as well as those imposed by the particular filter (e.g. thresholds). The list of unmapped members is then refreshed and all mapping candidates (a, b) where both members already form mappings with other structures are removed. For instance, imagine that the mapping (a_1, b_1) has been created in the n-th and the mapping (a_2, b_2) in the $n+k$-th step of the algorithm. Structures a_1, a_2, b_1 and b_2 all participate in a mapping after the $n+k$-th step and the remaining candidates (a_1, b_2) and (a_2, b_1) are therefore removed from the candidate list as redundant and "worse" than the already created mappings, according to the calculated similarity values.

Our implementation of the *best sum* filter shows at their best the features of a greedy algorithm. The algorithm always puts the pair with the largest similarity coefficient into the list of mappings, then adds the one with the second highest similarity, etc. It continues, step by step, until there are no unmatched structures left in at least one of the match target sets. Thus, it returns the first satisfactory solution able to be created, although it may not be the one with really the highest possible sum of the similarity coefficients. For instance, given the simple example in Figure 5 and also including monogamy as a mapping condition, there are only two possible mapping solutions: M_1 = $\{(a_1, b_1), (a_2, b_2)\}$ and M_2 = $\{(a_1, b_2), (a_2, b_1)\}$. Our implementation of the *best sum* algorithm chooses

Figure 7. Inability to produce a correct mapping after an earlier wrong step

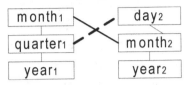

the solution M_1 with sum 1.04 and not M_2, whose sum is 1.20. For larger sets, with many possible solutions, there is a high percentage of correctly created mappings and the *best sum* algorithm is even more efficient when additional restrictions (as for aggregation levels) are introduced.

EVALUATION OF ALGORITHM PERFORMANCE

The quality of the automated matching process is measured by its *accuracy*, as defined by Melnik et al. (2002). This measure estimates how much effort it costs the warehouse designer to modify the automatically proposed match result $P=\{(x_1, y_1),\ldots,(x_n, y_n)\}$ into the intended result $I=\{(a_1, b_1), \ldots,(a_m, b_m)\}$, i.e. how many deletions of incorrectly suggested map pairs and insertions of missing pairs have to be made. Let $c=|P \cap I|$ be the number of correct suggestions (n and m are the sizes of P and I, respectively). The difference $(n–c)$ is the number of false positives (incorrect suggestions) to be removed from P, and $(m–c)$ the number of missing matches that need to be added. Assuming (for reasons of simplicity) that deletions and additions of map pairs require the same amount of effort, accuracy (i.e. the labor savings obtained by using our matching technique) is defined as:

$$A = 1 - \frac{(n-c)+(m-c)}{m} \qquad (7)$$

In a perfect match (i.e. P = I), $n = m = c$, the resulting accuracy is 1. Negative accuracy (for $c/n < 0.5$ i.e. when more than half of the created matches are wrong) suggests that it would take the user more effort to correct the automatically proposed mappings than to perform the matching manually from scratch. Thus, whenever accuracy is higher than 0, the automatic method saves time.

We evaluate the proposed algorithm by matching the schema of the federated data warehouse for health insurance organizations developed in our previous work for the purpose of evidence-based medicine (Banek et al., 2006; Stolba et al., 2006) to the local warehouse of one of the organizations participating in the federation project. Both warehouses consist of mutually compatible three facts representing patient encounters, performed therapies and medicine prescriptions. In both cases the facts share dimensions (many, but not all of which are compatible).

The goal of the experiments was to determine the parameter values in the similarity function formulas for different types of multidimensional structures (the formulas are given in Equations 1, 3, 4, 5), as well as to make the decision which of the three filters should be applied to map each of the five multidimensional structure types. There are five similarity function parameters: $texp, w_{lname},$ w_{dname}, w_{fname} and w_m. The range of values for $texp$ is $[0,\infty)$, while the values of the other parameters are within the interval $[0,1]$. The five parameters are independent of each other, with the exception of w_{fname} and w_m, whose sum must not exceed one (see Equation 5). Since none of the parameters is discrete, we have to empirically choose some representative values that will be tested. The values are shown in Table 3. Due to the fact that $w_{fname} + w_m \leq 1$, those two parameters actually produce 7 valid combinations (of 25 possible). In total, there are $7 \cdot 5 \cdot 5 \cdot 5 = 875$ independent combinations for the five parameters.

All three filters will be tested using threshold values 1, 0.8, 0.6, 0.4 and 0.2. For the *threshold* and the *outer* filter, the value of the threshold refers to relative similarity, while for the *best sum* filter it refers to absolute similarity. Thus, there are $3 \cdot 5 = 15$ possible filter options. Since filters

Table 3. Values of similarity parameters used for testing

Parameter	Values				
texp	0	0.5	1	3	5
w_{lname}	0	0.25	0.5	0.75	1
w_{dname}	0	0.25	0.5	0.75	1
w_{fname}	0	0.17	0.33	0.66	1
w_m	0	0.17	0.33	0.66	1

are independent of the similarity function parameters and since the choice of filter for one type of multidimensional structures is independent of the choices for the other four types, the number of combination rises to $875 \cdot 15^5 \approx 6.64 \cdot 10^8$.

The number of experiments that need to be performed can be reduced by many times following the notion that a good match is needed for all levels, while all combinations with a bad match for at least one level can be discarded. On the other hand, since we first map more complex structures, examination of different filters' performance to less complex structures (e.g. aggregation levels) will not influence the results that were previously obtained for more complex structures (facts and dimensions). Thus, we adopt the following strategy of performing the experiments. First, we combine different filters and similarity function parameters for fact mapping. Its result influences the match candidates for measure and dimension mapping. All combinations that do not produce a high, probably best possible accuracy (for the given combination of similarity function parameters) are removed from further experiments. Next, we test filters for measure and dimension mapping alternating the similarity function parameters simultaneously. Again, we remove unsuccessful combinations and proceed with aggregation levels, and then, finally, with dimensional attributes.

The values of match accuracy for each of the three filters are given in Table 4. The rather small number of facts enabled all three filters to make a perfect match (the first row of Table 4). *Threshold* (*thr* = 1) and *best sum* proved to be more successful for measure matching than *outer*, although neither of them succeeded in creating a perfect match (the second row of Table 4). Only the *threshold* filter with the threshold parameter set to 1 was able to create a perfect match for dimensions. *Outer* (*thr* = 0.6) and *best sum* (*thr* = 0.2) showed an almost equally good performance when matching aggregation levels; they outperformed the *threshold* filter. The *threshold* filter (*thr* = 1) slightly outperforms the *best sum* filter for attribute matching while the accuracy of the *outer* filter is much worse. As a conclusion to the performed experiments, we recommend the usage of the *outer* or *best sum* filter for aggregation level matching (Table 5). On the other hand, *threshold* should be used for all other multidimensional structures.

The optimal values of the five tested similarity function parameters are shown in Table 6. There are two particularly interesting issues concerning the parameters. First, there is an extremely large

Table 4. Comparison of three mapping selection metrics (filters)

	OUTER				THRESHOLD				BEST SUM			
	n	m	c	acc	n	m	c	acc	n	m	c	acc
facts	3	3	3	**1.000**	3	3	3	**1.000**	3	3	3	**1.000**
measures	10	11	9	0.727	9	11	9	**0.818**	9	11	9	**0.818**
dimensions	21	21	20	0.904	21	21	21	**1.000**	19	21	18	0.810
agg. levels	29	28	27	**0.893**	28	28	24	0.715	28	28	26	**0.857**
dim. attrib.	92	74	51	0.135	51	74	63	**0.473**	57	74	45	**0.446**

Table 5. Filters recommended to be used for mapping multidimensional structures

Facts	Measures	Dimensions	Aggr. levels	Dim. attributes
threshold, thr=0.8	*threshold, thr=1*	*threshold, thr=1*	*outer, thr=0.6; best sum, thr=0.2*	*threshold, thr=1*

Table 6. Optimal values of similarity function parameters

texp	w_{lname}	w_{dname}	w_{fname}	w_m
0, 0.5, 1, 3, 5	0.75	0.5	0.17	0.66

influence of measures to similarity between facts (w_m = 0.66). Second, *texp* does not significantly influence the mapping results: the equation system consisting of the four structure similarity formulas (Equations 1, 3, 4, 5) is robust enough not to be influenced to a great extent by measure and attribute data types i.e. the change of measure and attribute similarity values caused by different values of *texp*. The choice of different values of *texp* causes a change of measure and attribute similarity values. However, the change of the values refers to all measure and attribute pairs and hence the mutual relations between the pairs mostly remain unchanged. For instance, let the initial values $sim_{atomic}(S_1, S_{2a})$ = 0.2643 and $sim_{atomic}(S_1, S_{2b})$ = 0.2084 be replaced by new values $sim'_{atomic}(S_1, S_{2a})$ = 0.2928 and $sim'_{atomic}(S_1, S_{2b})$ = 0.2484 due to the change of *texp*. This change has no impact on the fact that $sim_{atomic}(S_1, S_{2a})$ > $sim_{atomic}(S_1, S_{2b})$, which actually determines the calculation of relative similarities for the *threshold* and the *outer* filter, as well as the creation of the lists needed by the *best sum* filter.

As mentioned before, none of the existing frameworks for automated schema matching has been successfully applied to match data warehouses. Therefore, we can only compare the results of our match discovery procedure with the results of the existing techniques for matching database schemas, XML Schemas and ontologies. However, we must be aware that the

complexity of the match is not equal, so that the comparison of the results can be understood only as an illustration. A thorough quantitative comparison can be performed only with the similarity flooding technique, whose accuracy measure is also adopted in our approach. Other approaches (ARTEMIS/ MOMIS, DIKE) do not define quantitative measures of their performance, except for Cupid, where recall percentages are given.

Similarity flooding performs three XML Schema matching tasks with an average accuracy of 0.5 achieved by the *threshold* filter. Three tasks concerning relational database schemas are performed with an average accuracy of 0.57, *threshold* being again the most successful filter. The accuracy of the *best sum* filter is worse (about 0.4), while the *outer* filter performed with a negative accuracy (-0.08). Considering only attributes, which give the worst performance in our approach, their accuracy of 0.47 (see Table 4) is approximately equal to the accuracy of similarity flooding with XML Schemas, but worse than with relational databases. However, since our approach is aimed at matching all multidimensional structures and works successfully with facts, measures, dimensions and aggregation levels, we define the *average accuracy* resulting from matching all five types of multidimensional structures: facts, measures, dimensions, aggregation levels and attributes. For each of the five structure types, average accuracy calculation considers the results obtained by using the proposed optimal filter (both *best sum* and *outer* were proposed for mapping aggregation levels, thus we take their average; accuracies produced using *threshold* are selected for other multidimensional structures). Each structure contributes to the average accuracy value according to its proportion in the intended, human-designed mapping solution I (the contribution of attributes is most significant, the contribution of facts least significant):

$$A_{avg} =$$
$$\frac{m_F \cdot A_F + m_M \cdot A_M + m_D \cdot A_D + m_L \cdot A_L + m_A \cdot A_A}{m_F + m_M + m_D + m_L + m_A}. \quad (8)$$

Given the accuracy values from Table 4, the average accuracy for our case study example is 0.675, which is significantly higher than the accuracy achieved by similarity flooding, both for XML Schemas and relational schemas.

Cupid performs a match between a star schema and a corresponding non-multidimensional relational structure, creating 68% of the correct mappings (the proportion of correct mappings corresponds to the ratio c/m). This result is similar to 71.6% in our approach, when the comparison is performed only with respect to facts, measures and attributes (Cupid cannot deal with dimensions and aggregation levels). The proportion of correct mappings obtained in our approach considering all five types of multidimensional structures is much higher, 80.2%.

CONCLUSION

This article presents an approach to automating the schema matching process for heterogeneous data warehouses in order to shorten the warehouse integration process. The approach is based on analyzing warehouse schemas and can be used when the access to data content is restricted. We defined a match discovery procedure capable of solving heterogeneities among data warehouse-specific structures: facts, measures, dimensions, aggregation levels and dimensional attributes.

The match discovery procedure consists of two basic phases. In the first phase all multidimensional structures belonging to the same type are mutually compared and their similarity is expressed by means of a probability function (called similarity function) using different heuristic formulas. In the second phase, heuristic mapping algorithms (also called filters) are applied to determine which structures should be mapped as equivalent, among a much larger number of possible match candidates. The result of the automated matching process must as much as possible be commensurate with the solution that a data warehouse designer would produce manually. First, the most complex structures (facts) are mapped. When mapping dimensions and measures, only candidates that belong to already mapped facts are considered. Such a procedure continues recursively until the attributes are mapped. Particular relevance was given to aggregation level matching, as the partial order in dimension hierarchies must be preserved. We proposed three additional restriction rules needed to perform that part of the matching process successfully. We implemented three different filters, *best sum*, *threshold* and *outer*, all of them as greedy algorithms.

A Java-based prototype tool has been developed to test and verify the presented match methodology. Experiments were performed on a case study example. The manually created schema of a federated data warehouse for the purpose of evidence-based medicine was matched to one of the component warehouses that take part in the federation project. While the *best sum* and *outer* filter are recommended for aggregation level mapping, the *threshold* filter is the best solution for other multidimensional structures.

REFERENCES

Aumueller, D., Do, H.H., Massmann, S., & Rahm, E. (2005). Schema and Ontology Matching with COMA++. In F. Özcan (Ed.), *Proc. ACM SIGMOD Int. Conf. on Management of Data* (pp. 906-908). New York: ACM Press.

Banek, M., Tjoa, A. M., & Stolba, N. (2006). Integrating Different Grain Levels in a Medical Data Warehouse Federation. In A. M. Tjoa & J. Trujillo (Eds.), *Proc. 8th Int. Conf. on Data Warehousing and Knowledge Discovery. Lecture Notes in Computer Science, 4081*, 185-194.

Banek, M., Vrdoljak, B., Tjoa, A. M., & Skočir, Z. (2007). Automating the Schema Matching Process for Heterogeneous Data Warehouses. In I. Y. Song, J. Eder & T. Manh Nguyen (Eds.), *Proc. 9th Int. Conf. on Data Warehousing and Knowledge Discovery. Lecture Notes in Computer Science, 4654*, 45-54.

Beneventano D., Bergamaschi S., Guerra F., & Vincini M. (2003). Synthesizing an Integrated Ontology. *IEEE Internet Computing Magazine, 7* (5), 42-51.

Beneventano D., & Bergamaschi S. (2006). Semantic Search Engines based on Data Integration Systems. In J. Cardoso (Ed.), *Semantic Web: Theory, Tools and Applications* (pp. 317-341). Hershey, PA, USA: IGI Publishing.

Bergamaschi, S., Castano, S., & Vincini, M. (1999). Semantic Integration of Semistructured and Structured Data Sources. *SIGMOD Record 28* (1), 54-59.

Berger S., & Schrefl, M. (2006). Analysing Multidimensional Data accross Autonomous Data Warehouses. In A. M. Tjoa & J. Trujillo (Eds.), *Proc. 8th Int. Conf. on Data Warehousing and Knowledge Discovery. Lecture Notes in Computer Science, 4081*, 120-133.

Cabibbo, L., & Torlone, R. (2005). Integrating Heterogeneous Multidimensional Databases. In J. Frew (Ed.), *Proc. 17th Int. Conf. Scientific and Statistical Database Management* (pp. 205-214).

Dhamankar, R., Lee, Y., Doan, A-H., Halevy, A. Y., & Domingos, P. (2004). iMAP: Discovering Complex Mappings between Database Schemas. In G. Weikum, A. C. König, S. Deßloch (Eds.), *Proc. ACM SIGMOD Int. Conf. on Management of Data* (pp. 383-394). New York: ACM Press.

Doan A., & Halevi, A. Y. (2005). Semantic integration research in the database community: A Brief Survey. *AI Magazine, 26* (1), 83-94.

Doan, A., Lu, Y., Lee, Y., & Han, J. (2003). Profile-Based Object Matching for Information Integration. *IEEE Intelligent Systems, 18* (5), 54-59.

Euzenat, J., & Valtchev, P. (2004). Similarity-Based Ontology Alignment in OWL-Lite. In: R. López de Mántaras, L. Saitta (Eds.), *Proc. 16th European Conf. on Artificial Intelligence,* (pp. 333-337). Amsterdam: IOS Press.

Embley, D. W., Xu, L., & Ding Y. (2004). Automatic Direct and Indirect Schema Mapping: Experiences and Lessons Learned. *SIGMOD Record 33* (4), 14-19.

Golfarelli, M., Maio, D. & Rizzi, S. (1998). The Dimensional Fact Model: a Conceptual Model for Data Warehouses. *International Journal of Cooperative Information Systems, 7*, 215-247.

Hackney, D. (1997). *Understanding and Implementing Successful Data Marts*. Reading, MA, USA: Addison-Wesley.

Halevy, A. Y. (2001). Answering queries using views: A survey. *VLDB J., 10*, 270-294.

Health Level Seven – HL7 (2008). Retrieved February 25, 2008 from the World Wide Web: http://www.hl7.org

Inmon, W. H. (1996). *Building the Data Warehouse* (2nd ed.). New York: John Wiley & Sons.

Jindal, R. & Acharya, A. (2004). Federated Data Warehouse Architecture. Wipro Technologies – white paper. Retrieved October 10, 2007 from the World Wide Web: http://hosteddocs.ittoolbox.com/Federated%20data%20Warehouse%20Architecture.pdf

Kim, W., & Seo, J. (1991). Classifying Semantic and Data Heterogeneity in Multidatabase Systems. *IEEE Computer, 24* (12), 12-18.

Levenshtein, V. I. (1966). Binary Codes Capable of Correcting Deletions, Insertions, and Reversals. *Cybernetics and Control Theory, 10* (8), 707–710.

Lovàsz, L. & Plummer, M. D. (1986). *Matching Theory.* Amsterdam: North-Holland.

Madhavan, J., Bernstein, P. A., & Rahm, E. (2001). Generic Schema Matching with Cupid. In P. M. G. Apers, P. Atzeni, S. Ceri, S. Paraboschi, K. Ramamohanarao, R. T. Snodgrass (Eds.) *Proc. 27ʰ Int. Conf. on Very Large Data Bases* (pp. 49-58). San Francisco: Morgan Kaufmann.

Mansmann, S., & Scholl, M. H. (2006). Extending Visual OLAP for Handling Irregular Dimensional Hierarchies. In A. M. Tjoa & J. Trujillo (Eds.), *Proc. 8ʰ Int. Conf. on Data Warehousing and Knowledge Discovery. Lecture Notes in Computer Science, 4081,* 95-105.

Melnik, S., Garcia-Molina, H., & Rahm, E. (2002). Similarity Flooding: A Versatile Graph Matching Algorithm and Its Application to Schema Matching. In *Proc. 18ʰ Int. Conf. on Data Engineering* (pp. 117-128). IEEE Computer Society.

Palopoli, L., Saccà, D., Terracina, G., & Ursino, D. (2003). Uniform Techniques for Deriving Similarities of Objects and Subschemes in Heterogeneous Databases. *IEEE Transactions on Knowledge and Data Engineering, 15,* 271-294.

Rahm, E., & Bernstein, P. A. (2001). A survey of approaches to automatic schema matching. *VLDB Journal, 10,* 334-350.

Rahm, E., Do, H., & Massmann, S. (2004). Matching Large XML Schemas. *SIGMOD Record, 33* (4), 26-31.

Resnik, P. (1999). Semantic Similarity in a Taxonomy: An Information-Based Measure and its Application to Problems of Ambiguity in Natural Language. *J. Artificial. Intelligence Research, 11,* 95-130.

Rodríguez, M. A., & Egenhofer, M.J. (2003). Determining Semantic Similarity among Entity Classes from Different Ontologies. *IEEE Transactions on Knowledge and Data Engineering, 15,* 442-456.

Sackett, D. L., Rosenberg, W. M. C., Muir Gray, J. A., Haynes, R. B., & Richardson, W. S. (1996). Evidence-Based Medicine: What It Is and What It Isn't. *British Medical Journal, 312,* 71-72.

Sheth, A. P., & Larson, J. A. (1990). Federated Database Systems for Managing Distributed, Heterogeneous, and Autonomous Databases. *ACM Computing Surveys, 22,* 183-236.

Stolba, N., Banek, M., & Tjoa, A. M. (2006). The Security Issue of Federated Data Warehouses in the Area of Evidence-Based Medicine, In Proceedings of 1st Int. Conf. on Availability, Reliability and Security (pp. 329-339). Los Alamitos, CA, USA: IEEE Computer Society.

Stumme, G., & Maedche, A. (2001). FCA-Merge: Bottom-up Merging of Ontologies. In B. Nebel (Ed.), *Proc. 7th Int. Conf. on Artificial Intelligence,* (pp. 225–230). San Francisco: Morgan Kaufmann.

Ullman, J.D. (1997). Information Integration Using Logical Views, In F. N. Afrati, P. G. Kolaitis (Eds.), *Proc. 6ʰ Int. Conf. on Data Database Theory. Lecture Notes in Computer Science, 1186,* 19-40.

WordNet, a lexical database for English Language (2007). Retrieved October 10, 2007 from http://wordnet.princeton.edu/5papers.pdf

Yang, D., Powers, D. M. W. (2005). Measuring Semantic Similarity in the Taxonomy of WordNet. In V. Estivill-Castro (Ed.), *Proc. 28th Australasian Computer Science Conference* (pp. 315-322). Australian Computer Society.

Chapter 4
Algebraic and Graphic Languages for OLAP Manipulations

Franck Ravat
Université Toulouse I, France

Olivier Teste
Université Toulouse III, France

Ronan Tournier
Université Toulouse III, France

Gilles Zurfluh
Université Toulouse I, France

ABSTRACT

This article deals with multidimensional analyses. Analyzed data are designed according to a conceptual model as a constellation of facts and dimensions, which are composed of multi-hierarchies. This model supports a query algebra defining a minimal core of operators, which produce multidimensional tables for displaying analyzed data. This user-oriented algebra supports complex analyses through advanced operators and binary operators. A graphical language, based on this algebra, is also provided to ease the specification of multidimensional queries. These graphical manipulations are expressed from a constellation schema and they produce multidimensional tables.

INTRODUCTION

As competitiveness increases in the business world, and as faster reactivity is required more than ever, the decision-making process has become a major focus of research and is increasingly assisted with information technologies. OLAP (Online Analytical Processing) systems, aim to ease the decision-making process with a multidimensional data presentation. The use of Multidimensional DataBases (MDB) provides a global view of company data, and enables decision-makers to gain insight into an enterprise performance through fast and interactive access to data (Colliat, 1996). Unfortunately, in spite of a decade of research in OLAP systems, concepts and systems exist without uniform theoretical basis (Niemi et al., 2003; Rizzi et al., 2006).

Context and Related Works

Without a model based on a consensus for multidimensional data, many propositions have been made. Multidimensional models rest upon cube or hyper-cube metaphor. Several surveys may be found in Chaudhuri and Dayal (1997), Blaschka et al. (1998), Vassiliadis and Sellis (1999), Pedersen et al., (2001), Torlone (2003) and Abelló et al. (2006).

The first works, based on a "cube model" that present data in the form of n-dimensional cubes (Li and Wang, 1996; Agrawal et al., 1997; Gyssens & Lakshmanan, 1997; Datta & Thomas, 1999), have the following drawbacks:

1. Weakness in modeling the fact (subject of analysis) and its Key Performance Indicators (KPI or measures)
2. Little or no conceptual modeling of dimensions (analysis axes) with no explicit capture of their hierarchical structure
3. No separation between structure and content

The second category called "multidimensional model" overcomes these drawbacks and it is semantically richer. It allows a precise specification of each multidimensional component (Lehner, 1998; Pedersen et al., 2001; Abelló et al., 2003; Trujillo et al., 2003; Abelló et al., 2006). Models of this category are based on the concepts of fact and dimension. Dimension attributes are organized in hierarchies. A hierarchy defines a point of view (or analysis perspective) of an analysis axis and is composed of the different aggregation levels of the measures. To our knowledge, hardly any multidimensional model provides a combined multi-fact and multi-hierarchy representation.

From a manipulation point of view, the first works on OLAP manipulation algebras extended relational algebra operators for the cube model (Gray et al., 1996; Li & Wang, 1996; Agrawal et al., 1997; Gyssens & Lakshmanan, 1997; Rafanelli, 2003). To counter the inadaptability of relational algebra for manipulating multidimensional structures in an OLAP context, numerous works provided operations for specifying and manipulating a cube (Cabibbo & Torlone, 1997; 1998; Pedersen et al., 2001; Abelló et al., 2003; Franconi & Kamble, 2004). These works are not user-oriented (Abelló et al., 2003) for the following reasons: 1) they do not define an adapted structure for displaying decisional data to the user; 2) they are based on partial sets of OLAP operations; and 3) the defined operations do not easily represent OLAP manipulations of decision-makers (Ravat et al., 2006a).

Multidimensional OLAP analyses consist in exploring interactively multidimensional databases by drilling, rotating, selecting and displaying data. Although there is no consensus on a common core of a minimal set of operations for a multidimensional algebra, most papers offer a support of these operation categories:

*   **Drilling:** these operations allow navigating through the hierarchical structure of the analysis axes, in order to analyze a measure

Table 1. A comparison of different multidimensional languages

Operations		(Grouping Algebra) Li and Wang 1996	Agrawal et al., 1997	Gyssens and Lakshmanan, 1997	(MD) Cabibbo and Torlone 1997, 1998	Lehner, 1998	Pedersen et al., 2001	(YAM²) Abelló et al., 2003	(GMD) Franconi et al., 2004	Ravat et al., 2006
Drilling	Finer level	Roll ,Cube	Join			DrillDown[2], Split		DrillDown		Drill Down
	Coarser level	Roll, Aggregation	Merge	Summerization	RollUp, Aggregation	RollUp, Merge, Aggregation	Aggregation	RollUp		RollUp
Selection	Factual values				Slice (Selection)	Selection		Dice, Projection		
	Dimensional values		Restriction		Dice (Selection)	Selection	Selection	Slice, Multi-Slice[3]		
Rotation	Fact Dimension Hierarchy							DrillAcross ChangeBase		FRotate DRotate HRotate
Fact Modification	Adding a measure		Projection	Projection					Derived measures	
	Suppress a measure		Projection	Projection						
Dimension Modification	Reducing dimensions	Cube Aggregation	Projection, Destroy-Dimension		Simple Projection			Projection	Projection	
Ordering	Push		Push	Fold[4]						
	Pull		Pull	Unfold						
	Ordering			Classification						
	Nesting	Transfer								Nest
Set operators	Union	Union[6]		Union[6]	Union[6]		Union[5]	Union[6]	Union[6]	
	Intersect			Intersection	Intersection				Intersection	
	Difference			Difference	Difference		difference		Difference	
	Join	RC-Join (Relation to dimension)		join cubes	join cubes	Join[1]		Identity-based Join, Group	join cubes	
Model Structure		Cube	Cube	2D-Table	MD (f-table)	MD	MD	Cube	Cube	2D-Table (MT)
Other Operations		Add dimension		cartesian product	cartesian product					
Comments				provides calculus language	provides graphic laguage, query calculus			provides SQL translation		provides assertional language

MD=Multidimensional; [1]=no restriction; [2]=no hierarchy conservation; [3]=specified on a range; [4]=generalized push; [5]=on dimensions; [6]=identical cubes only;

with more or less precision. Drilling upwards (*roll-up*) consists in displaying the data with a coarser level of detail; for example. rollup allows changing corporate sales initially displayed by months into sales displayed by years. The opposite, drilling downwards (*drill-down*) consists in displaying the data with a finer level of detail.

- **Selections:** these operations allow the user to work on a subset of the available data. *Slice* specifies a restriction predicate on dimension data while *Dice* specifies a restriction predicate on fact data.
- **Rotations:** these operations allow changing analysis axes (rotation of dimensions), changing the subject of analysis (rotation of facts or drill-across), or changing an analysis perspective within the same dimension (rotation of hierarchies).

Some authors have also presented additional operations:

- **Fact modification:** these operations allow decision-makers to add and to remove a measure (analysis indicator or KPI) in the current analysis.
- **Dimension modification:** these operations enable the insertion of dimensional attributes into a fact (push operation) or measures into a dimension (pull operation).
- **Ordering:** these operations allow decision-makers to change the order of the values of dimension parameters or to insert a parameter in another place in a hierarchy (nest operation).
- **Set operations:** some authors offer to use union, difference and intersection operations.

The following table summarizes the available operations in various propositions. It also gives the authors' specific names for these operations.

Without a complete column, Table 1 shows that current research works are incomplete with regard to the different operation categories.

Figure 1. Graphical formalism of dimensions and hierarchies

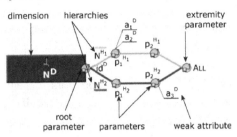

Expressing queries with these algebraic operators is a difficult task for decision-makers. As a consequence, more adapted languages have to be defined. Graphical languages used to specify multidimensional analyses are very present in commercial tools, but despite this, very little attention has been drawn on graphical languages within research on decision support systems. In Cabbibo and Torlone (1998), the authors present a graphical multidimensional manipulation language associated to a conceptual representation of the multidimensional structures. Although the authors define a manipulation algebra and calculus, the high level graphical language offers very limited manipulations in comparison. In Böhnlein et al. (2002), the authors offer an intermediate solution with more manipulations, but the system uses complex forms for query specifications. Neither of these two solutions provides a restitution interface. Stolte et al. (2002) and Sifer (2003) are advanced restitution tools. The first one offers an impressive pivot table that adapts its display according to the analyzed data type, whereas the second offers an arborescent view with multiple scales and very specific manipulations. Neither proposition provides a formal description of the manipulation language.

Microsoft Excel Pivot tables (or DynamiCube from Data Dynamics), although very expressive restitution interfaces, do not provide many dynamic manipulations (especially rotations). On the other hand, other commercial tools offer extensive manipulations (Business Objects[1], Cognos BI[2], Tableau[3], Targit[4]...). But all these tools display the multidimensional structures of the MDB within an arborescent view, rendering impossible comparative analyses between different subjects sharing analysis axes. Moreover, the representation used mixes completely MDB structures and content. The user completely lacks an adapted conceptual view of the MBD concepts for the specification analyses (Rizzi et al., 2006). Moreover, commercial tools lack formal manipulation languages and these languages are not complete with regard to the different operation categories previously described.

Nowadays, decision-makers wish to perform their own analyses, but they lack the knowledge to manipulate multidimensional structures with the use of multidimensional query algebras or with adapted procedural query languages. On the other hand, commercial tools provide adapted manipulation languages but lack: 1) rigorous reference to multidimensional operations, 2) a uniform theoretical basis (Niemi et al., 2003) as well as 3) an adapted conceptual view of the multidimensional elements of the underlying MDB (Rizzi et al., 2006). Moreover, these tools sacrifice analysis coherence for analysis flexibility.

Motivation

In this context, in order to ensure access to multidimensional OLAP analyses of company data, we intend to define a user-oriented query language composed of a formalized algebra and a graphic language. The query language has to be based upon: 1) data structures of the MDB close to the user's point of view and an adapted display structure for multidimensional data; 2) algebraic operators allowing the expression of multidimensional OLAP analyses; and 3) an incremental graphic query specification. These requirements are detailed in the following:

1.   Being user-oriented (Abelló et al., 2003), this language has to be based on a model disregarding implementation issues. We intend to define a multidimensional conceptual model, semantically richer than cube models. In order to facilitate correlations between analysis subjects and to analyze measures through different aggregation levels, the model will support multi-fact and multi-hierarchy representations. Contrary to previous works, our objective is also to offer an adapted structure to return analysis data to decision-makers. An n-dimensional cube (n>2) is hardly workable by decision-makers (Gyssens & Lakshmanan, 1997; Maniatis et al., 2005) and disregards the dimension's hierarchical structure.

2.   The algebra should provide a set of operators expressing all operations that an analyst may perform. In order to ensure complex OLAP analyses, the algebra must also support operator combinations.

3.   The use of graphic query languages ease query specifications for the end-user compared with algebraic expressions. Contrary to commercial software that provides an arborescent view of the multidimensional elements, the graphic language should operate on an explicit graphic view of the multidimensional conceptual schema. In the same way, OLAP analysis queries should be expressed directly on the graphic representation in an incremental way.

Article Contributions and Outline

In order to fulfil our goals, we define in the next section, a conceptual multidimensional model used as a basis for our query language. Section 3 introduces a formal algebraic language allowing the restitution of analyses in a multidimensional table (MT). In the manner of the relational algebra, we define a minimal core of multidimensional OLAP operators that may be combined together, expressing complex queries. This core is extended by the adjunction of second level operators and binary operators presented in sections 4 and 5. Finally, section 6 specifies an incremental graphic language, which is complete with regard to the algebra core and it operates directly on the conceptual elements of a multidimensional schema.

CONCEPTUAL MODELING

In this section, the model we define is close to the user's point of view and it is independent of implementation choices. This conceptual Multidimensional DataBase (MDB) model is based on facts, dimensions and hierarchies. This model facilitates correlations between several subjects of analysis through a constellation of facts and dimensions and it supports several data granularities according to which subjects may be analyzed.

Concepts

A constellation regroups several subjects of analysis (facts), which are studied according to several analysis axes (dimensions) possibly shared between facts. A constellation extends star schemas (Kimball, 1996), which are commonly used in the multidimensional context.

Definition. A *constellation* Cs is defined as (N^{Cs}, F^{Cs}, D^{Cs}, $Star^{Cs}$) where:

-   N^{Cs} is a constellation name
-   $F^{Cs} = \{F_1, \ldots, F_m\}$ is a set of facts
-   $D^{Cs} = \{D_1, \ldots, D_n\}$ is a set of dimensions
-   $Star^{Cs} : F^{Cs} \rightarrow 2^{D^{Cs}}$ associates each fact to its linked dimensions

The notation 2^X represents the powerset of the set X.

A dimension models an analysis axis; for example,. it reflects information according to which subjects of analysis will be analyzed. A dimension is composed of attributes (dimension properties).

Definition. A *dimension*, noted $D \in D^{Cs}$, is defined as (N^D, A^D, H^D, I^D) where:

- N^D is a dimension name
- $A^D = \{a^D_1,\ldots, a^D_u\} \cup \{id^D, All\}$ is a set of attributes
- $H^D = \{H^D_1,\ldots, H^D_v\}$ is a set of hierarchies
- $I^D = \{i^D_1,\ldots, i^D_p\}$ is a set of *dimension instances*

Dimension attributes (also called parameters or levels) are organized according to one or more hierarchies. Hierarchies represent a particular vision (perspective) of a dimension. Each attribute represents one data granularity according to which measures could be analyzed; for example, along the *store* dimension, a hierarchy could group *individual stores* into *cities* and *cities* into *countries*. Weak attributes (attributive properties) complete the parameter semantics, for example, the *name* of an *individual store*.

Definition. A *hierarchy* of a dimension D, noted $H_i \in H^D$, is defined as $(N^{Hi}, Param^{Hi}, Weak^{Hi})$ where:

- N^{Hi} is a hierarchy name
- $Param^{Hi} = <id^D, p^{Hi}_1,\ldots, p^{Hi}_{vi}, All>$ is an ordered set of attributes, called *parameters*, which represent useful graduations along the dimension, $\forall k \in [1..v_i], p^{Hi}_k \in A^D$
- $Weak^{Hi} : Param^{Hi} \to 2^{A^D} - Param^H$ is a function possibly associating each parameter to one or several *weak attributes*

For a hierarchy H_i we introduce

$$A^{Hi} = Param^{Hi} \cup (\bigcup_{j=1}^{j=vi} Weak^{Hi}(p^{Hj}))$$

the set of the hierarchy attributes, $A^{Hi} \subseteq A^D$. We also define the function level: $A^D \to \mathbb{N}^+$, noted $level^{Hi}(a_i)$, which returns the order of a_i in the list $Param^{Hi}$ (note that the level of a weak attribute is the level of its associated parameter).

All hierarchies in one dimension start with a same parameter, noted id^D called *root parameter*. All of these hierarchies end with a same parameter, noted All called *extremity parameter*. We represent dimensions using a graphical formalism, which extends notations introduced in (Golfarelli et al., 1998). Each path starting from Id and ending by All represents a hierarchy.

A fact reflects information that has to be analyzed according to dimensions. This analyzed information is modeled through one or several indicators, called measures; for example, a fact data may be *sale amounts* occurring in shops every day. The notation $D_i \in Star^{Cs}(F)$ represents that the dimension D_i is linked to the fact F_j.

Definition. A *fact*, noted $F \in F^{Cs}$, is defined as $(N^F, M^F, I^F, IStar^F)$ where:

- N^F is a name of fact
- $M^F = \{f_1(m^F_1),\ldots,f_w(m^F_w)\}$ is a set of *measures* associated with an aggregate function
- $I^F = \{i^F_1,\ldots, i^F_q\}$ is a set of *fact instances*
- $IStar^F : I^F \to I^{D1}x\ldots xI^{Dn}$ is a function $(\forall k \in [1..n], D_k \in Star^{Cs}(F))$, which respectively associates fact instances to their linked dimension instances

Figure 2 illustrates graphical notations used to represent facts.

Case Study

The case we study is taken from the meteorology domain. We define a multidimensional database, which allows users to analyze weather forecasts (atmospheric measures and forecasted measures) according to dates, geographic locations, sensor devices and forecast models.

Figure 2. Graphical formalism of facts

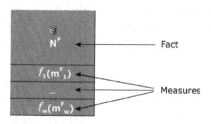

Figure 3. Example of constellation schema

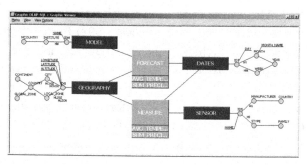

Figure 3 shows a constellation, which supports analyses about weather forecasts. It is composed of two facts, named *Forecast* and *Measures*, and four dimensions, named *Model*, *Dates*, *Geography*, and *Sensor*. Note that the extremity parameter (All) is not displayed in the graphical representation as this parameter tends to confuse users (Malinowsky & Zimányi, 2006).

The dimension named Geography, which represents geographic information, is defined by (N^{GEO}, A^{GEO}, H^{GEO}, I^{GEO}) where:

- N^{GEO} = 'Geography'
- A^{GEO} = {Latitude, Longitude, Altitude, City, Local_Zone, Country, Continent, Global_Zone} ∪ {IdG, All}
- H^{GEO} = {H_{COGZ}, H_{COCN}, H_{LZGZ}, H_{LZCN}}
- I^{GEO} = {i^{GEO}_1, i^{GEO}_2 ... i^{GEO}_p}

Examples of dimension instances are presented in the next table.

This dimension is composed of four hierarchies, noted H_{COGZ} = (N^{HCOGZ}, $Param^{HCOGZ}$, $Weak^{HCOGZ}$); H_{LZCN} = (N^{HLZCN}, $Param^{HLZCN}$, $Weak^{HLZCN}$); H_{LZGZ} = (N^{HLZGZ}, $Param^{HLZGZ}$, $Weak^{HLZGZ}$); and H_{COCN} = (N^{HCOCN}, $Param^{HCOCN}$, $Weak^{COCN}$).

The hierarchy named H_{COGZ} is specified by:

- N^{HCOGZ} = 'HCOGZ'
- $Param^{HCOGZ}$ = < IdG, City, Country, Global_Zone, All>
- $Weak^{HCOGZ}$ = { IdG → {Latitude, Longitude, Altitude}}

We shall only present $Param^{Hx}$ for the three other hierarchies: $Param^{HCOCN}$ =< IdG, City, Country, Continent, All>; $Param^{HLZCN}$ = <IdG, Local_Zone, Country, Continent, All>; and $Param^{HLZGZ}$ =<IdG, Local_Zone, Country, Global_Zone, All>.

Weather forecasts may be analyzed thought the fact noted FORC = (N^{FORC}, M^{FORC}, I^{FORC}, $IStar^{FORC}$) where:

- N^{FORC} = 'Forecast'
- M^{FORC} = {SUM(Precipitation), AVG(Temperature)}
- I^{FORC} = {i^{FORC}_1, i^{FORC}_2 ... i^{FORC}_q}

Table 2. Example of dimension instances

IdG	Latitude	Longitude	Altitude	City	Local_Zone	Country	Continent	Global_Zone	All
i^{GEO}_1	N43.36	E1.26	145M	Toulouse	MP	France	Europe	North	All
i^{GEO}_2	S34.0	E151.0	0M	Sydney	NSW	Australia	Oceania	South	All
…	…	…	…	…	…	…	…	…	…

- $IStar^{FORC} = \{i^{FORC}_k \rightarrow (i^{MOD}_{rk}, i^{DAT}_{sk}, i^{GEO}_{tk})$
  $\mid \forall k \in [1..q], i^{FORC}_k \in I^{FORC} \wedge \exists i^{MOD}_{rk} \in I^{MOD} \wedge$
  $\exists i^{DAT}_{sk} \in I^{DAT} \wedge \exists i^{GEO}_{tk} \in I^{GEO}\}$

Examples of fact instances are presented in the next table.

Multidimensional Table Structure

Constellation schemas depict MDB structures whereas user analyses are based on tabular representations (Gyssens & Lakshmanan, 1997) where structures and data are displayed. The visualization structure that we define is a multidimensional table (MT), which displays data from one fact and two of its linked dimensions.

Definition. A *multidimensional table* T is defined as (S, L, C, R) where:

- $S=(F^S, M^S)$ represents the analysed subject through a fact $F^S \in F^{Cs}$ and a set of projected measures $M^S=\{f_1(m_1),..., f_x(m_x)\}$ where $\forall i \in [1..x], m_i \in M^{Fs}$
- L=(DL, HL, PL) represents the horizontal analysis axis where $PL=<All, p^{HL}_{max},... p^{HL}_{min}>$, $HL \in H^{DL}$ and $DL \in Star^{Cs}(F^S)$, HL is the *current hierarchy* of DL
- C=(DC, HC, PC) represents the vertical analysis axis where $PC=<All, p^{HC}_{max},... p^{HC}_{min}>$, $HC \in H^{DC}$ and $DC \in Star^{Cs}(F^S)$, HC is the *current hierarchy* of DC
- R=$pred_1 \wedge ... \wedge pred_t$ is a normalized conjunction of predicates (restrictions of dimension data and fact data)

Figure 4 depicts an example of MT, which displays precipitation forecasts according to the temporal axis and the geographic axis. Note that a MT represents an excerpt of data recorded in a constellation.

$T_1 = (S_1, L_1, C_1, R_1)$ with:

- $S_1=(FORC, \{SUM(\text{Precipitation}), AVG(\text{Temperature})\})$
- $L_1=(GEO, HCOCN, <All, Continent>)$
- $C_1=(DAT, HY, <All, Year>)$
- $R_1=GEOGRAPHY.All = \text{'all'} \wedge DATES.All = \text{'all'} \wedge MODEL.All = \text{'all'}$)

A MT is built from a constellation using the operator named DISPLAY.

Definition. DISPLAY(N^{Cs}, F^S, M^S, DL, HL, DC, HC) = T_{RES} where:

- N^{Cs} is the constellation name
- $F^S \in F^{Cs}$ is the displayed fact
- $M^S=\{f_1(M_1),..., f_x(M_x)\}$, where $\forall i \in [1..x]$, $M_i \in M^{FS}$ is a measure of F^S to be displayed in the MT
- $DL \in Star^{Cs}(F^S)$ and $DC \in Star^{Cs}(F^S)$ are respectively the horizontal and vertical dimensions
- $HL \in H^{DL}$ and $HC \in H^{DC}$ are selected hierarchies, which are used to display parameters
- $T_{RES} = (S_{RES}, L_{RES}, C_{RES}, R_{RES})$ is the resulting multidimensional table, where: $S_{RES} = (F, \{f_1(M_1),..., f_x(M_x)\})$; $L_{RES} = (DL, HL, <All, p^{HL}_{vL}>)$; $C_{RES}=(DC, HC, <All, p^{HC}_{vC}>)$ $R_{RES} = \bigwedge_{\forall i, D_i \in Star^C(F^S)} D_i.ALL = \text{'all'}$.

Figure 4. Example of a MT (textual definition and graphic representation)

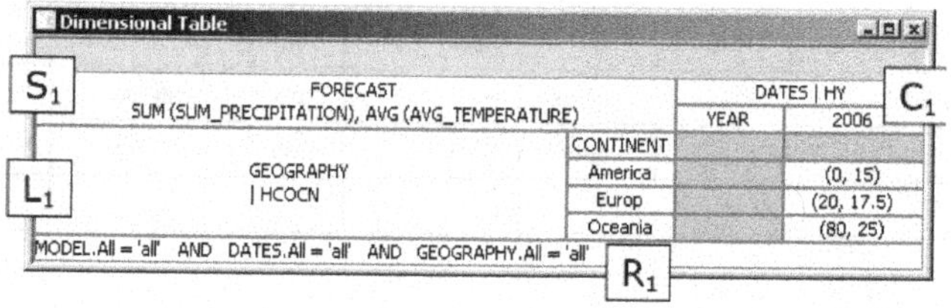

Example 1. Let us consider users who whish to display precipitation forecasts according to months grouped into years and according to cities grouped into countries and continents. This OLAP analysis is calculated according to the following algebraic expression: DISPLAY('Weather Constellation', FORC, {SUM(Precipitation), AVG(Temperature)}, GEO, H_{COCN}, DAT, H_Y) = T_1. The resulting MT (T_1) is displayed in Figure 4.

MINIMAL CORE OF THE OLAP ALGEBRA

In relational databases, the relational algebra is a procedural query language composed of operators. Queries are specified by sequences of relational algebraic operators that manipulate relations (database components). This language is a closed set of operators. Each one operates on one or more relations and yields a relation. More elaborated languages (e.g., SQL) are built on this algebra.

In the same way, our objective is to provide an algebra and an associated, more elaborated language. The OLAP algebra we define is associated to the multidimensional conceptual model described above. This algebra is a "procedural" query language that allows manipulation and retrieval of data from a MDB through nested expressions of multidimensional algebraic operators. It provides a stable basis for the specification of more elaborated languages, notably languages adapted to decision-makers such as graphical query language. Moreover, the algebra represents

also specific algorithms corresponding to each elementary operator.

Formally, the algebraic operations take as input a source MT, noted T_{SRC}=(S_{SRC}, L_{SRC}, C_{SRC}, R_{SRC}), and producing as output a new MT, noted T_{RES}=(S_{RES}, L_{RES}, C_{RES}, R_{RES}). Each output MT can further be manipulated using operations of the same algebra. This property is called closure. As relational algebra, we specify a minimal core of operators and a set of advanced operators composed of combined core operators.

The minimal core is a small set of *operators* that allows the analyst to manipulate MT in useful ways. We define three categories of multidimensional OLAP manipulation operators:

- **Modifying analysis precision:** It consists in moving the analysis details along a hierarchy (DRILLDOWN or ROLLUP) or selecting data of a multidimensional schema (SELECT).
- **Changing analysis criteria:** It consists in: 1) replacing an analysis axis by another one (ROTATE); 2) transforming the subject of the analysis (ADDM/DELM); 3) transforming an analysis axis by adding or removing a dimension attribute (PUSH/PULL); and 4) adding attributes from external dimensions in a displayed analysis axis (NEST).
- **Changing MT presentation:** It consists in: 1) switching parameter values of a displayed dimension; 2) add totals and subtotals in a MT.

Each operation has the following input: $T_{SRC}=(S_{SRC}, L_{SRC}, C_{SRC}, R_{SRC})$ where:

- $S_{SRC}=(F^S, \{f_1(m_1),\ldots, f_x(m_x)\})$, $\forall i$, $1\leq i\leq x$, $m_i\in M^S$
- $L_{SRC}=(DL, HL, <All, p^{HL}_{max},\ldots,p^{HL}_{min}>)$, $DL\in Star(F^S)$
- $C_{SRC}=(DC, HC, <All, p^{HC}_{max},\ldots, p^{HC}_{min}>)$, $DC\in Star(F^S)$
- $R_{SRC}=(pred_1 \wedge\ldots\wedge pred_t)$

Modifying the Analysis Precision

The operation called DRILLDOWN consists in moving from coarser-granularity data to finer-granularity data. The opposite operator, which modifies the analysis from finer-granularity data to a coarser granularity, is called ROLLUP.

Definition. DRILLDOWN(T_{SRC}, D, $Lvl_{inf}^{(*)}$) = T_{RES}.
Input:

- $D\in\{DC, DL\}$ is the dimension, on which the drilling downward operation is applied
- Lvl_{inf} is a lower attribute in the current hierarchy of D. The intermediate graduation levels between the finer graduation of T_{SRC} and the new graduation are not displayed

Output: $T_{RES}=(S_{SRC}, L_{RES}, C_{RES}, R_{SRC})$ is the resulting multidimensional table such as:

- If D=DL then $L_{RES}=(DL, HL, <All, p^{HL}_{max},\ldots, p^{HL}_{min}, Lvl_{inf}>)$ and $C_{RES}=C_{SRC}$
- If D=DC then $L_{RES}=L_{SRC}$ and $C_{RES}=(DC, HC, <All, p^{HC}_{max},\ldots p^{HC}_{min}, Lvl_{inf}>)$

$^{(*)}$ A level, noted Lvl, may represent a parameter p^D, a parameter with a list of weak attributes $p^D(a^D_1, a^D_2,\ldots)$, or a list of weak attributes $(a^D_1, a^D_2,\ldots)$ of p^D, which is not displayed.

Definition. ROLLUP(T_{SRC}, D, Lvl_{sup}) = T_{RES}
where:
Input:

- $D\in\{DC, DL\}$ is the dimension, on which the drilling upward operation is applied
- Lvl_{sup} is a coarser-graduation level used in T_{RES}, the finer graduations are deleted

Output: $T_{RES}=(S_{SRC}, L_{RES}, C_{RES}, R_{SRC})$ is the resulting multidimensional table such as:

- If D=DL then $L_{RES}=(DL, HL, <All, p^{HL}_{max},\ldots, Lvl_{sup}>)$ and $C_{RES}=C_{SRC}$
- If D=DC then $L_{RES}=L_{SRC}$ and $C_{RES}=(DC, HC, <All, p^{HC}_{max},\ldots, Lvl_{sup}>)$

The selection, noted SELECT, operates on a MT and removes the data that do not satisfy the condition. This condition may be expressed on dimension attribute values as well as on fact measure values. Note that this operator realizes "slicing/dicing" manipulations in a MDB terminology (Agrawal et al., 1997).

Definition. SELECT(T_{SRC}, pred) = T_{RES} where:
Input: pred= $pred_1 \wedge\ldots\wedge pred_t$ is a normalized selection predicate (conjunction of disjunctions) on the fact F^S and/or its linked dimensions (D_i | $D_i\in Star^{Cs}(F^S)$).

Output: $T_{RES}=(S_{SRC}, L_{SRC}, C_{SRC}, R_{RES})$ is the resulting MT where R_{RES} = pred.

Example 2. From the previous example in Figure 4, decision-makers change the precision of forecast analysis. The focus is on European continent (European countries and cities). Three operators compose the algebraic expression (output MT in Figure 5):

DRILLDOWN(DRILLDOWN(SELECT(T_1, Geography.Continent = 'Europ'), Geography, Country), Geography, City) = T_2.

Figure 5. Multidimensional table (T$_2$) resulting from three algebra operators

Dimensional Table						_ □ x
	FORECAST				DATES | HY	
	SUM (SUM_PRECIPITATION), AVG (AVG_TEMPERATURE)				YEAR	2006
	GEOGRAPHY	CONTINENT	COUNTRY	CITY		
	| HCOCN	Europ	France	Toulouse		(20, 17.5)
MODEL.All = 'all' AND DATES.All = 'all' AND GEOGRAPHY.CONTINENT = 'Europ'						

$T_2 = ($ (FORC, $\{SUM(Precipitation),$ $AVG(Temperature)\}),$
(GEO, HCO, <All, Continent, Country, City>),
(DAT, HY, <All, Year>),
GEOGRAPHY.Continent = 'Europ' $\wedge$ DATES.All = 'all' $\wedge$ MODEL.All = 'all').

Changing Analysis Criteria

The rotation, noted ROTATE, allows changing one analysis axis by another one in a MT. It also may be used to change the current hierarchy by another one belonging to the same dimension.

Definition. ROTATE(T_{SRC}, D_{old}, D_{new}, H^{Dnew}_k) = T_{RES} where:
Input:

- $D_{old} \in \{DC, DL\}$ is a dimension of T_{SRC} to be replaced
- D_{new} is the dimension replacing $D_{old} \in \{DC, DL\}$ in the resulting multidimensional table
- H^{Dnew}_k is the current hierarchy of D_{new} (positioned on the coarser-granularity parameter)

Output: $T_{RES} = (S_{SRC}, L_{RES}, C_{RES}, R_{SRC})$ is the resulting multidimensional table such as:

- If $D_{old} = DL$ then $L_{RES} = (D_{new}, H^{Dnew}_k, <All, p^{HDnew}_{vl}>)$ and $C_{RES} = C_{SRC}$
- If $D_{old} = DC$ then $L_{RES} = L_{SRC}$ and $C_{RES} = (D_{new}, H^{Dnew}_k, <All, p^{HDnew}_{vc}>)$

The operation that adds a measure, noted ADDM and the operation that deletes a measure, noted DELM, allow the modification of the analyzed measure set.

Definition. ADDM($T_{SRC}, f_i(m_i)$) = T_{RES} where:

Input: $f_i(m_i) \notin M^S = \{f_1(m_1),...,f_x(m_x)\}$ is a measure of F^S ($f_i(m_i) \in M^{FS}$) to be added to T_{SRC}

Output: $T_{RES} = (S_{RES}, L_{SRC}, C_{SRC}, R_{SRC})$ is the resulting multidimensional table where

$S_{RES} = (F^S, \{f_1(m_1),...,f_x(m_x),f_i(m_i)\})$.

Definition. DELM($T_{SRC}, f_i(m_i)$) = T_{RES} where:

Input: $f_i(m_i) \in M^S$ is a measure to be suppressed from T_{SRC},

Output: $T_{RES} = (S_{RES}, L_{SRC}, C_{SRC}, R_{SRC})$ is the resulting multidimensional table where:

$S_{RES} = (F^S, \{f_1(m_1),...,f_{i-1}(m_{i-1}),f_{i+1}(m_{i+1}),...,f_x(m_x)\})$. Note that this operator may not remove the last measure of T_{SRC}.

Example 3. Now, decision-makers complete the previous analysis by changing the analysis criteria; fo example, they change temporal granularity by the dimension named MODEL and they focus their analysis by deleting unnecessary measure. The algebraic expression is ROTATE(DELM(T_2, SUM(Precipitation)), DATES, MODEL, HM) = T_3 and Figure 6 displays the output MT.

Figure 6. Multidimensional table resulting from OLAP algebra manipulations

Dimensional Table						
					MODEL | HM	
FORECAST				MCOUNTRY	France	UK
AVG (AVG_TEMPERATURE)						
GEOGRAPHY	CONTINENT	COUNTRY	CITY			
| HCOCN	Europ	France	Toulouse		(17.5)	(15)
DATES.All = 'all' AND MODEL.All = 'all' AND GEOGRAPHY.CONTINENT = 'Europ'						

T_3 = ((FORC, {*AVG(Temperature)*}),
(GEO, HCO, <All, Continent, Country, City>),
(MOD, HM, <All, MCountry>),
GEOGRAPHY.Continent = 'Europ' $\wedge$ DATES.
All = 'all' $\wedge$ MODEL.All = 'all').

The restructuring operations, noted PUSH and PULL, consist in combining the dimension attributes with the measures. The PUSH operator converts dimension attributes into measures. The PULL operator is the converse of the PUSH operator; it converts measures into parameters.

Definition. $PUSH(T_{SRC}, D, p) = T_{RES}$ where:

Input:
- $D \in Star^{Cs}(F^S)$ is a dimension,
- $p \in H^D_k$ is the parameter of D to be converted into a measure

Output: $T_{RES}=(S_{RES}, L_{SRC}, C_{SRC}, R_{SRC})$ is the resulting multidimensional table where $S_{RES}=(F^S, \{f_1(m_1),...,f_x(m_x), p\})$.

Definition. $PULL(T_{SRC}, f_i(m_i), D) = T_{RES}$ where:

Input:
- $f_i(m_i) \in M^S$ is a measure of the current fact to be converted into a parameter of D
- $D \in \{DC, DL\}$ is the dimension, which is extended with the new converted parameter

Output: $T_{RES}=(S_{RES}, L_{RES}, C_{RES}, R_{SRC})$ is the resulting multidimensional table such as:

$S_{RES}=S_{SRC}-\{f_i(m_i)\}$

- If D=DL then $L_{RES}=(DL, HL, <All, p^{HL}_{max},...$
  $,p^{HL}_{min}, f_i(m_i)>) \wedge C_{RES}=C_{SRC}$
- If D=DC then $L_{RES}=L_{SRC} \wedge C_{RES}=(DC, HC, <All, p^{HC}_{max},..., p^{HC}_{min}, f_i(m_i)>)$

The nesting operator, noted NEST, allows the user to include dimension attributes of dimensions that are not displayed in the displayed dimensions of a multidimensional table. This operation enables the use of parameters from several dimensions in the 2D space of the MT.

Definition. $NEST(T_{SRC}, D, Lvl, D_{nested}, Lvl_{nested})$ $= T_{RES}$ where:

Input:
- $D \in \{DC, DL\}$ is a dimension and Lvl is its level
- $D_{nested} \in Star^{Cs}(F^S)$ is the dimension from which the nested level is taken
- Lvl_{nested} is the nested level of D_{nested}

Output: $T_{RES}=(S_{SRC}, L_{RES}, C_{RES}, R_{SRC})$ is the resulting multidimensional table such as:
- If D=DL then $L_{RES}=(DL, HL, <All, p^{HL}_{max},..., Lvl, Lvl_{nested},..., p^{HL}_{min}>) \wedge C_{RES}=C_{SRC}$
- If D=DC then $L_{RES}=L_{SRC} \wedge C_{RES}=(DL, HD, <All, p^{HC}_{max},..., Lvl, Lvl_{nested},..., p^{HC}_{min}>)$

Example 4. Decision-makers complete the previous analysis; they change the MT presentation by nesting year into Geography dimension. They also modify analysis precision by rolling up to continents and countries. The algebraic expression is NEST(ROLLUP(T_3, GEOGRAPHY, Country),

Figure 7. Multidimensional table resulting from nest operator

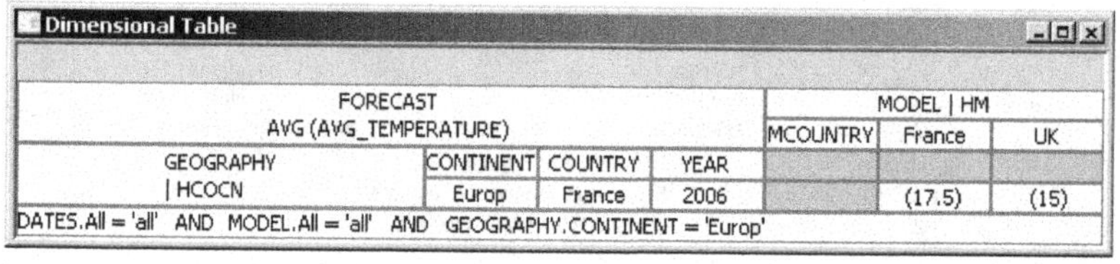

GEOGRAPHY, Country, DATES, Year) = T_4 and Figure 7 displays the output MT.

T_4 = ((FORC, {$AVG(Temperature)$}),
(GEO, HCO, <All, Continent, Country, Year>),
(MOD, HM, <All, MCountry>),
GEOGRAPHY.Continent = 'Europ' $\wedge$ DATES.
All = 'all' $\wedge$ MODEL.All = 'all').

Changing the Multidimensional Table Presentation

The switching operation, noted SWITCH, permutes two values of a parameter from a dimension allowing a specific order in the displayed values.

Definition. SWITCH(T_{SRC}, D, att, v_1, v_2) = T_{RES} where:

Input:

- $D \in \{DC, DL\}$ is a displayed dimension
- att $\in A^D$ is an attribute of the dimension D, on which the switching of the values v_1 and v_2 is applied. Note that dom(att)=$<...v_1,...v_2,...>$ in T_{SRC}

Output: T_{RES}=(S_{SRC}, L_{SRC}, C_{SRC}, R_{SRC}) is the resulting multidimensional table where dom(att)=$<...v_2,...v_1,...>$.

The operation to calculate aggregates, noted AGGRE-GATE, allows aggregating values in line or column of a multidimensional table. This operation realizes the Cube operator defined by (Gray et al., 1996).

Definition. AGGREGATE(T_{SRC}, D, f(att)) = T_{RES} where:

Input:

- $D \in \{DC, DL\}$ is a dimension.
- att is the attribute of D on which applies the aggregation function f (sum, avg,...) with dom(att)=$<v_1,...,v_x>$ in T_{SRC}.

Output: T_{RES}=(S_{SRC}, L_{SRC}, C_{SRC}, R_{SRC}) is the resulting multidimensional table where:

$\forall i \in [1..x]$, dom(att)=$<v_1, f(v_1),...,v_x, f(v_x)>$. Each initial value is completed by the aggregation value.

Summary

In this section, we have defined a core of eleven operators, dispatched in three categories. The following table summarizes this proposal. These operators may be combined together.

ADVANCED OPERATORS OF THE OLAP ALGEBRA

The minimal core of the algebra allows the expression of more or less complex analyses on constellation data. However, some analyses demand numerous combinations of different basic operators. In order to improve the processing of complex queries, we define a set of advanced operations (created by combinations of basic operators). The interest is twofold: the analysis query specification is simplified and the system processing of advanced operations may be optimized in relation to the equivalent combination of basic operators.

[*] History(T_{old}, obj, T_{new})=T_R represents the history of operations that were applied in T_{old} on obj (dimension or fact) and that must be applied

Table 4. OLAP Algebra core

Categories	Operators
modifying analysis precision	DRILLDOWN/ROLLUP SELECT
changing analysis criteria	ROTATE PUSH/PULL ADDM/DELM NEST
changing MT presentation	SWITCH AGGREGATE

on T_{new}. Note that the fact rotation operation, noted FROTATE, is equivalent to the Drill-Across operation (Abelló et al., 2003).

BINARY OPERATORS OF THE OLAP ALGEBRA

All previously defined operations are unary operators. In order to manipulate two MT, we provide a set of binary operators. From two MT, a binary operator builds a third MT by applying a union, an intersection or a difference operation. In order to be applied, these operations need compatible or semi-compatible MT as inputs. The following sections present the compatibility of input tables and the set of binary operators.

Compatibility of Input Tables

Input MT, which are noted $T_{SRC1}=(S_{SRC1}, L_{SRC1}, C_{SRC1}, R_{SRC1})$ and $T_{SRC2}=(S_{SRC2}, L_{SRC2}, C_{SRC2}, R_{SRC2})$, must be compatibles to applied binary operators. Note that $\forall i \in [1..2]$,

- $S_{SRCi} = (F, \{m^{SRCi}_1,..., m^{SRCi}_s\})$
- $L_{SRCi} = (DL^{SRCi}, HL^{SRCi}, <All, p^{DL/SRCi}_1,..., p^{DL/SRCi}_{cl}>)$
- $C_{SRCi} = (DC^{SRCi}, HC^{SRCi}, <All, p^{DC/SRCi}_1,..., p^{DC/SRCi}_{cc}>)$
- $R^{SRCi} = pred^{SRCi}_1 \wedge ... \wedge pred^{SRCi}_t$

Definition. Two tables T_{SRC1} and T_{SRC2} are *compatible tables* if and only if:

- S_{SRC1} and S_{SRC2} are compatibles; for example, they have the same number of measures, noted $\{m^{SRC1}_1,..., m^{SRC1}_s\}$ and $\{m^{SRC2}_1,..., m^{SRC2}_s\}$, and the type[*] of corresponding measures is the same in both S_{SRC1} and S_{SRC2}, $\forall i \in [1..s]$, type(m^{SRC1}_i) = type(m^{SRC2}_i),
- L_{SRC1} and L_{SRC2} are compatibles; for example, they have same structure (same dimension $DL^{SRC1}=DL^{SRC2}$, same hierarchy $HL^{SRC1}=HL^{SRC2}$, same ordered set of displayed dimension attributes $<All, p^{DL\ SRC1}_1,..., p^{DL\ SRC1}_{cl}>=<All, p^{DL\ SRC2}_1,..., p^{DL\ SRC2}_{cl}>)$. Notice that domains of dimension attributes are not necessarily equals.
- C_{SRC1} and C_{SRC2} are compatibles; for example, they have same structure.

[*] Note that type(att) gives the set of all possible values of the attribute whereas dom(att) gives the set of attribute values (dom(Att)$\subseteq$type(Att)).

We introduce the semi-compatibility property allowing binary operations between two MT, which are not strictly compatibles.

Definition. Two tables T_{SRC1} and T_{SRC2} are *semi-compatible tables* if and only if:

- L_{SRC1} and L_{SRC2} are compatibles
- C_{SRC1} and C_{SRC2} are compatibles

Example 5. In the following table, we display three MT noted T_a, T_b, and T_c.

Table 5. Advanced operators

Operator	Description	Syntax and its translation
FROTATE	This operation consists in using a new fact in the MT while preserving the characteristics of the current analysis axes (DC and DL). The new fact must share at least the two selected dimensions with the initial fact.	FROTATE(T_{SRC}, F_{new}, $\{f_1(m_1),...f_x(m_x)\}$) = History$^{(*)}$(T_{SRC}, DL, History(T_{SRC}, DC, DISPLAY(N^{CS}, F_{new}, $\{f_1(m_1),f_2(m_2),...\}$, DL, HL, DC, HC)))
HROTATE	The rotation of hierarchies in a MT consists in changing the current hierarchy in line or column.	HROTATE(T_{SRC}, D, H^D_k) = ROTATE(T_{SRC},D,D,H^D_k)
ORDER	This operation consists in ordering values of parameters in an ascending or descending order (ord∈{'asc', 'dsc'}).	ORDER(T_{SRC}, D, p, ord) = SWITCH(... (SWITCH(T_{SRC}, D, p, v_1, v_2), ...), D, p, v_a, v_b)
PLOT	This operation consists in displaying data according to a unique parameter of a dimension.	PLOT(T_{SRC}, D, Lvl) = DRILLDOWN(ROLLUP (T_{SRC},D,All),D, Lvl)
UNSELECT	The unselecting operation consists in canceling all selections on dimensions and facts. This operation builds a MT starting from all the characteristics of an initial MT but withdrawing all restrictions on the domain values.	UNSELECT(T_{SRC}) = SELECT(T_{SRC}, F^S.All='all' $\wedge$ ($\bigwedge_{D_i \in Star^{Cs}(F^S)} D_i.All = 'all'$)

- T_a is not compatible with T_b and T_c because $C_a \neq C_b$ and $C_a \neq C_c$ while
- T_b and T_c are compatibles because $S_b = S_c$, $L_b = L_c$ and $C_b = C_c$. Note that dom(Continent) in T_b is not equal to dom(Continent) in T_c.

Set Operators

Set operators can be applied between two tables, which may be compatibles or semi-compatibles. These operations consist in combining two MT using union, intersection or minus operations (Agrawal et al., 1997; Gyssens & Lakshmanan, 1997).

Definition. SET(T_{SRC1}, T_{SRC2} [,*fn*]) = T_{RES} where SET∈{UNION, INTERSECT, MINUS}.

Input: T_{SRC1} and T_{SRC2} are two compatible or semi-compatible MT, and *fn* is an optional calculus function, which is applied on corresponding measures from both T_{SRC1} and T_{SRC2}.

Output: T_{RES} is the resulting multidimensional table such as:

- If *fn* is specified, $S_{RES} = (F^{SRC1}, \{m^{SRC1}_1,..., m^{SRC1}_s\})$, else if *fn* is not specified, $S_{RES} = (F^{SRC1}, \{m^{SRC1}_1,..., m^{SRC1}_{s1}, m^{SRC2}_1,..., m^{SRC2}_{s2}\})$; *e.g.* measures from T_{SRC1} and T_{SRC2} are not regrouped into T_{RES}.
- $L_{RES} = (DL^{SRC1}, HL^{SRC1}, <All, p^{DL RES}_1,..., p^{DL RES}_{cl}>)$ where $\forall i \in [1..cl]$,
  - If SET=UNION, dom($p^{DL RES}_i$)=dom($p^{DL SRC1}_i$) $\cup$ dom($p^{DL SRC2}_i$),
  - If SET = INTERSECT, dom($p^{DL RES}_i$) = dom($p^{DL SRC1}_i$) $\cap$ dom($p^{DL SRC2}_i$),
  - If SET=MINUS, dom($p^{DL RES}_i$)=dom($p^{DL SRC1}_i$) \ dom($p^{DL SRC2}_i$),
- $C_{RES} = (DC^{SRC1}, HC^{SRC1}, <All, p^{DC RES}_1,..., p^{DC RES}_{cc}>)$ where $\forall i \in [1..cc]$,
  - If SET=UNION, dom($p^{DL RES}_i$)=dom($p^{DL SRC1}_i$) $\cup$ dom($p^{DL SRC2}_i$),
  - If SET = INTERSECT, dom($p^{DL RES}_i$) = dom($p^{DL SRC1}_i$) $\cap$ dom($p^{DL SRC2}_i$),

Table 6. Compatibilities between MT

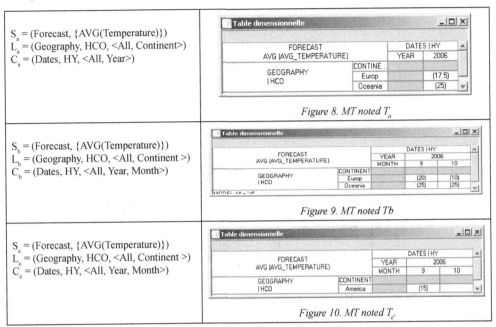

S_a = (Forecast, {AVG(Temperature)}) L_a = (Geography, HCO, <All, Continent>) C_a = (Dates, HY, <All, Year>)	*Figure 8. MT noted T_a*
S_b = (Forecast, {AVG(Temperature)}) L_b = (Geography, HCO, <All, Continent >) C_b = (Dates, HY, <All, Year, Month>)	*Figure 9. MT noted Tb*
S_c = (Forecast, {AVG(Temperature)}) L_c = (Geography, HCO, <All, Continent >) C_c = (Dates, HY, <All, Year, Month>)	*Figure 10. MT noted T_c.*

○   If SET = MINUS, dom($p^{DL\,RES}_i$) = dom($p^{DL\,SRC1}_i$) \ dom($p^{DL\,SRC2}_i$),

•   If SET = UNION, $R_{RES} = R_{SRC1} \vee R_{SRC2}$, if SET = INTERSECT, $R_{RES} = R_{SRC1} \wedge R_{SRC2}$, if SET = INTERSECT, $R_{RES} = R_{SRC1} \wedge \neg R_{SRC2}$.

Note that both union and intersection are commutative and associative operations whereas the minus operation is neither commutative nor associative.

Example 6. Decision-makers want to analyze data from T_b with data from T_c. The expression UNION(T_b, T_c) produces T_{R1} = ((Forecast, {AVG(Temperature)}),(Geography, HCO, <All, Continent>),(Dates, HY, <All, Year, Month>), Model.All='all') with dom(Continent) = {Europ, Oceania, America}.

GRAPHICAL QUERY LANGUAGE

Although the algebra is a powerful tool, it may not be directly used by a decision-maker. We provide a user-oriented graphic language avoiding the specification of long tedious textual queries. The graphic language is based on the algebraic operations. With this language the user expresses the different OLAP manipulations disregarding the algebraic syntax.

This section starts by defining the principles of the language. The second part provides formal specifications and the third focuses on the completeness with regard to the algebraic core.

Principles

The graphic language is based on an environment providing a display of the conceptual multidimensional elements and an analysis display interface presenting the results of the multidimensional OLAP analysis. Query specification uses both interfaces.

Constellation Display Interface

This interface presents to the user the schema of a MDB, with a graph (see Figure 3). In this graph,

Figure 11. Multidimensional table resulting from union

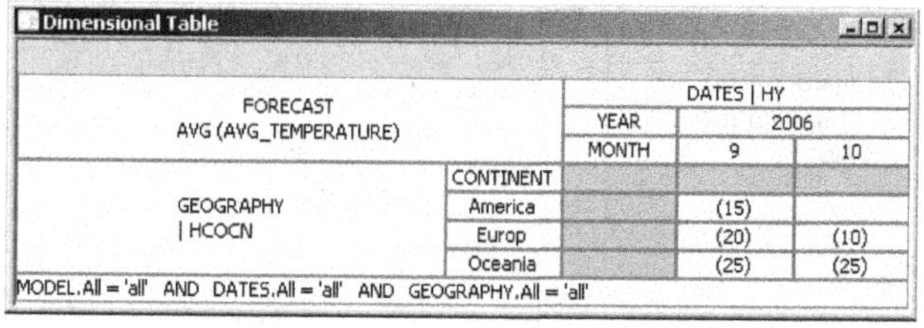

Figure 12. MT zones

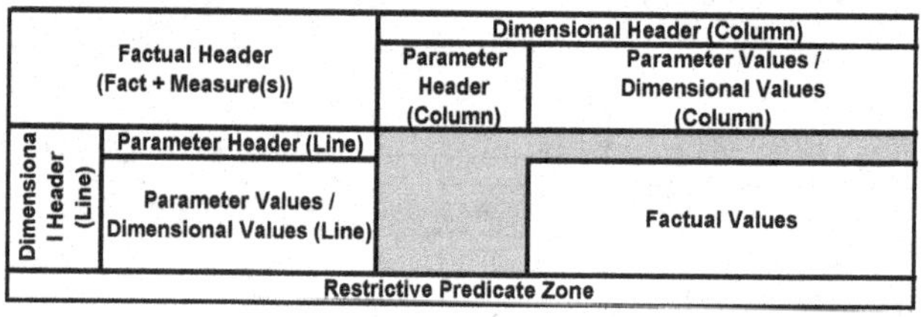

notations are inspired by (Golfarelli et al., 1998), each node is a fact (green) or a dimension (red) whereas links between facts and dimensions are represented by edges. Measures are directly associated to fact nodes. Each dimension is represented by a sub-tree of parameters (yellow circles) and weak attributes (underlined texts). Additional visualizations are provided for special cases (see Appendix A).

Analysis Display Interface

This interface is a bi-dimensional table representing a multidimensional table defined in section 2.3. This interface, called MT, is composed of eight "drop zones" that may be used for query specification. These zones are depicted in the following table. It evolves incrementally, according to decision-maker manipulations.

Query Specification

In order to specify multidimensional OLAP analyses, the decision-maker expresses his queries with the use of the two previously defined interfaces:

- Users may drag elements from the graph displayed in the constellation display interface onto a MT drop zone. He may also drag elements from a MT zone to another one.
- Alternatively, users may call a contextual menu on elements of the graph or on the elements in the MT. They then select the item in the menu corresponding to the desired operation.

In order to ensure consistency during the specification of the analyses, the user is guided along the query specification process: incompatible operations with the ongoing analysis are deactivated. As a consequence, the user cannot create erroneous analyses. Each operation takes as input a multidimensional element and is applied to the current MT. If complementary information is needed by the system, the user specifies it through dialog boxes.

Formal Specification of the Graphic Operations

The system provides users with a set of operations for specifying graphically multidimensional OLAP analyses. Users start by defining a MT

Figure 13. Example of a graphical definition of an MT

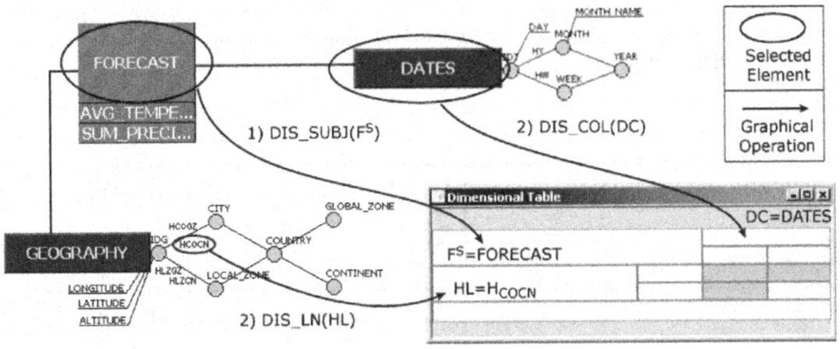

and employ the manipulation language to modify the MT.

Formal specifications of graphical operations are as follows: OPERATION(E), where E is a multidimensional element. This element may be: a fact (F), a measure ($f_i(m_i^F)$ or $f_i(m_i)$), a dimension (D), a hierarchy (H^D_i or H) or a parameter (p^D_i or p_i). This element may be either in the constellation display interface or in a MT, for example, the column dimension DC is in the graph representation, but also in the column dimensional header. Notation: $p_i \in H \Leftrightarrow (p_i \in Param^H \vee (\exists p_j \in Param^H \mid p_i \in Weak^H(p_j)))$

MT Definition

A MT may be in two different modes: definition mode where only a few graphic operations are available; and **alteration mode** where all other operations are available.

In definition mode, graphic manipulations are limited to those that may specify the DISPLAY operation in order to define the initial display of the MT: DIS_SUBJ to specify the displayed subject, DIS_COL and DIS_LN for the specification of the line and column axis. The MT stays in definition mode as long as the displayed fact and the column and line dimensions are not all specified, that is, for a MT noted T=(S, L, C, R) as long as (S=∅∨L=∅∨C=∅).

Example. The following algebraic expression permits to display the multidimensional table T_1 (see example.1):

Ex1: DISPLAY('Weather Constellation', FORC, {SUM(Precipitation), AVG(Temperature)}, GEO, H_{COCN}, DAT, H_Y) = T_1

Within the graphical context, T_1 (displayed in Figure 4) is defined by a sequence of three graphic actions which may be executed in any order. The MT is built incrementally and the display is updated with each new instruction. The following steps (1, 2 and 3) are displayed in Figure 13:

1. **Subject selection (DIS_SUBJ):** The user selects the fact FORECAST, drags its graphic icon and drops it in the factual header of the MT. This action defines F^S, and automatically selects all its measures in M^S, that is, the two measures SUM(Precipitation) and AVG(Temperature). Alternatively, the user may drag each measure one after the other and drop them in the factual header. The user may also use contextual menus to select a fact and/or its measures.

2. **Column dimension selection:** The user selects the dimension DATES and drags its graphic icon and drops it in the column dimensional header, defining DC. If a dimension is composed of a single hierarchy, this latest is automatically selected and the parameter of highest level which is just

Table 7. Graphical specifications of the algebraic DISPLAY operator

Source element of the action (and conditions)		Algebraic equivalent
Subject specification : DIS_SUBJ(E)		
1.	$E=F \mid F \in F^{Cs}$	DISPLAY(N^{Cs}, F^S, M^S, DL, HL, DC, HC) with: $F^S=F$, $M^S=M^F$
2.	$E=f_i(m_i) \mid f_i(m_i) \in M^F \wedge F \in F^{Cs}$	DISPLAY(N^{Cs}, F^S, M^S, DL, HL, DC, HC) with: $F^S=F$, $M^S=\{f_i(m_i)\}$
Column specification: DIS_COL(E)		
3.	$E=D \mid \exists\, H \in H^D \wedge D \in D^{Cs}$	DISPLAY(N^{Cs}, F^S, M^S, DL, HL, DC, HC) with: DC=D, HC=H**?**
4.	$E=H \mid H \in H^D \wedge D \in D^{Cs}$	DISPLAY(N^{Cs}, F^S, M^S, DL, HL, DC, HC) with: DC=D, HC=H
5.	$E=p_i \mid p_i \in H \wedge H \in H^D \wedge D \in D^{Cs}$	DISPLAY(N^{Cs}, F^S, M^S, DL, HL, DC, HC) with: DC=D, HC=H**?**
6.	$E=p_i \mid p_i \in H \wedge H \in H^D \wedge D \in D^{Cs} \wedge$ $level^{HC}(p_i)<level^{HC}(p_{vc})$	PLOT(DISPLAY(N^{Cs}, F^S, M^S, DL, HL, DC, HC), DC, p_i) with: DC=D, HC=H**?**
Line specification: DIS_LN(E), identical to columns for selecting DL and HL.		

If $(DC \neq \varnothing \wedge F^S \neq \varnothing)$ then $DC \in Star^{Cs}(F^S)$ and If $(DL \neq \varnothing \wedge F^S \neq \varnothing)$ then $DL \in Star^{Cs}(F^S)$

below the extremity parameter "All": p^{HC}_{vc} is displayed. If the system may not isolate this current hierarchy, automatic selection fails, which is the case here. The user is then prompted to select the correct hierarchy: HY. Alternatively, the user may drag the hierarchy edge or the desired parameter p_i. As above, the user may rely on contextual menus.

3. **Line dimension selection:** The user operates as previously described. In the example, the user drags the hierarchy edge HCOCN. In the end, the user obtains T_1, displayed in Figure 4.

The next table presents the different possibilities to define a MT with the graphic instructions. In the table (as in all other tables of this section), detailed instructions are presented only for the column definition (DC, HC,...), as they are identical to lines (DL, HL,...). "**?**" stands for an element that the user may have to select through a user prompt. In the DISPLAY case, this happens if: 1) DC is selected and DC has more than one hierarchy, that is, $\|H^{DC}\|>1$; 2) p_i is selected and it belongs to more

than one hierarchy, that is, $\exists\, H \in H^{DC}$, $H \neq HC \mid p_i \in H$ $\wedge p_i \in HC$; or 3) the edge between p_i and p_{i+1} represents more than one hierarchy, that is, $\exists\, H \in H^{DC}$, $H \neq HC \mid p_i \in H \wedge p_i \in HC \wedge p_{i+1} \in H \wedge p_{i+1} \in HC$.

Notice that the user may also directly select a parameter p_i which is not the highest parameter in the hierarchy, that is $level^{HC}(p_i)<level^{HC}(p_{vc})$.

Figure 14 presents the graphical "drag and drop" actions that may be used to define a MT. In order to specify the analysis subject, the user drags the graphic icon representing the subject from the constellation graph, onto the MT and drops it in the factual header zone (executing a DIS-SUBJ operation). To specify an analysis axis, the user has to drop the element in a dimensional header zone (executing a DIS_COL on the column header and a DIS_LN on the line header). In the following figure, operations numbered from 1 to 6 correspond to the six lines of Table 7.

Once a fact has been designated as a subject and two dimensions have been specified as line and column axes, the MT switches to alteration mode, authorizing all the other operations.

Figure 14. Actions that may be used to define a MT

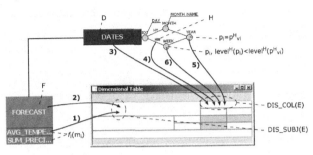

Figure 15. Correspondence between graphic operations and drag and drop actions

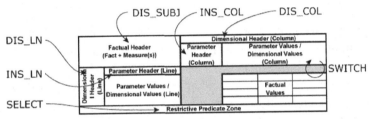

MT Manipulations

In alteration mode, a MT may be modified by the use of operations of the following sets:

- **A set of six display-oriented operations.** The three operations previously defined display an element as subject, in lines or in columns (DIS_SUBJ, DIS_LN, and DIS_COL). In addition to these three operations, the set is enriched by two "insertion" operations. These operations allow decision-makers to "insert" an element in the current line or column (INS_LN and INS_COL) of the analysis display interface. Moreover, a deletion operation is provided (DEL).

- **A set of specific operations**: these operations allow the execution of specific algebraic operators. In order to ease understanding, they have the same name as their algebraic equivalent. These operations allow the restriction of the displayed data (SELECT), the inversion of two displayed values (SWITCH), the addition of aggregated data (AGGREGATE),

the removal of previously aggregated data (UNAGGREGATE) and the inversion of all displayed values (ORDER).

- **A set of two drilling operations:** DRILL-DOWN, ROLLUP. As all drilling operations may not be expressed by the use of the graphic-oriented operations, these two operations are defined.

Each of these graphic operations executes a sequence of core and/or advanced algebraic operations.

The display operations are the equivalent of dropping elements into the factual header or the two dimensional headers; the insert operations are the equivalent of dropping elements into the parameter headers; and the delete operation is the equivalent of dragging an element which is in the MT and drop it out of the MT. The following figure summarizes the different correspondences between graphic operations and "drag and drop" actions on a particular drop zone.

Figure 16. Example of a graphical definition of an MT

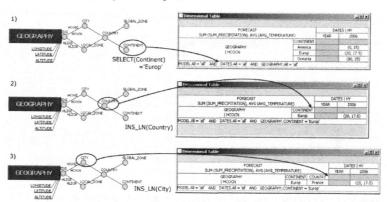

Example. The following algebraic expression permits to display the multidimensional table T_1 (see example.2):

Ex2: DRILLDOWN(DRILLDOWN(SELECT(T_1, Geography.Continent = 'Europ'), Geography, Country), Geography, City) = T_2

Within the graphical context, T_2 (displayed in Figure 5) is defined by a sequence of three graphic actions. A MT is built incrementally and the display is updated with each new graphic action. These actions are described below (see Figure 16):

1. **Restriction of the line values**: The user selects the parameter on which he wishes to add a predicate. He drags the parameter graphic icon from the graph and drops it in the restriction zone of the MT, thus executing a SELECT(Continent). He will be prompted to specify the restriction predicate which will be applied: "=Europ".
2. **Adding to the display parameters**: The user selects the graphic icon representing the parameter Country, drags it onto the MT and drops it in the line parameter header, thus executing INS_LN(Country).
3. **Adding to the display parameters**: The user repeats the operation with the parameter City: INS_LN(City). Alternatively,

the decision-maker could have used the contextual menus in order to execute two DRILLDOWN operations on GEOGRAPHY dimension. In the end, decision-makers obtain T_2 displayed in Figure 5.

The next paragraphs present complete formal specification of graphic instructions of display-oriented operations and their translation in algebraic language (see tables). These formal specifications are followed by their equivalent graphic "drag and drop" manipulations. Other specifications (specific operations and drilling operations) are in Appendix B.

Display-Oriented Operations: DIS_ SUBJ, DIS_LN and DIS_COL

The graphic instruction DIS_SUBJ is used to designate an element that will be displayed as a subject of a MT. Formal specifications may be found in Table 8. Its corresponding "drag and drop" actions are displayed in Figure 17. In this figure, the numbers from 1 to 5 correspond to each line of Table 8.

The graphic instruction DIS_COL (respectively DIS_LN) is used to replace the elements currently displayed in columns (resp. lines). Formal specifications of DIS_COL may be found in Table 9 and corresponding "drag and drop" ac-

Figure 17. Possible drag and drop manipulations for the instruction DIS_SUBJ(E)

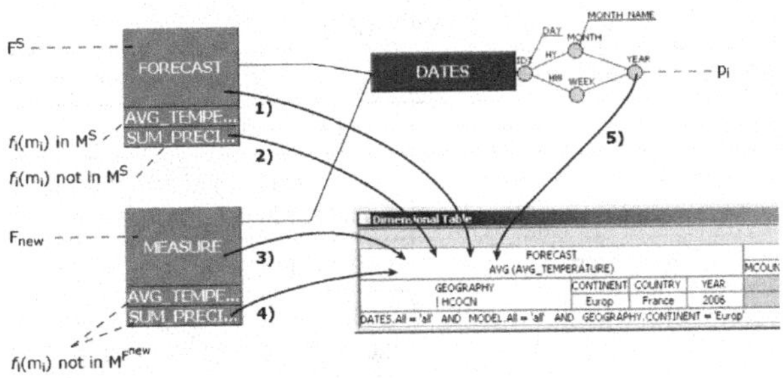

Table 8. Formal specification of DIS_SUBJ(E)

DIS_SUBJ(E)		
Source element of the action (and conditions)		**Algebraic equivalent (T_{RES})**
1.	$E=F^S$	History(T_{SRC}, DL, History(T_{SRC}, DC, DISPLAY(N^{CS}, F^S, $\{f_1(m_1),\dots f_w(m_w)\}$, DL, HL, DC, HC))), $\forall i \in [1..w], f_i(m_i) \in M^{FS}$
2.	$E=F_{new} \mid F_{new} \neq F^S \wedge$ $DC \in Star^{Cs}(F^{new}) \wedge DL \in Star^{Cs}(F^{new})$	FROTATE(T_{SRC}, F_{new}, $\{f_1(M_1),\dots f_w(M_w)\}$), $\forall i \in [1..w], M_i \in M^{Fnew}$
3.	$E=f_i(m_i) \mid f_i(m_i) \notin M^S \wedge f_i(m_i) \in M^{FS}$	ADDM($T_{SRC}, f_i(m_i)$)
4.	$E=f_i(m_i) \mid f_i(m_i) \notin M^{FS} \wedge f_i(m_i) \in M^{Fnew} \wedge$ $DC \in Star^{Cs}(F^{new}) \wedge DL \in Star^{Cs}(F^{new})$	FROTATE(T_{SRC}, F_{new}, $\{f_i(m_i)\}$)
5.	$E=p_i \mid \forall p_i \in A^{Dnew} \wedge D_{new} \in Star^{Cs}(F^S)$	PUSH(T_{SRC}, D_{new}, p_i)

tions are displayed in Figure 18. Like before, the specification of DIS_LN is not presented.

Display-Oriented Operations: INS_LN, INS_COL and DEL

The graphic instruction INS_COL (respectively INS_LN) is used to insert an element into a column (respectively a line). Formal specification for INS_COL may be found in Table 10. As before, INS_LN is not presented. The corresponding "drag and drop" actions are presented in Figure 19. Notice that actions represented by dashed arrows take into account the exact position where the drop action took place. For example, if the element is dropped between Year and Month, the element is inserted between both. More details are available in Appendix B.

The graphic instruction DEL is used to remove a displayed element in a MT. When removing all the elements of a MT zone such as the fact, the user is prompted to designate a new one. Formal specifications are provided in Table 11 and "drag and drop" actions are described in Figure 20.

Completeness of the Language

The graphic OLAP query language rests upon two possible user interactions: drag and drop (DnD) or contextual menus. The DnD actions may be executed from the conceptual graph towards the MT, or from the MT to the same MT, or from the MT to outside the MT. The contextual menu may be called on the conceptual graph elements or on the elements in the MT. Manipulations with the contextual menus assist with dialog boxes. It is easy to understand that the contextual menus have

Table 9. Formal specification of DIS_COL(E), DIS_LN for lines

DIS_COL(E)	
Source element of the action (and conditions)	**Algebraic equivalent (T_{RES})**
1)	$E=f_i(m_i) \mid f_i(m_i) \in M^{FS}$	PULL($T_{SRC}, f_i(m_i)$, DC)
2)	$E=DC$	ROLLUP(T_{SRC}, DC, p^{DC}_{vc}) the display of HC is reset on the most general parameter: $p_{Cmin} = p_{Cmax} = p^{DC}_{vc}$
3)	$E=D_{new} \mid D_{new} \neq DC, D_{new} \in Star^{Cs}(F^S)$	ROTATE(T_{SRC}, DC, D_{new}, H_{new}?), with $H_{new} \in H^{Dnew}$
4)	$E=HC$	ROLLUP(T_{SRC}, DC, p^{DC}_{vc}) the display of HC is reset on the most general parameter: $p_{Cmin} = p_{Cmax} = p^{DC}_{vc}$
5)	$E=H_{new} \mid H_{new} \neq HC \wedge H_{new} \in H^{DC}$	HROTATE(T_{SRC}, DC, H_{new})
6)	$E=H_{new} \mid H_{new} \notin H^{DC} \wedge H_{new} \in H^{Dnew} \wedge D_{new} \in Star^{Cs}(F^S)$	ROTATE(T_{SRC}, DC, D_{new}, H_{new})
7)	$E=p_i \mid p_i \in PC \vee (p_i \notin PC \wedge p_i \in HC)$	PLOT(T_{SRC}, DC, p_i)
8)	$E=p_i \mid p_i \notin HC \wedge p_i \in H_{new} \wedge H \in H^{DC}$	PLOT(HROTATE(T_{SRC}, DC, H_{new}), DC, p_i)
9)	$E=p_i \mid p_i \notin A^{DC} \wedge p_i \in A^{Dnew} \wedge D_{new} \in Star^{Cs}(F^S)$	PLOT(ROTATE(T_{SRC}, DC, D_{new}, H_{new}?), D_{new}, p_i), with $H_{new} \in H^{Dnew}, p_i \in H_{new}$

Figure 18. Possible drag and drop manipulations for the instruction DIS_COL(E)

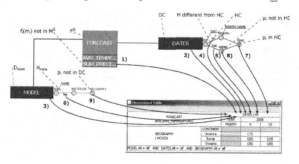

a greater expressive power in the number of different operations that they may allow. As specified in the following table, graphical manipulations are complete with regard to the algebraic operators.

Implementation

Our prototype is built using Java JDK 1.5 on top of the Oracle *10g* DBMS. Composed of a hundred classes, it allows the definition and manipulation of a R-OLAP constellation as well as visualizing and querying the multidimensional data with the use of a graph and an MT (the figures illustrating the present article are screenshots from the prototype).

The visual interface allows decision-makers to specify analysis queries with the constellation dis-

play interface as well as with the analysis display interface. The constellation display is done with the use of meta-data describing the R-OLAP data warehouse architecture.

Graphic queries are then translated into algebraic expressions, which are in turn, translated into SQL queries. Correctness of query expressions is validated through meta-data. These SQL queries are sent to the R-OLAP data warehouse and results are sent back to the MT which updates its display. Algebraic translation between graphic and algebraic expressions is done according to tables throughout this section and in Appendices.

Table 10. Formal specification of INS_COL(E), INS_LN for lines

INS_COL(E)	
Source element of the action (and conditions)	**Algebraic equivalent (T_{RES})**
1.	$E=f_i(m_i) \mid f_i(m_i) \in M^{FS}$	PULL($T_{SRC}, f_i(m_i)$, DC)
2.	E=DC	DRILLDOWN(...(DRILLDOWN(ROLLUP(T_{SRC}, DC, p^{DC}_{vc}), DC, p^{DC}_{vc-1})...), DC, p^{DC}_1) all parameters of HC are displayed: PC = Param^{HC}
3.	E=HC	DRILLDOWN(...(DRILLDOWN(ROLLUP(T_{SRC}, DC, p^{DC}_{vc}), DC, p^{DC}_{vc-1})...), DC, p^{DC}_1) all parameters of HC are displayed: PC = Param^{HC}
4.	$E=p_i \mid p_i \in PC$	NEST(DELETE(T_{SRC}, DC, p_i), DC, p_j?, DC, p_i), with $p_j \in PC$
5.	$E=p_i \mid p_i \notin PC \wedge p_i \in HC$	DRILLDOWN(T_{SRC}, DC, p_i), if level$^{HC}(p_i)$<level$^{HC}(p_{Cmin})$ DRILLDOWN(...(DRILLDOWN(ROLLUP(T_{SRC}, DC, p_i), DC, p_{i+1})...), DC, p_{Cmin}), if level$^{HC}(p_i)$>level$^{HC}(p_{Cmin})$ [1]
6.	$E=p_i \mid p_i \notin HC \wedge p_i \in H \wedge H \in H^{DC}$	NEST(T_{SRC}, DC, p_j?, DC, p_i), with $p_j \in PC$
7.	$E=p_i \mid p_i \notin A^{DC} \wedge p_i \in A^{Dnew} \wedge D_{new} \in Star^{Cs}(F^S)$	NEST(T_{SRC}, DC, p_j?, D_{new}, p_i), with $p_j \in PC$
[1]= p_i not displayed ($p_i \notin PC \wedge p_i \in HC$), p_{Ci+1} (respectively p_{Ci-1}) is the attribute immediately inferior (resp. superior) to p_i in PC: level$^{HC}(p_{Ci+1})$=level$^{HC}(p_i)$-1 (resp. level$^{HC}(p_{Ci+1})$ =level$^{HC}(p_i)$+1)	

Figure 19. Possible drag and drop manipulations for the instruction INS_COL(E)

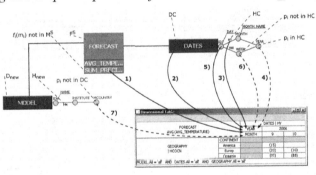

Table 11. Formal specification of DEL(E)

DEL(E)	
Source element of the action (and conditions)	**Algebraic equivalent (T_{RES})**
1.	E=F^S	FROTATE(T_{SRC}, F_{new}?, {$f_1(m_1),...,f_w(m_w)$}), $\forall i \in [1..w]$ $m_i \in M^{Fnew}$
2.	$E=f_i(m_i) \mid f_i(m_i) \in M^S$	DELM($T_{SRC}, f_i(m_i)$)
3.	E=DC	ROTATE(T_{SRC}, DC, D_{new}?, H?), $D_{new} \in Star^{Cs}(F^S)$, $H \in H^{Dnew}$
4.	E=HC	ditto above: DEL(DC)
5.	$E=p_i \mid p_i \in PC$	DELETE(DC, p_i)
6.	E=R (zone de restriction) [1]	UNSELECT(T_{SRC})
[1]= This operation is done on the restriction zone (R) of the MT.	

Figure 20. Possible drag and drop manipulations for the instruction INS_COL(E)

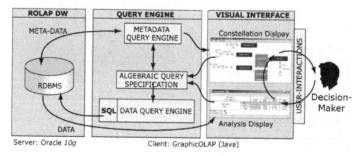

Table 12. Graphic actions for each operator/operation

		Core Operators											
		Rotate	DrillDown	RollUp	Nest	Switch	Aggregate	Unaggregate	Push	Pull	AddM	DelM	Select
Drag and Drop	Graph-mTable	x	x	x	x				x	x	x		x
	mTable-mTable			o	x				o	o			o
	mTable-outside	x		o				x				x	
Contextual Menu	Graph	x	x	x	x		x	x	x	x	x	x	x
	mTable	x	x	x		x	x	x	x	x	x	x	x
	Graphic support of the operations	x	x	x	x	x	x	x	x	x	x	x	x

o = partial support of the operator; p=complete support of the operator

Figure 21. Prototype architecture

![Prototype architecture figure]

Server: Oracle 10g   Client: GraphicOLAP (Java)

CONCLUDING REMARKS

The goal of this article is to provide a user-oriented OLAP environment. The provided solution is based on three points: a conceptual model that disregards implementation issues, an OLAP query algebra that provides formal specifications of manipulation operators and a graphic language easing graphic multidimensional OLAP analyses.

The conceptual model we define allows a multidimensional representation of the available data. This model represents a constellation of facts, dimensions, and hierarchies. The constellation has the advantage to ease correlations between analysis subjects (multi-fact modeling). The model, based on multi-hierarchical analysis axes, provides multiple data analysis perspectives. This model acts as a basis for of OLAP manipulation languages.

To formalize multidimensional OLAP analyses, we first define a query algebra. It allows the selection of analysis data to be displayed from a multidimensional schema (operator Display). This algebra uses a decisional analysis display structure adapted to decision-makers: a multidimensional table (MT), that is, a hierarchical bi-dimensional table. This algebra allows decision-makers to express the different operations, which may be performed during an analysis. Query correctness is guaranteed through the closure property supported by the algebra. Each operator produces as output a multidimensional table that is a compatible input for the other operators.

We defined a minimal core and advanced operations. The core operators allow the following modifications:

- The data granularity or the analysis precision (Drilldown, Rollup and Select)
- The analysis criteria (Rotate, Push, Pull, Nest, AddM and DelM)
- The structure of the resulting table (Switch, Aggregate)

In order to simplify complex OLAP query expression and to improve query processing, we provide a set of advanced operators defined by combinations of the core algebra operators. Finally to analyze two MT, we provide three set operators based on compatible or semi-compatible tables.

Although user-oriented, our algebra is difficult for decision-makers. As a consequence, we have defined a graphic language. This language is based on two interfaces. The first one displays the graphical schema of a multidimensional database and the second displays the resulting multidimensional table. To perform a multidimensional OLAP analysis, the decision-maker selects directly an element of the multidimensional schema and drags it in the result MT. These drag and drop actions

may be completed by a set of menus that specify the analysis elements. The graphic language allows the definition of an analysis in an incremental way and at each step, the decision-maker visualizes the resulting MT. The graphic language is complete with regard to the algebraic core. For each graphic instruction, we have specified the equivalent combination of algebraic operators. Finally, the language has been validated by its implementation in a prototype (figures throughout this article are screen captures). The prototype is based on an implementation of the multidimensional concepts in a ROLAP environment with the DBMS Oracle. The graphic language is composed of a hundred java classes and other components.

The next step of these works is to take into account multidimensional schema data evolutions. Versions could be used for the data evolution tracking (Ravat et al., 2006b), and within this framework, OLAP manipulation operators should be revised. Another step in OLAP systems is the integration of XML data. This will require adapted multidimensional models and methodologies (Nassis et al., 2005; Rusu et al., 2005; Messaoud et al., 2006) as well as adapted analysis operators (Ravat et al., 2007).

REFERENCES

Abelló, A., Samos, J., & Saltor, F. (2003). Implementing operations to navigate semantic star schemas. In *Proceedings of the 6th ACM international workshop on Data Warehousing and OLAP (DOLAP2003)* (pp. 56-62). ACM.

Abelló, A., Samos, J., & Saltor, F. (2006). YAM²: A multidimensional conceptual model extending UML. *Journal of Information Systems (IS)*, *31*(6), 541-556.

Agrawal, R., Gupta, A., & Sarawagi, S. (1997). Modeling multidimensional databases. In *Proceedings of the 13th Int. Conf. Data Engineering (ICDE)*, IEEE Computer Society, pp. 232–243.

Blaschka, M., Sapia, C., Höfling, G., & Dinter, B. (1998). Finding your way through multidimensional data models. In *Proceedings of the 9th Int. Workshop on Database and Expert Systems Applications: Data Warehouse Design and OLAP Technology (DWDOT'98)* (pp.198-203). IEEE Computer Society.

Böhnlein, M., Plaha, M.. & Ulbrich-vom Ende, A. (2002). Visual specification of multidimensional queries based on a semantic data model. *Vom Data Warehouse zum Corporate Knowledge Center (DW2002)* (pp.379-397). Physica-Verlag.

Cabibbo, L., & Torlone, R. (1998). From a procedural to a visual query language for OLAP. In *Proceedings of the 10th Int. Conf. on Scientific and Statistical Database Management (SSDBM 1998)*, IEEE Computer Society, pp. 74-83.

Cabibbo L., & Torlone R. (1997). Querying multidimensional databases. *Database Programming Languages, 6th International Workshop (DBPL-6)* (pp. 319-335). Springer.

Chaudhuri, S., & Dayal, U. (1997). An overview of data warehousing and OLAP technology. *SIGMOD Record*, 26(1), 65-74.

Colliat, G. (1996). OLAP, relational, and multidimensional database systems. *SIGMOD Record*, 25(3), 64-69.

Datta, A., & Thomas, H. (1999). The cube data model: A conceptual model and algebra for on-line analytical processing in data warehouses. *Journal of Decision Support Systems*, 27(3), 289-301.

Franconni, E., & Kamble, A. (2004). The GMD Data model and algebra for multidimensional information. In *Proceedings of the 16th Int. Conf. on Advanced Information Systems Engineering (CAiSE)* (pp. 446-462). Springer.

Golfarelli, M., Maio, D. & Rizzi, S. (1998). Conceptual design of data warehouses from E/R schemes. In *Proceedings of the 31st Hawaii Int. Conf. on System Sciences*.

Gray, J., Bosworth, A., Layman, A., & Pirahesh, H. (1996). Data cube: A relational aggregation operator generalizing group-by, cross-tab, and sub-total. In *Proceedings of the 12th Int. Conf. on Data Engineering (ICDE)* (pp. 152-159). IEEE Computer Society.

Gyssen, M., & Lakshmanan, L. (1997). A foundation for multi-dimensional databases. In *Proceedings of the 23rd Int. Conf. on Very Large Data Bases (VLDB'97)* (pp. 106-115). Morgan Kaufmann.

Kimball, R. (1996). *The data warehouse toolkit: Practical techniques for building dimensional data warehouses*, 2nd ed. John Wiley & Sons Inc.

Lamping, J., & Rao R. (1994). Laying out and visualizing large trees using a hyperbolic space. In *Proceedings of the 7th ACM Symposium on User Interface Software and Technology (UIST'94)* (pp. 13-14). ACM.

Lehner, W. (1998). Modeling large scale OLAP scenarios. In *Proceedings of the 6th Int. Conf. on Extending Database Technology (EDBT'98)* (pp. 153-167). Springer.

Li, C., & Wang, X.S. (1996). A Data Model for Supporting On-Line Analytical Processing. In *Proceedings of the 5th Int. Conf. on Information and Knowledge Management (CIKM'96)* (pp. 81-88). ACM.

Malinowski, E., & Zimányi, E. (2006). Hierarchies in a multidimensional model: From conceptual modeling to logical representation. *Journal of Data & Knowledge Engineering*, 59(2), 348-377.

Maniatis, A., Vassiliadis, P., Skiadopoulos, S., Vassiliou, Y., Mavrogonatos, G., & Michalarias, I. (2005). A presentation model & non-traditional visualization for OLAP. *International Journal of Data Warehousing & Mining*, 1(1), 1-36.

Messaoud, R., Boussaid, O., & Rabaséda, S. (2006). A data mining-based olap aggregation of complex data: Application on XML documents. *International Journal of Data Warehousing & Mining, 2*(4), 1-26.

Nassis, V., Rajagopalapillai, R., Dillon, T., & Rahayu, W. (2005). Conceptual and systematic design approach for XML document warehouses. *International Journal of Data Warehousing & Mining, 1*(3), 63-87.

Niemi, T., Hirvonen, L., & Jarvelin, K. (2003). Multidimensional data model and query language for informetrics. *Journal of the American Society for Information Science and Technology, 54*(10), 939-951.

Pedersen, T., Jensen, C., & Dyreson, C. (2001). A foundation for capturing and querying complex multidimensional data. *Journal of Information Systems, 26*(5), 383-423.

Rafanelli, M. (2003). Operators for Multidimensional Aggregate Data. In M. Rafanelli (Ed.), *Multidimensional databases: Problems and solutions* (pp. 116-165). Idea Group Publishing.

Ravat, F., Teste, O., & Zurfluh, G. (2006). Constraint-based multi-dimensional databases. In Zongmin Ma (Ed.), Chap. XI of *Database Modeling for Industrial Data Management* (pp. 323-368). Idea Group Publishing.

Ravat, F., Teste, O., & Zurfluh, G. (2006). A multiversion-based multidimensional model. In *Proceedings of the 8th Int. Conf. on Data Warehousing and Knowledge Discovery (DaWaK 2006)* (pp. 65-74). Springer.

Ravat, F., Teste, O., & Tournier, R. (2007). OLAP aggregation function for textual data warehouse. In *Proceedings of the International Conference on Enterprise Information Systems (ICEIS 2007)*, INSTICC Press.

Rizzi, S., Abelló, A., Lechtenbörger, J., & Trujillo, J. (2006). Research in data warehouse modeling and design: Dead or alive? In *Proceedings of the 9th ACM International Workshop on Data Warehousing and OLAP (DOLAP 2006)* (pp.3-10). ACM.

Rusu, L., Rahayu, J., & Taniar, D. (2005). A methodology for building XML data warehouses. *International Journal of Data Warehousing & Mining, 1*(2), 23-48.

Stolte, C., Tang, D., & Hanrahan, P. (2002). Polaris: A System for Query, Analysis, and Visualization of Multidimensional Relational Databases. *IEEE Trans. on Visualization and Computer Graphics, 8*(1), 52-65.

Torlone, R. (2003). Conceptual Multidimensional Models. In M. Rafanelli (Ed.), *Multidimensional databases: Problems and solutions*, (pp. 69-90). Idea Group Publishing.

Trujillo, J., Luján-Mora, S., & Song I. (2003). Applying UML for designing multidimensional databases and OLAP applications. In K. Siau (Ed.), *Advanced topics in database research Volume 2* (pp. 13-36). Idea Group Publishing.

Vassiliadis, P. & Sellis, T. (1999). A survey of logical models for OLAP databases. *SIGMOD Record, 28*(4), 64-69.

ENDNOTES

[1] Business Objects XI from http://www.businessobjects.com/

[2] Cognos Business Intelligence 8 from http://www.cognos.com/

[3] Tableau 2 from http://www.tableausoftware.com/

[4] Targit Business Intelligence Suite from http://www.targit.com/

APPENDIX-A:
CONSTELLATION GRAPHICAL VISUALIZATION

If a dimension is composed of a complex hierarchical structure, the structure may be exploded, in order to easily see the different parameters of each hierarchy. This is useful as drilling operations follow the hierarchical order of the dimensional parameters. For example in Figure 22, the dimension named GEOGRAPHY is composed of six parameters spread over four different hierarchies.

It is not exceptional that a corporate multidimensional database holds several facts and numerous dimensions. Users may be lost in large constellations. An alternative visualization is provided in order to focus on relevant parts of the constellation graph. The constellation graph is projected on a hyperbolic space (Lamping & Rao, 1994) and decision-makers "move" quickly through the graph in order to see relevant nodes.

Figure 22. The GEOGRAPHY dimension in (top) compact version and (bottom) split version

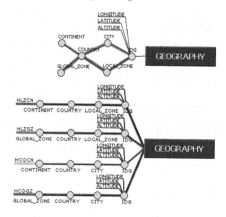

Figure 23. Hyperbolic view of a constellation

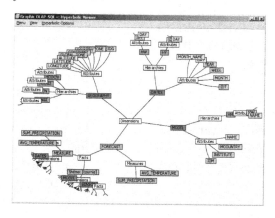

APPENDIX-B:
COMPLEMENTARY FORMAL SPECIFICATIONS

The following table presents specific operations that modify the MT display.

Table 14 presents the formal specification of the two drilling operations.

Figure 24 illustrates some graphic drag and drop operations that may be used on a parameter header zone. These graphic manipulations consist in "inserting in line" (INS_LN). The position of drop actions determines the equivalent algebraic operations; for example, in Figure 23, the parameter noted Global_Zone is dropped between Country and City, thus this action is translated in a nest operator NEST(T, GEOGRAPHY, Country, GEOGRAPHY, Global_Zone).

Table 13. Formal specification of the algebra-oriented graphic operations

Source element of the action (and conditions)	Algebraic equivalent (T_{RES})
SELECT(E)	
$E=f_i(m_i) \mid f_i(m_i) \in M^{FS}$	SELECT(pred?), pred is a predicate on $dom(f_i(m_i))$
$E=p_i \mid p_i \in A^D, D \in Star^{Cs}(F^S)$	SELECT(pred?), pred is a predicate on $dom(p_i)$
SWITCH(X) [1]	
$X=val_x \mid val_x \in dom(p_i), p_i \in PC$	SWITCH(T_{SRC}, DC, p_i, val_x, val_y?), with $val_y \in dom(p_i)$
AGGREGATE(E) and UNAGGREGATE(E)	
$E=p_i \mid p_i \in PC, dom(p_i)=<v_1,...,v_x>$	AGGREGATE(T_{SRC}, DC, f_i?(p_i))
$E=p_i \mid p_i \in PC, dom(p_i)=<v_1,f_i(v_1),...,v_x,f_i(v_x)>$	UNAGGREGATE(T_{SRC})
ORDER(E)	
$E=p_i \mid p_i \in PC$	ORDER(T_{SRC}, DC, p_i, ord?)

Table 14. Formal specification of the graphic drilling operations

Source element of the action (and conditions)	Algebraic equivalent (T_{RES})
DRILLDOWN(E)	
$E=DC \mid \exists p_i \in HC, level^{HC}(p_i)=level^{HC}(p_{Cmin})-1$	DRILLDOWN(T_{SRC}, DC, p_{Cmin-1}) [1]
$E=HC \mid \exists p_i \in HC, level^{HC}(p_i)=level^{HC}(p_{Cmin})-1$	DRILLDOWN(T_{SRC}, DC, p_{Cmin-1}) [1]
$E=p_i \mid level^{HC}(p_i)>level^{HC}(p_{Cmin})$	DRILLDOWN(T_{SRC}, DC, p_i)
ROLLUP(E)	
$E=DC \mid \exists p_i \in HC, level^{HC}(p_i)=level^{HC}(p_{Cmin})+1$	ROLLUP(T_{SRC}, DC, p_{Cmin+1}) [1]
$E=HC \mid \exists p_i \in HC, level^{HC}(p_i)=level^{HC}(p_{Cmin})+1$	ROLLUP(T_{SRC}, DC, p_{Cmin+1}) [1]
$E=p_i \mid level^{HC}(p_i)<level^{HC}(p_{Cmin})$	ROLLUP(T_{SRC}, DC, p_i)
[1] p_{Cmin-1} (resp. p_{Cmin+1}) is the parameter immediately inferior (resp. superior) to p_{Cmin} in the list $Param^{HC}$ (i.e. $level^{HC}(p_{Cmin-1})+1=level^{HC}(p_{Cmin})=level^{HC}(p_{Cmin+1})-1$).	

Figure 24. Some specific nesting and drilling interactions (INS_LN(E))

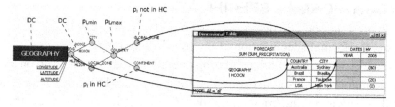

This work was previously published in International Journal of Data Warehousing and Mining, Vol. 4, Issue 1, edited by D. Taniar, pp. 17-46, copyright 2008 by IGI Publishing (an imprint of IGI Global).

Chapter 5
Dynamic View Selection for OLAP

Michael Lawrence
Dalhousie University, Canada

Andrew Rau-Chaplin
Dalhousie University, Canada

ABSTRACT

In a data warehousing environment, aggregate views are often materialized in order to speed up aggregate queries of online analytical processing (OLAP). Due to the increasing size of data warehouses, it is often infeasible to materialize all views. View selection, the task of selecting a subset of views to materialize based on updates and expectations of the query load, is an important and challenging problem. In this article, we explore dynamic view selection in which the distribution of queries changes over time and the set of materialized views must be tuned by replacing some of the previously materialized views with new ones.

INTRODUCTION

An online analytical processing (OLAP) data warehouse answers queries interactively posed by users, the answers to which are used to support data-driven decision making. Such queries usually make heavy use of aggregation, which may be realized using the group by clause in SQL. Since aggregate queries are so common in OLAP environments and their results are typically very expensive to compute, aggregate views

of the data are often pre-computed and stored in order to speed up future query processing. From the perspective of efficient query answering, ideally all views would be pre-computed and made available for answering aggregate queries. Realistically however, storage and computational constraints limit the number of views that are feasibly pre-materialized.

The problem of choosing a set of views for materialization is known as the *View Selection Problem*. In the view selection problem, one wishes to select a set of views for materialization which minimizes one or more objectives, possibly subject to one or more constraints. Many variants of the view selection problem have been studied including minimizing the query cost of a materialized view set subject to a storage size constraint (Harinarayan, Rajaraman & Ullman, 1996; Shukla, Deshpande & Naughton 1998; Chirkova, Halevy & Suciu, 2002; Kalnis, Mamoulis & Papadias, 2002; Nadeau & Teorey, 2002), minimizing a linear combination of query cost and maintenance cost of a materialized view set (Baralis, Paraboschi, & Teniente, 1997; Gupta, 1997; Gupta, Harinarayan, Rajaraman, & Ullman, 1997; Theodoratos & Sellis, 1997, 1999, 2000; Yang, Karlapalem, & Li, 1997a, 1997b; Horng, Chang, Liu, & Kao, 1999; Uchiyama, Runapongsa, & Teorey, 1999; Theodoratos, Dalmagas, Simitsis, & Stavropoulos, 2001; Theodoratos, Ligoudistianos, & Sellis, 2001; Zhang, Yao & Yang, 2001; Valluri, Vadapalli, & Karlapalem, 2002; Gupta & Mumick, 2005), minimizing both query and maintenance cost as separate objectives (Lawrence, 2006), and minimizing query cost under a maintenance cost constraint (Gupta & Mumick, 1999; Lee & Hammer, 2001; Liang, Wang, & Orlowska, 2001; Kalnis et al., 2002; Yu, Yao, Choi, & Gou, 2003).

Note, however, that in most of these cases the problem considered is *static* in that:

1. Query frequencies are assumed to be static (i.e., not changing over time)
2. It is assumed that the pool of materialized views is to be selected and computed from scratch rather than making use of a running OLAP system's pool of previously materialized views.

While the static view selection problem is important, it captures only the start-up phase of a OLAP system and does not address what is arguably in practice the more important dynamic question: how, given a running OLAP system with an existing pool of materialized views and a new vector of query frequencies, should we identify views that should be added to our materialized pool and views that should be removed in order to best minimize query times subject to a storage size constraint?

The need for dynamic view management was forcefully made by Kotidis and Roussopoulos (1999, 2001) in their DynaMat system. As they observe, "This static selection of views [...] contradicts the dynamic nature of decision support analysis." There are a number of ways to approach the dynamic view selection problem. Kotidis and Roussopoulos (1999, 2001) take a caching approach in which rather than a set of materialized views at the data warehouse, a pool of view *fragments* is maintained. A view fragment is a portion of a whole view which results from a range selection on its dimensions. The authors describe how to locate fragments to answer a query, and how to decide which fragments to admit to the cache based on bounds on the size or maintenance cost of the cached fragments. Another approach is to consider the view selection problem in the context of a *given set of queries* (Gupta, 1997; Yang et al., 1997a, 1997b; Gupta & Mumick, 1999, 2005; Horng et al., 1999; Zhang et al., 2001; Valluri et al., 2002). The idea is to construct a directed acyclic graph (DAG) representing a joint query processing plan and then to consider the view selection problem consisting of choosing a subset of the nodes in the plan DAG so query cost is minimized under some set of constraints.

In this article, we explore an alternative approach to *dynamic view selection*. We consider an OLAP system with two phases of operation: *Startup* and *Online*. In the Startup Phase, an initial set of views must be selected based on some estimated query probabilities. This is the classical (static) view selection problem. In the Online Phase, an "in use" OLAP system is considered, for which a set of views M has already been selected and materialized. Since over time the relative importance of each type of aggregate query may change due to the changing demands of its users, the system may elect to select a new set of views, *M'*, which better serves the incoming queries. However, view materialization is computationally expensive and the time window in which new views can be materialized may prohibit selection of an entirely new view set. Thus the problem becomes selecting a new view set *M'* by discarding some views from *M*, and adding new ones to be materialized. We refer to the problem of incrementally updating a view set as the *online view selection problem*. We believe that the online view selection problem is an important addition to the static variant, as OLAP systems in practice are restarted from scratch only infrequently and must be able to tune their performance to changing conditions on-the-fly.

Our approach to the online view selection problem is to adapt methods that have proven to be effective for the static variant. In this article, we develop online adaptations of the greedy heuristic, BPUS, introduced by Harinarayan et al. (1996) and three randomized techniques (iterative improvement, simulated annealing and two-phase optimization) initially proposed for static view selection by Kalnis et al. (2002). Our challenge is two-fold. For the static phase, the randomized methods must be adapted so as to take into account the maintenance cost constraint in addition to the space constraint and for the online phase all of the methods must be adapted to take into account the existing pool of previously materialized views.

We implement and evaluate these four strategies for dynamic view selection in the context of our cgmCube system (Chen, Dehne, Eavis, & Rau-Chaplin, 2004a, 2004b), a parallel OLAP system designed to address high-dimensional terabyte-sized data cubes. Our experimental evaluation of these techniques was performed on view selection problems ranging up to 16 dimensions in size and focused on both solution quality and efficiency and clearly point to best methods for both the Startup and Online phases of dynamic view selection.

The remainder of this article is structured as follows. The following section formulates the static and online phases of dynamic view selection in more detail and reviews related work. Following that, the application of randomized search to view selection is described, along with the modification to BPUS which allows it to solve the online view selection problem. The article concludes with experimental results of the algorithms' performance, and concluding remarks in the final section.

PROBLEM DEFINITION AND RELATED WORK

Static View Selection

A typical data warehouse stores its information according to a star schema having a central fact table with *d* feature attributes (dimensions), and some number of measure attributes. The dimensions of the fact table have a foreign-key/primary-key relationship with the dimension tables, so that each row in dimension table *i* gives detailed information about a particular value in the domain of the fact table's dimension *i*. Queries to the data warehouse request aggregated measures from the perspective of some subset of the dimensions of the joined fact and dimension tables. The aggregated table from which a query's results are collected is called a *view*, and is identified by the dimensions chosen from the fact table, as well as the corresponding dimensions in the dimension tables which determine the level of hierarchy that the dimension is viewed at. For example, the *customer* dimension of a data warehouse may have further attributes, birth year and city of residence which define a hierarchical organization of customers by birth year or city of residence. A user may wish to view the results based on individual customers, or at a coarser level of granularity higher up in the hierarchy. If the number of hierarchal levels of dimension i is H_{id}, then the total number of possible views is $\prod_{i=1}^{id} (2^{H_i} +1)$.

Harinarayan et al. (1996) introduced the data cube lattice, which expresses the relationship between views as a partial order. Each view corresponds to an answer to a particular aggregate query, and there is a path from a view v_1 to a view v_2 in the lattice if queries on v_2 can be answered also using v_1, although perhaps at a higher cost. For example a query grouping on the dimensions *time* and *customer* can be answered by aggregating the results of a query grouping on *time, customer,* and *item* (provided that the selected dimensions in this view are at lower levels of their respective hierarchies), although it will likely be more expensive than if the query were answered directly on the *time, customer* view.

The view selection problem can be formally defined as follows. For each view v in the lattice L, we have some estimate of the number of records r_v in v, and the frequency of queries f_v on v. As in most previous studies, we adopt the linear cost model presented in [11], where the cost of answering a query on a view v is r_v. The cost $q(v,M)$ of answering aggregate queries on view v using a materialized view set M is equal to the number of records in the smallest view in M which is an ancestor of v in the data cube lattice. The overall query time using M is a weighted sum of these terms

$$Q(M) = \sum_v f_v q(v,M),$$

and the size $S(M)$ of M is simply the sum of the sizes of each of the views in M. The update or maintenance cost $u(v,M)$ of a materialized view v in M is modeled based on a maintenance cost which is assigned to every edge (v_1, v_2) in the lattice. This represents the cost of maintaining v_2 using updates from v_1, and the maintenance cost $u(v,M)$ is the smallest maintenance cost over all paths from materialized ancestors of v_1 to v_2. Each node v also has an update frequency g_v,

and the total update cost for a set of materialized views M is

$$U(M) = \sum_{v \in M} g_v u(v,M)$$

This modeling of maintenance cost is essentially the same as in Gupta and Mumick (1999), Kalnis et al. (2002), Liang et al. (2001) and Yu et al. (2003), however, some studies (Baralis et al., 1997; Gupta, 1997; Horng et al., 1999; Zhang et al., 2001; Valluri et al., 2002) assume that $u(v,M)$ is part of the input to the problem. Note that while $Q(M)$ decreases when new views are added, $U(M)$ does not always increase, as the additional cost of maintaining a materialized view v might be outweighed by the benefit that v has in propagating smaller batches of updates to its children. Our goal for the static phase is as follows: to select a M which has the minimum $Q(M) + U(M)$ subject to the constraint $S(M) < S_{max}$ for some maximum size S_{max}.

In general, the input of the view selection problem is an AND/OR-DAG (Gupta, 1997; Gupta & Mumick, 1999; 2005), a directed acyclic graph where the outgoing edges of each node are partitioned into groups of AND edges, representing the fact that each node requires all of the vertices at the destination of only one of these groups of edges in order to be computed. Associated with each of the groups of AND edges are computation and maintenance costs, and associated with each node is a storage cost. A data cube can be represented by an OR-DAG, which is an AND/OR-DAG where each group of AND edges contains exactly one edge. The edge direction in a data cube is usually reversed to indicate that aggregation of the view at the tail of an edge results in the view at the head. Multiple View Processing Plans (MVPPs) (Yang et al., 1997a, 1997b) on the other hand are represented by an AND-DAG, which is an AND/OR-DAG where each group of AND edges for a node contains all outgoing edges from that node. An MVPP is usually organized with the base relations as sinks (no outgoing edges), a static set of queries Q as sources (no incoming edges), and intermediate nodes as the intermediate result sets computed during query answering. An MVPP can be constructed from the individual query processing graphs for each query in Q (Yang et al., 1997a, 1997b), which themselves can be produced by a query optimizer. The view selection problem consists of choosing a subset of the nodes in an AND/OR-DAG so that the total operational cost represented as the sum of view maintenance and query cost is minimized.

Numerous solutions have been proposed to the (static) view selection problem on data cubes. The first is a greedy algorithm presented by Harinarayan et al. (1996) which selects a fixed number of views to minimize query cost. It is proven to find a solution within 63% of optimal. In work by Gupta (1997) and Gupta and Mumick (2005), the same heuristic was extended to minimize sum of query and update cost in AND-OR/DAGs, as well as an algorithm given to include selection of indexes. Baralis et al. (1997) minimize the sum of query and update cost in a data cube lattice with respect to a fixed set of queries. Shukla et al. (1998) give a heuristic minimizing query cost under a size constraint which is asymptotically faster than that of Harinarayan et al. (1996), but achieves the same solution only under certain conditions. Uchiyama et al. (1999) give a greedy algorithm for minimizing the sum of query and update cost. They consider the cost of specific types of update operations on a view, but ignore the overall effect on update cost of a view set when adding a view v, focusing only on the update cost of v itself. Gupta and Mumick (1999) give the first solution to the view selection problem minimizing query cost under an update cost constraint. Agrawal, Chadhuri and Narasayya (2000) present a tool and algorithms for selecting a set of views based on a cost metric involving query cost, update cost, index construction and other factors. Liang et al. (2001) follow up on Gupta and Mumick (2005) by giving two algorithms minimizing query cost under an update cost constraint. Lee and Hammer (2001) and Yu et al. (2003) apply genetic algorithms to the same variant of the problem. Lawrence (2006) applies multi-objective evolutionary algorithms to minimize both query and update cost under a size constraint, achieving better solutions than Harinarayan et al.'s (1996) heuristic in a reasonable amount of time. Nadeau and Teorey (2002) give a greedy algorithm minimizing query cost under a space constraint which is polynomial in the number of dimensions. Although it does not do as well as other heuristics, it is able to tackle problems with a larger number of dimensions than feasible with previous algorithms. Kalnis et al. (2002) use randomized algorithms to search the solution space of view sets. Their algorithms minimize query cost, are constrained by space or update cost, and are evaluated against those of Harinarayan et al. (1996) and Shukla et al. (1998) under various conditions. They are shown to achieve solutions nearly as good in a smaller amount of time.

Online View Selection

For the online phase we consider a data warehousing system which has a fixed-sized time window to materialize new views which are not currently materialized, but are perhaps more beneficial to the changing query patterns of the users. However, because of the space constraint, a number of views may have to be discarded as well. Based on the size of the available time window for computing new views, the database administrator calculates how much of the materialized view set can be replaced. We do not consider update costs in online view selection because updates themselves are counter to the purpose of online view selection. Online view selection is an act which is typically performed at regular maintenance intervals, based on an observed or expected change in query probabilities. During these intervals, updates are applied to the views and so we do not expect updates to be applied between intervals, hence update cost is not our concern in online view selection. Hence we can define the online view selection problem as follows: Given a materialized view set M and new query frequencies $\mathbf{f'}$, find a M' which minimizes $Q(M')$ with respect to the new query frequencies, and such that

$$\sum_{v \in M \cap M'} r_v \geq (1-h) \cdot S_{max}$$

for some h which represents a percentage of M (in terms of size) for which the system has enough resources to materialize new views for. Our dynamic view selection involves an initial startup phase consisting of a static selection of views M_1, and multiple online phases where M_1 is updated to M_2, M_2 to M_3 and so on. The decision of when to select an M_{i+1} by updating M_i can be made in many ways, for example during a pre-allocated maintenance window, when average query time degrades past an unacceptable level, or based on measuring the difference between the current query distribution and the distribution at the last online phase.

Our formulation of dynamic view selection is different from that of other studies (Kotidis & Roussopoulos, 1999; Theodoratos & Sellis, 1999; 2000; Kotidis & Roussopoulos, 2001; Theodoratos et al., 2001). Theodoratos et al. (2001) and Theodoratos and Sellis (1999; 2000) consider what they call dynamic or incremental data warehouse design. In the static phase, they are given a fixed set of queries Q, and views must be selected from multi-query AND/OR-DAGs which answer the queries with minimum query and update cost. In the online phase, additional queries are added to the set Q, and new materialized views are added so that the new queries can be answered, while still minimizing the sum of query and update cost with respect to the updated set of queries. However, in practice there may not be extra space available for materializing new views and some previously materialized views must be discarded. Also, some of the original queries in Q may not

be posed again. In the dynamic view selection considered here, our materialized view set M is able to answer any possible aggregate query, and its size never increases beyond S_{max} over time. Later in the life of the system it may be the case that additional space is available for materialized views, which can easily be handled by our implementation of the algorithms.

Kotidis and Roussopoulos (1999; 2001) take a caching approach to dynamic view selection. Rather than a set of materialized views at the data warehouse, a pool of view *fragments* is maintained. A view fragment is a portion of a whole view which results from a range selection on its dimensions. The authors describe how to locate fragments to answer a query, and how to decide which fragments to admit to the cache based on bounds on the size or maintenance cost of the cached fragments. Their approach is fundamentally different from ours in that it can only choose to store aggregate data which has been requested from the user, where as pre-materializing a set of views is more flexible in that any aggregate data which can be produced is considered for storage. Also, their approach is in reaction to user's queries, where as a materialized view set approach aims to prepare the system for future queries. We believe ours to be a useful alternative approach to dynamic view selection for the following reasons:

1. As argued by Loukopoulos, Kalnis, Ahmad, and Papadias (2001), the ad-hoc nature of OLAP queries reduces the chance that stored fragments will be able to fully answer future queries. Storing whole views guarantees that any queries on the same or more highly aggregated views can be answered.

2. Knowledge giving an expectation of future query loads (e.g., daily reports) may be available, allowing advance preparations to be made by choosing an appropriate pre-materialized view set.

3. Multiple unrelated and popular aggregate queries may have a common ancestor which can answer all of them at a slightly higher cost. In DynaMat, this ancestor will never be considered for storage unless it is queried, where as a good approach to view selection, it will store this ancestor instead of the individual aggregates below it resulting in significant space savings which can be put to better use.

RANDOMIZED ALGORITHMS FOR DYNAMIC VIEW SELECTION

In order to apply randomized search to a problem, transitions between feasible solutions are required. Each search process moves stochastically through the graph of feasible solutions called the search space, which can be pictured as a topographical space where elevation represents objective value and locality represents connectivity of the solutions through the transitions defined. Since we are minimizing, the "lower" solutions in this space are the ones we desire. The effectiveness of a randomized search strategy depends on the shape of the search space and in what manner the search moves through it.

For the static phase we define two transitions based on those of Kalnis et al. (2002):

1. Add a random view which is not in the current solution and randomly remove selected views as necessary to satisfy the space constraint
2. Remove a randomly selected view

The second transition is different from that of Kalnis et al. (2002), which, after removing a view fills the rest of the available space with views. This is because our algorithms minimize both query and maintenance cost, as opposed to just maintenance cost. Under these conditions it is no longer safe to assume that the optimal view set

is a "full" one, and the randomized algorithms must adapt to the tradeoff between query and maintenance cost. We similarly modify Kalnis et al.'s (2002) method of generating a random solution, by repeatedly adding views to an initially empty view set until the addition of some view v causes a decrease in overall cost, and removing v. This method gave us better results in terms of generating solutions nearer to the favorable ones than another technique of generating random solutions, which was to randomly pick a size S_0 from a uniform distribution on $[0, S_{max}]$, and creating a view set no larger than S_0 by adding as many random views as possible.

The three randomized search algorithms considered here are iterative improvement (II), simulated annealing (SA) and two-phase optimization (2PO), as described by Kalnis et al. (2002).

- II makes a number of transitions, only accepting ones which lead to a better solution (downhill transitions). When a local minimum is detected, based on a number of unsuccessful attempts to transition from a state, II starts again from a random initial state. The search terminates after some maximum amount of time or number of local minima have been examined.
- SA is an analogy of the process a physical system undergoes as it is cooled. It works like II, except that transitions leading to a worse state may be accepted with some probability that is proportional to a "temperature" which decreases with time. The algorithm halts when the temperature reaches a fixed "freezing point", returning the best solution found during the process.
- 2PO combines II with SA. II is first applied to find a good local minimum, from which SA is applied with a small initial temperature to do a more thorough search of the surrounding area.

II tends to work well if the problem has structure so that good solutions are near each other in the search space. SA is more robust than II in that it can overcome the problem that good solutions may be near each other in search space, but separated by a small number of relatively worse solutions. 2PO attempts to combine the best of both II, which proceeds in a more direct manner towards a solution, and SA, which is able to more thoroughly explore an area.

We modify the transitions for online view selection as follows: If, while removing views to satisfy the space constraint, transition 1 violates the online constraint, then we add the previously removed view back to the solution, and continue only removing views in $M' - M$ from M' until the space constraint is satisfied. If transition 2 violates the online constraint, the removed view is re-added and a randomly selected view in $M' - M$ is removed instead.

GREEDY ALGORITHM FOR DYNAMIC VIEW SELECTION

For the static phase, the BPUS heuristic (Haranarayan et al., 1996) begins with an initially empty view set, and greedily adds views which maximize a benefit heuristic. If the currently selected view set is M, then the benefit per unit space of adding an unselected view v is defined as:

$$\frac{(Q(M) + U(M)) - (Q(M \cup \{v\}) + U(M \cup \{v\}))}{r_v},$$

that is, the reduction in overall cost achieved by adding v, scaled by size. The BPUS algorithm adds the view v with maximum benefit per unit space until either there is no more space for materialized views, or v has negative benefit (when $U(M \cup \{v\} - U(M) > Q(M) - Q(M \cup \{v\})$). To apply BPUS to online view selection, the same heuristic is "reversed", and the objective cost only considers query time of the materialized view set.

When deciding which views to remove from M, we choose the view v which minimizes:

$$\frac{Q(M - \{v\}) - Q(M)}{r_v},$$

the increase in average overall cost scaled to the size of v. Once a set of views totaling no more than $h \cdot S_{max}$ in size has been removed from M, we apply the BPUS heuristic (without update cost) to greedily select which views to replace them with, arriving at our solution M'.

EXPERIMENTAL RESULTS

We have implemented our approach to dynamic view selection in the context of the cgmCube system (Chen et al., 2004a, 2004b) and carefully evaluated the randomized search methods as applied in both the Startup Phase (static view selection) and the Online Phase (online view selection).

In our evaluation, we use a variety of synthetic data sets which we can control the properties of in terms of size, dimensionality, skew, and so forth. In particular, we focus on two classes of data sets: 1) *uniform*, where the cardinality of all dimensions are equal, representing data cube lattices with highly uniform view sizes, and 2) *2pow*, where the cardinality of the *i*-th dimension is 2^i, representing data cube lattices with highly skewed view sizes. In all cases, the number of rows in the data sets was set to one billion and S_{max} was set to be ten times this number of rows. Note that this is in contrast to Kalnis et al. (2002), in which S_{max} is proportional to the size of the full data cube (i.e., all 2^d views). The reason for this choice is that we believe that the amount of storage space available is more likely to be a constant factor of the size of the raw data regardless of dimensionality, rather than growing exponentially with dimensionality.

In evaluating the algorithms, we use two different types of query distributions: 1) *uniform random*, where query probabilities are assigned from a uniform random distribution, and 2) *hot regions* (Deshpande, Ramasamy, Shukla, & Naughton, 1998; Kalnis, Ng, Ooi, Papadias, & Tan, 2002), where 90% of the queries are distributed amongst a set of views (the "hot region") selected from the bottom 1/3 of the lattice and containing 10% of the total views. The remaining 10% of the queries are distributed uniformly amongst the other views. We believe this to be a realistic but very challenging scenario, due to the underlying semantics of the dimensions of the data warehouse in which some combinations of dimensions may not provide useful information, while others do, hence there may be a large number of views which are simply not interesting at all. The reason that views are selected from the bottom 1/3 of the lattice is that the results of aggregate queries on large numbers of dimensions are not easy to visualize, and would most likely require the user to simply read the results from the aggregated tables rather than display them graphically.

We assign maintenance costs to views the same as Kalnis et al. (2002), by associating with each view v an update probability u_v, and an update propagation factor p_v, representing the percentage of updates to v which propagate to v's children in the data cube lattice. The update cost to a view w resulting from a batch of updates of size x is xp_wu_v, where v is the materialized ancestor of w with the smallest such u_v. In all of the following experiments, we fix u_v at 10% for all v, and we adjust p_v and x for data set so that the overall cost the resulting solutions are balanced with respect to the relative proportions of query and update cost.

We tune the randomized algorithms similarly as Kalnis et al. (2002), although our final parameter selection is slightly different. Iterative improvement performs $cycles_{II}$ cycles, where each cycle ends at a local minimum. It considers at state a local minimum when $min.d_{II}$ unsuccessful downhill transitions have been attempted from it. At each stage, simulated annealing performs $cycles_{SA}$ transitions, accepting an uphill transition with probability $e^{-\Delta C/T}$, where ΔC is the cost difference between states and T is the current temperature. The temperature is initialized at T_{SA}, and decreases by a factor of Δt_{SA} between each stage. The algorithm halts when $T < 1$ and the last four stages have not produced a better local minimum. Two-phase optimization uses II with $min.d_{II} = min.d_{2PO}$ to find $cycles_{2PO}$ local minima. The best is used as a seed for SA, which is applied with an initial temperature of $T_{SA} = T_{2PO}$ and $\Delta t_{SA} = \Delta t_{2PO}$. The values for these parameters were chosen to achieve both reasonable run time and results. They are summarized in Table 1.

The Startup Phase: Static View Selection

In static view selection, we are primarily concerned with 1) Quality: the solution values achieved by the randomized algorithms versus that of BPUS, and 2) Efficiency: the amount of time it takes to converge on a solution. To maintain consistency with Kalnis et al. (2002), and since randomized algorithms are being considered as an alternative to BPUS, we express their solution quality as a factor of the solution quality of BPUS, called the *scaled solution* value. This is further motivated by the fact that on their own, absolute solution values provide little insight into solution quality outside of the context of a particular problem instance.

Figure 1 shows the running time of BPUS, and the time to convergence for all randomized algorithms as the number of dimensions is varied. As the plot shows, the randomized algorithms converge much faster than the BPUS heuristic for both uniform and highly skewed data, especially in larger dimensions.

Now that we have established the scalability benefits of the randomized techniques with regards to running time, we aim to establish their

Table 1. Selected parameters for the randomized algorithms applied to both the static and online phases of dynamic view selection.

	Static	Online
$cycles_{II}$	$50 \cdot 2^{d-10}$	$40 \cdot h \cdot 2^{3(d-10)/4}$
$min.d_{II}$	$7d$	$3d$
$cycles_{SA}$	$2^d/20$	$h / 30\% \cdot 2^d/20$
T_{SA}	10^7	10^3
Δt_{SA}	0.9	0.8
$cycles_{2PO}$	$cycles_{II}/4$	$cycles_{II}/2$
$min.d_{2PO}$	$min.d_{II}$	$2d$
T_{2PO}	10^5	10^2
Δt_{2PO}	0.9	0.64

scalability in terms of solution quality. Figure 2 shows the scaled cost of the solutions found by the randomized algorithms as the number of dimensions is increased. As can be seen in Figure 2, the randomized algorithms perform competitively against the BPUS heuristic, with their solutions falling typically within a few percent of it and being especially close with uniform data. Surprisingly, there are classes of problem instances where some of the randomized algorithms outperform the heuristic by as much as 15%. These problem instances are ones for which the update cost is

sufficiently prohibitive that the better solutions are ones which contain a small number of views. BPUS finds a maximal solution with respect to size, in that no more views can be added without increasing the overall cost. As a result, the randomized algorithms are able to find solutions with a much better update cost at the expense of a slightly higher query cost. Note that SA does particularly poorly on the low dimensional instances of both the uniform and skewed problems, while the other algorithms do particularly well. This is an indication that for these instances there is a

Figure 1. Running time vs. dimensionality for static view selection with 10^9 rows and $S_{max} = 10^{10}$. The mean of 20 independent trials is shown.

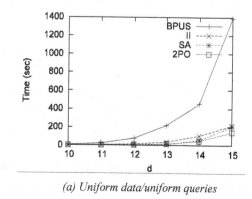

(a) Uniform data/uniform queries

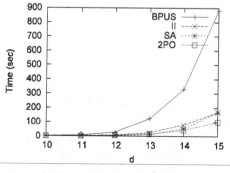

(b) Skewed data/hot regions

Figure 2. Scaled solution vs d for static view selection with 10^9 rows and $S_{max} = 10^{10}$. The mean of 20 independent trials is shown.

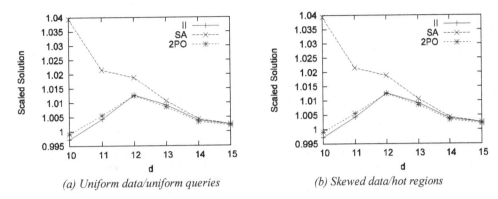

(a) *Uniform data/uniform queries*   (b) *Skewed data/hot regions*

Figure 3. Running time vs. dimensionality for online view selection with 10^9 rows, $S_{max} = 10^{10}$ and $h = 30\%$. The mean of 20 independent trials is shown.

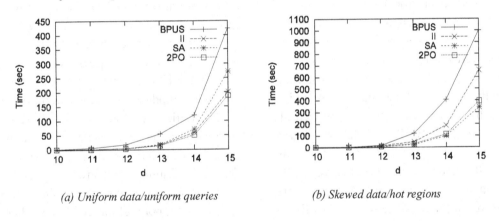

(a) *Uniform data/uniform queries*   (b) *Skewed data/hot regions*

Figure 4. Percent improvement (relative to that of a newly selected view set) as h is increased. A 12-dimensional data cube is used. The mean of 20 independent trials is shown.

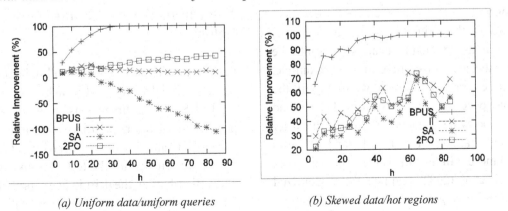

(a) *Uniform data/uniform queries*   (b) *Skewed data/hot regions*

Figure 5. Scaled solution over iterations of the online view selection problem with h = 30%. A 12-dimensional data cube is used. The mean of 20 independent trials is shown.

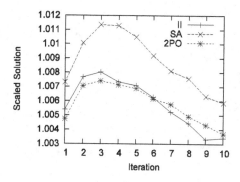

(a) Uniform data/uniform queries

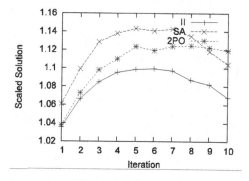

(b) Skewed data/hot regions

larger proportion of uphill transitions and that the downhill transitions are relatively steep.

Although the results from Figure 2 may suggest the randomized algorithms are more favorable for static view selection, we note that this performance is only observed for such problem instances where the query and update cost are relatively balanced. In fact, in the space of all possible view selection problems, this region where the randomized algorithms outperform BPUS is quite narrow, and most of our testing showed BPUS to significantly outperform the randomized algorithms, especially as maintenance cost decreases and on the more highly skewed instances. The reason for this, as opposed to the results of Kalnis et al. (2002) and our own experiments with the query cost only view selection problem, is that the addition of update cost adds another dimension of difficulty to the view selection problem. In the query cost only view selection problem, the optimal view set is a "full" one, which is an assumption that can be built into the design of the randomized algorithms. For example, to generate a random solution, we simply fill the available space with randomly selected views, and we can modify the second transition so that after removing a random view, it adds random views until no more will fit. This is the approach taken by Kalnis et al. (2002), and puts the randomized algorithms into a good locality in solution space.

However, in the presence of update cost optimization, we can no longer assume that a full view set is the optimal one, and the randomized algorithms have to navigate their way to a good locality in solution space. For the problems having a relatively equal balance between update and query cost, for which the solutions contain few views, this is easy. However, as update cost becomes more prohibitive, the randomized algorithms must travel a further "distance" to the good locality in solution space, facing a vastly larger number of downhill transitions and possibilities for bad choices along the way. This is not to say we recommend using BPUS when update cost is not prohibitive, rather, when this is the case, we recommend applying that knowledge to the design of the randomized algorithms by taking an approach as Kalnis et al. (2002).

The Online Phase: Online View Selection

In the following tests each algorithm begins with the same initial view set M, which is selected using BPUS. d = 12 dimensions are used, with the parameters of the randomized algorithms summarized in Table 1. Unless otherwise indicated, *h* = 30% was chosen for the tests. For the uniform query distribution, the drift in query probabilities for a single iteration was achieved by scaling each view's probability by a random factor chosen uniformly between 0 and 1, and re-normalizing them so that they sum to 1. Using this query drift model, the area between distribution curves on an iteration is generally in the range of 0.9 to 1.0 (with the maximum possible difference being 2). For the hot region query distribution, query drift was achieved by selecting both a beginning and ending hot region, and interpolating between the two over the iterations.

For performance on a single iteration, we are concerned with the improvement in query time. We measure the percent improvement of an online iteration from M to M' as:

$$Imp(M,M') = 100 \frac{Q(M) - Q(M')}{Q(M)}.$$

Note that the percent improvement not only depends on algorithm performance but also the amount that query distribution shifts.

First, we examine the scalability of the algorithms in terms of running time. Figure 3 shows the results as we increase the dimensionality of the data sets. As in the case of static view selection, the randomized techniques are significantly faster than BPUS, especially with higher dimensions.

One question which is pertinent to online view selection is how much can we improve the current materialized view set given that we only have time to replace $h\%$ of it, or how much of the view set must be replaced to achieve a given improvement in query time. Figure 4 shows the relative improvement in query time as h is increased. The relative improvement is the percent improvement $Imp(M,M')$ achieved relative to the percent improvement $Imp(M,M^{new})$ which can be achieved if an entirely new set of views M^{new} were selected with BPUS. 0% means that $Q(M') = Q(M)$ (no improvement), 100% means $Q(M') = Q(M^{new})$, and < 0% means that $Q(M') > Q(M)$ (negative improvement). From the figure we can see that the online version of BPUS is a very strong performer for both uniform and skewed data, able to make 95% of the improvement of

a newly chosen view set by replacing as little as 30% of it. A larger improvement with smaller h is possible for the skewed instance. This is likely due to the hot regions themselves, since the drift in query probabilities for this distribution goes from one small hot region to the next, exchanging a small number of views (those in the hot region) is sufficient for a large improvement in query time.

The final experiments examine the scaled solution of the algorithms over a number of consecutive iterations. All algorithms begin with the same initial view set M, on each iteration the query probabilities drift by some amount, and each algorithm must update its current materialized view set by solving the online phase of view selection. For example, after the first iteration, each algorithm obtains its own updated viewset M', which is used as the starting point for the next iteration. Our goal is to examine how much the algorithms' solutions diverge after a number of iterations, in order to assess the long-term impact of choosing one algorithm over the other, after multiple iterations of online view selection have been performed. The scaled solution values at each iteration are plotted in Figure 5. In both the uniform and skewed problem instances, there is an initial divergence with the randomized algorithms becoming a fraction of a percent, or a few percent worse than BPUS respectively. However, in later iterations, their solutions converge again.

CONCLUSION AND FUTURE WORK

In this article, we have described a new approach to dynamic view selection which recognizes that in practice OLAP systems are restarted from scratch only infrequently and must be able to tune their performance to changing conditions on the fly. We have described a greedy and three randomized methods for dynamic view selection and implemented and evaluated them in the context of a large-scale OLAP system. Overall, in terms of solution quality, our BPUS-online adaptation appears to outperform the three randomized methods studied. However, as the number of dimensions grows, the computational cost of BPUS-online may become impractically large and in this case the randomized methods presented here offer an attractive alternative. One important area of future work is to consider how best the dynamic view selection method proposed here can be combined with established caching and batch query optimization approaches.

REFERENCES

Agrawal, S., Chaudhuri, S., & Narasayya, V. (2000). Automated selection of materialized views and indexes in sql databases. In A. Abbadi, M. Brodie, S. Chakravarthy, U. Dayal, N. Kamel, G. Schlageter, & K. Whang (Eds.), *Proceedings of the InternationalConference on Very Large Data Base* (pp. 496-505). San Francisco: Morgan Kaufmann Publishers Inc.

Baralis, E., Paraboschi, S., & Teniente, E. (1997). Materialized viewsselection in a multidimensional database. In M. Jarke, M. Carey, K. Dittrich, F. Lochovsky, P. Loucopoulos, & M. Jeusfeld (Eds.), *Proceedings of the International Conference on Very Large Data Bases* (pp. 156-165). San Francisco: Morgan Kaufmann Publishers Inc.

Chen, Y., Dehne, F., Eavis, T., & Rau-Chaplin, A. (2004). Building large ROLAP data cubes in parallel. In *Proceedings of the International Database Engineering and Applications Symposium* (pp. 367-377). Coimbra, Portugal: IEEE.

Chirkova, R., Halevy, A., & Suciu, D. (2002). A formal perspective on the view selection problem. *The VLDB Journal, 11*(3), 216-237.

Dehne, F., Eavis, T., & Rau-Chaplin, A. (2006). The cgmCUBE project: Optimizing parallel data cube generation for ROLAP. *Distributed and Parallel Databases, 19*(1), 29-62.

Deshpande, P., Ramasamy, K., Shukla, A., & Naughton, J. (1998). Caching multidimensional queries using chunks. In L. Haas & A. Tiwary (Eds.), *ACM SIGMOD International Conference on Management of Data* (pp. 259-270). New York: ACM Press.

Gupta, H. (1997). Selection of views to materialize in a data warehouse. In F. Afrati & P. Kolaitis (Eds.), *Proceedings of the International Conference on Database Theory* (pp. 98-112). Delphi, Greece: Springer.

Gupta, H., & Mumick, I. (1999). Selection of views to materialize under a maintenance cost constraint. In C. Beeri & P. Buneman (Eds.), *Proceedings of the International Conference on Database Theory* (pp. 453-470). Jerusalem, Israel: Springer-Verlag.

Gupta, H. & Mumick, I. (2005). Selection of views to materialize in a data warehouse. *IEEE Transactions on Knowledge and Data Engineering, 17*(1), 24-43.

Gupta, H., Harinarayan, V., Rajaraman, A., & Ullman, J. (1997). Index selection for OLAP. In: W. Gray & P. Larson (Eds.), *Proceedings of the International conference on data engineering* (pp. 208-219). Birmingham, UK: IEEE.

Harinarayan, V., Rajaraman, A., & Ullman, J. (1996). Implementing data cubes efficiently. In H. Jagadish & I. Mumick (Eds.), *ACM SIGMOD international conference on management of data* (pp. 205-216). Montreal, Canada: ACM Press.

Horng, J., Chang, Y., Liu, B., & Kao, C. (1999). Materialized view selection using genetic algorithms in a data warehouse system. In *Proceedings of Congress on evolutionary computation* (pp. 2221-2227). Washington DC: IEEE.

Kalnis, P., Mamoulis, N., & Papadias, D. (2002a). View selection using randomized search. *Data Knowledge and Engineering, 42*(1), 89-111.

Kalnis, P., Ng, W., Ooi, B., Papadias, D., & Tan, K. (2002b). An adaptive peer-to-peer network for distributed caching of olap results. In M. Franklin, B. Moon & A. Ailamaki (Eds.), *ACM SIGMOD international conference on management of data* (pp. 25-36). Madison, USA: ACM Press.

Kotidis, Y. & Roussopoulos, N. (1999). Dynamat: A dynamic view management system for data warehouses. In: A. Delis, C. Faloutsos & S. Ghandeharizadeh (Eds.), *ACM SIGMOD international conference on management of data* (pp. 371-382). Philadelphia: ACM Press.

Kotidis, Y. & Roussopoulos, N. (2001). A case for dynamic view management. *ACM Transactions on Database Systems, 26*(4), 388-423.

Lawrence, M. (2006). Multiobjective genetic algorithms for materialized view selection in olap data warehouses. In M. Cattolico (Ed.), *Proceeding of the Genetic and evolutionary computation conference* (pp. 699-706). Seattle, USA: ACM Press.

Lee, M., & Hammer, J. (2001). Speeding up materialized view selection in data warehouses using a randomized algorithm. *International Journal of Cooperative Information Systems, 10*(3), 327-353.

Liang, W., Wang, H., & Orlowska, M. (2001). Materialized view selection under the maintenance time constraint. *Data & Knowledge Engineering. 37*(2), 203-216.

Loukopoulos, T., Kalnis, P., Ahmad, I., & Papadias, D. (2001). Active caching of online analytical processing queries in www proxies. In *Proceedings of the International conference on parallel processing* (pp. 419-426). Columbus, USA: IEEE Computer Society.

Nadeau, T., & Teorey, T. (2002). Achieving scalability in OLAP materialized view selection. In I. Song & P. Vassiliadis (Eds.), *ACM international workshop on data warehousing and OLAP* (pp. 28-34). Arlington, USA: ACM Press.

Shukla, A., Deshpande, P., & Naughton, J. (1998). Materialized view selection for multidimensional datasets. In: A. Gupta, O. Shmueli & J. Widom (Eds.), *Proceedings of the International Conference on Very Large Data Bases* (pp. 488-499). New York: Morgan Kaufmann.

Theodoratos, D., & Sellis, T. (2000). Incremental design of a data warehouse. *Journal of Intelligent Information Systems, 15*(1), 7-27.

Theodoratos, D., & Sellis, T. (1997). Data warehouse configuration. In M. Jarke, M. Carey, K. Dittrich, F. Lochovsky, P. Loucopoulos, & M. Jeusfeld (Eds.), *Proceedings of the International Conference on Very Large Data Bases* (pp. 126-135). Athens, Greece: Morgan Kaufmann.

Theodoratos, D., & Sellis, T. (1999). Dynamic data warehouse design. In M. Mohania & A. Tjoa (Eds.), *Proceedings of the International conference on data warehousing and knowledge discovery* (pp. 1-10). Florence, Italy: Springer-Verlag.

Theodoratos, D., Dalamagas, T., Simitsis, A., & Stavropoulos, M. (2001a). A randomized approach for the incremental design of an evolving data warehouse. In H. Kunii, S. Jajodia & A. Sϊlvberg (Eds.), *Proceedings of the International conference on conceptual modeling* (pp. 325-338). Yokohama, Japan: Springer-Verlag.

Theodoratos, D., Ligoudistianos, S., & Sellis, T. (2001b). View selection for designing the global data warehouse. *Data Knowledge & Engineering, 39*(3), 219-240.

Uchiyama, H., Runapongsa, K. & Teorey, T. (1999). A progressive view materialization algorithm. In *Proceedings of the International workshop on data warehousing and OLAP* (pp. 360-41). Kansas City, USA: ACM Press.

Valluri, S., Vadapalli, S. & Karlapalem, K. (2002). View relevance driven materialized view selection in data warehousing environment. In *Proceedings of the Australasian conference on database technologies* (pp. 187-196). Darlinghurst, Australia: ACM.

Yang, J., Karlapalem, K., & Li, Q. (1997a). Algorithms for materialized view design in data warehousing environment. In M. Jarke, M. Carey, K. Dittrich, F. Lochovsky, P. Loucopoulos, & M. Jeusfeld (Eds.), *Proceedings of the International Conference on Very Large Data Bases* (pp. 156-165). San Francisco: Morgan Kaufmann Publishers Inc.

Yang, J., Karlapalem, K., & Li, Q. (1997b). A framework for designing materialized views in data warehousing environment. In *Proceedings of the International conference on distributed computing systems* (p. 458). Baltimore: IEEE.

Yu, J., Yao, X., Choi, C., & Gou, G. (2003). Materialized view selection as constrained evolutionary optimization. *IEEE Transactions on Systems, Man and Cybernetics, 33*(4), 458-467.

Zhang, C., Yao, X., & Yang, J. (2001). An evolutionary approach to materialized views selection in a datawarehouse environment. *IEEE Transactions on Systems, Man and Cybernetics, 31*(3), 282-294.

This work was previously published in International Journal of Data Warehousing and Mining, Vol. 4, Issue 1, edited by D. Taniar, pp. 47-61, copyright 2008 by IGI Publishing (an imprint of IGI Global).

Chapter 6
RCUBE:
Parallel Multi-Dimensional ROLAP Indexing[1]

Frank Dehne
Carleton University, Canada

Todd Eavis
Concordia University, Canada

Andrew Rau-Chaplin
Dalhousie University, Canada

ABSTRACT

This chapter addresses the query performance issue for Relational OLAP (ROLAP) data cubes. The authors present RCUBE, a distributed multi-dimensional ROLAP indexing scheme which is practical to implement, requires only a small communication volume, and is fully adapted to distributed disks. Their solution is efficient for spatial searches in high dimensions and scalable in terms of data sizes, dimensions, and number of processors. Their method is also incrementally maintainable. Using "surrogate" group-bys, it allows for the efficient processing of arbitrary OLAP queries on partial cubes, where not all of the group-bys have been materialized. Experiments with RCUBE show that the ROLAP advantage of better scalability, in comparison to MOLAP, can be maintained while providing, at the same time, a fast and flexible index for OLAP queries.

INTRODUCTION

Online Analytical Processing (OLAP) has become a fundamental component of contemporary decision support systems. Gray et al. (1995) introduced the *data cube*, a relational operator used to compute summary views of data that can, in turn, signifi-cantly enhance the response time of core OLAP operations such as *roll-up*, *drill down*, and *slice and dice*. Typically constructed on top of relational data warehouses, these summary views (called *group-bys*) are formed by aggregating values across attribute combinations. For a d-dimensional input set R, there are 2^d possible group-bys. Figure 1 illustrates a data cube as well as a *lattice* which is often used to represent the inherent relationships between group-bys (Harinarayan, 1996).

DOI: 10.4018/978-1-60566-717-1.ch006

Figure 1. (a) A three dimensional data cube for automobile sales data. (b) The lattice corresponding to a four dimensional data cube with dimensions A, B, C and D

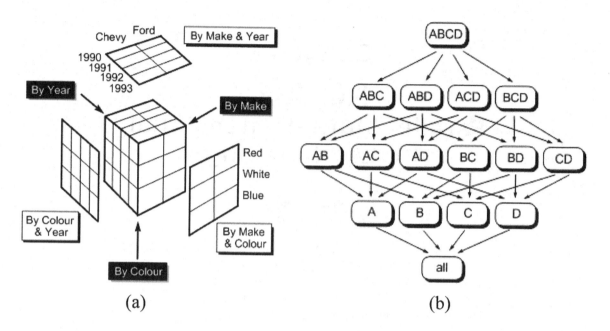

(a)   (b)

There are two standard data cube representations: MOLAP (multi-dimensional array) and ROLAP (set of relational tables). The array-based model, MOLAP (Multi-dimensional OLAP), has the advantage that native arrays provide an immediate form of indexing for cube queries. Interesting MOLAP based systems have been described and implemented in both the sequential and parallel settings; e.g. (Goil, 1997). However there is some evidence, that MOLAP based systems may encounter significant scalability problems (Pendse, 2002). For example, high-dimension data cubes represent extremely sparse spaces that are not easily adapted to the MOLAP paradigm. Hybrid indexing schemes are often used, significantly diminishing the power of the model. Moreover, since MOLAP needs to be integrated with standard relational databases, *middleware* of some form must be employed to handle the conversion between relational and array-based data representations. The relational model, ROLAP (Relational OLAP), does not suffer from such restrictions. Its summary records

are stored directly in standard relational tables without any need for data conversion. Its table based data representation does not pose scalability problems. Yet, many current commercial systems use the MOLAP approach (Pendse, 2002). The main reason, as outlined in (Pendse, 2002), is the indexing problem for the fast execution of OLAP queries. The problem for ROLAP is that it does not provide an immediate and fast index for OLAP queries. Many vendors have chosen to sacrifice scalability for performance. However, this path is becoming increasingly unsustainable. As outlined in the 2005 Winter Report (Winter Corp., 2005), the size of data warehouses grew exponentially during recent years. More precisely, between 2001 and 2005 the average size of data warehouses grew by 243%, and the size of the largest data warehouses grew by an astounding 578% (Winter Corp., 2005). Hence, there is an urgent need for scalable (i.e. ROLAP) and high performance data cube indexing methods.

This paper addresses the query performance issue for ROLAP and proposes a novel, distributed multi-dimensional ROLAP indexing scheme. We show that the ROLAP advantage of high scalability can be maintained, while at the same time providing a fast index for OLAP queries. We present RCUBE, a distributed indexing scheme which is a combination of packed R-trees with distributed disk striping and Hilbert curve based data ordering. Our method requires only very low communication volume between processors and works in "low bandwidth connectivity" multi-processor environments such as processor clusters or workstation farms. Our method does not require a shared disk and scales well with respect to the number of processors used. We also note that our implementation of our new distributed multi-dimensional ROLAP indexing scheme is based on standard R-trees. This is done to support maximum compatibility with standard database systems. Clearly, more sophisticated data structures such as the RA*-tree (Juergens, 1998) could be employed and possibly yield further improvements of our result.

To further improve the scalability of ROLAP with respect to the size and dimension of the data set (which was already better than MOLAP's scalability), we extend RCUBE to the *partial cube* case. The large number of group-bys, 2^d, is a significant problem in practice for any data cube method. We consider the case where we do not wish to build (materialize) all group-bys, but only a subset. For example, a user might want to only materialize those group-bys that are most frequently used, thereby saving disk space and time for the cube construction. The problem then is to find a way to answer effectively those less frequent OLAP queries which require group-bys that have not been materialized. We present an indexing scheme, based on "surrogate group-bys", which answers such queries efficiently. In fact, our experiments show that RCUBE queries are almost as efficient on "virtual" group-bys as on ones that actually exist.

In summary, our distributed RCUBE indexing method provides a framework for distributed high performance indexing of ROLAP cubes with the following properties:

- practical to implement,
- low communication volume,
- fully adapted to external memory (i.e. disks), no shared disk required,
- incrementally maintainable,
- efficient for spatial searches in high dimensions,
- scalable in terms of data sizes, dimensions, and number of processors.

We have implemented our distributed RCUBE indexing method in C++, STL and MPI, and tested it on a 17 node Beowulf cluster (a frontend and 16 compute nodes). While easily extendible to *shared everything* multi-processors, our algorithms perform well on these low-cost commodity-based systems. Our experiments show that for RCUBE index construction and updating, close to optimal speedup is achieved. An RCUBE index for a fully materialized data cube of ~640 million rows (17 Gigabytes) on a 16 processor cluster can be generated in just under 1 minute. Our method for distributed query resolution also exhibits good speedup achieving, for example, a speedup of 13.28 on 16 processors. For distributed query resolution in partial data cubes, our experiments show that searches against absent (i.e. non-materialized) group-bys can typically be resolved at only a small additional cost. Our results demonstrate that it is possible to build a ROLAP data cube that is scalable and tightly integrated with the standard relational database approach and, at the same time, provide an efficient index for OLAP queries.

The remainder of this paper is organized as follows. We first review some key research results from the sequential and parallel settings and describe our framework for distributed index generation, including mechanisms for building and updating the indexes. We then present the distributed query engine that is used to access the indexed group-bys and a performance analysis of our current prototype.

DISTRIBUTED INDEX CONSTRUCTION FOR ROLAP

Various methods have been proposed for building ROLAP data cubes (Agarwal, 1996; Beyer, 1999; Chen, 2006; Chen, 2004; Chen, 2005; Chen, 2006; Dehne, 2001; Dehne, 2001; Dehne, 2006; Gray, 1996; Harinarayan, 1996; Ross, 1997; Sarawagi 1996) but there are only very few results available for the indexing of such cubes. For sequential query processing, (Gupta, 1997) propose an indexing model composed of a collection of b-trees. While adequate for low-dimensional data cubes, b-trees are inappropriate for higher dimensions in that (a) their performance deteriorates rapidly with increased dimensionality and (b) multiple, redundant attribute orderings are required to support arbitrary user queries. Roussopoulos et al. (1997) propose the *cubetree*, a sequential indexing model based upon the concept of a *packed* R-tree (Roussopoulos, 1985). Cube compression methods such as Dwarf (Sismanis, 2002) also provide a "built-in" indexing framework, though it is not clear how gracefully these techniques scale.

For parallel query processing, a typical approach used by current commercial systems like ORACLE RAC is to improve throughput by distributing a stream of incoming queries over multiple processors and having each processor answer a subset of queries. Other relevant commercial systems include IBM DBs's multidimensional clustering, Transaction TransBase's Z-ordered B-trees (Padmanabhan, 2003; Ramsek, 2000). However, these approaches provide no speedup for each individual query. For OLAP queries, which can be time consuming, the parallelization of each individual query is important for the scalability of the entire OLAP system.

Recent academic research has investigated optimizations and extensions for the increasingly common shared nothing data management model. DeWitt et al. present Clustera, a cluster-oriented system designed specifically for extensibility in environments with a broad range of data management requirements (DeWitt, 2008). This "general purpose" approach also characterizes the work of Yang et al. (Yang, 2007). Here, the authors extend the Map-Reduce paradigm to include a merge operation that efficiently combines previously partitioned (and processed) local data.

With respect to the parallelization of R-tree queries, a number of researchers have presented solutions for general purpose environments. Koudas et.al. (1996) present a *Master R-tree* model that employs a centralized index and a collection of distributed data files. Schnitzer and Leutenegger's (1999) *Master-Client R-tree* improves upon the earlier model by partitioning the central index into a smaller master index and a set of associated client indexes. While offering significant performance advantages in generic indexing environments, neither approach is well-suited for OLAP systems. In addition to the sequential bottleneck on the main server node, both utilize partitioning schemes that can lead to the localization of searches. In addition, neither approach provides a mechanism for incremental updates.

More recent tree-based indexing efforts have often focused on loosely coupled peer-to-peer environments. Here, the focus is on the maintenance of dynamically updated, widely distributed datasets that have the potential to grow to vast sizes. Methods based upon the B+-tree (Crainiceanu, 2004), binary-tree (Jagadish, 2005), and the R-tree (du Mouza, 2007) have all been explored. Nevertheless, given the latency and connectivity issues associated with P2P settings, such systems are not well suited to the demands of high performance OLAP.

In the remainder of this section, we present the distributed RCUBE indexing method which has no sequential bottleneck, provides load balancing across the p processors during the resolution of each query (i.e. good parallelization), and allows for incremental updates.

Generating the Distributed RCUBE Index

The distributed RCUBE consists of a distributed data cube and a distributed RCUBE index which is used to answer multi-dimensional range queries on individual group-bys. The challenge is in how data ordering and partitioning can be used to help satisfy the following goals: 1) partition the data such that the number of records retrieved per node is as balanced as possible, thereby maximizing the simultaneous involvement of *all* processors for each query resolution, and 2) minimize the number of disk seeks required in order to retrieve the records returned by a query.

In the distributed RCUBE, as with the Master-Client technique, local partial R-tree indexes are constructed on each processor and used to resolve a portion of the query. However, for our distributed RCUBE, there is no global R-tree on the front-end. Instead, queries are passed directly to each processor in the cluster, via a single short message, and intermediate results remain distributed and available for further processing. For OLAP query results that are to be further processed, this also avoids the possible bottleneck of previous solutions where the results were always gathered on the front-end. Another difference to previous methods is that the distributed RCUBE index results in the generation of local packed R-tree *forests* rather than a single R-tree.

A further important difference between our distributed RCUBE index and the previous work in (Gupta, 1997; Roussopoulos, 1997; Schnitzer, 1999) is that our distributed RCUBE index method applies a novel combination of Hilbert-curve sort ordering and round robin disk striping for data partitioning. Previous approaches used *XYZ* (sometimes also called *lowX* or *nearest-X*) data ordering, which is simply the standard multi-dimensional sort ordering. The disadvantage of

that approach is that response time deteriorates rapidly when non-primary indices are required, since relevant points are dispersed broadly across the entire data set. Our approach applies a combination of Hilbert-curve sort ordering and round robin disk striping. Hilbert-curve orderings have been shown to be an effective tool for ordering data such that items that are close to each other in the original space are likely to be placed close to each other in the sorted order (Faloutsos, 1989; Kamel, 1993). Experimental evidence indicates a significant performance advantage over the XYZ ordering on sequential range queries (Kamel, 1993). Figure 2 illustrates a typical case. While XYZ is likely to be efficient for range queries with a large X component and a small Y component, queries with large Y components are likely to require an excessive number of disk accesses. In higher dimensions, the problem is exacerbated. Hilbert-based ordering, on the other hand, favors no single dimension and is therefore very well suited to arbitrary range queries. In the parallel environment, considered here for distributed RCUBE index construction, we have, however, the additional requirement that we seek to balance the retrieval times for arbitrary range queries across all p processors. Therefore, an effective data partitioning mechanism is essential. Our approach is to stripe the Hilbert-curve ordered data in a round robin fashion such that successive records are sent to successive processors. We then build local packed R-trees from the striped data. The motivation for this striping pattern is that it dramatically increases the likelihood that the space bounded by the hyper-rectangle of an arbitrary user query will be evenly distributed across the p processors. Figure 3 illustrates this argument. The diagram shows the effect of striping the original space across two processors. The user query (shown as a dashed rectangle) results in the retrieval of eight points, with each processor contributing four points from a pair of contiguous blocks. It is also worth noting that this example

Figure 2. Hilbert curve packing versus XYZ

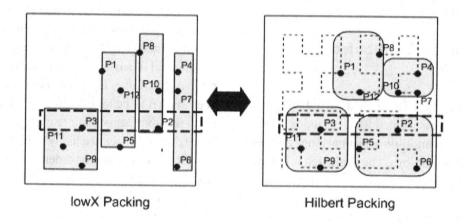

lowX Packing   Hilbert Packing

Figure 3. Striping the data across two processors. (Block capacity = 3)

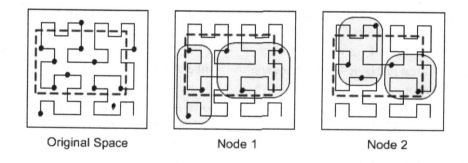

Original Space   Node 1   Node 2

would require four accesses with a sequential R-tree implementation.

Algorithm 1 presents an outline of our distributed RCUBE index generation method. Much of the communication complexity of the algorithm is associated with Step 2 which we will now discuss in more detail. In Step 1, the distributed data cube was generated using the parallel ROLAP data cube generation algorithms from (Chen, 2004) or (Dehne, 2001). Note that, in (Dehne, 2001) every group-by generated is entirely stored on one single processor, whereas in (Chen, 2004) every group-by is distributed evenly across the p processors. This implies different sort criteria for these two cases. The computation of the comparison function for the global sort ordering is a non trivial combination of the Hilbert curve

comparison function (in our implementation, we use code from Moore, 2002) and a comparison function representing round robin disk striping. Furthermore, we do not wish to execute a separate sort for each group-by, which could result in up to 2^d sort operations. Instead, we combine the comparison functions for all group-bys into one single global sort operation. As a result, we can implement Step 2 with only two h-relation (MPI_AllToAllv) operations.

Updating the Distributed RCUBE

An important advantage of our distributed RCUBE generation method is that it is easy to perform efficient cube updates. In typical data warehousing applications, updates consist of an accumulated

Algorithm 1. Outline of distributed RCUBE construction

Input: Raw data set R.

Output: A distributed data cube, C, distributed RCUBE index, I.

1. Using the parallel ROLAP data cube generation algorithms from (Chen, 2004) or (Dehne, 2001) generate the distributed data cube, C.

2. Using parallel sample sort (Li, 1993), order each group-by v of C in Hilbert order and stripe the result across the processors in a round-robin fashion such that each of the p processors receives a stripe of size $\lceil n/p \rceil$, where n is the number of records in v.

3. Each processor P_i, independently and in parallel, performs the following for each local data stripe for a group-by v: For a *disk block size* of m records, and a local record count k for the group-by v, associate a *bounding box* with each of the $\lceil k/m \rceil$ blocks in the stripe. Using these blocks as the *base* (for the leaves), build the packed R-tree in the usual bottom-up fashion. Write the disk blocks representing the R-tree to disk in level ordering, starting with the block representing the root.

Algorithm 2. Outline of distributed RCUBE query resolution

Input: A set S of indexed group-bys, striped evenly across p processors P_1, ... P_p, and a query Q.

Output: Query result deposited on front-end or distributed across the p processors.

1. Pass query Q to each of the p processors.

2. Locate target group-by T.

3. Transform Q into Q' according to the attribute ordering of the records in T.

4. In parallel, each processor P_j retrieves the record set R_j matching Q' for its local data and then reorders the values of each record of R_j to match the attribute ordering of Q.

5. Perform a parallel sample sort (Li, 1993) of $R_1 \cup R_2 \cup ... \cup R_p$ with respect to the attribute ordering of Q.

6. IF the query result is to be deposited on the front-end THEN collect the result via a MPI_AllGather.

---

additional data set R' that needs to be added to the original data set R. Such updates typically occur on a daily or monthly schedule.

In order to add R' to the data cube, our method constructs the data cube C' for R', sorts each group-by of C' in Hilbert-curve ordering and stripes it across the disk in round-robin fashion. Each processor performs, for each group-by v and received update v' of C' relevant for v, the following two operations: (1) it merges v' into v and agglomerates, and (2) it merges the two packed R-trees for v and v'.

DISTRIBUTED ROLAP QUERY ENGINE

Previous R-tree parallelization results have focused exclusively on the retrieval characteristics of R-trees (Gupta, 1997; Roussopoulos, 1997). However, in an OLAP environment, accessing disk blocks is only the first phase of query resolution. Typically, some form of post-processing is then required to fully resolve the original query.

An important example of this is partial cube extrapolation. The construction of a partial cube implies that some number of group-bys do not physically exist on disk. There needs to be an efficient mechanism for performing searches in these non-materialized group-bys.

In this section, we describe the implementation of a distributed data cube query engine. A general framework for post-processing is presented, along with a specific algorithm for handling partial cube indexing.

Distributed RCUBE Query Resolution

As discussed, our distributed RCUBE index has been designed to balance the retrieval of query records across all p processors. Once the records have been obtained, additional OLAP processing is often necessary. The fundamental model, outlined in Algorithm 2, provides the means by which both forms of computation may be carried out in an efficient, load balanced manner.

In Step 1, the query is distributed to all of the p processors, avoiding unnecessary bottlenecks on

Algorithm 3. Outline of distributed partial RCUBE query resolution

---

Input: A *partial* set S' of indexed group-bys, striped evenly across p processors P$_1$, ..., P$_p$, and a query Q.
Output: Query result deposited on front-end or distributed across the p processors.
1. Pass query Q to each of the p processors.
2. Locate a surrogate group-by T containing the attributes in Q and possibly some additional, *peripheral*, attributes. Among all possible such group-bys select as surrogate group-by T the one with smallest size.
3. Transform Q into Q' according to the attribute ordering of the records in T and add "*" values for the *peripheral* attributes.
4. In parallel, each processor P$_j$ retrieves the record set R$_j$ matching Q' for its local data and then reorders the values of each record of R$_j$ to match the attribute ordering of Q. While performing the re-ordering, processor P$_j$ removes from each record the redundant values for the peripheral attributes of T.
5. Perform a parallel sample sort (Li, 1993) of R$_1$ ∪ R$_2$ ∪ ... ∪ R$_p$ with respect to the attribute ordering of Q. While performing the sort, aggregate duplicate records that have been introduced by *peripheral* attributes of the surrogate group-by T.
6. IF the query result is to be deposited on the front-end THEN collect the result via a MPI_AllGather.

---

the frontend. The query usually cannot be executed in its *native* form, however, since the user's request is not likely to match the physical ordering of attributes that was determined by the original data cube build algorithm. For example, the user may request a three-dimensional group-by sorted and presented as A × B × C, while Algorithm 1 may have generated that group-by as C × A × B. In Steps 2 and 3, we identify the group-bys whose dimensions represent a valid permutation of the dimensions of the user request and then transform the original query to match the attribute order of the index/group-by. This transformed query is passed to the packed R-tree. Since the *retrieved* records are not guaranteed to have the right attribute ordering or the right ordering of records, further processing is necessary. In Step 4, the attributes of each record are permuted, if necessary, via a single linear scan of the query result. In Step 5, the query result is sorted. If the query result is to be deposited on the front-end, it is simply collected via a MPI_AllGather operation. Otherwise, the result remains distributed over the p processors for further parallel processing.

A number of additional performance improvements are included in our solution. Our packed R-tree implementation performs a *prefetch* on all parent pages in the group-by index. Because the pages of level i in the packed R-tree are written contiguously to disk prior to the pages in level i - 1 (Step 3 of Algorithm 1), the prefetch of all relevant parent pages allows the query engine to

minimize the seek time associated with traversing the index.

We also employ a *threshold factor* α to determine whether or not a full parallel sort is required. For very small result sets, a p processor sort would introduce unnecessary communication overhead. If the number of records in the result set is below α, then the partial result sets are sent directly to a single processor for sorting. The threshold factor can be tuned to the physical characteristics of the parallel machine.

Distributed Partial RCUBE Query Resolution

To further improve the scalability of ROLAP with respect to the size and dimension of the data set, we now consider the case where we do not wish to build all group-bys but only a subset. Since the computation of all 2^d group-bys can lead to unacceptable processing and storage requirements, particularly in higher dimensions, a user might want to only build those group-bys that are most frequently used, thereby saving disk space and time for the cube construction. The problem for OLAP query resolution is then to find a way to answer effectively those less frequent OLAP queries which require group-bys that have not been materialized.

It is important to observe that data cube construction costs are skewed heavily towards the upper (high dimensional) portion of the lattice.

For example, in a ten dimensional data cube, much of the weight is typically associated with group-bys of five to ten dimensions. In the upper portion of the lattice, little aggregation takes place and the group-bys are very similar to one another. For example, we measured the sizes of group-bys of a data cube for a 10 dimensional data set of 1 Million records. Most group-bys with 6 through 10 dimensions contain almost 97% of all records in the original input set. Therefore, it is not efficient to build all these very similar group-bys. Clearly, a *partial* cube construction and indexing method is required. However, the query engine must then be able to efficiently answer queries on group-bys that do not physically exist. In the following, we present a new method, based on ``surrogate group-bys'', which answers such queries efficiently. An outline of our method is given in Algorithm 3.

There are a number of key differences between Algorithm 3 and the previous Algorithm 2. First, a *surrogate* group-by T is used as the basis of query resolution for Q. A surrogate is an alternate group-by that will be used to answer the query on the group-by requested by the user, termed the *primary* group-by. To select a surrogate, each processor scans its local disk to find those group-bys whose dimensions represent a superset of the dimensions specified by the user. From the group-bys in this list, it selects the group-by of minimum size. Note that, since this surrogate group-by contains even more detailed information than the original group-by, we can answer *all* queries associated with the original group-by. Furthermore, we note that because Hilbert-based R-tree packing has been used, there is no performance problem due to the different ordering of the records in the group-by, since the Hilbert curve does not favor any particular order. In (Sismanis, 2002), the authors observe that when XYZ ordering is used, the only alternate group-bys that can be efficiently used for this purpose are the ones in which the attributes of Q represent a prefix of T. Since this situation is unlikely to occur in practice, XYZ ordering makes partial cube query resolution very costly. However, as shown in the experiments in Section 4, such problems do not occur with Hilbert ordering.

Once the surrogate group-by T has been determined, the query is transformed by (i) rearranging the attributes of the query to match the order of the surrogate and (ii) adding "*" values for the *peripheral* attributes of the surrogate to the original query. A peripheral attribute is a dimension that is not part of the user query but that must be passed to the packed R-tree query in order to resolve the query on the surrogate. The result of the packed R-tree query is a superset of the records that would have been retrieved had the primary group-by actually existed. However, we note that, since partial cube indexing is most attractive within environments in which data sparsity creates large group-bys of almost identical size, the difference between the sizes of the surrogate result and the actual result are likely to be small in such cases. In addition, since the disk blocks for the packed R-tree are arranged to support contiguous retrieval of disk blocks, the time taken to answer the query will be less influenced by the use of a surrogate because the additional blocks are likely to be accessed within the same disk scans rather than with costly additional disk seeks. These observations are consistent with our experimental results.

When the records have been retrieved, their values must be re-ordered to match the order of attribute values in Q. Furthermore, during this re-ordering, the redundant values for the peripheral attributes of T are removed. Thereby, no additional disk accesses are introduced for the removal of the redundant values.

During the final sort of the query result, it is easy to aggregate, at the same time, the duplicate records that have been introduced by the *peripheral* attributes of the surrogate group-by T. Again, no additional disk accesses are introduced for the removal of the redundant records.

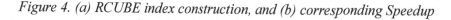

Figure 4. (a) RCUBE index construction, and (b) corresponding Speedup

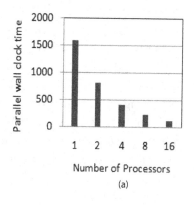 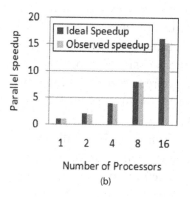

In summary, our partial cube query mechanism is build directly upon the method for completely built data cubes, requiring only very little additional computation. Our experiments, discussed in the following section, show that our distributed query engine is almost as efficient on ``virtual'' group-bys as it is on ones that actually exist.

PERFORMANCE ANALYSIS

We have implemented our distributed data cube indexing prototype using C++, STL and the LAM MPI communication library, version 6.5.6. The current prototype consists of approximately 8,000 lines of code (not including libraries) and was created by a single programmer over a seven month period.

Our experimental platform consisted of a 17 node Beowulf cluster (a frontend and 16 compute nodes), with 1.8 GHz Intel Xeon processors, 1 GB RAM per node and two 40 GB 7200 RPM IDE disk drives per node. Every node was running Linux Redhat 7.2 with gcc 2.95.3. All nodes were interconnected via an Intel 100 Megabyte Ethernet switch. Note that on this machine communication speed is quite slow in comparison to computation speed. We will shortly be replacing our 100 Megabyte interconnect with a 1 Gigabyte Ethernet interconnect and expect that this will

further improve performance results obtainable on this machine.

In the following experiments all sequential times were measured as wall clock times in seconds. All parallel times were measured as the wall clock time between the start of the first process and the termination of the last process. We will refer to the latter as *parallel* wall clock time. All times include the time taken to read the input from files and to write the output into files. Furthermore, all wall clock times were measured with no other users except us on the Beowulf cluster.

Figure 4 shows, for an input data set consisting of 10 dimensions and 1,000,000 records, the parallel wall clock time observed for *RCUBE index construction* as a function of the number of processors used. We observe that for index construction our method achieves close to optimal speedup; generating, on a 16 processor cluster, the RCUBE index for a fully materialized data cube of ~640 million rows (17 Gigabytes) in just under 1 minute.

Figure 5 shows the parallel wall clock time for *distributed query resolution* as a function of the number of processors used, and the corresponding speedup. In this experiment, batches of ten multidimensional queries were resolved against random views in a 10 dimensional data cube consisting of 1,000,000 records, where the queries were constructed to return approximately 15% of the

Figure 5. (a) Distributed query resolution, and (b) corresponding Speedup

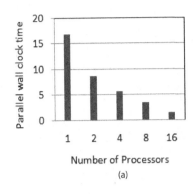

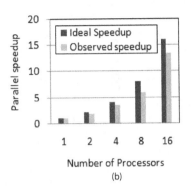

corresponding group-bys. We observe that for distributed query resolution our method achieves good speedup. For example, for 16 processors, a speedup of 13.28 is achieved. The source of the difference between this speedup and perfect speedup is interesting. Perhaps surprisingly, it does *not* arise from the queries returning different numbers of data points on different processors. Hilbert ordering combined with round-robin striping almost perfectly balances the query results evenly over the parallel machine. The small work imbalance observed results from the parallel sample sort used to order the query results. This suggests that these speedup results might be further improved by using a better sort code.

Figure 6a shows the number of *disk blocks retrieved and corresponding number of disk seeks required* in performing distributed query resolution on views of differing sparsity. Each point represents the average of 15 random queries, each of which returns between 5% and 15% of the associated view, drawn from the 10 dimensional data cube described above. The low density (i.e. sparse) views were typically views high in the lattice, while the high density views were typically views low in the lattice. Again, we observe the benefit of using Hilbert ordering combined with round-robin striping in our distributed RCUBE. Even when a large number of blocks need to be retrieved, the

number of disk seeks across our parallel machine is very small. This is crucial to achieving good performance, given that contiguous reads are an order of magnitude faster than reads that require an associated disk seek. Figure 6b shows the *relative record imbalance*, that is the maximum percentage variation between the sizes of query results on different processors computed over the experiments illustrated in Figure 6a. We observe that the Hilbert ordering combined with round-robin striping leads to a maximum imbalance of less than 0.3% with up to 16 processors.

Figure 7a compares parallel wall clock times for distributed query resolution in *primary and surrogate group-bys* as a function of the number of processors used. Figure 7b shows the corresponding relative cost of a surrogate-based query resolution over the same search in the corresponding materialized primary group-by. We observe from Figure 7a that the overhead of using surrogates, that is, performing query resolution against non-materialized views, is reasonable small, ranging from 3.5 seconds for a batch of 10 queries on a single processor to 0.12 seconds for the same queries on 16 processors. Figure 7b illustrates an interesting trend. As the number of processors grow, the relative cost of using surrogate group-bys decreases.

Figure 6. (a) Disk blocks received vs. number of disk seeks required on 16 processors, and (b) Relative record imbalance percentage

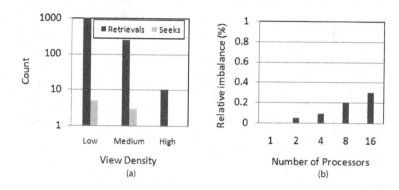

Figure 7. (a) Distributed query resolution in surrogate group-bys, and (b) Relative percentage cost of using surrogate view instead of materialized primary view

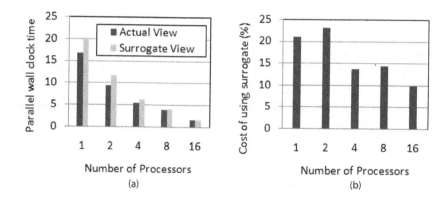

CONCLUSION

In this paper, we have shown that it is possible to build an efficient parallel ROLAP index that is scalable and tightly integrated with the standard relational database approach. Our parallel RCUBE index has the additional advantage of being able to process arbitrary queries on partial data cubes.

ACKNOWLEDGMENT

Research partially supported by the Natural Sciences and Engineering Research Council of Canada.

REFERENCES

Agarwal, S., Agrawal, R., Deshpande, P., Gupta, A., Naughton, J., Ramakrishnan, R., & Sarawagi, S. (1996). On the computation of multidimensional aggregates. In *Proceedings of the 22nd International VLDB Conference* (pp. 506-521).

Beyer, K., & Ramakrishnan, R. (1999). Bottom-up computation of sparse and iceberg cubes. In *Proceedings of the 1999 ACM SIGMOD Conference* (pp. 359-370).

Chen, Y., Dehne, F., Eavis, T., Green, D., Rau-Chaplin, A., & Sithirasenan, E. (2006). cgmOLAP: Efficient parallel generation and querying of terabyte size ROLAP data cubes. In *Proc. 22nd Int. Conf. on Data Engineering (ICDE)* (pp. 164-164). IEEE.

Chen, Y., Dehne, F., Eavis, T., & Rau-Chaplin, A. (2004). Parallel ROLAP data cube construction on shared-nothing multiprocessors. *Distributed and Parallel Databases*, *15*, 219–236. doi:10.1023/B:DAPD.0000018572.20283.e0

Chen, Y., Dehne, F., Eavis, T., & Rau-Chaplin, A. (2005). PnP: Parallel and external memory iceberg cube computation. In *Proc. 21st Int. Conf. on Data Engineering (ICDE)* (pp. 576-577). IEEE Comp. Soc. Dig. Library.

Chen, Y., Dehne, F., Eavis, T., & Rau-Chaplin, A. (2006). Improved data partitioning for building large ROLAP data cubes in parallel. *Journal of Data Warehousing and Mining*, *2*(1), 1–26.

Crainiceanu, A., Linga, P., Gehrke, J., & Shanmugasundaram, J. (2004). Querying peer-to-peer networks using P-Trees. In *WebDB '04: Proceedings of the 7th International Workshop on the Web and Databases* (pp. 25-30).

Dehne, F., Eavis, T., Hambrusch, S., & Rau-Chaplin, A. (2001). Parallelizing the datacube. [Special Issue on Parallel and Distributed Data Mining]. *Distributed and Parallel Databases*, *11*(2), 181–201.

Dehne, F., Eavis, T., & Rau-Chaplin, A. (2001). A cluster architecture for parallel data warehousing. IEEE International Symposium of Cluster Computing and the Grid (CCGRid'01), 2001

Dehne, F., Eavis, T., & Rau-Chaplin, A. (2006). The cgmCUBE project: Optimizing parallel data cube generation for ROLAP. *Distributed and Parallel Databases*, *19*(1), 29–62. doi:10.1007/s10619-006-6575-6

DeWitt, D., Paulson, E., Robinson, E., Naughton, J., Royalty, J., Shankar, S., & Krioukov, A. (2008). Clustera: an integrated computation and data management system. *VLDB*, *1*(1), 28–41.

du Mouza, C., Litwin, W., & Rigaux, P. (2007). SD-Rtree: A Scalable Distributed Rtree. *International Conference on Data Engineering (ICDE)* (pp. 296-305).

Faloutsos, C., & Roseman, S. (1989). Fractals for secondary key retrieval. *Symposium on Principles of Database Systems* (pp. 247-252).

Goil, S., & Choudhary, A. (1997). High performance olap and data mining on parallel computers. *Journal of Data Mining and Knowledge Discovery*, *1*(4). doi:10.1023/A:1009777418785

Gray, J., Bosworth, A., Layman, A., & Pirahesh, H. (1996). Data cube: A relational aggregation operator generalizing group-by, cross-tab, and sub-totals. In *Proceedings of the 12th International Conference On Data Engineering* (pp. 152-159).

Gupta, H., Harinarayan, V., Rajaraman, A., & Ullman, J. (1997). Index selection for olap. In *Proceedings of the 13th International Conference on Data Engineering* (pp. 208-219).

Harinarayan, V., Rajaraman, A., & Ullman, J. (1996). Implementing data cubes. In *Proceedings of the 1996 ACM SIGMOD Conference* (pp. 205-216).

Jagadish, H., Ooi, B. C., & Vu, Q. H. (2005). BATON: A Balanced Tree Structure for Peer-to-Peer Networks. In *VLDB* (pp. 661–672).

Juegens, M., & Lenz, H.-J. (1998). The Ra*-tree: An improved r-tree with materialized data for supporting range queries on OLAP-data. In *DEXA Workshop* (pp. 186-191).

Kamel, I., & Faloutsos, C. (1993). On packing r-trees. In *Proceedings of the Second International Conference on Information and Knowledge Management* (pp. 490-499).

Koudas, N., Faloutsos, C., & Kamel, I. (1996). Declustering spatial databases on a multi-computer architecture. In *Proceedings of Extended Database Technologies* (pp. 592-614).

Li, X., Lu, P., Schaefer, J., Shillington, J., Wong, P. S., & Shi, H. (1993). On the versatility of parallel sorting by regular sampling. *Parallel Computing*, *19*(10), 1079–1103. doi:10.1016/0167-8191(93)90019-H

Moore, D. (2002). *Fast hilbert curve generation, sorting, and range queries*. Retrieved from http://www.caam.rice.edu/~dougm/twiddle/Hilbert

Padmanabhan, S., Bhattacharjee, B., Malkemus, T., Cranston, L., & Huras, M. (2003). Multidimensional clustering: A new data layout scheme in DB2. In *ACM SIGMOD* (pp. 637-641).

Pendse, N., & Creeth, R. (2002). *The OLAP Report*. Retrieved from http://www.olapreport.com

Ramsak, F., Markl, V., Fenk, R., Zirkel, M., Elhardt, K., & Bayer, R. (2000). Integrating the UB-tree into a database system kernel. In *VLDB Conference* (pp. 263-272).

Ross, K., & Srivastava, D. (1997). Fast computation of sparse data cubes. In *Proceedings of the 23rd VLDB Conference* (pp. 116-125).

Roussopolis, N., & Leifker, D. (1985). Direct spatial search on pictorial databases using packed r-trees. In *Proceedings of the 1985 ACM SIGMOD Conference* (pp. 17-31).

Roussopoulos, N., Kotidis, Y., & Roussopolis, M. (1997). Cubetree: Organization of the bulk incremental updates on the data cube. In *Proceedings of the 1997 ACM SIGMOD Conference* (pp. 89-99).

Sarawagi, S., Agrawal, R., & Gupta, A. (1996). *On computing the data cube* (Technical Report RJ10026). IBM Almaden Research Center, San Jose, California.

Schnitzer, B., & Leutenegger, S. (1999). Master-client r-trees: a new parallel architecture. *11th International Conference of Scientiffic and Statistical Database Management* (pp. 68-77).

Sismanis, Y., Deligiannakis, A., Roussopoulos, N., & Kotidis, Y. (2002). Dwarf: shrinking the petacube. In *Proceedings of the 2002 ACM SIGMOD Conference* (pp. 464-475).

Winter Corporation. (2005). *Report*. Retrieved from http://www.wintercorp.com

Yang, H., Dasdan, A., Hsiao, R., & Parker, D. (2007). Map-reduce-merge: simplified relational data processing on large clusters. *International conference on Management of data SIGMOD)*, pp. 1029-1040, 2007.

ENDNOTE

[1]   Research partially supported by the Natural Sciences and Engineering Research Council of Canada.

This work was previously published in International Journal of Data Warehousing and Mining, Vol. 4, Issue 3, edited by D. Taniar, pp. 1-14, copyright 2008 by IGI Publishing (an imprint of IGI Global).

Chapter 7
Medical Document Clustering Using Ontology–Based Term Similarity Measures

Xiaodan Zhang
Drexel University, USA

Michael Ng
Hong Kong Baptist University, China

Liping Jing
The University of Hong Kong, China

Jiali Xia
Jiangxi University of Finance and Economics, China

Xiaohua Hu
Drexel University, USA

Xiaohua Zhou
Drexel University, USA

ABSTRACT

Recent research shows that ontology as background knowledge can improve document clustering quality with its concept hierarchy knowledge. Previous studies take term semantic similarity as an important measure to incorporate domain knowledge into clustering process such as clustering initialization and term re-weighting. However, not many studies have been focused on how different types of term similarity measures affect the clustering performance for a certain domain. In this article, we conduct a comparative study on how different term semantic similarity measures including path-based, information-content-based and feature-based similarity measure affect document clustering. Term re-weighting of document vector is an important method to integrate domain ontology to clustering process. In detail, the weight of a term is augmented by the weights of its co-occurred concepts. Spherical k-means are used for evaluate document vector re-weighting on two real-world datasets: Disease10 and OHSUMED23. Experimental results on nine different semantic measures have shown that: (1) there is no certain type of similarity measures that significantly outperforms the others; (2) Several similarity measures have rather more stable performance than the others; (3) term re-weighting has positive effects on medical document clustering, but might not be significant when documents are short of terms.

INTRODUCTION

Recent research has been focused on how to integrate domain ontology as background knowledge to document clustering process and shows that ontology can improve document clustering performance with its concept hierarchy knowledge (Hotho et. al., 2003; Jing et. al., 2006; Yoo et. al., 2006). Hotho, Staab and Stumme (2003) employed WordNet synsets to augment document vector and achieves better results than that of "bag of words" model on public domain. Yoo, Hu, and Song (2006) applied MeSH domain ontology to clustering initialization and achieved promising cluttering results. Terms are first clustered by calculating semantic similarity using MeSH ontology (http://www.nlm.nih.gov/mesh/) on PubMed document sets. Then the documents are mapped to the corresponding term cluster. Last, mutual reinforcement strategy is applied. Varelas et al. (2005) integrated domain ontology using term re-weighting for information retrieval application. Terms are assigned more weight if they are semantically similar with each other. Jing et al. (2006) adopted similar technique on document clustering.

Although existing approaches rely on term semantic similarity, not many studies have been done on evaluating the effects of different similarity measures on document clustering for a specific domain. Yoo, Hu, and Song (2006) employed one similarity measure that calculates the number of shared ancestor concepts and the number of co-occurred documents. Jing et al. (2006) compared two ontology-based term similarity measure. Even though these approaches heavily relied on term similarity information and all these similarity measures are domain independent, however, to date, relatively little work has been done on evaluating measures of term similarity for biomedical domain (where there are a growing number of ontologies that organize medical concepts into hierarchies such as MeSH ontology) on document clustering. In our pervious study (Zhang

et al., 2007), a comparative study is conducted on a selected PubMed document set. However, the conclusion on one dataset may not be very general. Moreover, the similarity score threshold applied in previous study brings unfairness to term re-weighting since the distribution of similarity scores are different in terms of different similarity measure. Therefore, for a fair comparison, we use the minimum path length between two documents as the threshold.

Clustering initialization and term re-weighting are two techniques adopted for integrating domain knowledge. In this article, term re-weighting is chosen because: (1) a document is often full of class-independent "general" terms, how to discount the effect of general terms is a central task. Term re-weighting is more possible to help discount the effects of class-independent general terms and thus aggravates the effects of class-specific "core" terms; (2) hierarchically clustering terms (Yoo, Hu, & Song, 2006) for clustering initialization is more computational, expensive and more lack of scalability than that of term re-weighting approach.

As a result, we evaluate the effects of different term semantic similarity measures on document clustering using term re-weighting, an important measure for integration domain knowledge. We examine four path-based similarity measures, three information content- based similarity measures, and two feature-based similarity measures for document clustering on two biomedical literature sets: Disease10 and OHSUMED23. The rest of the article is organized as follows: the "Term Semantic Similarity Measures" section describes term semantic similarity measures; the "Methodology" section shows document representation and defines the term re-weighting scheme. The "Datasets" section lists two biomedical data sets. In the "Experimental Results And Analysis" section, we present and discuss experiment results. The last section briefly concludes the article.

TERM SEMANTIC SIMILARITY MEASURES

Ontology-based similarity measure has some advantages over other measures. First, ontology is manually created by human beings for a domain and thus more precise; second, compared to other methods such as latent semantic indexing, it is much more computational efficient; Third, it helps integrate domain knowledge into the data mining process. Comparing two terms in a document using ontology information usually exploits the fact that their corresponding concepts within ontology usually have properties in the form of attributes, level of generality or specificity, and their relationships with other concepts (Pedersen et al., 2007). It is worth noting that there are many other term semantic similarity measures such as latent semantic indexing, but this is out of scope of this study and our focus is on term semantic similarity measure using ontology information. In the subsequent subsections, we classify the ontology-based semantic measures into the following three categories.

Path-Based Similarity Measure

Path-based similarity measure usually utilizes the information of the shortest path between two concepts, of the generality or specificity of both concepts in ontology hierarchy, and of their relationships with other concepts.

Wu and Palmer (1994) developed a similarity measure finding the most specific common concept that subsumes both of the concepts being measured. The path length from most specific shared concept is scaled by the sum of IS-A links from it to the compared two concepts.

$$S_{W\&P}(C_1, C_2) = \frac{2H}{N_1 + N_2 + 2H} \qquad (1)$$

In the Equation 1, N_1 and N_2 is the number of IS-A links from C_1, C_2 respectively to the most specific

common concept C, and H is the number of IS-A links from C to the root of ontology. The similarity score is between 1(for similar concepts) and 0. In practice, we set H to 1 when the parent of the most specific common concept C is the root node.

Li et al. (2003) combines the shortest path and the depth of ontology information in a non-linear function:

$$S_{Li}(C_1, C_2) = e^{-\alpha L} \frac{e^{\beta H} - e^{-\beta H}}{e^{\beta H} + e^{-\beta H}} \qquad (2)$$

where L stands for the shortest path between two concepts, α and β are parameters scaling the contribution of shortest path length and depth, respectively. The value is between 1(for similar concepts) and 0. In our experiment, we set α and β to 0.2 and 0.6, respectively for the best performance.

Leacock and Chodorow (1994) defined a similarity measure based on the shortest path $d(C_1, C_2)$ between two concepts and scaling that value by twice the maximum depth of the hierarchy, and then taking the logarithm to smooth the resulting score:

$$S_{L\&C}(C_1, C_2) = -\log\left(d(C_1, C_2)/2D\right) \qquad (3)$$

where D is the maximum depth of the ontology and similarity value. In practice, we add 1 to both $d(C_1, C_2)$ and $2D$ to avoid log (0) when the shortest path length is 0.

Mao and Chu (2002) presented a similarity measure using both shortest path information and number of descendents of compared concepts.

$$S_{Mao}(C_1, C_2) = \frac{\delta}{d(C_1, C_2)\log_2(1 + d(C_1) + d(C_2))} \qquad (4)$$

where $d(C_1, C_2)$ is the number of edges between C_1 and C_2, $d(C_1)$ is the number of C_1's descendants, which represents the generality of the concept. Here, the constant δ refers to a boundary case where C_1 is the only direct hypernym of C_2, C_2 is the only direct hyponym of C_1 and C_2 has no hyponym. In this case, because the concepts C_1 and C_2 are very close, δ should be chosen close to 1. In practice, we set it to 0.9.

Information Content-Based Measure

Information content-based measure associates probabilities with concepts in the ontology. The probability is defined in Equation 5, where *freq(C)* is the frequency of concept C, and *freq(Root)* is the frequency of root concept of the ontology (Pedersen et al., 2007). In this study, the frequency count assigned to a concept is the sum of the frequency counts of all the terms that map to the concept. Additionally, the frequency counts of every concept includes the frequency counts of subsumed concepts in an IS-A hierarchy.

$$IC(C) = -\log\left(\frac{freq(C)}{freq(Root)}\right) \qquad (5)$$

As there may be multiple parents for each concept, two concepts can share parents by multiple paths. We may take the minimum $IC(C)$ when there is more than one shared parents, and then we call concept C the most informative subsumer—IC_{mis} (C_1, C_2). In another word, $IC_{mis}(C_1, C_2)$ has the least probability among all shared subsumer between two concepts.

$$S_{Resnik}(C_1,C_2) = -\log IC_{mis}(C_1,C_2) \qquad (6)$$

$$S_{Jiang}(C_1,C_2) =$$
$$-\log IC(C_1) - \log IC(C_2) + 2\log IC_{mis}(C_1,C_2) \quad (7)$$

Resnik (1999) defined a similarity measure that signifies that the more information two terms share in common, the more similar they are, and the information shared by two terms is indicated by the information content of the term that subsume them in the ontology. The measure reveals information about the usage within corpus of the

part of the ontology queried. Jiang and Conrath (1998) included not only the shared information content between two terms, but also the information content each term contains.

Lin utilized both the information needed to state the commonality of two terms and the information needed to fully describe these two terms. Since $IC_{mis}(C_1, C_2) > = \log IC(C_1)$, $\log IC(C_2)$ the similarity value varies between 1 (for similar concepts) and 0.

$$S_{Lin}(C_1,C_2) = \frac{2\log IC_{mis}(C_1,C_2)}{\log IC(C_1) + \log IC(C_2)} \qquad (8)$$

Feature-Based Measure

Feature-based measure assumes that each term is described by a set of terms indicating its properties or features. Then, the more common characteristics two terms have and the less non-common characteristics they have, the more similar the terms are (Varelas et al., 2005). As there is no describing feature set for MeSH descriptor concepts, in our experimental study, we take all the ancestor nodes of each compared concept as their feature sets. The following measure is defined based on the discussion in Knappe et al. (2006) and Lin (1003):

$$S_{BasicFeature}(C_1,C_2) = \frac{|Ans(C_1) \cap Ans(C_2)|}{|Ans(C_1) \cup Ans(C_2)|} \qquad (9)$$

where $Ans(C_1)$ and $Ans(C_2)$ correspond to description sets (the ancestor nodes) of terms C_1 and C_2 respectively, $C_1 \cap C_2$ is the join of two parent node sets and $C_1 \cup C_2$ is the union of two parent node sets.

Knappe et al. (2006) developed a similarity measure, as seen below, using the information of generalization and specification of two compared concepts:

$$S_{Knappe}(C_1, C_2) = p \times \frac{|Ans(C_1) \cap Ans(C_2)|}{|Ans(C_1)|} +$$

$$(1-p) \times \frac{|Ans(C_1) \cap Ans(C_2)|}{|Ans(C_2)|} \qquad (10)$$

where p's range is [0, 1] that defines the relative importance of generalization versus specialization. This measure falls between 1 (for similar concepts) and 0. In our experiment, p is set to 0.5.

METHODOLOGY

Given a document set, our clustering method is composed of the following steps: (1) apply ontology to index whole document set; each document is thus represented as a vector of terms; (2) each term's weight is re-calculated by the proposed term re-weighting method; (3) Spherical K-means is run the on the dataset.

MeSH Ontology

Ontology is very important to biomedical documents clustering. First, biomedical literature is usually composed of many complicated biomedical concepts with name variations containing usually more than one word. Second, bag-of-words model suffers from "the curse of dimension" and lacks interpretation power to clustering results.

Therefore, MeSH ontology is applied to index biomedical literature in this article.

Medical Subject Headings (MeSH) [www.nlm.nih.gov./mesh] mainly consists of the controlled vocabulary and a MeSH Tree. The controlled vocabulary contains several different types of terms, such as Descriptor, Qualifiers, Publication Types, Geographics, and Entry terms. Descriptor terms are main concepts or main headings. Entry terms are the synonyms or the related terms to descriptors. For example, "Neoplasms" as a descriptor has the following entry terms {"Cancer," "Cancers," "Neoplasm," "Tumors", "Tumor", "Benign Neoplasm," "Neoplasm, Benign"}. As a result, descriptors terms are used in this research. MeSH descriptors are organized in a MeSH Tree, which can be seen as the *MeSH Concept Hierarchy*. In the MeSH Tree, there are 15 categories (e.g., category A for anatomic terms), and each category is further divided into subcategories. For each subcategory, corresponding descriptors are hierarchically arranged from most general to most specific. In addition to its ontology role, MeSH descriptors have been used to index PubMed articles. For this purpose, about 10 to 20 MeSH terms are manually assigned to each article (after reading full papers). On the assignment of MeSH terms to articles, about three to five MeSH terms are set as "MajorTopic" that primarily represent the article. This indicates that submitting Major Topic MeSH term query to PubMeD usually retrieves dataset with ground truth.

Figure 1. PubMed document indexing

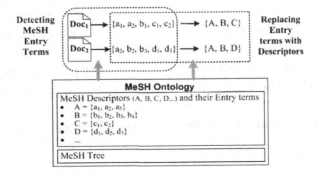

MeSH Concept Indexing

Terms in each document are mapped to the entry terms in MeSH and then maps the selected Entry terms into MeSH Descriptors to remove synonyms.

In detail, our indexing system matches the terms in each document to the entry terms in MeSH and then maps the selected entry terms into MeSH Descriptors. Instead of searching all entry terms in the MeSH against each document, we select 1- to 5-gram words as the candidates of MeSH Entry terms. Then, only those candidate terms are chosen that match with MeSH entry terms. We then replace those semantically similar entry terms with the Descriptor term to remove synonyms. Next, some MeSH Descriptors are filtered out that are too common or have nothing do with the contents of PubMed articles (e.g., ENGLISH ABSTRACT or Government supported); A stop term list is generated for this purpose by analyzing 10 years of PubMed documents (1995-2004). At the time of this writing, there are about 23,833 unique MeSH descriptor terms, 44,978 MeSH ontology nodes (one descriptor term might belong to more than one ontology nodes) and 593,626 MeSH entry terms.

MeSH entry term sets are detected from documents "Doc_1" and "Doc_2" using the MeSH ontology, and then the Entry terms are replaced with Descriptors based on the MeSH ontology. Both MeSH descriptors and entry terms are multi-grams.

Term Re-Weighting

A document is often full of class-independent "general" words and short of class-specific "core" words, which leads to the difficulty of document clustering. Steinbach et al. (2000) examined on the data that each class has a "core" vocabulary of words and remaining "general" words may have similar distributions on different classes. To solve this problem, we should "discount" general

words and "emphasize" more importance on core words in a vector. Jiang and Conrath (1998) and Varelas et al. (2005) define the term re-weighting scheme as below,

$$\tilde{x}_{ji1} = x_{ji1} + \sum_{\substack{i_2=1 \\ i_2 \neq i_1}}^{m} S\left(x_{ji1}, x_{ji2}\right) \cdot x_{ji2} \qquad (11)$$

where x stands for term weight, m stands for the number of co-occurred terms, and $S(x_{ji1}, x_{ji2})$ stands for the similarity score between two concepts. Through this re-weighting scheme, the weights of semantically similar terms will be co-augmented. Since we are only interested in re-weighting those terms that are more semantically similar with each other, it is necessary to set up a threshold value—the minimum similarity score or the minimum path length between compared concepts. In practice, document is first represented according to certain scheme such as TF-IDF. Then, each term's weight is augmented by Equation 11.

DATASETS

Disease10

Disease10 dataset is collected from PubMed (a Web interface of Medline documents) by submitting queries using "MajorTopic" tag along with the corresponding MeSH term of the disease name. For example, if the disease name's corresponding MeSH term is "Gout," then the query will become "Gout [Major Topic]." Table 1 shows the ten classes of document sets and their document numbers (24,566 documents). The document class name is the query name. The average document length for MeSH descriptor is 13 (as shown in Table 2). Compared to the average document length—81—when using bag of words representation, the dimension of clustering space is dramatically reduced. A general stop term list is applied to bag of words scheme.

Table 1. The document sets and their sizes

	Document Sets	No. of Docs
1	Gout	642
2	Chickenpox	1,083
3	Raynaud Disease	1,153
4	Jaundice	1,486
5	Hepatitis B	1,815
6	Hay Fever	2,632
7	Kidney Calculi	3,071
8	Age-related Macular Degeneration	3,277
9	Migraine	4,174
10	Otitis	5,233

Table 2. Document indexing schemes

Indexing Scheme	No. of term indexed	Avg. doc length
MeSH descriptor term	8829	13
Word	41,208	81

OHSUMED23

OHSUMED consists of scientific abstracts collected from Medline, an online medical information database. The selected OHSUMED corpus contains 13,929 Medline abstract of the year 1991, each of which was assigned with one or multiple labels out of 23 cardiovascular diseases categories. Excluding abstracts with multiple labels, we indexed the rest 7,400 abstracts belonging to 23 classes.

EXPERIMENTAL RESULTS AND ANALYSIS

Evaluation Methodology

Cluster quality is evaluated by four extrinsic measures, *entropy* (Steinbach, Karypis & Kumar, 2000), *F-measure* (Larsen & Aone, 1999), *purity* (Zhao & Karypis, 2001), and *normalized mutual information (NMI)* (Banerjee & Ghosh, 2002). NMI is defined as the mutual information between the cluster assignments and a pre-existing labeling of the dataset normalized by the arithmetic mean of the maximum possible entropies of the empirical marginal, that is,

$$NMI(X,Y) = \frac{I(X;Y)}{(\log k + \log c)/2} \qquad (12)$$

where X is a random variable for cluster assignments, Y is a random variable for the pre-existing labels on the same data, k is the number of clusters, and c is the number of pre-existing classes. NMI ranges from 0 to 1. The bigger the NMI is the higher quality the clustering is. NMI is better than other common extrinsic measures such as purity and entropy in the sense that it does not necessarily increase when the number of clusters increases. Purity can be interpreted as the classification rate under the assumption that all samples of a cluster are predicted to be members of the actual dominant class for that cluster. Entropy is a more comprehensive measure than purity since rather than just considering the number of objects "in" and "not in" the most frequent class, it considers the entire distribution. F-score combines the information of precision and recall which is the extensively applied in information retrieval, with values falling in [0, 1] and the larger is the value, the better is the cluster quality.

Experiment Settings

To improve the efficiency of the calculation of term-term similarity, a 44,978 term-term similarity matrix (including all MeSH descriptors) is constructed for each similarity measure before the document vector re-weighting.

The similarity score is disregarded between two terms of which minimal path length is larger than 3, since we are only interested in augmenting the weights of terms that are similar enough. This is better than setting a similarity score threshold and very important to evaluate different semantic similarity measures in a fair manner. The distributions of the similarity scores between documents are usually various in terms of different similarity measures. Setting one threshold to all similarity measures can make the results easily biased toward several measures and need time consuming tuning (Zhang et al., 2007). Therefore, we apply minimum length threshold instead of similarity score threshold. The minimum path length is defined as:

$$MinLen(C_1, C_2) =$$
$$Dep(C_1) + Dep(C_2) - 2 \cdot Dep(C_1, C_2) \qquad (13)$$

where $Dep(C_1)$ indicates the depth of concept C_1 within the ontology and $Dep(C_1, C_2)$ is the depth of the nearest co-parent of concept C_1, C_2.

Apparently, the similarity score range of $S_{L\&C}$, S_{Resnik} and S_{Jiang} is not within [0, 1]. For a fair comparison, their similarity matrices are normalized before they are applied to re-weighting document vector. In detail, each similarity score is denominated by the row sum. In this study, each document

is represented as TF-IDF vector since this scheme achieves much better performance than normalized term frequency and term frequency (Zhang, Zhou, & Hu, 2006). Each document vector is re-weighted using equation the equation by Pedersen, Pakhomov, Patwardhan, and Chute (2007) and the ontology term-term similarity matrix. Spherical K-means is used for documents clustering, for it is a well-known vector-based clustering algorithm. Documents are also indexed using unigram words for a more comprehensive comparison. Documents are not considered in our experiments if they contain fewer than five terms. The whole process is implemented using dragon toolkit (Zhou, Zhang, & Hu, 2006).

Result Analysis

Table 3 and 4 show the experimental results of document clustering on Disease10 and OHSUMED23 datasets, respectively. The nine ontology-based similarity measures are divided by their corresponding types including: path-based, information-content-based and feature-based. "MeSH descriptor" and "Word" indicate the type of document representation and they do not use term re-weighting scheme.

Comparison Between "Re-Weighting" and "None Re-Weighting"

The performance between re-weighting and none re-weighting varies in terms of the corresponding datasets. For Disease10 dataset, most similarity measures slightly outperform none re-weighting, that is, MeSH descriptor. For OHSUMED23 dataset, the results of different schemes are very close. Three measures including Li, Zuhair and McLean (2003), Leacock and Chodorow (1994) and Resnik (1999) have slightly better performances than none re-weighting scheme. These results show that the re-weighting scheme can slightly improve document clustering, but it is

Table 3. Clustering results of Disease10

Type of Measure	Measure Name	Entropy	F-Score	Purity	NMI
Path-based	Wu & Palmer	0.348	0.858	0.874	0.779
	Li et al.	0.304	0.834	0.901	0.799
	Leacock	0.276	0.853	**0.923**	**0.811**
	Mao et al.	0.342	0.830	0.875	0.782
Information-Content-based	Resink	0.295	0.856	0.906	0.802
	Jiang	0.300	0.848	0.905	0.800
	Lin	0.342	0.845	0.882	0.782
Feature-based	Basic Feature	0.358	0.818	0.872	0.775
	Knappe	0.350	0.834	0.876	0.778
MeSH descriptor		0.341	0.772	0.867	0.776
Word		0.245	0.755	0.908	0.820

Table 4. Clustering results of OHSUMED23

Type of Measure	Measure Name	Entropy	F-Score	Purity	NMI
Path-based	Wu & Palmer	2.209	0.244	0.347	0.165
	Li et al.	**2.181**	**0.253**	**0.356**	**0.174**
	Leacock	2.199	0.241	0.351	0.168
	Mao et al.	2.183	0.255	0.354	0.173
Information- Content-based	Resnik	2.194	0.252	0.352	0.170
	Jiang	2.199	0.251	0.351	0.168
	Lin	2.234	0.239	0.341	0.158
Feature-based	Basic Feature	2.219	0.241	0.344	0.162
	Knappe	2.226	0.239	0.340	0.160
MeSH descriptor		2.193	0.248	0.353	0.170
Word		2.321	0.200	0.302	0.130

not very significant. They also show that term re-weighting as a method of integrating domain ontology to clustering might not be a very effective approach when the documents are short of terms (Table 2), because when all these terms are very important core terms for the documents, ignoring the effects of some of them by re-weighting can cause serious information loss. This is on the contrary to the experiment results (Jing et al., 2006) in general domain where document length is relatively longer.

Comparison Between Different Similarity Measures

Experimental results on two datasets show that, among the three types of term similarity measures, there is no certain type of measure that significantly outperforms others. Interestingly, information-content-based measures, with the support of corpus statistics, have very similar performances with the other two types of measure. This may indicate that the corpus statistics is fit with ontology structure of MeSH and thus does not have better performance than path-based measures. Two path-based measures including Leacock and Chodorow (1994) and Li, Zuhair, and McLean (2003) achieve the best performance on both datasets, respectively. Both measures consider not only the shortest path and depth of two concepts. Judging from the overall performance on the two datasets, Li, Zuhair, and McLean (2003), Leacock and Chodorow (1994), Mao and Chu (2002), Resink (1999) and Jiang and Conrath (1998) have rather more stable performances than that of the other measures. Feature-based measures always have the worst performance. This shows that using parent concepts as features may have negative impact on term re-weighting.

Comparison Between Ontology-Based and Word-Based Document Representation

The performance of word scheme is significantly different on the two datasets. For Disease10 dataset, word scheme is slightly better than ontology-based scheme, but this is not significant. On OHSUMED23 dataset, word scheme performs significantly worse than the other schemes. The results show both advantage of ontology and the limitation of ontology. First, while keeping competitive or significantly better clustering results, not only the dimension of clustering space but also the computational cost are dramatically reduced especially when handling large datasets. Second, existing ontologies are under growing, they are still not enough for many text mining applications. For example, there are only about 44,000 unique MeSH descriptor terms for the time of writing. Third, there is also limitation of term extraction. So far, existing approaches usually use "exact match" to map abstract terms to entry terms. This will cause serious information loss. For example, when representing document as MeSH descriptor terms, the average document length is only 13 for Disease10, while the length of the corresponding word representation

is 81. Finally, if taking advantage of both medical concept representation and informative word representation, the results of text mining application can be more convincing.

CONCLUSION AND FUTURE WORK

In this article, we evaluate the effects of nine semantic similarity measures with a term re-weighting method on document clustering of PubMed document sets. The spherical k-means clustering experiment shows that term re-weighting has some positive effects on medical document clustering, but might not be very significant. In detail, we obtain following meaningful findings by comparing nine semantic similarity measures three types: path-based, information-content-based and feature-based measure with two indexing schemes—MeSH descriptor and Word: (1) term re-weighting achieves very similar clustering results with none term re-weighting. Some of them outperform none re-weighting, some of them do not and neither of them is very significant, which indicates that term re-weighting can be effective in a very limited degree when documents are short of terms because when most of these terms are distinguishable core terms for a document, ignoring some of them by re-weighting will cause information loss; more developed ontology and advanced term extraction technique may help term re-weighting achieve better results; (2) There is no certain type of measure that is significantly better than others; the best performance are achieved by two path-based measures including Leacock and Chodorow (1994) and Li, Zuhair, and McLean (2003) that consider both the closeness and the depth of the compared concepts; feature-based measures have the worst overall performance, which shows that using parent concepts as feature set is not effective for this application; although information- content-based measures consider both ontology and corpus statistics, they do not achieve better results than the other measure types;

(3) the performance of MeSH scheme is much better than that of word scheme on OHSUMED23 dataset and slightly worse than word scheme on Disease10 dataset, which demonstrates both the advantage and limitation of domain ontology; while keeping competitive or significantly better results, indexing using MeSH ontology dramatically reduces the dimension of clustering space and computational complexity; however, the limitation of ontology such as limited concepts and rough term extraction techniques can cause information loss easily and thus hurt the clustering performance. Furthermore, this finding indicates that there should be an approach taking advantage of both medical concept representation and informative word representation.

In our future work, we may consider other biomedical ontology such as Medical Language System (UMLS) and also expand this comparative study to some public domain.

ACKNOWLEDGMENT

This work is supported in part by NSF Career grant (NSF IIS 0448023), NSF CCF 0514679, PA Dept of Health Tobacco Settlement Formula Grant (No. 240205 and No. 240196), and PA Dept of Health Grant (No. 239667).

REFERENCES

Banerjee A., & Ghosh, J. (2002). Frequency sensitive competitive learning for clustering on high-dimensional hyperspheres. In *Proceedings of IEEE International Joint Conference on Neural Networks*, pp. 1590-1595.

Hotho, A., Staab, S., & Stumme, G. (2003). Wordnet improves text document clustering. In *Proceedings of the Semantic Web Workshop at 26th Annual International ACM SIGIR Conference*, Toronto, Canada.

Jiang, J., & Conrath, D. (1998). Semantic similarity based on corpus statistics and lexical taxonomy. In *Proceedings of the International Conference on Research in Computational Linguistic*, Taiwan.

Jing, J., Zhou, L., Ng, M., & Huang, Z. (2006). Ontology-based distance measure for text clustering. In *Proceedings of SIAM SDM workshop on text mining*. Bethesda, Maryland, USA.

Knappe, R., Bulskov, H., & Andreasen, T. (2006). Perspectives on ontology-based querying. *International Journal of Intelligent Systems*.

Larsen, B., & Aone, C. (1999). Fast and effective text mining using linear-time document clustering. *KDD-99* (pp. 16-22). San Diego, California.

Leacock, C., & Chodorow, M. (1994). Filling in a sparse training space for word sense identification. ms.

Li, Y., Zuhair, A., & McLean, D. (2003). An approach for measuring Semantic similarity between words using multiple information sources. *IEEE Transactions on Knowledge and Data Engineering, 15*(4), 871-882.

Lin, D. (1993). Principle-based parsing without over-generation. In *Proceedings of the 31st Annual Meeting of the Association for Computational Linguistics* (pp. 112-120). Columbus, Ohio.

Mao, W., & Chu, W. (2002). Free text medical document retrieval via phrased-based vector space model. In *Proceedings of AMIA'02*, San Antonio, TX.

Pedersen, T., Pakhomov, S., Patwardhan, S., & Chute, C. (2007). Measures of semantic similarity and relatedness in the biomedical domain. *Journal of Biomedical Informatics, 40*(3), 288-299.

Resnik, O. (1999). Semantic Similarity in Taxonomy: An Information-Based Measure and its Application to Problems of Ambiguity and Natural Language. *Journal of Artificial Intelligence Research, 11*, 95-130.

Steinbach, M., Karypis, G., & Kumar, V. (2000). *A comparison of document clustering techniques.* Technical Report #00-034, Department of Computer Science and Engineering, University of Minnesota.

Varelas, G., Voutsakis, E., Raftopoulou, P., Petrakis, E., & Milios, E. (2005). Semantic similarity methods in WordNet and their application to information retrieval on the Web. *WIDM '05* (pp. 10-16). New York: ACM Press.

Wu, Z., & Palmer, M. (1994). Verb Semantics and lexical selection. In *Proceedings of the 32nd Annual Meeting of the Associations for Computational Linguistics* (pp. 133-138), Las Cruces, New Mexico.

Yoo I., Hu X., & Song I-Y. (2006). Integration of Semantic-based bipartite graph representation and mutual refinement strategy for biomedical literature clustering. In *Proceedings of the 12th ACM SIGKDD International Conference on Knowledge Discovery and Data Mining*, pp. 791-796.

Zhao, Y., & Karypis, G (2001). *Criterion functions for document clustering: Experiments and analysis.* Technical Report, Department of Computer Science, University of Minnesota.

Zhang X., Zhou X., & Hu X. (2006). Semantic smoothing for model-based document clustering. *In Proceedings of the sixth IEEE International Conference on Data Mining.*

Zhang X., Jing L., Hu X., Ng M., & Zhou X. (2007). A comparative study of ontology based term similarity measures on document clustering. Accepted in the *12th International conference on Database Systems for Advanced Applications (DASFFA2007).*

Zhou, X., Zhang, X., & Hu, X. *The Dragon Toolkit, Data Mining & Bioinformatics Lab.* iSchool at Drexel University. Retrieved from http://www.dragontoolkit.org/

This work was previously published in International Journal of Data Warehousing and Mining, Vol. 4, Issue 1, edited by D. Taniar, pp. 47-61, copyright 2008 by IGI Publishing (an imprint of IGI Global).

Chapter 8
A Graph-Based Biomedical Literature Clustering Approach Utilizing Term's Global and Local Importance Information

Xiaodan Zhang
Drexel University, USA

Xiaohua Hu
Drexel University, USA & Jiangxi University of Finance and Economics, China

Jiali Xia
Jiangxi University of Finance and Economics, China

Xiaohua Zhou
Drexel University, USA

Palakorn Achananuparp
Drexel University, USA

ABSTRACT

In this article, we present a graph-based knowledge representation for biomedical digital library literature clustering. An efficient clustering method is developed to identify the ontology-enriched k-highest density term subgraphs that capture the core semantic relationship information about each document cluster. The distance between each document and the k term graph clusters is calculated. A document is then assigned to the closest term cluster. The extensive experimental results on two PubMed document sets (Disease10 and OHSUMED23) show that our approach is comparable to spherical k-means. The contributions of our approach are the following: (1) we provide two corpus-level graph representations to improve document clustering, a term co-occurrence graph and an abstract-title graph; (2) we develop an efficient and effective document clustering algorithm by identifying k distinguishable class-specific core term subgraphs using terms' global and local importance information; and (3) the identified term clusters give a meaningful explanation for the document clustering results.

INTRODUCTION

PubMed (www.ncbi.nlm.nih.gov/PubMed) is a service of the U.S. National Library of Medicine that includes more than 17 million citations from MEDLINE and other life science journals for biomedical articles back to the 1950s. As a large digital archive, PubMed is widely used by biomedical domain scientists. For such a large dataset, a nonspecific query can easily return more than 100,000 search results. Automatically clustering the search results and providing topic-specific core terms for each cluster can help domain experts concentrate on the relevant articles and disregard the nonrelevant ones. Therefore, we present an efficient and effective clustering method for this purpose.

Proper document representation is very important for document clustering. Conventional document clustering tends to represent a document as a bag of words and then cluster documents using vector cosine similarity or other similarity measures. One main limitation of these document clustering methods is that they are usually black box clustering, invisible to end users and lacking the ability to interpret clustering results.

Steinbach, et al. (2000) argue that each document class has a "core" vocabulary of words, and the remaining "general" words may have similar distributions in different classes. Thus, two documents from different classes can share many general words (i.e., stop words) and thus be treated similarly in terms of vector cosine similarity. The ideal situation is that we use only the distinguishable terms to cluster documents in a much lower dimensionality to improve accuracy and efficiency. However, to discover these distinguishable core terms is not a trivial problem when we have no knowledge about the document class in advance. If these class-specific core terms are successfully identified, they can be used not only for document clustering but also for the interpretation of document clustering results.

Motivated by this discussion, we develop an approach to represent a collection of documents as a term co-occurrence graph or an abstract-title term graph. Global ranking methods such as PageRank (Page, et al., 1998) and HITS (Kleinberg, 1999) are applied to the graph to detect the class-specific core terms. Then an efficient algorithm is designed to grow some semantic-related and graphically connected core term clusters from these top-ranked terms. A document is then assigned to its closest term cluster.

PageRank and HITS-based algorithms have been very popular for improving Web document retrieval (a directed hyperlink graph) and text summarization such as LexRank (Erkan & Radev, 2004) (an undirected sentence similarity graph). Take PageRank as an example. If a Web page has more in-links from the Web pages with a higher PageRank score, the Web page gets a higher PageRank score. However, when such algorithms are used to identify the globally important terms within an undirected term co-occurrence graph for a document collection, they face the problem of term noises. The top-ranked terms can be either class-specific core terms or class-unspecific general terms, because those general terms have very dense connections with other terms. Moreover, an undirected graph contains no reference information (i.e., who cites whom). Ideally, we should keep the links between the class-specific core terms and remove the links that are from the class-unspecific general terms. Therefore, we can remove the "noise" of the general terms and let the ranking of the class-unspecific general terms go down and the class-specific core terms go up. Then we simply pick up a set of the top-ranked terms to initialize the "core" of a cluster.

In this study, two types of term graph representations are presented to discount the effects of the general terms and to strengthen the impacts of the class-specific core terms. One approach is to construct an undirected corpus-level term co-occurrence graph, where each term is a vertex and each edge represents the frequency of co-occurrence. A corpus-level graph is a graph for an entire dataset, not for a single document. The frequency of co-occurrence is the number of documents where the two terms co-occur. Statistical filtering and semantic filtering are applied sequentially to remove the "noisy" co-occurrence edges. The edges between the two terms are thus filtered out if they are not statistically dependent on each other and semantically related. The other approach is to construct a directed corpus-level abstract-title term graph with the abstract terms pointing to the title terms. Title terms are usually more indicative of the class information than the abstract terms. By constructing the corpus-level term graphs this way, the class-specific core terms can have more in-links (edges) and thus have a better ranking by PageRank or HITS.

Moreover, we develop an efficient and effective algorithm to detect the k highest density term subgraphs from the top-ranked terms. Each dense term subgraph corresponds to one document cluster and captures the core semantic relationship information about the document cluster. Then the distance between each document and the k term subgraphs is calculated. A document is assigned to the closest term subgraph. Experiments are conducted on two PubMed document sets: Disease10 and OHSUMED23. In detail, we make the following three main comparisons and evaluations: (1) evaluation of term's global ranking: a filtered term co-occurrence graph v an abstract-title graph; (2) evaluation of the term clustering results: a filtered term co-occurrence graph v an abstract-title graph; and (3) evaluation of the document clustering results: a filtered term graph-based clustering v an abstract-title term graph-based clustering v a spherical k-means clustering.

From the experimental results, we have the following main findings: (1) the semantic and statistical filtering of a term co-occurrence graph improves both class-specific term global ranking and the corresponding document clustering results; (2) an abstract-title term graph is more

effective than a term co-occurrence term graph with statistical and semantic filtering for improving the class-specific core term global ranking score and the corresponding document clustering quality, because it encodes document's section importance information as the external knowledge; (3) clustering documents using an abstract-title graph achieves competitive results to those of the spherical k-means; and (4) our clustering method is more efficient than spherical k-means.

The rest of the article is organized as follows. Section 2 surveys the related work. In section 3, we present two graph-based document representations and provide an efficient and effective graph-based document-clustering algorithm. Section 4 introduces two datasets. Extensive experimental evaluations on PubMed articles are conducted, and the results are reported in Sections 5, 6, and 7. Finally, we conclude the article with our major findings and future work in Section 8.

RELATED WORK

Given the topic of representation of a group of documents or sentences as a graph, there are some emerging works on text classification, text clustering, and text summarization (Erkan & Radev, 2004; Markov et al., 2006; Yoo et al., 2006; Zhang et al., 2007).

Markov et al. (2006) represent a Web document as a graph using a certain heuristic with the consideration of semantic information and location of text and then using a frequent subgraph extraction algorithm (Kuramochi & Karypis, 2004) to extract the most frequent document subgraphs. Then these document subgraphs are used for document classification. However, in essence, this approach is equal to extracting one-gram, two-gram, tri-gram, and so forth, from a document. Though it considers the semantic information of text, each document is still represented by separated term graphs. In contrast, we represent the whole document set as a term graph. Based on this representation, both local and global importance of a term can be considered.

In our previous study (Zhang et al., 2007), we compare two different document graph representation schemes and their effects on a term rank-based document clustering algorithm. In this study, we focus on comparing more term noise reduction techniques and their influence on our revised term rank based clustering algorithm. Moreover, we give clear definitions on how to evaluate the performance of terms global and local ranking, the quality of a detected term cluster, and the clustering performance of our proposed algorithm.

Yoo, et al. (2006) presented a bipartite graph-based document clustering algorithm. Mutual reinforcement strategy is applied to iteratively assign terms and documents to their corresponding clusters. In their approach, a document is represented by co-occurrence concept pairs, which was demonstrated for dimension reduction. However, without very aggressive concept pair filtering, it would actually increase the dimension (square the number of concepts).

Hotho, et al. (2001) introduced the semantic document clustering approach that uses background knowledge. The authors apply a manually constructed ontology during the construction of vector space representation by mapping terms in documents to ontology concepts and then aggregating concepts based on the concept hierarchy, which is called concept selection and aggregation (COSA). As a result of COSA, they resolve the synonym problem and introduce more general concepts to vector space to identify related topics.

In Erkan and Radev (2004), a link is constructed if the similarity value between two sentences is over a threshold. Then the power method is applied to rank the sentences' global importance. The top-ranked sentences will be used for summarization.

There are some other related text mining applications on PubMed documents (Iliopoulos et al., 2001; Ontrup et al., 2004; Srinivasan, 2001; Srinivasan & Rindflesch, 2002).

Textquest (Iliopoulos et al., 2001) introduced a term clustering procedure. They first applied k-means clustering to a selected PubMed document set and then used many heuristic methods to extract topical terms from these document clusters. In contrast, our algorithm does not rely on other clustering algorithms. Moreover, our approach can cluster terms and documents at the same time. Srinivasan (2001) and Srinivasan and Rindflesch (2002) developed two applications for PubMed documents. One system extracted concept pairs from PubMed documents for summarization purpose. MeSHMap is another application for searches via PubMed followed by user-driven exploration of the MeSH terms and subheadings in the retrieved set. In Ontrup, et al. (2004), a non-Euclidean document distance measure was proposed based on MeSH tree structures, which was promising but surpassed by the vector space model.

As opposed to existing studies, our work focuses on the graph representation of a collection of documents and utilizing terms' global and local importance information for document clustering.

OUR METHOD

MeSH Ontology

Biomedical literature is usually composed of many complicated biomedical concepts with name variations. For example, a compound usually has more than 10 synonyms. Therefore, biomedical scientists manually developed an ontology called Medical Subject Headings (MeSH) (http://www.nlm.hih.gov/mesh).

MeSH consists mainly of a controlled vocabulary and a MeSH Tree. The controlled vocabulary contains several types of terms, such as Descriptor, Qualifiers, Publication Types, Geographics, and

Figure 1. The concept mapping from MeSH entry terms to MeSH descriptors. MeSH entry term sets are extracted from documents "Doc₁" and "Doc₂" using the MeSH ontology, and then the entry terms are replaced with descriptors based on the MeSH ontology. Both MeSH descriptors and entry terms are multigrams

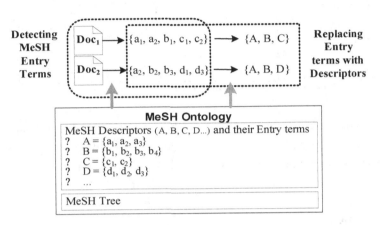

Entry terms. Descriptor terms are main concepts or main headings. Entry terms are the synonyms or terms related to descriptors. For example, "Neoplasms" as a descriptor has the following entry terms: {"Cancer," "Cancers," "Neoplasm," "Tumors," "Tumor," "Benign Neoplasm," "Neoplasm, Benign"}. As a result, descriptors terms are used in this research. MeSH descriptors are organized in a MeSH Tree, which can be seen as the MeSH Concept Hierarchy. In the MeSH Tree, there are 15 categories (e.g., category A for anatomic terms), and each category is further divided into subcategories. For each subcategory, corresponding descriptors are hierarchically arranged from most general to most specific. In addition to their ontology role, MeSH descriptors have been used to index PubMed articles. For this purpose, about 10 to 20 MeSH terms are manually assigned to each article (after reading full papers). On the assignment of MeSH terms to articles, about three to five MeSH terms are set as "Major Topics" that primarily represent the article. This indicates that submitting a Major Topic MeSH term query to PubMeD usually retrieves a dataset with ground truth.

MeSH Concept Indexing

The terms in each document are mapped to the Entry terms in MeSH, and then the selected Entry terms are mapped into MeSH Descriptors to remove synonyms.

In detail, our indexing system matches the terms in each document to the Entry terms in MeSH and then maps the selected Entry terms into MeSH Descriptors. Instead of searching all Entry terms in the MeSH against each document, we select 1- to 5-gram words as candidates for MeSH Entry terms. Then only those candidate terms are chosen that match with MeSH Entry terms. We then replace those semantically similar Entry terms with the Descriptor term to remove synonyms. Next, some MeSH Descriptors are filtered out that are too common or have nothing do with the contents of PubMed articles (e.g., ENGLISH ABSTRACT or Government supported); by automatically studying 10 years of PubMed abstracts from 1994 to 2003 using the zipf-law (Zipf, 1935), a stop term list is generated for this purpose. Figure 1 illustrates the mapping procedure.

Figure 2. A term co-occurrence graph between two documents: Doc1 and Doc2. The edge weight is the number of documents where two terms co-occur

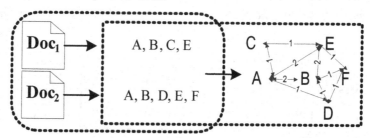

In short, the purpose of the two-step mapping is to remove synonyms, to solve name variations, and to reduce the dimension of a document representation.

MeSH Co-Occurrence Graph

Co-Occurrence Graph Construction

An edge is constructed if two concepts (MeSH descriptors) co-occur in a document. The edge weight is the number of documents in which the two concepts co-occur (Figure 2). Although the example in Figure 2 is only for the two documents, the method can be used to build a graph for a whole collection of documents.

Noise Reduction

The PageRank algorithm does well in identifying globally important Web pages on the World Wide Web since it ranks a Web page using its social reference information (i.e., it is cited by whom). However, when it is applied to a term co-occurrence graph, it faces the noise problem (i.e., the general terms can receive high ranking easily as they tend to co-occur with most of class-specific core terms). Should the impacts of "general terms" be discounted, it would contribute to strengthening the effects of "core terms." Therefore, the following two filtering strategies are applied sequentially. We first employ a chi-square statistical filtering to remove each edge

between nonsignificant concept pairs. Then we delete each edge between every two concepts that never appear in the same sentence clause. In detail, our statistical filtering and semantic filtering is defined as follows.

Statistical Filtering

In order to validate the strength of the relatedness of concept pairs, the edges are filtered out if their chi-square value falls below a critical value (P=0.001 with degree of freedom 1, 10.83). Other statistical measures such as mutual information are disregarded, as there is no critical value table to follow.

Semantic Filtering

A pair of two concepts is determined as semantic related if they appear in the same clause of an English sentence. An edge between two co-occurred concepts is thus filtered if they are not semantic related.

MeSH Abstract-Title Graph

As discussed in previous sections, how to discount the impacts of the general terms is essential to detecting the class-specific core terms. But filtering methods are not the only strategies that we can apply. If a term graph is well constructed, we may not need heuristics such as a filtering. We argue that the different sections of a document

Figure 3. An abstract-title term graph between two documents: Doc1 and Doc2 with abstract terms pointing to title terms. TI stands for title terms. AB means abstract terms. The edge weight is the number of documents where an abstract term co-occurs with a title term

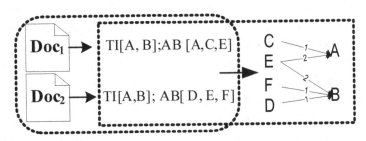

have different importance levels for assigning the terms' global ranking scores. For example, the terms in a document title usually contain a much bigger percentage of topical terms than those in a document abstract. Therefore, we view a document abstract as an explanation of a document title. In other words, an abstract term "cites" the title terms. Based on this intuition, a directed abstract-title term graph is constructed with each abstract term pointing to each title term (see Figure 3). This makes the class-specific core terms receive more in-links. In Figure 3, we explain how to construct an abstract-title graph using the two documents. An abstract term E co-occurs with the title term A and B in two documents. Thus, a directed edge is constructed with E pointing to A and B. Edge weight 2 means that {E} and {A, B} co-occur twice. It is possible that a term appears both in the title and abstract section, which is equivalent to an author's citing his or her own work. In practice, we find that many terms occur in both title and abstract, not necessarily simultaneously, which makes some abstract (title) terms receive in-links from other abstract (title) terms. This fact actually guarantees the run of PageRank-based algorithms because PageRank requires that the graph should not be a bipartite graph (i.e., there should be some links among abstract (title) terms).

Table 1 shows the rankings of the title terms (in bold font) and the abstract terms of a PubMed document belonging to the macular degeneration

Table 1. The ranking of title and abstract terms of a PubMed document calculated by PageRank

Term(T:Title;A:Abstract)	Ranking
Macular Degeneration (T, A)	**3**
Lithiasis (T)	**35**
Uric Acid (A)	36
Urinary Calculi (A)	37
Phosphorus (A)	756
Parathyroid Hormone (A)	981
Staining and Labeling (A)	2436
Microdissection (A)	3426
Anthraquinones (A)	5127

class. Apparently, the two terms in the title receive higher rankings, and they are very topic-specific. Note that although our method is quite effective to improve class-specific terms' ranking, it cannot make all general terms rank below class-specific terms since it is possible that a class-unspecific general term appears in both title and abstract. However, our approach takes the advantage of the fact that most title terms are topic-specific terms and therefore are effective to improve these terms' global ranking.

Term Global Importance

The ranking of terms by global ranking methods such as PageRank and HITS indicates their global importance. Ideally, we just pick the top-ranked class-specific core terms to initialize the "core" of clusters. The success of PageRank lies on its integration of human knowledge (in-links). Unless the graph is not a bipartite graph, PageRank can be applied. Therefore, they can be applied to both symmetric term co-occurrence graphs and asymmetric abstract-title graphs. However, when applied to a symmetric graph, they have to deal with the fact that the class-unspecific general terms tend to co-occur with most of the class-specific core terms and thus receive very high rankings. The function of these terms is very similar to a large portal Web site such as Yahoo that is cited by a great deal of other Web pages. How to discount the effects of these class-unspecific general terms can contribute to discovering the distinguishable class-specific core terms. We expect that a statistical filtering and a semantic filtering can help solve this problem. For example, which is the closer concept pair, {"Human," "Migraine Disorder"} or {"Headache," "Migraine Disorder"}? By chi-square, {"Headache," "Migraine Disorder"} is more significant than {"Human," "Migraine Disorder"}, because "Human" tends to co-occur with most other terms while "Headache" tends to co-occur with "Migraine Disorder." Therefore, if the chi-square value of {"Human," "Migraine Disorder"} is below the threshold, the edge between the two terms will be filtered out.

As discussed before, hyperlinks contain more useful information than undirected co-occurrence links because they encode human choices beyond the document content. Motivated from this observation, an abstract-title term graph with abstract terms pointing to title terms is constructed to integrate the document section importance information into the links between terms. As a result, title terms have more in-links than that of abstract terms and thus receive higher PageRank scores. Assigning title terms higher ranking scores is assigning topic-specific terms higher ranking scores, since a document title usually contains more topic-specific terms than a document abstract.

Term Local Importance

A term's local importance is defined as the density with which it connects to other terms. If a topic-specific term is densely connected, a number of other terms are also closely related to this topic. Then a core term cluster is formed.

We believe that the top-ranked terms form several dense areas within a co-occurrence term graph or an abstract-title term graph. Therefore, we start from the top-ranked terms to detect core term clusters.

For this purpose, we develop a measure called In_Cluster_Degree (ICD) (Equation 1) to calculate a term's local importance:

$$In\_Cluster\_Degree(t_i, C_k) = \frac{\sum Weight(Edge_{t_i, C_k})}{Num(Edge_{t_i, C_k})} \qquad (1)$$

where $\sum Weight(Edge_{t_i, C_k})$ is the sum of co-occurrences of term t_i with each connected term in term cluster C_k, and $Num(Edge_{t_i, C_k})$ means the number of links connecting term t_i to cluster C_k.

In practice, the top-ranked terms by PageRank are selected sequentially to detect k core term subgraphs (clusters). For a top-ranked term t_i, our algorithm first generates a term list where all the terms are linked to term t_i. This term list forms a temporary term cluster (subgraph) and is sorted in a descending order based on their ICD values (i.e., the link frequency to other terms). Terms below a predefined threshold are put back into the term pool for reassignment. Terms over the threshold and term t_i are kept to form a core term cluster. If no term is over the threshold, term t_i will be put back to the term pool. Once K core term clusters are detected, the remaining terms are assigned to the k term clusters according to their ICD values. The details of calculating a term's local importance and its corresponding term cluster's density will be explained in Section 3.8 with a solid example.

Document Clustering

After k term clusters are identified, each document is assigned to its closest term cluster by maximizing (2):

$$DocClusterCloseness(d_j, C_k)$$
$$= \sum In\_Cluster\_Degree(t_{i,d_j}, C_k) \qquad (2)$$

In equation (2), the closeness between document d_j and cluster C_k is calculated by summing up the In_Cluster_Degree of each term t_{i,d_j}.

An Efficient and Effective Algorithm for Identifying k Core Term Clusters and k Document Clusters

Figure 4 shows the procedure of document clustering. Next we explain each step in great detail. Compared to our previous algorithm (Zhang et al., 2007), which is designed for a title-abstract graph and its coreresponding term co-occurence graph, this algorithm is more general and suitable for any type of term graphs. Note that this algorithm requires only one term graph as input, while our previous algorithm uses two graphs as inputs. This change makes the algoritm more efficient, less effected by term noise in term co-occurence graph and achieve better performance.

Step 1 (lines 1-2): The global importance score of each term vertex is treated as its salience score. The larger the score, the higher the ranking. First, a global ranking algorithm such as PageRank is run on a term co-occurrence or an abstract-title term graph until it converges. Once the score is determined, terms are sorted in a descending order according to their salience scores—global importance.

Step 2 (lines 3-18): To detect K term clusters (as shown in Figure 4), our algorithm checks each term sequentially from the sorted list generated from Step 1. Herein, the procedure is explained by a detailed example. If the No. 1 top-ranked term

is "Hepatitis B, Chronic," then all the terms that have links to term "Hepatitis B, Chronic," including the term itself, are treated as a candidate term cluster. These terms are further sorted by their In_Cluster_Degree (ICD) in descending order (Ti_list) (line 9). Starting from the lowest ranked term (line 10), the ICD of each term in Ti_list is denominated by the *ICD* of the term with the largest *ICD* value, the *ICD* of "Hepatitis B, Chronic (that connects to every other term)." This value is then checked against a predefined threshold Q, say 0.5 (line 11). If this value is over 0.5, then the current term and all the terms ranking above it form a new term cluster (lines 12-14). If only the terms including "Lamivudine," "Hepatitis B virus," and "Hepatitis B, Antigens" are over the threshold, then these terms, together with the term "Hepatitis B, Chronic," form a new core dense subgraph (core term cluster). The terms below the threshold Q are put back into the term pool. Furthermore, we require the number of core terms in this term cluster be over a predefined number M, say 3. In other words, if the size of the detected term cluster is too small, it will not be treated as a term cluster, and all the terms in the list will be put back for future reassignment (lines 15-17). Our example term cluster satisfies all the criteria; therefore, the system will stop here and start to detect the other *K-1* term clusters. The algorithm loops until it finds all K core term clusters.

Finally, after K term clusters are detected, all the remaining terms, including those that have not been clustered, are assigned to their closest term cluster by the maximization of Equation (1) (line 18).

Step 3 (lines 19-21): We match each document efficiently to its closest term cluster by just adding up its terms' ICD value (i.e., the maximization of equation (2)).

It deserves mentioning that the convergence of the algorithm is dependent on the term cluster threshold Q and the minimum core terms number M. We find our algorithms converge when Q is

Figure 3. Term global ranking

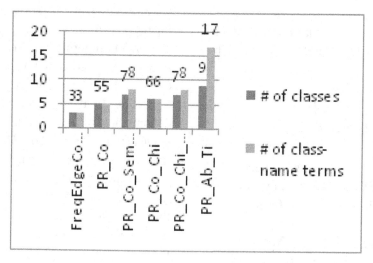

less than and equal to 0.5 and M is less than and equal to 5 on the two experimental datasets. In our experiment, the threshold Q is set to 0.5 for the larger dataset (Disease10) where terms have very dense connectivity and to 0.3 for the smaller dataset (OHSUMED23) where terms are relatively sparsely connected; M is set to 3 for both datasets. Both Q and M guarantee that the identified core term clusters are densely connected, and these terms are semantically related to each other.

In summary, we present an efficient clustering algorithm based on terms' global and local importance information. The detected core term clusters can be further used for annotating document clusters. Although existing model-based clustering methods (Zhang et al., 2006) can choose the most probable terms of a document cluster to interpret the corresponding document clustering, these terms can be lack of interpretation power because they are not required to be semantically and graphically related to each other.

DATA SETS

Disease10

The Disease10 dataset is collected from PubMed by submitting queries using the "MajorTopic" tag along with the corresponding MeSH term of the disease name. For example, if the disease name's corresponding MeSH term is "Gout," then the query will become "Gout [Major Topic]." Table 2 shows the 10 classes of document sets and their document numbers. The document class name is the query name. Each class is named using a disease name; namely, a class-name term.

OHSUMED23

OHSUMED consists of scientific abstracts collected from MEDLINE, an online medical information database. The selected OHSUMED corpus contains 13,929 MEDLINE abstracts from the year 1991, each of which was assigned one or multiple labels out of 23 cardiovascular disease categories. Excluding abstracts with multiple labels, we indexed the remaining 7,400 abstracts belonging to 23 classes.

TERM GLOBAL RANKING EVALUATION

Evaluation Method

The evaluation of term ranking is conducted on the Disease10 dataset. We evaluate terms' global ranking by checking how many different classes (in Table 2) are found within the top 40 ranked terms. The terms are counted as class-specific core terms if they are the class-name terms or the class-name terms' synonyms (as shown in Table 2). If two methods happen to identify an equal number of classes within the top 40 terms, the one with more class-name terms is deemed to have a better performance. For example, if both methods detect six classes, and if one method has 10 class-name terms in total and the other method has seven class-name terms in total, then the one with 10 class-name terms has a better performance.

Term Ranking Results and Analysis

Although we compare both PageRank and HITS on ranking terms in our experiments, we only show PageRank ranking results since they perform very similarly to each other. The PageRank algorithm requires a damping factor or "Jump-out" factor. In our experiment, we set it to 0.85, which achieves relatively better results. For details about the damping factor, please refer to Page et al., 1998).

"FreqEdgeCount" indicates ranking term by edge frequency; "PR" is PageRank; "Co" means term co-occurrence graph; "Semantic" is semantic filtering; "Chi" is chi-square filtering; "Ab_Ti" means abstract-title graph. For example, PR_Co_Chi_Semantic means PageRank on a term co-occurrence graph with chi-square and semantic filtering.

Apart from PageRank, we introduce a baseline ranking method called FreqEdgeCount. The FreqEdgeCount method is based on terms' edge frequency. The edge frequency of a term is the number of terms connecting to it. A term with

Table 2. The document sets and their sizes

Document Class	#. of Docs
Gout	642
Chickenpox	1,083
Raynaud Disease	1,153
Jaundice	1,486
Hepatitis B	1,815
Hay Fever	2,632
Kidney Calculi	3,071
Age-related Macular Degeneration	3,277
Migraine	4,174
Otitis	5,233

a higher edge frequency value receives a higher ranking score. Accordingly, FreqEdgeCount_co in Figure 3 and Table 3 stands for a FreqEdgeCount ranking on a term co-occurrence graph without filtering.

We compare the performances of the PageRank algorithm on four different term graphs: a term co-occurrence graph without filtering (PR_Co), a term co-occurrence graph with chi-square filtering (PR_Co_Chi), a term co-occurrence graph with semantic filtering (PR_Co_Semantic), a term co-occurrence graph with both chi-square filtering and semantic filtering (PR_Co_Chi_Semantic), and an abstract-tittle term graph. The shorthand scheme symbols are listed in Figure 3 and Table 3. Among all these schemes, PR_Ab_Ti identify the most classes, and FreqEdgeCount detects the least number of classes. Observe that PR_Co_Chi_Semantic achieves a better result than that of PR_Co_Chi and PR_Co_Semantic, which performs better than PR_Co.

The identified class-name terms and their synonyms are shown in Table 3 in bold font. FreqEdgeCount_Co has only three class-name terms: "Migraine Disorders," "Otitis," and "Macular Degeneration." PR_Co detects two more class-name terms: "Kidney Calculi" and "Hepatitis B, Chronic." Moreover, semantic filtering performs slightly better than chi-square filtering, which gets

Figure 4. Term rank-based document clustering

Algorithm:

Input:
G : a term graph,
  D: a document set.
  K: a pre-defined cluster number.
  M: the minimum number of core terms in each cluster.
  Q: a term cluster quality threshold.
  Output: *K* core term clusters and their corresponding *K* document clusters.

/* calculate term salient score and assign to a term vertex list *v_list* and sort the *v_list* in a descending order by terms' salience score */ 1:   *v_list* <- globalRank (*G*); 2:   *v_list* <- sort (*v_list*, *SalienceScore*, *des*);

/* Detecting *K*core term clusters */
3: while (*the number of detected term clusters is less than K*) do
4:        for each term vertex *Ti* in *v_list* do   *//start from the first term in v_list*
              //get a non-used term cluster from clusterPool
5:            cluster_k <- getFreeTermCluster(*clusterPool*);
6:            if (*cluster_k* is nil) return // *all k clusters are detected*
7:            cluster_k.add(*Ti*);
8:            *Ti_list* <- findConnectedTerms (*Ti*);
  //sort terms in Ti_list descendingly by In_Cluster_Degree(ICD)
9:        *Ti_list* <-Sort (*Ti_list, ICDScore,des*)
10:        for each Tj in *Ti_list* do //start from the last term
11:            if (ICD(*Tj*)/ICD(*Ti*)>= *Q*) do
12:              *cutoff_index* <- *j*;
13:              break for loop;
  //add all the terms over cutoff_index in Ti_list to cluster_k;
14:            cluster_k.add(getTermsOver (*cutoff_index*));
  // if the detected term cluster is too small, it will not be counted.
15:            if (size(*cluster_k*) < *M*) do
16:              cluster_k.clear();
17:              free(*cluster_k*); //put back *cluster_k to cluster-Pool*
18: assign remaining terms to k term clusters by maximizing ICD.

/*match each document to its closest term cluster by the maximization of equation(2) */ 19:   For each document *dm* in *D* do 20:   cluster_k<-findClosestCluster(*dm*) 21:   cluster_k.add(*dm*);

a better result than that of FreqEdgeCount_Co. By applying chi-square and semantic filtering sequentially on a term co-occurrence graph, PageRank identifies three more class-name terms: "Hepatitis B, Virus"; "Chickenpox"; and ""Rhinitis, Allergic, Seasonal (Hay Fever)."

The last row of Table 3 shows the terms' PageRank ranking on an abstract-title term graph. Apparently, many more class-name terms are identified by PR_AB_Ti than by the other schemes.

Table 3. Schemes and top 40 ranked terms. "FreqEdgeCount" indicates rank term by edge frequency; "PR" indicates PageRank; "Co" means term co-occurrence graph; "Semantic" is semantic filtering; "Chi" is chi-square filtering; "Ab_Ti" means abstract-title graph. Terms in boldface indicate class related terms

Top 40 ranked MeSH descriptor terms
Scheme: FreqEdgeCount_Co Patients; Therapeutics; **Migraine Disorders;** Child; **Otitis;** Disease; Cells; Infection; Attention; Serum; Time; Role; Ear, Middle; Ear; Humans; Headache; Risk; History; Blood; Eye; Diagnosis; Plasma; Rats; Population; Research Design; Tissues; Organization and Administration; **Macular Degeneration;** Pain; Evaluation Studies; Genes; Prevalence; Surgery; Syndrome; Incidence; **Rhinitis;** Pollen; Economics; Association; Family
Scheme: PR_Co Patients; Therapeutics; Disease; Child; **Otitis;** Time; Infection; **Migraine Disorders;** Serum; Role; Diagnosis; Risk; Population; Attention; History; Headache; Cells; Ear, Middle; Incidence; Blood; Evaluation Studies; Ear; Eye; Research Design; **Macular Degeneration;** Adult; Prevalence; Association; Pain; Surgery; Humans; **Rhinitis;** Women; Methods; **Kidney Calculi; Hepatitis B, Chronic;** Hospitals; Antigens; Life; Review
Scheme: PR_Co_Semantic Patients; Therapeutics; **Migraine Disorders;** Child; **Otitis;** Serum; Infection; Disease; **Hepatitis B virus;** Headache; Ear, Middle; Cells; Eye; Attention; **Chickenpox;** Pollen; Time; **Macular Degeneration;** Risk; Rhinitis; **Hepatitis B, Chronic;** Blood; Ear; History; **Rhinitis, Allergic, Seasonal;** Prevalence; DNA; Diagnosis; Incidence; Population; Epilepsy; Role; Bilirubin; Infant; Calcium; Pain; **Kidney Calculi;** Antigens; Adult; Liver
Scheme: PR_Co_Chi Patients; Therapeutics; Disease; Child; **Otitis;** Time; Infection; **Migraine Disorders;** Serum; Role; Diagnosis; Risk; Population; Headache; Ear, Middle; Attention; Cells; History; Incidence; Blood; Eye; Ear; **Macular Degeneration;** Evaluation Studies; Research Design; Prevalence; Rhinitis; Association; **Hepatitis B, Chronic;** Surgery; Adult; Humans; Antigens; **Kidney Calculi;** Methods; **Rhinitis, Allergic, Seasonal;** Pain; Pollen; Hospitals; Women
Scheme: PR_Co_Chi_Semantic Patients; Therapeutics; **Migraine Disorders;** Child; **Otitis;** Serum; Infection; Disease; **Hepatitis B virus;** Headache; Ear, Middle; Eye; **Chickenpox;** Pollen; Cells; Attention; **Macular Degeneration;** Time; Rhinitis; **Hepatitis B, Chronic;** Risk; Ear; **Rhinitis, Allergic, Seasonal;** Blood; DNA; History; Prevalence; Epilepsy; Diagnosis; Bilirubin; Incidence; Calcium; Population; Infant; **Kidney Calculi;** Pain; Antigens; Role; Liver; Immunoglobulin E
Scheme: PR_Ab_Ti **Migraine Disorders; Otitis; Macular Degeneration; Kidney Calculi; Hepatitis B, Chronic; Chickenpox;** Rhinitis; **Rhinitis, Allergic, Seasonal;** Lithotripsy; Review [Publication Type]; **Jaundice;** Shock; **Gout;** Pollen; **Hepatitis B virus;** Viruses; Herpesvirus 3, Human; Sumatriptan; Epilepsy; **Calculi;** Lamivudine; **Hepatitis B; Jaundice, Neonatal; Otitis Media with Effusion;** Infection; Hypersensitivity; Immunotherapy; Calcium Oxalate; Urinary Calculi; Safety; **Macular Edema, Cystoid;** Visually Impaired Persons; **Hepatitis; Otitis Externa;** Life; Antigens; Edema; Vaccination; Membranes; Costs and Cost Analysis

Table 4. Term cluster identified by our algorithm and the PageRank ranking on a filtered term co-occurrence graph

	Term cluster (corresponding class name)
1	Plasma; Epilepsy; Migraine Disorders (**Migraine Disorders**)
2	Epilepsy; Migraine Disorders; Sumatriptan (**Migraine Disorders**)
3	Mucous Membrane; Otitis; Otitis Media with Effusion (**Otitis**)
4	Hepatitis B virus; Hepatitis B, Chronic; Lamivudine (**Hepatitis B**)
5	Serotonin, Tryptamines, Triazoles
6	Membranes; Choroidal Neovascularization; Macular Degeneration (**Macular Degeneration**)
7	Poaceae; Rhinitis; Pollen (**Hay fever**)
8	Amoxicillin; Clavulanic Acid; Cephalosporins
9	Calcium Oxalate, Citric Acid, Kidney Calculi (**Kidney Calculi**)
10	Chickenpox; Herpes Zoster; Herpesvirus 3, Human (**Chickenpox**)

Table 5. Term cluster identified by our algorithm using the PageRank ranking on abstract-title graph

	Term cluster(corresponding class name)
1	Kidney Calculi, Shock, Lithotripsy (**Kidney Calculi**)
2	Macular Degeneration, Visual Acuity, Vision (**Macular Degeneration**)
3	Chickenpox, Viruses, Herpesvirus 3, Human (**Chickenpox**)
4	Migraine Disorders, Epilepsy, Women (**Migraine Disorders**)
5	Otitis Media with Effusion, Otitis, Observation (**Otitis**)
6	Hepatitis B, Chronic, Lamivudine, Hepatitis B virus, Hepatitis B, Antigens(**Hepatitis B**)
7	Kidney Calculi, Calcium Oxalate, Chickenpox (**Kidney Calculi**)
8	Jaundice, "Jaundice, Neonatal," Bilirubin, Life (**Jaundice**)
9	Rhinitis, Pollen, Immunotherapy (**Hay Fever**)
10	Macular Edema, Cystoid, Visual Acuity, Edema (**Macular Degeneration**)

PR_Ab_Ti has nine more class-specific core terms than PR_Co_Semantic_Chi. Except for the term "Raynaud Disease," all the other nine disease names are shown in the top 40 term list. The experimental results confirm our expectation that class-specific core terms receive higher ranking scores on an abstract-title term graph than the other term graphs. This infers that the document section importance information as external knowledge is integrated into the graph and thus gives title class-specific core terms a higher ranking score than the class-unspecific general terms.

As discussed before, our method to a certain degree decreases the ranking of the general terms, but it cannot make all the general terms receive lower ranking scores than the class-specific core terms. For example, a general term can also appear frequently in the document titles. However, a document title usually contains more class-specific core terms than general terms. Therefore, we observe that the PR_Ab_Ti attains a better performance.

TERM CLUSTERING EVALUATION

An evaluation of a term cluster is also conducted on the Disease10 dataset. The quality of a term cluster is judged by whether it contains class-name terms or their synonyms.

Table 4 shows the term cluster results of our algorithm using PageRank on a term co-occurrence graph with a chi-square and semantic filtering. Eight out of 10 term clusters contain class-name terms or their synonyms. Since cluster 1 and cluster 2 correspond to the same class—"Migraine Disorder"—seven classes are identified in total. In Table 5, using an abstract-title graph, niine out of 10 term clusters contain class-name terms. Cluster 2 and cluster 10 are two identical term clusters. Thus, eight classes are discovered. Obviously, clustering using an abstract-title graph identifies more core term clusters than a filtered term co-occurrence graph. Although the experiments of other schemes are also conducted, for saving space, we only show these two better schemes.

DOCUMENT CLUSTERING EVALUATION

Evaluation Method

Cluster quality is evaluated by four extrinsic measures: *entropy* (Zhao & Karypis, 2001), *F-score* (Zhao & Karypis, 2001), *purity* (Zhao & Karypis, 2001), and *normalized mutual information (NMI)* (Zhong & Ghosh, 2003). NMI is defined as the mutual information between the cluster assignments and a pre-existing labeling of the dataset normalized by the arithmetic mean of the maximum possible entropies of the empirical marginals (i.e.,

$$NMI(X,Y) = \frac{I(X;Y)}{(\log k + \log c)/2} \qquad (3)$$

where X is a random variable for cluster assignments, Y is a random variable for the pre-existing labels on the same data, k is the number of clusters, and c is the number of pre-existing classes). NMI ranges from 0 to 1. The bigger the NMI, the higher quality the clustering. NMI is better than other common extrinsic measures such as purity and entropy in the sense that it does not necessarily increase when the number of clusters increases. Purity can be interpreted as the classification rate under the assumption that all samples of a cluster are predicted to be members of the actual dominant class for that cluster. Entropy is a more comprehensive measure than purity since rather than just considering the number of objects "in" and "not in" the most frequent class, it considers the entire distribution. F-score combines the information of precision and recall, which is extensively applied in information retrieval, with values falling in [0, 1], and the larger the value, the better the cluster quality.

Table 6. The clustering results on disease10 (PageRank); node: minimum number of nodes for detecting 10 term cluster; secs: the number of seconds; co: term co-occurrence graph without filtering; co_ilter: semantically and statistically filtered term co-occurrence graph; Ab_Ti: abstract-title graph; k-means: spherical k-means the TF*IDF

	Node	Secs	Entropy	FScore	Purity	NMI
Co	100	30	0.76	0.66	0.79	0.60
Co_filter	90	9	0.65	0.66	0.81	0.65
Ab_Ti	**58**	**7**	0.36	0.75	**0.89**	**0.75**
K-means	N/A	39	**0.35**	**0.77**	0.87	0.75

Table 7. The clustering results on OHSUMED23 (PageRank); the notations are the same as in Table 6

	Nodes	Secs	Entropy	FScore	Purity	NMI
Co	600	20	2.20	0.22	0.34	0.16
Co_filter	551	6	2.10	0.23	0.35	0.17
Ab_ti	**330**	**3**	**2.07**	**0.28**	**0.38**	**0.20**
K-means	N/A	26	2.28	0.21	0.33	0.15

Clustering Results and Analysis

Although both PageRank and HITS are applied to our clustering algorithm, we only present the clustering results using PageRank since their performances are very close. All the experiments are conducted on a Lenovo T60 laptop with a dual-core 1.83GHZ CPU, a 1GB memory, and an 80GB 5400RPM hard drive.

Tables 6 and 7 show the document clustering results on the Disease10 and OHSUMED23 datasets, respectively. "Co," "Co_filter," and "Ab_Ti" stand for term co-occurrence graph without filtering, term co-occurrence graph with chi-square and semantic filtering, and abstract-title term graph. The performance of our algorithm is compared to that of spherical k-means using the TF*IDF scheme, because spherical k-means is a very widely used clustering algorithm in the data mining community, and spherical k-means using the TF*IDF as representation scheme has continuously better performance than other schemes such

as term frequency and normalized term frequency (Zhang et al., 2006). Since the results of k-means clustering vary with initialization, we run it 10 times with random initialization and take the average as the result.

In Tables 6 and 7, the "secs" indicates the number of seconds that the algorithm consumes. For our approach, it includes ranking terms, detecting core term clusters, and matching documents to their closest term clusters.

To compare the performance between using term co-occurrence graph (co, co_filter) and using abstract-title graph (Ab_Ti), we also check the number of term node used for detecting k core term clusters. If only a very small number of terms can detect all K core term clusters, these terms are very class-specific, which indicates the corresponding graph representation makes PageRank assign higher rankings to class-specific terms. Therefore, the fewer the term vertices (node), the better the graph representation.

As shown in Tables 6 and 7, "Co_filter" has slightly better performance and uses fewer term nodes to detect core term clusters than "Co." The used time is also dramatically reduced from 30 to nine seconds and from 20 to six seconds on the Disease10 and OHSUMED23, respectively. This shows that our semantic and statistical filtering strategy on the term co-occurrence graph has a very positive effect on document clustering.

Compared to other graph representations, "Ab_Ti" has the best overall performance. It uses seven seconds to cluster 24,566 documents from the Disease10 dataset and three seconds to cluster the 7,400 documents from the OHSUMED23 dataset. Moreover, judging by the four extrinsic evaluation measures, it significantly outperforms "Co" and "Co_filter." This indicates that encoding document section importance information into a graph is better than a postfiltering on a term co-occurrence graph.

In Tables 6 and 7, we also see that compared with the spherical k-means, our algorithm performs similarly on Disease10 but better on OHSUMED23. However, just one run of k-means uses more seconds than our algorithm. This indicates our algorithm is efficient and more scalable. Notice that our algorithm has a better performance on the "noisy" dataset OHSUMED23 (with 23 classes and each of them containing a limited number of documents). In short, while performing more efficiently, our algorithm is comparable to k-means. However, this is not our only contribution. The byproducts of our clustering algorithm are the class-specific core term clusters that provide the annotation of clustering results.

CONCLUSION AND FUTURE WORK

In this article, we present a graph-based biomedical literature clustering approach utilizing terms' global and local importance information. The advantages of our approach are the following: (1) we develop two types of corpus-level graph representations to improve topic-specific terms' global rankings and the corresponding document clus-

tering quality: a term co-occurrence graph with statistical and semantic filtering and an abstract-title term graph; (2) we identify distinguishable class-specific core term subbraphs (clusters) using terms' global and local importance information; and (3) our approach provides a meaningful explanation for document clustering through its generated core term subgraphs, which is crucial for users to have an overview of clustering results, picking only the interested document clusters and disregarding the noninterested ones.

In detail, we have the following main findings: (1) semantic and statistical filtering do have positive effects on improving both the class-specific terms' global ranking score and the corresponding document clustering performance; (2) an abstract-title graph representation is more effective than a term co-occurrence graph representation with semantic and statistical filtering in improving class-specific terms' global ranking score, as well as the document clustering quality, because it encodes documents' section importance information as external knowledge; and (3) clustering using an abstract-title graph achieves competitive results to spherical k-means using the TF*IDF scheme, but is more efficient.

In short, our ontology-enriched and graph-based approach is very effective for clustering biomedical literature while providing interpretation for the clustering results.

In the future, we would extend our work to other text mining applications, such as feature selection, classification, and text summarization.

ACKNOWLEDGMENT

This research work is supported in part by NSF career grant (NSF IIS 0448023), NSF CCF 0514679, and a research grant from the Pennsylvania Department of Health.

REFERENCES

Erkan, G., & Radev, D.R. (2004). LexRank: Graph-based lexical centrality as salience in text summarization. *Journal of Artificial Intelligence Research, 22*, 457–479.

Hotho, A., et al. (2001). Text clustering based on good aggregations. *Proceedings of the 2001 IEEE International Conference on Data Mining.*

Iliopoulos, I., et al. (2001). Textquest: Document clustering of Medline abstracts for concept discovery in molecular biology. *Pac Symp Biocomput,* 384–395.

Kleinberg, J.M. (1999). Authoritative sources in a hyperlinked environment. *J. ACM 46*(5), 604–632.

Kuramochi, M., & Karypis, G. (2004). An efficient algorithm for discovering frequent subgraphs. *IEEE Transactions on Knowledge and Data Engineering, 16*(9), 1038–1051.

Markov, A., et al. (2006). Model-based classification of Web documents represented by graphs. *Proceedings of the WebKDD 2006: KDD Workshop on Web Mining and Web Usage Analysis, in conjunction with the 12th ACM SIGKDD International Conference on Knowledge Discovery and Data Mining (KDD 2006).* Philadelphia, Pennsylvania.

Ontrup, J., et al. (2004). A MeSH term based distance measure for document retrieval and labeling assistance. *Proceedings of the 25th Annual International Conference of the IEEE, 2,* 1303–1306.

Page, L., et al. (1998). The PageRank citation ranking: Bringing order to the Web. Technical Report, Stanford Digital Library Technologies Project.

Srinivasan, P. (2001). MeSHmap: A text mining tool for MEDLINE. *Proceedings of the AMIA Symposium,* 642–646.

Srinivasan, P., & Rindflesch, T. (2002). Exploring text mining from MEDLINE. *Proceedings of the AMIA Symposium,* 722–726.

Steinbach, M., et al. (2000). A comparison of document clusteirng techniques. Technique Report, #00-034. Minnesota.

Yoo, I., et al. (2006). Integration of semantic-based bipartite graph representation and mutual refinement strategy for biomedical literature clustering. *Proceedings of the 12th ACM SIGKDD International Conference on Knowledge Discovery and Data Mining.* Philadelphia, Pennsylvania.

Zhang, X., et al. (2006). Semantic smoothing for model-based document clustering. *Proceedings of the Sixth International Conference on Data Mining.*

Zhang, X., et al. (2007). Utilization of global ranking information in graph- based biomedical literature clustering. *Proceedings of the 9th International Conference on Data Warehousing and Knowledge Discovery (DAWAK).* Regensburg, Germany.

Zhao, Y., & Karypis, G. (2001). Criterion functions for document clustering: Experiments and analysis. Technique Report.

Zhong, S., & Ghosh, J. (2003). A comparative study of generative models for document clustering. *Proceedings of the Workshop on Clustering High Dimensional Data and Its Applications in SIAM Data Mining Conference.*

Zipf, G.K. (1935). *The psycho-biology of language; an introduction to dynamic philology.* Boston: Houghton Mifflin.

This work was previously published inInternational Journal of Data Warehousing and Mining, Vol. 4, Issue 4, edited by D. Taniar, pp. 84-101, copyright 2008 by IGI Publishing (an imprint of IGI Global).

Chapter 9
An Integrated Framework for Fuzzy Classification and Analysis of Gene Expression Data

Mohammad Khabbaz
University of Calgary, Canada

Keivan Kianmehr
University of Calgary, Canada

Mohammad Alshalalfa
University of Calgary, Canada

Reda Alhajj
University of Calgary, Canada

ABSTRACT

*This chapter takes advantage of using **fuzzy classifier rule**s to capture the correlations between genes. The main motivation to conduct this study is that a **fuzzy classifier rule** is essentially an "if-then" rule that contains linguistic terms to represent the feature values. This representation of a rule that demonstrates the correlations among the genes is very simple to understand and interpret for domain experts. In this proposed gene selection procedure, instead of measuring the effectiveness of every single gene for building the classifier model, the authors incorporate the impotence of a gene correlation with other existing genes in the process of gene selection. That is, a gene is rejected if it is not in a significant correlation with other genes in the dataset. Furthermore, in order to improve the reliability of this approach, the process is repeated several times in these experiments, and the genes reported as the result are the genes selected in most experiments. This chapter reports test results on five datasets and analyzes the achieved results from biological perspective.*

DOI: 10.4018/978-1-60566-717-1.ch009

Table 1. Example gene expression data

Sample	G1	G2	G3	G4
Sample1	52	39	59	16
Sample2	57	32	64	21
Sample3	30	76	61	65
Sample4	52	39	59	16
Sample5	18	79	56	64
Sample6	65	81	59	70
Sample7	41	83	21	23

INTRODUCTION

Gene expression analysis is the use of quantitative RNA measurements of **gene expression** in order to characterize biological processes and clarify the mechanisms of gene transcription. The microarray technology makes it possible to monitor the expression levels of tens of thousands of genes in parallel. It measures the relative RNA levels of genes and produces high dimensional dataset, which is in turn a highly informative source for **gene expression** analysis. The microarray data from a series of N experiments may be represented as N×M **gene expression** matrix in which each of the N rows consists of an M-element expression vector. The latter vector represents the **gene expression** level of the genes for a single experiment.

Table 1 displays an example matrix for **gene expression** data, where the rows denote different samples or conditions (such as the same cell type among different samples), while the columns denote genes; F [*Sample* 3, G_4] denotes the quantitative expression of gene G_4 in *Sample* 3.

These samples may correlate with different time points taken during a biological process or with different tissue types, such as normal cells and **cancer** cells Aas (2001). To this end, data mining techniques have been widely applied to **gene expression** data for conducting analysis in gaining insight into the functional behavior of genes as well as to correlate structural information with functional information. The main methods

of microarray data analysis include Piatetsky-Shapiro & Tamayo (2003):

- **Cluster Analysis:** This can be performed to identify genes that reveal similar functionalities under a number of experimental conditions.
- **Discriminant Analysis (Classification and prediction):** This can potentially yield useful diagnostic tools for classifying samples on the basis of their **gene expression** patterns.
- *Gene Selection*: This can yield a small fraction of genes that are informative in discriminant analysis problems.

Although microarray provides considerable flexibility for **gene expression** analysis, there are several general issues in using microarray data. First, the datasets are usually complex and noisy. The noise and complexity in experimental protocols strongly limit data integration. Another important issue is the fact that currently available datasets typically contain fewer than one hundred instances, though each instance quantifies the expression levels of several thousands of genes (*i.e.*, high dimensionality). For instance in **gene expression classification**, due to the high dimensionality and the small sample size of the experimental data, it is often possible to find a large number of classifiers that can separate the training data perfectly, but their diagnostic accuracy on unseen test samples is quite poor and different. Therefore, traditional methods for data mining can not be effectively applied to **gene expression classification** Li et al. (2003), and there is a need for more dedicated techniques to handle this problem. As one solution, feature construction and **feature selection** have been applied to pre-process the **gene expression** data in a way to overcome the high dimensionality problem Li et al. (2003); Zeng et al. (2002).

Many supervised machine learning algorithms such as neural networks, Bayesian networks and **support vector machine** (SVM), combined with **feature selection** techniques, have been previously applied to microarray **gene expression**. In the work described in Kianmehr et al. (2005), we achieved outstanding accuracy in **gene expression classification** by combining neural networks learning and SVM-based **feature selection** into an integrated approach. However, the most existing gene selection approaches employed in the integrated solutions use a common technique based on removing or adding features from the train dataset to a smaller train dataset, and then measuring the quality of features one by one. They basically do not consider the correlation existing among genes while removing them. Furthermore, some of the genes selected by these methods are not irrelevant to the disease under consideration, even though they result in building an accurate classifier model. Some other techniques that take the correlations among the genes into account suffer from unreliability. That is, each run of the algorithm results in different genes extracted from the dataset, and this really degrades the reliability of the approach. To biologists, **gene expression** data can be a valuable source for understanding the biological associations between genes. The relevant associations among different genes can be discovered by using rule mining techniques.

In this paper, we take advantage of using **fuzzy classifier rules** to capture the correlations between genes; a preliminary version of this study already appeared in Khabbaz et al. (2007). In here, we provide a better cover of the approach and report more extensive testing to highlight the different aspects of the model. The motivation is that a **fuzzy classifier rule** is essentially an "if-then" rule that contains linguistic terms to represent the feature values. This representation of a rule that demonstrates the correlations among the genes is very simple to understand and interpret for domain experts. In our proposed gene selection procedure, instead of measuring the effectiveness of every single gene for building the classifier model, we incorporate the impotence of a gene correlation with other existing genes in the process of gene selection. That is, we reject a gene if it is not in a significant correlation with other genes in the dataset. Furthermore, in order to improve the reliability of our approach, we repeat the process several times in our experiments, and the genes reported as the result are the genes selected in most experiments.

The rest of the paper is organized as follows. Section provides an overview of **feature selection** concepts and techniques. Section presents a review of some existing gene selection methods. Our approach for discovering the correlation among the genes is presented in Section . Section describes the procedure in which we employ a **frequent pattern** mining technique to extract the most important genes from the dataset. Section provides detailed explanation on the selected evaluation model, the conducted experiments and the achieved results. Section is summary and conclusions.

FEATURE SELECTION

Gene expression data are characterized by their high dimensionality, which brings many challenges for methods dealing with gene analysis problems. Therefore, it is important to pre-process a **gene expression** dataset and reduce its size in order to facilitate better analysis by concentrating on a manageable relevant subset of features.

The **feature selection** problem in general, and gene subset selection in particular, is to select a small subset of genes which are informative and relevant to **classification** problems. Gene subset selection results in computational cost reduction as a result of problem dimensionality reduction. It also prevents the danger of the irrelevant genes overshadowing the contribution of the relevant ones. Furthermore, identification of the informative genes may be beneficial in that it could reveal genes of particular importance in a biological process. The basic **feature selection** methods may be categorized into three broad groups: filter Dash et al. (2002); Hall (2000), wrapper Caruana & Freitag (1994); Dy & Brodley (2000) and embedded Das (2001); Ng (1998) methods.

In the filter method, **feature selection** is considered as a preprocessing task, separate from the classifier algorithm. A subset of features are extracted based on the general characteristics of the data. The wrapper model uses a predetermined **classification** algorithm to search for an optimal subset of features aiming to improve **classification** performance. The quality of a particular subset of features is evaluated by measuring the accuracy of the classifier model (the model is built using the predetermined **classification** algorithm and a particular subset of features). The embedded method attempts to make the **feature selection** task more efficient by taking advantages of the two models and incorporating **feature selection** as part of the training process.

The Filter Method

The filter method is essentially a data pre-processing method where features are selected based on their ability to discriminate the target classes relying on their special characteristics, not on the classifier algorithm. A statistical evaluation criterion is usually applied to rank features based on the discriminative power of every individual feature. Then, a subset of top ranked features at a specified importance level is selected as the result of the **feature selection** process. Since filter method is a completely encapsulated and independent component from the classifier algorithm, it does not involve any bias of the **classification** algorithm and it is also computationally efficient. The major weakness of the filter method is that it only relies on the characteristics of the individual features, and not on the correlation among features. The correlation between features may have a significant effect on building an efficient and accurate classifier. A set of low ranked features, which are naturally ignored by the filter method, may result in a good classifier model when combined together.

The Wrapper Method

Compared to the filter approach, the wrapper method uses a predefined **classification** algorithm to assess (by measuring the prediction accuracy of the classifier) the quality of subsets of features instead of an independent measurement for subset evaluation. Many candidate feature sets are evaluated using the training set of data samples to tune the **feature selection** process for the **classification** method. The aim is to choose the subset which can be best used in the **classification** process. Although the wrapper method overcomes the drawback of the filter method that ignores the correlation between features, the implementation of the wrapper approach is more difficult because of the interaction between the **feature selection** process and the **classification** algorithm. One drawback of the wrapper method is that it can be computationally intensive in cases where there exist a huge number of features, such as **gene expression** data. Therefore, efficient search algorithms, such as Greedy search strategies, are usually used to improve the efficiency of the process.

The Embedded Method

Embedded methods incorporate **feature selection** as part of the training process to take advantages of the above two models and to provide more efficient model. The embedded method has been recently proposed to deal with large data sets Das (2001); Xing et al. (2001). An embedded algorithm uses both an independent measure and a **classification** algorithm to evaluate different feature subsets: the best subsets for a given level of significance are determined by the independent measure, and **classification** algorithm is used to choose the final best subset among the best subsets. Thus, the stopping criterion in the embedded model is provided by the **classification** algorithm based on the prediction power of different classifier models resulted from the best subsets.

RELATED WORK

In this study, to evaluate our method for relevant gene selection against existing ones, we mainly focus on the SVM-RFE Guyon et al. (2002) based gene selection approach, namely r-GeneSelect Fu & Youn (2003). The SVM-RFE **feature selection** method proposed by Guyon *et al* Guyon et al. (2002) has been recognized as a powerful wrapper approach to conduct relevant gene selection for **cancer classification**. All of the methods previously proposed for **gene expression** analysis use score-based **feature selection** methods, such as the signal-to-noise ratio and NBR score to choose important genes. A major drawback of these metrics is that they treat each gene independently, i.e., they ignore the important correlations between the genes that may exist in the data. SVM-RFE has been proposed to deal with this issue. The main idea is that the orientation of the separating hyperplane found by the SVM algorithm Vapnik (1998) can be used to discriminate between relevant and irrelevant genes (features), *i.e.*, if the plane is orthogonal to a particular feature dimension, then

that feature is informative, otherwise the feature in not relative to the **classification** problem. However, the major concern with SVM-RFE may be stated as follows: *there is no guarantee that the same set of genes is extracted in every run of the algorithm*. This may reduce the reliability of the genes selected to be used as informative genes in the **classification** task. r-GeneSelect is a SVM-RFE gene selection method that has been proposed in Fu & Youn (2003) to address this issue by assessing the reliability of the selected genes based on error and repeatability within the context of 10-fold cross validation. The steps of this approach are highlighted in the following subsections.

Gene Selection

The gene dataset is divided into ten subsets of equal size. Nine of these subsets are used by the gene selection algorithm for gene selection. Then, a classifier model is built using only the selected genes. The predictive error rate of the model is evaluated using only the selected genes from the remaining set, called the validation set. This process is repeated a total of 10 times, as each group in turn is set aside because the validation set for model evaluation and the other nine sets are used by the **feature selection** algorithm. Finally, the mean of the 10 independent error rate predictions is used as the error rate for cross validation. The basic algorithm used for gene selection in each cycle of cross validation is SVM-RFE. It first builds a rank-ordered list of genes using a sequential backward elimination approach. The ranking process starts with all the genes. Gene ranks are determined by the coefficients of the weight vector calculated in the learning process of the SVM algorithm over the dataset. The larger the weight magnitude, the higher is the rank of the associated gene. The least important gene, the one having the smallest weight magnitude, is identified and removed from the feature vector and added to the ranked-list at each step. At the beginning of the next step, the remaining genes are re-ranked based on the associated weight in the trained SVM, where the feature vector of each training instance given to the SVM algorithm represents only the remaining genes. The recursive elimination of genes runs until no more gene is available in the feature vector. After building the ranked list of genes, gene selection is performed by iteratively training the SVM, while adding one top-ranked gene at a time from the ordered list. The process stops when the minimum prediction rate is achieved on the training data. The genes describing the feature vectors used in the learning process of the best achieved SVM model are introduced as the selected genes.

Reliability Assessment

Recall that the SVM-RFE algorithm does not select the same subset of genes in each individual run, as so in the case of 10 fold cross validation. However, if a single gene is selected by the algorithm in a steady manner, it can be considered as important gene. The target of reliability assessment is to distinguish genes with the greater repeatability in 10 subsets of the selected genes obtained from 10 fold cross validation. This approach is designed to combine the genes obtained in each iteration of the cross validation and to include those genes whose repeatability values are not less than a threshold in the final gene set. A possible threshold for repeatability can take a value from 1 to 10, since a gene can appear at most in all subsets, *i.e.*, 10 times. In order to find the best possible threshold, the second 10 fold cross validation is performed by using every possible threshold at a time. The cross validation error is used to evaluate the goodness of the selected threshold. The best repeatability threshold is the one associated with the most accurate classifier model obtained by cross validation technique.

We obtained the source code of the r-Gene-Select method from Fu (2007); it was developed by the authors of the paper Fu & Youn (2003).

After conducting very precise biological analysis on several **gene expression** datasets, we noticed that some of the genes selected by this method are not biologically significant. That is, even though the selected genes resulted in building a highly accurate classifier, they are irrelevant to **cancer**. We will show that, using our method for gene selection, we are also able to build an accurate classifier mostly with fewer number of genes compared with r-GeneSelect. Furthermore, we argue that our genes are more related to **cancer** disease. We demonstrate this by performing a comprehensive biological analysis on the functionality of the genes selected by our method.

CONSTRUCTING THE CORRELATION DATASET

The first step in the proposed gene selection involves creating from the training dataset a classifier fuzzy rule set that highlights important existing correlations between informative genes. This process is a mapping between the training dataset and a correlation dataset containing correlations between features. Since our main purpose here is not building a fuzzy rule based classifier, we propose an algorithm for creating fuzzy rules that rely on data samples in the training dataset. This approach may cause overfitting to the training dataset. However, we believe this overfitting is not an obstacle for gene selection because informative genes from both the training and test datasets are supposed to be identical. However, we already managed to remove this side effect by adding before rule creation a simple filtering step based on standard deviation; this filters genes with a flat like curve that could not be used earlier to distinguish between classes. The target rule set is generated through a number of iterations, while changing the minimum expected value for the standard deviation. The steps involved in each iteration are enumerated next:

1. For each gene, separate values of different classes and calculate the mean values.
2. Calculate the standard deviation of the mean values for each gene. Filter the gene out if its standard deviation is less that t, for a given threshold value t.
3. Start from the training dataset and the selected features in the previous step, randomly select a sample and create a fuzzy rule using the selected genes and gene values of the sample.
4. Evaluate the created fuzzy rule; if it does not satisfy the initial expectation then discard the rule and remove the sample from the list of candidate samples for generating rule in the dataset, otherwise generate a rule from the sample.
5. Reduce the fuzzy rule by changing the gene values to "don't care", which do not have any effect on the rule performance.
6. Add the rule to the rule set and remove from the training dataset all the data samples classified by the rule.
7. Continue generating rules; unless the set of existing data samples in the training dataset, which are candidate for rule creation is not empty, return to step 3.

The steps enumerated above are explained in detail in the following subsections. The threshold value t is variable in our final algorithm, *i.e.*, we create rule sets starting from low values of threshold and increase the threshold value by a step size in each subsequent step of the iterative process. We keep adding rules to the final rule set until the threshold is so high that no feature can pass the initial filter.

Filtering Genes by Standard Deviation

Useful genes from every dataset are supposed to be able to discriminate patterns from different classes. In order to improve the performance of our fuzzy rule set classifier, we have added a simple filtering step before creating rules from data samples in the training set. This filtering procedure works as follows.

Given a dataset and a threshold t, gene values for different classes are separated into different sets. Then, the mean value for each set is calculated, and the standard deviation of the mean values is computed. If the standard deviation is below the given threshold, the gene is filtered out without getting to the next step. To illustrate this, assume that the values of gene I for two classes of **cancer** and non-**cancer** are: **Cancer** –[0.12, 0.14, 0.33, 0.21] and Non-**cancer** – [0.66, 0.89, 0.77], i.e., we have 7 data samples in our training set, 4 belong to the **cancer** class and 3 are in the non-**cancer** class. Gene I has low values (closer to 0) for the **cancer** class and high values (closer to 1) for the non-**cancer** class. The gap between the values for the two classes indicates that gene I can play an important role in the **classification** process. The mean value for the **cancer** class is $\frac{0.12 + 0.14 + 0.33 + 0.21}{4} = 0.2$, and the mean value for the non-**cancer** class is $\frac{0.66 + 0.99 + 0.77}{3} = 0.77$. After calculating these two mean values, we can consider them as class representatives, and hence find the standard deviation. We keep the feature in the dataset if the standard deviation of the new data sequence [0.2, 0.77] is greater than the given threshold t, otherwise we filter it out. The only concern here is selecting the value of the threshold. This will be discussed further when we demonstrate the proposed algorithm in Section .

Filtering Genes Using t-test

The t-test assesses whether the means of two groups are statistically different from each other. Given the replicas of particular treatment and control samples, it is possible to compute the t-test for any gene g for differential expression by using the following formula under the assumption that

Figure 1. Fuzzy membership functions

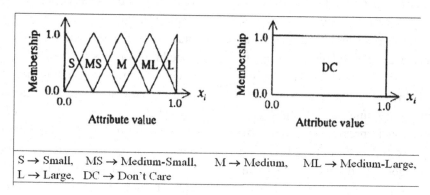

S → Small,   MS → Medium-Small,   M → Medium,   ML → Medium-Large,
L → Large,   DC → Don't Care

genes have differing standard deviation Dudoit et al. (2000).

$$t_g = \frac{\overline{x}_{g,t} - \overline{x}_{g,c}}{\sqrt{\dfrac{s_{g,t}^2}{n_t} + \dfrac{s_{g,c}^2}{n_c}}} \qquad (1)$$

where $\overline{x}_{g,t}$ and $\overline{x}_{g,c}$ are means of replicas of treatment and control conditions with respective standard deviations $s_{g,t}^2$ and $s_{g,c}^2$, and replica counts n_t and n_c for gene g. It is clear that t-test favors for large mean differences and small standard deviations and it is a good balance between them.

Filtering Genes Using SVD-Entropy

This is unsupervised feature filtering technique based on using SVD entropy for gene selection et al (2006). The genes are sorted by their relative contribution to the entropy. The genes are grouped into three groups; genes with high contribution to the entropy, genes with average contribution, and the third group is genes with low contribution. In this study, we are just interested in genes which have high entropy.

Creating Fuzzy Classifier Rule from Patterns Existing in Training Dataset

In this section, we explain how a **fuzzy classifier rule** could be created using the reduced set

of genes obtained after filtering genes which do not meet the initial criteria. A **fuzzy classifier rule** in our system is composed of a sequence of fuzzy linguistic values that indicate a class label. The employed fuzzy membership functions are shown in Figure 1.

For every normalized attribute in the dataset, each value in the range [0,1] indicates a degree of membership in one of the sets. A **fuzzy classifier rule** is a sequence of linguistic values of the same length as the number of genes. For instance, a **fuzzy classifier rule** with this format: (S, M, L, DC→Class0), means the current sample belongs to *class*0 when the values of the first three attributes are small, medium and large, respectively, regardless of the value of the fourth feature. A fuzzy rule set is composed of several **fuzzy classifier rule**s.

The construction of fuzzy rule set from the training set has already received considerable attention, e.g., Ishibuchi & Murata (1999); Cordon et al. (2004); Ishibuchi et al. (1999); Wangm & Mendel (1992); Ishibuchi et al. (1992); Abe & Lan (1995); Mitra & Pal (1994). One of the most common approaches described in the literature is based on genetic algorithms. However, genetic algorithms are slow and the convergence time is a real problem. In the proposed system, we use existing patterns in the training set in order to create the classifier rules. Algorithm 1 describes how a **fuzzy classifier rule** is created from the data sample.

Algorithm 1. Creating fuzzy classifier rule from the pattern existing in a data sample

```
1: CreateRule =(feature set, data sample)
2: Rule = Initialize an empty rule;
3: for i =1 to length(data sample) do
4: if data sample i is not in feature set then
5: Rule(i)= DC;
6: else
7: FuzzySet = GetMostMatchFuzzySet (MembershipFunctions, data sample(i));
8: Rule(i)= FuzzySet;
9: end if
10: end for
11: Return Rule;
```

Assigning the Class Label for the Rule

Not all the rules created as explained in the previous section are useful. To assign class labels to the generated rules, we take into account all the data samples present in the training set. The degree of compatibility between a fuzzy classifier and a data sample is defined as the minimum of all membership values for the corresponding feature (gene) values in the fuzzy rule and the data sample; it is computed using as follows:

$$\mu_j(x_p) = Min\{\mu_{j1}(x_{p1}),...,\mu_{jn}(x_{pn})\} \quad p = 1, 2,... \tag{2}$$

where $\mu_j(x_p)$ is the degree of compatibility between rule j and sample xp, and μ_{j1} is the membership function for the i-th attribute of the rule; p changes over the whole dataset for checking the compatibility of the rule with all samples in the dataset. After calculating the degree of compatibility between each rule and each sample, we determine the rule class using the sum of compatibility degrees for all classes using Equation 2.

Therefore, $\beta h(Rj)$ is the sum of all compatibility degrees of the j -th rule with samples of class h. Among all the classes, the one which achieves the maximum β value is the class selected for the newly created rule.

Evaluating the Effectiveness of Each Rule

Since our system works with individual rules created from data samples, we need a measure to separately evaluate each rule. The compatibility degree of each rule with each data sample is either 0 or a positive value. We compare the class labels of the rule and the data sample; if both class labels are the same, the sample is classified by the rule; otherwise, the sample is misclassified by the rule. Associated with each rule, we have 2 variables in our system: one is the number of samples classified by the rule and the other is the number of samples misclassified by the rule. The number of classified patterns by each rule indicates the strength of the rule in correctly classifying samples and the number of misclassified samples indicates the risk of future misclassifications by the rule. These two factors are used to evaluate the effectiveness of each rule.

Rule Creation Algorithm

In this section, we present the details of creating the rule set, which results in the construction of the correlation dataset. The process is outlined in Algorithm 2.

The functions invoked by Algorithm 2 are described next:

- *CandidateSamples* refers to the list of data samples, which are candidate patterns for

Algorithm 2. The process of creating rule set from a given training datase

```
1: GetRules(featureSet, trainingSet)
2: CandidateSamples = Copy(trainigSet);
3: RuleSet = Initialize Empty List;
4: while (CandidateSsamples > 0) do
5: CandidateSample = GetRandomSample(CandidateSamples)
6: if (Rule.classifiedSamples = 0) OR (Rule.misclassifiedSamples > 0) OR (Rule.classLabel ≠CandidateSample.classLabel) then
7: Rule = CreateRule(featureSet, CandidateSample);
8: DeretmineRuleClass(Rule);
9: EvaluateRule(Rule, trainingSet);
10: Remove(CandidateSamples, CandidateSample);
11: Break;
12: else
13: ReducedRule = Reduce(Rule, featureSet);
14: Add(RuleSet, Rule);
15: end if
16: end while
17: Return RuleSet;
```

rule generation. If a rule created from a candidate sample is not able to satisfy the initial criteria, the sample is removed from the list of candidate samples.

- *GetRandomSample* picks a data sample randomly and returns it as a candidate for rule generation. The selection is done randomly because there is no guarantee that creating the rule set starting from the beginning of the list gives the best order for creating the dataset. Due to this effect, the resulting rule set from the *GetRules* function does not return the same rule set each time. However, since there are some distinct genes which are important for the **classification**, important genes are identified by the algorithm regardless of the order of rule generation. To neutralize this randomness effect and improve the reliability, we have repeated the process several times in the experiments, and the genes reported in the result are those selected in most of the experiments. We will elaborate more on this in Section .

- *DetermineRuleClass* follows the procedure described in Section and determines the class label for the rule.

- *EvaluateRule* counts from the training set the number of data samples classified and

misclassified by the current rule. We use these values to make an initial decision, whether the rule is a good candidate for gene selection or not. No mis**classification** is allowed for the initial rule since we have enough candidate samples to generate rules, and hence do not want to take any risk in rule selection. After generating the initial rule, it is reduced using the *Reduce* function, and then it is added to the rule set. The *Reduce* function is basically the feature reduction unit; it is described in Algorithm 3.

Given the list of features other than the "don't care" ones, Algorithm 3 selects a random feature from the rule and changes it to *"don't care"*. If this does not affect the effectiveness in terms of the number of samples classified and misclassified by the rule, the change is committed, otherwise the feature is identified as playing an important role in the **classification** power of the rule, and hence we rollback the change.

Here, we still have the random selection for the order in which we remove the features because there is no guarantee that starting from the head of the list is the best order. This randomness effect for **feature selection** is natural. Other techniques which were attempted for gene selection also suffer

Algorithm 3. The Reduce function

```
1: Reduce(Rule, featureSet)
2: CandidateFeatures = Copy(featureSet);
3: while Size(CandidateFeatures > 0) do
4: CandidateFeature =RemoveRandomFeature(CandidateFeatures);
5: PrevClassified = Rule.classifiedSamples;
6: Rule.(CandidateFeature)= DC;
7: EvaluateRule(Rule);
8: if (Rule.classifiedSamples < prevClassified) OR (Rule.misclassifiedSamples > 0) then
9: RollBack(Rule);
10: else
11: CommitChange(Rule);
12: end if
13: end while
```

from this randomness. The SVM-RFE approach described in Guyon et al. (2002) extremely suffers from this randomness and each run of the algorithm returns different features extracted from the dataset. In Fu & Youn (2003), the authors tried to remove this randomness by reliability analysis using 10-fold cross validation. Although the most important genes reported from their approach are the same in all the experiments, their approach still suffers from randomness because there are some genes that change in the final result of each run. In this study, in order to resolve this problem, we repeat the experiment and report genes that appear in most experiments as the reliable genes.

Eventually, the algorithm that generates the final rule set is simply a loop over the *GetRules* function. Before the loop, we identify the maximum standard deviation among all genes. Then, we can define the step size for the threshold according to the number of times we want to repeat the algorithm with different thresholds for the initial filtering. We create the sub-rule sets starting from threshold 0, then change the threshold by the step size and add the sub-rule sets to the final rule set until the threshold value is so high that no gene can pass the filter. Using this approach in changing the value of the threshold, we consider the standard deviation as a factor for the effectiveness of individual genes and pay more attention to them, while at the same time we do not ignore the fact that some features that do not

have high standard deviation values could also be important due to their correlation with other genes. These genes are given the chance to show their importance in the first iterations of the algorithm; and as the algorithm proceeds to the next iteration more chance is given to genes with higher value of standard deviation because discovering correlations between extremely important genes is a priority.

Creating the Correlation Dataset from the Final Rule Set

The correlation dataset consists of correlations between genes, where each row of the dataset contains few genes which are highly correlated to each other in the **classification** process. The final rule set obtained from the previous phases basically consists of reduced rules, where each rule has the least number of relevant genes such that its efficiency is negatively affected by reducing any of its genes. So, each sequence of active (non-"don't care") attributes in the rule is a minimal set.

We create the correlation dataset using the final rule set. After evaluating each rule, it is associated with the samples it classifies. Here, it is worth noting that the number of misclassified samples for each rule is zero because we don't let any misclassification to happen by enforcing feature reduction when we generated the rule. The sequence of active features in the rule forms a correlation between them. The correlation appears in the correlation dataset the same number of times as the number of data samples classified by the rule. The process is explained via an example.

Assume that two rules $R1$ and $R2$ with the following characteristics are present in the dataset:

$R1$: (1, DC)-(2, DC)-. . . -(630, L)-(631, DC)-. . . -(7200, S)-(7201, DC)-. . . ;
$R1$.classifiedSamples = 5

$R2$: (1, DC)-(2, DC)-. . . -(630, ML)-(631, DC)-. . . -(1446, L)-. . . -(12153, S). . . ;
$R2$.classifiedSamples =2

Rule $R1$ has only two active features (630, 7200); other features have the *"don't care"* value; it is able to correctly classify 5 data samples from the training set. Similarly, the features (630, 1446, 12153) are active in rule $R2$, and the rule can achieve the **classification** of two data samples. According to these two rules, the following correlations will be added to the correlation dataset:

(630, 7200); (630, 7200); (630, 7200); (630, 7200); (630, 7200); (630, 1446, 12153); (630, 1446, 12153).

Taking the number of classified data samples into account helps us to convey the importance of the correlation, and also the features present in the correlation to the final dataset. Because rule $R1$ performs better that rule $R2$ in terms of the number of classified samples, we conclude that the features present in this rule and their correlations must appear more in the correlation dataset than the features present in rule $R2$. We follow the same procedure for all of the rules in the final rule set.

MINING FREQUENT PATTERNS IN THE CORRELATION DATASET

After creating a correlation dataset that contains strong correlations between genes, it is time to take the last step and extract the most important genes from the dataset. In order to extract the **frequent patterns**, we use the Apriori algorithm Agrawal & Srikant (1994) to find the maximal frequent sets. Section explains how we find the final list of rules using the Apriori algorithm. Section provides suggestions for determining the value of support, which is one of the key parameters in the process.

Forming the Final List of Features

We use the Apriori algorithm in order to discover **frequent patterns** in the correlation dataset. Using Apriori algorithm requires setting two initial parameters, Support and Confidence. We don't care about the confidence because our purpose is discovering the **frequent patterns**, and we don't want to generate association rules; the confidence parameter is set to 0 for all experiments. Assuming the value ε as the support for the frequent itemsets, we extract all maximal frequent itemsets. Assuming we have N maximal frequent itemsets, the final list of genes is obtained using Equation 3.

$$FeatureSet = \bigcup_{i=1}^{N} \{MaximalSet_i \mid Size(MaximalSet_i) > 1\}$$

(3)

Final, the feature set is the union of all frequent itemsets extracted by the Apriori algorithm of length greater than one with respect to the value of support. We discard frequent sets of length less than two because we believe that frequency of individual features in rules should not be the only important factor, particularly for the case of gene selection. Any frequent itemset with size less that two does not indicate any correlation and the minimum accepted size that can indicate correlation between samples is two. The only concern is adjusting the value of support; one process is described in the next section.

Adjusting the Value of Support

Since we already reduced each rule to the shortest rule containing the minimal set of features that can represent its characteristics, we do not expect very high frequency for itemsets in the dataset. Furthermore, because we select frequent itemsets of length more that one, we need to select a small value for support that allows enough frequent itemsets to be selected. For most experiments, a value around 2% demonstrated to be a good selection. To better estimate the value of support, we can use two guidelines:

1. Using a user specified value based on the number of features we expect to select from the dataset: This value could be adjusted by domain experts in order to get the number of genes we expect from the dataset. Domain knowledge is not always available, and since the reason for gene selection is finding the least number of genes that can achieve a high **classification** rate, we decided not to use this approach. However, this approach could be used if the domain knowledge is available.

2. Selecting the value of support according to the ratio between the number of features in frequent itemsets larger than 1 and the number of all singleton frequent itemsets: Since we are only interested in maximal frequent itemsets of size greater than one, the value of support must be small enough to find useful existing correlations and in order not to miss some important correlations due to a very large value. On the other hand, it should be large enough in order not to accept infrequent itemsets. We observed that this balance is achieved when the number of features in the union of maximal itemsets

with length greater than one is equal to the number of frequent singleton itemsets. Since equal number of features in the two mentioned sets is not possible in all cases, we select the value of support that leads to the best balanced result in terms of the number of features in the two sides. When the support value is too small, the number of features that appear in maximal frequent itemsets of length greater than 2 is considerably greater than the number of singleton frequent itemsets. On the other hand, when the value of support is too large, the number of singleton frequent itemsets is considerably more that the number of features that appear in correlations. Therefore, a balance between these two numbers leading to close number of features in the two sets is the best choice.

Generally, these two guidelines could be used. Along with these two methods, the lower and upper bounds of the support could be derived easily using the statistics of the correlation dataset. In Section, we will elaborate more on the statistics, and we will discuss how we can use them in order to derive lower and upper bounds for the support. For instance, lower and upper bounds of the support for the **Leukemia** dataset are 0.3% and 2.8%, respectively.

EXPERIMENTAL RESULTS

In this section, first we describe the **Gene ontology** and datasets used in evaluating the proposed approach, then for each dataset, we provide some statistics about the generated correlation dataset, and we report the extracted genes. We used a simple classifier in order to classify the datasets because we believe that gene reduction reduces the complexity dramatically, even a simple classifier must be able to classify the samples. At the end of this section, we use features reported in similar previous works and use the same classifier to compare the accuracy of our approach with other approaches used for this purpose.

Gene Ontology

Gene ontology is one of the most important ontologies build within functional bioinformatics field developed by the GO consortium **gene ontology** consortium (2000). The goal of the GO is to provide a structured, controlled vocabulary to describe gene function and the process in which the genes are involved. GO has a hierarchical structure as a directed acyclic graph, where general terms are at the top, closer to the root, and more specific terms are closer to the leaves. **Gene ontology** has three categories. Biological process which refers to a biological object to which the gene contributes. Those biological objects can be a chemical or a physical transformation in the sense that something goes in and something comes out as a product. An example of biological process is cell cycle and signal transduction. The second category of GO is Molecular function. It is defined as the biochemical activity of the gene product. A general function is enzyme or transcription factor. A narrower function is kinase, which are the enzymes which add phosphate group to its targets. The third GO is the cellular component. It refers to the location in the cell in which the gene product is active.

In GO, terms are represented as nodes which are connected by two kind of relationships; the "is a" relationship and the "is part of" relationship.

The first type is defined when a child class is a subclass of a parent class. For example, "viral infection cycle" is a child of "viral life cycle". The second type is used when a parent has a child as its part. For example, "regulation of viral life infection" is part of "viral life cycle". GO annotations are very important for data analysis and biological interpretations. GO has many applications to functional genomics. Noor Speer *et al* et al (2005) has used GO to validate the gene clusters biologically.

Biological Datasets

Three biological datasets have been used in the experiments. The datasets are taken from [http://sdmc.lit.org.sg/GEDatasets/Datasets.html] (2007); the training and test sets are provided for all of them. First, we used the provided training set in order to extract useful genes and then we used the test set for the final evaluation. These three datasets are **Leukemia**, Lung and Prostate **cancer** datasets. Table 2 summarizes the characteristics of these datasets.

Gene Extraction

In this section, we explain how we applied our approach to extract significant features from each of the biological datasets. In order to achieve more reliability, we have repeated the algorithm a number of times for all the datasets. The experiments are repeated 10 times for Lung and Prostate datasets and 5 times for the **Leukemia**

Table 2. Gene expression datasets used for experiments

Dataset	Number of Genes	Number of Classes	Number of Training	Number of Test
ALL-AML Leukemia	7129	2: ALL/AML	38 (27 / 11)	34
Lung Cancer	12533	2: MPM/ADCA	32 (16 / 16)	149
Prostate Cancer	12600	2: tumor/normal	102 (52 / 50)	34
Colon Cancer	2000	2:tumor/normal	35(23/12)	30
Nervous System	7129	2: class0/class1	32(20/12)	28

dataset. Lung and Prostate datasets have considerably more genes than the **Leukemia** dataset, and because of the randomness effect included in the process as explained earlier, more experiments are required for these datasets in order to report more reliable genes.

Deriving the correlation dataset for each biological dataset. For each dataset, first the correlation dataset is extracted, and then the final set of genes is selected using the **frequent pattern** mining process. Tables 3, 4 and 5 summarize the statistics obtained after the first phase of the algorithm about correlation datasets. These statistics highlight the usefulness of the rule creation phase in creating rules. Statistics show that strong correlations between genes have appeared more frequent than the other correlations.

Next, we elaborate more on the different parameters reported in the three tables. Number of lines is the number of feature sequences added to the correlation dataset. Because more important sequences are repeated in the dataset, number of lines is generally more than the number of distinct lines in the correlation dataset. The difference between these two numbers indicates the generalization that the final rule set achieves, and means even our rules are started from specific data samples; after feature reduction, they become more general and can classify other similar samples as well. It is important to note that the final rule set is only created for the purpose of feature reduction, and creating the correlation dataset in our approach; this does not mean that the final rule set is the smallest possible rule set that could be used for the purpose of **classification**. We decided to leave as future work the process of creating a rule based fuzzy classifier by taking the same approach.

Total number of genes shows the feature reduction power of the first phase. For the **Leukemia** dataset, we started from 7129 genes, and

Table 3. Statistics of the Leukemia correlation dataset

Parameter	R1	R2	R3	R4	R5	Average
Number of lines(P1)	279	279	279	279	279	279
Number of distinct lines(P2)	210	216	211	220	225	216.4
Total number of genes appeared(P3)	374	390	375	372	392	380.6
Average line length(P4)	3.16	3	3.04	2.91	2.96	3.01
Number of binary correlations(P5)	1401	1203	1328	1138	1239	1261.8
Maximum repetition of a binary correlation(P6)	8	10	7	7	9	8.2
Number of correlations appeared only once(P7)	423	409	386	397	471	417.2

Table 4. Statistics for the Lung correlation dataset

Parameter	R1	R2	R3	R4	R5	R6	R7	R8	R9	R10	Average
P1	276	276	276	276	276	276	276	276	276	276	276
P2	211	200	199	194	201	202	204	190	203	193	199.7
P3	334	333	353	341	352	361	377	315	387	343	349.6
P4	2.77	2.88	2.93	2.93	2.88	2.91	2.93	2.85	2.96	3.07	2.91
P5	984	1145	1127	1124	1071	1093	1110	1067	1124	1274	111.9
P6	10	8	9	14	7	13	7	7	11	12	9.8
P7	322	278	290	309	369	399	375	271	380	292	328.5

Table 5. Statistics for the Prostate correlation dataset

Parameter	R1	R2	R3	R4	R5	R6	R7	R8	R9	R10	Average
P1	759	760	760	758	759	760	758	759	761	760	759
P2	443	448	464	469	462	460	454	469	460	467	459.6
P3	1200	1215	1281	1296	1293	1231	1230	1299	1264	1276	1258
P4	5.52	5.63	5.32	5.41	5.44	5.55	5.59	5.41	5.5	5.51	5.48
P5	12976	13915	11643	12225	12678	13247	13628	12291	12957	12944	12850
P6	23	17	21	16	17	20	20	15	21	16	18.6
P7	1682	1770	2001	1987	1808	1886	1845	1963	1983	2108	1903.3

after the first phase most of the redundant and unnecessary genes are removed; the number of genes is reduced to 380 genes on average for the **Leukemia** dataset. Average Line length shows the average reduction power of our Reduce function. The sequence length is 3.01 on average, which means each rule can maintain its classifier power and characteristics with this number of genes, and other genes are unnecessary for it. Number of binary correlations, which is the number of times a pair of features from the total remaining features has appeared together in the correlation dataset is 1401. Compared to the total number of possible combinations from the remaining genes (C(374,2) = 69751), this number is rather small and means the correlation matrix derived from the correlation dataset is a sparse matrix containing only strong correlations between genes.

Maximum repetition of binary correlations is the maximum number of times that two possible genes have appeared together in correlations. This number is 8.2 on average, and could be used, as explained earlier, as a guideline in order to adjust the value of support. Simply maximum support for the correlation dataset derived form the **Leukemia** dataset could be the maximum appearance over the number of lines, while the minimum support value is one over the total number of lines. Number of correlations appearing only once could be an indicator of the randomness attribute of the algorithm since a correlation that has appeared only once in the dataset is not definitely of great importance. Finally, the statistical interpretations for the other two datasets are similar to what we have done for the **Leukemia** dataset.

It is obvious from the statistics that the Prostate dataset is more complex that the other datasets. As we will see in the comparison, the number of features resulted from the algorithm presented in Fu & Youn (2003), (29) is considerably more that the number of features extracted from other datasets, which approves this fact.

Table 6. Results of running the Apriori algorithm and feature extraction on correlation dataset for Leukemia cancer

Experiment	Features
R1	6201-5688-1882-4342-5290-2592-4377-5552-758-4569-6224-1054- 2150-4237-4825-5163-5211
R2	5688-758-5290-6201-4342-1882-4680-5599-6277-2592-2830
R3	5688-5290-6201-758-1882-4342-6200
R4	5688-5290-4680-758-6201-5808-4342-2592-6277-3646-7001-5367-5712
R5	5688-5290-2642-6201-6606-2349-4342-4680-6277-5808-630-2592-5449-671-4409-4110-6806

Figure 2. Most frequent genes from Leukemia that appear in half or more of the results

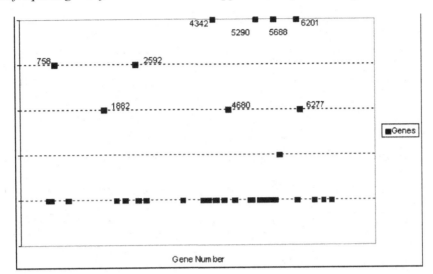

Gene Extraction. The final step is to extract genes which are repeated in most experiments from the correlation dataset. First, the lower and upper bounds of support were calculated for each correlation dataset using the statistics, and then genes were selected. Table 6 and Figure 2 demonstrate features extracted from the **Leukemia** dataset and the process of picking features that appear in most results as important features. Numbers that appear at the head of each sequence are gene numbers that had existed in more frequent item sets. Genes highlighted in bold font are frequent genes that have appeared in the results from most experiments (half or more of the experiments).

Tables 7 and 8 and Figures 2 and 3 report the genes extracted from each experiment as well as most frequent genes that appear in the results for Lung and Prostate **cancer** datasets, respectively.

In order to measure the **classification** power of our approach, we compare our results with the r-GeneSelect approach that uses SVM for gene

Table 7. Results of running the Apriori algorithm and feature extraction on correlation dataset for Lung cancer

Experiment	Features
R1	2378-630-8005-1464-3490-2549-3383-6571-7200-11485-7046-708-6658-7410-8697-8838 \par
R2	1464-630-4119-2378-4335-7059-7046
R3	1464-630-12153-7891-12200-1271-7046-3433-1401-6961-10643
R4	8005-630-1464-3389-4335-7444-7046-10619-2378-7765-7200-12114-4874-7048-8638-12153-522-2568-8886
R5	630-1464-4119-8005-12153-7046-7059-7200-3490-1246-7646-11857-12200-2378-8843-3916-3383-7605-11616-12198
R6	4335-630-7046-1464-6139-4119-8005-12153
R7	8005-630-3764-10619-7765-7046-2378-11245-3383-1271-1464-4243-8638-7444
R8	8005-630-1464-12153-7765-7059-12152-7046-3433-10458-5383-7048-7748
R9	3490-630-8005-4335-1464-3764-5853-2378-8638-7200-3433-12186-4119-5383-4243
R10	400-7046-7200-630-8005-1464-11507-7646-3508-12114-8180-10977

Table 8. Results of running the Apriori algorithm and feature extraction on correlation dataset for Prostate cancer

Experiment	Features
R1	6185-10996-6390-8878-9354-3417-6930-8850-9172-7826-288-5757-8058-2182-3879-5288
R2	10494-3417-10996-6185-6930-4208-288-8878-9354-8741-6390-6866-2182-8058-742-7905-11052-12185-7071
R3	6930-10996-3417-8878-9354-3879-9850-288-10494-2182-4208-375-4831-2046-4920
R4	10996-6185-9354-3417-6930-288-2182-10494-4208-8527-6866-11216-8850-9172-6390-11052-10833
R5	6185-9354-3417-10494-8878-6866-8527-2182-10241-348
R6	6930-9354-10996-3417-10494-2182-8527-8850-8878-8741-4690-6185-6866-6390-10837-12414-299-10550-12185-1032
R7	6930-3417-9354-6185-8741-10996-2182-10494-8878-8850-5288-8527-4365-6390-5757-12495-5923-12067-5909-4208
R8	3417-10996-8878-6185-9354-288-8850-2182-10494-6930-4365-6390-3879-9172-2791-9850-4920-3474-8123
R9	6185-6930-9354-3417-10996-8850-9850-8878-2182
R10	9354-6185-3417-6930-8878-10494-5909-6390

Figure 3. Most frequent genes from Lung that appear in half or more of the results

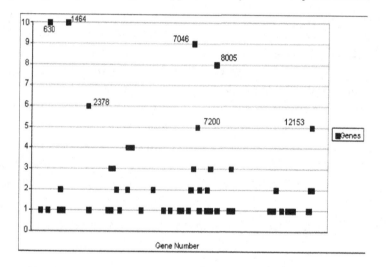

selection. To see which method achieves more general features, regardless of the approach used to extract genes, we use a third **classification** method based on feed forward back propagation network. Since the number of genes selected from the dataset decreases considerably and the number of data samples is small for all the datasets, a rather simple structure for the network must be able to achieve high **classification** rate. The network we used for **classification** has two middle layers each with two nodes and a single output layer. The transform function used in the middle layers is Tangent Sigmoid function, and since the problem is a binary **classification** problem, the output layer uses the Log Sigmoid function. We run the r-GeneSelect algorithm on all the three datasets and extracted the genes. Table 9 shows the comparison between the effectiveness of the two approaches.

Table 9. Comparison between our approach based on correlations between genes and the r-GeneSelect algorithm

Dataset	Approach	Number of Genes	Accuracy	Genes in Common
Leukemia	r-GeneSelect	5	88.23%	2
	Correlation	9	97.05%	
Lung	r-GeneSelect	9	99.3%	2
	Correlation	7	97.98%	
Prostate	r-GeneSelect	29	97.05%	0
	Correlation	11	97.05%	

Classification Results and Comparison

Accuracy of the two approaches is the same for the Prostate **cancer** dataset, however we achieve the same accuracy with only 11 features compared to the 29 features used by r-GeneSelect. For the **Leukemia** dataset, although r-GeneSelect achieves 97.05% accuracy using a specific implementation of SVM, **classification** using the described network does not achieve any accuracy better than 88.23% and our reported features seem to be more reliable than the features reported in the previous work. However, on the lung **cancer** dataset, the r-GeneSelect approach achieves a slightly better accuracy than our approach.

Extracted genes from the Prostate dataset are totally different using two different approaches, and it is probably due to the complexity of this dataset that two different approaches extract totally different genes. Genes numbered 1882 and 6201 are in common between the two approaches for the **Leukemia** dataset and also genes number 630 and 7200 are in common between the two approaches for the Lung **cancer** dataset. Biologists might find these features that are reported by both approaches and also other reported genes from our approach of great importance. This is highlighted further in the next section. We have also compared the efficiency of our algorithm with r-GeneSelect when we used t-test and SVD-entropy as initial filters. We have used **Support vector machine** and Neural Networks as **classification** tools. Table 10 and table 11 show the accuracy and reliability of our approach.

Biological Significance of the Extracted Genes

In this section, we focus on the biological Significance of the genes we have selected. We compare the results reported by the proposed method with the genes discovered by other methods described in the literature.

Leukemia Data

For the **Leukemia** dataset, our approach discovered nine genes, namely L33930, D88270, Y00787, X59871, L00058, U02020, X82240, M30703 and M27891, which have strong correlation with Lymphoma **cancer**. Gene L33930 is CD24 signal transducer; it codes for sialoglycoprotein that is expressed in B cells; CD24 regulates E-cadherin, which demonstrated to play a major role in cell-to-cell interaction and TGF-beta3 expression. Further, CD24 mediates apoptosis in precursore-B acute lymphoblastic **Leukemia** cell lines in the pro-B and pre-B stages accompanying activation of multiple caspases. Also, it is shown that CD24 expression is associated with breast and ovarian **cancer**.

Gene D88270 is Immunoglobin lambda gene; it encodes a protein with similarity to Human

Table 10. Comparison between our approach based on correlations between genes and the r-GeneSelect algorithm using t-test as gene filter. NN: Neural Networks, SVM: Support vector machine

Dataset	Approach	Most Reliable genes	NN Accuracy	SVM Accuracy	Reliability
Leukemia	r-GeneSelect	3847; 6539; 3320; 5039; 1779; 4196; 461; 1834	97.05%	85%	39.37%
	Correlation	3605; 1745; 1882; 2288; 6539; 6201; 1674; 3320; 6376; 2020	97.05%	91.7%	68.75%
Colon	r-GeneSelect	765;1094; 1993; 627; 1347; 1560; 47; 1325; 1772;493; 1985; 548; 1495; 527	83.3%	66.6%	44.65%
	Correlation	765; 15; 1094; 1993; 1668; 625; 1346; 249; 1423; 47; 1772; 26; 464; 1042; 377;548; 527	86.66%	70%	57.14%
Nervous System	r-GeneSelect	1352; 6164; 5061; 844; 4078; 2671; 3092;5073; 6252; 5653; 3389; 1715; 765; 3991; 1890; 2695; 5112; 3759; 61; 1877; 6425	80%	64%	35.77%
	Correlation	1352; 3991; 4971; 1698; 2695; 3759; 1847; 677; 3813; 1877; 2671; 4482;4415; 1715; 3977; 3645; 3120	80%	36%	63.57%

topisomerase (DNA) III beta, which is thought to relax supercoiled DNA upon replication and cell division. Moreover, this gene transduces signals for cell proliferation, differentiation from the pro-B cell to pre-B cell stage. Moreover, U02020, which is a pre-B-cell colony enhancing factor 1, is shown to be significant gene. This gene is upregulated in neutrophils by IL-1beta, and functions as a novel inhibitor of apoptosis in response to a variety of inflammatory stimuli. This gene is more expressed in ALL patients. X82240 has been identified by our method as significant gene. This gene is T-cell **Leukemia**/lymphoma 1 A(TCL1A). Increased TCL1 expression correlates with PBC-ALL progression. TCL1 expression is important for the maturation of precursor lymphocytes. It has also shown to be a proto-oncogene in some **cancer**s. This gene was overexpressed in ALL patients. These four genes are shown to be more expressed in acute lymphoblastic **Leukemia** (ALL) patients. However, the rest of our genes are more expressed in acute myeloid **Leukemia** (AML) patients.

Our fifth gene Y00787 encodes Interleukin-8, which is one of the mediators of the inflammatory response. Secretion levels of IL-8 and TNF-alpha are elevated in activated T-cells in large granual lymphocytic **Leukemia** associated with autoimmune disorders. IL-8 gene transcription is induced by p38 and NF-kB, which has shown to play role in different **cancer**s through degradation of IkB. Gene X59871 is a transcription factor 7 (T-cell factor1) involved in WNT signaling pathway. It does not only regulate T-cell development, but also peripheral T-cell differentiation. In addition, our method discovered an important gene, namely L00058. This gene encodes a multifunctional protein that plays a role in cell cycle progression, apoptosis. Mutations, overexpression, rearrangement and translocation of this gene have been associated with a variety of hematopietic tumors, **Leukemia**s and lumphomas. M30703 is another gene we discovered. This gene is amphiregulin (AREG), and it is a member of epidermal growth factor family. AREG gene expressed by purified primary myeloma cells. AREG plays an important role in biology of multiple myeloma. Finally, gene M27891 encodes a protein, which belongs to the cystatin superfamily; some members of those proteins are cysteine protease inhibitors.

Table 11. Comparison between our approach based on correlations between genes and the r-GeneSelect algorithm using SVD-Entropy as gene filter. NN: Neural Networks, SVM: Support vector machine

Dataset	Approach	Most Reliable genes	NN Accuracy	SVM Accuracy	Reliability
Leukemia	r-GeneSelect	3847- 6539- 3320- 5039- 1779- 4196- 461- 1834	97.05%	85%	39.37%
	Correlation	6766- 6201-1882- 6884- 6411- 5225- 2345- 5300-6200-2402- 2566- 5967- 6277-1779- 39	? %	94%	? %
Colon	r-GeneSelect	765- 1094- 1993- 627- 1347- 1560- 47- 1325- 1772-493- 1985- 548- 1495-527	83.3%	66.6%	44.65%
	Correlation	1967- 1714- 1387- 260- 1644- 1683- 1828-1272- 878- 1930- 1384- 493- 617- 1810-1967- 661	?%	93.3%	?%
Nervous System	r-GeneSelect	1352- 6164- 5061- 844- 4078- 2671- 3092-5073- 6252- 5653- 3389- 1715- 765- 3991- 1890- 2695- 5112- 3759- 61- 1877- 6425	80%	64%	35.77%
	Correlation	1322- 52- 549- 2965- 2656- 4068- 4701- 2377- 3704- 4622- 1054- 4892- 5002	?%	40%	?%

As a result, it can be easily seen that almost all of our genes play role in B and T cells proliferation and lymphocyte cells differentiation, besides their role in **cancer** and cell cycle regulation. Also, we see that the functions of our genes are related. For example, L33930 and X59871 are coregulated genes. Wnt genes encode for a large family of secreted Wnt proteins that act as extracellular signaling factors. Wnt genes function in several cellular activities such as cell fate determination, patterning, and migration in embryogenesis, apoptosis, etc. Beta-catenin is an intermediate at the center of the Wnt signaling pathway; it is located at the cytoplasmic domain of cadherin receptors, which determines cellular and tissue morphogenesis and regulate major processes likegrowth and differentiation. Another point is that CD24 and Immunoglobin lambda, and X59871 genes play role in pro-B to pre-B cell stage.

When we looked at the genes that were discovered by the other methods, they have discovered M19507, M27891, Y00787, M96326, and L20688. They claim that those genes are the most significant genes to distinguish between AML and ALL. When we looked into the functions of the genes they have discovered, we see that the function of the most significant gene they discovered (M19507) is Myeloperoxidase (MPO). MPO is a heme protein synthesized during myeloid differentiation. Although this protein is working in cell differentiation, there is no relation between MPO and cell cycle regulation. Both M27891 and Y00787 are in common with our genes. Although the former gene is kind of unrelated to **cancer**, the second one plays a role in inflammatory response.

M96326 and L20688 are Azurocidn and GDP, respectively. The former gene encodes an azurophil granule antibiotic protein, and the later has weak relation to **cancer**. Their method has considered FTH1 (L20941) as significant gene. This gene encodes the heavy subunit of ferritin, the major intracellular iron storage protein in prokaryotes and eukaryotes. A major function of ferritin is the storage of iron in a soluble and nontoxic state. Defects in ferritin proteins are associated with several neurodegenerative diseases. They reported Proteoglycan 1 gene was discovered as significant gene; however, there is no relation to cell cycle regulation. They also have discovered several genes like Enolase alpha and EIF4E. These genes showed to play role in cell cycle, but no specific study showed their role in Lymphocyte differentiation. In conclusion, we have seen that the genes we have discovered have strong relation to pre-B to Pro-B stage development, and we have seen that many studies showed the role of our genes in **Leukemia** as specific **cancer** and **cancer** in general. Some of the genes discovered by others were unrelated to **cancer** such Azurocidn and Cystatin. Some of them were related to **cancer**, but not related to **Leukemia** or lymphocyte development. Another point is that they have given the same weight for ENO1, EIF4E and FTH1. The former two have high expression in AML patients, but the later has a weak **ALL/AML** expression; we argue that their methods have to distinguish between such genes.

Lung Cancer

Related to the Lung **cancer** dataset, we have discovered 6 genes as significant. The most significant ones are M29540 and L08044. The former is carcinoembryonic antigen-related cell adhesion molecule 5 (CEACAM6); CEACAM6 expression is elevated in many solid tumors and may be a promising target for antibody-based therapy for **cancer**. There is a value of this tumor marker regarding relapse, metastasis and death in resectable non-small cell lung **cancer**. The latter gene is Human intestinal trefoil factor mRNA(TFF3). Results indicate that TFF3 is able to induce ciliogenesis and to promote airway epithelial ciliated cell differentiation, in part through an epidermal growth factor receptor-dependent pathway. Decreased expression of TFF3 mRNA is a marker of follicular thyroid carcinomas, especially those with a high risk of invasion or metastasis.

Another gene is Calbindin (calretinin); it is an intracellular calcium-binding protein belonging to the troponin C superfamily. E-cadherin and calretinin are sensitive and specific in differential

diagnosis of benign and malignant serous e□usion specimens. Calbindin is a tumor marker for cardiac myxoma. X16662 is another gene discovered by our method. This gene encodes a member of the annexin family of evolutionarily conserved Ca2+ and phospholipid binding proteins. Overexpression of this gene has been associated with acute myelocytic **Leukemia**. Annexin A8 is involved in mouse mammary gland involution and progression of human breast **cancer**. We also discovered J02761, which is Human pulmonary surfactant-associated protein B(SP-B). Examination of different immunohistochemical marker SP-B is helpful in the diagnosis and differential diagnosis of pulmonary sclerosing hemangioma. Our last reported gene is M22430 HUMRASFAB Human RASF-A PLA2 mRNA (PLA2G2A). The activity of PLA2G2A may suppress progression or metastasis of human gastric **cancer**. We see that all our genes are related to **cancer**, cell cycle and metastasis. The first two genes we have shown a very strong relation to lung **cancer**.

Other studies have shown that Calbindin and CEACAM6 are important for class prediction. They have also discovered genes like: Ig alpha 2=immunoglobulin A heavy chain allotype 2, Human complement factor B mRNA, which has weak relation to **cancer**. They have also found HUMLIC. This gene encodes a member of the annexin family. Members of this calcium-dependent phospholipid-binding protein family play role in the regulation of cellular growth and in signal transduction pathways. HUMGA7A08 is another gene discovered by their method. This 9-exon gene encodes a carcinoma-associated antigen; it is a member of a family that includes at least two type-I membrane proteins. This antigen is expressed on most normal epithelial cells and gastrointestinal carcinomas and functions as a homotypic calcium-independent cell adhesion molecule. The antigen is being used as a target for immunotherapy treatment of human carcinomas. Another gene is X77956: H.sapiens Id1 mRNA. The protein encoded by this gene is a helix-loop-helix (HLH) protein that can form heterodimers with members of the basic HLH family of transcription factors.

As a result, we can see that the genes we have discovered are important and have been shown to play role in **cancer**. However, not all the genes discovered by the others have showed Significance relation to the cell cycle. At the end, it is worth mentioning that all this information was obtained from the National Center for Biotechnology Information.

Prostate Cancer

We identified 10 significant genes in the prostate **cancer** data. We studied the biological function of these genes, and realized that there is high correlation between them and prostate **cancer**. In here, we will describe the function of the genes and see how their function is related to prostate **cancer**. AF038451, which is anterior gradient homolog 2(AGR2), is selected as marker gene. This gene showed to serve as a potential therapeutic target and a molecular marker for prostate **cancer**.

AF014794 is tumor necrosis factor receptor superfamily. This receptor contains an extracellular TRAIL-binding domain. It functions as an antagonistic receptor that protects cells from TRAIL-induced apoptosis. This gene was found to be a p53-regulated DNA damage-induced gene. In addition, the expression of this gene was detected in many normal, but not **cancer** tissues, this reflects what we saw in the profile of this gene in our data. Besides this, we have discovered X07732. This gene codes for Hepsin, which is a cell surface serine protease. Hepsin is functionally linked to hepatocyte growth factor/MET pathway, which contribute to prostate **cancer**. It is shown that a major 11-locus haplotype is significantly associated with prostate **cancer**, which provides further support that Hepsin is a potentially important candidate gene involved in prostate **cancer** susceptibility. Moreover, D83018 is gene that encodes a cytoplasmic protein that contains epi-

dermal growth factor-like repeats. This protein may be involved in cell growth regulation and differentiation. Further, we discovered AF061258, which is PDLIM5. The protein encoded by this gene is a LIM domain protein. LIM domains are cysteine-rich double zinc fingers that are involved in protein-protein interaction. Another important gene is M99487. It is a folate hydrolase, which is a prostate-specific membrane antigen. In prostate, this protein is up-regulated in **cancer**ous cells; it is used as an effective diagnostic and prognostic indicator of prostate **cancer**.

As a result of the above analysis, we can state that it is clear that almost all of the genes are prostate specific and it has been shown that they are correlated to prostate **cancer**.

Biological Interpretation of Extracted Genes Using Gene ontology Annotations

In this section we analyzed the GO terms associated with the genes extracted from **Leukemia**, colon, and nervous system data when we used t-test and SVD-entropy as initial gene filters.

Leukemia Data

In this section we have studied the GO annotations of the discovered genes by our algorithm, using t-test as initial gene filter, and r-gene using [www.geneontology.org]. We have seen that our genes participate in different processes and play different functions within the cell. Our genes are related to different GO terms which indicate that they cover many processes within the cell. Cell to cell communication is a well studied aspect in **cancer** . Three of our genes, CST3, IL8 and ITGAX, were related to cell adhesion term from three different angles. CST3(cystatin 3) showed to play role in cell migration. Decrease of cystatin C in the CSF might contribute in the process of metastasis and spread of the **cancer** cells in the leptomeningeal tissues. Cysteine was also related to protease inhibitor activity. IL8 showed to play role in negative regulation of cell proliferation by cell cycle arresting; beside, it play a role in inflammatory response. The third gene, ITGAX, showed to be related to integrin-mediated signaling pathway. Another gene we have discovered which play in inflammatory response is MGLL. This contribute to lipid metabolic process as well. The other genes we have discovered are LYN, involved in positive regulation of cell proliferation and protein-tyrosin kinase activity, CFD, involved in serine-type endopeptidase activity, STOM, involved in protein homooligomer biosynthetic process. In addition to that, we have discovered FTL, which is iron ion transport process related, LTC4s which is related to fatty acid leukotriene biosynthesis, and FAH, which is involved in the aromatic amino acid metabolic process. When we look at the genes discovered by R-gene, we see that we have two common genes, STOM and LTC4S. We also have similarities in GO annotations for some genes like SRGN which play a role in proteolysis, IL18 and CD33 which play role in cell adhesion regulation and negative regulation of cell proliferation. R-gene has discovered genes related to transcription factor activity, HOXA9, and hydrolase activity, LEPROT; and MPO which contributes to defense response. Our algorithm has discovered two genes, namely, CST3 (M27891) and IL8 (Y00787). Those gene were among the three genes (M27891, Y00787, X51521) which been used by Fan and Yang Li & Yang (2005) to get 100% **classification** accuracy. Those genes were also discovered by Golub et al et al (1999)

When we used SVD entropy we got different genes which are still related to cell cycle. We have extracted 10 genes. Three of them, Interleukin 8 precursor, interleukin 8 and CST3, were discovered as a significant when we used t-test as a filtering technique. The other genes, ALAS2, HBG2, MEF2C, were related to oxygen transportation, oxygen binding, erythrocyte differentiation and vessel development. The other genes were related to immune response, cell adhesion, and

anti-apoptosis. As a result we see that all of the discovered genes are related to **Leukemia** and they can be candidates to distinguish between two **Leukemia** types.

Colon Data

In this data we have identified a set of 17 genes which are able to classify colon **cancer** with 86% accuracy using t-test as initial filter. Through the study of the GO annotations of the discovered genes, we have seen that they are related to different GO terms, such zinc ion binding, signal transduction, cell cycle and RNA splicing. CSRP1 and GTF3A were related to zinc ion binding, but the later was also related to transcription from RNA polymerase III promoter. Our method has identified GRM1 and GRM2 which are related to G-protein coupled receptor protein signaling pathway. Moreover, we have identified three genes which are related to translation term. RPS9 has shown to play role in rRNA binding. RPL30 and C15irf15 play role in ribosome biosynthesis. Other important genes are PCNP which is related to cell cycle and protein ubiquitination, and HNRNPA1 which assist in RNA splicing and mRNA transport. The other genes we have discovered are LIPE, involved in lipid catabolic process and DES,involved in cytoskeleton organization, and MYL9,involved in regulation of muscle contration. We have CSRP1, LIPE, MEP50, WAS, and GRM1 in common with r-gene. The other genes discovered by r-gene are related to eye pigment biosynthesis, erythrocyte differentiation, and metal ion binding. Other terms were vesicle-mediated transport and translation. When we analyzed the significant genes using SVD-entropy as a filter, we observed that we have two genes which play a role in mRNA catabolic process. The first is AUH which plays a role in 3'-UTR binding. This process affects the stability of mRNA. The other gene is ZFP36 which showed to play a role in mRNA destabilizing by shortening polyA tail. This may affect the transport of mRNA to be translated as poly-A has a role in transporting mRNA from the nucleus to the cytoplasm. We have also discovered BST2 which contributes to cell proliferation and cell-cell signaling. Other genes, PCK1,IGHG3, which play a role in lipid metabolism and immune process, respectively. Another important gene is REG1A. It is a pancreatic thread protein act as a positive regulator of cell proliferation. REG expression was reported to be an independent predictor of overall gastric adenocarcinoma patient survival. REGI alpha protein may play a role in the development of gastric **cancer**s.

Nervous System Data

Through GO annotation analysis of the genes we discovered from this data, we observed that we got very specific terms related to cell cycle and cell division. HMGA1, which is involved in DNA unwinding during replication and nucleosome assembly, has shown to be an interesting gene according to our method. Nucleosome assembly is a hot subject to study change in **gene expression** and transcription and that showed to play a role in **cancer**. We also have discovered two important genes which play vital role in cell division. ABL1 showed to be related to S-phase-specific transcription in mitotic cell cycle, mismatch repair and actin cytoskeleton organization. The other gene is MRE11A, which involve in telomere maintenance via telomerase and regulation of mitotic recombination. Two genes we have discovered were related to G-protein mediated signal transduction. ARHGAP19 which is related to GTPase activator activity and OXTR, which is related to IP3 second messenger. The other gene were related to general terms like lipid metabolic and transport, THRSP and SLCO2A1, signal transduction, TNFRSF11b, translation, RPS18, and RNA binding, KIAA0430. Moreover, we have discovered ALPL which is related to hydrolase activity, DHX38 that involves in mRNA splicing, NKX3,involves in mutlicellular organisma; development and IL1R1 which is important in

inflammatory response. When we analyzed the GO terms of the genes discovered by r-gene, we did not see any specific term. We saw that the genes are related to general terms like, cell division, cell adhesion, immune response and apoptosis. After the analysis of the genes discovered from the NS data using SVD-entropy as a filter, we have seen that most of the genes are related to **cancer** but not specific to nervous system **cancer**. Many of the genes like, CTGF, CEACAM7, TPBG, Catenin, and SHROOM2, were related to cell adhesion. Other genes discovered were related to lipid metabolism like, AKR1D1, and APOD. This indicates that there is important effect of the mechanism of the phospholipid membrane on developing **cancer**. This may affect the mechanism of the receptors attached to the membrane. Among the genes discovered, three were strongly related to nervous system. GAP43 shown to playa role in nervous system development and cell differentiation, SHROOM2 shown to contribute to brain development and cell migration, and v-myc which induces CRABP-II transcription directly in neuroblastoma. Moreover, we have PAM gene which is related to mitotic chromosome condensation and protein modification, and SS18 which contributes to tumor development through catenin signaling. Other genes related to proteolysis, microtubulebased movement, regulation of apoptosis and ion binding were discovered.

CONCLUSION AND FUTURE WORK

In this study, we have demonstrated the power of generating **fuzzy classifier rule**s and using them for identifying relevant genes. We first applied different feature reduction methods to get a compact set of representative features. The process involves creating **fuzzy classifier rule** set, and then deriving a correlation matrix between the genes appearing in the rules. The correlation matrix is the input to the apriori algorithm to find frequent itemsets, which lead to the relevant genes. The proposed approach reported high accuracy on Four datasets: **ALL/AML Leukemia**, Lung, Prostate, and colon **cancer**. Also, the genes identified from each of the three datsets are highly significant from biological perspective; the same may not be said regarding our competitors. GO terms were very related to cell cycle and **cancer**. Several studies stressed the role of our genes in **Leukemia** in particular and **cancer** in general. Currently, we are conducting experiments on other **gene expression** datasets and we are working on a comprehensive self-adaptive fuzzy classifier. Our target is to develop a more comprehensive approach capable of analyzing a wide range of datasets from different domains and with different characteristics.

REFERENCES

Aas, K. (2001). *Microarray data mining: A survey* (Tech. rep., NR Note). SAMBA, Norwegian Computing Center.

Abe, S., & Lan, M.-S. (1995). A method for fuzzy rules extraction directly from numerical data and its application to pattern classification. *IEEE transactions on Fuzzy Systems, 3*(1), 18–28. doi:10.1109/91.366565

Agrawal, R., & Srikant, R. (1994). Fast algorithms for mining association rule. In *Proceedings of the International Conference on Very Large Databases* (pp. 487-499).

Caruana, R., & Freitag, D. (1994). Greedy attribute selection. In *Proceedings of the International Conference on Machine Learning* (pp. 28-36).

Cordon, O., Gomide, F., Herrera, F., Hoffmann, F., & Magdalena, L. (2004). Ten years of genetic fuzzy systems: Current framework and new trends. *Fuzzy Sets and Systems, 141*, 5–31. doi:10.1016/S0165-0114(03)00111-8

Das, S. (2001). Filters, wrappers and a boosting-based hybrid for feature selection. In *Proceedings of the International Conference on Machine Learning* (pp. 74–81).

Dash, M., Choi, K., Scheuermann, P., & Liu, H. (2002). Feature selection for clustering-a filter solution. In *Proceedings of IEEE International Conference on Data Mining* (pp. 115-122).

Dy, J. G., & Brodley, C. E. (2000). Feature subset selection and order identification for unsupervised learning. In *Proceedings of the International Conference on Machine Learning* (pp. 247–254).

Fu, L. (2007). *Cancer subtype classification based on gene expression signatures*. Retrieved from http://www.cise.ufl.edu/$\sim$fu/NSF/cancer_classify_GES.html

Fu, L. M., & Youn, E. S. (2003). Improving reliability of gene selection from microarray functional genomics data. *IEEE Transactions on Information Technology in Biomedicine, 7*(3). doi:10.1109/TITB.2003.816558

Golub, T. (1999). Molecular classification of cancer: class discovery and class prediction by gene expression monitoring. *Science, 286*, 531–537. doi:10.1126/science.286.5439.531

Guyon, I., Weston, J., Barnhill, S., & Vapnik, V. (2002). Gene selection for cancer classification using support vector machines. *Machine Learning, 46*(13), 389–422. doi:10.1023/A:1012487302797

Hall, M. A. (2000). Correlation-based feature selection for discrete and numeric class machine learning. In *Proceedings of the International Conference on Machine Learning* (pp. 359-366).

http://sdmc.lit.org.sg/GEDatasets/Datasets.html

Ishibuchi, H., & Murata, T. (1999). Techniques and applications of genetic algorithms-based methods for designing compact fuzzy classification systems. *Fuzzy Theory Systems Techniques & Applications, 3*(40), 1081–1109. doi:10.1016/B978-012443870-5.50042-3

Ishibuchi, H., Nakashima, T., & Muratam, T. (1999). Performance evaluation of fuzzy classifier systems for multi-dimensional pattern classification problems. *IEEE Trans. on Systems, Man, and Cybernetics – Part B, 29*(5), 601–618.

Ishibuchi, H., Nozaki, K., & Tanaka, H. (1992). Distributed representation of fuzzy rules and its application to pattern classification. *Fuzzy Sets and Systems, 52*(1), 21–32. doi:10.1016/0165-0114(92)90032-Y

Khabbaz, M., Kiamehr, K., Alshalalfa, M., & Alhajj, R. (2007). Fuzzy classifier based feature reduction for better gene selection. In *Proceedings of the International Conference on Data Warehouse and Knowledge Discovery* (LNCS). Regensburg, Germany: Springer-Verlag.

Kianmehr, K., Zhang, H., Nikolov, K., Ozyer, T., & Alhajj, R. (2005). Combining neural network and support vector machine into integrated approach for biodata mining. In *Proceedings of the International Conference on Enterprise Information Systems* (pp. 182–187). Miami, FL.

Li, F., & Yang, Y. (2005). Analysis of recursive gene selection approach from microarray data. *Bioinformatics (Oxford, England)*, 37–41.

Li, J., Ng, K.-S., & Wong, L. (2003). Bioinformatics adventures in database research. In *Proceedings of the International Conference on Database Theory* (pp. 31–46). Siena, Italy.

Mitra, S., & Pal, S. K. (1994). Self-organizing neural network as a fuzzy classifier. *IEEE Transactions on Systems, Man, and Cybernetics, 24*(3), 385–399. doi:10.1109/21.278989

Ng, A. Y. (1998). On feature selection: Learning with exponentially many irrelevant features as training examples. In *Proceedings of the International Conference on Machine Learning* (pp. 404–412).

Piatetsky-Shapiro, G., & Tamayo, P. (2003). Microarray data mining: facing the challenges. *SIGKDD Explorations, 5*, 2–5. doi:10.1145/980972.980974

Speer, N., et al. (2005). Functional grouping of genes using spectral clustering and gene ontology. In *Proceedings of the IEEE International Joint Conference on Neural Networks*.

The Gene Ontology Consortium. (2000). Gene ontology: tool for the unification of biology. *Nature Genetics, 25*, 25. doi:10.1038/75556

Vapnik, V. N. (1998). *Statistical Learning Theory*. New York: John Wiley.

Varshavsky, R. (2006). Novel unsupervised feature filtering of biological data. *Bioinformatics (Oxford, England)*, 507–513. doi:10.1093/bioinformatics/btl214

Wangm, L. X., & Mendel, J. M. (1992). Generating fuzzy rules by learning from examples. *IEEE Transactions on Systems, Man, and Cybernetics, 22*(6), 1414–1427. doi:10.1109/21.199466

Xing, E., Jordan, M., & Karp, R. (2001). Feature selection for high dimensional genomic microarray data. In *Proceedings of the International Conference on Machine Learning* (pp. 601–608).

Zeng, F., Yap, C. H. R., & Wong, L. (2002). Using feature generation and feature selection for accurate prediction of translation initiation sites. *Genome Informatics, 13*, 192–200.

This work was previously published in International Journal of Data Warehousing and Mining, Vol. 4, Issue 4, edited by D. Taniar, pp. 62-83, copyright 2008 by IGI Publishing (an imprint of IGI Global).

Chapter 10
Vertical Fragmentation in Databases Using Data–Mining Technique

Narasimhaiah Gorla
American University of Sharjah, UAE

Pang Wing Yan Betty
Hong Kong Polytechnic University, Hong Kong

ABSTRACT

A new approach to vertical fragmentation in relational databases is proposed using association rules, a data-mining technique. Vertical fragmentation can enhance the performance of database systems by reducing the number of disk accesses needed by transactions. By adapting Apriori algorithm, a design methodology for vertical partitioning is proposed. The heuristic methodology is tested using two real-life databases for various minimum support levels and minimum confidence levels. In the smaller database, the partitioning solution obtained matched the optimal solution using exhaustive enumeration. The application of our method on the larger database resulted in the partitioning solution that has an improvement of 41.05% over unpartitioned solution and took less than a second to produce the solution. We provide future research directions on extending the procedure to distributed and object-oriented database designs.

INTRODUCTION

Vertical fragmentation (or partitioning) is a physical database design technique that is aimed at improving the access performance of user transactions. In vertical partitioning, a relation is split into a set of smaller physical files, each with a subset of the attributes of the original rela-tion. The rationale is that database transactions normally require access only to subset of the attributes. Thus, if we can split the relation into sub files that closely match the requirements of user transactions, the access time for transactions reduces significantly.

The fragmentation problem is computation-ally complex. Consider a relational schema with

N relations, with A_i attributes for relation i. A relation with A attributes can be partitioned in B(A) different ways (Hammer & Niamir, 1979), where B(A) is the Ath Bell number (for A=30, B(A) $= 10^{15}$). Using exhaustive enumeration, the number of possible fragmentations for the N-relation schema is approximately $B(A_1)B(A_2)$ ... $B(A_N)$. Yu, Chen, Heiss, and Lee (1992) find out that the number of attributes for base tables and views in a typical relational environment are 18 and 41, respectively. Even if we consider a small schema of 10 relations with 15 attributes per relation, the number of possible fragments is approximately $(10^9)^{10} = 10^{90}$. Since the problem is intractable, solving large problems requires the use of heuristic techniques.

The objective of this research is to provide a general approach for vertically fragmenting a relation. Since the problem is computationally intractable, we use a heuristic procedure to solve the problem using association rules. Our approach is based on Apriori algorithm developed by Agarwal and Srikanth (1994). We believe that "association rules" provide a natural way to represent the linkage between attributes as implied by the database transactions, thus providing a convenient way of solving the problem. Though several authors have studied vertical partitioning problem in databases, there is no study that employed association rules approach. The objective of the research is to develop a methodology for attribute partitioning with the least database operating cost, given the characteristics of relations and database transactions. The application of our algorithm using standard database workload (Yu et al., 1992) on large database resulted in an improvement of 41% over unpartitioned solution. Our association rules-based algorithm took only a few second to produce the solution, since it is relatively less complex compared to other approaches. Furthermore, the application of our methodology on small problems yielded optimal solutions as obtained by exhaustive enumeration.

The organization of the article is as follows. Section 2 provides related research in database partitioning. Section 3 provides background on association rules. Section 4 has the methodology for vertical partitioning using association rules. Section 5 contains experiments using the proposed method employing two real life data sets for various support and confidence levels. Section 6 has discussion on effectiveness of the proposed method. Section 7 deals with discussion of results and section 8 contains future research directions.

RELATED WORK IN VERTICAL PARTITIONING

Because of the criticality of the database performance, several researchers have contributed enormously to vertical partitioning problem for over two decades. Database partitioning has been applied in centralized relational databases (Ceri, Navathe, & Wiederhold, 1983; Cornell & Yu, 1990; Hoffer & Severance, 1976; Ng, Gorla, Law, & Chan, 2003; Song & Gorla, 2000), distributed databases (Baiao et al, 2004; Cheng, Lee, & Wong, 2002; March & Rho, 1995; Ozsu & Valduriez, 1996;), Data Warehouse Design (Ezeife, 2001; Furtado, Lima, Pacitti, Valduriez, & Mattoso, 2005; Labio, Quass, & Adelberg, 1997), and Object-Oriented Database design (Fung, Karlapalem, & Li, 2002; Gorla, 2001).

Hoffer and Severance (1976) consider the vertical partitioning problem by applying bond energy algorithm on similarity of attributes, which are based on access patterns of transactions. Their work was extended by Navathe, Ceri, Wiederhold, and Dou (1984) by presenting vertical partitioning algorithms for three contexts: a database stored on devices of a single type; in different memory levels; and a distributed database. They used affinity between attributes for partitioning, which is based on the number of disk accesses. An alternate graphical approach was proposed by Navathe and

Ra (1989). Cornell and Yu (1990) use an optimal binary-partitioning algorithm to obtain vertical partitioning, which is iteratively applied to obtain more partitions. The study uses the number of data accesses to evaluate partitions. Chu and Leong (1993) develop a transaction-based approach to vertical partitioning, in which transaction rather than attribute is used as the unit of analysis. Song and Gorla (2000) used genetic algorithms to obtain solutions for vertical partitions and access paths simultaneously. They also use the number of disk accesses as the partitioning evaluation criterion. Ailamaki, Dewitt, Hill, adn Skounakis (2001) proposed Partition Attributes Across (PAX) model by improving cache performance, while Ramamurthy, Dewitt, and Su (2002) proposed fractured mirrors partitioning scheme based on Decomposition Storage Model and N-ary Storage Model. Ng et al (2003) propose genetic-algorithm based solution to the combined problem of vertical partitioning and tuple clustering in relational databases.

There are also studies that use data partitioning in distributed databases, object-oriented databases, and data warehouse designs. For example, Cheng et al. (2002) use genetic search-based clustering algorithm on traveling salesman problem to obtain vertical partitions in distributed databases. With reference to object-oriented database design, Gorla (2001) used genetic algorithm to determine the instance variables that should be stored in each class/subclass in a subclass hierarchy, so that the total cost of database operations is minimized. Fung et al. (2002) analyze vertical partitioning of classes/subclasses in object-oriented databases for class composition hierarchy and subclass hierarchy and develop the associated cost functions for query processing under the cases of large memory and small memory availability. Partitioning has been applied in data warehouses in order to optimize OLAP queries by designing parallel database clusters (Furtado et al., 2005) and to generate ROLAP data cubes based on optimized data partitioning technique (Chen, Dehne, Eavis,

& Rau-Chaplin, 2006). Methods for selecting and materializing horizontally partitioned data warehouse views have been proposed in order to speed up the query response time and reduce data warehouse maintenance costs (Ezeife, 2001).

While present research provides an association rules based methodology to solve vertical partitioning problem in centralized relational databases, the article also provides extension to apply the methodology to distributed and object-oriented database designs.

RELATED WORK IN ASSOCIATION RULES

Data mining is a process of extraction of implicit information from databases (Chen, Han, & Yu, 1996; Frawley, Piatesky-Shapiro, & Matheus, 1991). Association Rules, a data-mining technique (Agarwal & Srikant, 1994), the formal definition of which is given as (Agarwal, Mannila, Srikant, Toivonen, & Verkamo, 1996) "given a finite multiset of transactions D, the problem of mining association rules is to generate all association rules that have support and confidence at least equal to the user-specified minimum support threshold (min_sup) and minimum confidence threshold (min_conf) respectively" (Tzanis & Berberidis, 2007). In other words, association rules can be represented by an expression of the form $X \rightarrow Y$, where X, Y are sets of items and $X \cap Y = \emptyset$. The rule $X \rightarrow Y$ has a support of s if s% of transactions contain both X and Y. The rule $X \rightarrow Y$ has a confidence of c, if c% of transactions (T) that contain X also contain Y. Thus, the confidence of the rule is Freq $(X \cap Y)$ / Freq (X). Confidence denotes the strength of implication, while support indicates the frequencies of occurrence of the rule".

Several approaches have been devised to extract association rules, such as, Apriori algorithm (Agarwal & Srikant, 1994), DHP (Park, Chen, & Yu, 1995), graph-based approach (Yen & Chen,

2001), itemset lattice structures (Zaki, 2000; Zaki & Hsiao, 2005), and multiple-level association rules (Han & Fu, 1999). Association rules have been applied in several contexts. For example, Bagui (2006) used association rules to determine the crime patterns based on the datacubes created using Structured Query Language (SQL) on the crime data obtained from an U.S. state. Tjioe and Taniar (2005) developed methods to extract association rules in data warehouses by focusing on aggregate data and applied their algorithms on repeatable predicate and on non-repeatable predicate. Tzanis and Berberidis (2007) propose a mining algorithm to discover association rules for mutually exclusive items (the presence of one item excludes the other) in transaction databases

While the previous works related to association rules provides some background, we derive association rules from the transactions and use those rules to design partitioning schemes in databases so that minimum database operating cost is incurred by the transactions. We develop the corresponding cost function in order to assess the merit of the database partitions obtained using our algorithm.

METHODOLOGY

Our methodology consists of three steps: estimating the transaction load, deriving the cost formulae for transaction execution in a partitioned environment, and an algorithm to obtain vertical data partitioning. Based on the workload characteristics of relational databases (Yu, Chen, Heiss, & Lee, 1992), we generate the transaction load for our research. While the workload of a typical

database (Yu et al., 1992) has 75.9% SELECT, 4.7% DELETE, 7.7% UPDATE and 11.7% INSERT, the transaction set in our experiments closely match these percentages. The proportion of transactions that use 1-5, 6-10 and 11-15 attributes are around 65%, 24% and 11%, respectively. Furthermore, we consider basic predicate type since it is the most commonly used.

Cost Formula

The amount of data transferred and the number of disk accesses have been the most commonly used methods of evaluating partitioning schemes by previous researchers (e.g., Cheng et al, 2002; Cornell & Yu, 1990; Fung et al, 2002; Gorla, 2001). In our research, we do not include cost of index access and storage cost. We use the blocks estimate given in Yao (1977) as the basis for cost of query processing, in line with previous studies. If there are n records divided into m blocks and if k records satisfying a query are distributed uniformly among the m blocks, then the number of blocks accessed for the query = $m(1 - (1 - 1/m)^k)$ (Yao, 1977). In the partitioned database, we apply this formula for each $Segment_i$ accessed by the query q. Thus, the cost of processing a (retrieval) query q is estimated as shown in Box 1. Where

$freq_q$ = Frequency of query q
$Segment_{qj}$ = Number of partition j required by the query q.

$$M_i = \lceil T * L_i / BS \rceil$$

M_i = Number of blocks to be accessed in partition i.

Box 1.

$$freq_q * \left(\left(\sum_{i=1}^{Segment_{qj}} \lceil M_i(1 - (1 - 1/M_i)^{k_q}) \rceil \right) * \left(1 + \left(0.1 * (Segment_{qj} - 1) \right) \right) \right) \qquad (1)$$

k_q = Number of tuples satisfying a query q.
T = Total number of tuples
L_i = Size of a partition i in bytes
BS = Block Size

The first part computes the total number of blocks to be accessed from each of the $Segment_{qj}$ partitions. The second part indicates the overhead to concatenate $Segment_{qj}$ partitions in the memory. Similarly, the cost of processing an insert/delete transaction q is estimated as:

$$2 * freq_q * \left(\sum_{i=1}^{Segment_{qj}} \left\lceil M_i (1 - (1 - 1/M_i)^{k_q}) \right\rceil \right) \qquad (2)$$

As the insert/delete transactions involve two I/O times, the cost is multiplied by a 2.

Proposed Algorithm for Database Partitioning

The rationale behind our algorithm is as follows. Let A and B be the attributes in a relation. If the confidence value of the rule $A \rightarrow B$ is greater than the predefined minimum (min_conf), then the association between attributes A and B is strong enough that they can be grouped into one partition. Since order of attributes within the same partition is of no significance, confidence values

Figure 1. Database partitioning algorithm

Inputs: Database Transaction Set $T_1..T_m$ Frequencies of database transactions: $Freq_1..Freq_m$ Predetermined Minimum Support (min_supp) Predetermined Minimum Confidence (min_conf) **Outputs:** Optimal Database Partitioning Scheme p-opt
Step 1: DiscoverLargeItemsets ($T_1..T_m$, $Freq_1..Freq_m$, min_supp, $L_1 .. L_k$) Adapt Apriori Algorithm using $T_1..T_m$ and $Freq_1..Freq_m$ /* the frequencies are added to determine the support level Generate Large Itemsets $L_1 .. L_k$ with support values >= min_supp
Step 2: FilterLargeItemsets ($L_1 .. L_k$, min_conf, $L'_1 .. L'_k$) Do for each itemset i in $L_1 .. L_k$ Calculate all possible confidence values Find the lowest confidence ($LowConf_i$) IF $LowConf_i$ >= min_conf THEN retain itemset i   ELSE discard itemset i End-Do
Step 3: DeriveVerticalPartitions ($L'_1 .. L'_k$, Partioning schemes $P_1..P_s$) Do for the Itemsets $L'_k .. L'_1$ Choose a non-overlapping itemset with the highest support Keep into partitioning scheme P End-Do

Step 4: FindOptimalPartitioning ($T_1..T_m$, $P_1..P_s$, P_{opt})
 	
Do for each database partitioning scheme $P \in P_1..P_s$
   Compute Total-Cost (P) = $\sum_q$ Cost (q) for $q \in T_1..T_m$
 	
   /* Cost (q) uses [Eq1] if q is Retrieval and [Eq2] if q is Update
   IF Total-Cost (P) < Min-DBCost
      THEN Min-DBCost ← Total-Cost (P)
End-Do
Returns Partitioning scheme P_{opt}, a set of optimal database partitions

for $A \rightarrow B$ and $B \rightarrow A$ are calculated and the lower value will be selected to represent the association between attributes A and B, as a conservative approach. Thus, the confidence (A,B) = freq (A,B)/ Max (freq(A), freq(B)). The confidence value is higher when (i) there are fewer transactions requiring attribute A only or B only and/or (ii) there are more transactions requiring both A and B. Thus, confidence provides further justification, in addition to minimum support (min_supp) for storing attributes A and B in the same partition. The proposed algorithm (see Figure 1) has the following steps: discovering large itemsets, filtering the itemsets, generating data partitions, and selecting the best partitioning scheme.

Discovering Large Itemsets: Large itemsets are the combinations of attributes that have support above the predefined minimum support. For a retrieval transaction, the set of attributes in the SELECT clauses are considered; for an INSERT/DELETE transaction, all the attributes in the relation are used. Then large itemsets can be discovered by adapting the Apriori algorithm (Agarwal & Srikant, 1994) and adding transaction frequencies rather than counting transactions. The support of candidate in C_k is calculated by the sum of the frequency of queries that contain the candidate set. The set of large itemset L_k are derived that meet the predefined minimum support level (min_supp). Thus, inputs for this step are set of database transactions (retrievals and updates) $T_1..T_m$, the transaction frequencies $Freq_1..Freq_m$, and predetermined support level min_supp. The outputs of this module are Large Itemsets $L_1 .. L_k$.

Filter Large Itemsets: Large itemsets with confidence value smaller than the predetermined minimum confidence (min_conf) are discarded. For each itemset of Large itemsets L_k, all possible association rules are generated and the corresponding confidence levels are computed. For the Association rule LHS $\rightarrow$ RHS, the confidence level is computed as total frequency of transactions that have both LHS and RHS divided by total frequency of transactions that have only LHS. Thus this step takes Large Itemsets ($L_1 .. L_k$) and predetermined minimum confidence level (min_conf) as inputs and returns Filtered Large Itemsets ($L'_1 .. L'_k$).

Deriving Vertical Partitions: After we generate Filtered Large itemsets $L'_1 ...L'_k$, we start from the k-itemsets to determine the partitions. Make a partitioning scheme by picking an itemset from L'_k and then by picking other itemset from $L'_{k-1} ... L'_1$ in that order so that they are disjoint. Continue like this the last items are picked from L'_1. This makes one partitioning scheme. Repeat the above process until all possible partitioning schemes are derived. Thus, this module uses Filtered Large Itemsets $L'_1 ...L'_k$ as input and returns partitioning schemes $P_1..P_s$. It should be noted that each partitioning scheme may constitute several partitions.

Find the optimal partitioning scheme: Calculate the database operating cost for a partitioning scheme P by computing cost for each transaction, using Equation 1 if transaction is retrieval and Equation 2 if transaction is update. Select the partitioning scheme P_{opt} with the lowest database operating cost. Thus, the inputs for this module are partitioning schemes $P_1..P_s$ and transaction set $T_1..T_m$ and the output is the optimal partitioning scheme P_{opt}.

Table 1. Database transaction set

No	Transactions		Frequency
T1	SELECT	A, B, E	1
T2	SELECT	B, E	3
T3	SELECT	A, D, F	3
T4	INSERT SQL		2
T5	DELETE SQL		1

Illustration

The following illustrates the working of the partitioning algorithm. Consider the set of 5 transactions T1...T5 and their frequencies to operate on the relation with six attributes (see Table 1).

Generate Large Itemsets L_k

Assuming a predetermined minimum support of 40% (i.e., min_supp is 4), Large itemsets L_k are generated by adapting Apriori algorithm. First, the Candidate 1-itemset C_1 is derived by adding the frequencies of the transactions in which an attribute is used. For insert and delete transactions, it is assumed that all attributes are used since the entire row is to be accessed. For example, attribute A is used in transactions T1, T3, T4, and T5 with frequencies 1, 3, 2, and 1 respectively. Thus the support for attribute {A} is 7. Large 1-itemset L_1 is derived from Candidate 1-itemset C_1 by eliminating itemsets with support < 4.

The Candidate 2-itemset C_2 is derived by concatenating L_1 with L_1 and finding the support levels by scanning the Transaction Set. For example, from L_1, concatenating {A} and {B}, we find {A B} as one of the 2-itemsets C_2. The support level for {A B} is obtained by adding the frequencies of transactions in which both A and B are used. These transactions are T1, T4, and T5 with frequencies 1, 2, and 1, respectively, resulting in the support level of 4 for {A B}. The above process is repeated until all Large itemsets are derived.

Filtering with Predetermined Confidence levels

Each itemset in Large itemsets is kept only if the itemset has confidence level >= min_conf. As an example, consider the association {A,D,F}. The confidence value for the rule A→ DF is computed as the number of transactions in which all the attributes A,D, and F are used (i.e., 6) divided by

number of transactions in which A is used (i.e., 7). Thus, the confidence values for $A \rightarrow DF$, $D \rightarrow AF$ and $F \rightarrow AD$ are 6/7, 6/6, and 6/6, respectively. Similarly the confidence values for $DF \rightarrow A$, $AF \rightarrow D$ and $AD \rightarrow F$ are 6/6, 6/6, and 6/6, respectively. Since the lowest value (6/7 or 86%) is higher than the predefined minimum confidence level (say, min_conf is 30%), the association {A,D,F} is included in the Filtered Large 3-itemsets L'_3.

Deriving Vertical Partitions

The large itemset {A,D,F} is taken from L'_3 as the one of the partitions (see Figure 2); then we go to L_2 to scan 2-itemsets and find that there is only one {B E} that do not overlap with the existing partition. The remaining attribute {C} is taken from L_1, resulting in the partitioning scheme C BE ADF. Similarly, considering the other 3-item set {A,B,E} from L_3, we obtain C DF ABE as the other solution. Out of these two partitioning schemes, the one that has the least database operating costs using equations Equation 1 and Equation 2 is selected as the best database partitioning scheme.

IMPLEMENTATION

Experiments have been conducted using the proposed methodology with two real-life databases (UCI, 1999). The first experiment uses Teaching Assistant Education (TAE) dataset with 6 attributes and 151 tuples. The second experiment uses Adults database with 15 attributes and 30,162 tuples, which has been used in prior research (Sung, Li, Tan, & Ng, 2003).

First Experiment (with TAE Dataset)

As shown in Table 2, the attributes of the Teaching Assistant Education dataset (UCI, 1999) are Speaker (A), Course_instructor (B), Course (C),

Figure 2. Generation of candidate itemsets, large itemsets, and filtered large itemsets

Candidate 1-itemset C_1

Itemsets	Support
{A}	7
{B}	7
{C}	3
{D}	6
{E}	7
{F}	6

Large 1-itemset L_1

Itemsets	Support
{A}	7
{B}	7
{D}	6
{E}	7
{F}	6

Filtered Large L'_1

Itemsets	Support
{A}	7
{B}	7
{D}	6
{E}	7
{F}	6

C_2

Itemsets
{A B}
{A D}
{A E}
{A F}
{B D}
{B E}
{B F}
{D E}
{D F}
{E F}

C_2

Itemsets	Support
{A B}	4
{A D}	6
{A E}	4
{A F}	6
{B D}	3
{B E}	7
{B F}	3
{D E}	3
{D F}	6
{E F}	3

L_2

Itemsets	Support
(A B)	4
{A D}	6
{A E}	4
{A F}	6
{B E}	7
{D F}	6

Filtered Large L'_2

Itemsets	Support
(A B)	4
{A D}	6
{A E}	4
{A F}	6
{B E}	7
{D F}	6

C_3

Itemsets
{A D F}
{A B E}

C_3

Itemsets	Support
{A D F}	6
{A B E}	4

L_3

Itemsets	Support
{A D F}	6
{A B E}	4

Filtered Large L'_3

Itemsets	Support
{A D F}	6
{A B E}	4

Semester (D), Class_size (E), and Class_attribute (F).

The block size is assumed to be 100 bytes. We generated 10 SELECT SQL (retrieval), one INSERT SQL and one DELETE SQL (Appendix A). We derived partitions using predefined minimum support levels (20%, 30%, 40%, 50% and 60%) and the predefined confidence levels (20%, 30%, 40%, 50%, 60%, 70%, and 80%). Tables 3 through 7 have the results of partitioning schemes for 20% to 60% support for various confidence levels, while Table 8 has the best solutions for various support levels.

As can be seen from Table 8, the best partitioning design obtained by the proposed algorithm at 20% or 30% support levels, resulting in an improvement of 493 units or 13.62% over unpartitioned relation. Our solution matched the optimal design obtained by exhaustive enumeration, which also has a 13.62% improvement over unpartitioned solution. The optimal solution is:

{speaker, course, semester},
{course_instructor, class_size},
{class_attribute}

Table 2. TAE database description

Attributes	Type	Attribute Length (bytes)
speaker	Nominal: Non-english-speaker, English-speaker	19
course_instruc-tor	Categorical: Range from 1 – 25 categories	2
course	Categorical: Range from 1 – 26 categories	2
semester	Nominal: summer, regular	7
class_size	Numerical	2
class_attribute	Categorical: low, medium, high	6

Table 3. Result of TAE with minimum support of 20%

Confidence (%)	Attribute Partitioning	Cost	Cost Reduction
20	C ABDEF	3900.00	-7.85%
30	E ABCDF	3904.10	-7.97%
40	BE ACDF	3281.00	9.26%
50	F BE ACD	3123.40	13.62%
60	D BE ACF	3638.80	-0.63%
70	C F AD BE	3506.00	3.04%
80	B D E F AC	3731.10	-3.18%
Optimal Design	F BE ACD	**3123.40**	**13.62%**

Table 4. Results on TAE with minimum support of 30%

Minimum Confidence (%)	Attribute Partitioning	Cost	% Cost reduc-tion
20	BE ACDF	3281.00	9.26%
30	BE ACDF	3281.00	9.26%
40	BE ACDF	3281.00	9.26%
50	F BE ACD	3123.40	13.62%
60	D BE ACF	3638.80	-0.63%
70	C F AD BE	3506.00	3.04%
80	B D E F AC	3731.10	-3.18%
Optimal Design	F BE ACD	**3123.40**	**13.62%**

Table 5. Results on TAE with minimum support of 40%

Minimum Confidence (%)	Attribute Partitioning					Cost	% Cost reduction
20	C	BE	ADF			3566.50	1.37%
30	C	BE	ADF			3566.50	1.37%
40	C	BE	ADF			3566.50	1.37%
50	C	BE	ADF			3566.50	1.37%
60	D	BE	ACF			3638.80	-0.63%
70	C	F	AD	BE		3506.00	3.04%
80	B	D	E	F	AC	3731.10	-3.18%

Table 6. Results on TAE with minimum support of 50%

Minimum Confidence (%)	Attribute Partitioning					Cost	% Cost reduction
20	B	C	D	E	AF	3676.50	-1.67%
30	B	C	D	E	AF	3676.50	-1.67%
40	B	C	D	E	AF	3676.50	-1.67%
50	B	C	D	E	AF	3676.50	-1.67%
60	B	C	D	E	AF	3676.50	-1.67%
70	B	C	D	E	AF	3676.50	-1.67%
80	A	B	C	D	E F	3840.40	-6.21%

Table 7. Results on TAE with minimum support of 60%

Minimum Confidence (%)	Attribute Partitioning						Cost	% Cost reduction
20	A	B	C	D	E	F	3840.40	-6.21%
30	A	B	C	D	E	F	3840.40	-6.21%
40	A	B	C	D	E	F	3840.40	-6.21%
50	A	B	C	D	E	F	3840.40	-6.21%
60	A	B	C	D	E	F	3840.40	-6.21%
70	A	B	C	D	E	F	3840.40	-6.21%
80	A	B	C	D	E	F	3840.40	-6.21%

Table 8. Best partitioning designs for various support levels (TAE database)

Min Support	Best Partitioning Scheme	Total Cost	Cost Reduction
20%	F BE ACD	3123.40	13.62%
30%	F BE ACD	3123.40	13.62%
40%	C F AD BE	3506.00	3.04%
50%	B C D E AF	3676.50	-1.67%
60%	A B C D E F	3840.40	-6.21%
Optimal Design	F BE ACD	**3123.40**	**13.62%**
Without Partition	ABCDEF	**3616.00**	

Figure 3 shows the plot of number of partitions and percent cost savings at 20% minimum support level for various confidence levels on TAE database. It can be observed that as the minimum confidence level increases, there are more partitions, because higher confidence results in fewer higher level Large itemsets. Thus there will be several small fragments. It can also be observed that high-cost savings are achieved at 50% minimum confidence. At lower confidence levels, there are fewer fragments resulting in high database costs for retrieval transactions. Similarly, at higher confidence levels, there are many fragments resulting in high cost of insert/delete transactions.

Second Experiment (with Adults Database)

The block size of Adults DB (UCI, 1999) is assumed to be 4K. For ease of presentation, the attributes of age, workclass, final-weight, education, education-num, marital-status, occupation, relationship, race, sex, capital-gain, capital-loss, hours-per-week, native-country and class are

Figure 3. Partitions and cost savings at 20% support level varying confidence (TAE database)

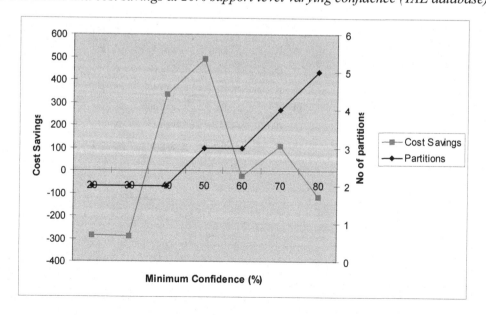

labeled as A through O. The Adults database description is given in Table 9. Based on the workload guidelines (Yu et al., 1992), we generate the transaction set for this database (Appendix B).

Our partitioning solution represents an enhancement of 41.05% over unpartitioned design (Table 10). The result shows the optimal solutions at 30% and 40% support levels have similar total cost of database operations. Though the total minimum cost should decrease with the increasing minimum support, the minor difference in costs may be attributed to the frequency of transactions. As can be seen from Table 10, the optimal partitioning scheme for Adults database is as follows:

{WorkClass}
{Final-Weight}
{Education}
{Marital Status}
{Occupation}
{Relationship}
{Race}
{Sex}
{Capital-Loss}
{Hours-per-week}
{Native Country}
{Age, Class}
{Education-num, Capital-Gain}

EFFECTIVENESS OF PROPOSED METHOD

The effectiveness of the proposed method is assessed using three ways: (1) How well the proposed-method generated vertical partitioning design solution reduces the database operating costs? (2) How efficient is the proposed method in terms of time of execution? (3) What is the computational complexity of the proposed partitioning algorithm and how does it compare with other algorithms used for vertical partitioning?

Database Operating Cost Reduction

As discussed in the previous section, the application of our method produced optimal vertical partitioning with the least database operating costs, as verified with exhaustive enumeration on the smaller database. Since vertical partitioning is an intractable problem, only heuristic solutions exist, as is the case with our proposed method. The application of our methodology on large database produced vertical partitions with database operating cost reductions of 41% compared to the unpartitioned database. Thus our approach shows that cost efficient database partitions can be obtained with association rules.

Time Performance

Programs were written in C and run on an IBM PC. Even after several hours of computer execution with Adults dataset with 15 attributes and 20 transactions, optimal solution could not be obtained with exhaustive enumeration as expected. With the proposed algorithm, the best design was obtained in less than a second. Figure 4 gives details of time taken to generate the best partition with the proposed algorithm for the Adults Database. As the support level decreases, there will be more k-itemsets qualify, thus requiring more time to process further itemsets. Similarly, as the confidence level increases, fewer associations qualify for higher levels of Large Itemsets, resulting in less execution time.

Computational Complexity

The time complexity of the proposed algorithm is computed as follows. Let there be n attributes and m transactions in the database. The first scan of 1-itemset contains n items to be scanned over the transaction set of m elements. The second scan of 2-itemsets needs n*n needs m*n*n scans over the transaction set. Beyond 2-itemsets the algorithm needs to compare only the common

Table 9. The adults database description (adapted from UCI, 1999)

Attribute	Letter	Data Type	Size in bytes
Age	A	Continuous: Range from 17 – 90	1
WorkClass	B	Nominal: Private, Self-emp-not-inc, Self-emp-inc, Federal-gov, Local-gov, State-gov	16
Final-weight	C	Continuous: Range from 21174 – 1033222	4
Education	D	Nominal: Bachelors, Some-college, 11th, HS-grad, Prof-school, Assoc-acdm, Assoc-voc, 9th, 7th-8th, 12th, Masters, 1st-4th, 10th, Doctorate, 5th-6th, Preschool	12
Education-num	E	Continuous: Range from 1 – 16	1
Marital-Status	F	Nominal: Married-civ-spouse, Divorced, Never-married, Seperated, Widowed, Married-spouse-absent, Married-AF-spouse.	21
Occupation	G	Nominal: Tech-support, Craft-repair, Other-service, Sales, Exec-managerial, Prof-specialty, Handlers-cleaners, Machine-op-inspct, Adm-clerical, Farming-fishing, Transport-moving, Priv-house-serv, Protective-serv, Adm-Forces.	17
Relationship	H	Nominal: Wife, Own-child, Husband, Not-in-family, Other-relative, Unmarried.	14
Race	I	Nominal: White, Asian-Pac-Islander, Amer-Indian-Eskimo, Other, Black.	18
Sex	J	Nominal: Female, Male	6
Capital-gain	K	Continuous: Range from 0 – 99999	3
Capital-loss	L	Continuous: Range from 0 – 4356	2
Hours-per-week	M	Continuous: Range from 1 – 99	1
Native-country	N	Norminal: Puerto-Rico, Canada, Germany, Outlying-US(Guam-USVI-etc), India, Japan, Greece, South, China, Cuba, Iran, Honduras, Philippines, Italy, Poland, Jamaica, Vietnam, Mexico, Portugal, Ireland, France, Dominican-Republic, Laos, Ecuador, Taiwan, Haiti, Columbia, Hungary, Guatemala, Nicaragua, Scotland, Thailand, Yugoslavia, El-Salvador, Trindad&Tobago, Peru, Hong, Holand-Netherlands.	26
Class	O	Nominal: >50, <=50K	5

Table 10. Result of the best case in each support group (Adults database)

Min Support	Attribute Partitioning	Total Cost	Cost reduction
30%	A C D F G H I J L M N BO EK	36920.60	40.84%
40%	B C D F G H I J L M N AO EK	36792.70	41.05%
Without Partition	ABCDEFGHIJKLMNO	**62409.00**	

elements on the left side of the itemsets (Chen et al. 1996). Assuming that about half the members in the k-itemset qualify for (k+1)-itemset, the number of elements to access in the itemsets become $n+n^2+n^2/2+n^2/4+n^2/8....$ These elements need to scan the transaction set of m elements each time, thus the computational complexity becomes $m*(n+n^2(1+1/2+1/4+1/8...))=m*(n+2n^2)$ approximately. Furthermore, steps 1 and 2 of the algorithm can be combined since both the min_supp and the min_conf can be checked at the same time for each Large k-itemset.

Considering the fact that commercial applications follow 80/20 rule for transaction set (Chu & Ieong, 1993) wherein 20% of database transactions are executed 80% of time, it should be sufficient to consider only these 20% high frequency transactions when designing physical database structures. These transactions can be maintained in memory as a binary file of (20%m transactions)*(n attributes), thus facilitating faster memory access. Furthermore, by providing indexed access or hashed access to these 20% transactions, the entire transaction table need not be scanned for each attribute. Thus, the computational complexity reduces to $c*(n+2n^2)$, where c is a constant (c=1 if hash file is used >1 if indexed file is used). Assuming c=2 on the average, the complexity becomes $2n+4n^2$. Furthermore, there will be additional accesses for creating partitions from the Large Itemsets: $n^2(1+1/2+1/4+1/8+...)$ or approximately $2n^2$. Thus the total computational complexity becomes $6n^2+2n$.

Thus our algorithm has a time complexity of $(O(n^2) + O(n))$, (where n is number of attributes). The complexity of our algorithm is comparable to or better than previous algorithms. For example, the bond energy algorithm (McCormick, Schweitzer, & White, 1972) has a complexity of $O(n^3)$, the graphical approach (Navathe & Ra, 1989) has a complexity of $O(n^2)$, and the binary partitioning approach (Chu & Ieong, 1993) has a complexity of $O(2^m)$, where m is the number of transactions.

DISCUSSION

A new method for attribute partitioning has been proposed based on association rules, which is applied to two real life data sets. In the smaller database (TAE), there is an improvement of 13.62% over unpartitioned relation, matching the optimal solution obtained by exhaustive enumeration. With the larger database (Adults), there is a cost savings of 41.05% over unpartitioned solution and has taken less than a second for the algorithm to find the best solution. Our results demonstrate the viability of *Association Rules* as an attribute partitioning technique.

Following are some remarks regarding the partitioning schemes. The optimal partitioning scheme depends on transaction mix and database characteristics. Fewer inserts/deletes in the transaction mix result in more fragmented solution, since the cost of these transactions is high on partitioned relations. Furthermore, higher the minimum support level, the resulting optimal solution is more fragmented. Higher the minimum confidence level, the more fragmented the partitioning scheme is, since a few items will qualify to next level itemsets (see Tables 2-7).

Our results using standard workloads indicate, optimal partitioning is obtained at around 30% support level and 40%-50% confidence level, which can be used by the database designer in real life. Optionally, the database designer may perform experiments around these support and confidence-levels using most frequent transactions (with 80/20 rule) and determine optimal fragmentation schemes. The later procedure is especially useful when the transaction mix is skewed.

The database designers in the real world can use the methodology suggested in this research to determine efficient partitioning schemes. In order to do that, the designer needs to collect data on the transactions (such as, type of transaction – retrievals and updates, frequency of transaction, set of attributes required, and the conditions of retrieval) and the database characteristics (such as, attribute lengths, selectivity of attributes, and number of tuples in each table, and block size). Transaction information may be obtained by studying the reports and screens used by the managers or operating staff in the organization.

FUTURE RESEARCH

Present research can be extended in the following directions. First, we use one table at a time for determining partitions, in line with most previous works on vertical partitioning. Join operations can be incorporated into the algorithm by converting those operations to corresponding operations on single tables and applying the algorithm on each table. Transactions using aggregate operators should be weighted more through frequency. Second, the present methodology can be extended to include other physical design techniques, such as access path selection (clustered index, unclustered index, or sequential scan) (Cornell & Yu, 1990; De, Park, & Pirkul, 1988; Song & Gorla, 2000). The cost function needs to be modified to incorporate the chosen access path. Third, we use number of disk accesses as the evaluating cost function in line with most previous research. A better partitioning solution can be obtained when physical characteristics of disk and access characteristics of transactions are incorporated in the cost function (Gorla & Boe, 1990). Fourth, while the scope of present research is determination of disjoint partitions, the research can be extended to include overlapping partitions.

While the present research deals with vertical partitioning solution in centralized relational databases using association rules, the research can be extended to distributed and object-oriented database designs. In distributed databases, user queries originate at various distribution sites and data resides at different locations. The present research can be extended to model the affinity between sites and the required data items using association rules, thereby solving data allocation

problems. The solution should provide optimal way to locate various tables and/or attributes across the nodes of a distributed network, so that the user transactions can be processed with the least data transmission costs. In a similar manner, horizontal partitioning of distributed databases can be derived modeling the affinity between tuples and user transactions using association rules. These horizontal partitions can be placed in the most optimal locations, so that communication costs are minimized and parallelism is achieved.

In object-oriented databases, the placement of attributes and instances across super type and sub types is a physical design problem (Gorla, 2001). By modeling the associations between instance variables required in the transactions with the subclasses, the physical location of the instance variables in the subclasses can be determined. Thus, by using the association-rule based heuristic, the optimal storage structures for object-oriented databases can be designed, which results in the least database costs of retrieval and update transactions.

REFERENCES

Agrawal, R., Mannila, H., Srikant, R., Toivonen, H., & Verkamo, A. I. (1996). Fast discovery of association rules. In *Advances in Knowledge Discovery and Data Mining.* AAAI/MIT Press.

Agrawal, R., & Srikant, R. (1994). Fast algorithms for mining association rules. In *Proceedings of the 20th International Conference on Very Large Databases.* Santiago, Chile.

Ailamaki, A., Dewitt, D. J., Hill, M. D., & Skounakis, M. (2001). Weaving relations for cache performance. In *Proceedings of the 27th VLDB Conference.*

Bagui, S. (2006). An approach to mining crime patterns. *International Journal of Data Warehousing and Mining, 2*(1), 50-80.

Ceri, S., Navathe, S., & Wiederhold, G. (1983). Distribution design of logical database schemas. *IEEE Transactions on Software Engineering,* SE-9(4).

Chen, M. S., Han, J., & Yu, P. S. (1996). Data mining: An overview from database perspective. *IEEE Transactions on Knowledge and Data Engineering, 8*(6), 866-883.

Chen, Y., Dehne, Y., Eavis, T., & Rau-Chaplin, A. (2006). Improved data partitioning for building large ROLAP data cubes in parallel. *International Journal of Data Warehousing and Mining, 2*(1),1-26.

Cheng, C-H., Lee, W-K., & Wong, K-F. (2002). A genetic algorithm-based clustering approach for database partitioning. *IEEE Transactions on Systems, Man, and Cybernetics, 32*(3), 215-230.

Chu, W. W. & Ieong, I. T. (1993). A transaction-based approach to vertical partitioning for relational database systems. *IEEE Transaction on Software Engineering, 19*(8), 804-812.

Cornell, D. W. & Yu, P. S. (1990). An effective approach to vertical partitioning for physical design of relational databases. *IEEE Transactions on Software Engineering, 16*(2), 248-258.

De, P., Park, J. S., & Pirkul, H. (1988). An integrated model of record segmentation and access path selection for databases. *Information Systems, 13*(1), 13-30.

Ezeife, C. I. (2001). Selecting and materializing horizontally partitioned warehouse views. *Data and Knowledge Engineering, 36,* 185-210.

Frawley, W. J., Piatetsky-Shapiro, G., & Matheus, C. J. (1991). Knowledge discovery in database: An overview. In G. Piatetsky-Shapiro & W. J. Frawley (Eds.), *Knowledge discovery databases.* AAAI/MIT Press.

Fung, C-W., Karlapalem, K., & Li, Q. (2002). An evaluation of vertical class partitioning for query processing in object-oriented databases. *IEEE Transactions on Knowledge and Data Engineering, 14*(5), 1095-1118.

Furtado, C., Lima, A., Pacitti, E., Valduriez, P., & Mattoso, M. (2005). Physical and virtual partitioning in OLAP database cluster. In *Proceedings of the 17th International Symposium on Computer Architecture and High Performance Computing* (pp. 143-150).

Gorla, N. (2001). An object-oriented database design for improved performance. *Data and Knowledge Engineering, 37,* 117-138.

Gorla, N., & Boe, W. (1990). Effect of schema size on fragmentation design in multirelational databases. *Information Systems, 15,* 291-301.

Hammer, M., & Niamir, B. (1979). A heuristic approach to attribute partitioning. *ACM SIGMOD International Conference on Management of Data.*

Han, J., & Fu, Y. (1999). Mining multiple-level association rules in large databases. *IEEE Transactions on Knowledge and Data Engineering, 11*(5), 798-805.

Hoffer, J. A. (1976). An integer programming formulation of computer database design problems. *Information Science,* 11, 29-48.

Hoffer, J. A., & Severance, D. G. (1975). The use of cluster analysis in physical data base design. *International Conference on Very large Databases.*

Labio, W. J., Quass, D., & Adelberg, B. (1997). Physical database design for data warehouses. In *Proceedings of the IEEE Conference on Data Engineering* (pp. 277-288).

March, S. T. (1983). Techniques in structuring database records. *ACM Computing Surveys, 15*(1).

March, S. T., & Rho, S. (1995). Allocating data and operations to nodes in distributed database design. *IEEE Trans. on Knowledge and Data Engineering, 7*(2).

McCormick, W. T., Jr., Schweitzer, P. J., & White, T. W. (1972). Problem decomposition and data organization by a clustering technique. *Operations Research, 20*(5), 993-1009.

Navathe, S., Ceri, S., Wiederhold, G., & Dou, J. (1984). Vertical partitioning algorithms for database design. *ACM Transactions on. Database Systems.*

Navathe, S., & Ra, M. (1989). Vertical partitioning for database design: A graphical algorithm. In *Proceedings of the 1989 ACM SIGMOD/*

Ng, V., Gorla, N., Law, D.M., & Chan, C. K. (2003). Applying genetic algorithms in database partitioning. In *Proceedings of the 2003 ACM Symposium on Applied Computing (SAC)* (pp. 544-549).

Ozsu, M., & Valduriez, P. (1996). *Principles of distributed database systems.* Prentice Hall.

Park, J-S., Chen, M-S., & Yu, P. S. (1995). *Mining association rules with adjustable accuracy* (IBM research report).

Ramamurthy, R., Dewitt, D. J., & Su, Q. (2002). A case for fractured mirrors. In *Proceedings of the 28th VLDB Conference.*

Song, S. K., & Gorla, N. (2000). A genetic algorithm for vertical fragmentation and access path selection. *The Computer Journal, 45*(1), 81-93.

Sung, S. Y., Li, Z., Tan, C. L., & Ng, P. A. (2003). Forecasting association rules using existing data sets. *IEEE Transactions on Knowledge and Data Engineering, 15*(6), 1448-1459.

Tjioe, H. C., & Taniar, D. (2005). Mining association rules in data warehouse. *International Journal of Data Warehousing and Mining, 1*(3), 28-62.

Tzanis, G., & Berberidis, C. (2007). Mining for mutually exclusive items in transaction databases. *International Journal of Data Warehousing and Mining, 3*(3).

Yao, S. B. (1977). Approximating block access in data-base organization. *Communications of the ACM, 20*(4), 260-261.

Yen, S-J., & Chen, A. L. P. (2001). A graph-based approach for discovering various types of association rules. *IEEE Transactions on Knowledge and Data Engineering, 12*(5), 839-845.

Yu, P. S., Chen, M. S., Heiss, H. U., & Lee, S. (1992). Workload characterization of relational database environments. *IEEE Transactions of Software Engineering, 18*(4), 347-355.

UCI. (1999). *Machine learning repository content summary.* Retrieved February 8, 2008, from http://www.ics.uci.edu/~mlearn/MLSummary.html

Zaki, M. J. (2000). Scalable Algorithms for association mining. *IEEE Transactions on Knowledge and Data Engineering, 12*(3), 372-390.

Zaki, M. J., & Hsiao, C-J. (2005). Efficient algorithms for mining closed itemsets and their lattice structures. *IEEE Transactions on Knowledge and Data Engineering, 17*(4), 462-478.

APPENDIX A. TRANSACTIONS FOR TAE DATABASE

No		Query	Freq
1	SELECT WHERE	speaker, course_instructor, course, semester, class_size class_size < 5	2
2	SELECT WHERE	speaker, course_instructor, semester, class_size, class_attribute course <= 20 AND class_size > 18	3
3	SELECT WHERE	speaker, course, class_attribute class_size <= 25 AND (course_instructor <= 9 OR semester = "regular")	13
4	SELECT WHERE	speaker, course_instructor, course, semester, class_attribute course_instructor < 10	15
5	SELECT WHERE	speaker, course_instructor, semester, class_size, class_attribute course_instructor < 15 AND (course >= 14 OR class_attribute > "low")	2
6	SELECT WHERE	speaker, course, semester, class_size, class_attribute class_size = 64 AND semester = "regular" AND course_instructor >= 5	7
7	SELECT WHERE	course_instructor, class_size course_instructor = 11 OR class_attribute > "low" OR semester <= "summer"	15
8	SELECT WHERE	speaker, course_instructor, semester, class_size, class_attribute speaker = "english-speaker" AND course < 5	6
9	SELECT WHERE	class_attribute class_instructor <> 25 OR class_attribute = "low"	18
10	SELECT WHERE	course_instructor, course, semester, class_size class_attribute <> "low" AND class_size >= 39	10
11	Number of tuples to be inserted : 1 INSERT SQL		6
12	Number of tuples to be deleted : 4 DELETE SQL		3

APPENDIX B: TRANSACTION SET FOR ADULTS DATABASE

No		Query	Frq
1	SELECT	Age, WorkClass, Final-weight, Education, Education-num, Occupation, Relationship, Race, Capital-gain, Hours-per-week, Native-country, Class	2
	WHERE	(Material-status = "Windowed" OR Marital-status = "Divorced") AND Sex = "Female"	
2	SELECT	Age, WorkClass, Final-weight, Education-num, Marital-status, Race, Sex, Capital-gain, Capitil-loss, Hours-per-week, Native-country, Class	5
	WHERE	Relationship = "Other-relative"	
3	SELECT	Age, WorkClass, Final-weight, Education-num, Marital-status, Relationship, Race, Sex, Capital-gain, Capital-loss, Hours-per-week	2
	WHERE	Sex = "Female"	
4	SELECT	Education, Occupation, Relationship, Race, Capital-gain, Hours-per-week	4
	WHERE	Native-country = "United-states"	
		Marital-status = "Divorced"	
5	SELECT	Age, WorkClass, Education, Relationship, Class	5
	WHERE	(Relationship = "Not-in family" OR Relationship = "Unmarried") AND Class = "<=50K" AND Sex = "Male"	
6	SELECT	Age, Final-Weight, Education, Education-num, Occupation, Relationship, Race, Capital-loss, Hours-per-week, Class	1
	WHERE	Age >= 50 AND (WorkClass = "Self-emp-not-inc" OR WorkClass = "Private")"	
7	SELECT	Age, WorkClass, Education, Marital-status, Hours-per-week, Class	7
	WHERE	Native-country = "South"	
8	SELECT	Age, Final-weight, Education-num, Occupation, Sex, Capital-gain, Capital-loss, Class	3
	WHERE	Education-num < 10 AND Hours-per-week >50	
9	SELECT	Education, Occupation, Capital-gain	4
	WHERE	Capital-gain > 1000	
10	SELECT	Age, Occupation, Capital-gain, Hours-per-week	6
	WHERE	Race = "White" AND Age <= 40	
11	SELECT	Education-num, Marital-status, Capital-gain	7
	WHERE	(WorkClass = "State-gov" OR WorkClass = "Federal-gov" OR WorkClass = "Local-gov") AND Class = "<=50K"	
12	SELECT	Education, Occupation, Capital-loss	3
	WHERE	Relationship = "Not-in family"AND Marital-status = "Divorced"	
13	SELECT	Age, Occupation	6
	WHERE	Marital-status = "Never-married"	
14	SELECT	Education, Education-num, Marital-Status, Capital-gain, Native-country	5
	WHERE	Occupation = "Farming-fishing" AND Class = "<=50K" AND Hours-per-week >=75	
15	SELECT	Occupation, Hours-per-week	3
	WHERE	Race = "Black" AND WorkClass = "Federal-gov"	
16	SELECT	Capital-loss, hours-per-week, Native-Country	3
	WHERE	Education = "Masters" AND Capital-loss > 0	

APPENDIX B: CONTINUED

17	SELECT	Marital-status, Race, Native-country	1
	WHERE	Occupation = "Armed-Forces" OR Occupation = "Protective-serv"	
18	SELECT	Hours-per-week, Native-country	8
	WHERE	WorkClass = "Private" AND Relationship = "Own-child" AND Sex = "Male"	
19	Number of tuples to be inserted : 1		13
	INSERT SQL		
20	Number of tuples to be deleted : 20		5
	DELETE SQL		

This work was previously published in International Journal of Data Warehousing and Mining, Vol. 4, Issue 3, edited by D. Taniar, pp. 35-53, copyright 2008 by IGI Publishing (an imprint of IGI Global).

Chapter 11
Introducing the Elasticity of Spatial Data

David A. Gadish
California State University Los Angeles, USA

ABSTRACT

The data quality of a vector spatial data can be assessed using the data contained within one or more data warehouses. Spatial consistency includes topological consistency, or the conformance to topological rules (Hadzilacos & Tryfona, 1992, Rodríguez, 2005). Detection of inconsistencies in vector spatial data is an important step for improvement of spatial data quality (Redman, 1992; Veregin, 1991). An approach for detecting topo-semantic inconsistencies in vector spatial data is presented. Inconsistencies between pairs of neighboring vector spatial objects are detected by comparing relations between spatial objects to rules (Klein, 2007). A property of spatial objects, called elasticity, has been defined to measure the contribution of each of the objects to inconsistent behavior. Grouping of multiple objects, which are inconsistent with one another, based on their elasticity is proposed. The ability to detect groups of neighboring objects that are inconsistent with one another can later serve as the basis of an effort to increase the quality of spatial data sets stored in data warehouses, as well as increase the quality of results of data-mining processes.

INTRODUCTION

Geographic Information Systems

Spatial databases, and most notably Geographic Information Systems (GIS) databases and data warehouses, have gained popularity in various business sectors in recent years. GIS or spatial databases may consist of vector, raster, and nonmapping business data (Abler, 1987). This article is focused on the vector data stored in these databases. GIS databases are comprised of vector-based data objects such as points, lines, and polygons (Aronoff, 1995). These elements are

Figure 1. Example of inconsistencies in spatial data

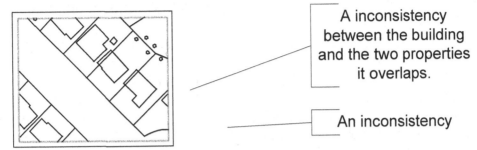

related to one another in terms of their location as well as in terms of their semantic interpretation (Clementini, Felice, & Van Ooserom, 1993; Egenhoffer, 1991).

Inconsistency of Spatial Data

Consistency is a measure of data quality of these databases and data warehouses. Inconsistency is the opposite of consistency (Kainz, 1991). Inconsistency can be measured in terms of the number of objects that relate to one or multiple objects that do not satisfy one or more rules that describe the data (Cockcroft, 2004; Lutz & Kolas, 2007; Xu, 2007). For example, it would be inconsistent to map a property boundary to the center of an adjacent road. Consistency is assessed using information contained within one or more databases. Spatial consistency includes topological consistency, or the conformance to topological rules (Kainz, 1991). An example of spatial inconsistency is illustrated in Figure 1, where two buildings slightly overlap their properties.

Detection of Inconsistencies in Spatial Data Warehouses

Detection of inconsistencies in spatial data is a key activity in an effort to manage the consistency of spatial data (Servigne, Ubeda, Zuricelli, & Laurini, 2000). It is useful for evaluating, maintaining, and enhancing spatial data quality in data warehouses. Since data in spatial databases is constantly evolving, there is an ongoing need for detection and adjustment of inconsistencies. This need is amplified as two or more spatial data sources are combined in a warehouse to increase the scope of data mining. It is also useful for enhancing the quality of results produced by data-mining operations.

Inconsistencies between pairs of neighboring spatial objects (consisting of spatial geometry and nonspatial attributes) are detected by comparing relations between spatial objects to rules. A property of spatial objects (or simply objects), called elasticity, is defined to indicate the contribution of each of the objects to inconsistent behavior. Grouping of multiple objects, which are inconsistent with one another, based on their elasticity, is proposed. These groupings become the basis for

Figure 2. The process of creating elasticity-based groupings

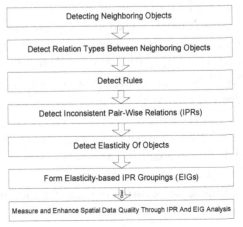

an effort to increase the quality of spatial data. This process is illustrated in Figure 2.

Determining Inconsistencies Between Pairs of Neighboring Objects

An object may be inconsistent with more than one of its neighbors. Detecting inconsistencies between pairs of neighboring objects in spatial databases is presented in this section.

First, objects that are neighbors with other objects are determined. The type of relations which exist between neighboring objects is essential (Mark et al., 1989). Rules that describe relations between neighboring objects as well as rules that govern the relations of an object with its neighbors are identified. These rules are then used to compare each object's relations to other objects. The comparison produces a list of objects that do not satisfy rules applicable to relationships with their neighboring objects.

Detecting Neighboring Objects

Neighboring objects are determined for each object in the database.

A layer in a spatial database is a subset of objects with a common semantic interpretation. Consider object i on layer L and another object j on layer M. Layers L and M may originate from different data sets, from the same data set. These objects i and j may also belong to the same layer L.

A threshold distance T between all objects on layers L and M is used to determine whether two objects are at a close proximity or not. If the minimal Euclidean distance between two objects is less than or equal to T, the two objects O_i and O_j are said to be *Neighboring Objects*; otherwise, they are not.

Each layer L, as well as each pair of layers L and M in a spatial database, is assigned a corresponding threshold T. The threshold T may be set to the same or different value for each pair of layers.

Detecting the Type of Relation between Neighboring Objects

The relation between each pair of neighboring objects is determined. The criteria that must be satisfied for a pair of neighboring objects to be considered of a particular relation type are based on the 9-Intersection model (Egenhofer et. al. 1991; Mark & Egenhofer, 1992) which classifies topological binary relations between spatial objects (Medeiros & Cilia,. 1995). The classification is based on the intersection of the boundaries, interiors and exteriors of object pairs (Egenhofer & Herring, 1990; Egenhofer et. al. 1991). These are represented as a 3x3 matrix:

$$\begin{bmatrix} \delta i \cap \delta j & \delta i \cap j^o & \delta i \cap j^{-1} \\ i^o \cap \delta j & i^o \cap j^o & i^o \cap j^{-1} \\ i^{-1} \cap \delta j & i^{-1} \cap j^o & i^{-1} \cap j^{-1} \end{bmatrix}$$

Each of these nine sets may be empty $\varnothing$ or nonempty $\neg\varnothing$. This results in a total of 9^2 possible combinations (Egenhofer & Herring, 1992; Egenhofer & Franzosa, 1995). Only eight of these combinations result in valid topological relations in R^2. The remaining combinations do not produce meaningful topological relations. The different relation types between pairs of spatial objects are:

$$\begin{bmatrix} \varnothing & \varnothing & \neg\varnothing \\ \varnothing & \varnothing & \neg\varnothing \\ \neg\varnothing & \neg\varnothing & \neg\varnothing \end{bmatrix} \rightarrow i \; Disjoint \; j \quad (1)$$

$$\begin{bmatrix} \varnothing & \varnothing & \neg\varnothing \\ \neg\varnothing & \neg\varnothing & \neg\varnothing \\ \varnothing & \varnothing & \neg\varnothing \end{bmatrix} \rightarrow i \; Contains \; j \quad (2)$$

$$\begin{bmatrix} \varnothing & \neg\varnothing & \varnothing \\ \varnothing & \neg\varnothing & \varnothing \\ \neg\varnothing & \neg\varnothing & \neg\varnothing \end{bmatrix} \rightarrow i \; Inside \; j \quad (3)$$

$$\begin{bmatrix} \neg\varnothing & \varnothing & \neg\varnothing \\ \varnothing & \varnothing & \neg\varnothing \\ \neg\varnothing & \neg\varnothing & \neg\varnothing \end{bmatrix} \rightarrow i \; Meet \; j \qquad (4)$$

$$\begin{bmatrix} \neg\varnothing & \varnothing & \varnothing \\ \varnothing & \neg\varnothing & \varnothing \\ \varnothing & \varnothing & \neg\varnothing \end{bmatrix} \rightarrow i \; Equal \; j \qquad (5)$$

$$\begin{bmatrix} \neg\varnothing & \varnothing & \neg\varnothing \\ \neg\varnothing & \neg\varnothing & \neg\varnothing \\ \varnothing & \varnothing & \neg\varnothing \end{bmatrix} \rightarrow i \; Covers \; j \qquad (6)$$

$$\begin{bmatrix} \neg\varnothing & \neg\varnothing & \varnothing \\ \varnothing & \neg\varnothing & \varnothing \\ \neg\varnothing & \neg\varnothing & \neg\varnothing \end{bmatrix} \rightarrow i \; Covered-by \; j \qquad (7)$$

$$\begin{bmatrix} \neg\varnothing & \neg\varnothing & \neg\varnothing \\ \neg\varnothing & \neg\varnothing & \neg\varnothing \\ \neg\varnothing & \neg\varnothing & \neg\varnothing \end{bmatrix} \rightarrow i \; Overlap \; j \qquad (8)$$

The relations *Disjoint, Contains, Inside, Meet, Equal, Covers, Covered-by,* and *Overlap* provide complete coverage for relations between pairs of spatial objects, and are mutually exclusive (i.e., exactly one of these topological relations holds true between any two spatial objects in R^2). Therefore the *observed relation* between object i on layer L and j on layer M takes one of eight relation type values: *Disjoint, Contains, Inside, Meet, Equal, Covers, Covered-by,* and *Overlap*.

To determine the relationship type of each pair of neighboring, it is necessary to analyze the content of databases or data warehouses.

Determine Rules That Manage the Relations Between Neighboring Objects

Rules that consider topological relations alone are based only on the shape of the object. This is not sufficient for detecting inconsistencies in spatial data, as this does not translate to a comprehensive description of real-world situations.

Semantic information is the meaning of real-world entities described by the objects. This information is combined with topological relations to discover rules.

Analyzing semantics of objects defines which topological relations are consistent and which are not. For example, a building inside a residential property is a permitted relation, while a building inside a road is not. In either case, the topology of the scenario is described as a polygon inside another polygon. Therefore the semantics of each object is required to determine which relationship is allowed and which is not.

Rules managing the relations between objects can be broadly classified based on the semantics of the real-world entities that these objects represent. Since each layer's objects correspond to real-world entities with a different semantic meaning, this discussion continues in terms of layers. Rules governing relations between objects are therefore determined based on the layers of corresponding objects. Rules can be manually provided or automatically detected.

Two types of rules are utilized in this article: (1) rules based on the analysis of the relation between each object and *each* of their neighbors, and (2) rules based on the analysis of the relations between each object and *all* of its neighboring objects.

The first type of rule, describing the relationship between a pair of objects is called a P-Rule. The aim is to determine rules such as "A tree is *Inside* a property" or "A road *Meets* a property."

The second type of rule, describing the relationship of an object with all its neighboring objects, is called an M-Rule. The goal is to determine rules such as "a Building is Inside a Property 1 time" or "A Property Meets a Road between 0 and 2 times." These rules are defined in terms of two layers, a relation type, and upper and lower bounds for the number of objects on the second layer that can be in the specified relation type with the object on the first layer.

These P-rules and M-rules play important roles in detection and adjustment of inconsistencies.

Figure 3. An IPR due to a violation of a P-rule

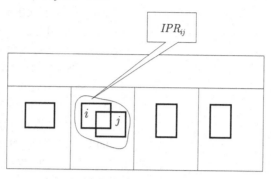

Figure 4. An IPR due to a violation of an M-rule

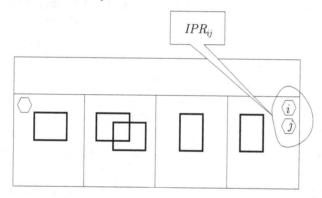

Detecting Inconsistent Pairwise Relations (IPR)

An inconsistent pairwise relation, or IPR, is an observed relation between two objects i and j which does not satisfy any of the P-Rules or M-Rules that correspond to layers L and M. It is denoted as $IPR_{ij} = T$. If the rules that correspond to these layers are satisfied, an IPR does not exist; this is denoted as $IPR_{ij} = F$.

Each object's relations to its neighboring objects are checked against P-rules and M-rules to determine if such an IPR exists.

Examples of IPRs

Consider the following two examples to illustrate this process. Assume the following two rules exist: (1) "House *Disjoint* House" (2) "Fire Hydrant *Inside* Property between 0 and 1 times." Then the

objects in Figure 3 violates the first rule, since there are two houses that overlap each other.

The objects in Figure 4 violates the second rule, since there are two fire hydrants inside one property.

Graphical Representation of an IPR

An IPR is schematically represented in Figure 5 as two "object" nodes linked with a gray line indicating that an inconsistency exists between them.

Having proposed a process for identification of inconsistencies between pairs of objects, the next task is to formulate the identification of inconsistencies among multiple objects. Before this can be accomplished, a property of objects is defined in the following section.

Figure 5. A schematic view of an IPR

DETERMINING ELASTICITY OF IPRs

The Elasticity Property of Objects

An inconsistency in a spatial database can involve two or more objects. A technique is proposed to characterize objects, which is then used to group all objects which form an inconsistency from multiple IPRs.

Consider an object that is inconsistent with one or more of its neighbors, that is, the object is involved in one or more IPRs. An example of this scenario is illustrated in Figure 6. In this case the inconsistency involves four objects, and three IPRs. They are: IPR_{ij}, IPR_{ik}, and IPR_{il}.

In this scenario, a number of objects may be inconsistent with one another. This may be due to an inaccurate position of only one, or possibly more than one, of these objects. That is, not all objects contribute to the existence of IPRs in this situation to the same extent. A weight is assigned to each object that is involved in one or more IPRs to reflect this disparity. This weight is the new elasticity property of an object, which is defined as follows:

Consider object i: Let I_i be the number of objects j that it is inconsistent with. Let N_i be the number of objects j that neighbor with it. Then the Elasticity property of object i is defined as:

$$ELS_i = \frac{I_i}{N_i}.$$

Characteristics of Elasticity

The Elasticity has lower and upper bounds, that is $0 \leq ELS \leq 1$. It exhibits the following five characteristics:

- Elasticity of a consistent object is zero. The elasticity of an object is zero if the object has no neighbors with which it is in an inconsistent binary relation. In this case, $ELS_i = 0$. This can only occur if

$$\frac{I_i}{N_i} = 0,$$

that is if $I_i = 0$ In other words i has no neighbors j such that IPR_{ij} exists.
- An object can not have negative elasticity. The elasticity of an object can not be less than zero. $ELS_i < 0$ would occur only if either I_i or N_i are negative values, which is not possible by their definition.
- The elasticity of an object can not be greater than 1. $ELS_i > 1$ would occur only if $I_i > N_i$, that is i has more inconsistent neighbors

Figure 6. An inconsistency involving four objects

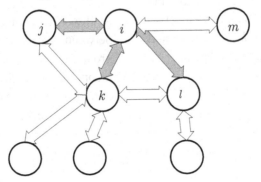

Figure 7. Example of elasticity calculation for objects

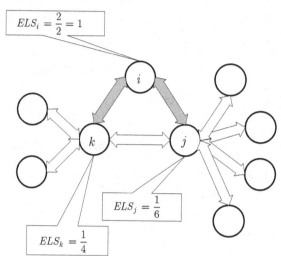

than neighbors. This is not possible by definition of I_i and N_i.

- The elasticity of an object may equal 1. ELS_i = 1 only when $I_i = N_i$, that is i is pairwise inconsistent with all its neighbors.
- The elasticity of an object may be a value between 0 and 1. $0 < ELS_i < 1$ only when $I_i < N_i$, that is i is pairwise inconsistent with at least one but not all of its neighbors.

Example of Elasticity

To understand the significance of the elasticity of an object, consider an example where two inconsistent pairwise relations are detected between three objects i, j, and k, which are neighbors with one another, such that $IPR_{ij} = T$ and $IPR_{ik} = T$. No IPR is detected between j, and k, and no additional IPRs are detected between i, j, and k and any other of their neighbors. Suppose i has two neighbors (j, and k), and j and k each have 6 and 4 neighboring objects, respectively. Then

$$ELS_i = \frac{2}{2} = 1,$$

$$ELS_j = \frac{1}{6},$$

and

$$ELS_k = \frac{1}{4}.$$

Since object i is inconsistent with all objects it is a neighbor of, it has a high elasticity value. This example is illustrated in Figure 7.

The higher the elasticity value, the more likely the object contributes to the inconsistency. This is the case since an object that is inconsistent with all or many of its neighbors is likely to be the source of the inconsistency more so than an object that is inconsistent with relatively few of its neighbors.

FORMATION OF ELASTICITY-BASED IPR GROUPINGS (EIGS)

Real-world inconsistencies are likely to occur between two or more objects. A technique to group the corresponding objects of a multiobject inconsistency in the spatial representation is required. This can be achieved by grouping objects using knowledge of the IPRs they are part of, as well as their elasticity.

Elasticity is used to group IPRs into multiobject structures that correspond to inconsistencies among multiple entities in the real world. The relative contribution of objects to these multiobject inconsistencies is established using elasticity.

Interpretation of IPRs in Terms of Elasticity

A number of observations can be made about an IPR by looking at the elasticity of its member objects. The observations are later used for grouping IPRs into multiobject inconsistencies. Consider a pair of objects i and j such that $IPR_{ij} = T$. In determining the elasticity of each of the two objects, two types of IPRs are distinguished.

If $ELS_i > ELS_j$ then object i is referred to as the higher elasticity object and j as the lower elasticity object. This occurs if one of the following conditions is satisfied:

- The objects are inconsistent with one another and with no other objects. Object i has fewer neighbors than j. In this scenario, we conclude that the object i that has fewer number of neighbors N is more likely to be used as the basis for grouping IPRs.
- Both objects have the same number of neighbors. Object i is inconsistent with more objects than j. In this scenario we conclude that the object, which is inconsistent with more of its neighbors, is more likely to be used as the basis for grouping IPRs.
- The rate of the number of objects i is inconsistent with, divided by the number of objects it is neighbors with, is greater than the rate of the number of objects j is inconsistent with, divided by the number of objects it is neighbors with. In this scenario we conclude that the object with the higher rate is more likely to be used as the basis for grouping IPRs.

If $ELS_i = ELS_j$ then objects i and j have the same level of elasticity. It occurs if:

- The objects are inconsistent with one another and with no other objects. Object i has the same number of neighbors as does j. In this scenario, no further grouping is required.
- Both objects have the same number of neighbors. Object i is inconsistent with the same number of objects as does j. In this scenario additional information is required to determine which object will be used as the basis for grouping IPRs.
- The number of objects i is inconsistent with, relative to the number of objects it is neighbors with, is the same as the number of objects j is inconsistent with, relative to the number of objects it is neighbors with. In this scenario the object that has a larger number of IPRs is more likely to be used as the starting point for grouping IPRs.

Defining EIGs

An elasticity-based IPR grouping (EIG) is a set of one or more objects where the object of highest elasticity in the group forms an IPR with each of the remaining objects in the group.

Example of an EIG

To clarify this definition, consider the following situation: Consider three objects i, j, and k that are neighbors with one another, but with no other objects. Let i and j form an inconsistent pairwise relation IPR_{ij} such that $ELS_i > ELS_j$. Let i and k form an inconsistent pairwise relation IPR_{ik} such that $ELS_i > ELS_k$. Objects i, j, k are said to constitute an inconsistent set since object i has the highest elasticity value among the three objects and it forms an IPR with each of the other two objects. This is referred to as an Elasticity-based

Figure 8. A schematic view of an EIG

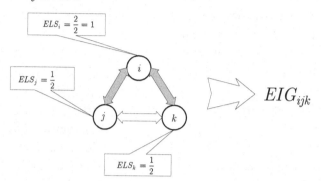

IPR Grouping (EIG) and denote it as ELS_{ijk}. This is illustrated in Figure 8.

Detecting EIGs

This is extended into a technique to analyze all IPRs in the database and group them into EIGs based on the elasticity of the objects which form the IPRs:

1. Determine all IPRs.
2. Extract a list of all objects in all IPRs and determine their elasticity values.
3. Sort the list of objects in descending order by elasticity.
4. Sort objects that have the same elasticity values by the number of IPRs they are a part of (I_j) in descending order.
5. Create the first empty EIG, to which objects will be assigned.
6. For each object in the sorted list (whether it has or has not yet been assigned to constructed EIGs):
   6.1. Determine all IPRs in which this object participates.
   6.2. For each such IPR:
   6.2.1. Identify the second object in the IPR.
       6.2.2. Check the remaining objects in the sorted list (those objects with the same or smaller elasticity values) for occurrence of the second object

regardless if they are already part of one or more EIGs.
       6.2.2.1. If the second object is found:
           6.2.2.1.1.Assign the first object to the current EIG (if not assigned before to this EIG).
           6.2.2.1.2. Assign the second object to the current EIG.
   6.3. If there are still objects that have not yet been assigned to any EIGs:
       6.3.1.Create the next empty EIG to which objects will be assigned.

This results in a list of multiobject inconsistencies (EIGs). Each object's elasticity helps form these inconsistencies. In future work we will explore how elasticity can be used to assist with object adjustment decisions that would eliminate or reduce the number and complexity of such multiobject inconsistencies.

INCORPORATING ELASTICITY INTO SPATIAL DATABASE MANAGEMENT PROCESSES

The proposed approach for detecting multiobject inconsistencies can be incorporated into the toolkits of database management systems that are capable of handling spatial data. Such a tool could be selected from the toolkit by the opera-

Table 1. Source data sets (SDS)

SDS ID	Geographic Coverage of Data Set	Data Source
SDS-1	Guelph	City of Guelph, Canada
SDS-2	Toronto (North York)	Teranet Inc., Canada
SDS-3	Toronto (North York)	North York Municipal Offices, Canada

Table 2. Experimental data set EDS-1

EDS ID	EDS-1		
Geographic Coverage	0.5 km by 0.6 km of Guelph.		
Number of Objects	749		
Layers			
Layer ID	**Layer Description**	**Source SDS**	**Number of Objects**
1	Residence	SDS-1	202
2	Shed	SDS-1	65
3	Property	SDS-1	201
4	Tree	SDS-1	281

tor, or configured to run automatically when the data is added to a data warehouse. It can also be configured to run during data mining operations on the data selected for analysis as part of the queries.

THE STUDY

Experiments were conducted on GIS data from a number of public and private sector organizations. These geographic information systems consist of a cross section of utility infrastructure, commercial, land, and taxation data.

A distinction is made between source data sets (SDS), which are the GIS data warehouse analyzed in this research, and experimental data sets (EDS), which are subsets of one or more SDS on which the experiments were conducted.

Source Data Sets (SDS)

Each SDS examined in this research consists of numerous layers of raw spatial data built and

maintained by highly qualified and experienced people engaged in commercial applications. Three of these SDS are discussed in this section. They are listed in Table 1.

Experimental Data Sets (EDS)

Experimental data sets were created from the source data sets and used throughout this study. This section describes two such EDS that were constructed from the three SDS described in the previous section. The first EDS, denoted EDS-1, was created by selecting a number of layers of SDS-1 in a geographic region, while the second EDS, denoted EDS-2 was formed by combining selected layers from SDS-2 and SDS-3 in a geographic region.

The first experimental data set EDS-1 covers a portion of Guelph, Ontario, Canada, and is discussed in Table 2.

The data in EDS-1 is shown graphically in Figure 9.

The second data set listed in Table 3 comprises of a portion of North York, which was created by

Figure 9. EDS 1

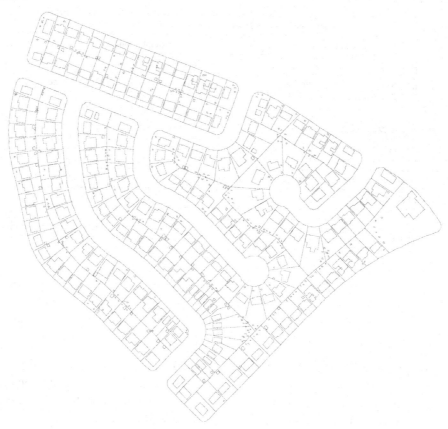

Table 3. Experimental data Set EDS-2

EDS ID	EDS-2		
Geographic Coverage	5,100 ft by 5,700 ft segment of North York		
Number of Objects	9,653		
Layers			
Layer ID	**Layer Description**	**Source SDS**	**Number of Objects**
1	Road	SDS-2	112
2	Property	SDS-2	3,437
3	Building	SDS-3	4,991
4	Water Pipe Junction	SDS-3	609
5	Sewer Manhole	SDS-3	504

Figure 10. EDS 2

combining data from two GIS data warehouses, and adjusting them to common control points.

The data in EDS-2 is shown graphically in Figure 10.

The Experiments

For each of these data sets (EDS-1 and EDS-2), the processing began with the detection of neighboring relations, followed by detection of relation types between neighboring objects. Rules were generated by the software and human experts confirmed the rules validity. Inconsistent Pairwise Relations (IPRs) were detected by comparing the relations to the rules. The elasticity of objects was determined, followed by formation of Elasticity-based IPR Groupings (EIGs).

The Results

The number of IPRs detected based on automatically observed relations that do not correspond to P-Rules or M-Rules are described in the first part of Table 4 and Table 5 for EDS-1 and EDS-2, respectively. Those automatically observed relations, that correspond to M-Rules but have a frequency that is either smaller than the lower bound or larger than the upper bound of the M-Rules, are presented in the second part of these tables.

Table 4. IPRs in EDS-1

EDS-1			
Observed Relation			**Number of IPRs based on Automatically Observed Relation**
Layer	**Layer**	**Relation**	
Residence	Property	Overlap	18
Shed	Property	Overlap	10
Tree	Residence	Overlap	4
Shed	Shed	Overlap	2
Tree	Tree	Overlap	6
Tree	Property	Overlap	1
M-Rule violated	**Nature of Violation**		**Number of IPRs based on Stationary M-Rules which were violated**
M-4 (1 shed in property)	2 sheds in property		4
M-15 (1 residence in property)	2 residences in property		2

Table 5. IPRs in EDS-2

EDS-2			
Observed Relation			**Number of IPRs based on Automatically Observed Relation**
Layer	**Layer**	**Relation**	
Building	Building	Overlap	27
Building	Property	Overlap	142
Building	Road	Overlap	56
Sewer	Road	Overlap	11
Sewer	Property	Overlap	11
Sewer	Building	Overlap	10
Water	Road	Overlap	20
Water	Property	Overlap	20
Water	Building	Overlap	16
M-Rule violated	**Nature of Violation**		**Number of IPRs based on Stationary M-Rules that were violated**
M-12 (property contains between 1 and 2 buildings)	Property contains 3 buildings.		24
M-12 (property contains between 1 and 2 buildings)	Property contains 4 buildings.		4
M-12 (property contains between 1 and 2 buildings)	Property contains 5 buildings.		5

Table 6. IPR summary

	Total IPRs	Number of Objects	IPR as Percent of Objects
EDS-1	47	749	6.27%
EDS-2	346	9653	3.58%

Table 7. Classification of EIGs in EDS-1

EDS-1		
Semantic Description of EIG	**Number of EIGs Automatically Detected**	**Number of EIGs Detected by Visual Inspection**
A Residence overlaps with one Property	2	2
A Residence overlaps with more then one Property	8	8
A Shed overlaps with more then one Property	3	3
A Tree overlaps with a Residence	4	4
A Shed inside one property overlaps with a second Shed. The second Shed overlaps two properties (show drawing here)	2	2
A Tree overlaps with more then one other Tree	1	1
A Tree overlaps with one Tree	3	3
A Tree overlaps with a Residence, and also with another Tree	1	1
A property contains two Sheds	4	4
A property contains two Residences	2	2

The number of IPRs detected in each EDS is listed in Table 6.

The EIGs which were detected by grouping IPRs based on their semantic structure are listed in Table 7 and Table 8 for EDS-1 and EDS-2, respectively, along with the count of the number of such EIGs formed.

The types of objects with highest elasticity in the EIGs are summarized in table 9 and Table 10 for EDS-1 and EDS-2, respectively.

The number of EIGs detected in each EDS is listed in Table 11.

The number of objects in EIGs, and the percent of objects that are in EIGs out of the total number of objects in each EDS are listed in Table 12.

DISCUSSION

The IPRs in EDS-1 listed in Table 4 indicate the existence of isolated incidents of IPRs of different types in very small quantities. This same situation is seen when observing the types of EIGs detected in Table 7. The only exception to this is the number of residences which overlap with more then one property, indicating a possibility of some pattern of inconsistent behavior depending on their proximity. This pattern, if exists, would not be extensive, and therefore, there is no need for clustering EDS-1 or applying a regional strategy to this data set.

The IPRs in EDS-2 listed in Table 5 and the corresponding EIGs in Table 8 indicate an appreciable number of inconsistencies involving buildings, and to a lesser extent inconsistencies involving sewers and water pipe junctions. This

Table 8. Classification of EIGs in EDS-2

EDS-2		
Semantic Description of EIG	**Number of EIGs Automatically Detected**	**Number of EIGs Detected by Visual Inspection**
Two buildings inside one property overlap one another.	14	14
Two buildings overlap one another. One of the buildings is inside a property, the other building overlaps this same property as well as and adjoining property (drawing goes here).	9	9
A building overlaps two properties.	34	34
A building overlaps a property, a second building inside the same property as well as the adjoining road (drawing goes here).	4	4
A building overlaps a property as well as the adjoining road.	26	26
A Sewer overlaps a road and the adjoining property.	7	7
A Building overlaps a property and an adjoining road, as well as a Sewer that overlaps the same road and property.	4	4
A building that overlaps a property and adjoining road, and a sewer that is inside the property.	6	6
A Water Pipe Junction overlaps a road and the adjoining property.	13	13
A Building overlaps a property and an adjoining road, as well as a Water Pipe Junction that overlaps the same road and property.	7	7
A building that overlaps a property and adjoining road, and a Water Pipe Junction that is inside the property.	9	9
A property contains three buildings.	24	24
A property contains four buildings.	4	4
A property contains five buildings.	5	5

Table 9. EIG analysis for EDS-1

EDS-1		
Layer	**Number of EIGs whose Highest Elasticity Object is on the Layer**	**Percent of Total EIGs**
Residence	12	40%
Shed	9	30%
Property	0	0%
Tree	9	30%

situation is clearly demonstrated in Table 10 which shows that 135 buildings require adjustment, as do 20 water pipe junctions and 11 sewer manholes. This same table shows that over 81% of the inconsistencies are due to building objects, with 12% and 7% due to water pipe junctions and sewer manholes respectively. The building layer in EDS-2, which originates from aerial photog-

raphy, is a likely cause of a significant number of the inconsistencies in EDS-2.

Both EDS-1 and EDS-2 were visually inspected for inconsistencies. All inconsistencies found during the visual inspection of the data sets were also automatically detected in terms of EIGs as seen in Table 7 and Table 8.

Table 10. EIG analysis for EDS-2

EDS-2		
Layer	Number of EIGs whose Highest Elasticity Object is on the Layer	Percent of Total EIGs
Road	0	0%
Property	0	0%
Building	135	81.32%
Water	20	12.04%
Sewer	11	6.62%

Table 11. EIG summary

	Total EIGs	Number of Objects	EIG as Percent of Objects
EDS-1	30	749	4.01%
EDS-2	166	9,653	1.72%

Table 12. Percentage of objects in EIGs

	Number of Objects	Number of Objects in EIGs	Percent of objects in EIGs
EDS-1	749	68	9.07%
EDS-2	9653	467	4.83%

A measure of consistency of spatial data is proposed in terms of the number of EIGs, as shown in Table 11, and in terms of objects in EIGs as shown in Table 12. It is apparent from both tables that while EDS-2 has 5 times as many EIGs as EDS-1, EDS-1 is nearly twice as inconsistent as is EDS-2. It therefore seems that the merger of SDS-2 and SDS-3 to form EDS-2 produced consistency levels that are higher than that of EDS-1.

CONCLUSION

A method for detecting inconsistencies between pairs of objects, or IPRs, based on a comparison of observed relations against P-rules and M-rules is presented.

Elasticity, a property of objects is introduced to capture the relative contribution of objects to IPRs. Elasticity is used to group IPRs into multiobject structures, called EIGs, that correspond to inconsistencies among multiple neighboring entities in the real world. The relative contribution of objects in EIGs was established using elasticity, and will be applied to the EIG adjustment process in future publications.

Having systematically formulated inconsistent behavior in spatial data warehouses, the regional aspects of some inconsistencies can be captured by clustering of EIGs. Future work is expected to discuss how elasticity and the clustering techniques are used in the process of finding local and global solutions to EIGs.

REFERENCES

Abler, R. (1987). The national science foundation national center for geographic information and analysis. *International Journal of Geographic Information Systems, 1*(4), 303-326.

Aronoff, S. (1995). *Geographic information systems: A management perspective.* WDL Publications.

Clementini, E., Felice, P. D., & Van Oosterom, P. (1993). A small set of formal topological relations suitable for end-user interaction. In *Advances in Spatial Databases (Third International Symposium, SSD'93),* Singapore (LNCS 692, pp. 277-295). New York: Springer-Verlag.

Cockcroft, S. (2004, March). The design and implementation of a repository for the management of spatial data integrity constraints. *8*(1), 49-69.

Davis, E. (1986). *Representing and acquiring geographic knowledge.* Los Altos, CA: Morgan Kaufmann.

Egenhofer, M. J. (1991). Reasoning about binary topological relations. In *Advances in Spatial Databases (Second Symposium, SDD'91),* Zurich, Switzerland (LNCS)

Egenhofer, M. J., & Franzosa, R. D. (1991). Point-set topological spatial relations. *International Journal of Geographic Information Systems, 5*(2), 161-174.

Egenhofer, M. J., & Franzosa, R. D. (1995). On equivalence of topological relations. *International Journal of Geographical Information Systems, 9*(2), 133-152.

Egenhofer, M., Herring, J. (1990). A mathematical framework for the definition of topological relations. In *Proceedings of the Fourth International Symposium on Spatial Data Handling* (pp. 803-813). Zurich, Switzerland:

Egenhofer, M. J., & Herring, J. R. (1991). *A mathematical framework for the definition of topological relations* (NCGIA Technical Paper, pp. 91-97).

Egenhofer, M. J., & Herring, J. R. (1992). *Categorizing binary topological relations between regions, lines, and points in geographic databases* (Tech. Rep.). Orono: University of Maine, Department of Survey Engineering,

Hadzilacos, T., & Tryfona, N. (1992). In A. Frank, I. Campari, & U. Formentini (Eds.), *A Model for Expressing Topological Integrity Constraints in Geographic Databases: Proceedings of the International Conference on Theories and Models of Spatio Temporal Reasoning in Geographic Space.* Pisa, Italy (LNCS 639, pp. 252-268). New York: Springer-Verlag

Kainz, W. (1991). Logical consistency. In Guptil & Morison (Eds.), *Elements of spatial data quality* (pp.109-137). Oxford, England.

Klien, A. (2007). A rule-based strategy for the semantic annotation of geodata. *Transactions in GIS, 11*(3), 437-452.

Lutz, M., & Kolas, D. (2007). Rule-based discovery in spatial data infrastructure. *Transactions in GIS, 11*(3), 317-336.

Mark, D. M., & Egenhofer, M. J. (1992). An evaluation of the 9-intersection for region line relations. In *Proceedings of GIS/LIS '93,*(pp. 513-521). San Jose, CA:

Mark, D., Frank, A., Egenhofer, M., Freundshuh, S., McGranghan, M., & White, R. M. (Eds.). (1989). *Languages of spatial relations: Report on the specialist meeting for NCGIA research initiative 2* (Tech. Rep. 89-2). National Center for Geographic Information and Analysis.

Medeiros, C. B., & Cilia, M. (1995). Maintenance of binary topological constraints through active databases. In *Proceedings of Third ACM Workshop on GIS.*

Redman, T. C. (1992). *Data quality.* Bantam.

Rodríguez, A. (2005). Inconsistency issues in spatial databases. (LNCS, pp. 237-269). Springer Berlin/Heidelberg.

Servigne, S., Ubeda, T., Zuricelli, A., & Laurini, R. (2000). A methodology for spatial consistency improvement of geographic databases. *GeoInformatica 4*(1), 7-34.

Veregin, H. (1991). *Data quality measurement and assessment.* NCGIA Core Curriculum in Geographic Information Science.

Xu, J. (2007). Formalizing natural-language spatial relations between linear objects with topological and metric properties. *International Journal of Geographical Information Science, 21*(4), pp. 377-395.

Chapter 12
Sequential Patterns Postprocessing for Structural Relation Patterns Mining

Jing Lu
Southampton Solent University, UK

Weiru Chen
Shenyang Institute of Chemical Technology, China

Osei Adjei
University of Bedfordshire, UK

Malcolm Keech
University of Bedfordshire, UK

ABSTRACT

Sequential patterns mining is an important data-mining technique used to identify frequently observed sequential occurrence of items across ordered transactions over time. It has been extensively studied in the literature, and there exists a diversity of algorithms. However, more complex structural patterns are often hidden behind sequences. This article begins with the introduction of a model for the representation of sequential patterns—Sequential Patterns Graph—which motivates the search for new structural relation patterns. An integrative framework for the discovery of these patterns—Postsequential Patterns Mining—is then described which underpins the postprocessing of sequential patterns. A corresponding data-mining method based on sequential patterns postprocessing is proposed and shown to be effective in the search for concurrent patterns. From experiments conducted on three component algorithms, it is demonstrated that sequential patterns-based concurrent patterns mining provides an efficient method for structural knowledge discovery.

INTRODUCTION

Sequential patterns mining is an important data-mining and pattern-discovery technique that aims to find the relationships between occurrences of sequential events and to find if there are any specific orders within these occurrences. It has been extensively studied and several methods have been proposed (Agrawal & Srikant, 1995; Pei, Han, Mortazavi-Asl, & Pinto, 2001; Zaki 2001). However, there are still some challenges within the conventional framework: most methods mine the complete set of sequential patterns and, in many cases, a large set of sequential patterns is not intuitive and not necessarily very easy to understand or use. Also, questions that are usually asked with respect to sequential patterns mining are: What is the inherent relation among sequential patterns? Is there a general representation of sequential patterns? Are there any other novel patterns that can be discovered based on sequential patterns?

These questions pointed out some obstacles within conventional sequential patterns mining methods and indicated further research directions associated with sequential patterns mining that has inspired this work. Since each sequence can be viewed as a partial order of a subset of events, any partial order can be represented by a directed acyclic graph (Mannila & Meek, 2000). It is then possible to describe a set of sequential patterns using a graphical model called Sequential Patterns Graph, or SPG (Lu, Adjei, Chen, & Liu, 2004; Lu, Adjei, Wang, & Hussain, 2004). SPG acts as a bridge between a discrete sequences set and a unified graphical structure. It is not only a minimal representation of sequential patterns mining results, but it also represents the potential interrelation among patterns such as *concurrent*, *exclusive* or *iterative* patterns. The framework for mining these new *structural relation patterns* has been called Postsequential Patterns Mining or PSPM (Lu, Wang, Adjei, & Hussain, 2004).

Figure 1 shows the levels of patterns ranging from a simple frequent itemset (Agrawal, Imielinski, & Swami, 1993), to sequential patterns (Agrawal & Srikant, 1995), to complex structures like graph patterns (Ivancsy & Vajk, 2005), tree patterns (Zaki 2002), partial order patterns (Mannila & Meek, 2000), and the proposed structural relation patterns. The shaded parts in the figure indicate the areas of new work in this article and elsewhere (Lu, Wang, et al., 2004; Lu 2006).

The objectives of the research, which has been undertaken (Lu, 2006), are as follows:

- Propose and construct Sequential Patterns Graph as a new model to represent the relations among sequential patterns.
- Define new structural relation patterns such as concurrent patterns, exclusive patterns, and iterative patterns.
- Elucidate the framework for Postsequential Patterns Mining as an extension of traditional sequential patterns mining.
- Devise methods and develop algorithms for mining structural relation patterns.
- Demonstrate the effectiveness of the method, and analyse the efficiency of the algorithms through experiments.

The remainder of the article is structured as follows: following a summary of sequential patterns mining, the Sequential Patterns Graph model is introduced to represent sequential patterns graphically. In the next section, structural relation patterns are defined formally and the Postsequential Patterns Mining architecture is described. The focus of this article is on *concurrent patterns* and an associated data-mining method, which is then specified along with its component algorithms. The penultimate section gives an experimental evaluation, using synthetic datasets, and the performance of the algorithms is presented in detail. The article draws to a close by making brief conclusions and indicating future research directions.

Figure 1. From frequent itemset to structural relation patterns

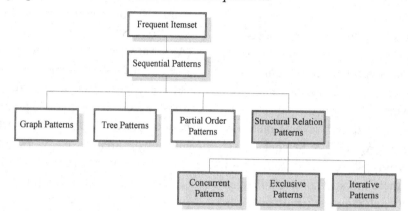

SEQUENTIAL PATTERNS MINING AND MODELLING

Sequential patterns mining aims to discover frequently occurring sequences (or sequential patterns) in a sequence database. It is important to understand the inherent relations among patterns as well as their general representation. Therefore, a graphical model called Sequential Patterns Graph (Lu, Adjei, Chen, et al., 2004; Lu, Adjei, Wang, et al., 2004) was proposed as a model to represent the relations among sequential patterns.

Sequential Patterns Mining

The sequential patterns mining referred to here is based on *frequent itemset mining*, which was originally defined by Agrawal et al. (1993) as follows. Let $I=\{i_1,i_2,...,i_l\}$ be a set of l items and let $TDB=<T_1,T_2,...,T_k>$ be a *transaction database*, where T_j $(1\leq j\leq k)$ is a transaction which contains a set of items in I. Suppose an *itemset*, denoted by $A=(x_1,x_2,...,x_q)$, is an unordered nonempty set of q items. The *support* (or occurrence frequency) of A is the number of transactions containing A in TDB. An itemset A is *frequent* if A's support is no less than a predefined *minimum support threshold*, ξ. Given a transaction database TDB and a minimum support threshold ξ, the problem

of finding the complete set of frequent itemsets is called *frequent itemset mining*.

Following the above concepts for frequent itemset mining, the problem of discovering sequential patterns was considered by Agrawal and Srikant (1995). Their approach introduced some of the most important and basic definitions in sequential patterns mining. A *sequence S*, denoted by $<e_1 e_2 ... e_k>$, is an ordered set of k elements where each element e_i $(1\leq i\leq k)$ is an itemset and k is called the *length* of the sequence. A *sequence database SDB* is considered to be a multiset of sequences or, more specifically, data sequences. A sequence $S_1=<X_1 X_2 ... X_n>$ is *contained* in another sequence $S_2=<Y_1 Y_2 ... Y_m>$ if $n\leq m$ and there exist integers $1\leq i_1<i_2<...<i_n\leq m$ such that $X_j\subseteq Y_{i_j} (1\leq j\leq n)$, and it is denoted by $S_1\angle S_2$. If sequence S_1 is contained in sequence S_2, then S_1 is called a subsequence of S_2 and S_2 a super-sequence of S_1.

The *absolute support* of sequence S in SDB is defined as the number of sequences belonging to SDB that contain S, and the *relative support* is defined as the percentage of sequences belonging to SDB that contain S. The *relative* measure of support will be used throughout this article, where the support of S in SDB is denoted by $S.sup$. The minimum support (*minsup*) is specified by the user and stands for the minimum fraction of total data sequences which support this sequence. A sequence S is called a *sequential pattern* in SDB

Table 1. Sequential patterns index list generated from prefixspan algorithm

SPI	SP	SPI	SP	SPI	SP	SPI	SP	SPI	SP
1	(a)	15	(b)(a)	29	(f)(c)	43	(a)(c)(b)	57	(f)(c)(b)
2	(b)	16	(b)(c)	30	(a)(a,c)	44	(a)(c)(c)	58	(a,b)(d)(c)
3	(c)	17	(b)(d)	31	(a,b)(c)	45	(a)(d)(c)	59	(a)(b)(a,c)
4	(d)	18	(b)(f)	32	(a,b)(d)	46	(b)(d)(c)	60	(a)(b,c)(a)
5	(e)	19	(c)(a)	33	(a,b)(f)	47	(c)(b)(c)	61	(a)(b,c)(c)
6	(f)	20	(c)(b)	34	(a)(b,c)	48	(c)(c)(c)	62	(a)(c)(a,c)
7	(a,b)	21	(c)(c)	35	(b)(a,c)	49	(d)(c)(b)	63	(a)(b,c)(a,c)
8	(a,c)	22	(d)(b)	36	(b,c)(a)	50	(e)(a)(b)	64	(a)(c)(b)(c)
9	(b,c)	23	(d)(c)	37	(b,c)(c)	51	(e)(a)(c)	65	(a)(c)(c)(c)
10	(a)(a)	24	(e)(a)	38	(c)(a,c)	52	(e)(b)(c)	66	(e)(a)(c)(b)
11	(a)(b)	25	(e)(b)	39	(b,c)(a,c)	53	(e)(c)(b)	67	(e)(f)(c)(b)
12	(a)(c)	26	(e)(c)	40	(a)(b)(a)	54	(e)(f)(b)		
13	(a)(d)	27	(e)(f)	41	(a)(b)(c)	55	(e)(f)(c)		
14	(a)(f)	28	(f)(b)	42	(a)(c)(a)	56	(f)(b)(c)		

if *S.sup≥minsup*. A sequential pattern is called a *maximal sequence* if it is not contained in any other sequential patterns.

Using the above definitions, Agrawal and Srikant (1995) proposed the problem of sequential patterns mining as follows: given a sequence database SDB, where each sequence consists of a list of elements and each element consists of a set of items, and given a minimum support threshold, sequential patterns mining aims to discover the set of all sequential patterns (*SP*) in SDB.

Example 1 Consider a sequential patterns mining example used in *PrefixSpan* (Pei et al., 2001): given SDB={<*a*(*a,b,c*)(*a,c*)*d*(*c,f*)>, <(*a,d*) *c* (*b,c*) (*a,c*)>, <(*e,f*) (*a,b*) (*d,f*) *c b*>, <*e g* (*a,f*) *c b c*>} with a minsup of 50%. Table 1 shows the set of all sequential patterns under this setup and the *Sequential Patterns Index, SPI*, is used for easy reference in the rest of the article.

Given a SDB and user specified minsup, a set of sequential patterns can be discovered from sequential patterns mining. All sequential patterns marked within the boxes in Table 1 are sub-sequences of maximal sequences.

Sequential Patterns Graph

The use of graphs to model complex datasets has been recognised by various researchers in different domains. In the field of Knowledge Discovery, using graphs is an expressive and versatile modelling technique that provides ways to reason about information implicit in the data (Cook & Holder, 2000; Garriga 2005; Lin & Lee, 2005). Typically, nodes of these graphs are sets of items, and edges represent the relationships of specificity among them. This has led to the development of a sequential patterns model that explores the inherent relationship among sequential patterns. All sequential patterns under minsup can be generated from the maximal sequences. Thus, a directed acyclic Sequential Patterns Graph or SPG [16,17] can be used to represent the maximal sequence sets. Figure 2 shows an SPG that corresponds to the set of maximal sequences and, therefore, the complete set of sequential patterns in Table 1.

With reference to Figure 2, it is seen that nodes (i.e., items or itemsets) of SPG correspond to elements in a sequential pattern and directed edges are used to denote the sequence relation between

Figure 2. A sequential patterns graph of sequential patterns in Table 1

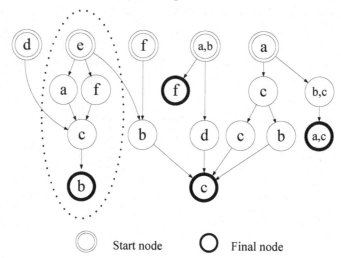

two elements. Any path from a start node to a final node corresponds to one maximal sequence. Two special types of nodes called the start node and the final node are used to indicate the beginning and end of maximal sequences.

As a further example, consider the segment circled by a dotted line above; it represents maximal sequences <eacb> and <efcb> in particular; it also represents other sequential patterns <e>, <a>, <c>, <f>, <b>, <ea>, <ef>, <ec>, <eb>, <ac>, <fc>, <ab>, <fb>, <cb>, <eac>, <efc>, <eab>, <efb> and <ecb>. Hence, SPG is a summary of sequential patterns, useful for representing results to users. The definition, properties and the construction method of SPG are developed systematically in (Lu, Adjei, Chen, et al., 2004; Lu, Adjei, Wang, et al., 2004).

The significance of SPG is not limited to the minimal representation of a collection of sequential patterns. It also motivates the further relationships among sequential patterns to be discovered. Some sequential patterns may be supported by the same data sequence, and these are called *concurrent patterns*; while some others may not possibly occur in the same data sequence, and these are called *exclusive patterns*. Furthermore, some

sequential patterns may occur more than once in a data sequence, such that an iterative relationship is expressed, and this is called an *iterative* pattern. This leads to more complex structured patterns called *structural relation patterns*, to be defined formally in the next section.

STRUCTURAL RELATION PATTERNS AND POSTSEQUENTIAL PATTERNS MINING

With the successful development of efficient and scalable algorithms for mining frequent itemsets and sequences, the literature has been extended to other structures like partial order (Atallah, Gwadera, & Szpankowski, 2004; Garriga & Balcazar, 2004; Mannila & Meek, 2000), graph (Cook & Holder, 2000; Han & Yan, 2004; Huan, Wang, Prins, & Yang, 2004) and tree (Zaki, 2002) patterns. The search for novel patterns defined here can be motivated using SPG and the framework to mine this new knowledge is known as Postsequential Patterns Mining (Lu, Adjei, Wang, et al., 2004).

Structural Relation Patterns

For the following definitions, it is assumed that $\{sp_1,sp_2,\ldots,sp_m\}$ is the set of m sequential patterns and they are *not* contained in each other.

Definition 1 Concurrence and Concurrent Patterns: *The concurrence of sequential patterns $sp_1,sp_2,\ldots,sp_k (1\leq k\leq m)$ is defined as the fraction of data sequences that contain all of the sequential patterns. This is denoted by*

$$concurrence(sp_1,sp_2,\ldots,sp_k)=|\{C:\forall i \ (i=1,2,\ldots,k)$$
$$sp_i \angle C, C \in SDB\}|/|SDB| \qquad (1)$$

where $sp_i \angle C$ represents sequential pattern sp_i contained in data sequence C and the symbol $|\ldots|$ denotes the number of data sequences.

Let *mincon* be the user specified minimum concurrence. If

$$concurrence(sp_1,sp_2,\ldots,sp_k)\geq mincon \qquad (2)$$

is satisfied, then $sp_1,sp_2,\ldots,sp_k$ are called *concurrent patterns*. This is represented by $ConP_k=[sp_1+sp_2+\ldots+sp_k]$ where k is the number of sequential patterns which occur together, and the notation '+' represents the concurrent relationship.

Example 2 Consider SDB=$\{<a (a,b,c) (a,c) d (c,f)>, <(a,d) c (b,c) (a,c)>, <(e,f) (a,b) (d,f) c b>, <e g (a,f) c b c>\}$ and assume a *mincon* of 50%. Since both data sequences $<(e,f) (a,b) (d,f) c b>$ and $<e g (a,f) c b c>$ support sequential patterns $<ebc>$, $<eacb>$ and $<efcb>$, then:

$$concurrence(<ebc>, <eacb>, <efcb>)=2/4=50\%.$$

Therefore, they constitute a concurrent pattern given by $ConP_3=[<ebc>+<eacb>+<efcb>]$.

The definition of a sequence contained in another sequence can be applied to concurrent patterns.

Definition 2 Maximal Concurrent Patterns: *Concurrent pattern $ConP_k=[a_1+a_2+\ldots+a_k]$ is contained in concurrent pattern $ConP_{(k+m)} =[b_1+b_2+\ldots +b_{k+m}]$ if $a_i \angle b_j$, for $1\leq i\leq k$ and $1\leq j\leq (k+m)$. This is denoted by $ConP_k \angle ConP_{(k+m)}$.*

Concurrent patterns are called *maximal* if they are not contained in any other concurrent patterns.

In a complementary manner, the relationship between sequential patterns that do *not* typically occur together in data sequences can be explored when a maximum exclusion degree *maxexc* is specified.

Definition 3: Exclusive Patterns: *Sequential patterns sp_1 and sp_2 are called exclusive patterns if*

$$concurrence(sp_1,sp_2)\leq maxexc \qquad (3)$$

is satisfied, and is represented by ExcP=$[sp_1-sp_2]$, where the notation '$-$' represents the exclusive relationship.

The maxexc degree is the extent that sequential patterns are allowed to occur together and remain exclusive. Consider the same sequence database SDB in Example 2 and assume a maxexc of 0. Any data sequence in SDB which contains $<a(b,c)(a,c)>$ does not contain $<efcb>$, and vice versa. Therefore, the concurrence is zero and an exclusive pattern ExcP=$[<a(b,c)(a,c)>-<efcb>]$ is obtained.

Definition 4: Iterative Patterns: *A sequential pattern sp is known as an iterative pattern if it appears within the same data sequence at least n times ($n \geq 2$) and at most m times ($m \geq n$). The expression $<\{sp\}_n^m>$ denotes the iterative pattern, where m and n represent the upper and lower*

Figure 3. Architecture of postsequential patterns mining

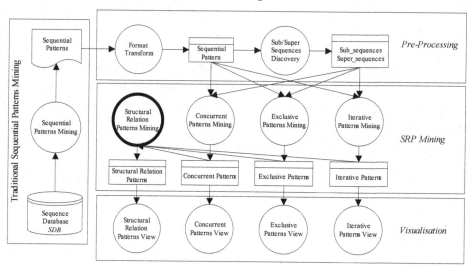

iteration bounds respectively, which means the maximal and minimal number of patterns appearing in a data sequence. If an iterative pattern has no upper iteration bound, then the parameter m is not required.

As an illustration, consider the SDB of Example 2 again and assume a minsup of 50%; then an iterative pattern $\{c\}_3$ can be obtained, where c is a sequence of length 1, which iterates three times in the first two data sequences.

Definition 5: Structural Relation Patterns (SRP): *A structural relation pattern (SRP) is a general designation of patterns that consists of sequential patterns, concurrent patterns, exclusive patterns, iterative patterns and their composition. That is, a concurrent pattern is an SRP. Similarly, an exclusive pattern and an iterative pattern are SRPs.*

Furthermore, the concurrent, exclusive or iterative combination of structural relation patterns constitutes new *SRPs*.

Postsequential Patterns Mining

Having defined structural relation patterns the main problem is to find a method to mine such patterns. This subsection will introduce a new approach called postsequential patterns mining, or PSPM (Lu, Adjei, Wang, et al., 2004), which is used to provide a framework for mining structural relation patterns.

It is interesting to note that structural relation patterns are often hidden within sequential patterns. With years of research and development, there have been many efficient and scalable sequential patterns mining methods devised. In order to capitalise on these pattern discovery techniques, sequential patterns mining is used to drive PSPM. Further analysis of the inherent relationships behind sequential patterns results in the identification of more complex structures—such as concurrent patterns, exclusive patterns or iterative patterns—to be discovered.

Figure 3 shows the architecture of PSPM and its relationship with traditional sequential patterns mining. It is clear that, in order to pursue postsequential patterns mining, the traditional sequential patterns mining should be performed first (as indicated to the left of the figure). A sequence database provides the input and sequential patterns are discovered after sequential patterns mining. Postsequential patterns mining can be viewed as a three-phase process: *Preprocessing*, *SRP Mining* and *Visualisation* (as indicated from the top to the bottom of the figure).

The first Preprocessing task transforms the result of sequential patterns mining into the appropriate format for the system. This phase also finds the subsequences and supersequences of each sequential pattern, which is straightforward and necessary for the following phase.

SRP Mining corresponds to the execution of the mining algorithm. This phase is complex and has several challenges that can be characterised in principle as follows:

i. Representation of structural relation patterns, including the formal (or logical) representation, computer internal representation and visual representation.
ii. Development of effective methods to discover structural relation patterns, based on sequential patterns post-processing.
iii. Adoption of appropriate data sequences to test the algorithms and analyse their performance for efficiency.
iv. Understanding of the actual meanings of structural relation patterns, related to the application area of real-world datasets.

During the final Visualisation phase, the mined structural relation patterns can be represented graphically, although it is not covered in this article.

CONCURRENT PATTERNS MINING METHOD AND ALGORITHMS

Concurrency is an important aspect of some system behaviour. For example, discovering patterns of concurrent behaviour from traces of system events is useful in a wide variety of software en-

gineering tasks, including architecture discovery, reengineering, user-interaction modelling, and software-process improvement. The structural relation patterns of particular interest here are concurrent patterns and this section will propose a corresponding data-mining method and its three component algorithms, indicating computational complexity.

Concurrent Patterns Mining Method

The three main steps in this method to mine concurrent patterns are described below:

1. Calculation of Sequential Patterns Supported by Data Sequences (*SuppSP*)

Sequential patterns which are supported by a sequence C (i.e., $C \in SDB$) are computed and denoted by:

$$SuppSP(C) = \{sp: sp \in SP \wedge sp \angle C\} \qquad (4)$$

The union of sets $SuppSP(C_1), SuppSP(C_2), \dots, SuppSP(C_n)$, where $C_i \in SDB$ ($1 \leq i \leq n$, n is the number of data sequences in SDB), are the sequential patterns supported by the sequence database SDB, denoted by:

$$SuppSp = \bigcup_{i-1}^{n} SuppSP(C_i) \qquad (5)$$

The detailed algorithms for this step will be defined in the next section.

2. Determination of Concurrent Patterns (*ConP*)

Each $SuppSP(C_i)$ can be viewed as a transaction (i.e., the unordered set of sequential patterns supported by data sequence C_i). Thus, the problem of finding the concurrent patterns which satisfy the user specified minimum concurrence (mincon) becomes one of mining frequent itemsets under

Table 2. Sequential patterns supported by each data sequence

DSI	SuppSP
1	1,2,3,4,6,8,9,10,11,12,15,16,19,20,21,22,23,30,34,35,36,37,38,39,40,41,42,43,44,47,48,49, 59,60,61,62,63,64,65
2	1,2,3,4,5,7,8,11,12,13,14,16,17,18,20,22,23,24,25,26,27,28,29,31,32,33,43,45,46,49,50,51,5 2,53,54,55,56,57,58,66,67
3	1,2,3,4,6,7,8,9,10,11,12,13,14,15,16,17,18,19,21,23,30,31,32,33,34,35,36,37,38,39,40,41,42 ,44,45,46,48,58,59,60,61,62,63,65
4	1,2,3,5,6,11,12,16,20,21,24,25,26,27,28,29,41,43,44,47,50,51,52,53,54,55,56,57,64,66,67

minsup. Therefore, the traditional frequent itemset mining approach can be adapted for this step.

3. Finding Maximal Concurrent Patterns (*Max-ConP*)

According to the containing relationship among sequences, the ConP need to be simplified in order to get the maximal concurrent patterns. This can be obtained using Definition 2 by:

a.   Deleting the concurrent patterns which are contained by other concurrent patterns;

b.   Deleting the sequential patterns in ConP which are contained by other sequential patterns of the ConP.

Example 3 An example is given to explain how to mine concurrent patterns based on traditional sequential patterns mining. In order to do this, the sequence database SDB in Example 1 and sequential patterns in Table 1 are considered again for illustration. The following steps correspond to the three described above and show the effectiveness of the method in a worked example.

Step 1. Using the results from Table 1, SuppSP are computed for every data sequence in order. These results are shown in Table 2, where the column SuppSP lists the sequential patterns index supported by the corresponding *Data Sequence Index, DSI.*

Step 2. To calculate concurrent patterns, consider mincon to be 50%, which means finding the groups of sequential patterns which occur together in more than 50% of the data sequences. Then the frequent itemset mining method is used to discover concurrent patterns with the minimum support threshold set to mincon. The results are listed below:

11 12 16 3 2 1: 4
11 12 16 3 2 1 21 23 41 44 4 65 63 62 61 60 59 48 15
    42 40 39 38 37 36 35 34 30 19 10 9 8 : 2
11 12 16 3 2 1 23 4 6 13 14 58 46 45 17 33 32 31
    18 7 : 2
11 12 16 3 2 1 20 23 43 4 49 22 : 2
11 12 16 3 2 1 20 43 6 67 66 57 56 55 54 53 52 51
    50 5 29 28 27 26 25 24 : 2
11 12 16 3 2 1 20 21 41 43 44 64 47 : 2
11 12 16 3 2 1 6 : 3
11 12 16 3 2 1 21 41 44 6 : 2
11 12 16 3 2 1 23 4 : 3
11 12 16 3 2 1 21 41 44 : 3
11 12 16 3 2 1 20 43 : 3

Each line above represents a concurrent pattern. For example,

11 12 16 3 2 1: 4

means concurrent pattern [11+12+16+3+2+1] and the value after the symbol ":" is the number of sequences which support this concurrent pattern.

Algorithm 1. FCmine (FC)

Input: Sequence database (SDB); sequential patterns (SP).

Output: Sequential patterns supported by data sequences (SuppSP).

Procedure:

(1) **For** each data sequence C_i in SDB

(2)   {SuppSP(C_i)=$\varnothing$ // SuppSP(C_i) is the pattern set supported by C_i

(3)   **For** each $sp_k \in$ SP   // k is the identifier of sp_k and ranges from 1 to the length of SP

(4)   {**If** $sp_k \angle C_i$ // sp_k is contained in data sequence C_i.

(5)   SuppSP(C_i)=SuppSP(C_i)+sp_k; }

(6)   SuppSP=SuppSP+SuppSP(C_i);}}

Step 3. In the above example, consider the three concurrent patterns underlined in step 2; since

$$[11+12+16+3+2+1] \angle [11+12+16+3+2+1+6] \angle [11+12+16+3+2+1+21+41+44+6],$$

then neither of the concurrent patterns [11+12+16+3+2+1] and [11+12+16+3+2+1+6] are maximal, and they can be deleted.

One can then ask: is $ConP_{10}$=[11+12+16+3+2+1+21+41+44+6] a maximal concurrent pattern now? Further work is still needed and, in this case, the sub-sequence which was calculated during the Preprocessing phase is useful. For example, for $ConP_{10}$ and referencing Table 1, the following contained relationships exist:

$$1\angle 11\angle 41,\ 2\angle 11\angle 41,\ 3\angle 11\angle 41 \text{ and } 1\angle 12\angle 41,$$
$$2\angle 12\angle 41, 3\angle 12\angle 41, 16\angle 41, 21\angle 44$$

Therefore 1,2,3,11,12,16,21 can be deleted from $ConP_{10}$, which results in $ConP_3$=[6+41+44].

Deleting all nonmaximal concurrent patterns gives the results below, which show the maximal concurrent patterns (MaxConP).

[23+63+65]
[52+56+66+67]
[11+33+58]

[16+43+49]
[6+41+44]

Using these results and Table 1, the patterns are represented as

[dc+a(b,c)(a,c)+accc]
[ebc+eacb+efcb+fbc]
[ab+(a,b)f+(a,b)dc]
[bc+acb+dcb]
[f+abc+acc]

Algorithms

The focus in this sub-section is on the first step of the concurrent patterns mining method—how to calculate sequential patterns supported by data sequence (i.e., SuppSP). Two categories of algorithms, called Full-Check (*FCmine*) and Partial-Check (*PCmine*), are developed for mining such sequential patterns. The FCmine algorithm is given below in pseudo-code.

Performance Analysis: Algorithm 1

In the FCmine algorithm, data sequences are compared with all the sequential patterns. Therefore, the complexity is O($m \times n$), where n is the

Algorithm 2. TopDown (TD)

Input: Sequence database (SDB); sequential patterns (SP)

Output: Sequential patterns supported by data sequences (SuppSP)

Procedure:

(1) **For** each data sequence C_i in SDB

(2) {Let SuppSP(C_i) be empty

(3) Clear marks of all sequential patterns

(4) **For** each $sp_k \in$ SP   // k is the identifier of sp_k and ranges from the length of SP to 1

(5)   {**If** (*no* mark on sp_k) and ($sp_k \angle C_i$)

(6)   {SuppSP(C_i)=SuppSP(C_i)+sp_k+SubSeq(sp_k);

(7)   **Mark**(sp_k,true);

(8)   **Mark**(SubSeq(sp_k),true);}

(9)   }

(10) SuppSP=SuppSP+SuppSP(C_i); }

---

number of data sequences and m is the number of sequential patterns.

An alternative category of algorithms, called Partial-Check (*PCmine*), is proposed to mine sequential patterns supported by data sequence. Before addressing this category concerning *SuppSP* mining, two lemmas are presented based on an antimonotone *Apriori* property, which states in Agrawal et a l. (1993) *if a pattern with k items is not frequent, any of its superpatterns with (k+1) or more items can never be frequent.*

Lemma 1 If a sequential pattern *sp* is supported by a data sequence *C*, then all the sub-sequences of *sp* must be supported by *C* too.

Lemma 2 If a sequential pattern *sp* is not supported by a data sequence *C*, then all the supersequences of *sp* cannot be supported by *C* either.

PCmine is similar to *FCmine* in that it also checks the relationship between data sequence and sequential pattern. But it is different from the latter in that *PCmine* utilises the above lemmas and is able to avoid some comparisons of sequential patterns.

Depending on different usage of the above two lemmas, the *PCmine* category can be divided into two algorithms:

TopDown Algorithm (i.e., Lemma1 is used);
BottomUp Algorithm (i.e., Lemma 2 is used).

Both of these algorithms require the use of subsequences or super-sequences of sequential patterns that are calculated during the Preprocessing phase. Since the sub-sequences or supersequences are also used in other phases of the mining, there is no extra computational cost in the use of the algorithms.

The following notation is used to make the proposed algorithm more concise and clear:

- **SubSeq***(sp_k)***:** Represents a set of sub-sequences of sequential patterns sp_k

- **SupSeq***(sp_k)***:** Represents a set of supersequences of sequential patterns sp_k

- **Mark***(sp_k,true)***:** Sets the mark of sp_k to be *true* (i.e., sequential pattern sp_k is supported by a data sequence)

- **Mark***(sp_k,false)***:** Sets the mark of sp_k to be *false* (i.e., sequential pattern sp_k is not supported by a data sequence)

Algorithm 3. BottomUp (BU)

Input: Sequence database (SDB); sequential patterns (SP)

Output: Sequential patterns supported by data sequences (SuppSP)

Procedure:

(1) **For** each data sequence C_i in SDB

(2)   {SuppSP(C_i)=$\varnothing$

(3)   Clear marks of all sequential patterns

(4)   **For** each $sp_k \in$ SP   // k is the identifier of sp_k and ranges from 1 to the length of SP

(5)   {**If** (*no* mark on sp_k)

(6)   {**If** ($sp_k \angle C_i$)

(7)   {SuppSP(C_i)=SuppSP(C_i)+sp_k;

(8)   **Mark**(sp_k,true);}

(9)   **else**

(10)   {**Mark**(sp_k,false);

(11)   **Mark**(SupSeq(sp_k),false);} }

(12)   SuppSP=SuppSP+SuppSP(C_i);}

Performance Analysis: Algorithm 2

The *TopDown* algorithm makes use of Lemma 1. That is, if a data sequence C_i supports a sequential pattern sp_k, then all sub-sequences of sp_k (i.e., SubSeq(sp_k)), are also supported by C_i (see rows (5) and (6) in Algorithm 2). These sub-sequences of sp_k need not be checked further. Therefore, in this approach, only the following two types of sequential pattern need to be checked in order to determine if they are supported by a data sequence:

a. sequential patterns whose supersequences *are not* supported by the data sequence;

In this case, given a sequential pattern *sp* and for any data sequence *C*, the minimum support implies that the extent that *sp* is not supported by *C* is (1-*minsup*). Clearly for *m* sequential patterns the extent will be $m \times (1\text{-}minsup)$.

b. sequential patterns which have no super-sequences (i.e., maximal sequences)

Compared with the number of sequential patterns, the number of maximal sequences is small. For example, consider a maximal sequence of length L, where there are 2^{L-1} sub-sequences and the maximal sequence is just the fraction $1/(2^{L-1}+1)$ of these patterns.

So, generally speaking, most sequential patterns which need to be checked are from case a). This means that the number of sequential patterns may be computed as $m \times (1\text{-}minsup)$ times. On the whole, the complexity of the *TopDown* algorithm is $O(n \times m \times (1\text{-}minsup))$ and it is efficient when minsup is greater than 0.5 and approaches 1.

Performance Analysis: Algorithm 3

In the *BottomUp* approach, only the following two types of sequential pattern need to be checked in order to determine if they are supported by a data sequence:

a. sequential patterns which have no sub-sequence.

b. sequential patterns whose sub-sequences *are* supported by the data sequence.

If a sequential pattern is *not* supported by a data sequence, then its supersequences are not either and therefore do not need to be compared against the data sequence.

The complexity of this algorithm is $O(n \times m \times minsup)$ and it is more efficient when minsup is smaller, especially when minsup is less than 0.5 and approaches 0. A small minsup means lower support for sequential patterns from data sequences (i.e., most of the data sequences will not support a sequential pattern and therefore will not support its supersequences, which is often the case for real applications).

It can be concluded that the complexities of algorithms 1, 2 and 3 increase as the number of data sequences (n) and the number of sequential patterns (m) increase. In algorithms 2 and 3 the complexities depend on the factors (1-*minsup*) and *minsup* respectively; therefore the *TopDown* and *BottomUp* algorithms of *PCmine* are likely to be more efficient than *FCmine*.

The three algorithms described above correspond to step 1 of the data-mining method specified in the previous subsection—the calculation of sequential patterns supported by data sequences (i.e., *SuppSP*). Any frequent itemset mining can be used in step 2 to generate concurrent patterns so long as all of the SuppSP have been discovered. SuppSP(C_i), ($1 \leq i \leq n$), is an unordered set and can be considered as a transaction T_i in TDB. The minimum support threshold is taken to be the minimum concurrent threshold *mincon* and the results of this mining—frequent itemsets—are the concurrent patterns required. An efficient mining technique called CLOSET (Pei, Han, & Mao, 2000) can for example be used in this step. It is worth noting that the data reduction from step 1 to step 2 is from $O(n \times m)$ to at most $O(n)$.

Finally, maximal concurrent patterns need to be discovered. The key requirement in step 3 is checking the *containing* relationship between sequences, which is straightforward in principle.

EXPERIMENTS

To evaluate the efficiency of the algorithms, experiments were performed on large-scale synthetic datasets that show consistent and promising results. The performance of the algorithms was measured by comparing their running time on a dedicated computer.

Experimental Set-Up and Datasets

The experiments for concurrent patterns mining were performed on a 2.4GHz Pentium PC, with 1.0GB main memory, running under Microsoft Windows 2000. To make the time measurements more reliable, no other application was allowed to run on the system while the experiments were running.

Synthetic sequence data used in this experiment were generated using the IBM data generator, which has been used in most sequential patterns mining studies (Agrawal & Srikant, 1995; Pei et al., 2001; Zaki 2001). The particular software was retrieved in July 2007 from IBM Almaden (http://www.almaden.ibm.com/cs/projects/iis/hdb/Projects/data_mining/datasets/syndata.html).

The datasets consist of sequences of itemsets, where each itemset represents a market basket transaction.

This synthetic dataset generator produces a database of data sequences whose characteristics can easily be controlled by the user. The generator allows one to specify the number of data sequences |**D**|, the average number of transactions in a sequence |**C**|, the average length of maximal potentially large sequences |**S**|, the average number of items in a transaction |**T**|, and the number of

Table 3. Parameter settings of datasets

Name	$\|C\|$	$\|T\|$	$\|S\|$	$\|N\|$	$\|D\|$	Size (KB)
C10-T8-S8-N1K-D10K	10	8	8	1,000	10,000	2540
C50-T2.5-S4-N1K-D1K	50	2.5	4	1,000	1,000	635
C200-T2.5-S4-N1K-D1K	200	2.5	4	1,000	1,000	2520
C100-T4-S4-N100-D100	100	4	4	100	100	193

different items $\|N\|$. Table 3 characterises the test datasets appropriate to this article.

The convention for the datasets can be described as follows: dataset *C10-T8-S8-N1K-D10K*, for example, means that the dataset contains 10,000 (i.e., 10K) data sequences and the number of items is 1,000 (i.e., 1K). The average number of items in a transaction (i.e., event) is set to 8, and the average number of transactions per data sequence is set to 10. Using the same convention as noted previously, it is straightforward to deduce the meanings of the other datasets in Table 3. These four synthetic datasets are used to compare the performance of algorithms in mining concurrent patterns.

Calculation of Sequential Patterns Supported by Data Sequence

The respective performance is considered here for the three algorithms proposed in the previous section for mining *SuppSP*; that is, the *FC* (Full Check mining), *TD* (TopDown Partial mining) and *BU* (BottomUp Partial mining) algorithms. The experiments use the four synthetic datasets *C10-T8-S8-N1K-D10K*, *C100-T4-S4-N100-D100*, *C100-T4-S4-N100-D100* and *C50-T2.5-S4-N1K-D1K*, which are described in Table 3. The corresponding pattern distributions resulting from mining the above datasets are listed in Figure 4 (from *a* to *d*), which shows the number of sequential patterns of different lengths for various levels of minsup.

To explain the experimental results, one may distinguish between "dense" datasets and "sparse" datasets. A dense dataset has many frequent patterns of larger size and higher support, while datasets with mainly short patterns are called sparse. Longer patterns may exist in sparse datasets, but only with very low support.

It can be seen from Figure 4(*a*) that the sequence database *C10-T8-S8-N1K-D10K* is sparse. For example, when minsup is 1% or more, the length of sequential patterns is very short (only 2 or 3). From the data distributions which are shown in Figure 4 (*b* to *d*), one may conclude that datasets *C100-T4-S4-N100-D100*, *C100-T4-S4-N100-D100* and *C50-T2.5-S4-N1K-D1K* are relatively dense.

The three algorithms *FC*, *TD* and *BU* were all found to be effective in calculation of the sequential patterns supported by data sequences, so the analysis presented below is comparing their efficiency. Figure 5(a-d) demonstrates the relationship between the running time and the minimum support (minsup) on the four datasets respectively. Note that the running time excludes the data reading time and the result writing time.

The following conclusions are drawn from the experiments on the four datasets.

1. The test results demonstrate that the three algorithms are able to discover all sequential patterns supported by data sequences (SuppSP) to varying levels of efficiency, depending on the minimum support (minsup).

Figure 4. Pattern distributions from mining synthetic datasets

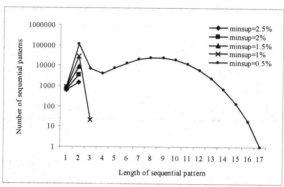

(a) Dataset **C***10***-T***8***-S***8***-N***1K***-D***10K*

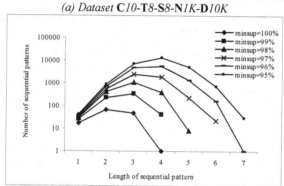

(b) Dataset **C***100***-T***4***-S***4***-N***100***-D***100*

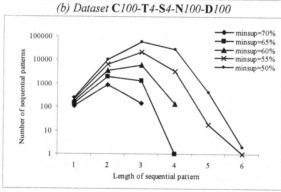

(c) Dataset **C***200***-T***2.5***-S***4***-N***1K***-D***1K*

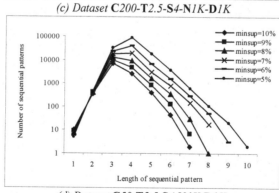

(d) Dataset **C***50***-T***2.5***-S***4***-N***1K***-D***1K*

Figure 5. Performance of algorithms FC, TD and BU on four datasets

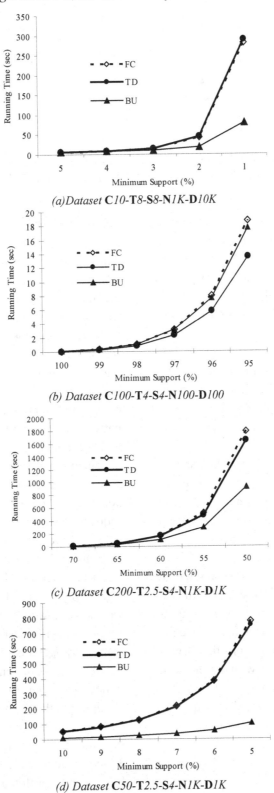

(a)Dataset **C***10-***T***8-***S***8-***N***1K-***D***10K*

(b) Dataset **C***100-***T***4-***S***4-***N***100-***D***100*

(c) Dataset **C***200-***T***2.5-***S***4-***N***1K-***D***1K*

(d) Dataset **C***50-***T***2.5-***S***4-***N***1K-***D***1K*

Figure 6. From concurrent patterns to concurrent branch patterns

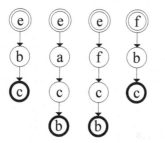

(a) Concurrent Pattern
[ebc+eacb+efcb+fbc]

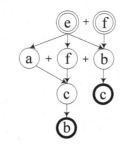

(b) Concurrent Branch Pattern
[<e[<bc>+<[a+f]cb>]>+<[e+f]bc>]

2. The FC algorithm is generally less efficient than the TD and BU algorithms. The reason is that FC is based on a full checking approach; therefore, each sequential pattern is compared to every data sequence in the database in order to determine if it is supported.

3. The TD algorithm is most efficient (see Figure 5 (b)) only when minsup is large, for example as it approaches 1. This confirms its computational complexity of O(n×m×(1-minsup)) discussed in the previous section.

4. The BU algorithm is most efficient (see Figures 5 (a), (c) and (d)) as minsup becomes smaller. Computational complexity of O(n×m×minsup) is again confirmed from before.

Clearly, the BU algorithm is of most practical value from the above results, especially in real large-scale applications where minsup is typically small. It is also worth noting that, while the TD algorithm starts checking from the largest sequential patterns, BU begins with the shortest, and larger sequential patterns require more items to be compared within the same data sequence and, hence, need more time in general.

CONCLUSION AND FUTURE WORK

The challenge of mining patterns not only relates to the search for frequent itemsets, but also more and more complex patterns. The work described in this article is intended to develop data-mining techniques in order to discover new structural relations through the postprocessing of sequential patterns. Thus, the main contributions of this article are drawn from three key areas that encompass sequential patterns graph, postsequential patterns mining, and a novel data-mining method and component algorithms for the discovery of concurrent patterns.

The concurrent patterns mining method has been shown to be effective in the calculation of sequential patterns supported by data sequences, which leads on to the determination of concurrent patterns and the maximal concurrent patterns contained therein. The performance of the three algorithms proposed was analysed and found to vary according to the minimum support threshold, enabling an efficient mining approach to be taken across a range of cases.

In order to extend the current research, an indication of some further work is outlined below. To highlight this with an example, the concurrent pattern $ConP_4$ = [ebc+eacb+efcb+fbc]—one of the patterns resulting from mining in Example 3—can be represented graphically by Figure 6(a). It is clear from this graph that some sequential patterns have a common prefix (i.e., *<ebc>*, *<eacb>* and *<efcb>* share *e*) and some have a common postfix (i.e., *<eacb>* and *<efcb>* share *cb*). Taking out the common prefix and/or postfix leads to another new type of pattern called a *Concurrent Branch Pattern* or *CBP* (Lu, 2006), represented graphically in Figure 6(b).

The expression and construction method of SPG can be adapted to concurrent branch patterns representation, and characterised as *Concurrent Branch Patterns (CBP) Graph*. The formal definition and method for this is the subject of another piece of work, which extends the PSPM framework to CBP mining. In addition, there is potential for future work to cover other forms of structural patterns—such as exclusive patterns and iterative patterns—to fulfil the complete mining of structural relation patterns.

ACKNOWLEDGMENT

This work was supported by Liaoning (China) Education Office, Science Technology and Research Project No.20040287. Thanks to Professor Jiawei Han of University of Illinois at Urbana-Champaign, particularly for his kind suggestions for this work.

REFERENCES

Agrawal, R., Imielinski, T., & Swami, A. (1993). Mining association rules between sets of items in large databases. In *Proceedings of the 1993 ACM SIGMOD* (pp. 207-216).

Agrawal, R., & Srikant, R. (1995). Mining sequential patterns. In *Proceedings of 11th International Conference on Data Engineering* (pp. 3-14). Taipei, Taiwan: IEEE Computer Society Press.

Atallah, M. J., Gwadera, R., & Szpankowski, W. (2004). Detection of significant sets of episodes in event sequences. In *Proceedings of the Fourth International Conference on Data Mining* (pp. 3-10).

Cook, D. J., & Holder, L. B. (2000). Graph-based data mining. *IEEE Intelligent Systems, 15*(2), 32-41.

Garriga, G. C. (2005). Summarizing sequential data with closed partial orders. In *Proceedings of the SIAM International Conference on Data Mining, California* (pp. 380-391).

Garriga, G. C., & Balcazar, J. L. (2004). Coproduct transformations on lattices closed partial orders. In *Proceedings of the Second International Conference on Graph Transformation* (pp. 336-351). Rome, Italy, .

Han, J. W., & Yan, X. F. (2004). From sequential patterns mining to structured pattern mining: A pattern-growth approach. *Journal of Computer Science and Technology, 19*(3), 257-279.

Huan, J., Wang, W., Prins, J., & Yang, J. (2004). SPIN: Mining maximal frequent subgraphs from graph databases. In *Proceedings of the 10th ACM SIGKDD* (pp. 581-586). Seattle, WA:

Ivancsy, R., & Vajk, I. (2005). A survey of discovering frequent patterns in graph. In *Proceedings of Databases and Applications* (pp. 60-72). ACTA Press.

Lin, M. Y., & Lee, S. Y. (2005). Fast discovery of sequential patterns through memory indexing and database partitioning. *Journal of Information Science and Engineering, 21,* 109-128.

Lu, J. (2006). *From sequential patterns to concurrent branch patterns: A new post sequential patterns mining approach.* Unpublished doctoral dissertation, University of Bedfordshire, UK.

Lu, J., Adjei, O., Chen, W.R., & Liu, J. (2004). Post sequential patterns mining: A new method for discovering structural patterns. In *Proceedings of the Second International Conference on Intelligent Information Processing* (pp. 239-250). Beijing, China: Springer-Verlag.

Lu, J., Adjei, O., Wang, X. F., & Hussain, F. (2004). Sequential patterns modelling and graph pattern mining. In *Proceedings of the 10th International Conference IPMU* (Vol. 2, pp. 755-761). Perugia, Italy.

Lu, J., Wang, X. F., Adjei, O., & Hussain, F. (2004). Sequential patterns graph and its construction algorithm. *Chinese Journal of Computers, 27*(6), 782-788.

Mannila, H., & Meek, C. (2000). Global partial orders from sequential data. In *Proceedings of the 6th Annual Conference on Knowledge Discovery and Data Mining (KDD-2000)* (pp. 161-168).

Pei, J., Han, J. W., & Mao, R. (2000). CLOSET: An efficient algorithm for mining frequent closed itemsets. In *Proceedings of the 2000 ACM-SIGMOD International Workshop Data Mining and Knowledge Discovery* (pp. 11-20).

Pei, J., Han J. W., Mortazavi-Asl, B., & Pinto, H. (2001). PrefixSpan: Mining sequential patterns efficiently by prefix-projected pattern growth. In *Proceedings of the Seventh International Conference on Data Engineering* (pp. 215-224). Heidelberg, Germany.

Zaki, M. J. (2001). SPADE: An efficient algorithm for mining frequent sequences. *Machine Learning, 42*(1/2), 31-60.

Zaki, M. J. (2002). Efficiently mining frequent trees in a forest. In *Proceedings of the SIGKDD* (pp. 71-78).

This work was previously published in International Journal of Data Warehousing and Mining, Vol. 4, Issue 3, edited by D. Taniar, pp. 71-89, copyright 2008 by IGI Publishing (an imprint of IGI Global).

Chapter 13
MILPRIT*:
A Constraint–Based Algorithm for Mining Temporal Relational Patterns

Sandra de Amo
Universidade Federal de Uberlândia, Brazil

Waldecir P. Junior
Universidade Federal de Uberlândia, Brazil

Arnaud Giacometti
Université François Rabelais de Tours, France

ABSTRACT

In this article, we consider a new kind of temporal pattern where both interval and punctual time representation are considered. These patterns, which we call temporal point-interval patterns, aim at capturing how events taking place during different time periods or at different time instants relate to each other. The datasets where these kinds of patterns may appear are temporal relational databases whose relations contain point or interval timestamps. We use a simple extension of Allen's Temporal Interval Logic as a formalism for specifying these temporal patterns. We also present the algorithm MILPRIT* for mining temporal point-interval patterns, which uses variants of the classical levelwise search algorithms. In addition, MILPRIT* allows a broad spectrum of constraints to be incorporated into the mining process. An extensive set of experiments of MILPRIT* executed over synthetic and real data is presented, showing its effectiveness for mining temporal relational patterns.

INTRODUCTION AND MOTIVATION

The problem of discovering sequential patterns in temporal data has been studied extensively in the past years (Pei et al., 2004; Srikant & Agrawal, 1996; Zaki, 2001), and its importance is fully justified by the great number of potential application domains where mining sequential pat-terns appears as a crucial issue, such as financial market (evolution of stock market shares quotations), retailing (evolution of clients purchases), medicine (evolution of patient symptoms), local weather forecast, telecommunication (sequences of alarms output by network switches), and so forth. Most of these patterns are specified by formalisms, which are, to some extent, reducible to Propositional Linear Temporal Logic, where time is represented by points in a straight line. For instance, let us consider a classical sequential pattern of the form $s = <\{a,b\}, \{c,d\}>$ (where $\{a,b\}$ and $\{c,d\}$ are sets of items purchased by a client. This sequential pattern can be expressed in the Propositional Linear Temporal Logic by the formula $P_a \wedge P_b \wedge \Diamond (P_c \wedge P_d)$, where for each $i \in \{a, b, c, d\}$, P_i is a propositional symbol standing for "client buys item i." The symbol $\Diamond$ stands for the temporal operator *sometimes in the future* (for a comprehensive survey on Linear Temporal Logic (Emerson, 1990)). The need for a more expressive kind of temporal patterns arises, for instance, when modeling Unix users' behavior (Jacobs & Blockeel, 2001). Consider, for instance[1], the following sequence of commands related to latex users: *ls, vi paper.tex, latex paper.tex, dvips paper. dvi, lpr paper.ps*. This sequence of commands can be represented as a sequence of relational (or first-order) atoms of the form: *ls, vi(paper:tex), latex(paper:tex), dvips(paper: dvi), lpr(paper:ps)*. Within such a database of sequences of relational atoms, it would be possible to discover that the relational sequence pattern *vi(X), latex(X)* is frequent. Notice that this pattern tells us that the sequence of commands (predicates) *vi, latex* is frequently requested by users. In order to specify this kind of sequential patterns, we need a more powerful logical formalism, the First-Order Linear Temporal Logic, since the elements involved in the patterns include both predicates and their parameters.

In all the previous examples illustrating the propositional and relational settings of the sequential pattern mining problem, the events are instantaneous; that is, the time when they happen is represented as a point (instant) in a straight line. The sequence of events corresponds to a sequence of instants when these events take place. However, there are many situations where events have a certain *duration*, and thus, the underlying time is measured in terms of *intervals* instead of points. In this article, we propose a new temporal pattern in-

volving a hybrid representation for time and a new algorithm (MILPRIT*) for mining them. These patterns, which we call *temporal point-interval patterns* (or pi-patterns for short), aim at capturing how events taking place in time intervals or time instants relate to each other. For instance, (1) in a medical application, we could be interested in discovering if patients who take some medicine X during a certain period of time P, and in some moment m in P undergo a stomach surgery, will present the symptom Z *during* a period of time beginning *right after* the surgery and *finishing* as soon as they stop taking the medicine X; (2) in an agricultural application, we could be interested in discovering if the use of some organic fertilizer *during* a period of time has an effect on the way a plant grows *during* and *after* the fertilizer application. The following example illustrates the medical application in more detail.

Example 1 (Running Example): *Let us consider the database schema* **R** = *{ Patient, Med, Symp, Hist } and the relational database instance D over* **R** *illustrated in Figure 1. Notice that the following behavior is verified by 50% of the patients (two patients out of four in the Patient relation verified it; namely, Paul and Sarah): the patient takes penicillin during a certain period of time e; during a period of time f following his taking the medicine, he feels dizzy and undergoes a stomach surgery someday t during f.*

Temporal pi-patterns are specified as a set of atomic first-order formulae where time is represented by an interval-time variable or by a point-time variable, together with a set of temporal predicates *{ before, meets, overlaps, during, starts, finishes }*. Our logical formalism for specifying pi-patterns is based on Allen's First Order Interval Logic (Allen & Ferguson, 1994). For instance, the temporal pattern described in Example 1 is specified by the triple $(K, \mathcal{D}, \mathcal{T})$ where: $K =$ *Patient(x)* (where x is a registered patient), $\mathcal{D} = \{$ *Med(x, penicillin, e), Symp(x, dizziness, f), Hist(x,*

Figure 1. A temporal relational database instance

Patient

Pname
Paul
Charles
Mary
Sarah

Med

Pname	Mname	T_{int}
Paul	penicillin	[1,3]
Charles	tetracyclin	[4,7]
Mary	penicillin	[8,10]
Sarah	penicillin	[4,6]

Symp

Pname	Sname	T_{int}
Paul	dizziness	[4,6]
Charles	dizziness	[5,6]
John	fever	[8,10]
Sarah	dizziness	[8,10]

Hist

Pname	Event	T_{point}
Paul	stomach surgery	[5]
Mary	childbirth	[3]
Sarah	stomach surgery	[9]

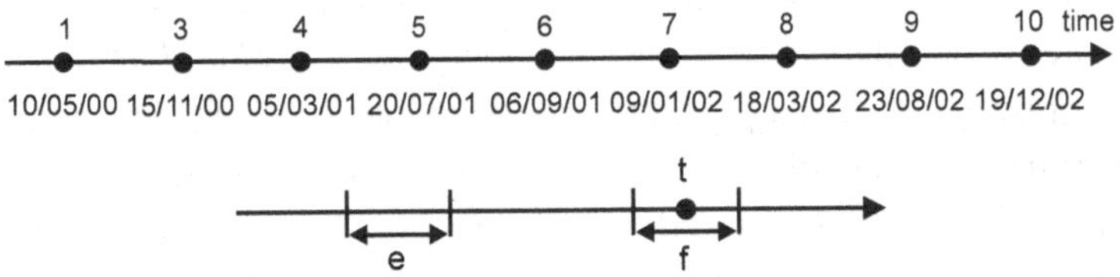

st.surgery, t) } (representing the events that take place in the pattern), $\mathcal{T}$ = *{ before(e,f), during(t,f) }* (representing the relationships verified by the time parameters associated to the pattern events).

In most applications, the lack of user control for specifying the kind of patterns he or she would find interesting can lead to tedious and computationally costly postprocessing phases. In this article, we use a formalism based on regular expression in order to allow users to specify the *shape* of potentially interesting patterns. Our temporal mining method MILPRIT* is constraint-based; it incorporates constraints inside the mining process.

Doing so, it accomplishes two goals: it saves a lot of calculation in the postprocessing phase, and it allows a non-negligent reduction in the search space of potential patterns. The following example illustrates the idea of using regular expressions to specify constraints on sequential patterns.

Example 2 (Running Example): *Let us consider the same situation depicted in Example 1. Users could be interested only in discovering pi-patterns where patients take some medicine (maybe more than one) and at the end present some symptom. Roughly speaking, we can say that these patterns fit into the regular expression format Med*Symp. In this case, it would be important that patterns representing situations where patients present a list of symptoms and after that take some medicine are not generated in the mining process since such patterns do not fit in the given regular expression format.*

Usually in real-world applications, it is important to allow different time granularities to be considered when evaluating pattern support; otherwise, some interesting patterns will not be mined. For instance, let us consider a database schema ***R*** = *{ R(A,T), S(B,T) }*, where *T* is an interval-time attribute. If the values of the temporal attributes in the database are dates (day/month/year), the temporal predicate *meets(e,f)* will be true in this database only if *e* and *f* are mapped into time intervals $[d_1,d_2]$, $[d_3,d_4]$, respectively, where d_1, d_2, d_3, d_4 are dates, and $d_2 = d_3$. If there are very few pairs of tuples $R(a,[d_1,d_2])$, $S(a, [d_2,d_4])$, we are unable to mine patterns of the form *(K(x), { R(x,e), S(x,f) }, { meets(e,f) })*. On the other hand, we can have a lot of pairs of tuples $R(a, [d_1,d_2])$, $S(a, [d_3,d_4])$ where d_2 and d_3 are different days but belong to the same week in the year. In this case, if we relax the time granularity and consider *week* to be the time unity, then d_2 and d_3 will be considered identical, and hence, the pattern *(K(x),* *{ R(x,e), S(x,f) }, { meets(e,f) })* will be mined. The algorithm MILPRIT* we present in this article allows users to specify different time granularities when evaluating the pattern support.

Related Work

A lot of studies on constrained-based temporal mining, in a propositional context, have been investigated in order to reduce the huge amount of patterns that are generated in the relational mining context. (Srikant & Agrawal, 1996) is a pioneer work introducing constraints in sequential pattern mining in order to reduce execution time and the number of discovered patterns. In this work, the constraints (minmax, slide-window) are related to the way the support of patterns is counted and not to the format of patterns. Recently, many works on constrained-based temporal mining have investigated formalisms to specify constraints over the pattern format. Regular expressions have been adopted in many of these proposals as a very general mechanism to specify user constraints. Garofalakis, Rastogi & Shim (1999) was a pioneer work in this field, introducing the SPIRIT family of algorithms for constraint-based sequential pattern mining. Lorincza and Boulicaut (2003) and Pei, Han, and Wang (2002) extended this pioneer work by proposing new and more efficient algorithms (RE-Hackle and Prefix-Growth, respectively) for sequential pattern mining where regular expressions are used to specify useful patterns beforehand. Such constraints are pushed inside the mining process instead of being verified only in a postprocessing phase. Antunes and Oliveira (2004), following the lines of Garofalakis, et al. (1999), proposed a more general formalism based on context-free grammars in order to specify constraints over sequential patterns.

In de Amo and Furtado (2007), we tackled the constraint-based temporal mining problem in the relational context by proposing a formalism to specify constraints over the temporal patterns we

had introduced in de Amo, Giacometti, Furtado, and Laurent (2004). In Lee and De Raedt (2002), the algorithm SeqLog, based on Inductive Logic Programming, was introduced for discovering relational sequential patterns with constraints. In Masson and Jacquenet (2003), the algorithm Spirit-Log, designed to mine relational temporal patterns was introduced. Spirit-Log extends SeqLog (where time is punctual), by pushing regular expression constraints inside the mining process. A comprehensive text about constraint-based temporal *relational* pattern mining following an inductive database approach can be found in Boulicaut, De Raedt, and Mannila (2006). In all these works, time is represented by points in a straight line. The approach we propose in this article is more general since it allows mining relational temporal patterns where time is represented by *points* as well as by *intervals*. We notice that most real-world applications involve both kinds of time representation.

In Hoppner (2001), Allen's Propositional Interval Logic has been used for the first time to treat the problem of discovering association rules over time series (Allen & Ferguson, 1994). In Lattner and Herzog (2005), an approach similar to ours is presented for temporal relational pattern mining where time is represented as intervals. However, this approach is not constraint-based like ours. Moreover, no experimental results concerning the performance of the proposed method are provided, which makes difficult a comparative analysis with our approach.

The issue of allowing user-specified different time granularities during support counting has been treated in the pioneer work of Srikant and Agrawal (1996) and Bettini, Wang, Jajodia, and Lin (1998) in the context of sequential pattern mining and time series. Here, patterns were specified in a formalism equivalent to propositional temporal logic. Moreover, time attributes are *point*-valued. We emphasize that our approach is more general since it is developed in a temporal *relational* database context where time attributes may be *point*-valued as well as *interval*-valued.

Our Contribution

We can summarize our main contributions as follows: (1) the introduction of a new temporal relational pattern allowing interval and point-based time representation in relations, as well as a logical formalism to specify these patterns; (2) the introduction of pattern constraints in the mining process, more precisely during the candidate generation phase; (3) the possibility of considering different user-specified time granularities during the support count phase; (4) the design and implementation of an algorithm (MILPRIT*) to mine such constrained temporal patterns; and (5) an extensive set of experiments over synthetic and real datasets. This is an extended version of the paper (de Amo, Giacometti, & Pereira, 2007). In that paper, we had only considered interval-based time representation in relations, and we had not treated user-specified time granularities. MILPRIT* is a generalization of the MILPRIT algorithm presented in de Amo, et al. (2007), designed to mine point-interval patterns with user-specified time granularities. The introduction of point-based time representation required considering a broader set of temporal predicates in the generation phase. We took care to consider a minimal set of new temporal predicates in order to simplify the generation phase without losing completeness. MILPRIT* can be considered as a general algorithm for temporal relational pattern mining since it can be executed over a dataset of multiple tables with point-based and interval-based timestamps. It can be applied in any situation that can be modeled by a temporal relational database involving point-valued and interval-valued attributes. Medical applications, for instance, are typical applications where both time representations (point-based and interval-based) must be considered. In this article, we focus

on this kind of application when evaluating the efficiency of our algorithm (see Section 5.2).

Article Organization

This article is organized as follows. In Section 2, we formalize the main concepts related to the problem of mining pi-patterns. In Section 3, we propose a constraint-based framework for mining pi-patterns and formalize all the concepts involved in the presentation of the main algorithm (MIL-PRIT*). Section 4 is dedicated to the presentation of MILPRIT*, an algorithm for mining pi-patterns with constraints. In Section 5, we present and analyze some experimental results obtained by executing MILPRIT* over synthetic data as well as over real data related to a medical application. Finally, in Section 6, we present our concluding remarks and discuss some future research on the subject.

PROBLEM FORMALIZATION

In this section, we introduce the main concepts related to the problem of discovering temporal point-interval patterns.

The Dataset

First, let us describe the datasets where the discovery procedure will be executed later on. We assume a set of attributes symbols $A_1, A_2, ...,$ called *data attributes*, and two special attribute symbols T_{it} and T_{pt}, called *interval-time attribute* and *point-time attribute*, respectively. Let $\boldsymbol{R} = \{ K, R_1, ..., R_n \}$ be a database schema such that each relational schema R_i is of the form $R_i(A^i_p, ..., A^i_{k(i)}, T_{pt})$ or $R_i(A^i_p, ..., A^i_{k(i)}, T_{it})$, and relational schema K (called the *reference relation*) is of the form $K(A_p, ..., A_m)$. The attributes appearing in K (all data attributes) are called *reference attributes*.

The values for data attributes A_i are taken within a set $\boldsymbol{Dom}$, called the *data domain*. The attribute T_{it} takes values in the set $I = \{\ [i,j]\ |\ i,\ j \in \mathbb{N},\ i < j\ \}$. The elements of I are intervals $[i, j]$ where i and j are natural numbers mapping dates: i is the starting date and j is the ending date of the interval $[i,j]$. The attribute T_{pt} takes values in the set $\mathbb{N}$. Elements of T_{pt} are natural numbers mapping dates. Naturally, a *point* can be viewed as an interval $[i,j]$ where $i = j$. In our approach, in order to optimize the generation phase of the algorithm MILPRIT*, we treat interval and points as distinct entities, emphasizing that the starting and ending points of an interval are different.

A *temporal dataset* over $\boldsymbol{R}$ is a set of temporal relations $\{\ k,\ r_1,\ ...,\ r_n\ \}$ where each r_i is a set of tuples $(a_1,\ ...,\ a_{n(i)},\ e)$ over R_i and k is a set of tuples over K. We will assume that the relations r_i with interval-valued timestamp are *coalesced* (Böhlen, Snodgrass & Soo, 1996); that is, if $(a_1,\ ...,\ a_k,\ e)$ and $(a_1,\ ...,\ a_k,\ f) \in r_i$, then $e \cap f = \varnothing$, (i.e., intervals associated to a same tuple are maximal). The dataset depicted in Figure 1 is a temporal dataset with the following schema:

$\boldsymbol{R} = \{$ *Patient(PName), Med(PName, MName, T_{it}), Symp(PName, SName, T_{it}), Hist(PName, Event, T_{pt})* $\}$.

Temporal pi-Patterns

Let $\boldsymbol{R} = \{\ K,\ R_1,\ ...,\ R_n\ \}$ be a database schema. Let us suppose four disjoints sets $\mathcal{V}$ (data variables, denoted by $x, y, z, x_1, ...$), C (data constants, denoted by $a, b, c, a_1, ...$), $\mathcal{V}_{it}$ (interval-time variables, denoted by $e, f, g, e_1, ...$), and $\mathcal{V}_{pt}$ (point-time variables, denoted by $t, s, t_1, s_1, ...$). Let us also assume the set of temporal predicates $\mathcal{P}_T = \{$ *before, meets, overlaps, during, finishes, starts* $\}$, as in Allen's Interval Logic (Allen & Ferguson, 1994). A *data atom* over the database schema $\boldsymbol{R}$ is an expression of the form $R(x_1, ..., x_n, e)$ where $R \in \boldsymbol{R}$, $(R \neq K)$, each x_i is a data variable or a data constant, and e is an interval-time or point-time variable (depending on the time attribute of R). A *temporal atom* is an expression of the form

Figure 2. Semantics of temporal predicates

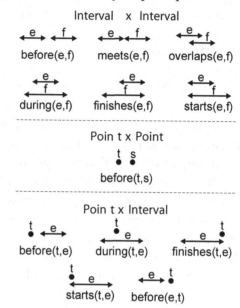

$r(e,f)$, where r is one of the temporal predicates in $\mathcal{P}_T$ and e, f are interval-time or point-time variables. If $r \in \{$ *overlaps, meets* $\}$, then e and f are interval-time variables. For the temporal predicates *before, during, starts, finishes*, we may have different temporal atoms: *before(e,f), before(t,e), before(e,t), before(t,s), during(e,f), during(t,e), starts(e,f), starts(t,e), finishes(e,f), finishes(t,e)*, where e, f are interval-time variables and t, s are point-time variables. Figure 2 illustrates the semantics of the temporal predicates. For instance, the formula *before(e,f)* is true if the variables e and f are evaluated as $[4,6]$ and $[8,9]$, respectively. The formula *before(t,e)* is true if t is evaluated as 5 and e as $[6,7]$. The formula *during(e,f)* is true if the variables e and f are evaluated as $[5,7]$ and $[4,9]$, respectively.

Definition 1 (Temporal pi-Pattern): *A temporal pi-pattern (temporal point-interval pattern) is a triple $(K, \mathcal{D}, \mathcal{T})$ where (1) $\mathcal{D}$ is a set of data atoms, (2) $\mathcal{T}$ is a set of temporal atoms, and (3) K is a special data atom $K(x_1, ..., x_n)$ whose variables $x_1, ..., x_n$ appear in $\mathcal{D}$. The data atom K is called the reference query of the pi-pattern $(K, \mathcal{D}, \mathcal{T})$. It* *is essential in the definition of a pi-pattern, since it specifies what is counted. It plays the same role in our setting as the atom key in the Datalog patterns of Dehaspe and Toivonnen (1999).*

Example 3 (Running Example): *Let us consider the temporal pi-pattern (Patient(x), $\mathcal{D}$, $\mathcal{T}$) where $\mathcal{D}$ = { Med(x,y,e), Symp(x,z,f) } and $\mathcal{T}$ = { before(e,f) }. Intuitively, this temporal pattern translates the fact that a patient x takes a medicine y (not specified) during a period of time e and during a further period of time f (after he or she has stopped taking the medicine y) presents a symptom z (not specified). Note that we are always interested in analyzing the behavior of patients registered in the relation Patient, even though relations Med and Symp may contain data related to other patients (not only those registered in Patient). For this reason, Patient(x) is called the reference query.*

An *instantiation* of an interval-time variable e (resp. a point-time variable t) is a mapping v associating an interval $v(e) = [i,j]$ to e (resp. a point i to t), where i and j are natural numbers (mapping dates). A *ground temporal atom* is the temporal atom obtained by instantiating its interval-time and point-time variables.

Definition 2 (Support and Frequency of a pi-Pattern): *Let D be a temporal database over the schema $\mathbf{R}$ = { K, R_1, ..., R_n } and M = (K(x_1, ..., x_m), { D_1, ...,D_s}, { T_1,...,T_l}) be a temporal pi-pattern over $\mathbf{R}$. The support of M with respect to D, denoted by sup(M) (omitting the dataset D, for the sake of simplifying the notation), is defined by sup(M) = |{ u∈K | u ⊨ Q_M}| / |K| where Q_M is the relational calculus query $\exists y_1 \exists y_2... \exists y_k K(x_1, ..., x_m)(D_1 \wedge D_2 \wedge ... \wedge D_s \wedge T_1 \wedge ... \wedge T_l)$, and $y_1, ..., y_k$ are the data variables not appearing in the reference query K(x_1,...,x_m). The expression u ⊨ Q_M means that u is an answer to the query Q_M when executed over D. Given $0 \leq \alpha \leq 1$, we say that the temporal*

pi-pattern M is frequent with respect to D and α if sup(M) ≥ α.

Example 4 (Running Example): *Let us consider the temporal pi-pattern M = (Patient(x), { Med(x,y,e), Symp(x,z,f) },{before(e,f) }). Let D be the temporal database instance illustrated in Figure 1. The relational query Q_M can be specified in the relational algebra formalism by the expression π_{PName}(Patient ⋈ Med ⋈ Symp). The answer of Q_M is {(Paul), (Sarah)}. Note that Charles is not an answer. Indeed, Charles has taken tetracycline and was dizzy during (and not after) the time he was taking this medicine. John is not an answer either, because he has not taken any medicine at all. So, the support of M w.r.t. D is 1/2.*

In what follows, we suppose that the set of temporal atoms $\mathcal{T}$ is *consistent* (i.e., the temporal variables can be instantiated in a consistent way). Formally, a set of temporal atoms $\mathcal{T}$ is *consistent* if there is an instantiation v of the set of temporal variables appearing in $\mathcal{T}$, such that the ground atoms obtained are simultaneously true. We denote this by $v \models \mathcal{T}$. For instance, the set of temporal atoms { before(e,f), before(f,g), before(g,e) } is not consistent, because the first two atoms imply that e comes before g, and thus, there is no way to instantiate the temporal variables e, f, and g in order to make the three temporal formulae simultaneously true. We also suppose that the set $\mathcal{T}$ is *complete* (i.e., for each pair of temporal variables e, f appearing in $\mathcal{T}$, it is possible to infer a unique temporal relationship between e and f.) For instance, the set { before(e,f), meets(f,g) } is complete because the relationship between e and g is completely determined (even though it does not appear explicitly in the set); the only possibility is before(e,g). On the other hand, { during(e,f), overlaps(f,g) } is not complete, since the relationship between e and g is not deterministically implied by the two relationships during(e,f), overlaps(f,g); it could be (1) before(e,g), (2) meets(e,g), (3) overlaps(e,g), (4) during(e,g), or (5) starts(e,g). That is, for each one of the five temporal atoms *(I)* (where *(I)* ∈ { *(1), (2), (3), (4), (5)* }), the set { *during(e,f), overlaps(f,g), (I)* } is consistent.

Representing Temporal pi-Patterns as Sequences

The notion of consistency and completeness of a set of temporal atoms is essential in our approach. As we will see next, given a consistent and complete set of temporal atoms, its temporal variables can be ordered in a natural way. This implies that a pi-pattern can be viewed as *a sequence of data atoms*. And so, we can naturally think about *regular expressions* as a formalism for specifying special sets of pi-patterns. Due to space limitation, we will only give an informal definition of the order relation $<_T$ over the set of temporal variables appearing in a pi-pattern. The idea can be easily formalized.

Let us consider the domain I for the interval-time variables and the domain $\mathbb{N}$ for the point-time variables. We can view a natural number n as an interval *[n,n]*. So, we consider the set $I^* = I \cup \mathbb{N}$ as being constituted of intervals *[i,j]*, with $i \leq j$. Let *[a,b]* and *[c,d]* in I^*. We say that *[a,b] < [c,d]* if and only if one and only one of the following conditions is verified: (1) $b < d$ or (2) $b = d$ and $a < c$. It can easily be shown that < is a (strict) total order over the set I^*.

The (strict) ordering < over the interval structure I^* naturally induces an ordering $<_T$ over the set of temporal variables (interval-time and point-time) appearing in the set of temporal predicates T of a pi-pattern. The following example illustrates the idea: let T = { *before(e,f), starts(f,g)* }. Then the induced ordering over the set of temporal variables *{e, f, g}* appearing in T is $e <_T f <_T g$. Indeed, for **all** instantiation v of the temporal variables, $v(e) = [a_e, b_e]$, $v(f) = [a_f, b_f]$, $v(g) = [a_g, b_g]$, such that the predicates in T are simultaneously true, the ending points b_e, b_f, b_g satisfy $b_e < b_f < b_g$. That is, for **all** instantiation v, we have $v(e) < v(f) < v(g)$.

The following theorem guarantees that the relation $<_T$ is well-defined and also an order relation.

Theorem 1. *Let T be a complete and consistent set of temporal atoms. Then (1) the definition of $<_T$ does not depend on the particular instantiation v of the temporal variables appearing in T and (2) $<_T$ is a strict order relation over the set of temporal variables appearing in T.*

Proof (Sketch). *In order to simplify the presentation, we suppose that we have only interval-time variables. The case where one has interval-time and point-time variables is treated in a similar way. (1) By the fact that T is consistent, we can affirm that there exists a valuation v of the temporal variables appearing in T such that $v \vDash T$. If v is unique, then $<_T$ is well-defined, since there is a unique way to define it through the valuation v. Now, let us suppose that such valuation is not unique; that is, let us suppose that v and v' are two valuations of temporal variables of T such that $v \vDash T$ and $v' \vDash T$. From the fact that T is complete, we can affirm without loss of generality that there exists a temporal predicate r such that $v \vDash r(e,f)$ and $v' \vDash r(e,f)$. So, $v(e) < v(f)$ if and only if $r(e,f)$ is either before(e,f) or during(e,f) or meets(e,f) or overlaps(e,f) or finishes(e,f) or starts(e,f). In each one of these cases, from the fact that $v' \vDash r(e,f)$, we conclude that $v'(e) < v'(f)$. (2) In order to prove that $<_T$ is a strict order over the temporal variables appearing in T, we must show that it satisfies the irreflexivity and transitivity properties. It is obvious that $<_T$ is irreflexive. Let $e <_T f$ and $f <_T g$, where e, f, g are temporal variables appearing in T. Let $r(e,f)$, $r'(f,g)$ and $r''(e,g)$ be the unique temporal relationship inferred from T for the pair of variables (e,f), (f,g), and (e,g), respectively. We can guarantee this by using the fact that T is complete. As T is consistent, there exists a valuation v of the temporal variables e, f, g such that $v \vDash r(e,f) \wedge r'(f,g) \wedge r''(e,g)$. Now, using the fact that $e <_T f$ and $f <_T g$, and considering all the possibilities for the temporal predicates r, r',* *and r ", it is not difficult to show that $v(e) < v(g)$ in all cases.*

The induced order $<_\mathcal{T}$ over the temporal variables appearing in a temporal pi-pattern M allows us to view M as a sequence of data atoms. Indeed, let $M = (K, \mathcal{D}, \mathcal{T})$ where $\mathcal{D} = \{ p_1(x^1_1, ... , x^1_{n(1)}, e_1), ..., p_k(x^k_1, ..., x^k_{n(k)}, e_k)\}$. Since we are assuming that $\mathcal{T}$ is complete and consistent, then, according to Theorem 1, its temporal variables are ordered by the order $<_\mathcal{T}$. Let us suppose, without loss of generality, that $e_1 <_\mathcal{T} e_2 <_\mathcal{T} ... <_\mathcal{T} e_k$. So, the set $\mathcal{D}$ can be viewed as the sequence $< p_1(x^1_1, ..., x^1_{n(1)}, e_1), ..., p_k(x^k_1, ..., x^k_{n(k)}, e_k) >$.

TEMPORAL PI-PATTERNS WITH RESTRICTIONS

In an application where the user has a previous idea of some specific characteristics of the patterns he or she is searching, the user can be overwhelmed with uninteresting patterns. In this section, we propose to use regular expressions as a formalism to specify a broad spectrum of constraints over pi-patterns in order to better satisfy user requirements as well as to reduce the search space of patterns.

A *mode* over a temporal database $\boldsymbol{R} = \{ K, R_1, ..., R_n \}$ is an expression of the form $R(u_1, ..., u_s, \#)$, where each u_i is a data variable or the (new) symbol *, # is a new symbol, and $R(A_1, ..., A_k, T)$ is one of the predicates $R \in \boldsymbol{R}$, $T \in \{ T_{it}, T_{pt} \}$. We say that a data atom $R(y_1, ..., y_s, e)$ is in accord with the mode $R(u_1, ..., u_s, \#)$, if for each $i = 1, ..., s$ we have: (1) If u_i is a variable then $y_i = u_i$; (2) If $u_i = $ *, then y_i is a variable or a constant; and (3) e is a interval-time variable if $T = T_{it}$ or a point-time variable if $T = T_{pt}$. For instance, *Med(x, *, #)* is a mode and the atom *Med(x, penicillin, e)* is in accord with *Med(x, *, #)*. On the other hand, the atom *Med(y, penicillin, e)* is not in accord with the mode *Med(x, z, #)*.

Let Σ be a set of modes over $\boldsymbol{R} = \{ K, R_1, ..., R_n \}$. In what follows, we will consider regular languages (sets of strings) over the alphabet Σ. These languages are specified by regular expressions. Given a regular expression E over the alphabet Σ, we denote by $W(E)$ the set of strings (words) verifying E. We denote by $P(E)$ the set of prefixes of strings in $W(E)$. We will need this notation later.

Definition 3 (The Search Space): *Let $\boldsymbol{R} = \{ K, R_1, ..., R_n \}$ be a database schema, Σ a set of modes over $\boldsymbol{R}$, and E a regular expression over Σ. The search space defined by E is the set of temporal pi-patterns $(K(x_1, ..., x_m), \mathcal{D}, \mathcal{T})$ such that $\mathcal{D} = < p_1(t^1_1, ..., t^1_{l(1)}, e_1), ..., p_n(t^n_1, ..., t^n_{l(n)}, e_n) >$ satisfies the following properties: (1) There exists a string $w_1 w_2 ... w_n \in W(E)$, such that p_i is in accord with w_i for each $i = 1, ..., n$; (2) For each data atom $p_i(x^i_1, ..., x^i_{l(i)}, e_i) \in \mathcal{D}$ let $w_i = p_i(u_1, ..., u_{l(i)}, e_i)$ be its associated mode; if $u_j = $ * and x_j is a variable, then x_j has only one occurrence in $\mathcal{D}$ (a data variable symbol x_j can be used to replace a symbol * in a mode only once). We denote by $\mathcal{W}(E)$ the search space specified by E. We denote by $\mathcal{P}(E)$ the set of pi-patterns defined in a similar way as $\mathcal{W}(E)$ by considering strings $w_1 w_2 ... w_n \in P(E)$ instead of $W(E)$ in condition (1). Patterns in $\mathcal{W}(E)$ are called valid. Patterns in $\mathcal{P}(E)$ are called prefix valid.* □

As we will see in the next section, in the generation phase of our algorithm, only pi-patterns in $\mathcal{P}(E)$ (prefixes) will be generated. The reason we generate prefix-valid patterns (p-valid patterns for short) rather than valid patterns will be clearer later.

Example 5 (Running Example): *Let $E = Med(x, *, \#) Med(x, *, \#)^* Symp(x, *, \#)$. The pi-pattern $M_1 = (Patient(x), \{ Med(x, penicillin, e), Med(x, tetracycline, f), Symp(x, diarrhea, g) \}, \{ before(e,f), overlaps(f,g) \})$ belongs to $\mathcal{W}(E)$. The pattern $M_2 = (Patient(x), \{ Med(x, penicillin, e),$*

Med(x,tetracycline,f) }, { before(e, f) }) belongs to P(E). The pattern M_3 = (Patient(x), { Med(x,y ,e), Symp(x,y,f) }, {before(e,f) }) does not belong to P(E), since property (2) of Definition 3 is not verified. Intuitively, the regular expression E captures the temporal pi-patterns corresponding to a patient x taking certain medicines during successive periods of time and eventually presenting some symptom.

Our mining task: Given a temporal database D, a minimum support threshold α, $0 \leq \alpha \leq 1$, and a regular expression E over Σ, find all temporal pi-patterns in $W(E)$ which are frequent with respect to D and α.

THE ALGORITHM MILPRIT*

In this section, we present the algorithm MIL-PRIT* (**M**ining **I**nterval **L**ogic **P**atterns with **R**egular express**I**ons cons**T**raints), which generalizes the idea of the SPIRIT algorithm introduced in Garofalakis, et al. (1999). In a high level, it follows the general Apriori strategy of Srikant and Agrawal (1996), working in passes and each pass producing patterns more specific than those produced in the previous pass. The classical Apriori strategy uses a Pruning Phase, where generated patterns that are more specific than a nonfrequent pattern p are pruned. This pruning strategy relies on the Antimonotonic Property: "*a frequent pattern cannot be more specific than a nonfrequent pattern.*"

At first glance, a way of conceiving a method for mining pi-patterns following the Apriori strategy would be: (1) at each pass k, one combines frequent and valid patterns in the set F_{k-1} obtained in the previous pass in order to generate the set of candidates C_k. One takes care to produce only valid patterns in this combination, pushing the regular expression E in the generation process; (2) one prunes those patterns in C_k containing a subpattern that is valid and that is not in $\cup_{i=1,...,k-1} F_i$ (this pattern surely is not frequent!); (3) one scans

the database in order to count the support of the remaining patterns. In this method, the number of generated patterns is in direct proportion to the restrictiveness of E. In the pruning phase, however, all patterns that are more specific than a pattern satisfying E and not belonging to F_{k-1} should be pruned. In this case, the size of the set of pruned patterns is in inverse proportion to the restrictiveness of the constraint E. Such trade-offs are due to the fact that regular expression constraints are not antimonotone; that is, if a pattern satisfies E, it may have some subpattern not satisfying E^2.

In order to find a suitable trade-off, we use a relaxation of the constraint E (i.e., a less restrictive one), the prefix constraint associated to E, according to which only frequent p-valid pi-patterns will be produced in the mining process. A postprocessing phase will filter the valid patterns.

The general structure of the algorithm MIL-PRIT* is depicted next:

Procedure MILPRIT*(D, α, E, δ)
D is a temporal dataset over $R = \{ K, R_1, ..., R_n\}$, E is a regular expression over the alphabet of modes Σ over R, α is a minimum support threshold, and δ is the time granularity (day, week, fortnight, month, bimester, trimester, semester, year). Let M_i be the set of data atoms $R_i(x_1, ..., x_{n(i)}, e)$, where e is a interval-time or a point-time variable, depending on the sort of the temporal attribute appearing in R_i.

   begin
1. $F := F_1 = \{M \in M_1 \mid M$ is frequent and $M \in P(E)\}$
2. $k := 2$
3.   **repeat**
4. $C_k := Gen(F_{k-1}, E)$ (**Generation Phase**)
5. $P := \{ M \in C_k \mid \exists N \in P(E)$, such that $N \notin F$ and M is more specific than $N \}$
6. $C_k := C_k - P$ (**Pruning Phase**)
7. $F_k := \{ M \in C_k \mid sup(M,D,\delta) \geq \alpha\}$ (**Validation Phase**)

8. $F := F \cup F_k$
9. $k := k + 1$
10. **until** $F_{k-1} = \varnothing$
11. $F := \{ M \in F \mid M \in \mathcal{W}(E) \}$ *(Post-Processing Phase)*

The function $sup(M,D,\delta)$ is defined as follows: First, each date appearing in some tuple in D is associated to the corresponding time value determined by the time granularity δ. For instance, if $\delta = month$ and date is *20/09/2007* and the minimum date appearing in D is *28/07/2006*, then *20/09/2007* is mapped into *15*, since date *20/09/2007* occurs in the *15th* month relatively to the first month *July 2006*. Let D' be the database obtained from D after this transformation. The support $sup(M,D,\delta)$ is obtained by calculating $sup(M)$ with respect to D' as in Definition 2.

The Generation Phase

MILPRIT* works in passes, each pass k producing patterns of "level" k. The "level" of a temporal pi-pattern M is measured in terms of the refinement vector associated to M as defined next.

Definition 4: *The refinement vector associated to $M = (K, \mathcal{D}, \mathcal{T})$ is $v(M) = (n,c)$, where n is the size of $\mathcal{D}$ and c is the number of constants appearing in $\mathcal{D}$. The refinement level of M, denoted by $l(M)$, is defined as $n+c$ where $(n,c) = v(M)$.*

For instance, let M be the temporal i-pattern *(Patient(x), { Med(x,penicillin,e), Symp(x,z,f) }, { before(e,f) })*. Then $v(M) = (2,1)$ and $l(M) = 3$.

The procedure $Gen(F_{k-1}, E)$ is designed to generate temporal pi-patterns whose refinement level is k, by specializing the frequent temporal pi-patterns of F_{k-1} (whose refinement level is k-1) in such a way that the patterns produced are in $\mathcal{P}(E)$. The core of procedure Gen is the two specialization operators (ρ_E and ρ_I) defined next.

Definition 5 (Extension): *Let E be a regular expression and $M \in \mathcal{P}(E)$, $M = (K(x_1,...,x_n), \mathcal{D}, \mathcal{T})$. The extension operator ρ_E executed over M is defined as follows: (a) if $v(M) = (n,c)$ with $c > 0$, then $\rho_E(M) = \varnothing$ (b) if $v(M) = (n,0)$ then $\rho_E(M)$ is the set of temporal pi-patterns $M' = (K(x_1,...,x_n), \mathcal{D}', \mathcal{T}') \in \mathcal{P}(E)$ such that $\mathcal{D}' = \mathcal{D} \cup \{ p_{n+1}(z_1,...,z_l, e_{n+1}) \}$ where $p_{n+1} \in \mathbf{R}$, $z_1, ..., z_l$ are data variables and e_{n+1} is a interval-time or a point-time variable (according to the sort of the time attribute of p_{n+1}) and $\mathcal{T}' = \mathcal{T} \cup \{ r_1(e_1, e_{n+1}), ... , r_n(e_n, e_{n+1}) \}$ where r_i are temporal predicates, and $\mathcal{T}'$ is complete and consistent. Clearly, for each $i=1,...,n$, the temporal predicates r_i are taken according to the type of the time variables e_i, e_{n+1} (point or interval) (see Figure 2). For instance, if both e_i and e_{n+1} are point-time, r_i must be the temporal predicate before. The following example illustrates the operator ρ_E:*

Example 6 (Running Example): *Let E be the regular expression $Hist(x,*,\#)^* Med(x,*,\#)^*$. The pi-pattern $M=(Patient(x),\{ Hist(x,y,t_1) \},\varnothing)$ belongs to $\mathcal{P}(E)$. Let us consider the following pi-patterns:*

$M_1 = (Patient(x), \{ Hist(x,y_1,t_1), Hist(x,y_2,t_2) \}, \{ before(t_1, t_2) \})$

$M_2 = (Patient(x), \{ Hist(x,y_1,t_1), Hist(x,y_2,t_2), Med(x,z,e_3) \}, \{ before(t_1,t_2), meets(t_2,e_3) \})$

$M_3 = (Patient(x), \{ Hist(x,y_1,t_1), Hist(x,y_2,t_2), Med(x,z, e_3) \}, \{ before(t_1,t_2), starts(t_1,e_3), during(t_2,e_3) \})$

$M_4 = (Patient(x), \{ Hist(x,y_1,t_1), Hist(x,y_2,t_2), Med(x,z_1,e_3), Med(x,z_2,e_4) \}, \{ before(t_1,t_2), starts(t_1,e_3), overlaps(e_3,e_4) \})$

M_1 *is in* $\rho_E(M)$, *but* M_2 *is not in* $\rho_E(M_1)$, *because meets is not a valid relationship between* t_2 *and* e_3. *The pattern* M_3 *is in* $\rho_E(M_1)$, *but* M_4 *is not in* $\rho_E(M_3)$, *because there is no explicit nor implicit relationship between the temporal variables* e_4 *and* t_2; *that is, the set of temporal predicates in* M_4 *is not complete.*

Definition 6 (Instantiation): *Let E be a regular expression and $M \in \mathcal{P}(E)$, $M = (K(x_1,...,x_n), \mathcal{D}, \mathcal{T})$ where $\mathcal{D} = < D_1, ...,D_m >$. The instantiation operator executed over M produces the set $\rho_I(M)$ of temporal pi-patterns $M' = (K(x_1,...,x_n),\mathcal{D}',\mathcal{T}')$, where $\mathcal{D}'$ is obtained by replacing some variable y_k ($y_k \neq x_l$ for $l \in [1,n]$) occurring in some $D_i = p(y_1,...,y_p,e)$ by a constant c in such a way that if the string of modes corresponding to $\mathcal{D}$ is $w_1 w_2...w_m$ and $w_i = p(u_1,...,u_p,\#)$, then: (a) $u_k = *$; (b) for every $l > k$, if $u_l = *$, then y_l is not a constant; (c) for every $j > i$, if $w_j = p'(v_1,...,v_q,\#)$, then for every $l \in [1,q]$, if $v_l = *$ and $D_j = p'(z_1,...,z_q,e)$, then z_l is not a constant.*

Intuitively, condition (b) states that if some variable in a data atom is instantiated, then no other variables on the left of this one in the atom can be instantiated in further steps of the candidate generation process. Condition (c) states that if some variable in a data atom p is instantiated, then no other variables appearing in data atoms coming before p in the pattern can be instantiated in the future. These conditions are necessary for assuring optimality of the specialization operators, as stated in the following Theorem 2. The following example illustrates the operator ρ_I:

Example 7 (Running Example): *Let E be the regular expression $E = Med(x, *, \#)^* Symp(x, *, \#)^*$. Consider the following pi-patterns in $\mathcal{P}(E)$:*

M_1 = (Patient(x), { Med(x,w,e$_1$), Symp(x,y,e$_2$) }, { before(e$_1$,e$_2$) })

M_2 = (Patient(x), { Med(x,w,e$_1$), Symp(x,dizziness,e$_2$) }, { before(e$_1$,e$_2$) })

M_3 = (Patient(x), { Med(x,penicillin,e$_1$), Symp(x,y,e$_2$) }, { before(e$_1$,e$_2$) })

M_4 = (Patient(x), { Med(x,penicillin,e$_1$), Symp(x, dizziness,e$_2$) }, { before(e$_1$,e$_2$) })

According to Definition 6, M_2 and M_3 are in $\rho_I(M_1)$ (i.e., are valid instantiations of M_1), $M_4 \notin \rho_I(M_1)$, $M_4 \notin \rho_I(M_2)$, $M_4 \in \rho_I(M_3)$.

Two temporal pi-patterns M and M' are said to be equivalent if M' is obtained from M by renaming its variables.

Theorem 2: *The specialization operator ρ defined as $\rho(M) = \rho_I(M) \cup \rho_E(M)$ satisfies the following properties:*

- **Completeness:** Every pi-pattern $M \in \mathcal{P}(E)$ can be obtained by successively applying ρ to some pi-pattern with the refinement level 1.
- **Optimality:** Suppose that the regular expression E verifies the following condition: for all distinct modes m_1 and m_2 appearing in E, associated to the same predicate p, the positions containing the symbol * are the same in both modes. Under this condition, the instantiation operator ρ is optimal in the sense that a pi-pattern cannot be obtained by specializing two nonequivalent pi-patterns.

Proof.

1. **Completeness:** Let $M = (K,\mathcal{D},\mathcal{T}) \in \mathcal{P}(E)$ and $v(M) = (n,c)$. We will show by induction on n that for all $c \geq 0$, M is obtained by successively applying ρ to some pi-pattern M_1 whose refinement level is 1.

   - *Let $n = 1$.* Let us show by induction on c that M is obtained by successively applying ρ to some pi-pattern M_1 with refinement level 1. For $c = 0$: the refinement level of M is 1 and $M = \rho^0(M)$ (we apply ρ "0 times" over M). Let $c \geq 1$ and let us suppose that the result is true for c-1. Let $p(t_1,...,t_k,e_n)$ the last atom in $\mathcal{D}$ where, for some $i \in \{1,...,k\}$, t_i is a constant in C. Let $m = max\{ i \mid 1 \leq i \leq k$ such that $t_i \in C \}$. Let M' be the pi-pattern obtained by replacing t_i by a new variable y in the atom $p(t_1,...,t_k,e_n)$. That is, we replace the data atom $p(t_1,...,t_i,...,t_k,e_n)$ by $p(t_1,...,y,...,t_k,e_n)$.

Figure 3. Candidate generation: Executing the specialization operators level by level

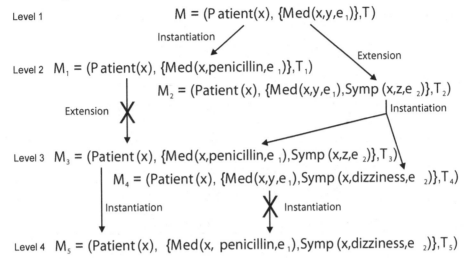

Then, M is obtained by applying ρ_I over M'. By the induction hypothesis, since $v(M') = (n,c\text{-}1)$, then M' is obtained by successively applying the specialization operator ρ over a pi-pattern M_I with refinement level I. Then, $M = \rho_I(M')$ is also obtained in such a way.

- Let us suppose the result is true for $n - 1$ and let us show it is true for $n \geq 2$. We will show that by induction on $c \geq 0$. For $c = 0$: $M = < p_1(t^I_{\ I}, t^I_{\ 2}, ..., t^I_{\ n(I)}, e_I), ..., p_m(t^m_{\ I}, t^m_{\ 2}, ..., t^m_{\ n(m)}, e_m) >$, and $t^i_{\ j}$ is a variable, for all i, j. It is easy to see that M is obtained by applying successively the operator ρ_E to the pi-pattern $< p_1(t^I_{\ I}, t^I_{\ 2}, ..., t^I_{\ n(I)}, e_I) >$ with refinement level I (the proof is achieved by induction on m, using the fact that each prefix of M is in $\mathcal{P}(E)$. For the case $c \geq I$, we employ the same argument used in the case $n = I$ and $c \geq I$.

2. **Optimality:** For lack of space the proof is given in the Appendix. □

Figure 3 illustrates the completeness and optimality of ρ. M_3 cannot be obtained by specializing both M_1 and M_2, since they are nonequivalent pi-patterns. In fact, ρ executed over M_1 does not produce M_3 since according to Definition 5(a),

each time a pi-pattern is instantiated, it cannot be extended any more. M_5 cannot be obtained by specializing both M_3 and M_4, since they are nonequivalent pi-patterns. In fact, ρ executed over M_4 does not produce M_5 since according to Definition 6(c), each time a position in a pi-pattern is instantiated, no positions at its left can be instantiated in future steps.

The Validation Phase

The support counting of the generated pi-patterns is a rather technical procedure, and its details are omitted here. Roughly speaking, an equivalence relation over the set of generated patterns is defined, depending on the sequence of modes appearing in the patterns. A SQL query $Q(C)$ is associated to each equivalence class C. Thus, to each equivalent class C, a database D_C is associated. An important point to make here is that the database D_C has a unique relation; namely, the answer of query $Q(C)$ executed over the input database D. Thus, in order to evaluate the support of the patterns in class C, the relation D_C is scanned once at each pass. A hash-tree structure is used for optimizing support counting in each equivalence class. The construction of these hash-trees has been inspired by the ones used in Srikant and Agrawal (1996).

Table 1. Parameters used for the synthetic data generation

	Parameters	Default
I	Number of tables with intervals	2
P	Number of tables with points	2
M	Number of attributes per table (not temporal)	2
U	Number of tuples per table - in '000s	5
S	Domain size of reference attributes - in '000s	2
D	Domain size of nonreference attributes - in '000s	1
F	Domain size of temporal attributes - in '000s	1
B	Number of blocks of regular expressions	2
T	Number of terms per blocks of regular expressions	2
V	Number of modes per term of regular expressions	1
Q	Minimum amount of pi-patterns - in '000s	1

The following result is a corollary of Theorem 2, which guarantees the soundness and completeness of MILPRIT*:

Corollary 1 (Soundness and Completeness). *Let $\mathcal{P}$ be the set of temporal pi-patterns returned by the algorithm MILPRIT*. Then (1) all patterns in $\mathcal{P}$ are frequent and satisfy the constraints enforced by the regular expression E, and (2) all frequent and valid patterns are in $\mathcal{P}$.*

Proof. *(1) If $P \in \mathcal{P}$, then P is frequent, since after the validation phase, only frequent patterns are returned. Besides, step 11 of MILPRIT* guarantees that only valid patterns (with respect to E) are returned. (2) Let P be a frequent and valid pattern. Then P is p-valid. By Theorem 2, P is obtained by applying the specialization operator ρ n times over a pi-pattern M in the refinement level 1. It is easy to prove, by induction on n, that P is obtained during the generation phase of MILPRIT* in the refinement level n + 1. Since P is frequent, it will be returned in step 7 of MILPRIT*. Since P is valid, it will be returned in step 11 of MILPRIT*.*

$\square$

EXPERIMENTAL RESULTS

In this section, we discuss the performance and scalability of algorithm MILPRIT* through a set of experiments using both synthetic and real-life datasets. Our experiments were performed on an IBM Super Workstation 7043A-8R with 2.4GHz and 4GB of main memory, running Linux. The DBMS PostgreSQL has been used to handle the SQL queries at the validation phase, as discussed before.

Synthetic Data

We have developed a synthetic data generator that generates regular expressions and temporal databases where pi-patterns satisfying a regular expression may appear. The regular expressions generated have the format $(B_1^* B_2^* \dots B_k^*)$, where each block B_i has the form $(T_1 \dots T_m)$, and each T_j (called *term*) has the form $(m_{i(1)}^j + \dots + m_{i(l)}^j)$, where m_p^j are modes. Thus, our generator can produce several types of regular expressions by varying the number of blocks (k), the maximum number of terms in each block (m), and the maximum number of modes appearing in the terms. For instance, one regular expression that fits into this format is $E = (Med(x,*,\#) \; Symp(x,*,\#))^* \; (Med(x,*,\#) \; Hist(x,*,\#))^*$. This expression has two blocks and two terms in each block. For each term, there is only one mode that can be chosen. In Table 1, we list the parameters used in the synthetic data generator, allowing a great variety of temporal databases and regular expressions to be produced. For the tests presented in this article, we use the following notation for the input datasets: *Ix-Py-Mz-Us-Bt-Tu-Vv-Qw*, where *x, y, z, s, t, u, v,* and *w* are values for the input parameters *I, P, M, U, B, T, V,* and *Q*, respectively. The remaining input parameters (*S, D* and *F*) are set as (*S = U/2.5, D = U/5 and F = U/5*). The parameter *Q* refers to the number of valid pi-patterns, which surely appear in the generated dataset.

Performance Analysis

Figure 4(a) shows the performance of MILPRIT* with respect to support variation. The tests have been executed over the dataset *I2-P2-M2-U5-B2-T2-V1-Q1*. As the minimum support is increased from *0.5%* to *3%*, the number of frequent patterns at each pass decreases, as expected. Thus, the execution time of the algorithm decreases, since few candidates are potentially frequent for high values of minimum support. Figures 4(b), (c), and (d) show how the algorithm performs with respect to variations in the regular expression. In these tests, the minimum support has been set as *2%*. The datasets used in these tests were *I2-P2-M2-U5-Bt-T2-V1-Q1*, where $t \in \{1, 2, 3, 4, 5\}$, *I2-P2-M2-U5-B2-Tu-V1-Q1*, where $u \in \{1, 2, 3, 4, 5\}$ and *I2-P2-M2-U5-B2-T2-Vv-Q1*, where $v \in \{1, 2, 3, 4, 5\}$. As the values of parameters *B, T,* or *V* (the number of blocks, the number of terms in each block, and the number of choices for modes in each term, respectively) increase, the number of *long* patterns potentially frequent increases as well. Thus, the execution time of the algorithm increases, too, since longer patterns have to be tested at the validation phase. Notice that the number of attributes of the table

Figure 4. Performance results

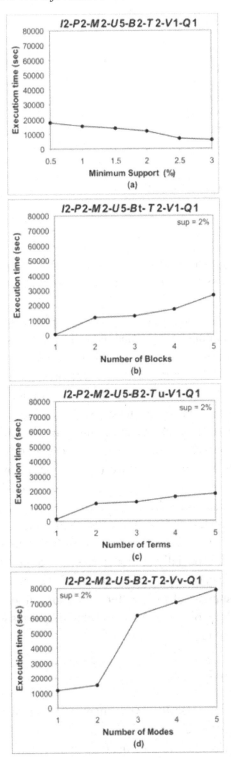

Figure 5(a). Number of generated and pruned pi-patterns

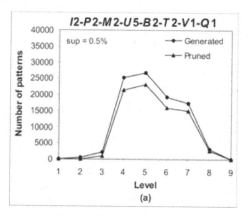

(a)

Figure 5(b). Time in each phase

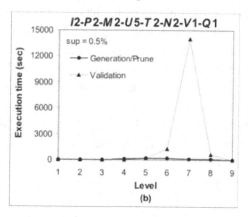

(b)

that is scanned to evaluate the support for these long patterns increases as the size of the patterns increases.

Figure 5(a) shows the relationship between the number of generated and pruned pi-patterns during the execution of MILPRIT* over the dataset *I2-P2-M2-U5-B2-T2-V1-Q1* with minimum support *0.5%*. Note that the number of pruned *pths* is quite expressive, and consequently, a smaller amount of pi-patterns are evaluated at the validation phase. Figure 5(b) shows the execution time associated to each phase (generation, pruning, and validation) at each refinement level. The tests also have been executed over the dataset *I2-P2-M2-U5-B2-T2-V1-Q1* with minimum support *0.5%*. The execution time at the validation phase, especially at higher levels, is quite high. This can be explained by the fact that calculating the support of long patterns at high refinement levels involves the execution of SQL queries with a high number of *joins*.

Scalability

For the scalability experiments, the parameters related to the database have been changed. In these experiments, we used the default parameters for the regular expression and fixed the minimum support as *2%*. We first show how MILPRIT*

performs as the number of tuples per table *(U)* increases. The datasets considered here were *I2-P2-M2-Us-B2-T2-V1-Q1*, where $s \in \{ 2000 0, 40000, 60000, 80000, 100000 \}$. Figure 6(a) shows the results of these tests. Clearly, the higher the number of tuples in the database tables, the longer the execution time of the algorithm, since the validation phase (the support evaluation) is the most computationally costly.

It can be noticed that MILPRIT* scales almost linearly with respect to the number of tuples in the dataset. Figure 6(b) shows how MILPRIT* scales up as the number of attributes per table *(M)* increases. We show the results for the datasets *I2-P2-Mz-U5-B2-T2-V1-Q1*, where $z \in \{ 2, 3, 4, 5 \}$. As the number of attributes in the base tables increases, the number of attributes of the table that is scanned in the validation phase[3] increases as well. Consequently, the execution time increases. Figure 6(c) shows how the execution time increases as the number of generated patterns increases. This experiment consisted in running the algorithm over datasets *I2-P2-M2-U5-B2-T2-V1-Qw*, for $w \in \{ 1000, 1500, 2000, 2500, 3000, 3500, 4000 \}$. In these three scalability tests, we can notice that MILPRIT* scales up almost linearly with respect to the corresponding parameters (number of tuples per table, number of attributes per table, and number of interesting patterns appearing in the dataset).

Figure 6. Scalability results

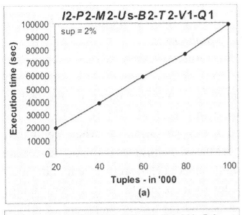

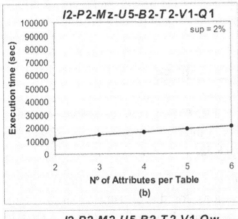

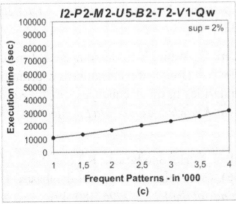

Real Data

The *AMDI* [4] is part of a project in our laboratory that aims at building a system supporting an indexed atlas of digital mammograms. This system intends to be used by radiologists as well as radiology students in order to help them in breast cancer diagnosis. The *AMDI* database[5]

stores for each patient a series of digital mammograms taken during its lifetime. Besides image data, some important temporal data are stored, related to the patient's habits and lifestyle (e.g., periods of time she smoked or took contraceptive drugs). The data used in our tests were supplied by Instituto Victorio Valeri de Diagnósticos Médicos, Ribeirão Preto-SP, Brazil. For the time being, the *AMDI* database stores information about *1,365* patients. In the future, as the system will be available online, it will be possible for radiologists to insert new patients' records and images.

The *AMDI* relational schema is $R = \{$
$Patient(PName),$
$Contraceptive(PName, CName, T_{it})$
$, Antidepressant(PName, AName, T_{it}),$
$Hormone(PName, HName, T_{it}),$
$Tobacco(PName, Amount, T_{it}),$
$Drink(PName, Type, T_{it}),$
$FirstPregnancy(PName, T_{pt}),$
$Menarche(PName, T_{pt}),$
$Menopause(PName, T_{pt}),$
$Birads(PName, Category, T_{pt}) \}.$

The relation *Birads* stores information related to the BIRADS classification, standard published by the American College of Radiology (ACR)[6]. The attribute *Category* may assume five different values, each one corresponding to a mammogram class. MILPRIT* has been executed over the *AMDI* database in order to find temporal pi-patterns relating the evolution of a breast cancer tumor and the patient's habits and lifestyle. For the experiment carried out over this database, we considered the time granularity $\delta = semester$.
Some of the patterns found were:

$P_1 = (Patient(x), \{ Menopause(x,YES,e_1),$
$Anti\text{-}depressant(x,fluoxetine,f_2) \},$
$\{ starts(e_1,f_2) \})$
$P_2 = (Patient(x), \{ Tobacco(x,20,e_1), Birads(x,$
$2,s_2) \}, \{ before(e_1,s_2) \})$

P_3 = (Patient(x), { FirstPregnancy(x,YES,e₁),
Menopause(x,YES,f₂), Birads(x,2,s₃)},
{ before(e₁,f₂), before(e₁,s₃), before(f₂,s₃) })

The pi-pattern P_1 can be interpreted as follows: *patients start taking the antidepressant fluoxetine as soon as they enter menopause.* This pi-pattern has been verified by *25* patients (support = *1.8%*). The pi-pattern P_2 has been verified by *14* patients (support = *1%*) and can be interpreted as follows: *patients who smoke 20 cigarettes per day stop smoking after their mammogram is classified with Birads 2.* The pi-pattern P_3 can be interpreted as follows: *patients who have already had children present mammograms with Birads 2 after entering menopause*; this pi-pattern has been verified in *177* patients (support = *12%*).

We notice that for the time being, MILPRIT* has not mined expressive patterns relating patients' lifestyles and cancer occurrences as we expected in the beginning of the project. Clearly, this is due to the fact that in the current stage of the *AMDI* database, with only *1,365* records, the Birads classification of the mammograms is almost unchanged. Moreover, there are no cases of mammograms with Birads 5 in our database. We hope that as the *AMDI* database gets more populated and diversified, MILPRIT* will be able to discover more interesting patterns.

CONCLUSION AND FURTHER WORK

In this article, we introduced a first-order (or relational) temporal pattern mining framework where time can be viewed as *intervals* as well as *points* in a straight line. We also proposed a formalism to specify a broad class of constraints over such temporal patterns. We developed and implemented the algorithm MILPRIT* designed to mining temporal patterns with constraints. For the time being, our temporal pattern formulation does not include a pattern where *several* data

atoms are related to the same temporal variable. For instance, we do not consider patterns such as (Patient(x), { Med(x,penicillin,e), Med(x,xanax, f) }, { equal(e,f) }).

Our future research focuses on three main targets: (1) the development of a second algorithm for mining pi-patterns based on the technique PrefixSpan (Pei et al., 2004), which presents a much better performance when compared to Apriori-based techniques in the sequence pattern mining context; (2) the refinement of the method in order to incorporate more general temporal patterns; and (3) the development of a tool for temporal relational pattern mining.

REFERENCES

Allen, J.F., & Ferguson, G. (1994). Actions and events in interval temporal logic. *Technical Report* TR521.

Antunes, C., & Oliveira, A.L. (2004). Constraint relaxations for discovering unknown sequential patterns. *Proceedings of the KDID'2002*, 11–32.

Bettini, C., Wang, X.S., Jajodia, S., & Lin, J.-L. Discovering frequent event patterns with multiple granularities in time sequences. *IEEE Transactions on Knowledge and Data Engineering, 10*(2), 222–237.

Böhlen, M.H., Snodgrass, R.T., & Soo, M.D. (1996). Coalescing in temporal databases. *Proceedings of the VLDB'1996*, 180–191.

Boulicaut, J.-F., De Raedt, L., & Mannila, H. (eds.) (2006). Constraint-based mining and inductive databases. *Lecture Notes in Computer Science, 3848.*

de Amo, S., & Furtado, D. (2007). First-order temporal pattern mining with regular expression constraints. *Data & Knowledge Engineering, 62*(3), 401-420.

de Amo, S., Giacometti, A., Furtado, D.A., & Laurent, D. (2004). An Apriori-based approach for first-order temporal pattern mining. *Proceedings of the 19th Brazilian Symposium on Databases*, 48–62.

de Amo, S., Giacometti, A., & Pereira Jr., W. (2007). Mining first-order temporal interval patterns with regular expression constraints. *Proceedings of the 9th International Conference on Data Warehousing and Knowledge Discovery (DaWaK 2007)*, LNCS, *4654*, 459–469.

Dehaspe, L., & Toivonnen, H. (1999). Discovery of frequent datalog patterns. *Data Mining and Knowledge Discovery*, *3*, 7–36.

Emerson, E.A. (1990). Temporal and modal logic. *Handbook of Theoretical Computer Science*, *B*, 995–1072.

Garofalakis, M.N., Rastogi, R., & Shim, K. (1999). SPIRIT: Sequential pattern mining with regular expression constraints. *The VLDB Journal*, 223–234.

Hoppner, F. (2001). Discovery of temporal patterns—Learning rules about the qualitative behavior of time series. *Proceedings of the 5th European Conference on Principles and Practice of Knowledge Discovery in Databases*, 192–203.

Jacobs, N., & Blockeel, H. (2001). From shell logs to shell scripts. *Proceedings of the 11th International Conference on Inductive Logic Programming*, LNAI, *2157*, 80–90.

Lattner, A., & Herzog, O. (2004). Unsupervised learning of sequential patterns. *Proceedings of the ICDM'2004 Workshop on Temporal Data Mining: Algorithms, Theory and Applications.*

Lattner, A., & Herzog, O. (2005). Mining temporal patterns from relational data. *Proceedings of LWA'2005*, 184–189.

Lee, S.D., & De Raedt, L. (2002). Constraint based mining of first order sequences in seqlog. *Proceedings of the KDID'02*, 76–92.

Lorincza, H.A., & Boulicaut, J.-F. (2003). Mining frequent sequential patterns under regular expressions: A highly adaptive strategy for pushing constraints. *Proceedings of the ICDM'03*, 316–320.

Masson, C., & Jacquenet, F. (2003). Mining frequent logical sequences with SPIRITLoG. *Proceedings of the 12th International Conference on Inductive Logic Programming*, LNCS, *2583*, 166–181.

Pei, J., et al. (2004). Mining sequential patterns by pattern-growth: The prefix-span approach. *IEEE Transactions on Knowledge and Data Engineering*, *16*(11), 1424-1440.

Pei, J., Han, J., & Wang, W. (2002). Mining sequential patterns with constraints in large databases. *Proceedings of the 2002 ACM CIKM Conference*, 18–25.

Srikant, R., & Agrawal, R. (1996). Mining sequential patterns: Generalizations and performance improvements. *Proceedings of the EDBT'96*, Avignon, France, 3–17.

Zaki, M.J. (2001). SPADE: An efficient algorithm for mining frequent sequences. *Machine Learning Journal*, *42*(1/2), 31–60.

ENDNOTES

[1] This example has been taken from Lee and De Raedt, 2002.

[2] For instance, the word *aba* verifies the regular expression $E = ab*a$, but its subword *ba* does not verify E.

[3] This table is obtained as the result of executing an SQL query over the temporal dataset.

[4] The *AMDI* system is available on www.lcc. ufu.br/ amdi.

[5] The *AMDI database is available on www. lsi.ufu.br.*

[6] Breast Imaging Reporting and Data System BIRADS. American College of Radiology, 2004.

[7] For the sake of simplifying the notation, we omitted the symbol # at the end of modes.

APPENDIX: PROOF OF THEOREM 2 *(OPTIMALITY)*

Let $M = (K, \mathcal{D}, \mathcal{T}) \in \mathcal{P}(E)$, $\mathcal{D} = \{p_1(t^1_1, ..., t^1_{l(1)}, e_1), ..., p_n(t^n_1, ..., t^n_{l(n)}, e_n)\}$ and let $v(M) = (n, c)$.

1. **Case 1:** if $c = 0$, then M must be generated by extension; that is, $M = \rho_E(M')$, for some pi-pattern M_1. Since the atoms in $\mathcal{D}$ are ordered according to the partial order introduced in Section 2, then $M' = (K, \mathcal{D}', \mathcal{T}') \in \mathcal{P}(E)$ with:
   - $\mathcal{D}' = \{p_1(t^1_1, ..., t^1_{l(1)}, e_1), ..., p_{n-1}(t^{n-1}_1, ..., t^{n-1}_{l(n-1)}, e_{n-1})\}$
   - $\mathcal{T}' = \{r(e_i, e_j) \in \mathcal{T} / i, j < n\}$

2. **Case 2:** if $c > 0$: Let us suppose that $M = \rho(M_1) = \rho(M_2)$. Notice that, since $c > 0$, it is not possible that M is obtained by extension from M_1 or M_2. Then, $M = \rho_I(M_1) = \rho_I(M_2)$. Let $M_1 = (K, \mathcal{D}_1, \mathcal{T}_1)$ and $M_2 = (K, \mathcal{D}_2, \mathcal{T}_2)$.
   - $\mathcal{D}_1 = \{p_1(x^1_1, ..., x^1_{l(1)}, e_1), ..., p_n(x^n_1, ..., x^n_{l(n)}, e_n)\}$
   - $\mathcal{D}_2 = \{p_1(y^1_1, ..., y^1_{l(1)}, e_1), ..., p_n(y^n_1, ..., y^n_{l(n)}, e_n)\}$

   The strings of modes associated to M_1 and M_2 are respectively[7]:
   - $W_1 = p_1(u^1_1, ..., u^1_{l(1)}), ..., p_n(u^n_1, ..., u^n_{l(n)})$
   - $W_2 = p_1(v^1_1, ..., v^1_{l(1)}), ..., p_n(v^n_1, ..., v^n_{l(n)})$

   I. Since $M = \rho_I(M_1)$ then there exists $i1, j1$ (uniquely determined) such that $u^{i1}_{j1} = *$, x^{i1}_{j1} is a variable and t^{i1}_{j1} is a constant. Moreover, for all i, j, if $i \neq i1$ and $j \neq j1$, then $x^i_j = t^i_j$.

   II. Since $M = \rho_I(M_2)$, then there exists $i2, j2$ (uniquely determined) such that $u^{i2}_{j2} = *$, x^{i2}_{j2} is a variable and t^{i2}_{j2} is a constant. Moreover, for all i, j, if $i \neq i2$ and $j \neq j2$, then $x^i_j = t^i_j$.

   We must consider three possibilities; namely:

   a. $i1 = i2$ and $j1 < j2$: in that case, both $t^{i1}j1$ and $t^{i2}j2$ are constants (according to points (I) and (II)). Moreover, since $M = \rho_I(M1)$ and $j1 < j2$, then M is obtained by instantiating a variable in position $j1$ in the $i1$-th atom.

   But in this *i1-th* atom, a variable in position $j2 > j1$ is already instantiated. Contradiction (see Definition 6(b)).

   b. $i1 < i2$: in that case, $v^{i2}j2 = u^{i1}j1 = *$ and $x^{i1}j1$, $y^{i2}j2$ are constants. That is impossible, since by Definition 6(c), a variable $x^{i1}j1$ cannot be instantiated if it appears in the $i1$-th atom and a variable $x^{i2}j2$ in the $i2$-th atom ($i2 > i1$) has already been instantiated.

   c. $i1 = i2$ and $j1 = j2$: in that case, we have $u^{i1}_{j1} = v^{i2}_{j2} = *$, and x^{i1}_{j1}, y^{i2}_{j2} are variables. So, M_1 and M_2 are equivalent (M_1 can be obtained from M_2 by renaming its variable x^{i1}_{j1} as y^{i2}_{j2}). $\square$

This work was previously published in International Journal of Data Warehousing and Mining, Vol. 4, Issue 4, edited by D. Taniar, pp. 42-61, copyright 2008 by IGI Publishing (an imprint of IGI Global).

Chapter 14
Computing Join Aggregates over Private Tables

Rong She
Simon Fraser University, Canada

Ke Wang
Simon Fraser University, Canada

Ada Waichee Fu
Chinese University of Hong Kong, Hong Kong

Yabo Xu
Simon Fraser University, Canada

ABSTRACT

We propose a privacy-preserving protocol for computing aggregation queries over the join of private tables. In this problem, several parties wish to share aggregated information over the join of their tables, but want to conceal the details that generate such information. The join operation presents a challenge to privacy preservation because it requires matching individual records from private tables without letting any non-owning party know the actual join values or make any inference about the data in other parties. We solve this problem by using a novel private sketching protocol that securely exchanges some randomized summary information about private tables. This protocol (1) conceals individual private values and their distributions from all non-owning parties, (2) works on many general forms of aggregation functions, (3) handles group-by aggregates, and (4) handles roll-up/drill-down operations. Previous works have not provided this level of privacy for such queries.

INTRODUCTION

With explosive growth in data storage and networking, collaboration among various data holders has become more and more important. Such collaboration frequently involves multiple private sources where free-access to private data is difficult or impossible due to privacy concerns. Therefore, techniques that address the need of privacy-preserving collaborative data analysis are critical (Clifton et al., 2004).

For example, a hospital maintains the medical histories of patients, denoted as table H, and a research institute maintains the records of patients' DNA samples, denoted as R. Both tables contain the attribute "Patient_Name" that is not necessarily a key attribute if a patient has several diseases or DNA samples. To establish the relationships between diseases and DNA anomalies, the research institute issues the following query that returns the aggregated number of occurrences for each combination of disease and DNA characteristics:

```
SELECT  H.Disease, R.DNA_Characteristics,
COUNT(*)
FROM  H, R
WHERE        H.Patient_Name=R.Patient_
Name
GROUP BY  H.Disease, R.DNA_Characteris-
tics
```

Such aggregate queries are fundamental for most statistical and trend analysis. For example, for a certain disease "d" and DNA characteristic "c", in the joined table, if the number of occurrences for <d,c> combination is 70, and the number of occurrences for <c> alone is 100, then it can be deduced that a patient with DNA characteristic "c" has 70% chance of having disease "d". Association and correlation analysis (Agrawal, Imielinski & Swami, 1993) is based on this idea.

On the other hand, due to privacy restrictions such as the HIPAA policies (http://www.hhs.gov/ocr/hipaa/), neither the hospital nor the research institute is willing to disclose its patient-specific information (such as patient names) to the other party. They wish to share the high level aggregated count, but want to conceal the low level details such as who contributed to the count. This is an example of private join aggregate queries that we will consider in this paper.

Private Join Aggregate Queries

Join Aggregate Queries

A join aggregate query has the following form:

```
SELECT      group-by-list, agg(exp)
FROM  T_1, ..., T_n
WHERE       A_1=A_1' and ... and A_m=A_m'
GROUP BY    group-by-list
```

where each T_i is a table; A_i and A_i' are join attributes from different tables; *group-by-list* is a list of group-by attributes possibly from different tables; *exp* is an arithmetic expression over aggregation attributes possibly from different tables; *agg* is an aggregation function. In this paper, we consider the aggregation functions COUNT and SUM. Conceptually, to answer such query, the tables in FROM are joined according to the predicates in WHERE, and the joined records are then grouped on the group-by-list. The query result contains one row for each group with agg(exp) being computed over the group. If the optional GROUP BY is missing, there is only one group and one row in the query result. We can assume that a table contains only join attributes and the attributes that occur in SELECT (including aggregation attributes and group-by attributes); all other attributes are invisible to the query and thus are safe to be ignored for our purpose.

Private Join Aggregate Queries

In a private join aggregate query, each T_i is a private table owned by a different party. These parties wish to compute and share the result of a join aggregate query, but no party should learn any information from other parties beyond the query result. The group-by attributes and their values are contained in the query result, thus they are not considered private. Our goal is to conceal all other private attribute values and their distributions. In particular, among other attributes, we want to protect $F(v)$ from any non-owning party, where $F(v)$ is the occurrence count of a join value v in a private table. This level of privacy has not been provided by previous solutions, which will be discussed in more details in the next section.

We assume the honest-but-curious behavior (Goldreich, 2001): The parties follow the protocol properly with the exception that they may keep track of all intermediate computations and received messages, and analyze the messages to try to learn additional information. Our focus is on privacy protection in the computation process, not against the answers to queries. The latter has been studied in statistical databases (Adam & Wortman, 1989). Our assumption is that, when the participating parties wish to share the query result, information inferred from such results is a fair game (Agrawal, Evfimievski & Srikant, 2003). Protection against query results and background knowledge in general requires additional mechanisms and is beyond the scope of this paper.

Challenges and Contributions

We present a novel solution to private join aggregate queries based on the sketching technique previously studied for join size estimation and aggregation for data streams (Alon, Gibbons, Matias & Szegedy, 1999; Dobra, Garofalakis, Gehrke & Rastogi, 2002; Ganguly, Garofalskis & Rastogi, 2004). However, none of these works involve privacy issues. The basic idea of sketching is that each table maintains a summary structure, called *atomic sketch*, which is later combined to produce an estimator of the query result. More details on sketching are given in a later section. A striking property of atomic sketches is that they are computed locally. Each party can compute its own atomic sketches without any knowledge of data in other parties. This localization property of atomic sketches inspired us to develop a solution for private join aggregate queries by making use of similar sketching techniques.

However, it is not straightforward to adapt the sketching techniques in our privacy-preservation scenario. We will show that a straightforward way of combining atomic sketches, when producing the query estimator, would allow a party to learn the distribution of join values owned by other parties. In the patient example, this means that the hospital or research institute could learn some patient names owned by the other party by examining atomic sketches. We will present a detailed analysis on the source of such privacy leakage and the types of information that need to be concealed in order to prevent such leakage. We then propose a *private sketching protocol* for computing the private join aggregate query. The key idea is that each party holds one "random share" of the same atomic sketch so that collectively they represent the atomic sketch, but individually they are useless. We show how the query can be estimated from such random shares in such a way that no party learns private information (both individual values and distribution of values) from other parties.

We then extend this protocol to multi-party queries, with general arithmetic expressions and group-by operator, and to support the roll-up/drill-down operations (Gray, Bosworth, Layman & Pirahesh, 1996). Typically, an interesting group-by-list is unknown in advance and must be discovered simultaneously as interesting aggregates are searched. With the roll-up and drill-down operations, the aggregates at a coarser level (with fewer group-by attributes) can be computed efficiently from the aggregates at a finer level (with more group-by attributes). However, supporting roll-up/drill-down operations at the same level of privacy protection as for basic queries requires an innovative work.

This paper is an extended version of our previous work (She, Wang, Fu & Xu, 2007) which gives a basic private sketching protocol for two-party COUNT queries. In this paper, we show how the protocol can be extended with some modifications to a lot more general aggregation queries and also present substantial experimental results.

RELATED WORK

Several models have been proposed for general secure computations. In the trusted third party model (Jefferies, Mitchell & Walker, 1995), all parties give the data to a "trusted" third party and have the third party do the computation. Such a third party has to be completely trusted and is difficult (often impossible) to find. In the secure multi-party model (Yao, 1986), given two parties with inputs x and y, the goal is to compute a function f(x,y) such that the two parties learn only f(x,y) and nothing else. In theory, any multi-party computation can be solved by building a combinatorial circuit, and simulating that circuit. However, the communication costs are impractical for data intensive problems such as the one considered here.

In Du & Atallah (2001), privacy-preserving cooperative statistical analysis was studied for vertically or horizontally partitioned data. With vertically partitioned data, n records $\{(x_1,y_1), ..., (x_n,y_n)\}$ are distributed at two parties such that Alice holds $\{x_1,...,x_n\}$ and Bob holds $\{y_1, ..., y_n\}$. In this case, the join relationship is one-to-one and is implicit by the sequential ordering of records. A similar data partition based on a common key identifier is assumed in Du & Zhan (2002) and Vaidya & Clifton (2002). In real world, it is odd that the data owned by two mutually untrusted

parties are about exactly same set of entities. In Agrawal, Srikant & Thomas (2005), horizontally partitioned data is considered where each party possesses some records from the same underlying table and the aggregation is over a specified range of attribute values. We consider general join relationships specified by a SQL statement, which cannot be implied by the sequential ordering of records. For example, the patient example has the many-to-many join relationship. Another example is the foreign-key based join. In these cases we have to protect the private join attributes.

Another recent work (Emekci, Agrawal, Abbadi & Gulbeden, 2006) also discussed aggregations such as SUM queries over several private databases; however, the problem it considers is also different. It assumes horizontally partitioned data with all parties having the same pair of attributes: a "key" and a "value" field. The aggregation query is defined to aggregate the values from all parties that correspond to the same key. In their scheme, all data sources send their data to multiple third party peers where the actual aggregations take place and obtain the final query result by assembling the intermediate results received back from the third parties. To prevent data from being leaked to the third parties, the data is disguised using a polynomial and distributed as random shares so that each third party only receives a random share and cannot figure out the original data without collusions among a majority of all third parties. However, it does not work on COUNT queries, because only the data values are disguised but the number of data records remains the same, so that the intermediate COUNT results obtained by the third parties will be the same as the final query result. In contrast, we can handle more general aggregations including COUNT and SUM queries. Our problem setting is also more general in that we deal with private tables with different schemas and general join relationships, where the aggregation query is defined over the joined table.

The closest work to ours is Agrawal et al. (2003) that studied the private equi-join size problem. It proposed a scheme for encrypting join values but required exchanging the frequency of encrypted join values. As pointed out in Agrawal et al. (2003), if the frequency of some join values is unique, the mapping of the encryption can be discovered by matching the frequency before and after the encryption. Thus the privacy of join values may be compromised. Our solution does not have such problem.

Another related problem is the restriction-based inference control in OLAP queries (Wang, Jajodia & Wijesekera, 2004; Zhang, Zhao & Chen, 2004). The goal of inference control is to prevent values of sensitive data from being inferred through answers to OLAP queries. These works mainly dealt with the privacy breaches that arise from the answers to multiple queries; they do not consider the privacy breaches during query processing. The inference control problem has been studied largely in statistical databases, for example, see Adam & Wortman (1989).

PRELIMINARIES

First, we give a brief review on two basic techniques that are the building blocks of our solution: the sketching technique and the private scalar product protocol.

Basic Sketching Technique

Sketching is a randomized algorithm that estimates the join aggregate result with an unbiased random variable, called sketch. The sketch is obtained by multiplying some atomic sketches, which are computed at each table. The expected value of the sketch is shown to be equal to the aggregate result with bounded variance (Alon et al. 1999; Dobra et al. 2002).

As an example, consider the query SUM(A) over 3 tables T_1, T_2 and T_3, with join conditions $T_1.J_1 = T_2.J_2$ and $T_2.J_3 = T_3.J_4$, where A is an aggregation attribute in T_1. The table containing A (in this case, T_1) will be called the aggregation table. Each pair of the join attributes (J_1, J_2) or (J_3, J_4) is called a join pair. J_2 and J_3 may be the same attribute in T_2, but conceptually they belong to different join pairs and are treated separately. Let D_i denote the domain of J_i. Each join pair shares the same domain. For simplicity, we assume $D_i = \{1, \ldots, |D_i|\}$. For any table T_i, let JS_i be the set of join attributes in T_i. Suppose JS_i contains m join attributes, then a value instance V on JS_i is a set that contains one value for each of the m attributes, i.e. $V = \{x_1, \ldots, x_m\}$ where each x_i is a value of a distinct join attribute in JS_i. Let $T_i(V)$ be the set of records in T_i having the value instance V on JS_i. For an aggregation table T_i, we define $S_i(V)$ to be the sum of aggregation attribute values over all records in $T_i(V)$; for any non-aggregation table T_i, we define $F_i(V)$ to be the number of records in $T_i(V)$. Thus, T_1 will have $S_1(V)$ defined; T_2 and T_3 will have $F_2(V)$ and $F_3(V)$ defined. The sketch is constructed as follows:

- *The ε family*: For each join pair (J_i, J_j), select a family of 4-wise independent binary random variables $\{\varepsilon_k, k=1, \ldots, |D_i|\}$, with each $\varepsilon_k \in \{1, -1\}$. That is, each join value k is associated with a variable ε_k whose value is randomly selected from $\{1, -1\}$ and any 4 tuple of such ε variables is jointly independent. The set of values for all ε_k variables is called a ε family. In this example, there are two independent ε families, one for each join pair. In table T_i, with a join value instance V, for each join value x in V (x is a value of some join attribute J), there is one ε_x variable from J's ε family. Let $E_i(V) = \Pi_{x \in V} \varepsilon_x$, i.e. the product of all such ε_x variables.

- *Atomic sketches*: There is one atomic sketch for each table. For the aggregation table T_1, its atomic sketch is $X_1 = \Sigma_V[S_1(V) \times E_1(V)]$, i.e. the sum of $S_1(V) \times E_1(V)$ over all distinct V in T_1, called *S-atomic sketch* (S for summary); the atomic sketches for T_2 and T_3 are $X_2=\Sigma_V[F_2(V)\times E_2(V)]$ and $X_3=\Sigma_V[F_3(V)\times E_3(V)]$, called *F-atomic sketches* (F for frequency). Hence there is exactly one atomic sketch for each table, either a S-atomic sketch or a F-atomic sketch, depending on whether the table contains aggregation attribute or not.

- *The sketch*: The sketch is defined as $\Pi_i(X_i)$, the multiplication of atomic sketches over all tables. The expected value of the sketch can be shown to be equal to SUM(A) with bounded variance. We refer interested readers to Alon et al. (1999) and Dobra et al. (2002) for details.

Because sketch is a random variable, the above computation must be repeated many times to get a good average. Alon, Matias & Szegedy (1996) suggests a procedure of boosting where the number of trials is $\alpha\times\beta$. For every α trials, the average of their sketches is computed, resulting in β averages. The final estimator is the median of these β averages. Note the ε families are chosen independently in each trial. We will refer to this process as $\alpha\beta$-boosting. The time complexity of sketching with $\alpha\beta$-boosting is $O(\alpha\times\beta\times\Sigma_i|T_i|)$, where $|T_i|$ denotes the number of records in table T_i. Experiments from previous works and our experiences show it is usually accurate (error rate < 5%) with moderate size of α (~50) and β (~5).

Sketching is suitable when the join size is larger than a certain "sanity bound" (Alon et al. 1999; Ganguly et al. 2004). This condition typically holds for aggregation queries in data mining applications where data volume is large.

Private Shared Scalar Products

The private scalar product protocol was first discussed in Du & Atallah (2001). Given two d-dimensional vectors $\vec{U} =<U_1,...,U_d>$ and $\vec{V} = <V_1,...,V_d>$ owned by two honest-but-curious parties, this protocol computes

$\vec{U}\times\vec{V} = \sum_{i=1,d} U_i\times V_i$, such that the two parties obtain no additional knowledge other than $\vec{U}\times\vec{V}$. In other words, the inputs $\vec{U}$ and $\vec{V}$ are concealed from the non-owning parties.

In some applications, a scalar product $\vec{U}\times\vec{V}$ is needed as a part of the entire computation, but the value of $\vec{U}\times\vec{V}$ needs to be concealed in the process from all parties. Such problems can be addressed by the private shared scalar product (SSP) protocol (Goethals, Laur, Lipmaa & Mielikainen, 2004), or SSP protocol subsequently. With this protocol, each party obtains one random share of $\vec{U}\times\vec{V}$, denoted as R_1 and R_2, such that $R_1+R_2= \vec{U}\times\vec{V}$, but (R_1+R_2) is concealed from both parties. R_1 and R_2 are complementary in that they are random shares of the same scalar product $\vec{U}\times\vec{V}$ and only knowing both can infer the result of the scalar product, thus the value of $\vec{U}\times\vec{V}$ is unknown to both parties. Note that a random share can be positive or negative and their range can be the real domain which has nothing to do with the value of $\vec{U}\times\vec{V}$, thus it is impossible to guess from any single share. Several two-party SSP protocols with linear complexity have been proposed (Clifton, Kantarcioglu, Vaidya, Lin & Zhu, 2002; Du & Atallah, 2001; Du & Zhan, 2002). The SSP protocol for multi-parties was studied in Goethals et al. (2004). In the rest of this paper, we use SSP$(\vec{V}_1,...,\vec{V}_k)$ to denote the SSP protocol on input vectors $\vec{V}_1,...,\vec{V}_k$.

METHOD

We start with analyzing the privacy breaches in the standard sketching process. The purpose is to derive the requirements on the types of information that must be concealed in the query computation. We then show how to conceal such information using our protocol. For illustration purposes, we first consider the basic join aggregate COUNT(*) over two private tables (i.e., computing the join size of two tables). The analysis can be extended to general join aggregates over multiple tables in a similar way.

Assume that Alice holds table T_1 and Bob holds T_2 with one common join attribute J. Let D_1 be the set of distinct join values in T_1 and D_2 be the set of join values in T_2. Thus, J's active domain $D=D_1 \cup D_2$. First, a ε family of binary random variables for J is selected. Both parties use this same ε family to compute their atomic sketches. For simplicity, assume that D has two values, v_1 and v_2 (thus $|D|=2$); there are two variables $\{\varepsilon_1, \varepsilon_2\}$ in the ε family. Let $F_i(v)$ denote the number of records having the join value v in table T_i, i.e. $F_i(v)$ values represent the distribution of join values. $F_1(v)$ belongs to Alice and should be concealed from Bob; $F_2(v)$ belongs to Bob and should be concealed from Alice.

The two parties compute their atomic sketches X_i as follows:

Alice: $X_1 = F_1(v_1) \times \varepsilon_1 + F_1(v_2) \times \varepsilon_2,$ (1)

Bob: $X_2 = F_2(v_1) \times \varepsilon_1 + F_2(v_2) \times \varepsilon_2.$ (2)

So far, the computation of X_1 and X_2 is done locally, using the shared ε family and locally owned $F_i(v_j)$ values ($\{F_1(v_1), F_1(v_2)\}$ for Alice and $\{F_2(v_1),F_2(v_2)\}$ for Bob). Because the ε family is just some random value, knowing it will not lead to any private information about the other party.

Next, the sketch $X_1 \times X_2$ needs to be computed. Unfortunately the standard sketching technique will disclose information about $F_i(v)$ in this computation process, and thus fail on privacy protection. To see this, suppose that Alice sends her atomic sketch X_1 to Bob. Now, Bob knows X_1, his own X_2, and the ε family. In Equation (1) and (2), with only $F_1(v_1)$ and $F_1(v_2)$ being unknown, Bob can infer some knowledge about $F_1(v_j)$ using Equation (1). For example, knowing $\varepsilon_1=1$ and $\varepsilon_2=-1$, if X_1 is positive, Bob knows that v_1 is more frequent than v_2 by a margin of X_1 in Alice's table. The problem may be less obvious when there are more than two values in D, however, it still leaks non-zero

knowledge about $F_1(v_j)$ values. Furthermore, in the $\alpha\beta$-boosting process, the above computation is repeated $\alpha \times \beta$ times and there will be one pair of Equation (1) and (2) for each of the $\alpha \times \beta$ trials. With the ε family being independently chosen in each trial, each pair of these equations provides a new constraint on the unknown $F_1(v_j)$ values. If the number of trials is equal to or greater than $|D|$, Bob will have a sufficient number of Equation (1) to solve all $F_1(v_j)$ values owned by Alice. Therefore, even for a large domain D, the privacy breach is severe if Bob knows both atomic sketches.

On the other hand, even if Bob knows only his own X_2, given the result of $X_1 \times X_2$, he can easily get X_1. Now, if the individual sketch $X_1 \times X_2$ in each trial is also concealed from Bob, because both parties agree to share the final result which is an average of $X_1 \times X_2$, by comparing the final result with his own X_2's, Bob may still infer some approximate knowledge on X_1, allowing him to find the approximate values of $F_1(v_j)$ as described above. The situation is symmetric with Alice. Therefore, to prevent any inference on other party's $F_i(v_j)$, all atomic sketches should be unknown to all parties, which implies that the ε families should also be concealed from all parties.

Suppose that all of atomic sketches X_i and ε families are concealed from all parties. If the sketch $X_1 \times X_2$ is known to Bob, Bob may still succeed in inferring X_1 in some extreme cases. For example, knowing $X_1 \times X_2 = 0$, and $F_2(v_1)=10$ and $F_2(v_2)=5$, since $X_2 \neq 0$ for any value of ε_1 and ε_2, Bob can infer that $X_1=0$. Additionally, from Equation (1), $X_1=0$ holds only if $F_1(v_1)=F_1(v_2)$ (because ε_1 and ε_2 are from $\{1,-1\}$). Consequently, Bob learns that the two join values are equally frequent in Alice's table. Therefore, to prevent the above inference, the individual sketch $X_1 \times X_2$ in each trial should be concealed from all parties.

Therefore, the only non-local information that a party is allowed to know is the final query result which will be shared at the end. Because the final result is something that has been averaged over many independent trials, disclosing one average will not let any party infer the individual sketches or underlying atomic sketches. Note that with the current problem definition where parties agree to share the final result, we cannot do better than this.

Since the ε families must be concealed from Alice and Bob, we need to use a semi-trusted third party (Kantarcioglu & Vaidya, 2002), called Tim, to generate the ε families. To fulfill its job, Tim must also be an honest-but-curious party who does not collude with Alice or Bob. In real world, finding such a third party is much easier than finding a trusted third party. Now we have three parties: Alice, Bob and Tim. The protocol needs to make sure that Tim cannot learn private information about Alice or Bob or the final query result, i.e. Tim knows nothing about atomic sketches, sketches or $F_i(v_j)$ values. The only thing Tim knows is the ε families which are just some random variables. On the other hand, Alice owns $F_1(v_j)$ and Bob owns $F_2(v_j)$, both should know nothing about the other party's $F_i(v_j)$, the ε families, atomic sketches or individual sketches. These requirements are summarized in the following definition.

Definition 1. Information Concealing (IC-conforming): *Sketching Protocol. Let Y denote an average of sketches over α trials in the αβ-boosting. There will be β number of such Y's in total. A sketching protocol satisfying the following requirements is said to be an Information Concealing sketching protocol, or we say that the sketching protocol is IC-conforming: Alice learns only Y and local $F_1(v_j)$; Bob learns only Y and local $F_2(v_j)$; Tim learns only the ε families; atomic sketches X_i and individual sketches $X_1 \times X_2$ are concealed from all parties.* ■

Theorem 1. *The computations in an IC-conforming sketching protocol conceals $F_i(v)$ from all non-owning parties throughout the computation process.*

Proof: *First, Tim knows only the ε families and nothing about $F_i(v)$. Consider Alice and Bob. From*

the IC-conformity, Alice knows only Y and $F_1(v_j)$ and Bob knows only Y and $F_2(v_j)$, where Y is the average of sketches over α trials. $F_1(v_j)$ and $F_2(v_j)$ does not go beyond the information derived from the local table. An average Y of sketches $X_1 \times X_2$ over α trials, where α≥2, provides no clue on an individual sketch $X_1 \times X_2$ and whether $X_1 \times X_2$ is equal to 0 because each sketch is a signed quantity and is computed with a ε family that is independently and randomly chosen in each trial. Even if there is a non-zero chance that Tim chooses the same ε family in all α trials, therefore Y is equal to each individual sketch, Alice and Bob will never know that this actually happens because the ε families are unknown to them.

The only additional knowledge gained by Alice and Bob is the value of Y, which may approximate the query result $F_1(v_1) \times F_2(v_1) + \ldots + F_1(v_k) \times F_2(v_k)$. However, this approximation alone does not allow any party to solve the other party's $F_i(v)$ because there are many solutions for the unknown $F_i(v)$. It does not help to use different averages Y in the αβ-boosting because they are instances of a random variable and do not act as independent constraints. ■

Basic IC-Conforming Sketching Protocol for Two-Party COUNT(*) Queries

We now present a IC-conforming protocol for two-party COUNT(*) queries. More general queries will be considered in the next section.

Let Bob be the querying party. The overall computation with αβ-boosting is as follows:

1. for i=1 to β do
2.   for j=1 to α do
3.   ε-phase;
4.   S-phase;
5.   α-phase;
6. β-phase;

The $\alpha\times\beta$ trials are divided into β groups with each group containing α trials. Each trial has the *ε-phase* and the *S-phase* (line 3 and 4). The ε-phase generates the ε family and the S-phase computes atomic sketches. For each group, the *α-phase* computes the average of the sketches in the α trials (line 5). Finally the *β-phase* finds the median of the β averages (line 6), which is the query estimator. Below, we explain each phase.

ε-phase

In this phase, Tim generates the ε family. Let D_1 be the set of join values in T_1 (Alice's table) and D_2 be the set of join values in T_2 (Bob's table). $D=D_1 \cup D_2$. To generate the ε family, Tim needs to know $|D|$, $|D_1|$ and $|D_2|$, and the correspondence between the ε variables and the join values. Alice and Bob can hash their join values by a *cryptographic hash function* (Stinson, 2006) such that Tim does not need to know the actual join values in D. A cryptographic hash function H has the following properties: (1) *pre-image resistant*: given a hash value H(v), it is computationally infeasible to find v; (2) *collision resistant*: it is computationally infeasible to find two different inputs v_1 and v_2 with $H(v_1)=H(v_2)$. In real life, industrial-strength cryptographic hash functions with these properties are available (NIST, 2002). The ε-phase is given as follows. Alice and Bob create two hashed sets, S_1 and S_2, of their join values using a shared cryptographic hash function H, and send the hashed sets to Tim separately (line 1 and 2). Tim then generates a ε family $\vec{E}_1$ for Alice and another ε family $\vec{E}_2$ for Bob.

1. Alice and Bob compute locally the hashed sets $S_1 = \{H(v) \mid v \in D_1\}$ and $S_2 = \{H(v) \mid v \in D_2\}$ where H is concealed from Tim.
2. Alice and Bob send S_1 and S_2 to Tim.
3. Tim computes $S=S_1 \cup S_2$.
4. Tim assigns a unique ε variable to each value in S, generating a ε family $\vec{E}_1$ from S_1 and a ε family $\vec{E}_2$ from S_2.

Security Analysis

Alice and Bob do not receive information from any party. With the cryptographic hash function H, Tim will not be able to learn original join values from the hashed sets. Since Tim does not know H, it is impossible for Tim to infer whether a join value exists in T_1 or T_2 by enumerating all possible values. This scenario is different from Agrawal et al. (2003) where all parties know the hash functions. What Tim does learn is the domain size like $|D_1|$, $|D_2|$, $|D_1 \cup D_2|$ and $|D_1 \cap D_2|$. But such general knowledge will not help Tim to infer atomic sketches or the sketches. Therefore, this phase is IC-conforming.

S-Phase

In this phase, we compute the atomic sketches X_1 for T_1 (or for Alice) and X_2 for T_2 (or for Bob). For i=1,2, let $\vec{F}_i$ denote the vector of $F_i(v)$ values for all distinct v from D_i, arranged in the same order as in $\vec{E}_i$. X_i is given by the scalar product $\vec{F}_i \times \vec{E}_i$, where $\vec{F}_i$ is owned by T_i and $\vec{E}_i$ is owned by Tim. To conceal $\vec{E}_i$, $\vec{F}_i$ and X_i, Alice and Tim compute $\vec{F}_1 \times \vec{E}_1$ using the SSP protocol; similarly, Bob and Tim compute $\vec{F}_2 \times \vec{E}_2$ using the SSP protocol. This is shown as follows.

1. Alice and Tim compute $SSP(\vec{E}_1, \vec{F}_1)$. Alice obtains RA and Tim obtains TA, where $RA+TA=X_1$, the atomic sketch for Alice.
2. Bob and Tim compute $SSP(\vec{E}_2, \vec{F}_2)$. Bob obtains RB and Tim obtains TB, where $RB+TB=X_2$, the atomic sketch for Bob.

At the end of this phase, Alice obtains one random share RA, Bob obtains one random share RB, Tim obtains two random shares TA and TB, such that $RA+TA=X_1$ and $RB+TB=X_2$, where X_1 and X_2 are the atomic sketches for Alice and Bob.

Security Analysis

The SSP protocol ensures that $\vec{F}_i$, $\vec{E}_i$, and X_i are concealed as required. Tim obtains two non-complementary random shares from *different* atomic sketches, which are not useful to infer any atomic sketch. Thus, this phase is IC-conforming.

α-Phase

In this phase, we compute the average of the sketches for every α trials. In the jth trial, the sketch is given by $X_{1j} \times X_{2j}$, where X_{1j} and X_{2j} are the atomic sketches for T_1 (Alice) and T_2 (Bob). However, at the end of S-phase, no party obtains X_{1j} or X_{2j}; rather, Tim obtains TA_j and TB_j, Alice obtains RA_j and Bob obtains RB_j, such that $X_{1j} = TA_j + RA_j$ and $X_{2j} = TB_j + RB_j$. In addition, the IC-conformity requires concealing the individual sketches (i.e. $X_{1j} \times X_{2j}$) from all parties. Our approach is to compute the average directly from these random shares while preventing any party from obtaining both complementary random shares.

After α trials, let $\overline{RA}$ be the vector of $<RA_1,\ldots,RA_\alpha>$ and let $\overline{RB}$, $\overline{TA}$, $\overline{TB}$ be defined analogously. Alice owns $\overline{RA}$, Bob owns $\overline{RB}$ and Tim owns $\overline{TA}$ and $\overline{TB}$. The average over the α trials is:

$$Y = \frac{\sum_{j=1}^{\alpha}(X_{1j} \times X_{2j})}{\alpha} =$$

$$\frac{\sum_{j=1}^{\alpha}[(RA_j + TA_j) \times (RB_j + TB_j)]}{\alpha}$$

$$= \frac{\sum_{j=1}^{\alpha}(RA_j \times RB_j + TA_j \times RB_j + RA_j \times TB_j + TA_j \times TB_j)}{\alpha}$$

$$= \frac{\overline{RA} \times \overline{RB} + \overline{TA} \times \overline{RB} + \overline{RA} \times \overline{TB} + \overline{TA} \times \overline{TB}}{\alpha}$$

The numerator is the sum of several scalar products of the random share vectors possibly owned by different parties. To compute these scalar products, if we allow the input vectors to be exchanged among parties, a party obtaining both complementary random shares immediately learns the atomic sketch, thereby violating the

IC-conformity. To conceal the input vectors, we use the SSP protocol again to compute these scalar products.

1. Alice and Bob compute SSP($\overline{RA}$, $\overline{RB}$);
2. Tim and Bob compute SSP($\overline{TA}$, $\overline{RB}$);
3. Tim and Alice compute SSP($\overline{TB}$, $\overline{RA}$);
4. Tim computes $\overline{TA} \times \overline{TB}$ (no SSP is needed);
5. Tim sums all his random shares and $\overline{TA} \times \overline{TB}$, send the result to Alice;
6. Alice adds all her random shares to the sum from Tim, forwards the result to Bob;
7. Bob adds all his random shares to the sum from Alice, divides it by α.

On line 1-3, each party obtains two non-complementary random shares. Then, these random shares and $\overline{TA} \times \overline{TB}$ are summed in a forwarding chain (line 5-7), starting from Tim and ending at the querying party Bob. In the end, Bob has the average Y over the α trials.

Security analysis. The SSP protocols ensure that $\overline{RA}$, $\overline{RB}$, $\overline{TA}$, $\overline{TB}$ are concealed from a non-owning party; therefore, no party learns atomic sketches. After SSP computations, a party may obtain several non-complementary random shares. For example, Alice obtains one random share of $\overline{RA} \times \overline{RB}$ and one random share of $\overline{TB} \times \overline{RA}$, which together does not help her learn anything. A party may receive a partial sum during sum forwarding. However, each partial sum always contains two or more non-complementary random shares. It is not possible for the receiver to deduce individual contributing random shares from such a sum. Therefore, this phase is IC-conforming.

β-Phase

Repeating the α-phase β times would yield the averages $Y_1, \ldots, Y_\beta$ at Bob. In the β-phase, Bob finds the median of $Y_1, \ldots, Y_\beta$, which is the estimator of the query result.

Security Analysis

This phase is done entirely by Bob alone and there is no information exchange at all. Thus the level of privacy at all parties is unchanged.

Since all phases of our sketching protocol are IC-conforming, we conclude that our protocol is a private sketching protocol that is IC-conforming.

IC-Conforming Sketching Protocol for Multi-Party COUNT(*) Queries

Consider n parties $P_1, \ldots, P_n$, where each party P_i holds one private table T_i. Let JS_i be the set of join attributes in T_i. Let $v_i=(x_1,\ldots,x_k)$ be a vector of join values on JS_i in T_i such that each x_i is from a distinct join attribute in JS_i. $F_i(v_i)$ denotes the frequency count of v_i in T_i and $E_i(v_i)=\prod_{x\in v_i} \varepsilon_x$. With each distinct v_i on JS_i corresponding to one dimension, $\vec{F}_i$ and $\vec{E}_i$ denote the vectors of $F_i(v_i)$ and $E_i(v_i)$. The atomic sketch for T_i is given by $\vec{F}_i \times \vec{E}_i$. The sketch, i.e. the multiplication of the atomic sketches for all T_i, is then given by:

$$\sum_{(v_1,\cdots,v_n)} Q(v_1,\cdots,v_n) \tag{3}$$

where,
$$Q(v_1,\cdots,v_n) = F_1(v_1)\times\cdots\times F_n(v_n)\times E_1(v_1)\times\cdots\times E_n(v_n)$$

and $(v_1,\ldots,v_n)$ represents all possible combinations of $v_1,\ldots,v_n$ values.

We can show that the expected value of expression (3) equals to COUNT(*), which is the query result. Let $\sigma(v_1,\ldots,v_n)$ denote the function of whether $(v_1,\ldots,v_n)$ satisfies the equi-join conditions, i.e., $\sigma(v_1,\ldots,v_n)$=true if and only if $(v_1,\ldots,v_n)$ belongs to a tuple in the joined table. The expression (3) can be separated into two parts:

$$\sum_{\sigma(v_1,\ldots,v_n)=true} Q(v_1,\cdots,v_n),$$

and

$$\sum_{\sigma(v_1,\ldots,v_n)=false} Q(v_1,\cdots,v_n).$$

Similar to the proof in Alon et al. (1999), the first part is equal to COUNT(*) because $E_1(v_1)\times\ldots\times E_n(v_n)=1$ for $\sigma(v_1,\ldots,v_n)$=true, and the expected value of the second part is 0 since $E_1(v_1)\times\ldots\times E_n(v_n)$ has the expected value of 0 for $\sigma(v_1,\ldots,v_n)$=false. This shows that expression (3) is an unbiased estimator of the query result. Therefore it can be used to estimate the query. Below, we extend our IC-conforming protocol to compute this estimator in a privacy preserving manner.

The ε-phase is similarly done as in the two-party computations, except that $\vec{F}_i$ is owned by P_i and $\vec{E}_i$ is owned by Tim. In the S-phase, we use $SSP(\vec{F}_i, \vec{E}_i)$ to compute the atomic sketch $\vec{F}_i \times \vec{E}_i$. At the jth trial, P_i obtains the random share R_{ij} and Tim obtains the random share RT_{ij} such that $\vec{F}_i \times \vec{E}_i = R_{ij}+RT_{ij}$. The average of the sketches over α trials is:

$$Y = \frac{\sum_{j=1}^{\alpha}[(R_{1j}+RT_{1j})\times\cdots\times(R_{nj}+RT_{nj})]}{\alpha}$$

The numerator is the sum of 2^n scalar products of the form: $\vec{W}_1\ldots\vec{W}_n$, where $\vec{W}_i$ is either $\vec{R}_i = (R_{i1},\ldots,R_{i\alpha})$ owned by P_i, or $\vec{RT}=(RT_{i1},\ldots,RT_{i\alpha})$ owned by Tim. In the α-phase, we can use the SSP protocol to securely compute each of these 2^n scalar products, except that we need to use the n-party SSP protocol such as the one in Goethals et al. (2004). The steps afterwards are the same as in the two-party case, and the security analysis can be similarly done and the same level of security is achieved.

Cost Analysis

1. **Running time:** Let $|T_i|$ be the number of records in table T_i. Let $|C_i|$ be the number of distinct vectors v on JS_i in T_i. Let $|D|$ be

the total number of distinct join values (on single join attributes) from all tables. Let C_H denote the computation cost of one hash operation. Let $C_{SP}(d)$ denote the computation cost and $S(d)$ denote the communication cost for executing the SSP protocol on d-dimensional vectors. For example, for the two-party SSP protocol in Du & Zhan (2002), $S(d)$ is $4d$ and $C_{SP}(d)$ is $O(d)$. The total running time of our n-party IC-conforming sketching protocol (with $\alpha\beta$-boosting) is as follows. Note such running time is the total time for computations in all parties.

- *ε-phase.* Hashing and generating the ε families takes $O(C_H \times |D| + \Sigma_i |T_i| + \alpha \times \beta \times |D|)$ time. Note that the hashing is done only once for all trials, but the ε family is generated independently in each trial.

- *S-phase.* Computing atomic sketches takes $O(\alpha \times \beta \times \Sigma_i C_{SP}(|C_i|))$ time.

- *α-phase.* Computing the β averages takes $O(\beta \times 2^n \times C_{SP}(\alpha))$ time as each average involves 2^n calls to the SSP protocol, where n is the number of parties. Note that the factor 2^n usually does not impose an efficiency problem because n is typically very small, say 2-3. In our problem setting, each party refers to an individual or organization that owns some private tables. In most applications, a join aggregate query joins only a small number of tables. This is different from a large number of "record owners" where each owner owns only one record.

- *β-phase.* finding the median of β averages takes $O(n \times \beta)$ time.

2. **Space requirements:** The storage space for keeping $\vec{F}_i$ and $\vec{E}_i$ is proportional to the dimensionality of these vectors, which is $|C_i|$ for party P_i. This space is reused in every trial. The space required in the α-phase is $O(\alpha)$ because α is now the dimensionality of the input vectors to the SSP protocols. The space required in the β-phase is $O(\beta)$.

3. **Communication cost:** The communication cost is $n \times |D|$ for the n parties sending hashed sets to Tim, $\alpha \times \beta \times \Sigma_i S(|C_i|)$ for computing atomic sketches, $\beta \times 2^n \times S(\alpha)$ for computing all β averages.

EXTENSIONS

Join Aggregates on General Attribute Expressions

SUM(A) Queries

So far, we have presented the protocol for computing the COUNT(*) query defined on the joined table. Note such protocol can be easily adapted to SUM(A) query on a single aggregation attribute A, since sketch techniques have been shown applicable to SUM(A) in a very similar way, as discussed in the third section where the preliminaries of sketching techniques are discussed. The only difference is that the table with the aggregation attribute A will maintain a S-atomic sketch instead of a F-atomic sketch. Such change only influences the local computations of the atomic sketch in that table. All later computations that are based on atomic sketches are the same.

SUM($A_1 \times \ldots \times A_m$) Queries

For join aggregates of the form SUM($A_1 \times \ldots \times A_m$), where A_1 through A_m are aggregation attributes from different tables, the simple approach of creating a new attribute to store $A_1 \times \ldots \times A_m$ requires joining all tables, therefore, violates our security claims. For this case, our private sketching protocol can be used where the sketch is still computed by multiplication of atomic sketches, only that every table containing an aggregation attribute will contribute a S-atomic sketch, and every other table will contribute a F-atomic sketch. It can be shown that such sketch estimator converges to SUM($A_1 \times \ldots \times A_m$), by following a similar analysis as in the previous section where multi-party COUNT(*) queries are analyzed.

SUM($A_1 \pm \ldots \pm A_m$) Queries

Now let us consider a join aggregate of the form SUM($A_1 \theta \ldots \theta A_m$), where each θ is either "+" or "–". We can rewrite this query into SUM(A_1)$\theta \ldots$ θSUM(A_m) such that each SUM(A_i) is a sub-query over the original join. For each table containing an aggregation attribute A_i, we now construct one F-atomic sketch and one S-atomic sketch; only one ε family needs to be maintained for both atomic sketches. For all other tables, we construct only the F-atomic sketch. The sketch for each sub-query SUM(A_i) is computed using the S-atomic sketch for the table containing A_i and the F-atomic sketches for all other tables, as described above in the paragraph for the basic type of SUM(A) queries. Then the estimator for the entire SUM($A_1 \theta \ldots \theta A_m$) query can be obtained by summing the estimators for all SUM(A_i) sub-queries.

One subtlety, however, is that each party should learn only the final estimator of SUM($A_1 \theta \ldots \theta A_m$), not the estimator of an intermediate subquery SUM(A_i). In order to achieve this, we need to conceal the estimator of SUM(A_i) from all parties. Let us consider two parties Alice and Bob. The ε-phase and the S-phase can be shared by all sub-queries because these phases produce only random shares. At the end of the S-phase, for each sub-query SUM(A_i), Alice and Bob each obtain one random share, and Tim obtains two random shares that are complementary to Alice's and Bob's share, respectively. The subsequent α-phase and β-phase are separately computed for each sub-query, as explained below.

In the α-phase, each party computes SSPs for each sub-query SUM(A_i). Additionally, to conceal the estimator of SUM(A_i), Tim generates a secret random number R_i. R_i is generated independently for each sub-query but stays the same in each

repeated α-phase for the same sub-query. We modify the α-phase as follows:

1-4. are the same as in the α-phase of the basic IC-conforming sketching protocol as discussed in the previous section.
5. Tim generates a random number R_i. This is done once for SUM(A_i).
6. Tim sums all his random shares and R_i, and send the result to Alice.
7. Alice adds all her random shares to the sum and forwards it to Bob.
8. Bob adds all his random shares to the sum, divide the sum by α.

Essentially, we use R_i to disguise the average over the α trials for SUM(A_i) in this modified α-phase.

The β-phase for SUM(A_i) then computes the median of these averages. Let TS_i denote the true estimator of SUM(A_i). At the end of the β-phase for SUM(A_i), the result obtained by Bob is not TS_i, but rather a modified estimator that is equal to ($TS_i + R_i/\alpha$). Since R_i is unknown to Bob, Bob cannot deduce TS_i.

With m sub-queries, all following the same modified α-phases, Tim generates m secret random numbers $\{R_1, \ldots, R_m\}$ and Bob obtains m modified estimators $\{S_1, \ldots, S_m\}$. After all sub-queries are done, Tim computes ($R_1 \theta \ldots \theta R_m$)/$\alpha$, where each operator θ follows exactly as in SUM($A_1 \theta \ldots \theta A_m$), and sends the result to Bob, who can then compute the estimator of SUM($A_1 \theta \ldots \theta A_m$) as ($S_1 \theta \ldots \theta S_m$)-($R_1 \theta \ldots \theta R_m$)/$\alpha$. Since each R_i is an independently-generated random number and is only known to Tim, ($R_1 \theta \ldots \theta R_m$)/$\alpha$ provides no clue to Bob on the value of individual R_i. Therefore, the true estimator of each SUM(A_i) is concealed from Bob (as well as from Alice).

General Expressions

In general, in the aggregate function *agg*(*exp*) of the join aggregate query, the attribute expres-

Figure 1. Join aggregates with group-by

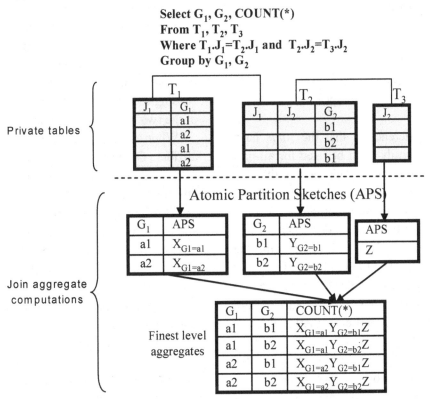

sion *exp* can be any arithmetic of aggregation attributes, as long as there is no division with the denominator that involves addition or subtraction of attributes from different tables. For example, $SUM(A_1+A_2 \times A_3 -1/A_4)$ can be separated into subqueries $SUM(A_1)$, $SUM(A_2 \times A_3)$, $SUM(1/A_4)$, and the final aggregate is the sum of all sub-queries and can be computed using modified α-phases as described above. Note that $SUM(1/A_4)$ can be computed by $SUM(A_5)$, where the new attribute A_5 is equal to $1/A_4$. The only case where our private sketching protocol cannot be applied, is when the denominator involves additions or subtractions of attributes from different tables, such as $SUM(A_1/(A_2+A_3))$, where A_2 and A_3 are from different tables. Such aggregations cannot be estimated using sketches because the join relationship needs to be maintained at the record level.

Group-by Operations

In the presence of the group-by operator, the join can be considered as being partitioned on the group-by attributes. Each table with a group-by attribute consists of disjoint *partitions* corresponding to the group-by attribute values in the table. Each table without group-by attributes consists of only one partition, i.e., the table itself. Let $p(T,c)$ denote the partition on a table T that satisfies a condition c. In Figure 1, T_1 consists of two partitions: $p(T_1,G_1=a1)$ and $p(T_1,G_1=a2)$; T_3 consists of one partition $p(T_3,*)$ because T_3 has no group-by attribute, where * denotes the trivial "true". All join values are omitted.

The query can be computed by applying the protocol discussed earlier to each combination of partitions from different tables, called a *partition combination*. Each partition combination produces one row in the result. In Figure 1, the protocol can be applied to each of the following partition combinations:

$p(T_1,G_1{=}a1)$, $p(T_2,G_2{=}b1)$ and $p(T_3,*)$
$p(T_1,G_1{=}a1)$, $p(T_2,G_2{=}b2)$ and $p(T_3,*)$
$p(T_1,G_1{=}a2)$, $p(T_2,G_2{=}b1)$ and $p(T_3,*)$
$p(T_1,G_1{=}a2)$, $p(T_2,G_2{=}b2)$ and $p(T_3,*)$

The only difference is that the *same* hash function and ε family must be used for all partitions of the same table. This means that the same atomic sketch for a partition, called *atomic partition sketch (APS)*, will be used for all partition combinations that contain this partition. For example, with $X_{G1=a1}$, $X_{G2=b1}$, $X_{G2=b2}$, Z being the APSs for $p(T_1,G_1{=}a1)$, $p(T_2,G_2{=}b1)$, $p(T_2,G_2{=}b2)$ and $p(T_3,*)$, respectively, COUNT(*) for the first combination is computed by $X_{G1=a1}X_{G2=b1}Z$, and COUNT(*) for the second combination is computed by $X_{G1=a1}X_{G2=b2}Z$.

There is one sketch for every partition combination and each party obtains one random share of every sketch. Since the random shares at a single party are for different partition combinations, they are non-complementary and do not infer anything. Thus the protocol extended to the group-by operator remains IC-conforming. In the case that all attributes of some table are in the group-by list, the full detail of the table may be leaked in the query result. But this leakage is through the query result, not through computations. A party can always reject such queries or impose a minimum size on the partitions that participate in a query.

Roll-Up/Drill-Down Operations

To support roll-up/drill-down operations, in a straightforward implementation, the aggregates at the finest level are first computed and subsequently are used for roll-up/drill-down. This means that the parties that maintain such aggregates will know the most detailed aggregates. For preserving the privacy, however, aggregates should be known to a party only at the requested level and only if the participating parties honor the request. In order to achieve this protection, for each partition at the finest level, its owning party maintains one random share of the APS for the partition, whereas the third party Tim maintains the other random share. No single party can learn the APS from only one of the two complementary random shares.

When a roll-up is requested on some group-by attribute G, the party P that owns G sums up the local random shares for all partitions that differ only on the dimension of G, so does Tim. For each "rolled-up" partition p, the sum at party P and the sum at Tim are the two complementary random shares of the APS for the partition p. The subsequent α-phase will use these random shares in the computation that involves p. In $\alpha\beta$-boosting, each trial maintains a separate set of random shares.

As an example, in the previous Figure 1, suppose that the roll-up is requested by some party P on the group-by attribute G_1, i.e., the roll-up is along G_2 from the finest aggregates on $<G_1,G_2>$. Essentially, it requires computing the sketches:

$$X_{G1=a1}(Y_{G2=b1}{+}Y_{G2=b2})Z \qquad \text{for } G_1{=}a1$$
$$X_{G1=a2}(Y_{G2=b1}{+}Y_{G2=b2})Z \qquad \text{for } G_1{=}a2$$

where $Y{=}Y_{G2=b1}{+}Y_{G2=b2}$ is the APS for the rolled-up partition $p(T_2,*)$. Before the roll-up, the party P_2 has the random shares of $Y_{G2=b1}$ and $Y_{G2=b2}$, denoted as R_1 and R_2; Tim has the other random shares of $Y_{G2=b1}$ and $Y_{G2=b2}$, denoted as $R_1{}'$ and $R_2{}'$. Note that $Y_{G2=b1}{=}R_1{+}R_1{}'$ and $Y_{G2=b2}{=}R_2{+}R_2{}'$. Then, P_2 obtains one random share of Y by $R_1{+}R_2$ and Tim obtains the other random share of Y by $R_1{}'{+}R_2{}'$.

Thus, by maintaining only one set of random shares for the APSs at the finest level, the random shares at a coarser level can be computed incrementally and locally at each party. Essentially, the roll-up/drill-down is now performed on local random shares, not on sketches that involve all parties. The major benefit is that the random shares at a single party provide no clue on the APSs or sketches, as required by the IC-conformity. Only by an honored roll-up/drill-down request, do all parties collaborate to compute the sketches from local random shares (as in the α-phase and β-phase). Therefore, our protocol supports the roll-up/drill-down operations at the same level of privacy protection as specified by the IC-conformity.

It is true that both group-by operations and roll-up/drill operations add more complexity and cost to the basic protocol. But some of this added cost is due to the increase of query power itself even without the privacy consideration.

EXPERIMENTS

We implemented the basic two-party join size estimation protocol on three PCs that simulate Alice, Bob and Tim, all connected through a LAN with 100Mbps network cables. All PCs have Pentium IV 2.4GHz CPU and 512M RAM and Windows XP. The cryptographic hash function was implemented using the QuickHash library 3.0 ("The QuickHash Library", online source) and the two-party SSP protocol in Du & Zhan (2002) was used.

Tests were done on synthetic datasets with various table sizes and join characteristics: Alice and Bob each own a private table T_1 and T_2 with one join attribute J. The cardinality of J, denoted

as $|D|$, varies from 100 to 10,000. The number of records in T_1, $|T_1|$, was varied from 10,000 to 1,000,000 with the values of J generated following the zipf distribution. T_2 was generated such that for every distinct join value in T_1, a certain B number (B varies from 1 to 10) of records are generated in T_2 with the same join value. Thus, the size of table T_2 is B*$|D|$ and the join size $|T_1 \infty T_2|$ is B*$|T_1|$.

We evaluated our algorithm in terms of both accuracy and efficiency. Since sketching is a randomized algorithm, each reported result is an average over 5 runs, where each run uses exactly the same parameters.

Accuracy

We define the error rate as $|F-E|/E$, where F is the approximated count computed by our algorithm and E is the true count. In each run, the query result was computed by the αβ-boosting where the number of trials is α×β. In general, a larger number of trials will produce a smaller error rate.

Figure 2 shows the error rate vs. different choices of α and β in the case of $|T_1|$=1,000,000, $|D|$=100, B=1. The results in other cases show similar trends. Generally, when β is small (<15), the error rate shows random fluctuations with different choices of α, due to the fact that the sketch is constructed on random variables and does not necessarily converge when β is small. As β gets

Figure 2. The effect of α and β on error rate

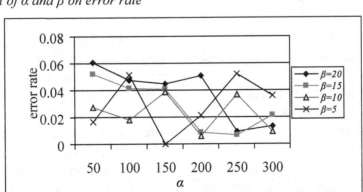

Figure 3. Error rate w.r.t. |T1| and B (|D|=100)

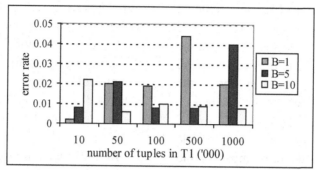

Figure 4. Error rate w.r.t. |D| and B (|T1|=10k)

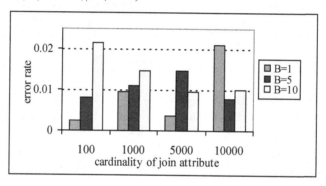

Figure 5. ε-phase running time (B=5)

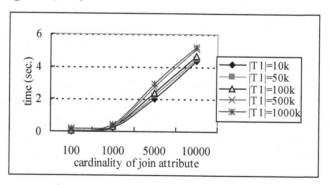

bigger, the error rate tends to be decreased with increasing α, as expected. Note that because sketching is a randomized algorithm, there are always random variations observed; nevertheless, bigger β values generally show smoother trends. We observed that with α ranging from 50 to 300 and β ranging from 5 to 20, the error rate in all runs is no more than 6%. For large α and β, the error is frequently less than 2%. This shows that the approximation provided by sketching is in general sufficient for most data mining applications where the focus is on trends and patterns, instead of exact counts.

With α=200 and β=15, Figure 3 shows the error rate for different $|T_1|$ and B while fixing |D|=100. In general, the error rate is low (<5%). There is no clear trend observed with regard to either $|T_1|$ or B. Figure 4 shows the error rate for different

Figure 6. S-phase running time (B=5)

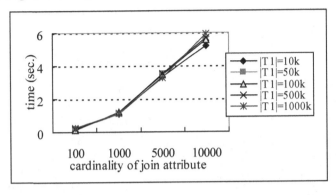

Figure 7. Message size w.r.t. |D| (B=5)

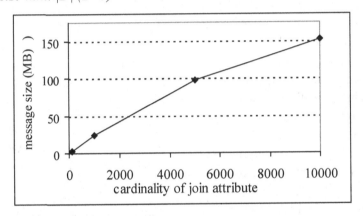

|D| and B while fixing |T₁|=10,000. Again, the error rate fluctuates in a small range, i.e., 2%. We believe such randomness is a natural behavior of the sketching algorithm, irrelevant with any other parameter.

Efficiency

Our protocol has a linear complexity in terms of the table size, because (1) both the basic sketching algorithm and the SSP protocol have a linear complexity and (2) these procedures are called only a constant number of times. As a representing case, we report the results on efficiency for the case of α=200 and β=15. With other α and β settings, the efficiency analysis stays the same.

Figure 5 shows the running time of the ε-phase with regard to $|T_1|$ and $|D|$. This time increases linearly with increasing $|T_1|$ and $|D|$.

Figure 6 gives the running time of the S-phase. It shows a linear increase with regard to the join cardinality and does not change with $|T_i|$.

In all experiments, the running time of α-phase and β-phase is almost ignorable as there are only two tables involved. In general, with more than two tables, the running time will increase, but typically the number of tables, which is the number of parties involved in a join query, is small.

Note that the reported running time is the aggregated time spent on local computations at all parties and does not include the time spent on message transmissions, since the latter depends on transmission media, network protocol, traffic etc. To measure the communication cost in an implementation-independent manner, we collected the total size of messages transmitted among all parties, as shown in Figure 7. We can see that the message size increases with increasing $|D|$. As analyzed in Section 6.1, because we used only one join attribute in our experiments, the number of join value combinations $|C_i|$ in a table is the same as $|D|$. Thus, the communication cost depends only on $|D|$. If there are more join attributes in table T_i, $|C_i|$ may be much larger than $|D|$, but no more than $|T_i|$. Note that the message size is independent of the size of tables or the join size.

The experiments show that the running time depends mainly on the join cardinality and only the first phase involves scanning the tables. The tables are scanned only once with hash functions applied to each distinct join value, thus this first phase is very efficient. The subsequent phases depend only on the join cardinality and parameters α and β. Thus, the proposed approach is highly suitable for the trend and pattern analysis on large and private databases while scalability and privacy are major concerns. In all our experiments, the total running time is less than 20 seconds for all computations and less than 5 seconds for network communications.

DISCUSSIONS

The capabilities of computing join aggregate queries over private tables are essential for collaborative data analysis that involves multiple private sources. In this paper, we proposed an efficient privacy-preserving protocol for computing join aggregate queries over private tables. By a novel use of the sketching technique and the private scalar product protocol, we achieve a level of protection not provided by the previous encryption technique. The key idea is locally maintaining random shares of atomic sketches that provide no clue on the data owned by other parties. This protocol can be naturally extended for handling group-by aggregations and OLAP roll-up/drill-down operations, while maintaining the same level of privacy protection.

REFERENCES

Adam, N. R., & Wortman, J. C. (1989). Security-Control Methods for Statistical Databases. *ACM Computing Surveys*, 21 (4), 515-556.

Agrawal, R., Evfimievski, A., & Srikant, R. (2003). Information Sharing Across Private Databases. In *Proceedings of 2003 ACM SIGMOD International Conference on Management of Data*.

Agrawal, R., Imielinski, T., & Swami, A. (1993). Mining Association Rules between Sets of Items in Large Databases. In *Proceedings of 1993 ACM SIGMOD International Conference on Management of Data*.

Agrawal, R., Srikant, R., & Thomas, D. (2005). Privacy Preserving OLAP. In *Proceedings of 2005 ACM SIGMOD International Conference on Management of Data*.

Alon, N., Gibbons, P. B., Matias, Y., & Szegedy, M. (1999). Tracking Join and Self-Join Sizes in Limited Storage. In *Proceedings of 1999 ACM PODS Principles of Database Systems*.

Alon, N., Matias, Y., & Szegedy, M. (1996). The Space Complexity of Approximating the Frequency Moments. In *Proceedings of 1996 ACM STOC Symposium on Theory of Computing*.

Clifton, C., Doan, A., Elmagarmid, A., Kantarcioglu, M., Schadow, G., Suciu, D., & Vaidya, J. (2004). Privacy-Preserving Data Integration and Sharing. In *ACM SIGMOD Workshop on Research issues in Data Mining and Knowledge Discovery*.

Clifton, C., Kantarcioglu, M., Vaidya, J., Lin, X., & Zhu, M. Y. (2002). Tools for Privacy Preserving Distributed Data Mining. In *SIGKDD Explorations*, 4 (2), 28-34.

Cormode, G., & Muthukrishnan, S. (2004). An Improved Data Stream Summary: the Count-Min Sketch and Its Applications. In *Latin American Symposium on Theoretical Informatics, Lecture Notes in Computer Science* (Vol. 2976, pp. 29-38). Berlin / Heidelberg: Springer.

Dobra, A., Garofalakis, M., Gehrke, J., & Rastogi, R. (2002). Processing Complex Aggregate Queries over Data Streams. In *Proceedings of 2002 ACM SIGMOD International Conference on Management of Data.*

Du, W., & Atallah, M. J. (2001). Privacy-Preserving Cooperative Statistical Analysis. In *Proceedings of 2001 Computer Security Applications Conference.*

Du, W., & Zhan, Z. (2002). Building Decision Tree Classifier on Private Data. In *ICDM Workshop on Privacy, Security, and Data Mining.*

Emekci, F., Agrawal, D., Abbadi, A. E., & Gulbeden, A. (2006). Privacy Preserving Query Processing Using Third Parties. In *Proceedings of 2006 ICDE International Conference on Data Engineering.*

Ganguly, S., Garofalskis, M., & Rastogi, R. (2004). Processing data-stream join aggregates using skimmed sketches. EDBT International Conference on Extending Database Technology.

Goethals, B., Laur, S., Lipmaa, H., & Mielikainen, T. (2004). On Private Scalar Product Computation for Privacy-Preserving Data Mining. In *Proceedings of 2004 ICISC International Conference in Information Security and Cryptology.*

Goldreich, O. (2001). Secure Multi-Party Computation. *The Foundations of Cryptography* (Vol. 2, Chapter 7). Cambridge University Press.

Gray, J., Bosworth, A., Layman, A., & Pirahesh, H. (1996). Data Cube: a Relational Aggregation Operator Generalizing Group-by, Cross-tab, and Sub-totals. In *Proceedings of 1996 ICDE International Conference on Data Engineering.*

Jefferies, N., Mitchell, C., & Walker, M. (1995). A Proposed Architecture for Trusted Third Party Services. In *Proceedings of 1995 Cryptography Policy and Algorithms Conference.*

Kantarcioglu, M., & Vaidya, J. (2002). An Architecture for Privacy-Preserving Mining of Client Information. In *ICDM IEEE Conference on Data Mining Workshop on Privacy, Security and Data Mining.*

National Institute of Standards and Technology (NIST). (2002). Secure Hash Standard. *Federal Information Processing Standards 180-2.*

She, R., Wang, K., Fu, A., & Xu, Y. (2007). Computing Join Aggregates over Private Tables. In *Proceedings of 9th International Conference on Data Warehousing and Knowledge Discovery*, Regensburg, Germany.

Stinson, D. R. (2006). *Cryptography: Theory and Practice* (3rd ed.). Chapter 4. Chapman & Hall/CRC.

The QuickHash Library. (2006). Retrieved from the World Wide Web: http://www.slavasoft.com/quickhash/

Vaidya, J. S., & Clifton, C. (2002). Privacy Preserving Association Rule Mining in Vertically Partitioned Data. In *Proceedings of 2002 ACM SIGKDD International Conference on Knowledge Discovery and Data Mining.*

Wang, L., Jajodia, S., & Wijesekera, D. (2004). Securing OLAP Data Cubes against Privacy Breaches. In *Proceedings of 2004 IEEE Symposium on Security and Privacy.*

Yao, A. C. (1986). How to Generate and Exchange Secrets. In *Proceedings of 1986 Symposium on Foundations of Computer Science*.

Zhang, N., Zhao, W., & Chen, J. (2004). Cardinality-Based Inference Control in OLAP Systems: an Information Theoretical Approach. In *ACM DOLAP International Workshop on Date Warehousing and OLAP*.

Chapter 15
Overview of
PAKDD Competition 2007

Junping Zhang
Fudan University, China

Guo-Zheng Li
Shanghai University, China

ABSTRACT

The PAKDD Competition 2007 involved the problem of predicting customers' propensity to take up a home loan when a collection of data from credit card users are provided. It is rather difficult to address the problem because 1) the data set is extremely imbalanced; 2) the features are mixture types; and 3) there are many missing values. This article gives an overview on the competition, mainly consisting of three parts: 1) The background of the database and some statistical results of participants are introduced; 2) An analysis from the viewpoint of data preparation, resampling/reweighting and ensemble learning employed by different participants is given; and 3) Finally, some business insights are highlighted.

INTRODUCTION

The PAKDD Competition 2007 is about finding better solutions for a cross-selling business problem donated by a consumer finance company. In one of their markets, the company currently has a credit card customer base and a housing loan (mortgage) customer base with few customers overlapping between the two. The company would like to make use of this opportunity to cross-sell home loans to its credit card customers.

In the problem setting of the competition, a modeling database of 40,700 customers with 40 modeling features plus a binary target feature is provided to the participants. This is a sample of customers who opened a new credit card with the company within a specific 2-year period, while they did not have an existing home loan with the company. In the database, 700 cases that the customer opened a home loan with the company within 12 months after opening the credit card are assumed to be positive examples, and the other 40,000 cases are assumed to be negative. Participants were tasked to create cross selling response scores to predict the propensity of 8,000 customers to take up a mortgage. Data are made up of large imbalanced distribution and small absolute number of positive cases, as well as a mixture of feature types. Furthermore, there are a large number of missing data, invalid data and special values in the database. These problems result in a formidable challenge to participants. A more detailed introduction of the data set can be found in the Web site (PAKDD Competition, 2007).

Moreover, the AUC (area under the curve) value, which is the area under the ROC curve (Receiver Operating Characteristic)[1], was used as the evaluation criterion for the competition. The AUC calculated from a team's submission for the prediction set was regarded as a major factor for determining the winners; the higher, the better.

This overview is organized as follows. In Section 2, participation and competition results are reported. A survey on data preparation and resampling (or reweighting) techniques, as well as ensemble approaches, are given in Section 3. Business insights into the problem provided by the participants are summarized in Section 4. Finally, Section 5 concludes.

PARTICIPATION AND RESULTS

In this competition, 47 entries from 12 countries submitted their write-ups and predictive results for the 8,000 observations in the unlabelled prediction set. There are 7,650 negatives and 350 positives in the prediction set. A set of comparisons on geographic distributions, participant types and modeling techniques between participants in 2006 and participants in 2007 are tabulated in Table 1 to Table 4.

Compared with the PAKDD 2006 Data Mining Competition (Noriel & Tan , 2007), the number of entries slightly increased. Secondly, the entries

Table 1. A comparison of geographic distributions by regions

Affiliation Region	2006 All	2007 All	Top20	Top10
North America	18	19	7	3
East Asia	18	18	9	4
South Asia	3	3	1	
West Asia		1		
South America		2	1	1
Europe	4	3	1	1
ANZ	2	1	1	1
Total	45	47	20	10

from industry in 2007 is nearly twice as those in 2006, indicating that the competition has received more attention from industry this year. The percentage of entries from industry are also high in the Top 10 and the Top 20. It shows that entries from industry benefit from their professional experiences and knowledge on how to address data mining problems.

For determining who are the champion and first runner up, the AUC values using trapezoidal rule are computed for all the submitted predictive results. The evaluation results are summarized, as in Figure 1. From the figure, it can be found that the highest AUC is 70.01%, and the lowest AUC is 47.73%. The top four entries in terms of AUC values, together with modeling techniques, are reported in Table 5.

DISCUSSION

The participants make use of different ways for processing the data set provided by the competition. These steps can be mainly categorized into three levels: data preparation, resampling/ reweighting and ensemble learning techniques. Here, we would like to give an in-depth analysis on the approaches used for each of these three levels.

Table 2. A comparison of geographic distributions by locations

Affiliation Location	2006 All	2007 All	Top20	Top10	Affiliation Location	2006 All	2007 All	Top20	Top10
USA	16	18	7	3	China	3	13	7	3
Singapore	14	4	2	1	India	3	3	1	
Russia	1	2			Argentina		1		
Australia	1	1	1	1	Belgium		1	1	1
Brazil		1	1	1	Canada	2	1		
Jordan		1			Taiwan		1		
Italy		1			New Zealand	1			
Portugal	1				Thailand	1			
UK	1				Total	45	47		

Table 3. A comparison of participant types

	All Entries (2006)	All Entries (2007)	Top 20(2007)	Top 10(2007)
Affiliation Type	Count (%)	Count (%)	Count (%)	Count (%)
Industry	8(17%)	14(30%)	12(60%)	8(80%)
Academia	38(83%)	29(61%)	6(30%)	2(20%)
Unknown	0(0%)	4(9%)	2(10%)	0(0%)

Table 4. A comparison of modeling techniques and implementations

	2006		2007	
Modeling Technique	Count	%	Count	%
Linear/Polynomial/Spline/Logistic Regression	12	19%	15	23 %
Trees and Forests (including stumps)	20	32 %	22	34 %
Neural Networks (excluding probabilistic)	10	16 %	12	19 %
Naive Bayes/Bayesian Networks	4	6 %	2	3 %
Support Vector Machines	6	10%	3	5 %
K Nearest Neighbors	2	3%	1	2 %
Others	9	14%	9	14%
Total	63	100 %	64	100 %

Data Preparation

In this competition, mixture types of features, such as ordinal, binary, nominal and interval features, are concurrently present in the cross-sell data set. Specifically, the database is made up of 24 nu- merical and 16 categorical features. Due to some reasons, missing values also exist in some features. To address the two issues, missing values should be either removed or imputed before performing modeling. Meanwhile, some important features

Figure 1. The AUC values of the results provided by the participants

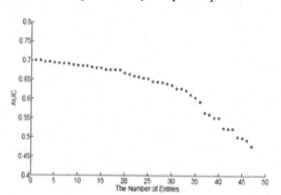

Table 5. Top teams with overall rankings and model techniques

Team	AUC(Rank)	Modeling Techniques
Lei Chai, Mingjun Wei Sherpa Consulting Inc.	70.01%(1)	TreeNet + Logistic Regression
Hualin Wang, Yan Yu, Kaixia Zhang Alliance Data	69.99%(1)	Probit Regression
Paulo J. L. Adeodato, Germano C. Vasconcelos Adrian L. Arnaud, Rodrigo C. L. V. Cunha Domingos S. M. P. Monteiro, Rosalvo F. Oliveira Neto Neurotech	69.62%(3)	MLP +n_Tuple Classifier
Dan Steinberg, Nicholas Scott Cardell, John Ries Mikhaylo Golovnya, Don Cozine Salford Systems	69.61%(2)	TreeNet

as well as correlation among features should be extracted from the training data.

Feature Selection and Extraction

Feature selection and extraction procedures were widely used for capturing important features which are highly related to predictive accuracy, removing some irrelevant features, and extracting highly correlated features from a set of features (Guyon & Elisseeff, 2003).

To capture important features, a large number of feature selection approaches are employed by entries. Several typical ways include: 1) TreeNet from Salford System for computing importance scores for all the predictors used in the models; 2) c-statistics for adaptively controlling the number of features; 3) classical forward and backward-based feature selection techniques; and 4) analyzing statistical properties such as chi-square, information gain, and gain ratio. With feature selection, the number of features is reduced to 17 features or so on average.

Besides capturing important features, some entries also focus their attention on the creation of new features which reflect the correlation among the original features. For example, one champion and first runner up regrouped or binned categorical features into several clusters (PAKDD Competition, 2007). The advantage is that new features can either represent the weighted combination of the original features or emphasize some features in the original database. The other advantage is to extract domain knowledge that may be embedded into the data set. It is noted that while two winners employed these strategies, most of the entries did not consider the issue of generating new features (PAKDD Competition, 2007).

Missing Values

\

By scrutinizing the database, we can find that the feature values of some examples are missing. These missing values are potentially influential on predictive accuracy. One simple but effective way is to fill the missing values with mean values or modes based on statistical properties of databases. The disadvantage here is that they would be assuming that missing values are not implicitly biased as compared to the responding sample. A second way is to remove the feature which has missing values from the database. The disadvantage of this is that the feature to be removed may be important to the prediction. The third way is to ignore the processing of missing values and leave it for the subsequent classifiers. The disadvantage of this is that the performance of classifiers may strongly suffer from incorrect or abnormal inputs.

In the competition, several effective approaches include: 1) One champion makes imputations for the missing values with CART from Salford Systems; 2) One first runner-up converts the features which have missing values into a binary one; 3) Some entries create new features for identifying missing values; and 4) The other entries replace missing values with the mode (or mean/frequency) of the corresponding features (PAKDD Competition, 2007).

In summary, to build a good model for beating the cross-sell problem, data preparation, including feature selection and missing values processing is necessary. Actually, some entries who assumed the database was good enough and paid little attention on the data preparation often failed.

Resampling

One important difficulty is that the data distribution is extremely skewed. The ratio of positives to negatives in the training data is equal to 1.75%. It is clear that if this skewness problem is not considered, than an inefficient predictive model will be generated.

To address the issue, a lot of resampling approaches are considered. One strategy is to undersample the positive samples many times so that the number of positives is the same as that of negatives. However, this strategy hasn't been applied by the entries because of high imbalance. The second strategy is to extract key examples from a pool of negatives so that the ratio between two classes is close to 1:1. For example, an entry decreases the number of negative examples through randomly sampling from the negatives (PAKDD Competition, 2007).

Furthermore, some entries attempt to combine the undersampling with oversampling for obtaining a more reasonable training set. An advantage is that the combination cannot only reduce some redundancy information in the negatives but also approximate the real distribution of positives. For example, an entry employed both SMOTE, which is an interpolation technique for oversampling the positive sample and bootstrap for undersampling the negative sample (PAKDD Competition, 2007).

The fourth strategy is to partition a class being of large examples into several subclasses. Each subclass has as many negatives as positives. For instance, an entry employed the grouping method to divide negative sample into several subsets with equal size, and then combine the positive sample set into these component sets (PAKDD Competition, 2007). In the other entry, N models were developed on N subsets in which each contains 80% of observations randomly selected from the modeling dataset. This approach can be regarded as a kind of bootstrapping approach. An advantage of the fourth strategy is that classifier can be independently built based on each component training set and therefore the computational complexity is low. Actually, many entries incline to apply the strategy in the competition.

It is noted that in the field of machine learning and data mining, cost-sensitive learning is also a powerful tool for processing and analyzing the imbalanced data. Due to the fact that the distribution of training data is too skew, however, it is impractical to employ the techniques for addressing the problem. As a result, only two entries had tried the cost-sensitive learning in the competition.

Ensemble Learning

Modeling is crucial to predictive accuracy. Tree-based and regression-based models were two major tools considered by the entries. Some entries selected the tree-based approach or its variants, such as TreeNet from Salford system, CART algorithm, decision Tree with CHAID, or exhaustive CHAID. An advantage of these approaches is that they are insensitive to feature types. Others employed regression-based techniques such as logistical regression, which is a nonlinear regression applied in cases where the dependent feature is discrete. Furthermore, PROBIT regression modeling by one champion, as well as ridge regression and 2-layered linear regression analysis for overcoming the sparseness of the data were also some of the variants of regression models considered (PAKDD Competition, 2007).

While each mentioned model was able to achieve good accuracy, we found that ensembling these approaches are a powerful way to further improve performance. Some approaches might focus on specific local solutions for the problems being studied. Under certain conditions, ensemble learning is capable of discovering global and reasonable solutions that are more stable and with higher accuracy. Almost each entry had tried at least one ensemble learning method for the prediction set. For examples, one champion

proposed the combination of TreeNet models and logistical regression models. One champion used ensembles of PROBIT models. Furthermore, many entries had employed random forest and its variants (Breiman, 2001; Chen, Liaw, & Breiman, 2004). Though different ensemble approaches are employed, a common and implicit rule is to guarantee the diversity among component learners. In the write-up of one of the champions, they pointed out that the correlation of TreeNet and logistical regression model is not high. It means that the predictive performance could benefit from the diversity between the two models. Also, one first runner-up emphasized that the n-tuple classifier is a complementary to the multilayer perceptron in the aspect of using validation data and universal function approximation. They therefore decided to stack a multilayer perceptron together with an n-tuple classifier (PAKDD Competition, 2007).

From the results it can be concluded that in normal datasets, perhaps the incremental gain from ensembles might not be much when compared to only using single learning machines, but in this competition where we have a small number of positive targets, the incremental learning gain from using ensembles becomes even more noticeable and important for squeezing out as much learning as possible from the small-size cases. With post-competition checks, we also observe that doing further ensembles of the top competition entries can interestingly improve AUC in the prediction set. A problem easily being neglected is overfitting. Analyzing the accuracy of models on the training data, it can be found that most of the entries that had lower ranks paid less attention to the problem. Meanwhile, some entries had higher AUC values for the prediction dataset and usually paid more in-depth analysis on how to address the overfitting. For instances, the eighth ranked entry selected their component learners by removing classifiers having a risk of overfitting. In the ninth ranked entry, the participants introduced the mean-variance filtering (MVF) technique for reducing overfitting (PAKDD Competition, 2007).

Also, we found that not many participants employed SVM (support vector machine), a state-of-the-art algorithm, for the competition. Meanwhile, the evaluation results showed that those participants using SVM did not get a good AUC value for the prediction data set.

Evaluation Criteria

To evaluate whether the difference in AUCs derived from the same prediction dataset is random or real, one possible criterion is to calculate a critical ratio z based on the AUCs and their respective standard errors as well as the correlation between the two AUCs (Hanley & McNeil, 1982, 1983). If the ratio z is greater than some cutoff, for example, $z \geq 1.96$, then it would indicate that the two models being compared are different. We investigated the results of a simple confidence interval check $[AUC\text{-}1.96 \times AUCse, AUC + 1.96 \times AUCse]$ which does not factor in correlation of AUCs. Here $AUCse$ denotes the standard error of AUCs. Furthermore, we also attempt to evaluate these submissions with a more complex index, the Hanley-Mcneil statistic (Hanley & McNeil, 1983).

Both tests unfortunately didn't help much in determining winners. A lot of the top entries were supposedly not statistically different from each other, but at the same time there's the issue that probably the power of the tests might be low because of the large imbalance and small number of positive target examples. In the end, the champions and the first runner ups were evaluated based on their AUC values.

BUSINESS INSIGHTS

In business, even a slight gain in performance could give a significant gain in terms of profits

(Neslin, Gupta, Kamakura, Lu, & Mason, 2006). While most participants didn't have a background in the banking domain, potential business insights can be discovered by analyzing the correlation of features and studying the influence of different features on the model accuracy.

First of all, the feature *B_ENQ_L6M_GR*3, which indicates the customers' interests in mortgages, is commonly regarded as an important predictor. It means that the number of times the customer enquired through various channels about a mortgage loan is helpful in determining potential users to send promotional offers to. Secondly, one first runner up thinks that the district of residence of the applicant is the single most important predictor.

Thirdly, some redundant features have little influence on accuracy and thus can be removed. For example, one first runner up pointed out that "the RESYRS (total number of years in their current residence and their last residence) and *RENT_BUY_CODE* (categorical feature with levels RENT, MORTGAGE, OWNER, PARENTS, and BOARD) are virtually tied as the next two most important predictors." Meanwhile, the seventh ranked entry revealed that "for people who lived at their previous residence less than 4 months, number of dependents had no effect on the outcome, And, for people who lived at their previous residence for 4 months or more, people with more than 3 dependents had significantly lower rate of cross-selling."

Finally, some entries also suggest that adding several operational features will be helpful to the design of a good questionnaire and the quality of the modeling procedure. For examples, the sixth ranked entry proposed that several new features, such as age of the card, outstanding balance, and number of purchases done with the card, should be considered as a set of reasonable features (PAKDD Competition, 2007).

CONCLUSION

In the article, we give an overview on the PAKDD Competition 2007, report the evaluation results and several statistical distributions of participants. Pointing to the cross-sell problem, some aspects including data preparation, resampling, ensemble learning and business insights were discussed. The fact that the cross-selling dataset was highly imbalanced and of mixed features made it a big challenge to the participants. As a result, the issues of overfitting, feature selection and extraction, and diversity of component learners became very critical for solving the tasks.

Furthermore, the evaluation results reveal that TreeNet and logistic regression can be considered as two good component learners for building a powerful ensemble learner.

ACKNOWLEDGMENT

The authors wish to express their thanks to the anonymous dataset sponsor, and also to the competition prize sponsor, SAS institute (China). Many thanks also go to N.B. Noriel from GE Money (China), he conceived and guided this competition. The first author acknowledges the NSFC for its sponsorship with contracts NSFC 60635030, 60505002. The second author acknowledges the NSFC for its sponsorship with contract no. 20503015.

REFERENCES

Breiman, L. (2001). Random forests. *Machine Learning, 45*(1), 5C32.

Chen, C., Liaw, A., & Breiman, L. (2004). *Using random forest to learn imbalanced data* (Tech. Rep.). Berkeley, CA: Department of Statistics, UC Berkeley.

Guyon. I., & Elisseeff, A. (2003). An introduction to variable and feature selection. Special issue on variable and feature selection. In I. Guyon & A. Elisseeff (Eds.), *Journal of Machine Learning Research, 3*, 1157-1182.

Hanley, J. A., & McNeil, B. J. (1982). The meaning and use of the area under a receiver operating characteristic (ROC) curve. *Radiology, 143,* 29-36.

Hanley, J. A., & Mcneil, B. J. (1983). A method of comparing the areas under receiver operating characteristic curves derived from the same cases. *Radiology, 148,* 839-843.

Neslin, S. A., Gupta, S., Kamakura, W., Lu, J., & Mason, C. H. (2006). Defection detection: Measuring and understanding the predictive accuracy of customer churn models. *Journal of Marketing Research, 43*(5), 204-211.

Noriel, N. B., & Tan, C. L. (2007). A look back at the PAKDD data mining competition 2006. *International Journal of Data Warehousing and Mining, 3*(2), 1-11.

PAKDD Competition. (2007). Retrieved November 8, 2007, from http://lamda.nju.edu.cn/conf/pakdd07/dmc07/

ENDNOTE

[1]   A ROC curve is a plot of true positive rate vs. false positive rate as the prediction threshold sweeps through all the possible values. The area under the curve has the nice property that it specifies the probability that, when we draw one positive and one negative example at random, the decision function assigns a higher value to the positive than to the negative example Hanley & McNeil, 1982).

Chapter 16
A Solution to the Cross–Selling Problem of PAKDD–2007:
Ensemble Model of TreeNet and Logistic Regression

Mingjun Wei
Zhejiang University and Sherpa Consulting, China

Lei Chai
Sherpa Consulting, China

Renying Wei
China Mobile Group Zhejiang Co., China

Wang Huo
China Mobile Group Zhejiang Co., China

ABSTRACT

Our team has won the Grand Champion (Tie) of PAKDD-2007 data mining competition. The data mining task is to score credit card customers of a consumer finance company according to the likelihood that customers take up the home loans offered by the company. This report presents our solution for this business problem. TreeNet and logistic regression are the data mining algorithms used in this project. The final score is based on the cross-algorithm ensemble of two within-algorithm ensembles of TreeNet and logistic regression. Finally, some discussions from our solution are presented.

INTRODUCTION

The PAKDD-2007 competition requires development of a cross-selling model for a financial services company offering both credit cards and home loans. The main challenge we face is high class imbalance, and the low incidence rate of the target class in the overall population. In the modeling dataset, the number of target class is extremely small, only 700 records out of 40,700.

The imbalance ratio is as high as 57.143. To deal with such class imbalance, certain data partition strategy and ensemble method are employed to effectively improve the performance of predictive models. TreeNet and logistic regression are the data mining algorithms used in this project. The final score is based on the cross-algorithm ensemble of two within-algorithm ensembles of TreeNet and logistic regression.

SOFTWARE

To achieve the analysis objectives, we used the following tools:

- Weka
- CART
- TreeNet

The data mining package Weka (Witten & Frank, 2005) is used to carry out logistic regression modeling task. CART® is the decision tree tool developed by Breiman, Friedman, Olshen and Stone (1984) and exclusively licensed to Salford systems. CART® can automatically sift large, complex databases, searching for significant patterns and relationships. TreeNet® is the tool developed by Friedman (1999) and exclusively licensed to Salford systems. TreeNet® uses Stochastic Gradient Boosting to develop hundreds of small trees, each of which contributes just a tiny adjustment to the overall mode. TreeNet is a breakthrough technology that can offer surprisingly high accuracy while remaining remarkably robust in the presence of common data problems such as missing values and misrecorded training data.

DATA PREPROCESSING

There is a need to preprocess the original modeling data into data used for modeling.

Data Preparation

The supplied dataset went through a standard series of data preparation steps including:

- Study the univariate and bivariate analysis and frequency tables;
- Handle missing values and potential outliers;
- Create new variables from the original ones;
- Compress categorical variables, and so forth.

There were 40 candidate predictors, plus a target variable in the raw forms. Only a couple of predictors had a severe missing problem. B_DEF_UNPD_L12M was excluded from our analysis because it was equal to 0 for all the records. MVIs (Missing Value Indicators) were created for all the predictors with missing values. Using CART, we also made imputations for the missing values. In addition, there were inconsistent values in the categorical variable ANNUAL INCOME RANGE. In the data there was a value "\00K-<30K". We deleted the preceding "0" in "\00K-<30K," making it consistent with "\0K-<30K" in the data dictionary.

Data Partition via 5-Fold Cross-Validation Method

We adopted the 5-fold cross-validation (CV) method that evenly and randomly partitioned the modeling dataset (40,700 records) into 5 nonoverlapping subsets (CV1, CV2, CV3, CV4 and CV5), each of which was approximately as big as the prediction dataset (8,000 records). CV parameter is usually set to 10, but in this case, 10-fold CV would make each fold contain too few positives. Hence, we reduced the CV parameter to 5. Each of 5 subsets was used as a testing dataset, while the rest of 4 subsets were merged and used as a learning dataset. Therefore, every observation could make its contribution to ensemble models in a way that it was used as learning data 4 times and as testing data once in each within-algorithm ensemble.

MODELING

We use an ensemble method of TreeNet and logistic regression.

Ensemble Method

In our solution, there are two kinds of ensembles, **within-algorithm ensemble** and **cross-algorithm ensemble**. The process of the ensemble method based on our data partition strategy is shown as follows:

- **Step1:** (Within-algorithm ensemble of TreeNet). We built five models on five different combinations of datasets using TreeNet. We scored the prediction datasets using these five different models. Then, five scores from the five models for each prediction record were averaged to give a score to each record.
- **Step2:** (Within-algorithm ensemble of logistic regression). We repeated the process described above except that we replaced TreeNet by logistic regression and finally obtained the logistic regression ensemble.
- **Step3:** (Cross-algorithm ensemble of TreeNet and logistic regression). The final score is based on a two-algorithm ensemble of TreeNet and logistic regression.

Variable Selection

To optimize the model, we need to pick out a final set of predictors from 40 candidates. TreeNet gives importance scores to all the predictors used in the models so that we could obtain the ranking of all the predictors. Then, we compared the per-

formance of models of different combinations of variables with the consideration of their ranking. Finally, we determined 17 variables which would be contained in our final model.

When building logistic regression models, we also employed chi-square test on individual variable to do the selection. Interestingly, similar variables with imputation and MIVs (Missing Value Indicators) stood out.

Building Models and Evaluation

With these 17 predictors, we built five TreeNet models on five different combinations of datasets. Similarly, logistic regression models were also built with imputed variables. We compared the Area Under the receiver operating characteristic Curve (AUC) (Fawcett, 2003) of different models on five testing datasets, all of which are around 0.7, shown in Figure 1.

TreeNet performs slightly better than logistic regression, although the correlations of their predictions are not very high (about 0.73, shown in Figure 2). This means that TreeNet and logistic regression don't agree with each other on some of the predictions, while their overall performances are close. Hence, we decided to combine the results of the two different models in hopes of making the models complement each other. Here, it was seen that the ensemble model has a more stable performance than the individual TreeNet and logistic regression model.

FINAL SCORES FOR PREDICTION DATASET

We scored the prediction datasets using the five TreeNet models on five different combinations of datasets. Then, the TreeNet scores from the five TreeNet models for each prediction record were averaged to form the TreeNet ensemble score for each record. We repeated this process with logistic regression and finally obtained the logistic regression ensemble score. The correlation between the score of TreeNet ensemble and the score of logistic regression ensemble is 0.75.

Two ranks generated from the two scores were assigned to each prediction record. The transformed average rank for each record was the final score of the cross-algorithm ensemble for that record. Therefore, the final score is based on the cross-algorithm ensemble of two within-algorithm ensembles of TreeNet and logistic regression.

DISCUSSION

Within-Algorithm Ensemble vs. Cross-Algorithm Ensemble

In our solution, there are two kinds of ensembles, within-algorithm ensemble and cross-algorithm ensemble. The other two of our entries in the competition (TreeNet ensemble and logistic regression ensemble) are within-algorithm ensembles, while our champion entry is the cross-algorithm ensemble based on these two within-algorithm ensembles.

The predictions of the five TreeNet models or the five logistic regression models that form our within-algorithm ensemble entries correlate with each other very well (all the correlation coefficients are about 0.9), whereas the average correlations between TreeNet models and logistic regression models are only near 0.73. We thought that the minor disagreement of the predictions among the models in within-algorithm ensembles is mostly due to the variation of modeling datasets, whereas the underlying different natures of different algorithms are the main factor that leads to the higher inconsistency of the predictions between models in cross-algorithm ensemble.

Given the close overall performances of different models in cross-algorithm ensemble, the significant inconsistency of the predictions indicates that each model in the cross-algorithm ensemble has its own advantages and disadvantages on predicting certain portions of the observations. The ensemble of these models with different algorithms could make the models complement each other with their respective advantages. As for within-algorithm ensembles, due to the higher correlations among the predications of the models, the effect of the ensemble might not work as well as the cross-algorithm ensemble.

To examine our thinking, we submitted all three ensembles. By comparing all these models, we are able to investigate the effect of two different types of ensembles. Apparently, cross-algorithm ensemble gives us a better result, as expected.

One of our reflections on the final result is that, because the models in within-algorithm ensembles are from the same model families and all these models share the similar basic structures, it is likely for them to have similar perspectives. When it comes to cross-algorithm ensemble, however, because logistic regression and TreeNet are so different in their intrinsic structures, they might tend to have different perspectives on some observations. In our case, combining these different perspectives could work very well. However, all the discussion above is based on experiences and intuitive thinking. This discussion is subject to further theoretical proof, although there are obviously many challenges for this work.

Accuracy vs. Efficiency

When accuracy can be boosted via ensembles, there is also a tradeoff we need to deal with, which is the lower efficiency of ensembles in terms of scoring speed and modeling time. To obtain optimal models in real world applications, we need to balance between the accuracy and efficiency of ensembles.

Interpretability

Another tradeoff for ensemble is the sacrifice of some interpretability. Due to the complexity of the model, not many understandable insights could be obtained from the model except some kind of variable importance ranking. For the further understanding of the business insights, CART tree can be used to give rule-based interpretation.

Deployment

We think that the deployment of ensemble models is an issue worth a little discussion here. In our ensemble models, the averaged ranks of the observations in different models are the final scores. The ranks are the relative scores in each model. But this scoring strategy might not be able to be directly implemented in the real world business environment. If the records that need to be scored come in the form of batches that contain enough records, the scoring process used in this study could be similarly implemented. However, if the records come individually or separately, it will be difficult to obtain their meaningful relative scores. One solution we propose is first we set up a dataset containing enough records that will be given the absolute scores by the different models in ensemble, and then these scores will be transformed to their relative scores, namely their ranks in each model. This dataset containing all the score information will be kept as a reference dataset. Once a new record comes, it will receive its absolute scores, and then the relative scores of the new record in each model could be found by

checking with the reference dataset. The process described above can be automated.

ACKNOWLEDGMENT

We thank Salford Systems for kindly allowing us to use CART and TreeNet. We also want to thank the organizers of PAKDD-2007 for providing us with this competition opportunity.

REFERENCES

Breiman, L., Friedman, J.H., Olshen, R.A., & Stone, C.J. (1984). *Classification and regression trees*. Belmont: CRC Press.

Fawcett, T. (2003). *ROC graphs: Notes and practical considerations for data mining researchers*. Retrieved November 8, 2007, from http://citeseer. nj.nec.com/fawcett03roc.html

Friedman, J. H. (1999). *Stochastic gradient boosting*. Retrieved November 8, 2007, from http://www-stat.stanford.edu/~jhf/

Witten, I. H., & Frank, E. (2005). *Data mining: Practical machine learning tools and techniques* (2nd ed.). San Francisco: Morgan Kaufmann.

This work was previously published in International Journal of Data Warehousing and Mining, Vol. 4, Issue 2, edited by D. Taniar, pp. 9-14, copyright 2008 by IGI Publishing (an imprint of IGI Global).

Chapter 17
Bagging Probit Models for Unbalanced Classification

Hualin Wang
AllianceData, USA

Xiaogang Su
University of Central Florida, USA

ABSTRACT

This chapter presents an award-winning algorithm for the data mining competition of PAKDD 2007, in which the goal is to help a financial company to predict the likelihood of taking up a home loan for their credit card based customers. The involved data are very limited and characterized by very low buying rate. To tackle such an unbalanced classification problem, the authors apply a bagging algorithm based on probit model ensembles. One integral element of the algorithm is a special way of conducting the resampling in forming bootstrap samples. A brief justification is provided. This method offers a feasible and robust way to solve this difficult yet very common business problem.

INTRODUCTION

The 11th Pacific-Asia Knowledge Discovery and Data Mining Conference (PAKDD 2007) hosted a data mining competition, co-organized by the Singapore Institute of Statistics. The data set is from a consumer finance company with the aim of finding solutions for a cross-selling business problem. The company currently has two databases, one for credit card holders and the other for home loan (mortgage) customers and they would like to make use of this opportunity to cross-sell home loans to its credit card holders. Thus, it is of their keen interest to have an effective scoring model for predicting potential cross-sell take-ups.

The training dataset contains information on 40,700 customers with 40 input variables, most of which are related to the point of application for the company's credit card, plus a binary target variable indicating the home loan take-up status. This is a sample of customers who opened a new credit card with the company within a specific 2-year period and did not have an existing home loan with the company. The binary target variable has a value of 1 if the customer then opened a home loan with the company within 12 months after opening the credit

DOI: 10.4018/978-1-60566-717-1.ch017

card (700 customers), and will have a value of 0 if otherwise (40,000 customers). Another test dataset containing 8,000 sampled cases is also available with same input variables but withholding the target variable. The data mining task is to produce a score for each customer in the test dataset, indicating his/her propensity to take up a home loan with the company within 12 months after opening the credit card. More detailed information on the competition can be found at http://lamda.nju.edu.cn/conf/pakdd07/dmc07/.

Clearly, it is a classification problem. However, the main challenge of the analysis stems from the vey unbalanced distribution of the target variable. Namely, the proportion of 1's is only 700/40,000 = 1.72%. This is a very common problem seen in many application areas such as fraud detection, rare disease studies, marketing strategic modeling, network intrusion analysis, and others. The problem, generally termed as *unbalanced classification* in data mining practices, is characterized by the fact that one class of the response variable is very much underrepresented in the data. When working directly with severely unbalanced data, most classifiers will encounter numerical problems and yield poor performance.

BAGGING WITH WEIGHTED RESAMPLING

The common approach to unbalanced classification is to modify the weights, borrowing the idea from retrospective designs (see, e.g., Agrestri, 1990). This amounts to either decreasing the weight for the majority class by under-sampling or increasing the weight for the minority class by over-sampling. However, how to adjust the weights is quite an art. In the following, we shall present our procedure with justification and compare it with some alternative approaches.

To proceed, we first introduce some notations to set up the problem. Let

$$L_0 = \left\{ \left(y_i, \underline{x}_i \right) : i = 1, \ldots, n_0 \right\}$$

denote the training sample, where y_i is the i-th binary 0-1 outcome with Class 1 severely underrepresented and $\underline{x}_i$ is the associated input vector. Let $L_1 = \left\{ \underline{x}_p : p = 1, \ldots, n_1 \right\}$ denote the test sample that contains the input information only.

Let D denote the distribution underlying the data. What is under modeling is the conditional probability that y is equal to 1 conditioning on $\underline{x}$, i.e.,

$$\pi = \Pr \left\{ y = 1 \mid \underline{x} \right\}. \tag{1}$$

There are various modeling tools or classifiers available for modeling this probability, e.g., logistic regression, decision trees, neural networks, support vector machine, to name a few. One is referred to Hastie, Tibshirani, and Friedman (2001) for a full account of different modeling or learning processes.

Our procedure is outlined in Algorithm 1. First, we generate B *bootstrap* samples, denoted by $L^{(b)}$ for $b = 1, \ldots, B$, from the training sample L_0 by oversampling the minority class. More specifically, let $\lambda > 1$ denote the ratio of sampling probabilities for the two classes. In other words, we randomly select an observation from Class 1 with a higher sampling probability $\lambda / (1 + \lambda)$, while selecting an observation from Class 0 with a lower probability $1 / (1 + \lambda)$. A bootstrap sample $L^{(b)}$ has the same sample size as L_0 does. For more background information about bootstrap, see Efron and Tibshirani (1998). With the oversampling strategy, the proportions of 1's and 0's will become more balanced in the resultant bootstrap sample $L^{(b)}$. To prepare for the inference below, we introduce a binary indicator variable s to indicate whether or not an observation is selected by this resampling scheme.

Algorithm 1: Outline of the algorithm

Do $b = 1, \ldots, B$

- <u>Weighted Resampling</u>:
  - Pick up a number $\lambda_b > 1$.
  - generate bootstrap sample $L^{(b)}$ from L_0, with λ_b being the ratio of sampling probabilities for Class 1 observations versus Class 0 observations.
- <u>Prediction</u>:
  - Based on $L^{(b)}$, apply a modeling process, e.g., the probit regression model, to develop a classifier $\hat{f}_b(\cdot)$. Note that this is no longer an unbalanced classification problem.
  - Apply the developed classifier to each observation in the test sample and obtain a predicted probability as $\tilde{\pi}_p^{(b)} = \hat{f}_b(\underline{x}_p)$.
  - <u>Probability Adjustment</u>: compute
  $$\hat{\pi}_p^{(b)} = \frac{\tilde{\pi}_p^{(b)} / \left(1 - \tilde{\pi}_p^{(b)}\right)}{\lambda_b + \tilde{\pi}_p^{(b)} / \left(1 - \tilde{\pi}_p^{(b)}\right)}$$

End do

<u>Model Ensemble</u>: Average $\hat{\pi}_p = \sum_b \hat{\pi}_p^{(b)} / B$.

Next, we can employ any modeling or learning algorithm, e.g., logistic regression, on the bootstrap sample $L^{(b)}$ without much difficulty as the problem has reduced to balanced classification. Let $\hat{f}_b(\cdot)$ denote the ensuing classifier. Then apply the classifier to calculate a predicted probability for each individual in the test sample L_1.

However, one should note that, when working with the bootstrap sample $L^{(b)}$, the probability under modeling or prediction is the conditional probability of y for the selected data, that is,

$$\pi^* = \Pr\left\{y = 1 \mid \underline{x}, s = 1\right\}. \tag{2}$$

Adjustment is needed in order to obtain estimates of $\pi = \Pr\left\{y = 1 \mid \underline{x}\right\}$. Applying the Bayes rule yields that

$$\pi^* = \Pr\left\{y = 1 \mid \underline{x}, s = 1\right\} = \frac{\Pr\left\{y = 1, s = 1 \mid \underline{x}\right\}}{\Pr\left\{s = 1 \mid \underline{x}\right\}}$$
$$= \frac{\Pr\left\{y = 1 \mid \underline{x}\right\} \Pr\left\{s = 1 \mid y = 1, \underline{x}\right\}}{\Pr\left\{y = 0 \mid \underline{x}\right\} \Pr\left\{s = 1 \mid y = 0, \underline{x}\right\} + \Pr\left\{y = 1 \mid \underline{x}\right\} \Pr\left\{s = 1 \mid y = 1, \underline{x}\right\}}$$
$$\tag{3}$$

Assume that the selection scheme is independent of covariates $\underline{x}$, which is reasonable. Then

$$\Pr\left\{s = 1 \mid y = 1, \underline{x}\right\} = \Pr\left\{s = 1 \mid y = 1\right\} \text{ and }$$
$$\Pr\left\{s = 0 \mid y = 1, \underline{x}\right\} = \Pr\left\{s = 0 \mid y = 1\right\}.$$

Note that

$$\lambda_b = \frac{\Pr\left\{s = 1 \mid y = 1\right\}}{\Pr\left\{s = 1 \mid y = 0\right\}}, \ \pi = \Pr\left\{y = 1 \mid \underline{x}\right\},$$

and $1 - \pi = \Pr\left\{y = 0 \mid \underline{x}\right\}$.

Bringing these into (3) gives that

$$\pi^* = \frac{\Pr\left\{y = 1 \mid \underline{x}\right\} \Pr\left\{s = 1 \mid y = 1\right\}}{\Pr\left\{y = 0 \mid \underline{x}\right\} \Pr\left\{s = 1 \mid y = 0\right\} + \Pr\left\{y = 1 \mid \underline{x}\right\} \Pr\left\{s = 1 \mid y = 1\right\}}$$
$$= \frac{\lambda_b \cdot \pi}{(1 - \pi) + \lambda_b \cdot \pi} \quad \text{or} \quad \frac{\lambda_b \cdot \pi / (1 - \pi)}{1 + \lambda_b \cdot \pi / (1 - \pi)}.$$

Inversely, we have

$$\pi = \frac{\pi^* / (1 - \pi^*)}{\lambda_b + \pi^* / (1 - \pi^*)}. \tag{4}$$

Equation (4) has several implications. First it provides a way of adjusting the predicted probabilities from modeling the bootstrap sample $L^{(b)}$, as given in Algorithm 1. This adjustment is necessary for many purposes when the predicted probabilities are in need. Secondly, it can be easily seen that π is a monotone increasing function of π^*. If the goal of the analysis is to give a ranking of individuals in order of the predicted probability π, this ranking should be same as that based on π^*, even with difference values of sampling ratio λ_b. There is no adjustment necessary and one may use π^* directly. Same strategy applies to situations where the goal of the analysis is aimed to obtain predictions that yield the largest C-statistics, i.e., area under the receiver *operating characteristic (ROC)* curve, or to capture as many as possible cross-sell take-ups among top percentiles of predicted propensity scores. Recall that the computation of the C-statistics can be based on the number of discordant and concordant pairs formed by observed responses and predicted probabilities. What matters in this definition of concordance and discordance is the ranking among the predicted probabilities. Thus one can proceed with π^* for the calculation. Thirdly, the quantity $\pi^* / (1 - \pi^*)$ is referred to the odds, which is an important concept in classification. According to Equation (4), it is easy to verify that

$$\frac{\pi}{1 - \pi} = \frac{1}{\lambda_b} \cdot \frac{\pi^*}{1 - \pi^*}.$$

Namely, the odds based on π^* are proportional to the odds based on π, which, consequently, results in the same ratio of odds or *odds ratio*. If the logistic regression model, which models the odds, is used in particular, then the sampling ratio λ_b in the equation can be absorbed into the intercept term. Furthermore, the logistic model for π^* gives the same slope parameter, which are log of odds ratio, as the logistic model for π, an observation owing to Breslow (1976).

Finally, the predicted probabilities are averaged, yielding the ensemble model prediction. In order for model ensemble or bagging to work better, an important factor is the stability of base modeling process (Breiman, 1996). According to Breiman, "neural nets, classification and regression trees, and subset selection in linear or logistic regression were unstable, while k-nearest neighbor methods were stable." Another important factor

is to have reduced correlation among predictions from individual models is important, as indicated by Breiman (2001) in his proposal of the random forests. Thus the scheme of applying different λ_b values in resampling would be helpful in giving de-correlated predictions. Besides, trying different types of modeling processes with different bootstrap samples might be helpful as well, yet at the cost of computational complexity.

Several comments are listed in order. First, an alternative approach is to follow the same idea as in 1-M *matched case-control studies* (Breslow and Day, 1980). In this method, one takes all observations in Class 1 and then for each observations in Class 1, find M matches from Class 0. It is essentially under-sampling the majority class, i.e., Class 0, and results in much smaller samples. The problem with this method is loss of information. If combined with the model ensemble method, it would take a lot more iterations to have prediction of same quality as our method. Secondly, we would like to comment that model ensemble seems itself seems critical for handling unbalanced classification. It helps prevent loss of information and yields better predictions.

DATA ANALYSIS AND MODEL SELECTION

Since the target is 0 or 1 valued, a natural candidate for modeling the cross-selling propensity is the class of PROBIT regression models:

$$p = \text{probability } (Y = 0) = C + (1 - C) * F(X'\beta)$$

where p is the probability for the response to be 0; C the natural response rate; X a set of explanatory variables; β a vector of parameter estimates; and F a link function, usually a cumulative distribution function, such as the normal, logistic function or extreme value.

When the link function is the logistic function, this is usually called logistic regression; and when the link function is the cumulative distribution function of the normal distribution, it's called PROBIT regression. For more information about PROBIT regression, see 'Probit Analysis' by Finney, D.J. (1971).

Some believe that PROBIT tends to outperform logistic regression if there is an underlying function with thresholds that correspond to outcome categories (0 and 1 in this problem). Our belief for the current question is that the underlying function is the tradeoffs made by consumers in order to make their decision on whether or not to buy home loans from the company. Factors that influence their decision include whether they own a home, how much mortgages they have, financial charges by candidate companies, etc. Since there is no clear and obvious answer to which approach to take, we decided to conduct some comparative studies. Our analyses show that PROBIT tends to have higher and more stable c-statistics for simply random sub-samples as well as bootstrapping samples.

Other analysis helps to determine the range of weights for the PROBIT model. The weights that we proposed are not related to sampling per se, but to assigning different weights for different outcomes in the likelihood function while estimating the parameters. Practically, we observe that models have 'optimal' target rate for best performance. For example, logistic regression performs well when the target rates are around 18%. Put another way, the logistic regression does only marginally better than ordinary least linear regression if the target rates are around 50%. The weights can virtually change the target rates in the sample. With some trial and errors and comparisons of results, we find that using weights from 3 to 12 produces ideal results. The default value of natural response for all models is to be 0.

With these factors, the final model is built by following these 2 steps:

1. Pick any integer for weight between 3 and 12, build an ensemble of 10 PROBIT models using 10 bootstrapped samples and average the 10 obtained probabilities. This is the model for the selected weight. At the end of this process, there are 10 ensemble models corresponding to the 10 different weights (from 3 through 12). For more information about ensemble model, see 'Solving Regression Problems Using Competitive Ensemble Models' by Frayman, Rolfe, and Webb (2002).

2. For each observation, remove the largest as well as the smallest probabilities and compute the mean probability of the remaining 8 probabilities. This average probability based on a scoring mechanism similar to a diving scoring system is the final predicted value.

To create variables, select set of weights for sampling, determine number of samples, choose the type of models and validate models, there are series of analyses to conduct. One is referred to the previous published paper, Wang, Yu and Zhang (2008), for details. It may worth to reiterate here is the effort made to minimize over-fitting in this case. We gradually increase the number of variables in the model and compare value drop of c-statistics from modeling to validation datasets. An example of these charts is shown in Figure 1 below. Four models are under consideration corresponding to four sets of variables which have different numbers of variables. It can be seen that the c-statistics on modeling datasets are very close, and it is the values on validation datasets that determine the number of variables for the model. Through gradually expanding sets of variables, we find that when the number of variables in the model is about 16, which has about 1.6% drop in c-statistic from a modeling dataset to a validation one, the over-fitting is not serious and the model can achieve the largest c-statistics on validations. In short, the key idea is to compare the changes in c-statistic on modeling datasets with those on validation datasets. As the number of variables in

Figure 1.

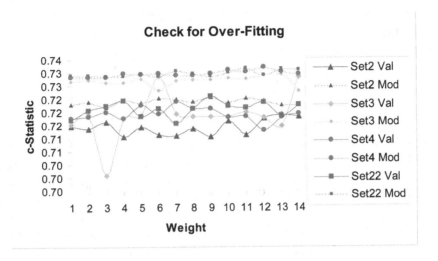

a model increases, the c-statistics on validation increase diminishingly or even start to decrease. The criterion for selecting which variable to enter is based on bootstrapping variable selection results. Those with higher percentages of being selected by bootstrapping samples enter earlier.

APPLICATION AND TECHNICAL DISCUSSIONS

This is a typical business problem: low response rates with many data problems. With this model, the company can develop a marketing program such as a direct mail campaign to target selected customers. The company can contact the top deciles with higher propensity to buy home loans; the company can also test the next a couple of deciles that currently do not have the highest rates of buying home loans from the company, but contacting them may generate highest lift therefore produce the maximal incremental ROI. The remaining few deciles are identified to have lowest response rates. However, there might be still some sub-segments that are profitable to the company. A thorough profit & loss (P&L) analysis should be conducted as the basis for developing any profitable marketing campaigns. Due to the

uniqueness of the type of the loan, customer segmentation using salient or latent classes may reveal heterogeneity which allows for customizing the loan terms and conditions.

NOTES

1. Hualin Wang works in the Advanced Analytics group within Retail Services, one of the major businesses of Alliance Data (www.alliancedata.com). They work for more than 100 clients whose businesses include, but are not limited to, specialty retail & department stores, healthcare, furniture, home improvement, and jewelers. Their work includes private label and co-brand credit card acquisition, portfolio management, marketing campaign design and analysis, customer segmentation, retention and re-activation.

2. Xiaogang Su is associate professor of statistics in the department of statistics & actuarial science at the University of Central Florida.

3. SAS® is a registered trademark of SAS Institute Inc. in USA.

REFERENCES

Agresti, A. (1990). *Categorical Data Analysis* (2nd ed.). New York: John Wiley & Sons.

Breiman, L. (1996). Bagging predictors. *Machine Learning, 24,* 123–140.

Breiman, L. (2001). Random Forests. *Machine Learning, 45,* 5–32. doi:10.1023/A:1010933404324

Breslow, N. E. (1976). Regression analysis of the log odds ratio: a method for retrospective studies. *Biometrics, 32,* 409–416. doi:10.2307/2529508

Breslow, N. E., & Day, N. E. (1980). Classical Methods of Analysis of Matched Data. In *Statistical Methods in Cancer Research, Volume I - The Analysis of Case-Control Studies.* Lyon, France: IARC Scientific Publications, No. 32. International Agency for Research on Cancer.

Efron, B., & Tibshirani, R. J. (1998). *An Introduction to the Bootstrap.* CRC Press LLC.

Finney, D. J. (1971). *Probit Analysis* (3rd ed.). London, UK: Cambridge University Press.

Frayman, Y., Rolfe, S., & Webb, G. (2002). Solving Regression Problems Using Competitive Ensemble Models. *AI 2002: Advances in Artificial Intelligence: Proceedings of the 15th Australian Joint Conference on Artificial Intelligence* (pp. 511-522). Berlin: Springer-Verlag.

Hastie, T., Tibshirani, R., & Friedman, J. (2001). *The Elements of Statistical Learning: Data Mining, Inference, and Prediction.* New York: Springer.

Wang, H., Yu, A., & Zhang, K. (2008). Ensemble PROBIT Models to Predict Cross Selling of Home Loans for Credit Card Customers. *International Journal of Data Warehousing and Mining, 4*(2), 15–21.

Chapter 18
The Power of Sampling and Stacking for the PAKDD-2007 Cross-Selling Problem

Paulo J.L. Adeodato
NeuroTech Ltd. and Federal University of Pernambuco, Brazil

Germano C. Vasconcelos
NeuroTech Ltd. and Federal University of Pernambuco, Brazil

Adrian L. Arnaud
NeuroTech Ltd. and Federal University of Pernambuco, Brazil

Rodrigo C.L.V. Cunha
NeuroTech Ltd. and Federal University of Pernambuco, Brazil

Domingos S.M.P. Monteiro
NeuroTech Ltd. and Federal University of Pernambuco, Brazil

Rosalvo F. Oliveira Neto
NeuroTech Ltd. and Federal University of Pernambuco, Brazil

ABSTRACT

This article presents an efficient solution for the PAKDD-2007 Competition cross-selling problem. The solution is based on a thorough approach which involves the creation of new input variables, efficient data preparation and transformation, adequate data sampling strategy and a combination of two of the most robust modeling techniques. Due to the complexity imposed by the very small amount of examples in the target class, the approach for model robustness was to produce the median score of the 11 models developed with an adapted version of the 11-fold cross-validation process and the use of a combination of two robust techniques via stacking, the MLP neural network and the n-tuple classifier. Despite the problem complexity, the performance on the prediction data set (unlabeled samples), measured through KS2 and ROC curves was shown to be very effective and finished as the first runner-up solution of the competition.

INTRODUCTION

The Pacific-Asian Conference on Knowledge Discovery in Databases (PAKDD) has been organizing open competitions on real world problems for stimulating the development of effective business solutions. This year the PAKDD-2007 Competition presented the challenging cross-selling business problem of a consumer finance company for developing a propensity scoring model. The goal was to point out the credit card customers who would be more likely to accept a home loan (mortgage) offer.

The task was to produce a propensity score for each customer in an independent prediction dataset, separated for performance evaluation, indicating how likely he or she would be for taking up a home loan with the company, with higher scores meaning higher propensity.

In this particular problem, the overlap between the portfolio of credit card customers and the base of home loan (mortgage) customers was very small. In the dataset of 40,700 customers made available for modeling, only 700 belonged to both bases and were labeled with the target for having higher scores in the propensity model. The prediction set consisted of 8,000 customers with both the target labels and the proportion of mortgage offer acceptance undisclosed. For all the data (modeling *plus* prediction sets) employed, there were 40 modeling variables with information collected at the credit card application moment.

These data referred to a random sample of customers who had opened a new credit card with the company within a specific 2-year period but did not have an existing home loan with the company. The target variable has the value 1 if the customer opened a home loan with the company within 12 months after opening the credit card account and the value 0 if otherwise.

Two main challenges were present in this cross-selling problem, the first being the small amount of data from the positive class in the modeling set, and the second being the unknown proportion of each class in the prediction set. As a matter of fact, there was 4.375% of the positive class in the prediction set representing more than 2.5 times the 1.72% proportion found in the modeling set. Therefore, the problem solving task involved much more complexity than the simple application of classification techniques, as will be described in the next sections.

This article is organized as follows. Section 2 presents the technical approach taken. Section 3 presents the creation of new modeling variables. Section 4 describes the data preparation. Section 5 presents the *k*-fold cross-validation sampling strategy. The modeling system is described in Section 6. The performance evaluation and methodology is described in Section 7 and the results and comparisons are presented in Section 8. Section 9 points out the most relevant aspects of the research carried out.

TECHNICAL APPROACH

As mentioned in the previous section, the main challenges of this cross-selling problem were the small amount of data from the positive class in the modeling data set and the unknown proportion of classes in the prediction data set. The employment of an efficient sampling strategy and the choice of robust modeling techniques were the approach taken for dealing with the situation.

Independent of the amount of data available, a complementary idea applied was to use additional information from the application domain based on expert knowledge representation to boost the solution performance. That was accomplished by applying the expertise of domain professionals supported by data analysis.

The work conducted here presents not only the solution developed for the competition, but also its performance evaluation on the prediction data set made available after the competition results were released. The solution development approach was decomposed in *stages* for extracting the most out of the available modeling data while allowing a reliable estimation of the scoring system quality. This consisted of the following technical tasks:

1. Creation of new input variables
2. Data preparation
3. Stage 1: Modeling with a single technique (MLP) on a single sample with a statistically independent hold-out set for defining the minimum performance expected for the solution
   3.1. Standard division of the data set for MLP network modeling (50% for training, 25% for validating, 25% for testing)
   3.2. MLP training
   3.3. Performance evaluation on the statistically independent test set
4. Stage 2: Modeling with stacked techniques on data strategically sampled for data modeling maximization (at the risk of compromising its performance evaluation)
   4.1. Set partition in k=11 folds and aggregation in 11 modeling data sets
   4.2. Training of 11 systems combined via stacking of RAM-based nets and Multi-layer perceptrons
   4.3. Production of the stacked scores for the 11 validation sets.
   4.4. Performance evaluation on the incompletely statistically independent validation sets
5. Stage 3: Submission of the competition scores (performance evaluation of the solution on a statistically independent set).
   5.1. Production of 11 sets of stacked scores for the competition prediction data set
   5.2. Choice of the median rank among them for each example
   5.3. Performance evaluation on the **statistically independent prediction set**

EMBEDDING EXPERT'S KNOWLEDGE IN NEW VARIABLES

The first step taken was the creation of new input variables. This is an important way to embed experts' knowledge into a solution by systematic data transformation for each sample taken from the business operation (Han & Kamber, 2006; Witten & Frank, 2005). In this direction, the following new variables were created from the original information available.

1. Flag for having major credit cards
2. Number of major credit cards owned
3. Flag for neither being a house owner nor having a mortgage
4. Flag for neither being married nor *de facto*
5. Flag for combining the two previous flags
6. Flag for having previously applied for mortgage
7. Available income/Annual income ratio
8. Total balance/Available income ratio

As all the above variables were verified to be significant through statistical analysis, they were kept as inputs for the modeling stage. In fact, in the modeling stage, each data sample had a different variable influence map, once that there were 11 modeling data sets and the amount of positive examples was very small.

After initial analyses, some original variables were discarded or transformed. The variable *B_DEF_UNPD_L12M* was discarded for having all values zero and the variables *CUSTOMER_SEGMENT* and *DISP_INCOME_CODE* were discarded for providing roughly no univariate information gain (Han & Kamber, 2006). The variable *ANNUAL_INCOME_RANGE* was converted to numeric type with its middle point as the new variable.

DATA PREPARATION

The data were prepared according to the typical recommendations employed in data mining processes (Han & Kamber, 2006; Witten & Frank, 2005). Missing data were completed with the average value for numeric variables without any special processing. There was no need to either encode them as missing values or to eliminate the corresponding variable from the modeling process. Numeric data were normalized having their 1st and the 99th percentiles as lower and upper normalization limits, respectively. Categorical variables were binary encoded with predefined and target independent sparse codes according to the number of categories present in that variable.

STRATIFIED SAMPLING STRATEGY

The labeled sample (modeling data set) was partitioned for producing $k=11$ data sets, which were aggregated for training 11 stacked systems in a fashion suited to the modeling techniques being applied. In this sense, the MLP network had 9/11 partitions as training set, the other 2/11 partitions as validation set, and no test set. In the merging process for generating the data sets, each partition was included in only two validation sets. Pragmatically, the partitions were called P1, P2 …P11 and the validation sets were denoted P1∪P2, P2∪P3… P11∪P1. The training sets were the complement set of each validation set.

This data sampling procedure for generating modeling data sets is particularly important here due to the very small amount of data for the target class and can be seen as an adapted version of the k-fold cross-validation method (Jain, Duin & Mao, 2000) to the modeling data. Sampling strategies with multiple data aggregates are very effective in reducing the variability in the final solution for such a small sample of the target class. The final score can be obtained either by averaging or by taking the median of the scores of the k models.

The main drawback of this approach is the computational cost, if the modeling techniques are expensive. For these reasons, we have chosen a small amount of folds (parameter $k=11$) and the median instead of the average due to its greater robustness.

The folds were randomly sampled from the modeling data set in a stratified manner. The 11 folds had 3,700 examples each (=40,700/11) with 7 of them having a proportion of 64:3,700 of positive examples, while the remaining 4 folds had a 63:3,700 proportion.

MODELING SYSTEM

Considering the complexity of modeling imposed by such a small quantity of examples of the target class and the lack of knowledge about the proportion of positive examples on the prediction data set, robustness and performance were the main features the system should have. For that, the decision of stacking (Wolpert, 1992) two techniques of very different nature and high performance was the approach taken.

MultiLayer Perceptron (MLP)

The well-known multilayer perceptron (MLP) trained with the back propagation algorithm (Rumelhart & McClelland, 1986) was one of the techniques used. The MLP has been one of the neural network models most frequently used in pattern classification for its generalization capacity, simplicity of operation and ability to perform universal function approximation (Hornik, Stinchcombe, & White, 1989). It is also a robust model (Kiang, 2003) and has been successfully used in credit risk applications (Amorim, Vasconcelos, & Brasil, 2007; West, 2000). However, one drawback of this technique is the need of a validation (hold-out) data set for preventing over fitting, which is critical here.

The MLPs had a single hidden layer with three neurons and trained with the standard error back propagation algorithm at a learning rate of 0.001, having the minimum squared error on the validation set as the training stopping criterion.

The n-Tuple Classifier

The second technique chosen was the n-tuple classifier (Bledsoe & Browning, 1959; Aleksander, Thomas, & Bowden, 1984) for having two main complementary features in relation to the MLP and because of its assured performance (Rohwer & Morciniec, 1996). First, it is composed of a set of universal function approximators (Anthony & Biggs, 1992; Al-Alawi & Stonham, 1992) working on input subspace samples of variables combined by a simple sum of their outputs. Secondly, because it allows the use of all the data available for training without the need for holding out a validation data set (a feature particularly relevant in the case studied here).

Further data preparation was needed for the n-tuple classifier modeling. The numeric values were discretized in at most 64 levels and were binary encoded according to the successful procedure used by Rohwer and Morceniec (1996).

Another data preparation carried out was the selection of the appropriate training examples from each of the 11 fold aggregates for generating the balanced examples for each class. The negative class had a reduction in the number of examples by random sampling according to a uniform distribution and the positive class had to match the number of examples by replicating the original data with added Gaussian noise with zero mean and standard deviation of 10% of the range for the numeric variables (Adeodato, 1997). The aim of this procedure is twofold: balancing the data and setting the appropriate amount of examples for preventing the well-known memory saturation problem in the n-tuple classifier (Rohwer & Morciniec, 1996). Each training set became a balanced 2,000-example dataset, according to the neuron size of the classifier (ten-input neurons).

The n-tuple classifier had one discriminator per class, each one having 1,000 ten-input neurons randomly connected to the input space. The outputs of the neurons were summed up and normalized per discriminator and then transformed into a score.

Stacking

The lack of data for training the second stage of a stacked solution required a simple and predefined form of combining the techniques. Initial performance evaluation of each isolated technique showed their score correlation was around 0.8, which in one side is a high level of correlation but on the other side has still something complementary.

Therefore, the scores of the MLP and the n-tuple classifier were combined as the weighed sum of their scores according to their performance on each fold aggregate measured by the maximum AUC_ROC (metrics described in the next section). As the initial performance comparison of each isolated technique also showed an equivalent quality, the weighed sum of their scores was reduced to the simple average of the MLP and the n-tuple classifier scores.

The production of the scores for the 8,000 examples of the competition data set was defined as the median score obtained for each unlabeled example among the k stacked systems (trained with the k fold aggregate).

PERFORMANCE EVALUATION AND METHODOLOGY

For systems that produce a continuous output for binary decision making, performance comparisons are more appropriately carried out when executed throughout the whole continuous domain of decision (the score range). Despite the final evaluation of the competition being on the Area Under the Receiver Operating Characteristic Curve (AUC_ROC) criterion (Fawcett, 2003; Provost & Fawcett, 1998), the modeling process performance was also evaluated by the maximum value of the Kolmogorov-Smirnov curve (KS2) (Conover, 1999), the area under the KS curve (AUC_KS) and the Gini coefficient. Those are all widely accepted performance metrics for binary classification based on continuous output and represent similar forms of performance evaluation with slightly different points of view.

ROC Curve and Minimum Distance to Optimum

The Receiver Operating Characteristic Curve (ROC Curve) (Fawcett, 2003) is a widely used tool whose plot represents the compromise between the true positive and the false positive example classifications based on a continuous output along all its possible decision threshold values (the score). The closer the ROC curve is to the upper left corner (optimum point), the better the decision system is. In this context, the minimum distance of the curve to this point is an important metric and assessing the performance throughout the whole X-axis range consists of calculating the area under the ROC curve (AUC) (Fawcett, 2003). The bigger the area, the closer the system is to the optimum decision. If the ROC curve of a classifier appears above that of another classifier along the entire domain of variation, the former system is better than the latter. The ideal decision system would have the AUC_ROC equal to one (1).

Kolmogorov-Smirnov Curve and its Maximum

The KS statistical method is a traditional non-parametric tool used for measuring the adherence of a cumulative distribution function (CDF) to the cumulative representation of the actual data (Conover, 1999). In binary decision systems, this metric is applied for assessing the lack of

adherence between the data sets from the two classes, having the score as independent variable. The Kolmogorov-Smirnov Curves are the difference between the CDFs of the data sets of the two classes and the higher the curve, the better the system. The point of maximum value is particularly important for the performance evaluation in credit risk analysis. The area under the curve metrics (AUC_ROC) is very relevant but can only be used when the horizontal axis is the proportion of the population sorted by the score. The larger the AUC_KS, the better the system is for class separability throughout the whole score range. The ideal decision system would have the AUC_ROC equal to ½.

Gini Curve and its Coefficient

The Gini curve is a statistical tool widely used for assessing the uneven distribution (inequity) of a given characteristic in a population. The population is sorted according to a certain criterion. The Gini curve represents the cumulative proportion of the population with the target characteristic plotted against the proportion of the population itself. In this cross-selling problem, the propensity score is the population sorting criterion and the target characteristic is the acceptance by a costumer of the home loan offer. The area under the curve (AUC_Gini) assesses the quality of the scoring system with the Gini coefficient defined as (2*AUC_Gini − 1) (Han & Kamber, 2006). Once again, the larger the AUC_Gini, the better the system is for class separability. The ideal decision system would have the AUC_ROC equal to one *minus* the proportion of the target class in the population.

EXPERIMENTAL RESULTS AND COMPARISONS

The results presented here refer to three stages of the solution development process assessed with the several metrics described above.

The first stage refers to the performance on the test set of a simple random standard division of the data set for MLP network modeling (25% of the modeling sample, statistically independent hold-out set) for defining the minimum expected performance (lower limit).

The second stage refers to the stacking of the MLP on the validation set (used for early stopping training) and the *n*-tuple classifier on the same set (completely statistically independent).

The third stage refers to the median score of the 11 systems computed by stacking the MLP and the *n*-tuple classifier scores on the examples of the competition prediction set whose target labels had been disclosed right after the competi-

tion ended. This was the actual result achieved on the competition.

If on one hand, the second stage had a positively biased performance estimation because it was partly assessed on the validation sets, on the other hand, the third stage took into account the stacking architecture and benefited from the influence of the sampling strategy, with the median result boosting the performance on the prediction data set of the competition.

The ROC, KS and Gini curves are shown below in Figures 1, 2 and 3, respectively.

It is interesting to observe that the simplest model (stage 1) defined the worst case along all the score range indeed. Another interesting aspect

Figure 1. ROC Curves for the 3 stages of the solution development

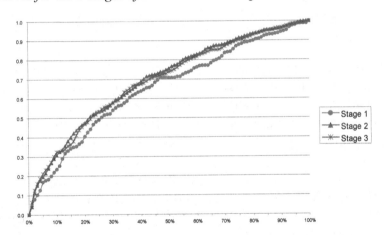

Figure 2. KS Curves for the 3 stages of the solution development

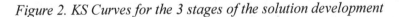

Figure 3. Gini Curves for the 3 stages of the solution development

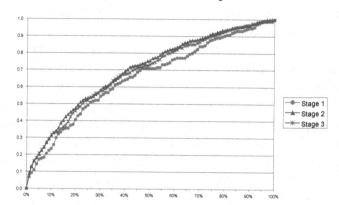

Table 1. Comparative performance metrics for the 3 stages of the solution development

	AUC_ROC	AUC_KS	GINI_Coeff.	Max_KS
Stage 1	0.657	0.157	0.308	0.252
Stage 2	0.703	0.203	0.399	0.295
Stage 3	0.696	0.196	0.375	0.299

is that the final solution (stage 3) achieves roughly the same performance as the optimistic results of stage 2 on the validation data set. These relationships are observed on the three curves above and quantified in the comparative Table 1.

CONCLUDING REMARKS

This article has presented relevant results in terms of statistical methodology and modeling performance on a real-world problem with challenging constraints. The solution proposed for this cross-selling business problem was very robust and achieved good standard, even facing the constraints imposed by the data sets. As a result, the approach taken successfully produced one of the Top 3 best solutions of the PAKDD-2007 Competition.

The solution showed the effectiveness of sampling strategies for modeling and stacking of techniques of different nature. The effectiveness of combining techniques has also been noticed in the overall PAKDD competition results (PAKDD, 2007) because it was the strategy used by the top ranked solutions.

The several metrics used for performance evaluation showed similar and consistent results. The results of the PAKDD-2007 Competition (PAKDD, 2007) offer several metrics beyond the AUC_ROC used as performance evaluation criterion, and all of them are consistent as well.

The combination of the MLP network and the *n*-tuple classifier through stacking was particularly interesting because much was gained from associating their complementary characteristics. The (linear) correlation of around 0.8 between their responses suggested that a linear combination would provide a better response without the need of reserving a data sample exclusively for training the second level classifier of the stacked architecture.

Improvements can be further accomplished if a refined solution is developed based on the CRISP-DM methodology (**CR**oss-**I**ndustry **S**tandard **P**rocess for **D**ata **M**ining) (Reinartz, et al.,

1998; Shearer, 2000). Much more of the experts' knowledge present in the context of the company being studied could be captured during the *"Business Understanding"* stage, and this would lead to the creation of new relevant input variables.

REFERENCES

Adeodato, P. J. L. (1997). *Theoretical investigations on RAM-based neural networks*. Doctoral Dissertation, Department of Mathematics, King's College London, UK.

Al-Alawi, R., & Stonham, T. J. (1992). A training strategy and functionality analysis of digital multi-layer neural networks. *Journal of Intelligent Systems, 2*, 53-93.

Aleksander, I., Thomas, W. V., & Bowden, P. A. (1984). WISARD, a radical step forward in image recognition. *Sensor Review, 4*, 120-124.

Amorim, B., Vasconcelos, G. C., & Brasil, L. (2007, September). Hybrid neural systems for large scale credit risk assessment. *Journal of Intelligent and Fuzzy Systems (JIFS), 18*(5).

Anthony, M., & Biggs, N. (1992). *Computational learning theory*. UK: Cambridge University Press.

Bledsoe, W. W., & Browning, I. (1959). Pattern recognition and reading by machine. In *Proceedings of the Eastern Joint Computer Conference*, (pp. 225-232).

Conover, W. J. (1999). *Practical nonparametric statistics* (3rd ed.). New York: John Wiley & Sons.

Fawcett, T. (2003). *ROC graphs: Notes and practical considerations for data mining researchers*. Retrieved November 9, 2007, from http://citeseer.comp.nus.edu.sg/fawcett03roc.html

Han, J., & Kamber, M. (2006). *Data mining: Concepts and techniques*. San Francisco: Morgan Kaufmann.

Hornik, K., Stinchcombe, M., & White, H. (1989). Multilayer feedforward networks are universal approximators. *Neural Networks, 2*, 359-366.

Jain, A. K., Duin, R. P. W., & Mao, J. (2000). Statistical pattern recognition: A review. *IEEE Transactions on Pattern Analysis and Machine Intelligence, 22*(1), 4-37.

Kiang, M. Y. (2003). A comparative assessment of classification methods. *Decision Support Systems, 35*, 441-454.

PAKDD-2007 Competition Web page. (2007). Retrieved November 9, 2007, from http://lamda.nju.edu.cn/conf/pakdd07/dmc07/

Provost F., & Fawcett, T. (1998). Robust classification systems for imprecise environments. In *Proceedings of the 15th National Conference on Artificial Intelligence*, AAAI-98, Menlo Park, CA, (pp. 706-713).

Reinartz, T., Wirth, R., Clinton, J., Khabaza, T., Hejlesen, J., Chapman, P., & Kerber, R. (1998). *The current CRISP-DM*. Retrieved November 9, 2007, from http://www.crisp-dm.org/

Rohwer, R., & Morciniec, M. (1996). A theoretical and experimental account of *n*-tuple classifier performance. *Neural Computation, 8*, 629-642.

Rumelhart, D. E., & McClelland, J. L. (1986). *Parallel distributed processing*. Cambridge, MA: The MIT Press.

Shearer, C. (2000). The CRISP-DM model: The new blueprint for data mining. *Journal of Data Warehousing, 5*(4), 13-22.

West, D. (2000). Neural network credit scoring models. *Computers and Operations Research, 27*, 1131-1152.

Witten, I. H., & Frank, E. (2005). *Data mining: Practical machine learning tools and techniques with Java implementations*. San Francisco: Morgan Kaufmann.

Wolpert, D.H. (1992). Stacked generalization. *Neural Networks, 5,* 241-259.

This work was previously published in International Journal of Data Warehousing and Mining, Vol. 4, Issue 2, edited by D. Taniar, pp. 9-14, copyright 2008 by IGI Publishing (an imprint of IGI Global).

Chapter 19
Using TreeNet to Cross-Sell Home Loans to Credit Card Holders

Dan Steinberg
Salford Systems, USA

Nicholas Scott Cardell
Salford Systems, USA

John Ries
Salford Systems, USA

Mykhaylo Golovnya
Salford Systems, USA

ABSTRACT

Today's credit card issuers are increasingly offering a broad range of products and services with separate lines of business responsible for different product groups. Too often, the separate lines of business operate independently and information available to one line of business may not be used productively by others. In this study, we examine the potential of using information from customers of multiple products to identify customers most likely to respond to cross-sell product offers. Specifically, we examine the potential for offering home loans to a population of credit card holders by studying individuals who do hold both a credit card and a mortgage with the card issuer. Using real world data provided to the 2007 PAKDD data mining competition, we employ Friedman's stochastic gradient boosting (MART™, TreeNet®) for the rapid development of a high performance cross-sell predictive model.

INTRODUCTION

This report describes our participation in the PAKDD 2007 data mining competition. The article is organized as follows. In Section 1 we offer our understanding of the competitive challenge, the data available, and how we framed the modeling objectives. In Section 2 we provide a summary of the key descriptive statistics that provide an initial picture of the nature of the data and its adequacy for modeling purposes. Section 3 describes our modeling methods and reports our results and performance based on the labeled data. Section 4 delves further into the results to examine specific findings at the predictor level. Finally, Section 5 summarizes our results and offers conclusions.

THE MODELING CONTEXT

The data provided for the PAKDD 2007 modeling competition consisted of historical records for each of 40,070 customers of a consumer finance company. The records included customer demographics, residential and employment history, income category, summaries of credit card use, and various components of credit bureau reports for the prior 3-, 6-, and 12-month periods. The training data came in the form of a flat file containing 40 modeling variables (columns) for customers who had opened a new credit card account in a 2-year observation window and who did not already have a home loan with the company. Seven hundred of these customers also signed up for a home loan within 12 months after opening their credit card account. The mortgage customers were flagged as "1," while the remaining customers were flagged as "0". Only 1.7% percent of these customers opened a home loan account, putting this problem into the category of "rare event modeling."

The organizers of this competition are to be commended for acquiring a substantial volume of real world customer data for public release. Such data can rarely be acquired without limitation. In this instance, the limitations pertain to the data fields made available, and to the descriptive information characterizing the data. We know that the data were drawn from a financial institution, but we are not given the time period from which the data were drawn, and several valuable fields are provided with partial information only. For example, an important variable CUSTOMER_SEGMENT with 11 categories was supplied without further elaboration on the actual meaning of those categories. We are provided with no information regarding the competitive landscape, the nature of the marketing campaigns, trends in the real estate market, or the overall market share in the country for the institution in question.

These informational limitations severely restrict both the business value of any models developed and our ability to extract real world insight into the workings of the marketplace or into consumer behavior.

Another fine point must be made concerning the actual loan application process. The mere fact that someone is looking for a home loan does not guarantee that the loan will be approved. The 700 loan holders in the learn data are the end result of a multistage process involving both consumer initiative as well as lender's decision making policies. Knowing the specifics of the process as well as time dimensions may in some cases drastically improve modeling solutions.

The formal description of the competition data was confined to one page. Therefore, we resorted to making plausible assumptions about its nature. Our tests (reported below) establish that the train and prediction sets were very likely drawn from the same customer population and from the same time period.

DATA OVERVIEW

To get a better grasp of the data, we grouped the available predictors into the following illustrative

Table 1. Grouping of predictors

Group	Variables
Demographics	Marital status, dependents, age, employment duration, residence duration and district, occupation, income
Self-Reported	Checking and savings account indicators, major credit card indicators
Bureau	Number of bureau inquiries in the last 3, 6 and 12 months for loans, mortgages, and consumer credit; default data

categories (not all variables are listed) shown in Table 1.

Based on our past experience, we expected the bureau and demographic groups to be more predictive than the self-reported application data, which seemed to be incomplete and may be susceptible to misrepresentation.

The modeling data, as received, included numerous variables that were not usable in their raw forms. In particular, the credit bureau variables had embedded codes signifying whether or not a credit bureau record was found (code=98) or whether a search was made (code=99). Because these codes were the same for all numeric credit bureau variables, we decided to create a new character variable, BUREAUSEARCH, defined as follows:

If B_ENQ_L6M_GR1=98 then
 bureausearch$="No match found"
else if B_ENQ_L6M_GR1=99 then
 bureausearch$="Did not go"
else bureausearch$="Match found"

New versions of the original credit bureau variables were created as follows:

For numeric variables:
Code 98 (no match found) recoded to 0
Code 99 (did not go) recoded to missing
For character variables:
All values other than "Y" or "N" recoded to
 missing

Because the sum of B_ENQ_L6M_GR1, B_ENQ_L6M_GR2, and B_ENQ_L6M_GR3 (number of bureau inquiries in the past 6 months for consumer credit, loans, and mortgages, correspondingly) was sometimes less than B_ENQ_L6M (number of bureau inquiries in the last 6 months), we assumed that there were some enquiries that did not fall into the three categories specified in the data dictionary. We therefore created a variable, B_ENQ_L6M_OTH, representing the difference.

Some variables were almost entirely missing or had degenerate distributions– Unpaid Defaults indicator (B_DEF_UNPD_IND) was zero on all records, while Paid Defaults indicator (B_DEF_PAID_IND) was either zero or "no match found" with the exception of just four records.

The self-reported account and credit card indicators included a number of values other than "Y," or "N." We therefore elected to create new versions of these variables as well, where miscellaneous values were recoded to missing.

We discovered 16 records in the modeling data set where CURR_EMPL_MTHS=1000; we took this as a code for "employment length unknown" and therefore created new versions of CURR_EMPL_MTHS and PREV_EMPL_MTHS (named CURR_EMPL_MTHS_v2, and PREV_EMPL_MTHS_v2). We also created a new variable EMPLYRS, defined as (CURR_EMPL_MTHS_v2+PREV_EMPL_MTHS_v2)/12 (number of years employed in the most recent two positions), and RESYRS, defined as (CURR_RES_MTHS+PREV_RES_MTHS)/12 (number of years resided at two most recent addresses).

There were also a few records where AGE_AT_APPLICATION was less than RESYRS by a small amount (1-2 years). In response, we created a new variable, APPAGE2, which was equal to AGE_AT_APPLICATION if greater than RESYRS; or RESYRS rounded down to the nearest unit otherwise.

Conventional inspection of the corrected data revealed no additional problems requiring repair prior to productive analysis. The 10 variables with missing values above 0.01% are listed below in Table 2. The disposable income code is heavily missing, as is typical for variables of this kind. We decided not to try to impute the income category, allowing our modeling algorithms to use their built-in missing value handling to process this data. The table of the missing value prevalence reveals that very few variables had any missings. The credit card indicators which record whether the customer had such an account proved to be of no value in the modeling, allowing us to conclude that missings were essentially a nonissue in this data.

Comparing Train and Prediction Sets via Modeling

In a predictive modeling assessment exercise it is always useful to know if the train and test data are drawn from the same population, and we prefer to test this hypothesis ourselves regardless of what the organizers of a competition advertise. For this test we concatenated the two data sets and used the sample indicator (PREDSET) as

Table 2. Missing value prevalence by variable

Variable	% Missing
DISP_INCOME_CODE	70.62
DINERS_CARD_V2	9.55
AMEX_CARD_V2	9.13
RETAIL_CARDS_V2	9.12
MASTERCARD_V2	7.25
VISA_CARD_V2	6.10
CUSTOMER_SEGMENT	4.28
CURR_EMPL_MTHS_V2	0.04
PREV_EMPL_MTHS_V2	0.04
EMPLYRS	0.04

the target in a multivariate modeling exercise. We used the CART decision tree (Breiman, Friedman, Olshen, & Stone, 1984; Steinberg & Colla, 1995) to automatically build this model and found virtual unpredictability: if we choose a record at a random from one of these two sets it is not possible to predict which set the record came from. Figure 1 displays the results of the CART analysis. The graph shows the relative test error for the train vs. predict set discrimination problem. The relative error never dips below .97, indicating an inability to discriminate between the two data sets. Table 3 shows the confusion matrix for the best of these models.

Testing was conducted by randomly dividing the data into equal-sized train and test partitions. The CART model shows negligible predictability at the optimal tree size, strongly supporting our hypothesis that both datasets come from the same population of customers.

Figure 1. CART test of ability to discriminate between train and prediction data

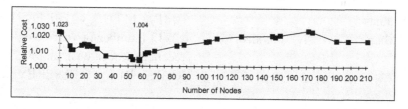

Table 3. Confusion Matrix: CART model to discriminate between train and prediction data

Actual Class	Total Cases	Percent Correct	0 N=9431	1 N=8583
0	15,061	52.29	7,875	7,186
1	2,953	47.31	1,556	1,397
Total:	18,014			
Average:		49.80		
Overall % Correct:		51.47		

MODELING

Single Tree CART Models

We began our analysis with CART trees to obtain initial insight into the data via its visual displays and variable importance rankings. A display of the tree pruned back to nine nodes is shown in Figure 2, where a *black* terminal node indicates above-average probability of home loan and a *gray* terminal node indicates below-average probability. The tree reveals that bureau activity variables, together with key demographic information, are the primary drivers here. While none of this is surprising, it is always reassuring to have core expectations ratified before moving on to more complex modeling methods.

Splitting the data into 70% learn and 30% test partitions yields a class average accuracy of 65.85%, and an area under the ROC curve (AUC) of .6941, as shown in Table 4.

We have also conducted repeated cross-validation experiment where the process of partitioning the training data into 10 bins is independently repeated 10 times with different random number seeds. The results are presented in Figure 3.

Apparently, natural variability in the CV estimates of AUC caused by the finiteness of the sample ranges between 0.66 and 0.69 with the average value of 0.675. As will be seen later, pushing modeling effort into the stochastic gradient boosting area (TreeNet) will further improve AUC by about six points, thus placing it far outside the upper boundary of the CART models. However,

Figure 2. Primary splitters in single CART tree to predict home loans

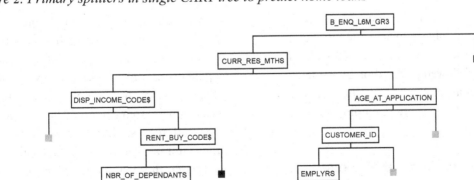

Table 4. Confusion Matrix: CART model to predict home loans. Cross-validation estimates.

Actual Class	Total Cases	Percent Correct	0 N=1945	1 N=1071
0	2,965	65.03	1,928	1,037
1	51	66.67	17	34
Total:	3,016.00			
Average:		65.85		
Overall % Correct:		65.05	ROC:	0.6941

Figure 3. Repeated CV battery (10 iterations) for CART model to predict home loans

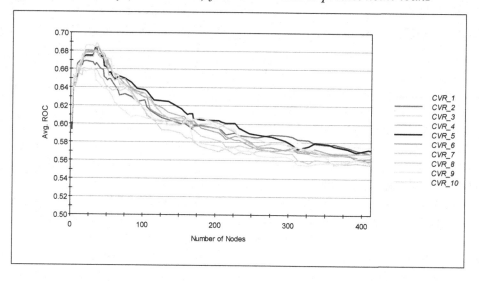

the biggest advantage of CART approach reigns in the simplicity of the solution, as well as ease with which it was obtained.

The most important variables as ranked by CART appear in Table 5, where the number of inquiries over the last 6 and 12 months clearly stand out. It is followed by duration of residence, number of bureau inquiries over the last three months, personal information, employment history, and others.

Boosted Trees: TreeNet Models

We next moved on to stochastic gradient boosting models (Friedman, 2001), using the TreeNet (Salford Systems, 2005) commercial release of Friedman's Multiple Additive Regression Trees (MART). Our primary reason for doing so was that tree ensembles often outperform single trees, and TreeNet in particular is able to work effectively with small data sets. In this example, the overall dataset is not small, but the number of responders is only 700, which will clearly limit the size of any single decision tree. TreeNet builds its models from a possibly large collection of very small trees, so that sample size is never a limiting factor in any one tree. TreeNet also tends to yield much more stable variable importance rankings and predictive scores than do single trees and TreeNet models can be tuned for AUC performance optimization.

Table 5. Variable importance rankings for CART model to predict home loans

Variable	Score
B_ENQ_L6M_GR3	100.00
B_ENQ_L12M_GR3	98.15
B_ENQ_L6M_MORT	93.65
CURR_RES_MTHS	92.05
B_ENQ_L12M_MORT	90.69
RENT_BUY_CODE$	54.80
PREV_RES_MTHS	52.36
B_ENQ_L3M	47.29
B_ENQ_L6M	47.23
DISP_INCOME_CODE$	37.51
NBR_OF_DEPENDANTS	36.23
EMPLYRS	35.50
AGE_AT_APPLICATION	32.44

Model Simplification

For interpretation purposes, it is often useful to try to reduce the number of predictors that appear in the model. We used "variable shaving" to accomplish model simplification, fitting a series of progressively smaller models to the data. Each new model is specified by dropping the least important predictor from the previous model in a pattern similar to backwards stepwise regression.

The graph shown in Figure 4 gives an example of the shaving process we conducted very early into our study using fast TreeNet models (small number of trees, explicit test sample, high learn rate).

The graph indexes each model by the number of predictors, while the model accuracy is reported in terms of the area under the ROC curve. We observe that a model with 11 predictors is sufficient to achieve an ROC not far below that of our "large scale" model.

We subsequently conducted a set of lengthy and exhaustive shaving runs using very large TreeNet models with low learn rates. During the process, we also selectively eliminated variables

that turned out to be minor variations of another. Our final best predictor set used 11 predictors.

Final Models

Based on the results of variable shaving described above, our final models used 11 ultimate predictors listed in Table 6.

The final set of scores was created by averaging the scores from two different TreeNet models. The first, consisting of 8,442 6-node decision trees, was estimated with a 70% learning sample and a 30% test sample. The second, consisting of 10,000 six-node decision trees, was estimated on the whole modeling data set. Because TreeNet is a nonparametric procedure, based on ensembles of decision trees, there are no parameters to report. The first of the final models is shown in Figure 5. It uses 6-node trees and a learn rate of 0.0012. We had to push model size toward the extreme (10,000 trees) because larger models tended to demonstrate marginal performance improvement, which always counts in a competition. In reality one could sacrifice a little bit of accuracy (within a single point) in favor of a more "lightweight"

Table 6. Final set of predictors

Variable	Description
B_ENQ_L3M_V2	# Bureau Enquiries in the last 3 months (codes removed)
B_ENQ_L12M_LOAN	# Bureau Enquiries in last 12 months for Loans (codes removed)
DISP_INCOME_CODE	Indicates monthly Disposable Income
AGE_AT_APPLICATION	Age at application time
MARITAL_STATUS	Marital status
CURR_EMPL_MTHS_V2	Indicates total number of months at Current Employment
B_ENQ_L6M_MORT	# Bureau Enquiries in last 6 months for Mortgages (codes removed)
RENT_BUY_CODE	Residential status code
A_DISTRICT_APPLICANT	District of Residence of the Applicant (using residential address)
RESYRS	Total # years at last two residences (current and previous)
CURR_RES_MTHS	Indicates total number of months at Current Residence

Figure 4. ROC as a function of the number of variables removed

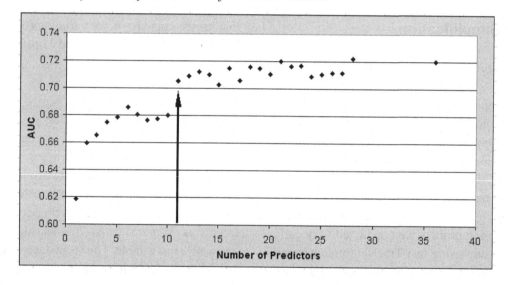

model. Still, obtaining the reported model took less than 5 minutes on a 1.73 GHz Centrino Duo Pentium processor with 2 GB of RAM.

The default tree size of six nodes is adequate for capturing 3-way (and possibly some 4- and 5-way) interactions and yields an area under the ROC curve of .714 on test data. Notice that this is far better than our best single decision tree model.

Assessment of Interactions

To test whether interactions are needed at all in this model, we re-ran our model restricting the tree size to two nodes, or "stumps" models. Because each tree can involve at most one predictor, and because the final prediction is based on a sum of scores across all trees, the stumps model is constrained to be additive (but possibly highly nonlinear) in the predictors. The model summary is shown in Figure 6.

Figure 5. Summary report for TreeNet model displaying model performance (ROC) vs. number of trees (Using 70% of data for learning)

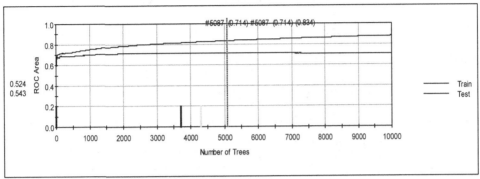

Figure 6. Additive TreeNet model displaying model performance vs. number of trees (Using 70% of data for learning)

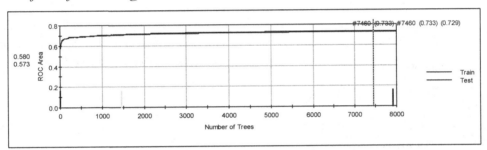

The additive model reaches an area under the ROC curve of 0.733, which is better than the performance of the unconstrained model (AUC = 0.714). Also note the striking absence of any overfitting in the new model as the train and test performance curves lie on top of each other.

Based on these, it became clear that interactions were not practically relevant to this model.

Distribution of Scores

To delve further into the details of the model, it is worth looking at the distribution of model scores on the train dataset where the actual response is known. When the objective function is the logistic regression, TreeNet scores are literally predicted logits (Friedman, Hastie, & Tibshirani, 2000) and a 0.0 score corresponds to a predicted probability of having a home loan account of 0.50. The greater the score, the greater the predicted probability of having a loan.

The distributions of TreeNet scores for each of the target classes are shown in Figure 7. The heavy black curve with the highest peak represents home loan customers, while the medium gray curve represents the remaining customers.

The graph shows a considerable overlap of scores for the two types of accounts, although home loan accounts generally have higher score values. All scores are negative (predicted probabilities are less than 0.5) as the probability of a cross-sell is a rare event.

Model Insights and Discussion

Table 7 lists the relative importance of the 11 predictors in the additive TreeNet model.

Figure 7. Distribution of TreeNet scores by target class (superimposed)

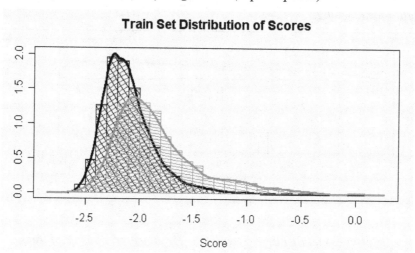

Table 7. Variable importance scores reported by TreeNet (Using 70% of data for learning)

Variable	Score
B_ENQ_L6M_MORT	100.00
RESYRS	70.70
CURR_RES_MTHS	51.28
AGE_AT_APPLICATION	49.84
A_DISTRICT_APPLICANT	47.42
RENT_BUY_CODE$	42.37
B_ENQ_L3M_V2	38.13
MARITAL_STATUS$	37.02
DISP_INCOME_CODE$	35.96
CURR_EMPL_MTHS_V2	33.34
B_ENQ_L12M_LOAN	32.75

Compared with earlier CART runs, some of the demographics have moved into higher positions, while bureau mortgage requests remains at the top. Also note how most of the previous "weak" variables show higher contribution scores. While similar in spirit to CART, the substantially increased complexity of TreeNet models accounts for a superior treatment of the available predictors, more information can be extracted from these predictors using multiple trees.

Figure 8. TreeNet partial dependency plot: Contribution of last 6 month mortgage inquiries to predicted log-odds of home loans

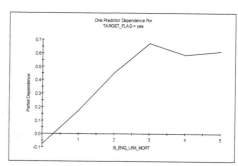

We now proceed by describing the effect each predictor appears to be making to the overall score produced by the additive TreeNet model.

The top-most important predictor is the number of bureau inquiries in the last 6 months for mortgages (Figure 8).

Naturally, the greater the number of mortgage inquiries, the higher the probability of having a home loan account. From the business point of view, this means that the customers are either in the process of shopping for a new mortgage or have recently acquired one. In any case, all such accounts appear to be likely candidates for a new offer.

Figure 9. TreeNet partial dependency plot: Contribution of total residence (years) and current residence (months) to predicted log-odds of home loans

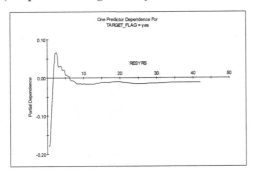
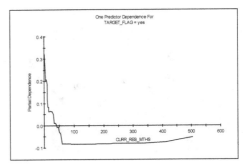

Figure 10. TreeNet partial dependency plot: Contribution of age at application and current employment months to predicted log-odds of home loans

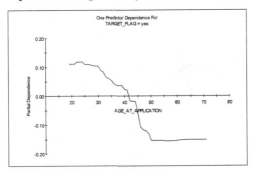
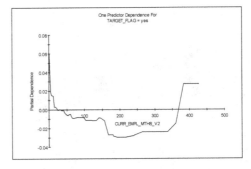

The contributions of total residence (measured in years and includes both current and previous residence) and current residence (measured in months) are shown in Figure 9.

Both plots resemble each other, emphasizing the higher likelihood of applying for a mortgage within the second or third year of residence. This is followed by a drastic decrease in response probability until the 5-year mark. The situation remains unchanged for another 10 years or so with a slight increase in probability around 15-year mark due to (possibly) expiration of the existing loans. The effect is most pronounced early in the customer's tenure in their home.

The contributions of related age at application and current employment months are shown in Figure 10.

Young applicants below 30 are more likely candidates for new loans, followed by a gradual decline up until the retirement threshold (55-60 years) with subsequent uprising after the retirement. Note the flat dip between 50 and 58 years: growing concern over the looming retirement probably pushes back acquiring new home loans and other concerns until the actual retirement.

In terms of employment history, there is a negative relationship (ignoring fluctuations) for the first 10 years (120 months), followed by a flat segment, followed by a positive relationship above 25 years (300 months). One possible explanation is that getting a new job may well be associated with buying a new home or refinancing, followed by a period of stability. The 25 years of employment mark may be also associated with another occasion to move or refinance in the country from which this data has been gathered.

Figure 11. TreeNet partial dependency plot: Contribution of geographic location and residence status to predicted log-odds of home loans

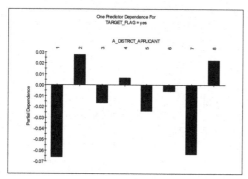
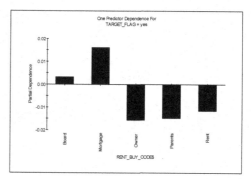

Figure 12. TreeNet partial dependency plot: Contribution of marital status and disposable income code to predicted log-odds of home loans

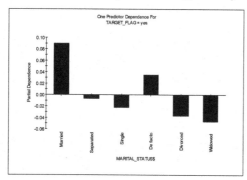
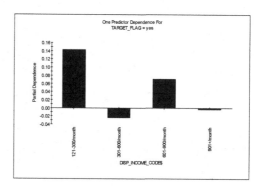

Figure 13. TreeNet partial dependency plot: Contribution of bureau inquiries over last 3 months and loan inquiries over last 12 months to Predicted Log-odds of Home Loans

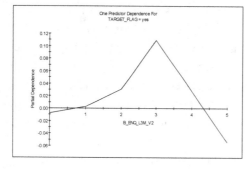
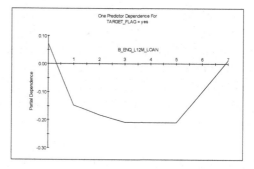

The next important variables (applicant's district and residential status) are shown in Figure 11.

Districts 2 and 8 have the highest odds of having a home loan, while districts 7 and 1 have the lowest odds. All the remaining districts show minor variation and can be safely pooled together.

In terms of the residence status, current mortgage owners are most likely to have a home loan account with the current company. In practice, the ultimate decision on whether to include such variable or not would ultimately rest on further clarification with the data supplier. Because including this variable does improve model performance, we made the decision to keep it.

Among the remaining levels, notably the "Owner" and (living with) "Parents" categories have the lowest odds followed by "Renters." "Board" category occupies the middle position and has higher likelihood of getting a new home loan than "Renters." Note that the magnitude of these effects is roughly one tenth of the magnitude of the effects described earlier, as evident from the vertical axis scaling.

The contributions of marital status and disposable income code are shown in Figure 12.

Married couples are most likely candidates, followed by "Defacto" group. In contrast, widowed group is strongly on the negative side, followed by divorced, single, and separated. Again, the conclusions appear to be quite logical but the magnitude of the effect is smaller than seen for the most important predictors.

Group "121-300/month" stands out with a strong positive contribution, but it represents just 66 records in the train data. Among the remaining categories the positive contribution of the "601-900/month" group is notable.

Two more bureau indicators, overall number of enquiries in the last 3 months and number of personal loan inquiries in the last 12 months, are shown in Figure 13.

It appears that the odds of having a home loan increase as the total number of overall bureau inquiries (last 3 months) increases. The contribution is maximal at 3 and then drops. In contrast, the number of personal loan inquiries (last 12 months) initially was negatively associated with the odds of having a home loan, attaining minimum at 5 with subsequent reversal of the trend.

CONCLUSION

Data mining competitions are inherently limited by the data and information that the proprietary data owners are prepared to release. In the PAKDD 2007 competition, the limitations permitted us to build a successful cross-sell model to identify likely candidates for a home loan from a list of existing credit card customers. Demographic measures combined with basic bureau data appeared to be most predictive. In contrast, self-reported application data showed no significant impact on the final solution. As the final model was strictly additive in the effects of the predictors, we were able to provide simple variable-by-variable insights into the workings of the constructed model. The results appear to be plausible and the model performed very well on unseen data.

REFERENCES

Breiman, L., Friedman, J., Olshen, R., & Stone, C. (1984). *Classification and regression trees.* Belmont, CA: Wadsworth.

Friedman, J. H. (2001). Greedy function approximation: A gradient boosting machine. *Annals of Statistics, 29,* 1189-1232.

Friedman, J. H., Hastie, T., & Tibshirani, R. (2000). Additive logistic regression: A statistical view of boosting (with discussion). *Annals of Statistics, 28,* 337-407.

Salford Systems. (2005). *TreeNet: Stochastic gradient boosting.* Version 2.0. Salford Systems.

Steinberg, D., & Colla, P. (1995). *CART: Tree structured non-parametric data analysis.* Salford Systems.

This work was previously published in International Journal of Data Warehousing and Mining, Vol. 4, Issue 2, edited by D. Taniar, pp. 32-45, copyright 2008 by IGI Publishing (an imprint of IGI Global).

Chapter 20
PAKDD-2007:
A Near-Linear Model for the Cross-Selling Problem

Thierry Van de Merckt
VADIS Consulting, Belgium

Jean-François Chevalier
VADIS Consulting, Belgium

ABSTRACT

This chapter presents VADIS Consulting's solution for the cross-selling problem of the PAKDD-2007 competition. For this competition, the authors have used their in-house developed tool RANK, which automates a lot of important tasks that must be done to provide a good solution for predictive modelling projects. It was for them a way of benchmarking their 3 years of investment effort against other tools and techniques. RANK encodes some important steps of the CRISP-DM methodology: Data Quality Audit, Data Transformation, Modelling, and Evaluation. The authors have used RANK as they would do in a normal project, however with much less access to the business information, and hence the task was quite elementary: they have audited the data quality and found some problems that were further corrected, they have then let RANK build a model by applying its standard recoding, and then applied automatic statistical evaluation for variable selection and pruning. The result was not extremely good in terms of prediction, but the model was extremely stable, which is what the authors were looking for.

The challenge proposed this year by the PAKDD is a good example of a usual predictive task in analytical CRM projects. It concerns a financial company having customers of credit card as well as of home loan (mortgage) products. Both of these products have been on the market for many years, although for some reason the overlap between these two customer bases is currently very small. The company would like to make use of this opportunity to cross-sell home loans to its credit card customers, but the small size of the overlap presents a challenge when trying to develop an effective scoring model to predict potential cross-sell take-ups – although this challenge is reduced when the right methods are used for building a model.

A modeling dataset of 40,700 customers with 40 modeling variables, plus a target variable, is

DOI: 10.4018/978-1-60566-717-1.ch020

Figure 1. Methodological steps & RANK contribution

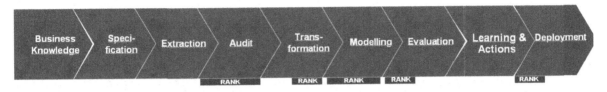

provided. This is a sample of customers who opened a new credit card with the company within a specific 2-year period and who did not have an existing home loan with the company. The target categorical variable "Target_Flag" has a value of 1 if the customer then opened a home loan with the company within 12 months after opening the credit card (700 random samples), and has a value of 0 if otherwise (40,000 random samples). A prediction dataset (8,000 sampled cases) is provided with similar variables but withholding the target variable, in order to judge the real performance of the model by the PAKDD contest committee. The data mining task is to produce a score for each customer in the prediction dataset, indicating a credit card customer's propensity to take up a home loan with the company.

Our goal in competing on this contest was to apply our standard processes and methods and to submit our solution without extensive search and tuning. We decided that the time spent should not be more than 1 man day in total, which was the case. On the technical side, our challenge – as usual – was to make sure that our model would be robust in order to avoid any bad surprise when applied on the prediction dataset.

APPLIED METHODOLOGY

Our methodology for building analytical solutions is based on CRISP-DM. In order to support our consultants in applying this methodology in a rigorous and consistent way, we have developed a platform called RANK that automates some

of the major steps of the process, as shown in figure 1.

Since PAKDD07 contest provides the data sets, the target, and the data dictionary, the first three steps are not applicable. Hence, the process is the following:

- **Audit** – Evaluation of the data quality, its consistency, etc.
- **Transformation** – Preparation of the data for modeling: defining types, binning, recoding, deriving new variables, linearization of the vector space, normalization, etc.
- **Modeling** – building the model itself, by choosing the best technique, the set of relevant variables, etc.
- **Evaluation** – asserting the model stability, its statistical relevance, etc. And reviewing the business relevance (this last important step is not applicable to the contest).

The last two steps (Learning and Deployment) are not applicable to the PAKDD07 contest.

RANK provides a great help for all these steps to the analyst.

Audit

The audit allows analyzing the distribution of the variables and to spot anomalies. An example is given in the next figure.

This variable indicates the Number of Bureau Enquiries in the last 6 months for Mortgages. Maximum actual value is 97. Special values are:

Figure 2. Anomaly for 98 & 98 modalities

	Count Univers	Count Client	% Univers	% RTT	Index	Z-Score
ORDINAL_RTT.B_ENQ_L6M_GR3						
0	33090	428	81.3	1.3	75.20	-4.76
1	4652	117	11.4	2.5	146.23	3.33
2	1666	77	4.1	4.6	268.73	5.60
3	554	42	1.4	7.6	440.79	5.20
4	202	17	0.5	8.4	489.32	3.43
5+6+7	119	11	0.3	9.2	537.45	2.83
8+9+10+12+98+99	417	8	1.0	1.9	111.55	0.29

- 98 = Went to bureau and no match found (new file created)
- 99 = Did not go to bureau

From the data dictionary, the distribution, and the output of Rank, we immediately see that there is a problem with value 98 & 99. Figure 2 shows for each modality (possibly grouped to form a statistically relevant sample of the data) the total number of cases, the number of clients (target), the equivalent percentages, the index which shows the target density compared to the total population, and the statistical significance of the modality in relation with the target density. We see that all modalities are significant and that the more a prospect enquires for mortgage, the more chances to sell one. However, when we look at the 8+9+ …+99 group of modalities, we see a decrease of the Index which does not make any business sense. This is just the side effect of the coding of "no match found" and "did not go to the bureau" into 98 and 99 values,

which are grouped with high values of enquiries. This has to be corrected.

Another example is the presence of un-documented modalities such as for MASTERCARD, where the modalities "2" and "1" are not described in the data dictionary. These values must be corrected as well.

The Audit takes less than 10 sec to be computed, and took minutes to analyze and spot anomalies (see Figure 3).

Transformation

The transformations involved the following:

- Correction of anomalies
- Re-coding of variables
- Linearization and normalization of the vector space
- Grouping of small modalities into statistically valid samples

Figure 3. Audit output

```
7) Name= MASTERCARD
   nModality= 6
   Modalities=
```

Name	#occ	%occ	#T	%RTT	Index	Score
MISSING	2937	7.2	60	2.0	118.78	0.38
N	36151	88.8	607	1.7	97.63	-1.55
Y	1597	3.9	33	2.1	120.14	0.22
2	1	0.0	0	0.0	-1.00	-99.99
X	1	0.0	0	0.0	-1.00	-99.99
1	13	0.0	0	0.0	-1.00	-99.99

Linearization of the vector space and the grouping of small modalities are done automatically by RANK. The linearization involves the creation of new variables that are linear w.r.t. the target distribution, and which are further normalized. The grouping is based on an algorithm that analyses, for each modality, its discriminative power w.r.t. the target and which groups modalities that would not give reliable samples. The test is based on classical statistical tests. An example is given in figure 2.

Corrections and Recoding

The following corrections have been applied.

- CUSTOMER_SEGMENT: 99 → Missing
- AMEX_CARD, VISA_CARD, DINERS_CARD, MASTERCARD, RETAIL_CARDS:
  ◦ 1 → Y
  ◦ 0 → N
  ◦ 1,2 → Y
  ◦ X → N

According the data dictionary, for the variables indicating the number of bureau enquiries, we observe two special values:

- 98: Went to bureau and no match found (new file created)
- 99: Did not go to bureau.

This was not totally appropriate for the modeling. Indeed, 99 and 98 interpretation is quite similar to the 0 one, whereas their values are far away from 0. Therefore the variables were recoded by, namely:

- 98 → -1
- 99 → 0.

Some variables were originally coded as nominal. However, since they present an order, we would rather use them as numeric. The reason

for that lies in the fact that RANK will eventually groups similar values together, taking into account their value as numerical variables (categorical would typically grouped into one single dummy value). The following recoding have then be done:

- ANNUAL_INCOME_RANGE:
  ◦ '0K -< 30K' → 15
  ◦ 00K -<30K → 15
  ◦ '30K -< 90K' → 60
  ◦ '90K -< 150K' → 120
  ◦ '150K -< 240K' → 195
  ◦ '240K -< 360K' → 300
  ◦ '360K+' → 500
- DISP_INCOME_CODE:
  ◦ 'A' → 120
  ◦ 'B' → 160
  ◦ 'C' → 450
  ◦ 'D' → 750
  ◦ 'E' → 1200

The re-coding performed automatically by RANK on the data set is the following:

- **Intelligent binning of the continuous variables** – We used a home made algorithm to analyze the distribution of each continuous variable in order to perform a binning which can deal with plateau effect, suddenly changes in distribution, etc.
- **Recoding in order to linearize the relation to the target** – Each modality is recoded to its relation to the target so that we can use them in linear regression algorithms.
- **Creation of additional dummy variables** – For nominal variables an additional dummy variable (flag) is created for each modality.
- **Missing value** – Depending of the re-coding schema, missing values can be treated in different ways. For PAKDD missing value is treated as a modality for all variables.

Modeling

The model has been created automatically by RANK, using most of default parameters. RANK builds a linear regression model, after automatic re-coding and linearization of the vector space. It automatically selects and prunes variables, in order to maximize the ROC surface (same measure as used for PAKDD to rank the results), and to improve model stability (no drop of the ROC among training, and validation sets). RANK loads all data in memory using a proprietary algorithm allowing gaining a factor between 5 to 10 in size compared to ASCII text file.

The variables selection has been done using a proprietary algorithm implementing a backward pruning. The algorithm uses cross-validation to evaluate the statistical relevance of a variable. In this run, we have used 5 folds for cross-validation. Because all data is in memory, RANK can compute many models per second.

Robustness and overfitting avoidance is done automatically by RANK using the following techniques:

- **Ridge Regression** – The algorithm uses a "Ridge Regression" technique. This technique introduced by Hoerl (Hoerl, 1970) and Andre Tikhonov (Tikhonov, 1977), and developed by M.J.L. Orr (Orr, 1995), add a regulation term to the normal equation.
- **Variables pruning** – The variables introducing noise and overfitting are dropped during the backward pruning process.
- **Systematic cross-validation** – The variable selection is done based on a 5 fold cross-validation which improves greatly the selection (Kohavi, 1995).
- **Bootstraps** – Bootstrap confidence intervals are computed for the test set in order to give an estimation of the model variance.

Evaluation

Evaluation on a statistical basis is automatically embedded in RANK's algorithms and its outputs.

To evaluate a model performance we usually observe the lift, which is quite similar to the ROC curve. It shows the percentage of customers

Figure 4. Performance of the model

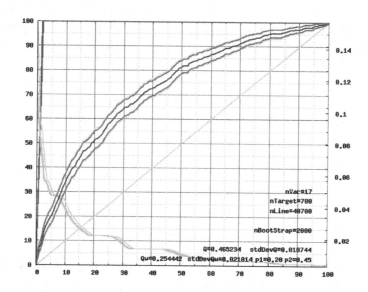

Figure 5. Importance of the variables

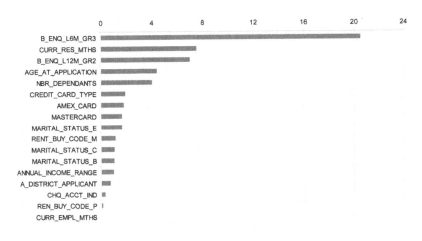

Figure 6. Variable weight

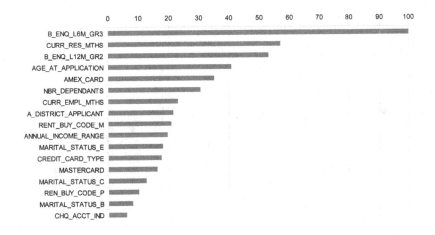

ranked by score against the percentage of target. It provides an easy interpretation: "if we take the top 10% of the population we will capture 35% of the target". The quality of the model is measured using the area under the lift curve. The graph on Figure 4 shows the lift (in dark blue) presented by the model on the modeling data set with a bootstrap confidence interval. The red curve shows the best lift we could obtain whereas the pink line gives the performance of a random model. The green curve represents the probability for a customer to take the product (with confidence interval). The quality of the model is 0.4652.

The final model is composed of 17 variables, which can be seen in the two graphs of Figure 5 and 6. We have basically two measures in order to evaluate the impact of the different variables:

• **The importance**: it indicates the lift percentage lost when a variable is removed.
• **The normalized weight**: this is simply the absolute normalized weight of the variables in the model.

In order to validate the model we looked at the variables distribution and relation to tar-

Figure 7.

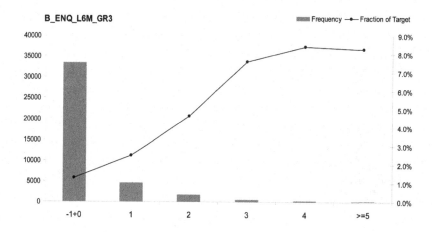

Figure 8.

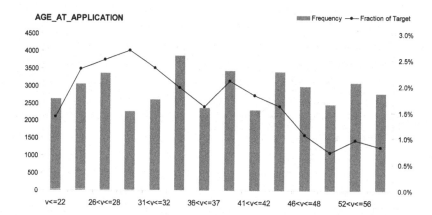

get. Here are the graphs of the most important variables:

- B_ENQ_L6M_GR3: Figure 7.
- AGE_AT_APPLICATION: Figure 8.
- MARITAL_STATUS: Figure 9.
- RENT_BUY_CODE: Figure 10.

The most important variables are B_ENQ_L6M, which indicates the number of times the customer came at an office for a mortgage loan, and CURR_RES_MTHS, which indicates the number of months the customer already spent at his current residence. These variables make a lot

of sense and let us think that the model is reliable. However, B_ENQ_L6M should be discussed with the company. Indeed, a customer who came at an office for a mortgage in the last 6 months might not present a great interest for company campaigns since he will probably come back himself or he has booked a mortgage meanwhile.

CONCLUSION

Our challenge was to benchmark our tool RANK against other teams and approaches to evaluate if our goal, having a tool that quickly builds good

Figure 9.

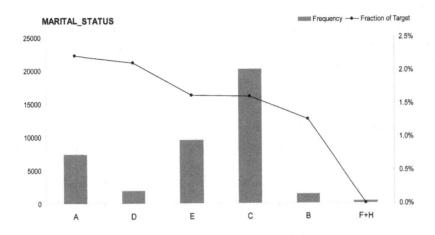

Figure 10.

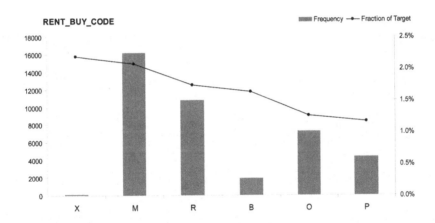

models, was achieved. We think the goal is met. Why RANK is able to get good results in just a few minutes? Because it embeds a methodology and processing steps reflecting many years of experience in modeling. However, one should not think that RANK solves the problem of making good models when one starts from a white page! By looking back at the methodological steps, we see that RANK helps only from the task "Audit". Before that, one must understand the business problem, do the specification, extract the data, and last but not least, understand how to design its models in order to really meet the business expectations. This is where "data mining projects" fails: even before you start the job of modeling. Of course, having a tool that implements best practices for modeling once the "business" side is properly done, helps a lot!

REFERENCES

Hoerl, A. E., & Kennard, R. W. (1970). Ridge regression: Biased estimation for nonorthogonal problems. *Technometrics*, *12*(3), 55–67. doi:10.2307/1267351

Kohavi, R. (1995). A study of cross-validation and bootstrap for accuracy estimation and model selection. *Proceedings of the Fourteenth International Joint Conference on Artificial Intelligence, 2*(12), 1137-1143. San Mateo: Morgan Kaufmann.

Tikhonov, A. N., & Arsenin, V. Y. (1977). *Solutions of Ill-Posed Problems*. Winston, Washington, Orr, M.J.L. (1995). Regularisation in the Selection of Radial Basis Function Centres. *Neural Computation, 7*(3), 606–623.

Chapter 21
Selecting Salient Features and Samples Simultaneously to Enhance Cross–Selling Model Performance

Dehong Qiu
Huazhong University of Science and Technology, China

Ye Wang
Huazhong University of Science and Technology, China

Qifeng Zhang
Huazhong University of Science and Technology, China

ABSTRACT

The task of the 2007 PAKDD competition was to help a finance company to build a cross-selling model to score the propensity of a credit card customer to take up a home loan. The present work tries to increase the prediction accuracy and enhance the model comprehensibility through efficiently selecting features and samples simultaneously. A new framework that coordinates feature selection and sample selection together is built. The criteria of optimal feature selection and the method of sample selection are designed. Experiments show that the new algorithm not only raises the value of the area under ROC curves, but also reveals more valuable business insights.

INTRODUCTION

The rapid growth in information science and technology has lead to generation of huge amount of valuable data in many areas. In finance for example, over the past five years, many banks have experienced exceptional growth in service and have built

up bank's Group Data Warehouse. In order to realize faster, more effective decisions and provide more excellent customer services, new technologies to handle or extract fully the latent knowledge within the data are urgently required. The finance company that donated the data for 2007 PAKDD competition would like to build a cross-selling model to predict the potential take-ups of cross-selling home loans to its credit card customers (Qiu, Wang & Bi, 2008).

DOI: 10.4018/978-1-60566-717-1.ch021

One critical issue in the building of cross-selling model is the processing of a huge amount of data having a high dimensionality. In the modeling dataset of 2007 PAKDD competition each sample is with 40 modeling feature variables and a categorical variable. Usually excessive features contain irrelevant or redundant features, which reduce the performance of data mining and increase computing costs. Feature selection, i.e., selecting an optimal subset of the features available for describing the data is an effective way to improve the performance of data mining (Hall, 2000; Peng, 2005). It has been proven in both theory and practice that there are many advantages of feature selection, such as the dimension reduction to reduce the computational cost, the improvement of predicative accuracy, and more interpretable business insights from the scoring cross-selling model.

Another problem in data mining is that the continued expansion of huge dataset contributes to the difficulty of obtaining a training sample set of good quality in appropriate size. The instances in huge dataset may come from a large variety of sources, be collected carefully or carelessly, be updated normally or not, satisfy the same distribution or not. In the modeling dataset of 2007 PAKDD competition, 40700 samples are provided, which come from a customer base of credit card customers as well as a customer base of home loan customers. The overlap between these two customer bases is very small. Obviously the training dataset is extremely class imbalanced, coming from different sources and may not satisfy the same distribution. In sample-based data mining, how well a predicting model eventually turns out depends heavily on the quality of training samples it receives. To use all training samples uniformly seems suboptimal. It is desirable to pick out training samples that are informative and representative for the final decision function.

Although there exists previous work addressing feature selection and sample selection respectively (Zadrozny, 2004; Liu, 2005; Huang, 2006; Zhang, 2008), there is relatively fewer work on combining them together into processing. In this paper, we first build up the criteria of feature selection and negative sample selection respectively, and then a uniform framework is build to select optimal features and informative samples efficiently and simultaneously. The remainder of this paper is organized as follows. Section 2 describes the problem of feature selection and sample selection respectively. In section 3, we set up the criteria for feature selection. Negative sample selection method is explained in section 4. In section 5, we propose a new framework that realizes feature selection and sample selection simultaneously and efficiently. Section 6 contains an empirical study of the new algorithm on the 2007 PAKDD competition dataset. Section 7 concludes this work.

PROBLEM DESCRIPTION

Feature Selection

Consider a given training set, in which an instance is typically described as $Z = [(x_1, x_2, \cdots x_N), c]$, where $(x_1, x_2, \cdots x_N)$ is one possible value of the vector $(X_1, X_2, \cdots X_N)$ with N features and c is one possible class of the categorical label C. Each sample in the dataset of 2007 PAKDD competition has 40 features. Feature selection is a process that selects a subset from the original features and ignoring others not in this set before applying data mining. The optimality of a feature subset is measured by an evaluation criterion. It is reasonable to believe that for a given problem under the same evaluation criterion, there may be several optimal feature subsets, as shown by figure 1. The entire feature set can be conceptually divided into several optimal feature subsets, an irrelevant feature set and a redundant feature set.

As one of the most important techniques in data preprocessing for data mining, feature selection has received lots of attentions as data mining is

Figure 1. Feature subset

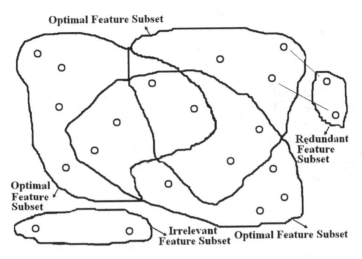

widely applied to many fields. According to the evaluation criteria, algorithms used for selecting features fall into two categories: the filter framework and the wrapper framework (Yu, 2003; Liu, 2005). The former relies on general characteristics of the data to evaluate and selects the optimal feature subset without involving any data mining algorithm, while the latter wraps a data mining algorithm into the procession of feature selection, whose performance is used as the evaluation criterion to select the optimal feature subset. Some researchers have attempted to take advantage of the two models by exploiting their different evaluation criteria in different search stages, resulted the hybrid framework.

Sample Selection

Given a set of M training samples, the data mining algorithm would require large memory and enormous amounts of training time when M is large. Sample selection is to select a subset of training examples to reduce the training set size and meanwhile to maintain the generalization performance of data mining algorithm. The training dataset of 2007 PAKDD competition contains 40700 samples, 40000 samples with categorical value of 0 and 700 samples with categorical value of 1. The training dataset is large and extremely class imbalanced. It is reasonable to imagine that the distribution of samples with class label 1, if compared with the distribution of samples with class label 0, would be very similar like some 'positive' mould just grows on large 'negative' bread, as figure 2(a) shows. In the literature (Qiu, Wang & Bi, 2008), the problem of large and class imbalance dataset was dealt with by a mix-resampling method. In this paper, we investigate a different approach to handling skewed class distribution. This approach selects a subset of negative instances from the training dataset, meanwhile keeps all positive instances as they are important and informative. The selected negative samples would be more representative and informative, as described by figure 2(b). The reduction of negative instances will not only reduce the training cost, but also improve the quality of training dataset.

There has been considerable research on sample selection. Heuristic approaches and active learning are two typical approaches to selecting samples. Heuristic approaches to selecting samples with an initial training set and add new training samples to the training set using heuristic method. For example in the literature (Qiu, Wang, Chen & Fang, 2008), training samples were selected

Figure 2. (a) Before sample selection; (b) After sample selection

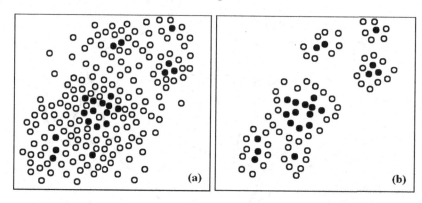

according to categorical sensitivity. In the literature (Koggalage, 2004), k-means clustering was employed to select samples from the training set. Random sampling (Qiu, Wang & Bi, 2008) was used to choose a subset of training samples. Active learning sample selection (Melville, 2005) starts with zero training samples. Input samples are selected according to quantitative criteria and be added to the training set to train the learner. The input samples continue to be added to the training set until the classifier is well trained.

CRITERION OF FEATURE SELECTION

In this section, we describe how to select the good features from the original 2007 PAKDD competition dataset. The good features are those that are relevant to the class label but are not redundant to any of the other relevant features. Therefore, the features are selected based on their relevance and redundancy to the class label.

Feature Relevance

Given a dataset of M samples, each sample is typically represented by a set of N features $X = (X_1, \cdots, X_N)$ and a class label C. Let $S_i = \left\{ X_1, \cdots, X_{i-1}, X_{i+1}, \cdots X_N \right\}$ be a feature set

containing all features of X except the feature X_i, $S_i' \subseteq S_i$ is a subset of S_i. Let s_i' be a possible value of S_i', x_i be a possible value of X_i and c_j be a possible class of C. X_i is a relevant feature if $p \left(X_i = x_i, S_i' = s_i' \right) > 0$ and there exists $\delta > 0$, satisfying

1) $\left| p \left(C = c_j \mid X_i = x_i \right) - p \left(C = c_j \right) \right| > \delta$,

and

2) $\left| p \left(C = c_j \mid X_i = x_i, S_i' = s_i' \right) - p \left(C = c_j \mid S_i' = s_i' \right) \right| > \delta$

If the feature X_i is relevant to the class and it is discrete and has possible K values $x_{i1}, \cdots, x_{iK}$, the relevance of feature X_i to the class label C could be defined by

$$rel \left(C \mid X_i \right) = \sum_{k=1}^{K} p \left(x_{ik} \right) \cdot \left\{ D \left(C \mid x_{ik} \right) \right\}^{\alpha}$$

where:

$\alpha \geq 1$,

$$D \left(C \mid x_{ik} \right) = \frac{\sum_{l=1}^{L} p^2 \left(c_l \mid x_{ik} \right)}{K} - \left(\frac{\sum_{l=1}^{L} p \left(c_l \mid x_{ik} \right)}{K} \right)^2$$

which measures the conditional unbalance of a class label C given a feature assignment x_{ik}. L is the number of class labels.

According to the definition of feature relevance, the features that are relevant to the class label stronger than a threshold could be picked out and simultaneously those are irrelevant to the class label could be removed. A feature X_i is an irrelevant feature, if the two equations below are satisfied.

1) $rel(C \mid X_i) = (D(C))^\alpha$
2) $rel(C \mid S_i', X_i) = rel(C \mid S_i')$

Feature Redundancy

Feature redundancy is measured based on the information-theoretical concept of entropy. For a pair of variables (X, C), the entropy of X is defined as

$$H(X) = -\sum_i p(x_i) \log_2(p(x_i))$$

where $p(x_i)$ is the prior probabilities for all values of X.

After observing the values of C, the entropy of X is defined as

$$H(X \mid C) = -\sum_l p(c_l) \sum_i p(x_i \mid c_l) \log_2(p(x_i \mid c_l))$$

where $p(x_i \mid c_l)$ is the posterior probabilities of X given the values of C.

Therefore, given the feature subset S_i', the conditional entropy of class variable C is $H(C \mid S_i')$; given the feature subset $S_i' \cup X_i$, the conditional entropy of class variable C is $H(C \mid S_i', X_i)$. The feature X_i is redundant to S_i' if the equation below is satisfied.

$$H(C \mid S_i', X_i) = H(C \mid S_i')$$

THE METHOD OF SAMPLE SELECTION

There has a large pool of negative training samples in the dataset of 2007 PAKDD competition. In this section, we describe the method that is used to select the representative and useful negative training samples. These more informative negative samples would not only enhance the performance of data mining model, but also reduce the cost of computing.

For each of negative training example Z_i^- (the upper mark '-' means the sample is a negative sample), we calculate its distance from each of the positive training sample. These distances are saved by a set named $Dis(Z_i^-)$. Obviously, the negative samples that are much far away from all positive training samples should be no useful in training. Meanwhile, the negative samples that are nearly overlapped on positive training sample should also be no useful in training, as they would worsen the generalization capability of data mining model. So we select the negative training samples satisfying the below criterion,

$$\lambda \leq \min(Dis(Z_i^-)) \leq \eta$$

where λ and η are the up and below threshold respectively.

Even after selecting negative samples according to the criterion $\lambda \leq \min(Dis(Z_i^-)) \leq \eta$, the problem of class imbalance is possibly still worse. So we select the negative samples once more time. Around each negative training example Z_i^-, we draw a sphere that is as large as possible without covering a positive training example and count the number of negative training examples that fall inside the sphere. The number is detonated by $N(Z_i^-)$. The larger the number $N(Z_i^-)$, the more negative training examples will be scattered around Z_i^-, the less likely Z_i^- will be representative. We sort the negative training samples according to the corresponding value of $N(Z_i^-)$ and choose a subset of them as the reduced negative training set that satisfied the criterion below

$$N(Z_i^-) \leq \omega$$

where ω is a selected threshold.

ALGORITHM COORDINATING FEATURE SELECTION AND SAMPLE SELECTION

Customarily, feature selection and sample selection have been treated as two different problems and been carried out separately. Here we coordinate feature selection and sample selection into a new framework to find the optimal subset of features and the optimal subset of training samples simultaneously. The new framework coordinating feature selection and sample selection is shown in figure 3, which composes of the following main steps: sorting the features according to their relevance to class label, removing irrelevant and redundant features, and then selecting the training samples. The candidate training subset with an optimal feature subset is evaluated and compared with the previous best one according to data mining model. If the new subset turns out to be better, it replaces the previous best subset. Otherwise, new set of threshold parameters is set and one more time of feature and sample selection and evaluation happens. The process is repeated until the iteration time is reached. The advantage of the new framework over the traditional framework lies in that the optimal subset of features and training samples can be obtained simultaneously and therefore it is possible to improve the performance of cross-selling model by the greatest extent.

The detailed procedure of the algorithm based on the new freamwork is summarized in Figure 4.

EXPERIMENT

In this section, we empirically evaluate the effectiveness of the algorithm in last section on the dataset of 2007 PAKDD competition and compare with the results in the literature (Qiu, Wang & Bi, 2008). In the modeling dataset there are 40700 samples with 40 modeling variables and a categorical variable. The categorical variable "Target_Flag" has a value of 1 if the customer opened a home loan with the company within 12 months after opening the credit card, and has a value of 0 if otherwise. A prediction dataset of 8,000 samples with the same 40 variables but without categorical variable is also provided. We are required to find each customer's propensity to purchase the cross selling home loan product. The accuracy of the results will be evaluated in terms of the area under ROC curves (AUC).

Through setting appropriate thresholds, the number of the negative samples we selected and used in training is about 4000, the number of the positive samples that were obtained through the over-sampling method in our previous work (Qiu, Wang & Bi, 2008) is about 3200. The number of selected optimal features is 12. For different thresholds, the AUC values obtained in cross-validate experiment are in the range of 0.674~0.71. Figure 5 shows the two ROC curves with the corresponding AUC value of 0.71 and 0.674 respectively by solid line. Meanwhile, the ROC curves with the maximum and minimum value of AUC respectively in the literature (Qiu, Wang & Bi, 2008) are also shown by dot line. It is easy to observe that the AUC value obtained through the new algorithm is better than that obtained through the old method.

Besides raising the AUC value, the new algorithm reveals useful business insights for cross-selling problem more directly and evidently after feature selection. The feature B_ENQ_L6M_GR3, CURR_RES_MTHS, AGE_AT_APPLICATION, B_ENQ_ L6M_GR2, B_ENQ_L12M_GR2, ANNUAL_INCOME_RANGE and CUR-

Figure 3. The framework coordinating feature selection and sample selection

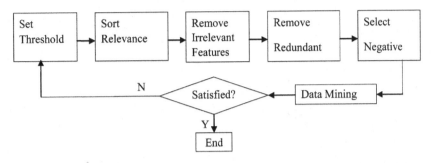

Figure 4.

> **Input:** Training set of M samples $Z_1, \cdots, Z_m$ and the iteration time T
>
> 1.   For t=1 to T do
> 2.   SetThreshold($\delta, \beta, \gamma, \lambda, \eta, \omega$)
> 3.   For n=1 to N
> 4.   Calculate $r_n = (rel(C \mid X_n) - (D(C))^\alpha)/(1 - (D(C))^\alpha)$;
> 5.   If $r_n < \delta$
> 6.   Remove the feature X_n from Z;
> 7. $Z \rightarrow Z'$;
> 8.   End
> 9.   End
> 10.   Let N' be the number of features of Z'
> 11.   For i=1 to N'
> 12.   For j=i+1 to N'
> 13.   If $(rel(C \mid X_i, X_j) - (D(C))^\alpha)/(1 - (D(C))^\alpha) < \beta$ and
>
> $(rel(C \mid X_i, X_j) - (D(C))^\alpha)/(rel(C \mid X_i) - (D(C))^\alpha) < \gamma$
>
> 14.   Remove the feature X_j from Z';
> 15. $Z' \rightarrow Z''$;
> 16.   End
> 17.   End
> 18.   End
> 19.   For m=1 to M
> 20.   If $\lambda \le \min(Dis(Z_m^{''})) \le \eta$ and $N(Z_m^{''}) \le \omega$
> 21.   Remove the sample $Z_m^{''}$ from Z'';
> 22. $Z'' \rightarrow Z'''$;
> 23.   End
> 24.   End
> 25. $P_t = CVHC(Z''')$; //Call the Cross-Validated Hybrid Classifier (CVHC)
>   in the literature (Qiu, Wang & Bi, 2008)
>
> 26. End
> 27. P

Figure 5. The ROC curves

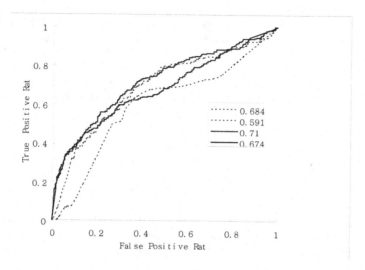

RENT_EMPL_MTHS are the most important attributes to predict potential customers. The feature B_ENQ_L6M_GR3 is especially effective attribute. If an instance's value of this attribute is bigger than 0, the instance is much likely to be a positive one. This means that a customer who has enquired about the mortgage at the bureau is muck likely to be a potential home buyer. An instance with the CURR_RES_MTH smaller than 30 months is likely to be a potential customer. This means a person who has lived in his or her current house no longer than two and a half years is more likely to be a mortgage buyer. The experimental results also tell us that an instance with the feature B_ENQ_GR2 bigger than 0 or the feature CURR_EMPL_MTHS smaller than 2 years is more likely to be a positive one, which means that a person who enquires for the loan or has not worked very long at current job is more likely to be a mortgage buyer. Besides, experimental results also show that people with higher annual income are more inclined to be a potential customer.

CONCLUSION

In this paper, we propose a new algorithm which coordinates feature selection and sample selection into a framework simultaneously to deal with the cross-selling problem of 2007 PAKDD competition. The new algorithm has shown very effective not only in removing irrelevant and redundant features and selecting more representative training samples, but also in increasing the accuracy of predicting potential home loan buyer and enhancing the comprehensibility of cross-selling model. The AUC value of the new algorithm is raised into the range of 0.674~0.71 comparing with that of 0.591~0.684 of our previous method. More valuable business insights are also obtained from the new cross-selling model.

REFERENCES

Hall, M. (2000). Correlation-based feature selection for discrete and numeric class machine learning. In *Proceedings of the Seventeenth International Conference on Machine Learning* (pp. 359-366).

Huang, J. Y., Smola, A. J., Gretton, A., Borgwardt, K. M., & Schölkopf, B. (2006). Correcting sample selection bias by unlabeled data. In *Proceedings of 20th Annual Conference on Neural Information Processing Systems* (pp. 601-608).

Koggalage, R., & Halgamuge, S. (2004). Reducing the number of training samples for fast support vector machine classification. *Neural Information Processing-Letters and Reviews*, 2(3), 57–65.

Liu, H., & Yu, L. (2005). Toward integrating feature selection algorithms for classification and clustering. *IEEE Transactions on Knowledge and Data Engineering*, 17(4), 491–502. doi:10.1109/TKDE.2005.66

Melville, P., Yang, S. M., Saar-Tsechansky, M., & Mooney, R. J. (2005). Active learning for probability estimation using Jensen-Shannon divergence. In *Proceedings of the 16th European Conference on Machine Learning* (pp. 268-279).

Peng, H. C., Long, F. H., & Ding, C. (2005). Feature selection based on mutual information: criteria of max-dependency, max-relevance, and min-redundancy. *IEEE Transactions on Pattern Analysis and Machine Intelligence*, 27(8), 1226–1238. doi:10.1109/TPAMI.2005.159

Qiu, D. H., Wang, Y., & Bi, B. (2008). Identify cross-selling opportunities via hybrid classifier. *International Journal of Data Warehousing and Mining*, 4(2), 55–62.

Qiu, D. H., Wang, Y., Chen, C. B., & Fang, S. H. (2008). Sample selection according to categorical sensitivity for building cross-sell model. *International of Computational Systems*, 4(2), 583–588.

Yu, L., & Liu, H. (2003). Feature selection for high-dimensional data: a fast correlation-based filter solution. In *Proceedings of the twentieth International Conference on Machine Learning* (pp. 856–863).

Zadrozny, B. (2004). Learning and evaluating classifiers under sample selection bias. In *Proceedings of the 21st International Conference on Machine Learning* (pp. 144-151).

Zhang, D. Q., Chen, S. C., & Zhou, Z. H. (2008). Constraint score: a new filter method for feature selection with pairwise constraints. *Pattern Recognition*, 41(5), 1440–1451. doi:10.1016/j.patcog,2007.10.009

Chapter 22
Classification of Imbalanced Data with Random Sets and Mean–Variance Filtering

Vladimir Nikulin
Suncorp, Australia

ABSTRACT

Imbalanced data represent a significant problem because the corresponding classifier has a tendency to ignore patterns which have smaller representation in the training set. We propose to consider a large number of balanced training subsets where representatives from the larger pattern are selected randomly. As an outcome, the system will produce a matrix of linear regression coefficients where rows represent random subsets and columns represent features. Based on the above matrix we make an assessment of the stability of the influence of the particular features. It is proposed to keep in the model only features with stable influence. The final model represents an average of the single models, which are not necessarily a linear regression. The above model had proven to be efficient and competitive during the PAKDD-2007 Data Mining Competition.

INTRODUCTION

We consider a standard binary classification applied to strongly imbalanced training data where we assume without loss of generality that a "positive" class represents a minority.

Ideally, our target is to find a transformation from a multidimensional space of features to one-dimensional Euclidean space in order to maximize the difference between different classes and minimize volatility inside classes (Huber, 1985).

Our approach was motivated by Breiman (1996, 2001) and represents a compromise between two major tendencies. On the one hand, we would like to deal with balanced data. On the other hand, we are interested in exploiting all available information. Respectively, we consider a large number n of balanced subsets of available data where any single subset includes two parts 1) all "positive" instances and 2) randomly selected "negative" instances.

Linear regression represents the simplest example of decision function. Combined with quadratic loss function, it has an essential advantage: using gradient-based search procedures, we can optimise the value of the step size. Consequently, we will observe rapid decline of the target function (Hastie, Tibshirani, & Friedman, 2001).

However, squared loss function excessively penalizes large values of the decision functions. In order to overcome this problem we can apply a generalised linear model with exponential loss function. Boosting algorithms (Friedman, Hastie, & Tibshirani, 2000) may be efficient in order to facilitate optimisation procedure. Furthermore, it appears to be natural to link any boosting iteration with randomly selected balanced subset.

By definition, regression coefficients may be regarded as natural measurements of influence of the corresponding features. In our case, we have n vectors of regression coefficients, and can investigate stability of the particular coefficients.

Feature selection problem is very important (Guyon, Weston, Barnhill, & Vapnik, 2002) in order to reduce overfitting. We remove features with unstable coefficients, and recompute classifiers. Note that stability of the coefficients may be measured using different methods. For example, we can apply t-statistic as a ratio of mean to standard deviation.

Clearly, selection of a linear regression as a base model is not necessary. Based on cross-validation experiments, we can apply another model such as decision trees, random forests or neural networks. The list of options is not limited and may be continued further (Guyon, Alamdari, Dror, & Buhmann, 2006). By definition, the final decision function represents a sample average of single decision functions.

The proposed approach is general and flexible. We cannot expect that a single algorithm will work optimally on all conceivable applications and, therefore, an opportunity of tuning and tailoring is very essential.

Experiments were conducted during the time of the PAKDD-2007 Data Mining Competition using real-world data, which were provided by a consumer finance company, with the aim of finding better solutions for a cross-selling problem. The data are strongly imbalanced, with a significantly smaller proportion of positive cases, which have the following practical interpretation: a customer opened a home loan with the company within 12 months after opening the credit card.

MODELING TECHNIQUE

Let $X = (x_t, y_t)$, $t = 1..m$, be a training sample of observations where $x_t \in R^\ell$ is a vector of features, and y_t is binary label: $y_t \in \{0, 1\}$.

In a practical situation, the label y_t may be hidden, and the task is to estimate it using a vector of features. Let us consider the most simple linear decision function

$$u_t = u(x_t) = \sum_{j=0}^{\ell} w_j \cdot x_{tj}, \qquad (1)$$

where x_{t0} is a constant term.

We can define the decision rule as a function of decision function and threshold parameter

$$f_t = f(u_t, \Delta) = \begin{cases} 1 & if \quad u_t \geq \Delta; \\ -1, & otherwise. \end{cases} \qquad (2)$$

We used the area under *ROC* curve (*AUC*) as an evaluation criterion. By definition, Receiver Operating Curve (*ROC*) is a graphical plot of True Positive Rates (*TPR*) against False Positive Rates (*FPR*) (see Figure 2(a, b)).

According to the proposed method, we consider large numbers of classifiers where any particular classifier is based on a relatively balanced subset with all "positive" and randomly selected (without replacement) "negative" data. The final decision function (*d.f.*) has a form of logistic average of the single decision functions.

Definition 1. *We call the above subsets as random sets RS(α, β, n) where α is a number of positive cases, β is a number of negative cases and n is the total number of random sets.*

This model includes two very important regulation parameters: 1) *n*, and 2)

$$q = \frac{\alpha}{\beta} \leq 1$$

-proportion of positive cases, where *n* must be big enough, and *q* cannot be too small.

We consider *n* subsets of *X* with α positive and $\beta = k \cdot \alpha$ negative data-instances where $k \geq 1$, $q = \frac{1}{k}$. Using gradient-based optimization (Nikulin, 2006b) we can compute the matrix of linear regression coefficients:

$$W = \{w_{ij}, i = 1..n, j = 1..\ell\}.$$

The mean-variance filtering (*MVF*) technique was introduced in Nikulin (2006a, 2006b), and may be efficient in order to reduce overfitting. Using the following ratios, we can measure the consistency of contributions of the particular features

$$r_j = \frac{|\mu_j|}{s_j}, j = 1..\ell, \qquad (3)$$

where μ_j and s_j are mean and standard deviation corresponding to the *j*-column of the matrix *W* (see Figure 1).

Low value of r_j indicates that influence of *j*-feature is not stable. Respectively, we conducted feature selection according to the condition:

$$r_j \geq \gamma > 0.$$

The final decision function (d.f.)

$$f_t = \frac{1}{n} \sum_{i=1}^{n} \frac{\exp\{\tau \cdot u_{ti}\}}{1 + \exp\{\tau \cdot u_{ti}\}}, \quad \tau > 0, \qquad (4)$$

was calculated as a logistic average of single decision functions

$$u_{ti} = \sum_{j=0}^{\ell} w_{ij} \cdot x_{tj},$$

where regression coefficients *w* were recomputed after feature reduction.

Remark 1. *We can expect that performance of the classifier will be improved if we will use in (4) nonlinear functions such as decision trees.*

Decision Trees

Decision Trees is a nonparametric tool of discriminant analysis, which is designed to represent decision rules in a form of so-called binary trees. Binary trees split training data imposing univariate linear restrictions and represent resulting clusters hierarchically starting from the root node for the whole training sample itself and ending with relatively homogenous small groups of observations. For each terminal node forecasted, value is assigned, and hence the resulting tree structure can be interpreted as a decision rule (Breiman, Freidman, Olshen, & Stone, 1984).

More specifically, we define a criterion in order to split R^ℓ-space into *m* Voronoi-regions V_i, *i* = 1 ...*m*, without intersection. Let us denote by $S_i = V_i \cup X$ the corresponding clusters. Assuming that clusters S_i are sufficiently large in order to ensure a proper level of confidence, we form the decision function:

$$u_t = u(x_t) = \sum_{i=1}^{m} \tilde{y}_i \cdot I\{x_t \in V_i\}, \quad \tilde{y}_i =$$

$$\frac{1}{\#S_i} \sum \{y_t \mid x_t \in S_i\}$$

where $I\{A\}$ is an indicator of the event A, and $\sum\{x \mid A\}$ sum of the elements x subject to the condition A.

We can apply *Gini* index in order to measure uniformity of any subset S

$$Gini(S) = 2 \cdot \tilde{y} \cdot (1 - \tilde{y}), \quad \tilde{y} =$$

$$\frac{1}{\#S} \sum \{y_t \mid x_t \in S\}.$$

Considering node S as a starting point we can continue construction of the tree deeper using feature j, which must be selected in order to maximize the following difference

$$Gini(S) - p \cdot Gini(S_L) - (1 - p) \cdot$$

$$Gini(S_R) \geq 0, \quad p = \frac{\#S_L}{\#S},$$

where $S = S_L \cup S_R, S_L \cap S_R = \varnothing$.

Note that two top performing submissions (NN 49 and 88) were produced using TreeNet from Salford Systems. A TreeNet model normally consists of from several hundred to several thousand small trees, each typically containing about six terminal nodes (see Figures 4-5). Each tree is devoted to contributing (or boosting) a small portion of the overall model and the final model prediction is constructed by adding up all of the individual tree contributions (Friedman, 1999a, 1999b). In the following section, we consider how boosting and *RS* may benefit each other.

BOOSTING ALGORITHMS

Boosting works by sequentially applying a classification algorithm to reweighted versions of the training data, and then taking a weighted majority vote of the sequence of classifiers thus produced. For many classification algorithms, this simple strategy results in dramatic improvements in performance.

An Exponential Criterion

The motivation in support of exponential target function is very simple and clear. Let us compare squared and exponential loss functions:

$$(y_t - u_t)^2; \tag{5a}$$

$$\exp\{-y_t \cdot u_t\}, \tag{5b}$$

using two data instances *{1, -1}* and *{1, 4}* where first and second values correspond to the label and decision function. The first example represents a misclassification, and exponential loss function (5b) detects this misclassification correctly in difference to the squared loss function (5a):

	{1,-1}	{1, 4}
squared	4	9
exponential	7.3891	0.0183

Similar to the Logit model (Nikulin, 2006b), we can not optimize step-size in the case of exponential target function. Respectively, we will need to maintain low value of the step-size in order to ensure stability of the algorithm. As a consequence, the whole optimization process may be very slow and time-consuming. Freund and Schapire (1997) introduced the following AdaBoost Algorithm in order to facilitate the optimization process.

AdaBoost ALGORITHM

Let us consider minimizing the criterion (Friedman et al., 2000)

$$\sum_{t=1}^{n} \xi(x_t, y_t) \cdot \exp(-y_t \cdot u(x_t)), \tag{6}$$

where

$$\xi(x_t, y_t) := \exp(-y_t \cdot F(x_t)). \tag{7}$$

We shall assume that initial values of $F(x_t)$ are set to zero.

The following Taylor-approximation is valid under assumption that values of $u(x_t)$ are small

$$\exp(-y_t \cdot u(x_t)) \approx \frac{1}{2}\left[(y_t - u(x_t))^2 + 1\right]. \qquad (8)$$

Therefore, we can apply quadratic-minimisation (QM) model in order to minimize (6). Then, we optimize value of the threshold parameter Δ for u_t, and find the corresponding decision rule $f_t \in \{-1, +1\}$.

Next, we will return to (6)

$$\sum \xi(x_t, y_t) \cdot \exp(-c \cdot y_t \cdot f(x_t)) \qquad (9)$$

where optimal value of the parameter c may be easily found

$$c = \frac{1}{2}\log(\frac{A}{B}), \qquad (10)$$

where

$$A = \sum \{\xi(x_t, y_t) \mid y_t = f(x_t)\},$$
$$B = \sum \{\xi(x_t, y_t) \mid y_t \neq f(x_t)\}.$$

Finally (for the current boosting iteration), we update function F:

$$F_{new}(x_t) \leftarrow F(x_t) + c \cdot f(x_t), \qquad (11)$$

and recompute weight coefficients ξ according to (7).

Remark 2. *Considering test dataset (labels are not available), we will not be able to optimize the value of the threshold parameter Δ. Respectively, we can use either an average (predicted) value of Δ in order to transform decision function into decision rule, or we can apply direct update:*

$$F_{new}(x_t) \leftarrow F(x_t) + c \cdot u(x_t), \qquad (12)$$

where value of the parameter $c \leq 1$ must be small enough in order to ensure stability of the algorithm.

Remark 3. *Boosting with RS represents a natural linkage, and it is proposed to apply any particular boosting iteration to the randomly selected balanced subset.*

LogitBoost Algorithm

Let us parameterize the binomial probabilities by

$$p(x_t) = \frac{\exp(2 \cdot F(x_t))}{1 + \exp(2 \cdot F(x_t))}.$$

The binomial log-likelihood is

$$y_t \cdot \log(p(x_t)) + (1 - y_t) \cdot \log(1 - p(x_t)) =$$
$$-\log(1 + \exp(-2 \cdot (2y_t - 1) \cdot F(x_t))). \qquad (13)$$

The following relation is valid

$$\exp(-2 \cdot (2y_t - 1) \cdot F(x_t)) = \xi(x_t)z_t^2, \qquad (14)$$

where

$$z_t = \frac{y_t - p(x_t)}{\xi(x_t)}, \quad \xi(x_t) = p(x_t)(1 - p(x_t)).$$

We can maximize (13) using method with Newton's step, which is based on the matrix of second derivatives (Nikulin, 2006b). As an alternative, we can consider the standard weighted QM-model:

$$\sum_{t=1}^{n} \xi(x_t)(z_t - u_t)^2. \qquad (15)$$

After solution $u(x_t)$ was found, we update function $p(x_t)$

$$p(x_t) \leftarrow \begin{cases} 1 & if \quad h_t \geq 1; \\ h_t & if \quad 0 < h_t < 1; \\ 0 & if \quad h_t \leq 0 \end{cases} \tag{16}$$

where $h_t = p(x_t) + \xi(x_t)u(x_t)$, Then, we recompute weight coefficients ξ, and return to the minimization criterion (15).

Let us consider an update of function F assuming that $0 < h_t < 1$. By definition,

$$F_{new}(x_t) = \frac{1}{2}\log(\frac{h_t}{1+h_t}) = \frac{1}{2}\log(\frac{p(x_t)}{1+p(x_t)}) +$$
$$\frac{1}{2}\log(1 + \frac{u(x_t)}{1-p(x_t)u(x_t)})$$
$$\approx F(x_t) + \nu \cdot u(x_t), \quad \nu = 0.5. \tag{17}$$

Remark 4. *Boosting trick (similar to the well-known kernel trick): as an alternative to QM-solution, we can apply in (12) or (17) decision function, which was produced by another method, for example, Naïve Bayes or Decision Trees (Lutz, 2006).*

Remark 5 *Approximation (17) coincides with the update formula of Friedman et al. (2000), and is valid under condition that value of $u(x_t)$ is small enough. Lutz (2006) suggests careful approach with the following range $0.1 \leq \nu \leq 0.3$ depending on the particular dataset. Also, it appears to be reasonable (Friedman et al., 2000) to restrict values of z_t in (15).*

LogitBoost2 Algorithm

Let us consider logit target function

$$L(w) = \sum_{t=1}^{n}(y_t - \varphi(u_t))^2, \quad \varphi(u) = \tanh(u). \tag{18}$$

The above target function appears to be more natural when comparing with squared loss, but (again as in the case of exponential loss function)

we cannot find an optimal value of the step-size in analytical form. Respectively, we will need to maintain low value of the step-size in order to ensure stability of the gradient-based algorithm.

The following simple boosting procedure may be efficient in order to facilitate optimization process. Essentially, the procedure includes 2 steps (NN2-3):

1:   Set initial values:
$j = 0, \quad z_t^{(j)} = y_t \quad and \quad p^{(j)}(x_t) = 0, \quad t = 1..n$;

2:   find solution of the standard QM-problem
$$L(w) = \sum_{t=1}^{n}\left(z_t^{(j)} - u_t^{(j)}\right)^2 \tag{19}$$

where j is a sequential number of iteration;

3:   recompute the target function

$$z_t^{(j+1)} = y_t - p^{(j+1)}(x_t),$$
$$p^{(j+1)}(x_t) \leftarrow \begin{cases} 1 & if \quad p^{(j)}(x_t) + u_t^{(j)} \geq 1; \\ p^{(j)}(x_t) + u_t^{(j)} & if \quad -1 < p^{(j)}(x_t) + u_t^{(j)} < 1; \\ -1 & if \quad p^{(j)}(x_t) + u_t^{(j)} \leq -1. \end{cases} \tag{20}$$

4:   $j \leftarrow j + 1$ and go to step 2.

Repeat K times above steps 2-4 and use $p^{(K)}(x_t)$ as a decision function.

Experience-Innovation Approach

The motivation for the *EI*-approach is very simple: assuming that overfitting is limited, we would be interested in improving training results under expectation that the corresponding test results will be better as well. This target may be pursued by the natural approach: we propose to increase attention to the misclassified patterns, and we can employ here two main methods: 1) increase weights (Algorithm 1), or 2) increase absolute values of the corresponding target functions (Algorithm 2).

Table 1. Results of the PAKDD-2007 Data-Mining Competition including Committee of Experts (CE) results (4th and 8th columns)

1	P049	0.7001	0.700164	25	P079	0.6528	0.704566
2	P085	0.6999	0.701932	26	P014	0.6453	0.70447
3	P212	0.6962	0.703745	27	P157	0.6445	0.704193
4	P054	0.6961	0.705702	28	P093	0.6426	0.702501
5	P088	0.6942	0.706291	29	P023	0.6395	0.702573
6	P248	0.6928	0.706095	30	P242	0.6357	0.702334
7	P134	0.6914	0.707132	31	P169	0.6273	0.70188
8	P126	0.691	0.70723	32	P125	0.6269	0.701949
9	P227	0.6885	**0.707231**	33	P135	0.6218	0.701566
10	P178	0.6869	0.707143	34	P220	0.611	0.701331
11	P249	0.6858	0.70551	35	P060	0.6037	0.701774
12	P056	0.6854	0.705428	36	P202	0.5926	0.700222
13	P041	0.6828	0.705707	37	P028	0.564	0.700332
14	P021	0.6804	0.705287	38	P160	0.5593	0.698843
15	P148	0.6802	0.704546	39	P251	0.5516	0.697067
16	P116	0.6758	0.704443	40	P080	0.551	0.697181
17	P149	0.6756	0.70355	41	P247	0.5243	0.697135
18	P083	0.6754	0.703332	42	P225	0.5226	0.696725
19	P172	0.675	0.703601	43	P123	0.5224	0.696157
20	P078	0.6671	0.702556	44	P128	0.5006	0.696373
21	P104	0.6636	0.701723	45	P071	0.4988	0.69641
22	P106	0.6595	0.704733	46	P211	0.4929	0.696172
23	P073	0.6569	0.704782	47	P216	0.4773	0.695359
24	P198	0.6542	0.70458				

Algorithm 1. EI-Boosting for the weight coefficients

1. Set initial weights $\xi^{(0)} = \xi$ as uniform.
2. Set initial value of optimal AUC $Q_0 = 0$, and
3. select values of parameters $\alpha > 1$ and $0 < \beta < 1$.
4. Repeat for $k = 1..K$ the following steps 5-7:
5. Evaluate QM model, and compute the corresponding value of AUC Q.
6. Make update $Q_0 = 0$, $\xi^{(0)} = \xi$ *if* $Q > Q_0$.
7. Boost misclassified patterns with probability β
   $\xi_t := \xi_t^{(0)} \cdot \alpha$ *if* $f_t \cdot y_t = -1$
8. Based on the above experiment select the optimal value of K.

Algorithm 2. EI-Boosting for the target function

1:	Set initial values of target function $z_t^{(0)} = z_t = y_t$, $t = 1..n$.
2:	Set initial value of optimal *AUC* $Q_0 = 0$, and
3:	select values of parameters $\alpha > 1$ and $0 < \beta < 1$.
4:	Repeat for $k = 1..K$ the following steps 5-7:
5:	Evaluate *QM* model, and compute the corresponding value of *AUC Q*.
6:	Make update $Q_0 = 0$, $z_t^{(0)} = z_t$, if $Q > Q_0$.
7:	Boost misclassified patterns with probability β. $z_t = z_t^{(0)} \cdot \alpha$ *iff* $f_t \cdot y_t = -1$
8:	Based on the above experiment select the optimal value of *K*.

EXPERIMENTAL RESULTS

Data Preparation

The given data includes two sets: 1) training-set with *700* positive and *40,000* negative instances, and 2) test-set with *8,000* instances. Any data-instance represents a vector of *40* continuous or categorical features. Using standard technique, we reduced categorical features to the numerical (dummy) values. Also, we normalized continuous values to the range *[0, 1]*. As a result of the above transformation we created totally numerical dataset with $\ell = 101$ features.

Simulation Results

Initial simulation results in the most simple case of linear regression against all training data was *AUC = 0.6553*.

The following parameters were used: $n = 1000$, $\alpha = 700$, $k = 1$, $\gamma = 1$, $\tau = 3$ (see Section "Modeling technique").

As a results of *MVF*, the number of features was reduced from *101* to *44*.

Then, we conducted *RS (700, 700, 1,000)* with the following results:

1:    0.7257 corresponds to the linear average d.f. in the case of all features;

2:    0.7311 corresponds to the logistic average d.f. (4) in the case of all features;

3:    0.7241 corresponds to the linear average d.f. in the case of selected *44* features; and

4:    **0.7253** corresponds to the logistic average d.f. (4) in the case of selected *44* features (used for the test-submission).

Test Results

Forty seven participants from various sources including academia, software vendors and consultancies submitted entries, with the range of results from 0.4778 to 0.701. Our result was 0.688 or ninth place (see Table 1).

The difference between simulation and test results in the case of 44 features appears to be quite significant. Respectively, initial thought (after results were published) was that there are problems with overfitting. Table 3 illustrates observed results where feature selection was conducted using mean-variance filtering against training set.

It is interesting to note that the winning submission was not the best in the sense of Balanced Error Rate (*BER*). The corresponding *BER*-trajectory is shown on the Figure 2(e). The main feature of this trajectory is a wide range of low values. Accordingly, it is not difficult to select the competitive value of the threshold parameter.

Table 2. List of the most significant features

N	Feature	μ	r
1	Bureau Enquiries for Morgages last 6 month	0.729	4
2	Age	-0.683	6.6
3	Bureau Enquiries for Loans last 12 month	-0.516	4.8
4	Bureau Enquiries last 3 month	0.342	2.54
5	Number of dependants	-0.322	3.82
6	Bureau Enquiries last month	0.299	1.92

Table 3. Number of the used features are given in the first column. The second column illustrates test results where training was conducted without test data. The third column illustrates test results where training was conducted using all data. The fourth column "Overfitting" represents the difference between values in the columns 3 and 2. The corresponding ranges of the training AUCs observed for the single classifiers are given in the columns 5 and 6. The particular meanings of the features in the cases of 4 and 17 features may be seen in the Tables 4 and 5.

N of features	Test-Train	Test-All	Overfitting	RS-Low	RS-High
44	0.688	0.702	0.014	0.698	0.743
30	0.689	0.695	0.006	0.689	0.739
17	0.688	0.691	0.003	0.683	0.731
4	0.6558	0.6564	0.0006	0.6379	0.69

Table 4. Values in the columns 2-4 were computed using all data, and values in the columns 5-7 were computed using training data only.

	All data			Training data		
Feature	μ	s	r	μ	s	r
Constant	0.7263	0.0288	25.2234	0.7422	0.0336	22.0691
N1 (see Table 2)	1.0926	0.0755	14.4711	1.1454	0.1011	11.3294
N3	-0.5727	0.0547	-10.4733	-0.6015	0.0663	-9.0751
N5	-0.1813	0.0634	-2.8602	-0.1587	0.0778	-2.0395
AGE	-0.6313	0.0709	-8.9079	-0.6831	0.0806	-8.4794

Figure 2(f) demonstrates another structure of *BER*-trajectories where a red dash-dot line corresponds to the absolutely best result in the sense of minimal *BER*. We can see that in this case, the selection task of the threshold parameter is much more difficult and risky.

Committee of Experts

Firstly, we normalised the available *47* solutions (vectors) to the range *[0, 1]* using linear transformation:

$$v_{new} = \frac{v_{old} - a}{b - a}$$

Table 5. Features were selected using MVF applied to all data. Then, we recomputed values of μ and s using the same random sets.

N	Feature	μ	s	r
1	MARITAL STATUS: married	0.0861	0.028	3.0723
2	MARITAL STATUS: single	0.0419	0.0236	1.7786
3	MARITAL STATUS: defacto	0.09	0.0438	2.0572
4	MARITAL STATUS: widowed	-0.2754	0.0766	3.594
5	RENT BUY CODE: mortgage	0.0609	0.0191	3.1838
6	RENT BUY CODE: parents	-0.1285	0.0341	3.7692
7	CURR RES MTHS	-0.0449	0.0101	4.4555
8	CURR EMPL MTHS	-0.0288	0.0111	2.586
9	NBR OF DEPENDANTS	-0.3298	0.0807	4.085
10	Bureau Enquiries last month	0.3245	0.183	1.7736
11	Bureau Enquiries last 3 month	0.1296	0.1338	0.9691
12	Bureau Enquiries for Morgages last 6 month	0.8696	0.1359	6.3982
13	Bureau Enquiries for Loans last 12 month	-0.6672	0.0795	8.3905
14	A DISTRICT APPLICANT=2	-0.1704	0.05	3.4067
15	A DISTRICT APPLICANT=8	-0.1216	0.0397	3.063
16	CUSTOMER SEGMENT=9	-0.0236	0.0317	0.7453
17	AGE	-0.654	0.0962	6.8015

where a is the minimal and b is the maximal values of the vector components.

Then, we considered an average of the first k solutions (see Table 1). It was found that a committee of experts will win the competition for all $k \leq 37$. The best result of $AUC = 0.707231$ corresponds to $k=9$.

Note that the same normalisation was used in order to produce Figures 2(c-f) and 3.

Figure 3 reflects similarities/differences between different solutions and was created using the function "agnes" from the R-package "cluster."

Discussion and Business Insights

RS-method provides good opportunities to evaluate the significance of the particular features. We can take into account 2 factors: 1) average values μ, and 2) *t*-statistic r, which are defined in (3).

Based on Tables 2 and 5, we can make a conclusion that younger people with a smaller number of dependants who made enquiries for mortgages during the last 6 months have a higher probability to take up a home loan.

On the other hand, enquiries for loans represent detrimental factor.

Considering such general characteristic as marital status, we can conclude that "widowed" people are less interested in applying for home loans.

Also, it is interesting to note that a stable job or long residence may be viewed as negative factors. Possibly, these people have already one or more homes and are reluctant to make further investments.

Remark 6. *Experiments with "tree" function (R-software, package "tree") had confirmed that the feature "Bureau enquiries for mortgages during last 6 month" is the most important (see Figures 4-5).*

Computation Time and Used Software

A Toshiba laptop, 2GHz, 1GB RAM, was used for computations, which were conducted using specially written C-programs.

Data transformation (all data 48,700 rows) to numerical values took about 5 seconds. Training in the case of 1,000 sets and 44 selected features was 811 seconds, and 78 seconds in the case of 4 selected features.

CONCLUDING REMARKS AND FURTHER DEVELOPMENTS

The proposed method is based on a large number of balanced random sets and includes 2 main steps: 1) feature selection and 2) training. During the PAKDD-2007 Data Mining Competition, we conducted both steps using linear regression. Obviously, this choice is far from optimal.

In general terms, feature selection may be done using different methods (Stoppiglia, Dreyfus, Dubois, & Oussar, 2003; Tuv, Borisov, & Torkkola, 2006). For example, we can apply R-package "varSelRF" or "randomForest" package, which include several functions for variable selection.

The final decision regarding feature selection may be calculated as an average of single selections.

Again, the final training may be conducted using different methods. For instance, we can mention trees or random forest as the most suitable models. Trees on Figures 4-5 were produced using different balanced random sets, and it is not difficult to see similarity between them. An average function will smooth random effects and will emphasise systematic factors.

We can expect similar outcomes if we will apply any boosting iteration not to the whole training set but to the randomly selected balanced subset. As a secondary important consequence, we will

reduce memory consumption and will increase speed of computation.

REFERENCES

Breiman, L. (1996). Bagging predictors. *Machine Learning, 24,* 123-140.

Breiman, L. (2001). Random forests. *Machine Learning, 45(1),* 5-32.

Breiman, L., Friedman, J., Olshen, R., & Stone, C. (1984). Classification and regression trees.

Freund, Y., & Schapire, R. (1997). A decision-theoretic generalization of online learning and an

application to boosting. *Journal of Computer System Sciences, 55,* 119-139.

Friedman, J. (1999a). *Greedy function approximation: A gradient boosting machine* (Tech. Rep.).

Department of Statistics, Stanford University.

Friedman, J. (1999b). *Stochastic gradient boosting* (Tech. Rep.). Department of Statistics, Stanford University.

Friedman, J., Hastie, T., & Tibshirani, R. (2000). Additive logistic regression: A statistical view of boosting. *Annals of Statistics, 28,* 337-374.

Guyon, I., Alamdari, A., Dror, G., & Buhmann, J. (2006, July 16-21). Performance prediction challenge. In *Proceedings of the International Joint Conference on Neural Networks,* Vancouver, BC, Canada, (pp. 2958-2965). IEEE.

Guyon, I., Weston, J., Barnhill, S., & Vapnik, V. (2002). Gene selection for cancer classification using support vector machines. *Machine Learning, 46,* 389-422.

Hastie, T., Tibshirani, R., & Friedman, J. (2001). *The elements of statistical learning.* Springer-Verlag.

Huber, P. (1985). Projection pursuit. *The Annals of Statistics, 13*(2), 435-475.

Lutz, R. (2006, July 16-21). LogitBoost with trees applied to the WCCI 2006 performance prediction challenge datasets. In *Proceedings of the International Joint Conference on Neural Networks,* Vancouver, BC, Canada, (pp. 2966-2969). IEEE.

Nikulin, V. (2006a). *Learning with gradient-based optimization, clustering-minimization and mean-*

variance filtering. PAKDD 2006 Data Mining Competition. Retrieved November 9, 2007, from http://www.ntu.edu.sg/sce/pakdd2006/competition/overview.htm

Nikulin, V. (2006b, July 16-21). Learning with mean-variance filtering, SVM and gradient-based optimization. In *Proceedings of the International Joint Conference on Neural Networks*, Vancouver, BC, Canada, (pp. 4195--4202). IEEE.

Stoppiglia, H., Dreyfus, G., Dubois, R., & Oussar, Y. (2003). Ranking a random feature for variable selection. *Journal of Machine Learning Research, 3,* 1399-1414.

Tuv, E., Borisov, A., & Torkkola, K. (2006, July 16-21). Feature selection using ensemble based ranking against artificial contrasts. In *Proceedings of the International Joint Conference on Neural Networks,* Vancouver, BC, Canada, (pp. 4183-4187). IEEE.

ENDNOTES

[1] Written at the request of the organisers of the PAKDD-2007 Data Mining Competition. Comments may be sent to the author at vladimir.nikulin@suncorp.com.au.

[2] Web site of the PAKDD-2007 Data Mining Competition: http://lamda.nju.edu.cn/conf/pakdd07/dmc07/

APPENDIX

Figure 1. Mean-variance filtering using RS(700,700,1000) where first feature is a constant; from top: an average values of regression coefficients (μ), standard deviations (s) and the ratios of μ to s

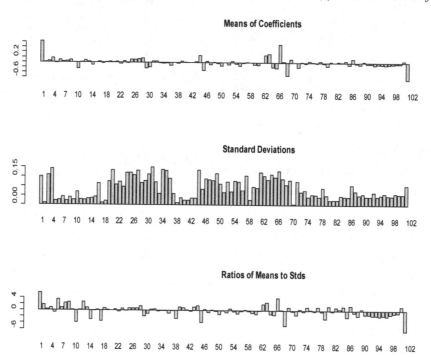

Figure 2. Top row, from left to right: ROC of the winners (red dash-dot line, papers N49 and N85); blue solid line repr

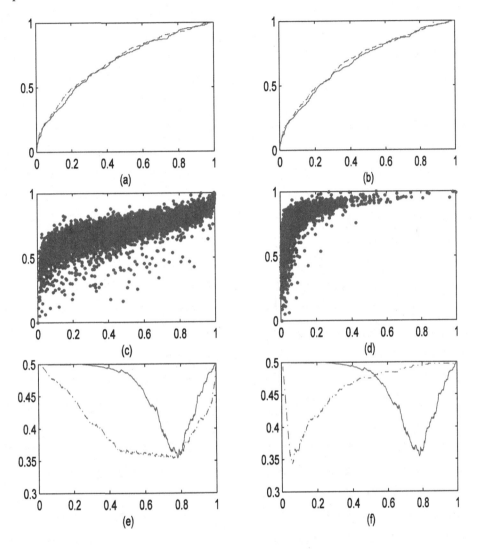

Figure 3. Hierarchical clustering of 47 submissions to PAKDD-2007 data mining competition

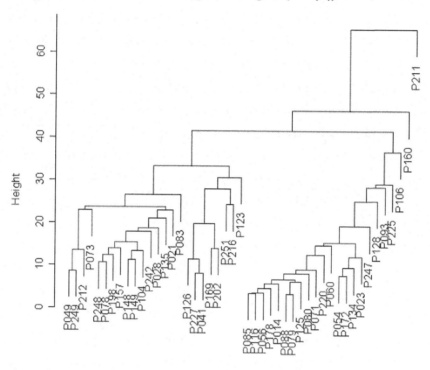

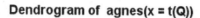

Figure 4. Decision tree ("yes" goes to the left from condition), which corresponds to one of the balanced random sets: meanings of the particular features are given in the Table 5

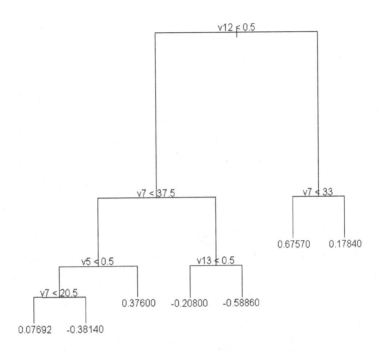

Figure 5. Second example of the RS-decision tree

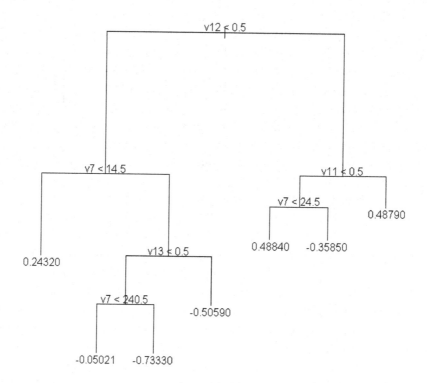

Chapter 23
Ranking Potential Customers Based on Group–Ensemble

Zhi-Zhuo Zhang
South China University of Technology, China

Qiong Chen
South China University of Technology, China

Shang-Fu Ke
South China University of Technology, China

Yi-Jun Wu
South China University of Technology, China

Fei Qi
South China University of Technology, China

Ying-Peng Zhang
South China University of Technology, China

ABSTRACT

Ranking potential customers has become an effective tool for company decision makers to design marketing strategies. The task of PAKDD competition 2007 is a cross-selling problem between credit card and home loan, which can also be treated as a ranking potential customers problem. This article proposes a 3-level ranking model, namely Group-Ensemble, to handle such kinds of problems. In our model, Bagging, RankBoost and Expending Regression Tree are applied to solve crucial data mining problems like data imbalance, missing value and time-variant distribution. The article verifies the model with data provided by PAKDD Competition 2007 and shows that Group-Ensemble can make selling strategy much more efficient.

INTRODUCTION

Data mining plays an increasingly important role in business application and practice. To maximize commercial profits, how to discover potential customers is one of the hottest topics in both data mining and e-business. Although huge amounts of commercial data provide good opportunities to approach the task more thoroughly and precisely, some difficult problems pop up. Among them, imbalance distribution of data, and existence of missing value and dynamic sample distribution are well-known ones, which also occur in the PAKDD Competition 2007. The detail about competition task can be found at the official Web site (LeVis Group, 2007).

The modeling dataset consists of 40,700 customers, only 700 of whom bought home loan as well as a credit card, that is, only 700 of them have a target flag of 1 with others having 0. Besides, among the 40 modeling variables, there exist many missing values. Nearly 90% of the sample more or less suffers this problem. The reason of overlap being small remained unknown, which excluded the possibility of additional assumptions. The provided dataset just gave us the information about whether customers have opened a home loan with the company within 12 months after opening the credit card. It would just so happen that the distribution of potential customers is different from distribution of customers who open a home loan account in the first year. What's more, it is better to treat this problem as a ranking problem, but not a classification problem described in Lecun, Chopra, Hadsell, Huang, and Ranzato (2006), because it would be more convenient for the company decision makers to put the limited resources to the most potential ones.

In this article, we proposed a 3-level learning model named Group-Ensemble to handle the potential ranking associating with data imbalance, missing value and time variant distribution. Different from other learning models, this model is designed for ranking which applies RankBoost as its subalgorithm. Moreover, we slightly modify the traditional bagging by reserving all minority class in each bag, which greatly improve the learners' performance in a serious imbalance case.

Group-Ensemble

After analyzing the problem, we think the task has the following difficulties which have to be tackled.

- **Distribution is time variant:** the target flag in the modeling dataset is based on the record within 1 year; however, the task is to predict the propensity of a customer not limited to 1 year.
- **Serious missing value problem:** the modeling dataset comes from the real world, so that nearly 90% of variables in the dataset encounter a serious missing value problem.
- **Serious data imbalance problem:** in the modeling dataset, the ratio of the positive class is only about 1.71%, which means the negative class dominates the whole dataset and causes poor performance in many traditional classifiers.

To handle the difficulties above, we introduce the 3-level Regression model. In the bottom level, ERTree (Expending Regression Tree) is applied to expand the probability distribution from 1 year to overall. Then in middle level, a metalearning method, RankBoost, presented in Freund, Iyer, Robert, Schapire, and Singer (1998), is used for optimizing the AUC value of the model to achieve the best ranking result (Ataman, Streets, & Zhang, 2006; Corinna & Mehryar, 2003). It is also helpful in the imbalance case. Finally, in the top level, a modified bagging method is used in dealing with the imbalance problem, which reduces the time complexity of the model.

Figure 1. Framework of group-ensemble

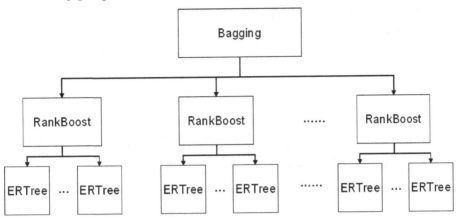

Expanding Regression Tree (The Bottom Level)

Expanding Regression Tree (ERTree) algorithm here, as shown in Table 1, updates the score iteratively, which is based on the REPTree in Weka, described in Witten and Frank (2005). The target flag is either 0 or 1 in the original data set and it is hard to rank. Therefore, we should find some way to make the weak positive class get a higher score than the strong negative class, and make the score distribute between 0 and 1, but not just two values. ERTree gradually enhances the score of the 0-label samples, meanwhile, and updates the score of 1-labels. As a result, the rank of positive samples and negative samples will both be updated: the weak positives will go down and the weak negatives will go up. This behavior of ERTree is due to REPTree taking the average value of incidents in a leaf as the prediction value of that leaf. To make the relabel process more reasonable, we introduce an Attenuation coefficient in step 5, as follows:

$$x.label \leftarrow (h(x) - x.label) \times attennuation + x.label \qquad (1)$$

For instance, supposing that Attenuation coefficient equals 0.2, and the labels of a leave are 1,0,0,0,0, then we know the average value of that leaf is 0.2, so h(x)=0.2 for each x in that leaf. According to step 5, origin 1-label samples will be relabeled to (0.2-1)*0.2+1=0.84. Similarly, other origin 0-label samples will be relabeled to 0.04. And refer to step 8; the Attenuation coefficient will be updated to its square value, which decreases its effect in each iteration gradually. Therefore, if a leaf contains many high-score samples, the low-score samples will be enhanced quickly during the iterations.

Another great advantage of using REPTree as a base model lies in its convenience of handling missing value samples in the tree model. However, ERTree has the same problem as GeTree in (LAMDAer Team, 2006), which can only expand the samples around the strong positive clusters, which is useless in the situation of positive samples scattering in the strong negative clusters. This disadvantage would be complemented in the RankBoost as a meta-algorithm of the upper level.

RankBoost Algorithm (The Middle Level)

As mentioned in Introduction section, the task of finding the potential customers can be regarded as a ranking problem, which is helpful for the company decision makers to decide how much

Table 1. Expand regression tree algorithm

Input: D: dataset; Learn: ERTree;

Process:

1.   hf $\leftarrow$ NULL, D' $\leftarrow$ D, $\text{avg}_{\text{error}}$ ' $\leftarrow \infty$, attenuation $\leftarrow 0.8$, $\text{avg}_{\text{error}} \leftarrow 0$

2.   **repeat**

3.   h $\leftarrow$ Learn(D');

4.   **for** (x $\in$ D') **do**

5.   x.label ($\leftarrow$ h(x) $-$ x.label) $\times$ attenuation $+$ x.label;

6. $\text{avg}_{\text{error}} \leftarrow \sum_{x \in D'} \dfrac{|h(x) - x.label|}{|D'|}$;

7.   **if** ($\text{avg}_{\text{error}} > \text{avg}_{\text{error}}$ ') **then** exit;

8.   **else** hf $\leftarrow$ h, $\text{avg}_{\text{error}} \leftarrow \text{avg}_{\text{error}}$ ', attenuation $\leftarrow$ attenuation^2

9.   **end of repeat**

Output: hf(x)

Table 2. RankBoost algorithm

RankBoost :

Input : D : dataset; Learn : ERTree; T : BaseLearnerNum

Process :

1.   Initialize: $D_1 \leftarrow (x \in D \mid x.label = 1)$, $D_0 \leftarrow (x \in D \mid x.label = 0)$

2.   **for** $(x \in D \mid x.label = 0)$ **do** $x\,weight \leftarrow 1/|D_0|$

3.   **for** $(x \in D \mid x.label = 1)$ **do** $x\,weight \leftarrow 1/|D_1|$

4.   **for** $t \in \{1, 2, ..., N\}$ **do**

5.   D' = a bootstrap sample of D according to weights;

6. $h_t \leftarrow$ learn(D');

7. $\text{SumWeight}_1 \leftarrow \sum_{x \in D \mid x.label = 1} x.weight$

8. $\text{SumWeight}_0 \leftarrow \sum_{x \in D \mid x.label = 0} x.weight$

9. $\text{RelativeError}_1 \leftarrow \sum_{x \in D \mid x.label = 1} (x.label \times SumWeight_0 \times h_t(x))$

10. $\text{RelativeError}_0 \leftarrow \sum_{x \in D \mid x.label = 0} (x.label \times SumWeight_1 \times h_t(x) \times (-1))$

11. $\varepsilon \leftarrow$ elativeError$_1$ +RelativeError$_0$

12. $\alpha_t \leftarrow n \dfrac{1 + \varepsilon}{1 - \varepsilon}$

13. $Z_0 \leftarrow \sum_{x \in D \mid x.label = 0} x.weight \times \exp(\alpha_t \times h_t(x))$

14. $Z_1 \leftarrow \sum_{x \in D \mid x.label = 1} x.weight \times \exp(-\alpha_t \times h_t(x))$

15.   **for** $(x \in D \mid x.label = 0)$. **o** $x\,weight \leftarrow \dfrac{x.weight \times \exp(\alpha_t \times h_t(x))}{Z_0}$

Table 3. Group-ensemble algorithm

Group Ensemble
Input: D: dataset; Learn: RankBoost; N: GroupNum;
1. $\{D_1, ..., D_N\}$ ← split the negative samples into N disjoint set, combine the positive set to construct new N datasets
2.   **for** t ∈ {1, ..., N} **do**
3. h_t ← learn(D_t)
4.   Output: $H(x) = \frac{1}{T}\sum_1^{t=T} h_t\ x)$

resources they need to invest on the potential customers in order to make them real customers.

Boosting is a well-known method to build a strong learner from a number of weak learners (Freund, 1990). RankBoost (Freund et al., 1998), as a special kind of boosting, whose objective is to achieve the better ranking result and higher AUC value, is more suitable in this task. Each Expanding Regression Tree (ERTree) is a weak learner, in which we use RankBoost to ensemble and rank the results of them. The pseudo code of RankBoost is shown in Table 2. Rankboost reweights every sample differently from Ada-Boost, which is proven to be more effective and have better generalized performance in Freund (1998) and can also help improve ranking the weak positive samples, which may also be effective to imbalanced problems.

Modified Bagging (The Top Level)

RankBoost is designed specifically for ranking, but its performance also degrades significantly in data imbalance situation according to our experiments. In fact, bagging has been proven effective in the serious imbalance case in Li (2007) and was used here to tackle seriously imbalanced problems and to reduce the time consumed in the training process. We modify the bagging method, which divides negative samples into several equal-size groups, and then combine the whole positive sample set with each of them. For instance, if 40 groups are applied in 40,700 samples, every

new dataset will contain 700 positive samples and 1,000 negative samples, so that each dataset seems much more balanced than before. What's more, in respect to training cost, splitting datasets can be used to train models in parallel. Even if in single-CPU computers, the time of training could also be reduced to

$$O(n^\alpha) > k \times O((\frac{n}{k})^\alpha)$$
(2)

where k is Group Number, n is scale of dataset, and *a* is the order of time complexity to the samples number, which is usually larger than 1.

Data Preparation

The modeling dataset included many unclear meaning values and some meaningless variables. The problems found in the dataset are listed as follow:

- Attribution B_DEF_PAID_L12M and B_DEF_UNPD_L12M are suffering a lack of representativeness. According to statistics of B_DEF_PAID, 3 samples took 1, 403 missed and all other 40,297 samples took 0. For B_DEF_UNPAID, all samples took identical value, which have no information according to entropy theories.
- Although in statement of Update 9, all attributes with bureau variables, which were begun with "B," special values 98 and 99

Figure 2. AUC values with different attenuation coefficient

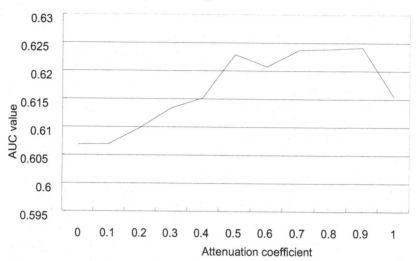

could be treated as missing values, as they were still different, because 99 indicated the customer didn't go to bureau, although 98 indicated positive. Thus, they may be treated separately.

- For attributes of CHQ_ACCT_IND, SAVE_ACCT_IND, AMEX_CARD, DINERS_CARD, VISA_CARD, MASTER_CARD, and RETAIL_CARDS (namely account attributes) invalid values existed and should be corrected into valid ones.
- All missing values are simply blank, which is incompatible with ARFF format.
- Some records have CURR_EMPL_MTHS=1000, which has unknown meaning.

According to the problems listed above, the modeling dataset went through following series of operations as our convenience:

- Kick B_DEF_PAID_L12M and B_DEF_UNPD_L12M out of the dataset.

- Add an attribute FlagNotBureau in each sample. For all samples, with value 99 in all remained bureau attributes, evaluate the flag with 1. Others take 0. Then transfer value 98 and 99 into blank ones, the identity of missing value.
- Transfer all values of account attributes into valid values: for missing values, transfer them to "X"; for all values besides "N," "Y," and "X," such as "0," "1," and "2," of which meaning are unknown, transfer them to "Z."
- Place a missing value flag "?" to all blanks in the dataset in order to make the format compatible to ARFF format.
- Place a missing value flag "?" to the variable CURR_EMPL_MTHS, when CURR_EMPL_MTHS=1000.

Parameter Selection

Three parameters should be considered in Group-Ensemble. The three parameters are: Attenuation coefficient, the number of weak learners and the number of groups.

Figure 3. AUC values with different numbers of weak learners

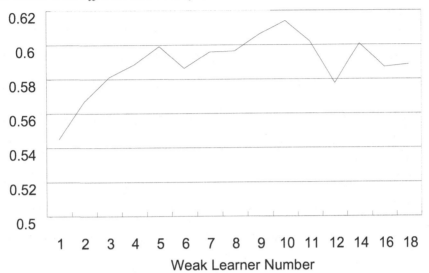

Attenuation Coefficient

Attenuation coefficient is the parameter in ERTree learning. As mentioned in the model description section, the functionality of Attenuation coefficient is to weaken the affection of the former iterations and meanwhile, maintain the rank in the suitable scale. It can be predicted that the Attenuation coefficient approach to 1, the dataset will become more unstable during the iterations; on the other side, if Attenuation coefficient approach to 0, the dataset will have no change and the ERTree becomes the REPTree described in Witten and Frank (2005). And we apply the ERTree as a predictor only, and try Attenuation coefficient from 0 to 1, the AUC value is shown in Figure 2. When Attenuation coefficient equals 0, ERTree is just a REPTree and has the worst performance. The best performance occurs at Attenuation coefficient =0.9.

Weak Learner Number

Weak learner number (WLN) is the parameter in level2, which indicates that the number of ERTree

in the schema of RankBoost. As common sense, the more weak learners that are in the boosting schema, the better training performance of the boosting learner. But what we really concern ourselves with is the performance on the unseen test data. According to Occam's razor principle, we choose the WLN carefully to avoid overfitting.

The AUC value varies with different WLN, as shown in Figure 5. And it achieves the best result 0.613 at 10 among 18 experiments. Thus, we select WLN = 10 to be the parameter in our final, which balances accuracy and the risk of overfitting.

Someone will find that the AUC of ERTree alone is 0.624, which is higher than 0.613 with RankBoost. In fact, we have done some experiments to compare bagging with and without RankBoost, and the result shows that applying RankBoost has significant better performance when the Group Number goes larger than 16. The fact suggests that serious imbalance data would weaken the performance of RankBoost significantly.

Figure 4. AUC values with different group numbers

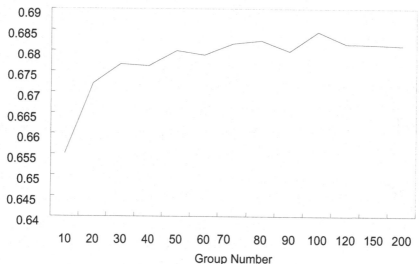

Table 4. AUC value of group-ensemble and other learners

Learner	AUC
Group-Ensemble	**0.684**
Modified Bagging-Linear Regression	0.671
Modified Bagging-RETree	0.661
RankBoost -J48	0.601
Adaboost-J48	0.530
J48	0.500
RETree	0.610

Group Number

Group Number is defined as the number of divisions in bagging (Top level), and we reserve all the positive class records in every group. With fixed parameters Attenuation=0.9 and WLN=10, we carry out the experiments according to various Group Numbers, as shown in Figure 4. When we don't apply bagging (Group Number=1), the AUC value is only 0.613. Dramatically, AUC value jumps to 0.655 when the Group Number equals 10, and becomes even higher as the Group Number increases. The fact indicates that the ratio of minority class in the training set plays a critical role in serious imbalance cases and the learner's performance can be enhanced significantly by adjusting the ratio to a reasonable level.

When the Group Number equals 100, the AUC value reaches its best (0.684), and the ratio of minority class in each group is 700/(700+400), about 63%. That is, the minority class becomes majority in each group, which reveals that a weak hypothesis on the minority class should be paid more special attention.

Model Evaluation and Insight

Model Evaluation

In the final model, the Group Number is 100, the Weak Learner Number is 10, and the Attenuation

Figure 5. Recall ratio-top percentage diagram of group-ensemble

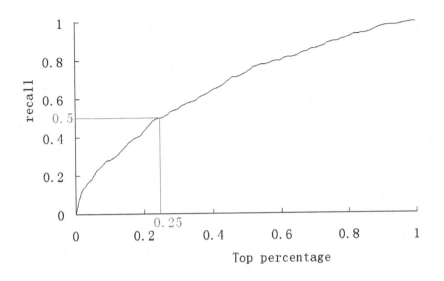

Figure 6. Results of JRip rules base on the output of group-ensemble

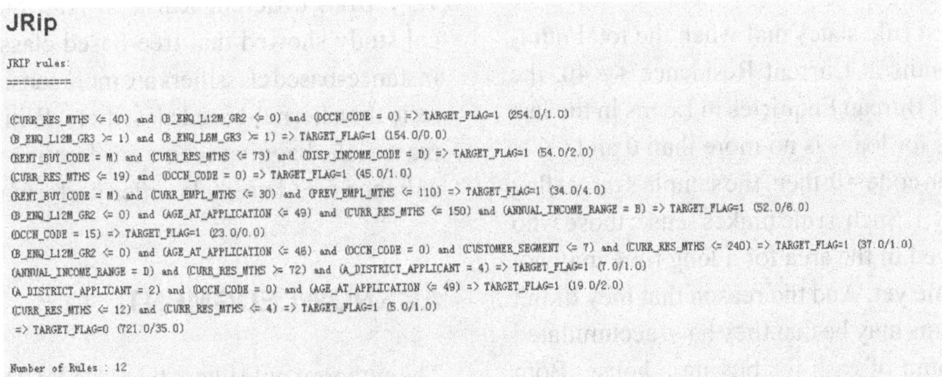

```
JRip

JRIP rules:
===========

(CURR_RES_MTHS <= 40) and (B_ENQ_L12M_GR2 <= 0) and (OCCN_CODE = 0) => TARGET_FLAG=1 (254.0/1.0)
(B_ENQ_L12M_GR3 >= 1) and (B_ENQ_L6M_GR3 >= 1) => TARGET_FLAG=1 (154.0/0.0)
(RENT_BUY_CODE = M) and (CURR_RES_MTHS <= 73) and (DISP_INCOME_CODE = D) => TARGET_FLAG=1 (54.0/2.0)
(CURR_RES_MTHS <= 19) and (OCCN_CODE = 0) => TARGET_FLAG=1 (45.0/1.0)
(RENT_BUY_CODE = M) and (CURR_EMPL_MTHS <= 30) and (PREV_EMPL_MTHS <= 110) => TARGET_FLAG=1 (34.0/4.0)
(B_ENQ_L12M_GR2 <= 0) and (AGE_AT_APPLICATION <= 49) and (CURR_RES_MTHS <= 150) and (ANNUAL_INCOME_RANGE = B) => TARGET_FLAG=1 (52.0/6.0)
(OCCN_CODE = 15) => TARGET_FLAG=1 (23.0/0.0)
(B_ENQ_L12M_GR2 <= 0) and (AGE_AT_APPLICATION <= 46) and (OCCN_CODE = 0) and (CUSTOMER_SEGMENT <= 7) and (CURR_RES_MTHS <= 240) => TARGET_FLAG=1 (37.0/1.0)
(ANNUAL_INCOME_RANGE = D) and (CURR_RES_MTHS >= 72) and (A_DISTRICT_APPLICANT = 4) => TARGET_FLAG=1 (7.0/1.0)
(A_DISTRICT_APPLICANT = 2) and (OCCN_CODE = 0) and (AGE_AT_APPLICATION <= 49) => TARGET_FLAG=1 (19.0/2.0)
(CURR_RES_MTHS <= 12) and (CURR_RES_MTHS <= 4) => TARGET_FLAG=1 (5.0/1.0)
=> TARGET_FLAG=0 (721.0/35.0)

Number of Rules : 12
```

coefficient is 0.9. The experimental results for the comparison with other traditional learning algorithms are the following:

From the view of the company, they are concerned with how much resources should be invested and how many valid customers should be collected. For this purpose, we draw a curve about recall ratio vs. top percentage in the ranking list, as shown as Figure 5:

recall ratio =

$$\frac{\text{the number of valid customers in top list}}{\text{the number of total valid customers}} \quad (3)$$

where the top list contains the customers in the top percentage of the ranking result.

Figure 5 shows the relationship between top percentage in the ranking list and the percent number of available potential customers it contains. For example, on the top 25% ranking list, there are 50% available potential customers, according to Figure 5. If we send ads for home loans to the top 25% ranking list customers, the customers who receive ads include 50% available potential customers. What's more, we find that the slope of the curve equals 1 at the point (0.51, 0.73), that is, on the top 0.73 percentage customers, 1% of resources can gain more than 1% of available customers with our ranking result, but after 73%, the gain can be worse than random guess.

Model Insight

Because the final output of Group-Ensemble is a score to a customer, although it is enough for ranking, little knowledge can be learned from this kind of output. Hence, we apply twice learning on the output with JRip in Weka (Witten & Frank, 2005).

Now, we can get some knowledge from the first and second rules in Figure 6 with high confidence:

The first rule states that when the total number of months at Current Residence <= 40, the Number of Bureau Enquiries in Loans in the last 12 months for loans is no more than 0 and CCN Occupation code = 0: then, the sample's target flag is probably 1. Such a rule makes sense: those who haven't lived in the area for a long time may not have a home yet. And the reason that they didn't require loans may be that they have accumulated some amount of cash for buying a house. Both of the conditions make the customer a potential home loan buyer.

The second rule states that if the Number of Bureau Enquiries in the last 12 months for Mortgages has been more than 1, the target flag of the sample would probably be 1 as well. This rule makes sense as well as the above one: a customer having inquired about a policy for mortgages is right for a home loan.

CONCLUSION AND FUTURE WORK

Ranking potential customers is a powerful new technology for extracting additional value for business from its user database. Our model can help the company invest their resources to the most potential customers. Twice learning helps the company decision maker gain the understandable knowledge before he or she makes any critical decision. On the other hand, Group-Ensemble does well in large database because it is trained on each group in parallel.

Further study can focus on how the bagging method works on imbalance problems The bagging method can be helpful to most imbalance problems of binary class, but multiclass problems will be more complicated, and some empirical results can be found in Zhou and Liu (2006). Moreover, the best ratio of minority class may vary from different learners. And our empirical study showed that tree-based classifiers and instance-based classifiers are more sensitive to that ratio than kernel-based classifiers. With the same reason, the bagging seems an effective method to enhance tree-based classifier performance.

ACKNOWLEDGMENT

The authors would like to thank PAKDD Competition 2007 Chair Nathaniel, who provided helpful and timely answers to our questions about the competition, and CS department of South China University of Technology, that provided much help for our experiments.

REFERENCES

Ataman, K., Streetr, W.N., & Zhang, Y. (2006). Learning to rank by maximizing AUC with linear programming. In *Proceedings of the International Joint Conference on Neural Networks*, (pp.123-129). Iowa City, IA, USA: IEEE Press.

Corinna, C., & Mehryar, M. (Eds.). (2003). AUC optimization vs. error rate minimization. *Advances in neural information processing systems* (Vol. 16). Cambridge, MA: MIT Press.

Freund, Y. (1990). Boosting a weak learning algorithm by majority. In *Proceedings of the Third Annual Workshop on Computational Learning Theory,* Rochester, NY, USA: Morgan Kaufmann.

Freund,Y., Iyer, R., Robert, E., Schapire, & Singer, Y. (1998). An efficient boosting algorithm for combining preferences. In *Machine Learning: Proceedings of the Fifteenth International Conference*, (pp. 170-178), San Francisco: Morgan Kaufmann.

LAMDAer Team. (2006). Predicting future customers via ensembling gradually expanded trees. PAKDD Competition 2006. *International Journal of Data Warehousing and Mining, 3*(2), 12-21.

Lecun, Y., Chopra, S., Hadsell, R., Huang, F.-J., & Ranzato, M.-A. (2006). *A tutorial on energy-based learning: Predicting structured outputs.* New York: MIT Press.

LeVis Group, Shanghai University. (2007). *PAKDD 2007 Data Mining Competition.* Retrieved November 9, 2007, from http://lamda.nju.edu.cn/conf/pakdd07/dmc07/

Li, C. (2007). Classifying imbalanced data using a bagging ensemble variation (BEV). In *Proceedings of the 45th Annual Southeast Regional Conference*, (pp. 203-208). New York: ACM Press.

Witten, I. H., & Frank (Eds.). (2005). *Data mining: Practical machine learning tools and techniques* (2nd ed.). San Francisco: Morgan Kaufmann.

Zhou, Z.-H. , & Liu, X.-Y. (2006). Training cost-sensitive neural networks with methods addressing the class imbalance problem. *IEEE Transactions on Knowledge and Data, Engineering, 18*(1), 63-77.

This work was previously published in International Journal of Data Warehousing and Mining, Vol. 4, Issue 2, edited by D. Taniar, pp. 79-89, copyright 2008 by IGI Publishing (an imprint of IGI Global).

Compilation of References

Aas, K. (2001). *Microarray data mining: A survey* (Tech. rep., NR Note). SAMBA, Norwegian Computing Center.

Abe, S., & Lan, M.-S. (1995). A method for fuzzy rules extraction directly from numerical data and its application to pattern classification. *IEEE transactions on Fuzzy Systems, 3*(1), 18–28. doi:10.1109/91.366565

Abelló, A., Samos, J., & Saltor, F. (2003). Implementing operations to navigate semantic star schemas. In *Proceedings of the 6th ACM international workshop on Data Warehousing and OLAP (DOLAP2003)* (pp. 56-62). ACM.

Abelló, A., Samos, J., & Saltor, F. (2006). YAM²: A multidimensional conceptual model extending UML. *Journal of Information Systems (IS), 31*(6), 541-556.

Abler, R. (1987). The national science foundation national center for geographic information and analysis. *International Journal of Geographic Information Systems, 1*(4), 303-326.

Adam, N. R., & Wortman, J. C. (1989). Security-Control Methods for Statistical Databases. *ACM Computing Surveys, 21* (4), 515-556.

Adeodato, P. J. L. (1997). *Theoretical investigations on RAM-based neural networks.* Doctoral Dissertation, Department of Mathematics, King's College London, UK.

Agrawal, S., Agrawal, R., Deshpande, P., Gupta, A., Naughton, J., Ramakrishnan, R., & Sarawagi, S. (1996). On the computation of multidimensional aggregates. In *Proceedings of the 22nd International VLDB Conference* (pp. 506-521).

Agrawal, R., & Srikant, R. (1994). Fast algorithms for mining association rule. In *Proceedings of the International Conference on Very Large Databases* (pp. 487-499).

Agrawal, R., & Srikant, R. (1995). Mining sequential patterns. In *Proceedings of 11th International Conference on Data Engineering* (pp. 3-14). Taipei, Taiwan: IEEE Computer Society Press.

Agrawal, R., Evfimievski, A., & Srikant, R. (2003). Information Sharing Across Private Databases. In *Proceedings of 2003 ACM SIGMOD International Conference on Management of Data.*

Agrawal, R., Gupta, A., & Sarawagi, S. (1997). Modeling multidimensional databases. In *Proceedings of the 13th Int. Conf. Data Engineering (ICDE)*, IEEE Computer Society, pp. 232–243.

Agrawal, R., Imielinski, T., & Swami, A. (1993). Mining Association Rules between Sets of Items in Large Databases. In *Proceedings of ACM SIGMOD International Conference on Management of Data, SIGMOD'93* (pp. 207-216), Washington DC, USA.

Agrawal, R., Mannila, H., Srikant, R., Toivonen, H., & Verkamo, A. I. (1996). Fast discovery of association rules. In *Advances in Knowledge Discovery and Data Mining.* AAAI/MIT Press.

Agrawal, R., Srikant, R., & Thomas, D. (2005). Privacy Preserving OLAP. In *Proceedings of 2005 ACM SIGMOD International Conference on Management of Data.*

Agrawal, S., Chaudhuri, S., & Narasayya, V. (2000). Automated selection of materialized views and indexes in sql databases. In A. Abbadi, M. Brodie, S. Chakravarthy,

U. Dayal, N. Kamel, G. Schlageter, & K. Whang (Eds.), *Proceedings of the InternationalConference on Very Large Data Base* (pp. 496-505). San Francisco: Morgan Kaufmann Publishers Inc.

Agresti, A. (1990). *Categorical Data Analysis* (2nd ed.). New York: John Wiley & Sons.

Ailamaki, A., Dewitt, D. J., Hill, M. D., & Skounakis, M. (2001). Weaving relations for cache performance. In *Proceedings of the 27th VLDB Conference.*

Al-Alawi, R., & Stonham, T. J. (1992). A training strategy and functionality analysis of digital multi-layer neural networks. *Journal of Intelligent Systems, 2*, 53-93.

Aleksander, I., Thomas, W. V., & Bowden, P. A. (1984). WISARD, a radical step forward in image recognition. *Sensor Review, 4*, 120-124.

Allen, J.F., & Ferguson, G. (1994). Actions and events in interval temporal logic. *Technical Report* TR521.

Alon, N., Gibbons, P. B., Matias, Y., & Szegedy, M. (1999). Tracking Join and Self-Join Sizes in Limited Storage. In *Proceedings of 1999 ACM PODS Principles of Database Systems.*

Alon, N., Matias, Y., & Szegedy, M. (1996). The Space Complexity of Approximating the Frequency Moments. In *Proceedings of 1996 ACM STOC Symposium on Theory of Computing.*

Amorim, B., Vasconcelos, G. C., & Brasil, L. (2007, September). Hybrid neural systems for large scale credit risk assessment. *Journal of Intelligent and Fuzzy Systems (JIFS), 18*(5).

Andrienko, G., & Andrienko N. (1999). Knowledge-based visualization to support spatial data mining. In *Proceedings of the 3rd Symposium on Intelligent Data Analysis, IDA'99*, Amsterdam, The Netherlands.

Anthony, M., & Biggs, N. (1992). *Computational learning theory.* UK: Cambridge University Press.

Antunes, C., & Oliveira, A.L. (2004). Constraint relaxations for discovering unknown sequential patterns. *Proceedings of the KDID'2002*, 11–32.

Aronoff, S. (1995). *Geographic information systems: A management perspective.* WDL Publications.

Atallah, M. J., Gwadera, R., & Szpankowski, W. (2004). Detection of significant sets of episodes in event sequences. In *Proceedings of the Fourth International Conference on Data Mining* (pp. 3-10).

Ataman, K., Streetr, W.N., & Zhang, Y. (2006). Learning to rank by maximizing AUC with linear programming. In *Proceedings of the International Joint Conference on Neural Networks*, (pp.123-129). Iowa City, IA, USA: IEEE Press.

Aumueller, D., Do, H.H., Massmann, S., & Rahm, E. (2005). Schema and Ontology Matching with COMA++. In F. Özcan (Ed.), *Proc. ACM SIGMOD Int. Conf. on Management of Data* (pp. 906-908). New York: ACM Press.

Bagui, S. (2006). An approach to mining crime patterns. *International Journal of Data Warehousing and Mining, 2*(1), 50-80.

Ballau, D. P, Wang, R. Y., Pazer, H. L., & Tayi G. K. (1998). Modelling information manufacturing systems to determine information product quality. *Management Science, 44*(4), 462-484.

Ballou, D. P., & Pazer, H. L. (1985). Modeling data and process quality in multi-input, multi-output information systems. *Management Science, 31*(2), 150-162.

Banek, M., Tjoa, A. M., & Stolba, N. (2006). Integrating Different Grain Levels in a Medical Data Warehouse Federation. In A. M. Tjoa & J. Trujillo (Eds.), *Proc. 8th Int. Conf. on Data Warehousing and Knowledge Discovery. Lecture Notes in Computer Science, 4081*, 185-194.

Banek, M., Vrdoljak, B., Tjoa, A. M., & Skočir, Z. (2007). Automating the Schema Matching Process for Heterogeneous Data Warehouses. In I. Y. Song, J. Eder & T. Manh Nguyen (Eds.), *Proc. 9th Int. Conf. on Data Warehousing and Knowledge Discovery. Lecture Notes in Computer Science, 4654*, 45-54.

Banerjee A., & Ghosh, J. (2002). Frequency sensitive competitive learning for clustering on high-dimensional hyperspheres. In *Proceedings of IEEE International Joint Conference on Neural Networks*, pp. 1590-1595.

Baralis, E., Paraboschi, S., & Teniente, E. (1997). Materialized viewsselection in a multidimensional database. In M. Jarke, M. Carey, K. Dittrich, F. Lochovsky, P. Loucopoulos, & M. Jeusfeld (Eds.), *Proceedings of the International Conference on Very Large Data Bases* (pp. 156-165). San Francisco: Morgan Kaufmann Publishers Inc.

Barry, R., Cavers, D., & Kneale, C. (1975). Recommended standards for digital tape formats. *Geophysics, 40*, 344-352.

Behnke, J., & Dobinson, E. (2000). NASA workshop on issues in the application of data mining to scientific data. *ACM SIGKDD Explorations Newsletter, 2*(1), 70-79.

Beneventano D., & Bergamaschi S. (2006). Semantic Search Engines based on Data Integration Systems. In J. Cardoso (Ed.), *Semantic Web: Theory, Tools and Applications* (pp. 317-341). Hershey, PA, USA: IGI Publishing.

Beneventano D., Bergamaschi S., Guerra F., & Vincini M. (2003). Synthesizing an Integrated Ontology. *IEEE Internet Computing Magazine, 7* (5), 42-51.

Bergamaschi, S., Castano, S., & Vincini, M. (1999). Semantic Integration of Semistructured and Structured Data Sources. *SIGMOD Record 28* (1), 54-59.

Berger S., & Schrefl, M. (2006). Analysing Multidimensional Data accross Autonomous Data Warehouses. In A. M. Tjoa & J. Trujillo (Eds.), *Proc. 8th Int. Conf. on Data Warehousing and Knowledge Discovery. Lecture Notes in Computer Science, 4081*, 120-133.

Bettini, C., Wang, X.S., Jajodia, S., & Lin, J.-L. Discovering frequent event patterns with multiple granularities in time sequences. *IEEE Transactions on Knowledge and Data Engineering, 10*(2), 222–237.

Beyer, K., & Ramakrishnan, R. (1999). Bottom-up computation of sparse and iceberg cubes. In *Proceedings of the 1999 ACM SIGMOD Conference* (pp. 359-370).

Blaschka, M., Sapia, C., Höfling, G., & Dinter, B. (1998). Finding your way through multidimensional data models.

In *Proceedings of the 9th Int. Workshop on Database and Expert Systems Applications: Data Warehouse Design and OLAP Technology (DWDOT'98)* (pp.198-203). IEEE Computer Society.

Bledsoe, W. W., & Browning, I. (1959). Pattern recognition and reading by machine. In *Proceedings of the Eastern Joint Computer Conference*, (pp. 225-232).

Böhlen, M.H., Snodgrass, R.T., & Soo, M.D. (1996). Coalescing in temporal databases. *Proceedings of the VLDB'1996*, 180–191.

Böhnlein, M., Plaha, M.. & Ulbrich-vom Ende, A. (2002). Visual specification of multidimensional queries based on a semantic data model. *Vom Data Warehouse zum Corporate Knowledge Center (DW2002)* (pp.379-397). Physica-Verlag.

Boulicaut, J.-F., De Raedt, L., & Mannila, H. (eds.) (2006). Constraint-based mining and inductive databases. *Lecture Notes in Computer Science, 3848*.

Breiman, L. (1996). Bagging predictors. *Machine Learning, 24*, 123-140.

Breiman, L. (2001). Random forests. *Machine Learning, 45*(1), 5C32.

Breiman, L., Friedman, J.H., Olshen, R.A., & Stone, C.J. (1984). *Classification and regression trees*. Belmont: CRC Press.

Breslow, N. E. (1976). Regression analysis of the log odds ratio: a method for retrospective studies. *Biometrics, 32*, 409–416. doi:10.2307/2529508

Breslow, N. E., & Day, N. E. (1980). Classical Methods of Analysis of Matched Data. In *Statistical Methods in Cancer Research, Volume I - The Analysis of Case-Control Studies*. Lyon, France: IARC Scientific Publications, No. 32. International Agency for Research on Cancer.

Cabibbo L., & Torlone R. (1997). Querying multidimensional databases. *Database Programming Languages, 6th International Workshop (DBPL-6)* (pp. 319-335). Springer.

Cabibbo, L., & Torlone, R. (1998). From a procedural to

a visual query language for OLAP. In *Proceedings of the 10th Int. Conf. on Scientific and Statistical Database Management (SSDBM 1998)*, IEEE Computer Society, pp. 74-83.

Cabibbo, L., & Torlone, R. (2005). Integrating Heterogeneous Multidimensional Databases. In J. Frew (Ed.), *Proc. 17th Int. Conf. Scientific and Statistical Database Management* (pp. 205-214).

Caruana, R., & Freitag, D. (1994). Greedy attribute selection. In *Proceedings of the International Conference on Machine Learning* (pp. 28-36).

Ceri, S., Navathe, S., & Wiederhold, G. (1983). Distribution design of logical database schemas. *IEEE Transactions on Software Engineering, SE-9*(4).

Chaudhuri, S., & Dayal, U. (1997). An overview of data warehousing and OLAP technology. *SIGMOD Record, 26*(1), 65-74.

Chen, C., Liaw, A., & Breiman, L. (2004). *Using random forest to learn imbalanced data* (Tech. Rep.). Berkeley, CA: Department of Statistics, UC Berkeley.

Chen, M. S., Han, J., & Yu, P. S. (1996). Data mining: An overview from database perspective. *IEEE Transactions on Knowledge and Data Engineering, 8*(6), 866-883.

Chen, Y., Dehne, F., Eavis, T., & Rau-Chaplin, A. (2004). Building large ROLAP data cubes in parallel. In *Proceedings of the International Database Engineering and Applications Symposium* (pp. 367-377). Coimbra, Portugal: IEEE.

Chen, Y., Dehne, F., Eavis, T., & Rau-Chaplin, A. (2004). Parallel ROLAP data cube construction on shared-nothing multiprocessors. *Distributed and Parallel Databases, 15*, 219–236. doi:10.1023/B:DAPD.0000018572.20283.e0

Chen, Y., Dehne, F., Eavis, T., & Rau-Chaplin, A. (2005). PnP: Parallel and external memory iceberg cube computation. In *Proc. 21st Int. Conf. on Data Engineering (ICDE)* (pp. 576-577). IEEE Comp. Soc. Dig. Library.

Chen, Y., Dehne, F., Eavis, T., Green, D., Rau-Chaplin, A., & Sithirasenan, E. (2006). cgmOLAP: Efficient parallel generation and querying of terabyte size ROLAP data cubes. In *Proc. 22nd Int. Conf. on Data Engineering (ICDE)* (pp. 164-164). IEEE.

Chen, Y., Dehne, Y., Eavis, T., & Rau-Chaplin, A. (2006). Improved data partitioning for building large ROLAP data cubes in parallel. *International Journal of Data Warehousing and Mining, 2*(1),1-26.

Cheng, C-H., Lee, W-K., & Wong, K-F. (2002). A genetic algorithm-based clustering approach for database partitioning. *IEEE Transactions on Systems, Man, and Cybernetics, 32*(3), 215-230.

Chengalur-Smith, I. N., Ballou, D. P., & Pazer H. L. (1999). The impact of data quality information on decision making: An exploratory analysis. *IEEE Transactions on Knowledge and Data Engineering, 11*(6), 853-864.

Chirkova, R., Halevy, A., & Suciu, D. (2002). A formal perspective on the view selection problem. *The VLDB Journal, 11*(3), 216-237.

Chu, W. W. & Ieong, I. T. (1993). A transaction-based approach to vertical partitioning for relational database systems. *IEEE Transaction on Software Engineering, 19*(8), 804-812.

Clementini, E., Felice, P. D., & Van Oosterom, P. (1993). A small set of formal topological relations suitable for end-user interaction. In *Advances in Spatial Databases (Third International Symposium, SSD'93)*, Singapore (LNCS 692, pp. 277-295). New York: Springer-Verlag.

Clifton, C., Doan, A., Elmagarmid, A., Kantarcioglu, M., Schadow, G., Suciu, D., & Vaidya, J. (2004). Privacy-Preserving Data Integration and Sharing. In *ACM SIGMOD Workshop on Research issues in Data Mining and Knowledge Discovery*.

Clifton, C., Kantarcioglu, M., Vaidya, J., Lin, X., & Zhu, M. Y. (2002). Tools for Privacy Preserving Distributed Data Mining. In *SIGKDD Explorations*, 4 (2), 28-34.

Cockcroft, S. (2004, March). The design and implementation of a repository for the management of spatial data integrity constraints. *8*(1), 49-69.

Colliat, G. (1996). OLAP, relational, and multidimensional database systems. *SIGMOD Record, 25*(3), 64-69.

CommonGIS. (2006). *GIS for everyone...everywhere!.* Retrieved from http://commongis.jrc.it/index.html

Conover, W. J. (1999). *Practical nonparametric statistics* (3rd ed.). New York: John Wiley & Sons.

Cook, D. J., & Holder, L. B. (2000). Graph-based data mining. *IEEE Intelligent Systems, 15*(2), 32-41.

Cordon, O., Gomide, F., Herrera, F., Hoffmann, F., & Magdalena, L. (2004). Ten years of genetic fuzzy systems: Current framework and new trends. *Fuzzy Sets and Systems, 141,* 5–31. doi:10.1016/S0165-0114(03)00111-8

Corinna, C., & Mehryar, M. (Eds.). (2003). AUC optimization vs. error rate minimization. *Advances in neural information processing systems* (Vol. 16). Cambridge, MA: MIT Press.

Cormode, G., & Muthukrishnan, S. (2004). An Improved Data Stream Summary: the Count-Min Sketch and Its Applications. In *Latin American Symposium on Theoretical Informatics, Lecture Notes in Computer Science* (Vol. 2976, pp. 29-38). Berlin / Heidelberg: Springer.

Cornell, D. W. & Yu, P. S. (1990). An effective approach to vertical partitioning for physical design of relational databases. *IEEE Transactions on Software Engineering, 16*(2), 248-258.

Crainiceanu, A., Linga, P., Gehrke, J., & Shanmugasundaram, J. (2004). Querying peer-to-peer networks using P-Trees. In *WebDB '04: Proceedings of the 7th International Workshop on the Web and Databases* (pp. 25-30).

Das, S. (2001). Filters, wrappers and a boosting-based hybrid for feature selection. In *Proceedings of the International Conference on Machine Learning* (pp. 74–81).

Dash, M., Choi, K., Scheuermann, P., & Liu, H. (2002). Feature selection for clustering-a filter solution. In *Proceedings of IEEE International Conference on Data Mining* (pp. 115-122).

Datta, A., & Thomas, H. (1999). The cube data model: A conceptual model and algebra for on-line analytical processing in data warehouses. *Journal of Decision Support Systems, 27*(3), 289-301.

Davis, E. (1986). *Representing and acquiring geographic knowledge.* Los Altos, CA: Morgan Kaufmann.

de Amo, S., & Furtado, D. (2007). First-order temporal pattern mining with regular expression constraints. *Data & Knowledge Engineering, 62*(3), 401-420.

de Amo, S., Giacometti, A., & Pereira Jr., W. (2007). Mining first-order temporal interval patterns with regular expression constraints. *Proceedings of the 9th International Conference on Data Warehousing and Knowledge Discovery (DaWaK 2007), LNCS, 4654,* 459–469.

de Amo, S., Giacometti, A., Furtado, D.A., & Laurent, D. (2004). An Apriori-based approach for first-order temporal pattern mining. *Proceedings of the 19th Brazilian Symposium on Databases,* 48–62.

De, P., Park, J. S., & Pirkul, H. (1988). An integrated model of record segmentation and access path selection for databases. *Information Systems, 13*(1), 13-30.

Dehaspe, L., & Toivonnen, H. (1999). Discovery of frequent datalog patterns. *Data Mining and Knowledge Discovery, 3,* 7–36.

Dehne, F., Eavis, T., & Rau-Chaplin, A. (2001). A cluster architecture for parallel data warehousing. IEEE International Symposium of Cluster Computing and the Grid (CCGRid'01), 2001

Dehne, F., Eavis, T., & Rau-Chaplin, A. (2006). The cgmCUBE project: Optimizing parallel data cube generation for ROLAP. *Distributed and Parallel Databases, 19*(1), 29-62.

Dehne, F., Eavis, T., Hambrusch, S., & Rau-Chaplin, A. (2001). Parallelizing the datacube. [Special Issue on Parallel and Distributed Data Mining]. *Distributed and Parallel Databases, 11*(2), 181–201.

Department of Statistics, Stanford University.

Deshpande, P., Ramasamy, K., Shukla, A., & Naughton, J. (1998). Caching multidimensional queries using chunks. In L. Haas & A. Tiwary (Eds.), *ACM SIGMOD International Conference on Management of Data* (pp. 259-270). New York: ACM Press.

DeWitt, D., Paulson, E., Robinson, E., Naughton, J., Royalty, J., Shankar, S., & Krioukov, A. (2008). Clustera: an integrated computation and data management system. *VLDB, 1*(1), 28–41.

Dhamankar, R., Lee, Y., Doan, A-H., Halevy, A. Y., & Domingos, P. (2004). iMAP: Discovering Complex Mappings between Database Schemas. In G. Weikum, A. C. König, S. Deßloch (Eds.), *Proc. ACM SIGMOD Int. Conf. on Management of Data* (pp. 383-394). New York: ACM Press.

Doan A., & Halevi, A. Y. (2005). Semantic integration research in the database community: A Brief Survey. *AI Magazine, 26* (1), 83-94.

Doan, A., Lu, Y., Lee, Y., & Han, J. (2003). Profile-Based Object Matching for Information Integration. *IEEE Intelligent Systems, 18* (5), 54-59.

Dobra, A., Garofalakis, M., Gehrke, J., & Rastogi, R. (2002). Processing Complex Aggregate Queries over Data Streams. In *Proceedings of 2002 ACM SIGMOD International Conference on Management of Data.*

du Mouza, C., Litwin, W., & Rigaux, P. (2007). SD-Rtree: A Scalable Distributed Rtree. *International Conference on Data Engineering (ICDE)* (pp. 296-305).

Du, W., & Atallah, M. J. (2001). Privacy-Preserving Cooperative Statistical Analysis. In *Proceedings of 2001 Computer Security Applications Conference.*

Du, W., & Zhan, Z. (2002). Building Decision Tree Classifier on Private Data. In *ICDM Workshop on Privacy, Security, and Data Mining.*

Dy, J. G., & Brodley, C. E. (2000). Feature subset selection and order identification for unsupervised learning. In *Proceedings of the International Conference on Machine Learning* (pp. 247–254).

Dzwinel, W., Yuen, D., Kaneko, Y., Boryczko, K., & Ben-Zion, Y. (2003). Multi-resolution clustering analysis and 3-D visualization of multitudinous synthetic earthquakes. *Visual Geosciences, 8*(1), 12-25.

Efron, B., & Tibshirani, R. J. (1998). *An Introduction to the Bootstrap.* CRC Press LLC.

Egenhofer, M. J. (1991). Reasoning about binary topological relations. In *Advances in Spatial Databases (Second Symposium, SDD'91),* Zurich, Switzerland (LNCS)

Egenhofer, M. J., & Franzosa, R. D. (1991). Point-set topological spatial relations. *International Journal of Geographic Information Systems, 5*(2), 161-174.

Egenhofer, M. J., & Franzosa, R. D. (1995). On equivalence of topological relations. *International Journal of Geographical Information Systems, 9*(2), 133-152.

Egenhofer, M. J., & Herring, J. R. (1991). *A mathematical framework for the definition of topological relations* (NCGIA Technical Paper, pp. 91-97).

Egenhofer, M. J., & Herring, J. R. (1992). *Categorizing binary topological relations between regions, lines, and points in geographic databases* (Tech. Rep.). Orono: University of Maine, Department of Survey Engineering,

Egenhofer, M., Herring, J. (1990). A mathematical framework for the definition of topological relations. In *Proceedings of the Fourth International Symposium on Spatial Data Handling* (pp. 803-813). Zurich, Switzerland:

Embley, D. W., Xu, L., & Ding Y. (2004). Automatic Direct and Indirect Schema Mapping: Experiences and Lessons Learned. *SIGMOD Record 33* (4), 14-19.

Emekci, F., Agrawal, D., Abbadi, A. E., & Gulbeden, A. (2006). Privacy Preserving Query Processing Using Third Parties. In *Proceedings of 2006 ICDE International Conference on Data Engineering.*

Emerson, E.A. (1990). Temporal and modal logic. *Handbook of Theoretical Computer Science, B,* 995–1072.

English, L. P. (1999). *Improving data warehouse & business information quality: Methods for reducing costs and increasing profits.* New York: Wiley.

Erkan, G., & Radev, D.R. (2004). LexRank: Graph-based lexical centrality as salience in text summarization. *Journal of Artificial Intelligence Research, 22,* 457–479.

Euzenat, J., & Valtchev, P. (2004). Similarity-Based Ontology Alignment in OWL-Lite. In: R. López de Mántaras,

L. Saitta (Eds.), *Proc. 16th European Conf. on Artificial Intelligence*, (pp. 333-337). Amsterdam: IOS Press.

Ezeife, C. I. (2001). Selecting and materializing horizontally partitioned warehouse views. *Data and Knowledge Engineering, 36,* 185-210.

Faloutsos, C., & Roseman, S. (1989). Fractals for secondary key retrieval. *Symposium on Principles of Database Systems* (pp. 247-252).

Fawcett, T. (2003). *ROC graphs: Notes and practical considerations for data mining researchers.* Retrieved November 9, 2007, from http://citeseer.comp.nus.edu. sg/fawcett03roc.html

Fayad, U., Piatetsky-Shapiro, G., Smith, P., & Uthurusami, R. (1996). *Advances in Knowledge Discovery and Data Mining.* MIT Press.

Finney, D. J. (1971). *Probit Analysis* (3rd ed.). London, UK: Cambridge University Press.

Franconni, E., & Kamble, A. (2004). The GMD Data model and algebra for multidimensional information. In *Proceedings of the 16th Int. Conf. on Advanced Information Systems Engineering (CAiSE)* (pp. 446-462). Springer.

Frawley, W. J., Piatetsky-Shapiro, G., & Matheus, C. J. (1991). Knowledge discovery in database: An overview. In G. Piatetsky-Shapiro & W. J. Frawley (Eds.), *Knowledge discovery databases.* AAAI/MIT Press.

Frayman, Y., Rolfe, S., & Webb, G. (2002). Solving Regression Problems Using Competitive Ensemble Models. *AI 2002: Advances in Artificial Intelligence: Proceedings of the 15th Australian Joint Conference on Artificial Intelligence* (pp. 511-522). Berlin: Springer-Verlag.

Freund, Y. (1990). Boosting a weak learning algorithm by majority. In *Proceedings of the Third Annual Workshop on Computational Learning Theory,* Rochester, NY, USA: Morgan Kaufmann.

Freund, Y., & Schapire, R. (1997). A decision-theoretic generalization of online learning and an application to boosting. *Journal of Computer System Sciences, 55,* 119-139.

Freund, Y., Iyer, R ., Robert, E., Schapire, & Singer, Y. (1998). An efficient boosting algorithm for combining preferences. In *Machine Learning: Proceedings of the Fifteenth International Conference,* (pp. 170-178), San Francisco: Morgan Kaufmann.

Friedman, J. (1999a). *Greedy function approximation: A gradient boosting machine* (Tech. Rep.).

Friedman, J. (1999b). *Stochastic gradient boosting* (Tech. Rep.). Department of Statistics, Stanford University.

Friedman, J. H. (2001). Greedy function approximation: A gradient boosting machine. *Annals of Statistics, 29,* 1189-1232.

Friedman, J. H., Hastie, T., & Tibshirani, R. (2000). Additive logistic regression: A statistical view of boosting (with discussion). *Annals of Statistics, 28,* 337-407.

Fu, L. (2007). *Cancer subtype classification based on gene expression signatures.* Retrieved from http://www.cise. ufl.edu/$\sim$fu/NSF/cancer_classify_GES.html

Fu, L. M., & Youn, E. S. (2003). Improving reliability of gene selection from microarray functional genomics data. *IEEE Transactions on Information Technology in Biomedicine, 7*(3). doi:10.1109/TITB.2003.816558

Fung, C-W., Karlapalem, K., & Li, Q. (2002). An evaluation of vertical class partitioning for query processing in object-oriented databases. *IEEE Transactions on Knowledge and Data Engineering, 14*(5), 1095-1118.

Furtado, C., Lima, A., Pacitti, E., Valduriez, P., & Mattoso, M. (2005). Physical and virtual partitioning in OLAP database cluster. In *Proceedings of the 17th International Symposium on Computer Architecture and High Performance Computing* (pp. 143-150).

Ganguly, S., Garofalskis, M., & Rastogi, R. (2004). Processing data-stream join aggregates using skimmed sketches. EDBT International Conference on Extending Database Technology.

Garofalakis, M.N., Rastogi, R., & Shim, K. (1999). SPIRIT: Sequential pattern mining with regular expression constraints. *The VLDB Journal,* 223–234.

Garriga, G. C. (2005). Summarizing sequential data with closed partial orders. In *Proceedings of the SIAM International Conference on Data Mining, California* (pp. 380-391).

Garriga, G. C., & Balcazar, J. L. (2004). Coproduct transformations on lattices closed partial orders. In *Proceedings of the Second International Conference on Graph Transformation* (pp. 336-351). Rome, Italy, .

Gerbesioti, A., Delis, V., Theodoridis, Y., & Anagnostopoulos, S. (2001). Developing decision support tools for confronting seismic hazards. In *Proceedings of the 8th Panhellenic Conference in Informatics, PCI'01*, Nicosia, Cyprus.

GI-NOA. (2006). *Earthquake catalog.* Retrieved from http://www.gein.noa.gr/services/cat.html

Goethals, B., Laur, S., Lipmaa, H., & Mielikainen, T. (2004). On Private Scalar Product Computation for Privacy-Preserving Data Mining. In *Proceedings of 2004 ICISC International Conference in Information Security and Cryptology.*

Goil, S., & Choudhary, A. (1997). High performance olap and data mining on parallel computers. *Journal of Data Mining and Knowledge Discovery, 1*(4). doi:10.1023/A:1009777418785

Goldreich, O. (2001). Secure Multi-Party Computation. *The Foundations of Cryptography* (Vol. 2, Chapter 7). Cambridge University Press.

Golfarelli, M., Maio, D. & Rizzi, S. (1998). Conceptual design of data warehouses from E/R schemes. In *Proceedings of the 31st Hawaii Int. Conf. on System Sciences.*

Golfarelli, M., Maio, D. & Rizzi, S. (1998). The Dimensional Fact Model: a Conceptual Model for Data Warehouses. *International Journal of Cooperative Information Systems, 7*, 215-247.

Golfarelli, M., Maio, D., & Rizzi, S. (1998). The dimensional fact model: A conceptual model for data warehouses. *International Journal of Cooperative Information Systems, 7*(2/3), 215-247.

Goltz, J., & Eisner R. (2003). Real-time emergency management decision support: The California integrated seismic network (CISN). In *Proceedings of the Disaster Resistant California 2003 Conference, DRC'03*, San Jose, CA, USA.

Golub, T. (1999). Molecular classification of cancer: class discovery and class prediction by gene expression monitoring. *Science, 286*, 531–537. doi:10.1126/science.286.5439.531

Gorla, N. (2001). An object-oriented database design for improved performance. *Data and Knowledge Engineering, 37*, 117-138.

Gorla, N., & Boe, W. (1990). Effect of schema size on fragmentation design in multirelational databases. *Information Systems, 15*, 291-301.

Gray, J., Bosworth, A., Layman, A., & Pirahesh, H. (1996). Data cube: A relational aggregation operator generalizing group-by, cross-tab, and sub-total. In *Proceedings of the 12th Int. Conf. on Data Engineering (ICDE)* (pp. 152-159). IEEE Computer Society.

Gray, J., Bosworth, A., Layman, A., & Pirahesh, H. (1996). Data Cube: a Relational Aggregation Operator Generalizing Group-by, Cross-tab, and Sub-totals. In *Proceedings of 1996 ICDE International Conference on Data Engineering.*

Guo, D., Peuquet D., & Gahegan, M. (2003). ICEAGE. Interactive clustering and exploration of large and high-dimensional geodata. *GeoInformatica, 7*(3), 229-253.

Gupta, H. & Mumick, I. (2005). Selection of views to materialize in a data warehouse. *IEEE Transactions on Knowledge and Data Engineering, 17*(1), 24-43.

Gupta, H. (1997). Selection of views to materialize in a data warehouse. In F. Afrati & P. Kolaitis (Eds.), *Proceedings of the International Conference on Database Theory* (pp. 98-112). Delphi, Greece: Springer.

Gupta, H., & Mumick, I. (1999). Selection of views to materialize under a maintenance cost constraint. In C. Beeri & P. Buneman (Eds.), *Proceedings of the International Conference on Database Theory* (pp. 453-470). Jerusalem, Israel: Springer-Verlag.

Gupta, H., Harinarayan, V., Rajaraman, A., & Ullman, J. (1997). Index selection for OLAP. In: W. Gray & P. Larson (Eds.), *Proceedings of the International conference on data engineering* (pp. 208-219). Birmingham, UK: IEEE.

Guyon, I., Alamdari, A., Dror, G., & Buhmann, J. (2006, July 16-21). Performance prediction challenge. In *Proceedings of the International Joint Conference on Neural Networks,* Vancouver, BC, Canada, (pp. 2958-2965). IEEE.

Guyon, I., Weston, J., Barnhill, S., & Vapnik, V. (2002). Gene selection for cancer classification using support vector machines. *Machine Learning, 46*(13), 389–422. doi:10.1023/A:1012487302797

Guyon. I., & Elisseeff, A. (2003). An introduction to variable and feature selection. Special issue on variable and feature selection. In I. Guyon & A. Elisseeff (Eds.), *Journal of Machine Learning Research, 3,* 1157-1182.

Gyssen, M., & Lakshmanan, L. (1997). A foundation for multi-dimensional databases. In *Proceedings of the 23rd Int. Conf. on Very Large Data Bases (VLDB'97)* (pp. 106-115). Morgan Kaufmann.

Hackney, D. (1997). *Understanding and Implementing Successful Data Marts.* Reading, MA, USA: Addison-Wesley.

Hadzilacos, T., & Tryfona, N. (1992). In A. Frank, I. Campari, & U. Formentini (Eds.), *A Model for Expressing Topological Integrity Constraints in Geographic Databases: Proceedings of the International Conference on Theories and Models of Spatio Temporal Reasoning in Geographic Space.* Pisa, Italy (LNCS 639, pp. 252-268). New York: Springer-Verlag

Halevy, A. Y. (2001). Answering queries using views: A survey. *VLDB J., 10,* 270-294.

Hall, M. A. (2000). Correlation-based feature selection for discrete and numeric class machine learning. In *Proceedings of the International Conference on Machine Learning* (pp. 359-366).

Hammer, M., & Niamir, B. (1979). A heuristic approach to attribute partitioning. *ACM SIGMOD International Conference on Management of Data.*

Han, J. W., & Yan, X. F. (2004). From sequential patterns mining to structured pattern mining: A pattern-growth approach. *Journal of Computer Science and Technology, 19*(3), 257-279.

Han, J., & Fu, Y. (1999). Mining multiple-level association rules in large databases. *IEEE Transactions on Knowledge and Data Engineering, 11*(5), 798-805.

Han, J., & Kamber, M. (2006). *Data mining: Concepts and techniques.* San Francisco: Morgan Kaufmann.

Hanley, J. A., & McNeil, B. J. (1982). The meaning and use of the area under a receiver operating characteristic (ROC) curve. *Radiology, 143,* 29-36.

Hanley, J. A., & Mcneil, B. J. (1983). A method of comparing the areas under receiver operating characteristic curves derived from the same cases. *Radiology, 148,* 839-843.

Harinarayan, V., Rajaraman, A., & Ullman, J. (1996). Implementing data cubes efficiently. In H. Jagadish & I. Mumick (Eds.), *ACM SIGMOD international conference on management of data* (pp. 205-216).Montreal, Canada: ACM Press.

Hastie, T., Tibshirani, R., & Friedman, J. (2001). *The Elements of Statistical Learning: Data Mining, Inference, and Prediction.* New York: Springer.

Health Level Seven – HL7 (2008). Retrieved February 25, 2008 from the World Wide Web: http://www.hl7.org

Hoerl, A. E., & Kennard, R. W. (1970). Ridge regression: Biased estimation for nonorthogonal problems. *Technometrics, 12*(3), 55–67. doi:10.2307/1267351

Hoffer, J. A. (1976). An integer programming formulation of computer database design problems. *Information Science, 11,* 29-48.

Hoffer, J. A., & Severance, D. G. (1975). The use of cluster analysis in physical data base design. *International Conference on Very large Databases.*

Hoppner, F. (2001). Discovery of temporal patterns—Learning rules about the qualitative behavior of time series. *Proceedings of the 5th European Conference on Principles and Practice of Knowledge Discovery in Databases, 192–203.*

Horng, J., Chang, Y., Liu, B., & Kao, C. (1999). Materialized view selection using genetic algorithms in a data warehouse system. In *Proceedings of Congress on evolutionary computation* (pp. 2221-2227). Washington DC: IEEE.

Hornik, K., Stinchcombe, M., & White, H. (1989). Multilayer feedforward networks are universal approximators. *Neural Networks, 2,* 359-366.

Hotho, A., et al. (2001). Text clustering based on good aggregations. *Proceedings of the 2001 IEEE International Conference on Data Mining.*

Hotho, A., Staab, S., & Stumme, G. (2003). Wordnet improves text document clustering. In *Proceedings of the Semantic Web Workshop at 26th Annual International ACM SIGIR Conference,* Toronto, Canada.

http://sdmc.lit.org.sg/GEDatasets/Datasets.html

Huan, J., Wang, W., Prins, J., & Yang, J. (2004). SPIN: Mining maximal frequent subgraphs from graph databases. In *Proceedings of the 10th ACM SIGKDD* (pp. 581-586). Seattle, WA:

Huang, J. Y., Smola, A. J., Gretton, A., Borgwardt, K. M., & Schölkopf, B. (2006). Correcting sample selection bias by unlabeled data. In *Proceedings of 20th Annual Conference on Neural Information Processing Systems* (pp. 601-608).

Huber, P. (1985). Projection pursuit. *The Annals of Statistics, 13*(2), 435-475.

Iliopoulos, I., et al. (2001). Textquest: Document clustering of Medline abstracts for concept discovery in molecular biology. *Pac Symp Biocomput,* 384–395.

Inmon, W. (1996). *Building the data warehouse,* 2nd ed. John Wiley & Sons.

Ishibuchi, H., & Murata, T. (1999). Techniques and applications of genetic algorithms-based methods for designing compact fuzzy classification systems. *Fuzzy Theory Systems Techniques & Applications, 3*(40), 1081–1109. doi:10.1016/B978-012443870-5.50042-3

Ishibuchi, H., Nakashima, T., & Muratam, T. (1999). Performance evaluation of fuzzy classifier systems for multi-dimensional pattern classification problems. *IEEE Trans. on Systems, Man, and Cybernetics – Part B, 29*(5), 601–618.

Ishibuchi, H., Nozaki, K., & Tanaka, H. (1992). Distributed representation of fuzzy rules and its application to pattern classification. *Fuzzy Sets and Systems, 52*(1), 21–32. doi:10.1016/0165-0114(92)90032-Y

Ivancsy, R., & Vajk, I. (2005). A survey of discovering frequent patterns in graph. In *Proceedings of Databases and Applications* (pp. 60-72). ACTA Press.

Jacobs, N., & Blockeel, H. (2001). From shell logs to shell scripts. *Proceedings of the 11th International Conference on Inductive Logic Programming,* LNAI, *2157,* 80–90.

Jagadish, H., Ooi, B. C., & Vu, Q. H. (2005). BATON: A Balanced Tree Structure for Peer-to-Peer Networks. In *VLDB* (pp. 661–672).

Jain, A. K., Duin, R. P. W., & Mao, J. (2000). Statistical pattern recognition: A review. *IEEE Transactions on Pattern Analysis and Machine Intelligence, 22*(1), 4-37.

Jain, A., Murty, M., & Flynn, P. (1999). Data clustering: A review. *ACM Computing Surveys, 31*(3), 264-323.

Jefferies, N., Mitchell, C., & Walker, M. (1995). A Proposed Architecture for Trusted Third Party Services. In *Proceedings of 1995 Cryptography Policy and Algorithms Conference.*

Jeusfeld, M. A., Quix, C., & Jarke, M. (1998). Design and analysis of quality information for data warehouses. In *Proceedings of the International Conference on Conceptual Modeling* (pp. 349-362).

Jiang, J., & Conrath, D. (1998). Semantic similarity based on corpus statistics and lexical taxonomy. In *Proceedings of the International Conference on Research in Computational Linguistic,* Taiwan.

Jindal, R. & Acharya, A. (2004). Federated Data Warehouse Architecture. Wipro Technologies – white paper. Retrieved October 10, 2007 from the World Wide Web: http://hosteddocs.ittoolbox.com/Federated%20data%20Warehouse%20Architecture.pdf

Jing, J., Zhou, L., Ng, M., & Huang, Z. (2006). Ontology-based distance measure for text clustering. In *Proceedings of SIAM SDM workshop on text mining.* Bethesda, Maryland, USA.

Juegens, M., & Lenz, H.-J. (1998). The Ra*-tree: An improved r-tree with materialized data for supporting range queries on OLAP-data. In *DEXA Workshop* (pp. 186-191).

Kainz, W. (1991). Logical consistency. In Guptil & Morison (Eds.), *Elements of spatial data quality* (pp.109-137). Oxford, England.

Kalnis, P., Mamoulis, N., & Papadias, D. (2002a). View selection using randomized search. *Data Knowledge and Engineering, 42*(1), 89-111.

Kalnis, P., Ng, W., Ooi, B., Papadias, D., & Tan, K. (2002b). An adaptive peer-to-peer network for distributed caching of olap results. In M. Franklin, B. Moon & A. Ailamaki (Eds.), *ACM SIGMOD international conference on management of data* (pp. 25-36). Madison, USA: ACM Press.

Kalogeras, I., Marketos, G., & Theodoridis, Y. (2004). A tool for collecting, querying, and mining macroseismic data. *Bulletin of the Geological Society of Greece, vol. XXXVI.*

Kamel, I., & Faloutsos, C. (1993). On packing r-trees. In *Proceedings of the Second International Conference on Information and Knowledge Management* (pp. 490-499).

Kantarcioglu, M., & Vaidya, J. (2002). An Architecture for Privacy-Preserving Mining of Client Information. In *ICDM IEEE Conference on Data Mining Workshop on Privacy, Security and Data Mining.*

Karr, A. F., Sanil, A. P., & Banks, D. L. (2006). Data quality: A statistical perspective. *Statistical Methodology, 3*(2), 137-173.

Kaufman, L. & Rousseeuw, P. (1990). *Finding Groups in Data: An Introduction to Cluster Analysis.* John Wiley & Sons.

Khabbaz, M., Kiamehr, K., Alshalalfa, M., & Alhajj, R. (2007). Fuzzy classifier based feature reduction for better gene selection. In *Proceedings of the International Conference on Data Warehouse and Knowledge Discovery* (LNCS). Regensburg, Germany: Springer-Verlag.

Kiang, M. Y. (2003). A comparative assessment of classification methods. *Decision Support Systems, 35,* 441-454.

Kianmehr, K., Zhang, H., Nikolov, K., Ozyer, T., & Alhajj, R. (2005). Combining neural network and support vector machine into integrated approach for biodata mining. In *Proceedings of the International Conference on Enterprise Information Systems* (pp. 182–187). Miami, FL.

Kim, W., & Seo, J. (1991). Classifying Semantic and Data Heterogeneity in Multidatabase Systems. *IEEE Computer, 24* (12), 12-18.

Kimball, R. (1996). *The data warehouse toolkit: Practical techniques for building dimensional data warehouses,* 2nd ed. John Wiley & Sons Inc.

Kiratzi, A., & Louvari, E. (2003). Focal mechanisms of shallow earthquakes in the aegean sea and the surrounding lands determined by waveform modeling: A new database. *Journal of Geodynamics, 36,* 251-274.

Kleinberg, J.M. (1999). Authoritative sources in a hyperlinked environment. *J. ACM 46*(5), 604–632.

Klien, A. (2007). A rule-based strategy for the semantic annotation of geodata. *Transactions in GIS, 11*(3), 437-452.

Knappe, R., Bulskov, H., & Andreasen, T. (2006). Perspectives on ontology-based querying. *International Journal of Intelligent Systems.*

Koggalage, R., & Halgamuge, S. (2004). Reducing the number of training samples for fast support vector machine classification. *Neural Information Processing Letters and Reviews, 2*(3), 57–65.

Kohavi, R. (1995). A study of cross-validation and bootstrap for accuracy estimation and model selection. *Proceedings of the Fourteenth International Joint Conference on Artificial Intelligence, 2*(12), 1137-1143. San Mateo: Morgan Kaufmann.

Koperski K., & Han J. (1995). Discovery of spatial association rules in geographic information databases. In *Proceedings of the 4th International Symposium on Large in Spatial Databases, SSD'95*, Portland, MA, USA.

Koperski, K., Han, J., & Adhikary, J. (1998). Mining knowledge in geographical data. *Communications of the ACM, 26*(1), 65-74.

Kotidis, Y. & Roussopoulos, N. (1999). Dynamat: A dynamic view management system for data warehouses. In: A. Delis, C. Faloutsos & S. Ghandeharizadeh (Eds.), *ACM SIGMOD international conference on management of data* (pp. 371-382). Philadelphia: ACM Press.

Kotidis, Y. & Roussopoulos, N. (2001). A case for dynamic view management. *ACM Transactions on Database Systems, 26*(4), 388-423.

Koudas, N., Faloutsos, C., & Kamel, I. (1996). Declustering spatial databases on a multi-computer architecture. In *Proceedings of Extended Database Technologies* (pp. 592-614).

Kretschmer, U., & Roccatagliata, E. (2000). CommonGIS: A European Project for an Easy Access to Geo-data. In *Proceedings of the 2nd European GIS Education Seminar, EUGISES'00*, Budapest, Hungary.

Kriebel, C. H. (1978). Evaluating the quality of information systems. In *Proceedings of the BIFOA Symposium* (pp. 18-20).

Kuramochi, M., & Karypis, G. (2004). An efficient algorithm for discovering frequent subgraphs. *IEEE Transactions on Knowledge and Data Engineering, 16*(9), 1038–1051.

Labio, W. J., Quass, D., & Adelberg, B. (1997). Physical database design for data warehouses. In *Proceedings of the IEEE Conference on Data Engineering* (pp. 277-288).

LAMDAer Team. (2006). Predicting future customers via ensembling gradually expanded trees. PAKDD Competition 2006. *International Journal of Data Warehousing and Mining, 3*(2), 12-21.

Lamping, J., & Rao R. (1994). Laying out and visualizing large trees using a hyperbolic space. In *Proceedings of the 7th ACM Symposium on User Interface Software and Technology (UIST'94)* (pp. 13-14). ACM.

Larsen, B., & Aone, C. (1999). Fast and effective text mining using linear-time document clustering. *KDD-99* (pp. 16-22). San Diego, California.

Lattner, A., & Herzog, O. (2004). Unsupervised learning of sequential patterns. *Proceedings of the ICDM'2004 Workshop on Temporal Data Mining: Algorithms, Theory and Applications.*

Lattner, A., & Herzog, O. (2005). Mining temporal patterns from relational data. *Proceedings of LWA'2005,* 184–189.

Lawrence, M. (2006). Multiobjective genetic algorithms for materialized view selection in olap data warehouses. In M. Cattolico (Ed.), *Proceeding of the Genetic and evolutionary computation conference* (pp. 699-706). Seattle, USA: ACM Press.

Leacock, C., & Chodorow, M. (1994). Filling in a sparse training space for word sense identification. ms.

Lecun, Y., Chopra, S., Hadsell, R., Huang, F.-J., & Ranzato, M.-A. (2006). *A tutorial on energy-based learning: Predicting structured outputs.* New York: MIT Press.

Lee, M., & Hammer, J. (2001). Speeding up materialized view selection in data warehouses using a randomized algorithm. *International Journal of Cooperative Information Systems, 10*(3), 327-353.

Lee, S.D., & De Raedt, L. (2002). Constraint based mining of first order sequences in seqlog. *Proceedings of the KDID'02,* 76–92.

Lehner, W. (1998). Modeling large scale OLAP scenarios. In *Proceedings of the 6th Int. Conf. on Extending Database Technology (EDBT'98)* (pp. 153-167). Springer.

Levenshtein, V. I. (1966). Binary Codes Capable of Correcting Deletions, Insertions, and Reversals. *Cybernetics and Control Theory, 10* (8), 707–710.

Levine, M., & Schultz, A. (2002). *GEODE (Geo-Data Explorer)—A U.S. geological survey application for data retrieval, display, and analysis through the Internet.* U.S. Geological Survey, Fact Sheet 132-01, Online Version 1.0. Retrieved from http://pubs.usgs.gov/fs/fs132-01/

LeVis Group, Shanghai University. (2007). *PAKDD 2007 Data Mining Competition.* Retrieved November 9, 2007, from http://lamda.nju.edu.cn/conf/pakdd07/dmc07/

Li, C. (2007). Classifying imbalanced data using a bagging ensemble variation (BEV). In *Proceedings of the 45th Annual Southeast Regional Conference*, (pp. 203-208). New York: ACM Press.

Li, C., & Wang, X.S. (1996). A Data Model for Supporting On-Line Analytical Processing. In *Proceedings of the 5th Int. Conf. on Information and Knowledge Management (CIKM'96)* (pp. 81-88). ACM.

Li, F., & Yang, Y. (2005). Analysis of recursive gene selection approach from microarray data. *Bioinformatics (Oxford, England)*, 37–41.

Li, J., Ng, K.-S., & Wong, L. (2003). Bioinformatics adventures in database research. In *Proceedings of the International Conference on Database Theory* (pp. 31–46). Siena, Italy.

Li, X., Lu, P., Schaefer, J., Shillington, J., Wong, P. S., & Shi, H. (1993). On the versatility of parallel sorting by regular sampling. *Parallel Computing, 19*(10), 1079–1103. doi:10.1016/0167-8191(93)90019-H

Li, Y., Zuhair, A., & McLean, D. (2003). An approach for measuring Semantic similarity between words using multiple information sources. *IEEE Transactions on Knowledge and Data Engineering, 15*(4), 871-882.

Liang, W., Wang, H., & Orlowska, M. (2001). Materialized view selection under the maintenance time constraint. *Data & Knowledge Engineering. 37*(2), 203-216.

Lin, D. (1993). Principle-based parsing without over-generation. In *Proceedings of the 31st Annual Meeting of the Association for Computational Linguistics* (pp. 112-120). Columbus, Ohio.

Lin, M. Y., & Lee, S. Y. (2005). Fast discovery of sequential patterns through memory indexing and database partitioning. *Journal of Information Science and Engineering, 21,* 109-128.

Liu, H., & Yu, L. (2005). Toward integrating feature selection algorithms for classification and clustering. *IEEE Transactions on Knowledge and Data Engineering, 17*(4), 491–502. doi:10.1109/TKDE.2005.66

Lorincza, H.A., & Boulicaut, J.-F. (2003). Mining frequent sequential patterns under regular expressions: A highly adaptive strategy for pushing constraints. *Proceedings of the ICDM'03*, 316–320.

Loukopoulos, T., Kalnis, P., Ahmad, I., & Papadias, D. (2001). Active caching of online analytical processing queries in www proxies. In *Proceedings of the International conference on parallel processing* (pp. 419-426). Columbus, USA: IEEE Computer Society.

Lovàsz, L. & Plummer, M. D. (1986). *Matching Theory.* Amsterdam: North-Holland.

Lu, J. (2006). *From sequential patterns to concurrent branch patterns: A new post sequential patterns mining approach.* Unpublished doctoral dissertation, University of Bedfordshire, UK.

Lu, J., Adjei, O., Chen, W.R., & Liu, J. (2004). Post sequential patterns mining: A new method for discovering structural patterns. In *Proceedings of the Second International Conference on Intelligent Information Processing* (pp. 239-250). Beijing, China: Springer-Verlag.

Lu, J., Adjei, O., Wang, X. F., & Hussain, F. (2004). Sequential patterns modelling and graph pattern mining. In *Proceedings of the 10th International Conference IPMU* (Vol. 2, pp. 755-761). Perugia, Italy.

Lu, J., Wang, X. F., Adjei, O., & Hussain, F. (2004). Sequential patterns graph and its construction algorithm. *Chinese Journal of Computers, 27*(6), 782-788.

Lutz, M., & Kolas, D. (2007). Rule-based discovery in spatial data infrastructure. *Transactions in GIS, 11*(3), 317-336.

Lutz, R. (2006, July 16-21). LogitBoost with trees applied to the WCCI 2006 performance prediction challenge datasets. In *Proceedings of the International Joint Conference on Neural Networks,* Vancouver, BC, Canada, (pp. 2966-2969). IEEE.

Madhavan, J., Bernstein, P. A., & Rahm, E. (2001). Generic Schema Matching with Cupid. In P. M. G. Apers, P. Atzeni, S. Ceri, S. Paraboschi, K. Ramamohanarao, R. T. Snodgrass (Eds.) *Proc. 27th Int. Conf. on Very Large Data Bases* (pp. 49-58). San Francisco: Morgan Kaufmann.

Malinowski, E., & Zimányi, E. (2006). Hierarchies in a multidimensional model: From conceptual modeling to logical representation. *Journal of Data & Knowledge Engineering, 59*(2), 348-377.

Maniatis, A., Vassiliadis, P., Skiadopoulos, S., Vassiliou, Y., Mavrogonatos, G., & Michalarias, I. (2005). A presentation model & non-traditional visualization for OLAP. *International Journal of Data Warehousing & Mining, 1*(1), 1-36.

Mannila, H., & Meek, C. (2000). Global partial orders from sequential data. In *Proceedings of the 6th Annual Conference on Knowledge Discovery and Data Mining (KDD-2000)* (pp. 161-168).

Mansmann, S., & Scholl, M. H. (2006). Extending Visual OLAP for Handling Irregular Dimensional Hierarchies. In A. M. Tjoa & J. Trujillo (Eds.), *Proc. 8th Int. Conf. on Data Warehousing and Knowledge Discovery. Lecture Notes in Computer Science, 4081,* 95-105.

Mao, W., & Chu, W. (2002). Free text medical document retrieval via phrased-based vector space model. In *Proceedings of AMIA'02*, San Antonio, TX.

March, S. T. (1983). Techniques in structuring database records. *ACM Computing Surveys, 15*(1).

March, S. T., & Rho, S. (1995). Allocating data and operations to nodes in distributed database design. *IEEE Trans. on Knowledge and Data Engineering, 7*(2).

Mark, D. M., & Egenhofer, M. J. (1992). An evaluation of the 9-intersection for region line relations. In *Proceedings of GIS/LIS '93*,(pp. 513-521). San Jose, CA:

Mark, D., Frank, A., Egenhofer, M., Freundshuh, S., McGranghan, M., & White, R. M. (Eds.). (1989). *Languages of spatial relations: Report on the specialist meeting for NCGIA research initiative 2* (Tech. Rep. 89-2). National Center for Geographic Information and Analysis.

Markov, A., et al. (2006). Model-based classification of Web documents represented by graphs. *Proceedings of the WebKDD 2006: KDD Workshop on Web Mining and Web Usage Analysis, in conjunction with the 12th ACM SIGKDD International Conference on Knowledge Discovery and Data Mining (KDD 2006).* Philadelphia, Pennsylvania.

Masson, C., & Jacquenet, F. (2003). Mining frequent logical sequences with SPIRITLoG. *Proceedings of the 12th International Conference on Inductive Logic Programming,* LNCS, *2583,* 166–181.

McCormick, W. T., Jr., Schweitzer, P. J., & White, T. W. (1972). Problem decomposition and data organization by a clustering technique. *Operations Research, 20*(5), 993-1009.

Medeiros, C. B., & Cilia, M. (1995). Maintenance of binary topological constraints through active databases. In *Proceedings of Third ACM Workshop on GIS.*

Melnik, S., Garcia-Molina, H., & Rahm, E. (2002). Similarity Flooding: A Versatile Graph Matching Algorithm and Its Application to Schema Matching. In *Proc. 18th Int. Conf. on Data Engineering* (pp. 117-128). IEEE Computer Society.

Melville, P., Yang, S. M., Saar-Tschansky, M., & Mooney, R. J. (2005). Active learning for probability estimation using Jensen-Shannon divergence. In *Proceedings of the 16th European Conference on Machine Learning* (pp. 268-279).

Messaoud, R., Boussaid, O., & Rabaséda, S. (2006). A data mining-based olap aggregation of complex data: Application on XML documents. *International Journal of Data Warehousing & Mining, 2*(4), 1-26.

Mitra, S., & Pal, S. K. (1994). Self-organizing neural network as a fuzzy classifier. *IEEE Transactions on Systems, Man, and Cybernetics, 24*(3), 385–399. doi:10.1109/21.278989

Moore, D. (2002). *Fast hilbert curve generation, sorting, and range queries.* Retrieved from http://www.caam.rice.edu/~dougm/twiddle/Hilbert

Nadeau, T., & Teorey, T. (2002). Achieving scalability in OLAP materialized view selection. In I. Song & P. Vassiliadis (Eds.), *ACM international workshop on data warehousing and OLAP* (pp. 28-34). Arlington, USA: ACM Press.

Nassis, V., Rajagopalapillai, R., Dillon, T., & Rahayu, W. (2005). Conceptual and systematic design approach for XML document warehouses. *International Journal of Data Warehousing & Mining, 1*(3), 63-87.

National Institute of Standards and Technology (NIST). (2002). Secure Hash Standard. *Federal Information Processing Standards 180-2.*

Navathe, S., & Ra, M. (1989). Vertical partitioning for database design: A graphical algorithm. In *Proceedings of the 1989 ACM SIGMOD/*

Navathe, S., Ceri, S., Wiederhold, G., & Dou, J. (1984). Vertical partitioning algorithms for database design. *ACM Transactions on. Database Systems.*

NEIC-USGS. *Earthquake search.* Retrieved from http://neic.usgs.gov/neis/epic/epic_global.html

Neslin, S. A., Gupta, S., Kamakura, W., Lu, J., & Mason, C. H. (2006). Defection detection: Measuring and understanding the predictive accuracy of customer churn models. *Journal of Marketing Research, 43*(5), 204-211.

Ng, A. Y. (1998). On feature selection: Learning with exponentially many irrelevant features as training examples. In *Proceedings of the International Conference on Machine Learning* (pp. 404–412).

Ng, V., Gorla, N., Law, D.M., & Chan, C. K. (2003). Applying genetic algorithms in database partitioning. In *Proceedings of the 2003 ACM Symposium on Applied Computing (SAC)* (pp. 544-549).

Niemi, T., Hirvonen, L., & Jarvelin, K. (2003). Multidimensional data model and query language for informetrics. *Journal of the American Society for Information Science and Technology, 54*(10), 939-951.

Nikulin, V. (2006a). *Learning with gradient-based optimization, clustering-minimization and mean-*

Nikulin, V. (2006b, July 16-21). Learning with mean-variance filtering, SVM and gradient-based optimization. In *Proceedings of the International Joint Conference on Neural Networks*, Vancouver, BC, Canada, (pp. 4195-4202). IEEE.

Noriel, N. B., & Tan, C. L. (2007). A look back at the PAKDD data mining competition 2006. *International Journal of Data Warehousing and Mining, 3*(2), 1-11.

Ontrup, J., et al. (2004). A MeSH term based distance measure for document retrieval and labeling assistance. *Proceedings of the 25th Annual International Conference of the IEEE, 2*, 1303–1306.

Ozsu, M., & Valduriez, P. (1996). *Principles of distributed database systems.* Prentice Hall.

Padmanabhan, S., Bhattacharjee, B., Malkemus, T., Cranston, L., & Huras, M. (2003). Multi-dimensional clustering: A new data layout scheme in DB2. In *ACM SIGMOD* (pp. 637-641).

Page, L., et al. (1998). The PageRank citation ranking: Bringing order to the Web. Technical Report, Stanford Digital Library Technologies Project.

PAKDD Competition. (2007). Retrieved November 8, 2007, from http://lamda.nju.edu.cn/conf/pakdd07/dmc07/

PAKDD-2007 Competition Web page. (2007). Retrieved November 9, 2007, from http://lamda.nju.edu.cn/conf/pakdd07/dmc07/

Palopoli, L., Saccà, D., Terracina, G., & Ursino, D. (2003). Uniform Techniques for Deriving Similarities of Objects and Subschemes in Heterogeneous Databases. *IEEE Transactions on Knowledge and Data Engineering, 15*, 271-294.

Park, J-S., Chen, M-S., & Yu, P. S. (1995). *Mining association rules with adjustable accuracy* (IBM research report).

PEADAB. (2006). *Post-earthquake assessment of building safety.* Retrieved from http://europa.eu.int/comm/ environment/ civil/prote/cpactiv/cpact08a.htm

Pedersen, T., Jensen, C., & Dyreson, C. (2001). A foundation for capturing and querying complex multidimensional data. *Journal of Information Systems, 26*(5), 383-423.

Pedersen, T., Pakhomov, S., Patwardhan, S., & Chute, C. (2007). Measures of semantic similarity and relatedness in the biomedical domain. *Journal of Biomedical Informatics, 40*(3), 288-299.

Pei, J., et al. (2004). Mining sequential patterns by pattern-growth: The prefix-span approach. *IEEE Transactions on Knowledge and Data Engineering, 16*(11), 1424-1440.

Pei, J., Han J. W., Mortazavi-Asl, B., & Pinto, H. (2001). PrefixSpan: Mining sequential patterns efficiently by prefix-projected pattern growth. In *Proceedings of the Seventh International Conference on Data Engineering* (pp. 215-224). Heidelberg, Germany.

Pei, J., Han, J. W., & Mao, R. (2000). CLOSET: An efficient algorithm for mining frequent closed itemsets. In *Proceedings of the 2000 ACM-SIGMOD International Workshop Data Mining and Knowledge Discovery* (pp. 11-20).

Pei, J., Han, J., & Wang, W. (2002). Mining sequential patterns with constraints in large databases. *Proceedings of the 2002 ACM CIKM Conference,* 18–25.

Pendse, N., & Creeth, R. (2002). *The OLAP Report.* Retrieved from http://www.olapreport.com

Peng, H. C., Long, F. H., & Ding, C. (2005). Feature selection based on mutual information: criteria of max-dependency, max-relevance, and min-redundancy. *IEEE Transactions on Pattern Analysis and Machine Intelligence, 27*(8), 1226–1238. doi:10.1109/TPAMI.2005.159

Pfoser, D., & Tryfona, N. (1998). Requirements, definitions and notations for spatiotemporal application environments. In *Proceedings of the 6th International Symposium on Advances in Geographic Information Systems, ACM-GIS'98,* (pp. 124-130). Washington DC, USA.

Phipps, C., & Davis, K. (2002). Automating data warehouse conceptual schema design and evaluation. In *Proceedings of DMDW* (pp. 23-32).

Piatetsky-Shapiro, G., & Tamayo, P. (2003). Microarray data mining: facing the challenges. *SIGKDD Explorations, 5,* 2–5. doi:10.1145/980972.980974

Pighin, M., & Ieronutti, L. (2007). From database to datawarehouses: A design quality evaluation. In *Proceedings of the International Conference on Enterprise Information Systems* (pp. 178-185).

PPDM. (2006). *The data exchange project.* Retrieved from http://www.ppdm.org/standards/exchange/index.html

Provost F., & Fawcett, T. (1998). Robust classification systems for imprecise environments. In *Proceedings of the 15th National Conference on Artificial Intelligence,* AAAI-98, Menlo Park, CA, (pp. 706-713).

Qiu, D. H., Wang, Y., & Bi, B. (2008). Identify cross-selling opportunities via hybrid classifier. *International Journal of Data Warehousing and Mining, 4*(2), 55–62.

Qiu, D. H., Wang, Y., Chen, C. B., & Fang, S. H. (2008). Sample selection according to categorical sensitivity for building cross-sell model. *International of Computational Systems, 4*(2), 583–588.

Rafanelli, M. (2003). Operators for Multidimensional Aggregate Data. In M. Rafanelli (Ed.), *Multidimensional databases: Problems and solutions* (pp. 116-165). Idea Group Publishing.

Rahm, E., & Bernstein, P. A. (2001). A survey of approaches to automatic schema matching. *VLDB Journal, 10,* 334-350.

Rahm, E., Do, H., & Massmann, S. (2004). Matching Large XML Schemas. *SIGMOD Record, 33* (4), 26-31.

Ramamurthy, R., Dewitt, D. J., & Su, Q. (2002). A case for fractured mirrors. In *Proceedings of the 28th VLDB Conference.*

Ramsak, F., Markl, V., Fenk, R., Zirkel, M., Elhardt, K., & Bayer, R. (2000). Integrating the UB-tree into a database system kernel. In *VLDB Conference* (pp. 263-272).

Ravat, F., Teste, O., & Tournier, R. (2007). OLAP aggregation function for textual data warehouse. In *Proceedings of the International Conference on Enterprise Information Systems (ICEIS 2007)*, INSTICC Press.

Ravat, F., Teste, O., & Zurfluh, G. (2006). A multiversion-based multidimensional model. In *Proceedings of the 8th Int. Conf. on Data Warehousing and Knowledge Discovery (DaWaK 2006)* (pp. 65-74). Springer.

Ravat, F., Teste, O., & Zurfluh, G. (2006). Constraint-based multi-dimensional databases. In Zongmin Ma (Ed.), Chap. XI of *Database Modeling for Industrial Data Management* (pp. 323-368). Idea Group Publishing.

Redman, T. C. (1992). *Data quality.* Bantam.

Redman, T. C. (1996). *Data quality for the information age.* Norwood, MA: Artech House.

Reinartz, T., Wirth, R., Clinton, J., Khabaza, T., Hejlesen, J., Chapman, P., & Kerber, R. (1998). *The current CRISP-DM.* Retrieved November 9, 2007, from http://www.crisp-dm.org/

Resnik, O. (1999). Semantic Similarity in Taxonomy: An Information-Based Measure and its Application to Problems of Ambiguity and Natural Language. *Journal of Artificial Intelligence Research, 11*, 95-130.

Resnik, P. (1999). Semantic Similarity in a Taxonomy: An Information-Based Measure and its Application to Problems of Ambiguity in Natural Language. *J. Artificial. Intelligence Research, 11*, 95-130.

Rizzi, S., Abelló, A., Lechtenbörger, J., & Trujillo, J. (2006). Research in data warehouse modeling and design: Dead or alive? In *Proceedings of the 9th ACM International Workshop on Data Warehousing and OLAP (DOLAP 2006)* (pp.3-10). ACM.

Rodríguez, A. (2005). Inconsistency issues in spatial databases. (LNCS, pp. 237-269). Springer Berlin/ Heidelberg.

Rodríguez, M. A., & Egenhofer, M.J. (2003). Determining Semantic Similarity among Entity Classes from Different Ontologies. *IEEE Transactions on Knowledge and Data Engineering, 15*, 442-456.

Rohwer, R., & Morciniec, M. (1996). A theoretical and experimental account of *n*-tuple classifier performance. *Neural Computation, 8*, 629-642.

Ross, K., & Srivastava, D. (1997). Fast computation of sparse data cubes. In *Proceedings of the 23rd VLDB Conference* (pp. 116-125).

Roussopolis, N., & Leifker, D. (1985). Direct spatial search on pictorial databases using packed r-trees. In *Proceedings of the 1985 ACM SIGMOD Conference* (pp. 17-31).

Roussopoulos, N., Kotidis, Y., & Roussopolis, M. (1997). Cubetree: Organization of the bulk incremental updates on the data cube. In *Proceedings of the 1997 ACM SIGMOD Conference* (pp. 89-99).

Rumelhart, D. E., & McClelland, J. L. (1986). *Parallel distributed processing.* Cambridge, MA: The MIT Press.

Rusu, L., Rahayu, J., & Taniar, D. (2005). A methodology for building XML data warehouses. *International Journal of Data Warehousing & Mining, 1*(2), 23-48.

Sackett, D. L., Rosenberg, W. M. C., Muir Gray, J. A., Haynes, R. B., & Richardson, W. S. (1996). Evidence-Based Medicine: What It Is and What It Isn't. *British Medical Journal, 312*, 71-72.

Salford Systems. (2005). *TreeNet: Stochastic gradient boosting.* Version 2.0. Salford Systems.

Sarawagi, S., Agrawal, R., & Gupta, A. (1996). *On computing the data cube* (Technical Report RJ10026). IBM Almaden Research Center, San Jose, California.

Scannapieco, M., Virgillito, A., Marchetti, C., Mecella, M., & Baldoni, R. (2004). The DaQuinCIS architecture: A platform for exchanging and improving data quality in cooperative information systems. *Information Systems, 29*(7), 551-582.

Schnitzer, B., & Leutenegger, S. (1999). Master-client r-trees: a new parallel architecture. *11th International Conference of Scientiffic and Statistical Database Management* (pp. 68-77).

SEG. (2006). The Society of Exploration Geophysicists. http://www.seg.org

Seismo-Surfer. (2006). Seismo-Surfer Project. http://www.seismo.gr

Servigne, S., Ubeda, T., Zuricelli, A., & Laurini, R. (2000). A methodology for spatial consistency improvement of geographic databases. *GeoInformatica 4*(1), 7-34.

She, R., Wang, K., Fu, A., & Xu, Y. (2007). Computing Join Aggregates over Private Tables. In *Proceedings of 9th International Conference on Data Warehousing and Knowledge Discovery*, Regensburg, Germany.

Shearer, C. (2000). The CRISP-DM model: The new blueprint for data mining. *Journal of Data Warehousing, 5*(4), 13-22.

Sheikholeslami, G., Chatterjee, S., & Zhang, A. (2000). WaveCluster: A Wavelet-based Clustering Approach for Spatial Data in Very Large Databases. *The VLDB Journal, 8*(3-4), 289-304.

Sheth, A. P., & Larson, J. A. (1990). Federated Database Systems for Managing Distributed, Heterogeneous, and Autonomous Databases. *ACM Computing Surveys, 22*, 183-236.

Shukla, A., Deshpande, P., & Naughton, J. (1998). Materialized view selection for multidimensional datasets. In: A. Gupta, O. Shmueli & J. Widom (Eds.), *Proceedings of the International Conference on Very Large Data Bases* (pp. 488-499). New York: Morgan Kaufmann.

Sismanis, Y., Deligiannakis, A., Roussopoulos, N., & Kotidis, Y. (2002). Dwarf: shrinking the petacube. In *Proceedings of the 2002 ACM SIGMOD Conference* (pp. 464-475).

Song, S. K., & Gorla, N. (2000). A genetic algorithm for vertical fragmentation and access path selection. *The Computer Journal, 45*(1), 81-93.

Speer, N., et al. (2005). Functional grouping of genes using spectral clustering and gene ontology. In *Proceedings of the IEEE International Joint Conference on Neural Networks*.

Srikant, R., & Agrawal, R. (1996). Mining sequential patterns: Generalizations and performance improvements. *Proceedings of* the *EDBT'96*, Avignon, France, 3–17.

Srinivasan, P. (2001). MeSHmap: A text mining tool for MEDLINE. *Proceedings of the AMIA Symposium*, 642–646.

Srinivasan, P., & Rindflesch, T. (2002). Exploring text mining from MEDLINE. *Proceedings of the AMIA Symposium*, 722–726.

Stefanovic, N., Han, J., & Koperski, K. (2000). Object-based selective materialization for efficient implementation of spatial data cubes. *IEEE Transactions on Knowledge and Data Engineering, 12*(6), 938-958.

Steinbach, M., Karypis, G., & Kumar, V. (2000). *A comparison of document clustering techniques.* Technical Report #00-034, Department of Computer Science and Engineering, University of Minnesota.

Steinberg, D., & Colla, P. (1995). *CART: Tree structured non-parametric data analysis.* Salford Systems.

Stinson, D. R. (2006). *Cryptography: Theory and Practice* (3rd ed.). Chapter 4. Chapman & Hall/CRC.

Stolba, N., Banek, M., & Tjoa, A. M. (2006). The Security Issue of Federated Data Warehouses in the Area of Evidence-Based Medicine, In Proceedings of 1st Int. Conf. on Availability, Reliability and Security (pp. 329-339). Los Alamitos, CA, USA: IEEE Computer Society.

Stolte, C., Tang, D., & Hanrahan, P. (2002). Polaris: A System for Query, Analysis, and Visualization of Multidimensional Relational Databases. *IEEE Trans. on Visualization and Computer Graphics, 8*(1), 52-65.

Stoppiglia, H., Dreyfus, G., Dubois, R., & Oussar, Y. (2003). Ranking a random feature for variable selection. *Journal of Machine Learning Research, 3*, 1399-1414.

Stumme, G., & Maedche, A. (2001). FCA-Merge: Bottom-up Merging of Ontologies. In B. Nebel (Ed.), *Proc. 7th Int. Conf. on Artificial Intelligence*, (pp. 225–230). San Francisco: Morgan Kaufmann.

Sung, S. Y., Li, Z., Tan, C. L., & Ng, P. A. (2003). Forecasting association rules using existing data sets. *IEEE Transactions on Knowledge and Data Engineering, 15*(6), 1448-1459.

The Gene Ontology Consortium. (2000). Gene ontology: tool for the unification of biology. *Nature Genetics, 25,* 25. doi:10.1038/75556

The QuickHash Library. (2006). Retrieved from the World Wide Web: http://www.slavasoft.com/quickhash/

Theodoratos, D., & Sellis, T. (1997). Data warehouse configuration. In M. Jarke, M. Carey, K. Dittrich, F. Lochovsky, P. Loucopoulos, & M. Jeusfeld (Eds.), *Proceedings of the International Conference on Very Large Data Bases* (pp. 126-135). Athens, Greece: Morgan Kaufmann.

Theodoratos, D., & Sellis, T. (1999). Dynamic data warehouse design. In M. Mohania & A. Tjoa (Eds.), *Proceedings of the International conference on data warehousing and knowledge discovery* (pp. 1-10). Florence, Italy: Springer-Verlag.

Theodoratos, D., & Sellis, T. (2000). Incremental design of a data warehouse. *Journal of Intelligent Information Systems, 15*(1), 7-27.

Theodoratos, D., Dalamagas, T., Simitsis, A., & Stavropoulos, M. (2001a). A randomized approach for the incremental design of an evolving data warehouse. In H. Kunii, S. Jajodia & A. Sølvberg (Eds.), *Proceedings of the International conference on conceptual modeling* (pp. 325-338).Yokohama, Japan: Springer-Verlag.

Theodoratos, D., Ligoudistianos, S., & Sellis, T. (2001b). View selection for designing the global data warehouse. *Data Knowledge & Engineering, 39*(3), 219-240.

Theodoridis, Y. (2003). Seismo-surfer: A prototype for collecting, querying and mining seismic data. In *Advances in Informatics—Post Proceedings of the 8th*

Panhellenic Conference in Informatics (pp. 159-171). Berlin: Springer Verlag.

Tikhonov, A. N., & Arsenin, V. Y. (1977). *Solutions of Ill-Posed Problems.* Winston, Washington, Orr, M.J.L. (1995). Regularisation in the Selection of Radial Basis Function Centres. *Neural Computation, 7*(3), 606–623.

Tjioe, H. C., & Taniar, D. (2005). Mining association rules in data warehouse. *International Journal of Data Warehousing and Mining, 1*(3), 28-62.

Torlone, R. (2003). Conceptual Multidimensional Models. In M. Rafanelli (Ed.), *Multidimensional databases: Problems and solutions*, (pp. 69-90). Idea Group Publishing.

Trujillo, J., Luján-Mora, S., & Song I. (2003). Applying UML for designing multidimensional databases and OLAP applications. In K. Siau (Ed.), *Advanced topics in database research Volume 2* (pp. 13-36). Idea Group Publishing.

Tuv, E., Borisov, A., & Torkkola, K. (2006, July 16-21). Feature selection using ensemble based ranking against artificial contrasts. In *Proceedings of the International Joint Conference on Neural Networks,* Vancouver, BC, Canada, (pp. 4183-4187). IEEE.

Tzanis, G., & Berberidis, C. (2007). Mining for mutually exclusive items in transaction databases. *International Journal of Data Warehousing and Mining, 3*(3).

Uchiyama, H., Runapongsa, K. & Teorey, T. (1999). A progressive view materialization algorithm. In *Proceedings of the International workshop on data warehousing and OLAP* (pp. 360-41). Kansas City, USA: ACM Press.

UCI. (1999). *Machine learning repository content summary.* Retrieved February 8, 2008, from http://www.ics.uci.edu/~mlearn/MLSummary.html

Ullman, J.D. (1997). Information Integration Using Logical Views, In F. N. Afrati, P. G. Kolaitis (Eds.), *Proc. 6th Int. Conf. on Data Database Theory. Lecture Notes in Computer Science, 1186*, 19-40.

Vaidya, J. S., & Clifton, C. (2002). Privacy Preserving Association Rule Mining in Vertically Partitioned Data.

In *Proceedings of 2002 ACM SIGKDD International Conference on Knowledge Discovery and Data Mining.*

Valluri, S., Vadapalli, S. & Karlapalem, K. (2002). View relevance driven materialized view selection in data warehousing environment. In *Proceedings of the Australasian conference on database technologies* (pp. 187-196). Darlinghurst, Australia: ACM.

Vapnik, V. N. (1998). *Statistical Learning Theory.* New York: John Wiley.

Varelas, G., Voutsakis, E., Raftopoulou, P., Petrakis, E., & Milios, E. (2005). Semantic similarity methods in WordNet and their application to information retrieval on the Web. *WIDM '05* (pp. 10-16). New York: ACM Press.

variance filtering. PAKDD 2006 Data Mining Competition. Retrieved November 9, 2007, from http://www.ntu.edu.sg/sce/pakdd2006/competition/overview.htm

Varshavsky, R. (2006). Novel unsupervised feature filtering of biological data. *Bioinformatics (Oxford, England),* 507–513. doi:10.1093/bioinformatics/btl214

Vassiliadis, P. & Sellis, T. (1999). A survey of logical models for OLAP databases. *SIGMOD Record, 28*(4), 64-69.

Veregin, H. (1991). *Data quality measurement and assessment.* NCGIA Core Curriculum in Geographic Information Science.

Wang, H., Yu, A., & Zhang, K. (2008). Ensemble PROBIT Models to Predict Cross Selling of Home Loans for Credit Card Customers. *International Journal of Data Warehousing and Mining, 4*(2), 15–21

Wang, L., Jajodia, S., & Wijesekera, D. (2004). Securing OLAP Data Cubes against Privacy Breaches. In *Proceedings of 2004 IEEE Symposium on Security and Privacy.*

Wang, R.Y., & Strong D. M. (1996a). Beyond accuracy: What data quality means to data consumers. *Journal of Management Information Systems, 12*(4), 5-33.

Wang, R.Y., & Strong D. M. (1996b). *Data quality systems evaluation and implementation.* London: Cambridge Market Intelligence Ltd.

Wang, R.Y., Storey, V. C., & Firth, C. P. (1995). A framework for analysis of data quality research. *IEEE Transactions on Knowledge and Data Engineering, 7*(4), 623-640.

Wangm, L. X., & Mendel, J. M. (1992). Generating fuzzy rules by learning from examples. *IEEE Transactions on Systems, Man, and Cybernetics, 22*(6), 1414–1427. doi:10.1109/21.199466

West, D. (2000). Neural network credit scoring models. *Computers and Operations Research, 27,* 1131-1152.

Winter Corporation. (2005). *Report.* Retrieved from http://www.wintercorp.com

Witten, I. H., & Frank (Eds.). (2005). *Data mining: Practical machine learning tools and techniques* (2nd ed.). San Francisco: Morgan Kaufmann.

Witten, I. H., & Frank, E. (2005). *Data mining: Practical machine learning tools and techniques* (2nd ed.). San Francisco: Morgan Kaufmann.

Witten, I. H., & Frank, E. (2005). *Data mining: Practical machine learning tools and techniques with Java implementations.* San Francisco: Morgan Kaufmann.

Wolpert, D.H. (1992). Stacked generalization. *Neural Networks, 5,* 241-259

WordNet, a lexical database for English Language (2007). Retrieved October 10, 2007 from http://wordnet.princeton.edu/5papers.pdf

Wu, Z., & Palmer, M. (1994). Verb Semantics and lexical selection. In *Proceedings of the 32nd Annual Meeting of the Associations for Computational Linguistics* (pp. 133-138), Las Cruces, New Mexico.

Xing, E., Jordan, M., & Karp, R. (2001). Feature selection for high dimensional genomic microarray data. In *Proceedings of the International Conference on Machine Learning* (pp. 601–608).

Xu, J. (2007). Formalizing natural-language spatial relations between linear objects with topological and metric properties. *International Journal of Geographical Information Science, 21*(4), pp. 377-395.

Yang, D., Powers, D. M. W. (2005). Measuring Semantic Similarity in the Taxonomy of WordNet. In V. Estivill-Castro (Ed.), *Proc. 28ᵗʰ Australasian Computer Science Conference* (pp. 315-322). Australian Computer Society.

Yang, H., Dasdan, A., Hsiao, R., & Parker, D. (2007). Map-reduce-merge: simplified relational data processing on large clusters. *International conference on Management of data SIGMOD)*, pp. 1029-1040, 2007.

Yang, J., Karlapalem, K., & Li, Q. (1997a). Algorithms for materialized view design in data warehousing environment. In M. Jarke, M. Carey, K. Dittrich, F. Lochovsky, P. Loucopoulos, & M. Jeusfeld (Eds.), *Proceedings of the International Conference on Very Large Data Bases* (pp. 156-165). San Francisco: Morgan Kaufmann Publishers Inc.

Yang, J., Karlapalem, K., & Li, Q. (1997b). A framework for designing materialized views in data warehousing environment. In *Proceedings of the International conference on distributed computing systems* (p. 458). Baltimore: IEEE.

Yao, A. C. (1986). How to Generate and Exchange Secrets. In *Proceedings of 1986 Symposium on Foundations of Computer Science*.

Yao, S. B. (1977). Approximating block access in database organization. *Communications of the ACM, 20*(4), 260-261.

Yen, S-J., & Chen, A. L. P. (2001). A graph-based approach for discovering various types of association rules. *IEEE Transactions on Knowledge and Data Engineering, 12*(5), 839-845.

Yoo I., Hu X., & Song I-Y. (2006). Integration of Semantic-based bipartite graph representation and mutual refinement strategy for biomedical literature clustering. In *Proceedings of the 12ᵗʰ ACM SIGKDD International Conference on Knowledge Discovery and Data Mining*, pp. 791-796.

Yoo, I., et al. (2006). Integration of semantic-based bipartite graph representation and mutual refinement strategy for biomedical literature clustering. *Proceedings of the 12th ACM SIGKDD International Conference on Knowledge Discovery and Data Mining*. Philadelphia, Pennsylvania.

Young, J., Presgrave, B., Aichele, H., Wiens, D., & Flinn, E. (1996). The Flinn-Engdahl Regionaligation Scheme: The 1995 Revision. *Physics of the Earth and Planetary Interiors, 96*, 223-297.

Yu, B. (2005). Mining earth science data for geophysical structure: A case study in cloud detection. In *Proceedings of 2005 SIAM International Conference on Data Mining, SIAM'05*, Newport Beach, CA, USA..

Yu, J., Yao, X., Choi, C., & Gou, G. (2003). Materialized view selection as constrained evolutionary optimization. *IEEE Transactions on Systems, Man and Cybernetics, 33*(4), 458-467.

Yu, L., & Liu, H. (2003). Feature selection for high-dimensional data: a fast correlation-based filter solution. In *Proceedings of the twentieth International Conference on Machine Learning* (pp. 856–863).

Yu, P. S., Chen, M. S., Heiss, H. U., & Lee, S. (1992). Workload characterization of relational database environments. *IEEE Transactions of Software Engineering, 18*(4), 347-355.

Zadrozny, B. (2004). Learning and evaluating classifiers under sample selection bias. In *Proceedings of the 21st International Conference on Machine Learning* (pp. 144-151).

Zaki, M. J. (2000). Scalable Algorithms for association mining. *IEEE Transactions on Knowledge and Data Engineering, 12*(3), 372-390.

Zaki, M. J. (2001). SPADE: An efficient algorithm for mining frequent sequences. *Machine Learning, 42*(1/2), 31-60.

Zaki, M. J. (2002). Efficiently mining frequent trees in a forest. In *Proceedings of the SIGKDD* (pp. 71-78).

Zaki, M. J., & Hsiao, C-J. (2005). Efficient algorithms for mining closed itemsets and their lattice structures. *IEEE Transactions on Knowledge and Data Engineering, 17*(4), 462-478.

Zaki, M.J. (2001). SPADE: An efficient algorithm for mining frequent sequences. *Machine Learning Journal, 42*(1/2), 31–60.

Zeng, F., Yap, C. H. R., & Wong, L. (2002). Using feature generation and feature selection for accurate prediction of translation initiation sites. *Genome Informatics, 13,* 192–200.

Zhang X., Jing L., Hu X., Ng M., & Zhou X. (2007). A comparative study of ontology based term similarity measures on document clustering. Accepted in the *12th International conference on Database Systems for Advanced Applications (DASFFA2007).*

Zhang X., Zhou X., & Hu X. (2006). Semantic smoothing for model-based document clustering. *In Proceedings of the sixth IEEE International Conference on Data Mining.*

Zhang, C., Yao, X., & Yang, J. (2001). An evolutionary approach to materialized views selection in a datawarehouse environment. *IEEE Transactions on Systems, Man and Cybernetics, 31*(3), 282-294.

Zhang, D. Q., Chen, S. C., & Zhou, Z. H. (2008). Constraint score: a new filter method for feature selection with pairwise constraints. *Pattern Recognition, 41*(5), 1440–1451. doi:10.1016/j.patcog.2007.10.009

Zhang, N., Zhao, W., & Chen, J. (2004). Cardinality-Based Inference Control in OLAP Systems: an Information Theoretical Approach. In *ACM DOLAP International Workshop on Date Warehousing and OLAP.*

Zhang, X., et al. (2006). Semantic smoothing for model-based document clustering. *Proceedings of the Sixth International Conference on Data Mining.*

Zhang, X., et al. (2007). Utilization of global ranking information in graph- based biomedical literature clustering. *Proceedings of the 9th International Conference on Data Warehousing and Knowledge Discovery (DAWAK).* Regensburg, Germany.

Zhao, Y., & Karypis, G (2001). *Criterion functions for document clustering: Experiments and analysis.* Technical Report, Department of Computer Science, University of Minnesota.

Zhong, S., & Ghosh, J. (2003). A comparative study of generative models for document clustering. *Proceedings of the Workshop on Clustering High Dimensional Data and Its Applications in SIAM Data Mining Conference.*

Zhou, X., Zhang, X., & Hu, X. *The Dragon Toolkit, Data Mining & Bioinformatics Lab.* iSchool at Drexel University. Retrieved from http://www.dragontoolkit.org/

Zhou, Z.-H., & Liu, X.-Y. (2006). Training cost-sensitive neural networks with methods addressing the class imbalance problem. *IEEE Transactions on Knowledge and Data, Engineering, 18*(1), 63-77.

Zipf, G.K. (1935). *The psycho-biology of language; an introduction to dynamic philology.* Boston: Houghton Mifflin.

About the Contributors

David Taniar holds Bachelor, Master, and PhD degrees - all in Computer Science, with a particular specialty in Databases. His current research is applying data management techniques to various domains, including mobile and geography information systems, parallel and grid computing, web engineering, and data mining. Every year he publishes extensively, including his recent co-authored book: High Performance Parallel Database Processing and Grid Databases (John Wiley & Sons, 2008). His list of publications can be viewed at the DBLP server (http://www.informatik.uni-trier.de/~ley/db/indices/a-tree/t/Taniar:David.html). He is a founding editor-in-chief of a number of international journals, including Intl. J. of Data Warehousing and Mining, Intl. J. of Business Intelligence and Data Mining, Mobile Information Systems, Journal of Mobile Multimedia, Intl. J. of Web Information Systems, and Intl. J. of Web and Grid Services. He is currently an Associate Professor at the Faculty of Information Technology, Monash University, Australia. He can be contacted at David.Taniar@infotech.monash.edu.au.

Laura Irina Rusu has completed her PhD in 2008 at La Trobe University, Australia, with a thesis on XML data warehousing and mining. Before that, she received a Master in Quantitative Economy degree (1997) and a Bachelor in Computer Science degree (1996), both from the Academy of Economic Sciences - Bucharest, Romania. Currently she is a Postdoctoral Research Fellow at La Trobe University, and her research interests are on dynamic XML data warehousing and mining, partitioning techniques for XML warehouses, and data migration to domain-specific XML standards.

* * *

Paulo Adeodato received his BSc in Electronics in 1982 and his MSc in Computer Science in 1991 from the Federal University of Pernambuco (Brazil), and his PhD in Mathematics from King's College London in 1997. He is Associate Professor at the Center for Informatics, Federal University of Pernambuco. He has published over 40 papers involving data mining, neural networks, pattern recognition and performance evaluation systems and has supervised several theses and dissertations. He is the Chief Scientist of NeuroTech where he has developed over 300 data mining solutions for market applications. He is also cofounder of NeuroTech and AILeader entrepreneurships.

Dr **Osei Adjei** received his MSc (CNAA) in Electronic Physics from Polytechnic of North London in 1978 and PhD in Computer Applications and Management Science from Cranfield University in 1996. He previously worked as an Antenna Systems Engineer at EMI SV& E Ltd, Hayes, Middlesex and as a Design and Development Engineer on aircraft engine control systems at Dowty Defence and Air Systems, Acton, London. He currently teaches Computer Science at the University of Bedfordshire, Luton campus. His research interests include artificial intelligence systems, quantum computation, robotics and data mining. Dr Adjei is a Chartered Engineer, a Chartered IT Practitioner and a full member of the Institution of Engineering & Technology (IET) and the British Computer Society (BCS). His hobbies are optical and radio astronomy and kit car construction.

Reda Alhajj received his B.Sc. degree in Computer Engineering in 1988 from Middle East Technical University, Ankara, Turkey. After he completed his BSc with distinction from METU, he was offered a full scholarship to join the graduate program in Computer Engineering and Information Sciences at Bilkent University in Ankara, where he received his M.Sc. and Ph.D. degrees in 1990 and 1993, respectively. Currently, he is Professor and Assistant Head for Graduate Affairs in the Department of Computer Science at the University of Calgary, Alberta, Canada. He published over 280 papers in refereed international journals and conferences. He served on the program committee of several international conferences including IEEE ICDE, IEEE ICDM, IEEE IAT, SIAM DM. He is associate editor of IEEE SMC- Part C. Dr. Alhajj's primary work and research interests are in the areas of biocomputing and biodata analysis, data mining, multiagent systems, schema integration and re-engineering, social networks and XML. He received Outstanding Achievements in Supervision Award from the Faculty of Graduate Studies at the University of Calgary. Dr. Alhajj recently received with Dr. Jon Rokne donation of equipment valued at $5 million from RBC and Teradata in support of their research on Computational Intelligence and Bioinformatics.

Mohammed Alshalalfa received his B.Sc. in Molecular Biology and Genetics from Middle East Technical University (METU), Ankara, Turkey. During his undergraduate studies, he worked in the Plant Biotechnology lab at METU. In the last year of his undergraduate studies, Mohammed visited the Department for Molecular Biomedical Research (DMBR), Ghent University, Belgium, for two months to study the effect of viral infection on transcription factors activity. In September 2006, Mohammed joined the graduate program in the Department of Computer Science at University of Calgary, Calgary, Canada, where he completed his M.Sc. degree in July 2008. Currently, Mohammed is a Ph.D. candidate in the Department of Computer Science at the University of Calgary under the supervision of Professor Reda Alhajj. So far Mohammed has published more than 20 papers in refereed international conferences and journals. Mohammed is focusing on Microarray data analysis and applications of data mining technique into Microarray data. His research interests are in the areas of genomics, proteomics, computational biology, social networks and bioinformatics, where is successfully adapting different machine learning and data mining techniques for modeling and analysis.

Adrian Arnaud received his BSc in 1996, his MSc in 2002, and his PhD in 2007, all in Computer Science from the Federal University of Pernambuco (Brazil). Since 2000, he has been developing data mining solutions for real world problems with large data sets and has also been supervising the development of software environments for data mining, time series prediction and On-Line Analytical Processing (OLAP). He is a senior developer in Borland Delphi 2006, certified by Borland and has been the team leader in several software engineering projects. His research interests include neural networks for classification and time series forecasting.

Marko Banek received his B.Sc. and M.Sc. degrees in Electrical Engineering (area Telecommunications) and his PhD degree in Computer Science from the University of Zagreb in 2003, 2005 and 2007, respectively. He has been working as a research assistant at the University of Zagreb, Faculty of Electrical Engineering and Computing, Croatia since 2003. His research interests include data warehousing, data integration, lexical databases, ontologies and semantic web.

Dr. Cardell specializes in econometrics, microeconomics, and economics of technological change, mathematical modeling and labor economics. He is currently the director of R&D at Salford Systems, a position he has held since June 1996. Dr Cardell has served as consultant to numerous organizations including The National Academy of Sciences Diesel Impact Study Committee and the National Economic Research Associates. He is the recipient of various awards including the Golden Key National Honor Society Advisor of the Year (1993), and won the best contributed paper in Statistics and Statistical Graphics, SAS Users' Group International, Orlando, March 1988.

Lei Chai is the data mining consultant of Sherpa Consulting Inc. in Hangzhou, China. The company is the reseller of Salford Systems' products in China. Before founding the company, he worked in Health Science Center of West Virginia University as a medical data analyst. He received his B.S. degree in Applied Mathematics in Zhejiang University and M.S. degree in Statistics in West Virginia University.

Qiong Chen received her PhD degree from South China University of Technology in 2001. Currently she is an Associate Professor at the school of computer science and engineering in South China university of Technology. Her research interests are in Artificial Intelligence, machine learning, data mining, pattern recognition, information extraction and neural computing. In these areas she has published 20 papers in journals or conference proceedings.

Professor **Weiru Chen** is the Dean of the Faculty of Computer Science and Technology at the Shenyang Institute of Chemical Technology (SYICT), China. He received his BSc in Computer Application (1985) from Dalian University of Technology, China, and MSc in Computer Science and Application (1988) from Northeastern University, China. He then joined SYICT as a Lecturer and has remained there ever since, becoming Dean of Faculty in 2004. His research interests include software architecture, software reliability engineering, biological information analysis, data mining and grid computing, and he is also a Director of the Liaoning Computer Federation in China. Professor Chen worked as an external supervisor for Jing Lu's PhD research from 2004 to 2006 and was invited to the University of Bedfordshire, UK in the summer of 2006.

Jean-François Chevalier is a consultant at VADIS Consulting. He has three years experience in analytical projects. He owns a mathematical degree from the Universté Catholique de Louvain (UCL), and a master in Statistics from UCL.

Rodrigo Cunha received his BSc in Statistics in 2002, honored as the BSc laureate that year, and his MSc in Computer Science in 2005 from the Federal University of Pernambuco (Brazil). Nowadays he is working on his PhD thesis also in Computer Science at the Federal University of Pernambuco focusing on the development of a framework for knowledge re-use in data mining solutions. His experience includes the application of data mining to real world problems with large data sets at NeuroTech where he has developed more than 200 data mining solutions for market applications.

Sandra de Amo received the PhD degree in computer science from the University of Paris 13, France, in 1995. She is an Associate Professor in the Faculty of Computer Science at the Federal University of Uberlândia, Brazil. In the past, she was an invited researcher in the Computer Science Laboratory (LABRI), at the University Bordeaux I. In the academic year 2001-2002, she was on sabbatical in the Computer Science Laboratory (LI) at the University of Tours, France. She is responsible for several research projects supported by Brazilian governmental research agencies. Her research interests include data mining, temporal databases, query languages, applications of logic in databases, inconsistent information management in databases. She has been often involved in the organization of important Brazilian conferences on Databases. Dr. Sandra de Amo is a member of the ACM since 1999.

Frank Dehne received a MCS degree (Dipl. Inform.) from the RWTH Aachen University, Germany and a PhD (Dr. Rer. Nat.) from the University of Würzburg, Germany. In 1986 he joined the School of Computer Science at Carleton University in Ottawa where he is now a Professor and Director of the School of Computer Science. His current research interests are in the areas of parallel computing, coarse grained parallel algorithms, parallel computational geometry, parallel data warehousing & OLAP, and parallel bioinformatics. Professor Dehne is a senior member of the IEEE, Vice-Chair of the IEEE Technical Committee on Parallel Processing, member of the ACM Symposium on Parallel Algorithms and Architectures Steering Committee, and editorial board member for IEEE Transaction on Computers, Information Processing Letters, Journal of Bioinformatics Research and Applications, and Int. Journal of Data Warehousing and Mining.

Todd Eavis received his PhD in computer science from the Faculty of Computer Science, Dalhousie University, Halifax, Canada, in 2003. Since 2004, he has been an assistant professor in the Department of Computer Science and Software Engineering, where he also holds a Tier II University Research Chair in Data Warehousing. Prior to his current appointment, he was an NSERC Postdoctoral fellow at Carleton University in Ottawa, Canada. His current research interests include data warehousing architectures, hierarchical data cubes, multi-dimensional indexing, parallel algorithms, and cluster computing.

Dr. **David Gadish** is a faculty member at the Information Systems Department at the College of Business and Economics, California State University Los Angeles. His research interests include GIS, Spatial data, Information Technology for Real Estate and Financial Sector organizations. Prof. Gadish has worked and consulted for government and industry since 1991 in GIS, Information Technology, and Business Process Management.

Arnaud Giacometti is Professor of Computer Science at the University François Rabelais of Tours (France) since September 1995, where he is heading the Computer Science Departement (since 2006). He is also Assistant Director of the Computer Science Laboratory (LI) at the University François Rabelais of Tours. His research interest includes data mining in relational databases, development of inductive databases, multi-dimensional databases and OLAP, user preference modelling and query personnalisation in databases. Arnaud Giacometti received his PhD in Computer Science from Ecole Nationale Supérieure des Télécommunications of Paris (ENST) in 1989.

Mykhaylo Golovnya was awarded a Master's of Science in Probability and Statistics Degree from the University of Central Florida in 2000 after successfully completing his Specialist Degree from

Kharkov State Polytechnic University in the Ukraine in 1995. Mr. Golovnya was employed by Salford Systems from 2000 to date in the position of Senior Scientist. Some of his duties include prototyping new algorithms in PERL, C, and FORTRAN, scripting automated procedures for scoring and analysis including multiple runs and conducting training sessions with prospects on the theory and applications of CART, MARS, TreeNet, and Random Forests.

Narasimhaiah Gorla is a Professor of MIS at the American University of Sharjah, UAE. He has a Ph.D. from the University of Iowa, USA and Post-graduation from Indian Institute of Management Calcutta. His articles have appeared in Communications of the ACM, Information & Management, IEEE Transactions on Software Engineering, Data and Knowledge Engineering etc. Pang Wing Yan Betty has graduated from the Department of Computing at Hong Kong Polytechnic University, Hung Hom, Kowloon in Hong Kong. Her specialization is database management and data mining.

Xiaohua Hu is currently an associate professor and the founding director of the Data Mining and Bioinformatics Laboratory in the College of Information Science and Technology at Drexel University. His current research interest includes biomedical literature data mining, bioinformatics, text mining, semantic Web mining and reasoning, rough set theory and application, information extraction, and information retrieval. He has published more than 140 peer reviewed research papers in various journals, conferences, and books, and co-edited nine books/proceedings. He has received a few prestigious awards, including the 2005 NSF Faculty Early Career Development (NSF Career) Award, the Best Paper Award from the 2007 International Conference on Artificial Intelligence, the Best Paper Award from the 2004 IEEE Symposium on Computational Intelligence in Bioinformatics and Computational Biology, the 2006 IEEE Granular Computing Outstanding Service Award, and the 2001 IEEE Data Mining Outstanding Service Award. He is the founding editor-in-chief of the International Journal of Data Mining and Bioinformatics, and associate editor/editorial board member of four international journals. His research projects are funded by the US National Science Foundation (NSF), US Department of Education, and the Pennsylvania Department of Health.

Wang Huo is a staff in the Dept. of New Business in China Mobile Zhejiang Co., Ltd. He received his Master Degree in International Marketing Management in Leeds University Business School, Leeds UK, and Bachelor Degree of Mechanical Engineering in ChongQing University, China.

Lucio Ieronutti received the PhD degree in Computer Science from the University of Udine, Italy, in 2006. Since 2003, he actively works at IS&SE-Lab (Information Systems and Software Engineering) and the HCI-Lab (Human Computer Interaction) of the University of Udine. His research interests are in information systems, Datawarehouses, 3D virtual environments and information visualization. He is author of 19 publications on these topics.

Liping Jing is a PhD student in the Department of Mathematics and E-Business Technology Institute at the University of Hong Kong. She received her Bachelor of Science and Master of Philosophy degrees in computer science from the Northern Jiaotong University, in 2000 and 2003, respectively. Her research interests are in the areas of data mining, subspace clustering algorithm, ontology-based programming and business intelligence.

Dr. **Ioannis Kalogeras** is senior researcher in the Institute of Geodynamics (IG), National Observatory of Athens. He was born in Athens in 1956 and he received his Diploma (1981) in Geology and PhD (1993) in Seismology both from the Athens University, Greece. In 2006 he received an MSc in geoinformatics from the National Technical University of Athens, Greece. His research interests include the strong ground motion study, the development of seismological databases, the seismic tomography and the development of strong motion networks. Since 1986 he is in charge of the strong motion networks of the IG. Recently he updated the macroseismic observation collection system of the IG. He is involved in various national and international research projects as scientific leader or as senior researcher. He has co-authored over 40 articles published in scientific journals (Natural Hazards, BSSA, SRL) and congress proceedings (EGS, IASPEI). He is member of SSA and AGU.

Shang-Fu Ke, senior student, studies in Computer Science and Engineer Department of South China University of Technology. His main research interests are the effective arithmetic using in software development. Also he is widely interesting in machine learning and data mining. His higher mathematics is very good, and he is specialize in using a mathematic model to figure out a truly question. Besides, he dose not just settle for theory research, he likes to do some experimentations to realize his ideas also.

Dr **Malcolm Keech** is the Associate Dean of Creative Arts, Technologies & Science at the University of Bedfordshire, UK. Before joining the University in 1999, Malcolm Keech had worked extensively in computing and IT development and management, both in the academic and industrial sectors. While his original academic background lies in mathematics (BA Oxford, MSc/PhD Manchester), Malcolm's professional experience includes periods at the London School of Economics, the Universities of London and Manchester, Florida State University, British Telecom and British Aerospace. He was Head of Computing & Information Systems at the Luton campus in Bedfordshire for 5 years before taking up his present position. Malcolm is both a Fellow of the Institute of Mathematics & its Applications (Chartered Mathematician) and a Fellow of the British Computer Society (Chartered IT Professional).

Mohammad Khabbaz received his B.Sc. degree in software engineering from Sharif University of Technology, Tehran, Iran; he received his M.Sc. degree in Computer Science from the University of Calgary. . Currently, Mohammad is a Ph.D. candidate in the Department of Computer Science at the University of British Columbia. He published papers in refereed international conferences and journals. His research interests are in the areas of data mining, bioinformatics and document clustering and classification.

Keivan Kianmehr received his B.Sc. degree in software engineering from IUST, Tehran, IRAN. After working as a computer engineer for six years, he joined the University of Calgary to pursue graduate studies. After spending over 5 years in the computer industry as software developer and project leader, Keivan joined the graduate program in the Department of Computer Science at the University of Calgary where he completed his M.Sc. degree in 2006. Currently, Keivan is a Ph.D. candidate in the Department of Computer Science at the University of Calgary under the supervision of Professor Reda Alhajj. He has published more than 20 papers in prestigious refereed international journals and conferences. He also received teaching excellence awards at the University of Calgary. He received several prestigious scholarships including NSERC CSD and AIF. He is a successful mentor for undergraduate and graduate students. His research focuses on machine learning techniques, data mining methodologies and bioinformatics.

Michael Lawrence received both bachelor's and master's degrees in computer science from Dalhousie University in 2004 and 2006, respectively, where he did research in applying parallel and distributed computing to online analytical processing. He is currently working towards a PhD in computer science at the University of British Columbia, where he is investigating integration and querying of data involved in large scale architecture, engineering and construction projects.

Guo-Zheng Li received his Ph.D. degree from Shanghai JiaoTong University. He is currently an Associate Professor in the School of Computer Science and Engineering at Shanghai University, China. He is also currently serving on the Committees at CAAI Machine Learning Society, CAS Pervasive Computing Society, International Society of Intelligent Biological Medicine and IEEE Computer Society. Dr. Li is a Principle Investigator of machine learning and bioinformatics research projects under the grants of Nature Science Foundation of China. Dr. Li has published more than 30 refereed papers in professional journals and conferences. He has written three book chapters and translated one professional book from English into Chinese. He is an Associate Editor of IJCIBSB and JCIB, Vice Chair of CSC07, ICAI07, and Program Committee Member of ICMLC07, IEEE 7th BIBE, IEEE BIBM07 and OSB07. He was a recipient of the Best Paper Awards at PRICAI 2006 and ICAI 2007.

Dr **Jing Lu** is a Post-Doctoral Enterprise Fellow at Southampton Solent University, UK. Jing Lu has been engaged in curriculum design, research and consultancy in knowledge management and intelligent systems at the University since the start of 2007. Jing was awarded her PhD in late 2006 from the University of Bedfordshire in the area of knowledge discovery and data mining. Prior to 2005, she had been working in China as an Associate Professor in the Faculty of Computer Science and Technology, Shenyang Institute of Chemical Technology. Jing was the academic leader for teaching and research in computer applications with a primary focus on the fields of artificial intelligence, data mining, database management and web-based systems.

Gerasimos Marketos is a PhD candidate at the Department of Informatics, University of Piraeus (UniPi), Greece. Born in 1981, he received his Bachelor of Science degree (2003) in informatics from University of Piraeus and his Master of Science degree (2004) in information systems engineering from University of Manchester Institute of Science and Technology (UMIST), UK. His research interests include spatiotemporal data warehousing and mining, pattern management and scientific databases. He is member of BCS.

Domingos Monteiro received his BSc in 1995 and MSc in 1999 in Computer Science from the Federal University of Pernambuco (Brazil), the latter focused on Neural Networks and Artificial Intelligence. He also received an MBA degree in 2005 from Dom Cabral Foundation. He has more than twelve years of experience in research and applications of Artificial Intelligence particularly to credit risk assessment. He is co-founder, partner and currently the Chief Executive Officer of NeuroTech, a leading company in Brazil specialized in the application of Data Mining to Business Applications with more than forty projects deployed in Brazil and United States.

Michael Ng is a professor in the Department of Mathematics at the Hong Kong Baptist University. As an applied mathematician, Michael's main research areas include bioinformatics, data mining, operations research and scientific computing. Michael has published and edited 5 books, published more than

160 journal papers. He is the principal editor of the Journal of Computational and Applied Mathematics, and the associate editor of SIAM Journal on Scientific Computing.

Vladimir Nikulin graduated from Perm State University (Russia) in 1981, and received a PhD in mathematical statistics from Moscow State University in February 1986. He was working in Russia as a Lecturer/Senior Lecturer at Vyatka State University. Since 1993 Dr Nikulin hold several research positions in Australia. The most recent appointments were Research Fellow at the Computer Science Laboratory, Australian National University, and Senior Analyst at the Airservices, Australia. Currently, Dr Nikulin works as a Senior Statistician at Suncorp in Brisbane (Suncorp Metway is one of the largest banks and insurance companies in Australia).Dr Nikulin participated successfully in several International data mining competitions, and published more than 50 research papers.

Rosalvo Oliveira Neto received his BSc in Information Systems in 2004 from the Integrated University of Recife (FIR), Brazil. Nowadays he is writing up his MSc dissertation in artificial intelligence from the Federal University of Pernambuco, Brazil. His experience includes the application of data mining to real world problems with large data sets and the development of software environments for On-Line Analytical Processing (OLAP) and data mining. He is senior developer in Borland Delphi 2006, certified by Borland and has solid knowledge in software engineering. His main research interests include artificial neural networks and data mining for real world applications.

Palakorn is a Ph.D. student in College of Information Science and Technology, Drexel University. He received his master degree in Information Systems Management (MISM) from Carnegie Mellon University in Pittsburgh, and a bachelor in Economics from Chulalongkorn University in Bangkok, Thailand. His current research interests include text mining, information retrieval, and natural language processing.

Waldecir Pereira Jr. received the MSc degree in Computer Science in 2007 from the Federal University of Uberlândia, Brazil. Since then, he has been working in the area of knowledge discovery in databases and temporal databases.

Maurizio Pighin is a Professor in the Department of Mathematics and Computer Science of the University of Udine, and currently teaches advanced courses of Software Engineering and Information Systems. His major research interests are in the area of Software Engineering and ERP and Datawarehouse Systems. He is the author of more than 60 scientific publications in international journals, books and refereed conference proceedings. He worked at several national and international research and development projects. He is a referee of various international journals. He has been involved in the organization of some important events in the fields of Software Engineering and Information Systems.

Fei Qi, senior student in mathematics department, He is mainly devoted to studies of pure mathematics, while also interested in a series of application topics, such as mathematical modeling, evolutionary computation, data mining, algorithm analysis and network security. As a mathematics student, he possesses a logical mind, which helps him to clarify problems and figure out the most possible breakthrough point, hence make critical suggestions. Meanwhile his mind is also fast and open, which made it more quickly for him to understand knowledge beyond his own study schedule. And he also own the ability of balancing intuition and preciseness.

Dehong Qiu received the BS degree and the MS degree in automation control engineering, both from the Huazhong University of Science and Technology (HUST), Wuhan, Chian in 1993 and 1995 respectively, the PhD degree in Electrical Engineering from the HongKong Polytechnic University in 2000. He is currently an associate professor in the School of Software Engineering at HUST. His research interests include machine learning, data mining, software engineering and digital media technology. He has published about 30 articles in scientific journals and conferences. He is a fellow of the CAAI Machine Learning Society.

Andrew Rau-Chaplin PhD is a professor of computer science at Dalhousie University, Canada. He is interested in the application of parallel computing to a wide range of problem domains including data warehousing and mining, computational geometry and GIS, and bioinformatics. His parallel computing research program tends to be almost evenly divided between theoretical studies, where the focus is on developing asymptotically optimal or near optimal algorithms in a given complexity model, and implementation work which is used to guide and "ground" the theoretical work. He has published more than 70 research articles which have appeared in international journals and conference proceedings.

Andrew Rau-Chaplin received a MCS and PhD from Carleton University in Ottawa Canada in 1990 and 1993, respectively. From 1993 to 1994 he was a Postdoctoral Fellow at DIMACS - a National Science Foundation center run by Princeton University, Rutgers, and AT&T Bell labs. In 1994 he joined the Technical University of Nova Scotia and is currently a professor in the Faculty of Computer Science at Dalhousie University. He is interested in the application of parallel computing to a wide range of problem domains including data warehousing & OLAP, bioinformatics, computational biochemistry, geographic information systems, and computational geometry/CAD. His parallel computing research program tends to be almost evenly divided between theoretical studies, where the focus is on developing asymptotically optimal or near optimal algorithms in a given complexity model, and implementation work which is used to guide and "ground" the theoretical work.

Franck Ravat (ravat@irit.fr) was born in 1968 in St. Michel de Fronsac (France). He obtained his PhD in computer science from the University of Toulouse 3, France, with a thesis on distributed databases in 1996. Since 1997, Dr. Franck Ravat is associate professor at the University of Toulouse 1 and researcher in the Generalised Information Systems/Data Warehouse research group (SIG/ED). His current research interests include all aspects of data warehouse design and languages. His publications appear in major national and international conferences, for which he also serves as reviewer.

John Ries. Data manager at Salford Systems in fifteen market research , data mining or biomedical consulting projects beginning in 1993. Developed simulation software for ten consulting projects. Developed numerous report generation and data analysis utilities for internal use. Other assignments include automation of data management and data manipulation tasks in SAS and Systat; development of SAS and Systat interfaces for various statistical procedures (including completion of PROC CART for VAX/VMS); analysis and documentation of source code acquired by Salford Systems from other sources; and pre-release testing of commercial software.

Rong She is currently a Ph.D. candidate in the School of Computing Science at Simon Fraser University in Canada. She received her degree of M.Sc. from Simon Fraser University in 2003. She is currently working with Prof. Ke Wang on a variety of topics in data mining and database techniques. Her research interests include data analysis and modeling with applications on biological databases, as well as privacy reservation in data mining.

Zoran Skočir is a full professor at the University of Zagreb, Faculty of Electrical Engineering and Computing, Croatia. He received his B.Sc., M.Sc. and Ph.D. degrees in Electrical Engineering from the University of Zagreb in 1974, 1979 and 1990, respectively. His research interests include database design, information systems implementation, application development and e-commerce.

Dan Steinberg, the President of Salford Systems, founded the company in 1982 just after receiving his Ph.D. in Economics at Harvard. He also served as a Member of Technical Staff at AT&T Bell Laboratories and Assistant Professor of Economics at the University of California, San Diego, and has participated in dozens of consulting projects for Fortune 100 clients. He has been honored by the SAS User's Group International (SUGI) and led the modeling teams that won the KDDCup 2000 and the 2002 Duke/Teradata Churn modeling competition. Dr. Steinberg has published articles in statistics, econometrics, computer science, and marketing journals, and has been a featured data mining issues speaker for the American Marketing Association, American Statistical Association, the Direct Marketing Association and the Casualty Actuarial Society.

Xiaogang Su is Associate Professor, Department of Statistics and Actuarial Science, University of Central Florida, Orlando, FL 32816. He got a PhD in statistics at University of California at Davis in 2001.

Olivier Teste (teste@irit.fr) was born in 1972 in Castres (France). He obtained his PhD in computer science from the University of Toulouse 3, France, with a thesis on data warehouse modelling in 2000. Since 2001, Dr. Olivier Teste is associate professor at the University of Toulouse 3 and researcher in the Generalised Information Systems/Data Warehouse research group (SIG/ED). His research interests include all aspects related to data warehousing, in particular multidimensional modelling and querying. He serves in the program comity of several national and international conferences. He has published over 30 papers in international and national conferences.

Dr. **Yannis Theodoridis** is assistant professor with the Department of Informatics, University of Piraeus (UniPi). Born in 1967, he received his Diploma (1990) and PhD (1996) in electrical and computer engineering, both from the National Technical University of Athens, Greece. His research interests include spatial and spatiotemporal databases, geographical information management, knowledge discovery and data mining. Currently, he is scientist in charge for UniPi in the EC-funded GeoPKDD project (2005-08) on geographic privacy-aware knowledge discovery and delivery, also involved in several national-level projects. He has co-authored three monographs and over 50 articles in scientific journals (including Algorithmica, ACM Multimedia and IEEE TKDE) and conferences (including ACM SIGMOD, PODS, VLDB and ICDE) with over 400 citations in his work. He participates in the steering committee for the Int'l Symposium on Spatial and Temporal Databases (SSTD) and in the editorial board for the Int'l Journal on Data Warehousing and Mining. He is member of ACM and IEEE.

A Min Tjoa is a full professor at the Vienna University of Technology. He received his M.Sc. degree in Computer Science and his PhD in Engineering from the University of Linz in 1979. He was a visiting professor at the Universities of Zurich, Kyushu and Wroclaw and the Technical Universities of Prague and Lausanne. He is a former president of the Austrian Computer Society. His current research interests include data warehousing, grid computing, semantic web, security and personal information management systems.

Ronan Tournier (tournier@irit.fr) was born in 1976 in Lannion (France). Formally computer technician and sales engineer for computer systems during four years, he received a research master's degree in computer science in 2004 from the University of Toulouse 3. He is currently a PhD student in the Generalised Information Systems/Data Warehouse research group (SIG/ED). His research interests include multidimensional modelling, algebras as well as the integration of text-rich documents within data warehouses and OLAP systems.

Thierry Van de Merckt is Managing Director and founder of VADIS Consulting. He owns a Ph.D. in Machine Learning from the Free University of Brussels, and has worked 2 years as a post-doc at the Basser Department of Computer Science with Ross Quinlan, in Sydney, Australia. He is professor in the MBA of the Solvay Business School, ULB. Thierry has 15 years experience in the field of Analytical Business Intelligence.

Germano Vasconcelos received his BSc and MSc in Computer Science from the Federal University of Pernambuco (Brazil), and his PhD in Artificial Intelligence from the University of Kent (United Kingdom) in 1995. He is an Associated Professor at the Center for Informatics at the Federal University of Pernambuco and an Adhoc Consultant of the Brazilian Research Council (CNPq). He has published more than 60 papers involving hybrid systems, data mining, neural networks and pattern recognition. He is also an INOVAR Entrepreneur from the Financer of Studies and Projects (FINEP), and has developed several real world solutions for market problems.

Boris Vrdoljak is an assistant professor at the University of Zagreb, Faculty of Electrical Engineering and Computing, Croatia. He received his B.Sc., M.Sc. and Ph.D. degrees in Electrical Engineering from the University of Zagreb in 1995, 1999 and 2004, respectively. From 2004 to 2005 he was a postdoctoral researcher at INRIA Futurs, France. His research interests include data warehousing, data integration, semistructured data, service-oriented architecture and semantic web.

Ada Waichee Fu received her B.Sc degree in computer science in the Chinese University of Hong Kong in 1983, and both M.Sc and Ph.D degrees in Computer Science in Simon Fraser University of Canada in 1986, 1990, respectively. She worked at Bell Northern Research in Ottawa, Canada from 1989 to 1993 on a wide-area distributed database project. In 1993, she joined the Chinese University of Hong Kong, where she is currently an associate professor in the Department of Computer Science & Engineering. Her research interests include issues in distributed databases, XML data, time series databases, data mining, content-based retrieval in multimedia databases, parallel and distributed systems.

Ye Wang received the BS degree from the School of Software Engineering at Huazhong University of Science and Technology (HUST), Wuhan, Chian. His research interests include data mining, machine learning and artificial intelligence. He was cultivated under the project of Cultivating High-quality Creative Talents of HUST.

Hualin Wang, a Senior Manager of Advanced Analytics in retail marketing at Alliance Data, Columbus Ohio, USA. My current responsibility includes private label and co-brand credit card acquisition, portfolio management, marketing campaign design and analysis, customer segmentation, retention and re-activation. My team also plans and designs marketing programs for some of our clients for their general customer relationship management. We provide statistical modeling, design of experiment, data mining, advanced market research and other quantitative and qualitative consulting services. With my leadership and direct participation, my team has won four national and international modeling / data mining competitions in the last two years. My work experiences have been focusing on applying statistical modeling and other analyses to solving diverse business problems and to driving business developments. The industries in which I have been working include credit and banking, auto and home insurance, and direct marketing. I have a Master's degree in Statistics from Stanford University and a PhD in Applied Mathematics from Iowa State University.

Ke Wang received Ph.D from Georgia Institute of Technology. He is currently a professor at School of Computing Science, Simon Fraser University. Ke Wang's research interests include database technology, data mining and knowledge discovery, machine learning, and emerging applications, with recent interests focusing on the end use of data mining. This includes explicitly modeling the business goal (such as profit mining, bio-mining and web mining) and exploiting user prior knowledge (such as extracting unexpected patterns and actionable knowledge). Ke Wang has published in database, information retrieval, and data mining conferences, including SIGMOD, SIGIR, PODS, VLDB, ICDE, EDBT, SIGKDD, SDM and ICDM. He is an associate editor of the IEEE TKDE journal, an editorial board member for Journal of Data Mining and Knowledge Discovery.

Mingjun Wei is a Ph.D. candidate in Zhejiang University since March 2005. He received his Master Science degree and Bachelor Science degree in mathematics from Zhejiang University. He is currently the data mining consultant of Sherpa Consulting Inc. in Hangzhou, China. His research interests include kinetic equation and data mining.

Renying Wei has been working for China Mobile since it was found. Now she is the general manager of Network Management Dept. of China Mobile Zhejiang Co., Ltd. From 1987 to 2000, she worked in the Network Management Dept of China Telcom Hangzhou Co., Ltd.

Yi-Jun Wu, senior student, studies in Computer Science and Engineer Department of South China University of Technology. He has wide research interests, mainly including java Web programming, P2P, C/S, B/S, MVC, Web Service using java C# python and Ruby etc, P2P Multimedia Stream, and web2.0 web3.0, netbeans and Eclipse's plug-in, among which P2P programming is his main research direction. Besides, he is a creative student who has won the honorable mention award in ICM2006 and second award in Challenging Cup. He is good at mathematics especially in Numerical Analysis, Number Theory and Riemann geometry.

Jiali Xia is a full professor and dean of the UFSoft School of Software, Jiangxi University of Finance & Economics. She obtaiend her BSc, MSc and PhD degrees all from the Computer Science Department of Huazhong University of Science and Technology in 1987, 1993, and 2003, respectively. Her research interest is real-time embedded database system. She has published many papers on top Chinese journals such as China Computer Transaction and China Software Transaction. She is the second-class prize winner of the Science and Technology Advancement Award from the Chinese Ministry of Education, in 2004 and third-class winner of the Science and Technology Advancement Award from Jiaxi Province in 2007.

Zhi-Zhuo Zhang, senior student, studies in Computer Science and Engineer Department of South China University of Technology. He has wide research interests, mainly including artificial intelligence, machine learning, data mining, information retrieval, pattern recognition, evolutionary computation, and neural computation, among which machine learning and data mining is his main research directions. Besides, he is a creative student who has won the honorable mention award in ICM2007 and outstanding award in Challenging Cup of Guangdong.

Ying-Ping Zhang, senior student, studies in Software Engineering Department of South China University of Technology. He is interested in artificial intelligence, machine learning, data mining, evolutionary computation, game theory and so on. Recently He made a deep study of the M2M algorithm model which propose by him. By the research of M2M and other domain he studied, he wins the outstanding award in Challenging Cup of Guangdong and publishes the paper to International Conference on Artificial Intelligence and Applications (ICAIA'07)

Xiaodan Zhang is a PhD candidate in College of Information Science and Technology, Drexel University. He received his B.S. in library and information science from Northeast Normal University, China in 1997 and M.S. in computer science from Jinan University, China in 2003. His current research interests include graph-based, ontology-based and model-based text data mining.

Qifeng Zhang is currently a postgraduate in the School of Software Engineering at Huazhong University of Science and Technology (HUST), Wuhan, Chian. His research interests include data mining, machine learning and autonomic computing.

Junping Zhang received the B.S. degree in automation from the XiangTan University, China, in 1992, the M.S. degree in control theory and control engineering from Hunan University, Changsha, China, in 1997, and the Ph.D. degree in pattern recognition and intelligent system from the Institute of Automation, Chinese Academy of Sciences, Beijing, China, in June 2003. Now he is an Associate Professor in the Shanghai Key Lab. of Intelligent Information Processing and the Department of Computer Sciences and Engineering, Fudan University, Shanghai, China. His research interests include pattern recognition, image processing, and machine learning.

Xiaohua Zhou is a PhD candidate in College of Information Science and Technology, Drexel University. He received his bachelor and master degree from Shanghai Jiao Tong University, China in 1999 and 2002, respectively. His current research interests include information retrieval, text data mining, and information extraction.

Gilles Zurfluh (zurfluh@irit.fr) is a professor of computer science at the University of Toulouse 1, France. He is a research staff member at the IRIT research centre (CNRS UMR 5505), where he manages the SIG/ED research group. His research interests span many aspects of non-traditional data management in databases, information systems and decisional systems.

Index

V

value-added 3

variable importance rankings 311, 312

vector-based data objects 198

vector cosine similarity 134

vector spatial data 198

vertical fragmentation 178, 194

vertical fragmentation in relational databases 178

vertical partitioning 178, 179, 180, 189, 192, 193

very large databases 1

view fragment 92, 96

View selection 91, 104, 105

"virtual" group-bys 109

Visualisation 223

W

Weak learner number (WLN) 361

Weka 286

within-algorithm ensemble 287, 288

WordNet synsets 122

workstation farms 109